Student Learning in South Asia

DIRECTIONS IN DEVELOPMENT
Human Development

Student Learning in South Asia

Challenges, Opportunities, and Policy Priorities

Halil Dundar, Tara Béteille, Michelle Riboud, and Anil Deolalikar

THE WORLD BANK
Washington, D.C.

1818 H Street NW, Washington DC 20433
Telephone: 202-473-1000; Internet: www.worldbank.org

1 2 3 4 17 16 15 14

ISBN (paper): 978-1-4648-0160-0
ISBN (electronic): 978-1-4648-0161-7
DOI: 10.1596/978-1-4648-0160-0

Cover photo: © Swati Sahni/World Bank. Used with the permission of Swati Sahni. Further permission required for reuse.
Cover design: Debra Naylor, Naylor Design

Library of Congress Cataloging-in-Publication Data

Dundar, Halil.
Student learning in South Asia: challenges, opportunities, and policy priorities / by Halil Dundar, Tara Béteille, Michelle Riboud, and Anil Deolalikar.
pages cm. — (Directions in development)
Includes bibliographical references.
ISBN 978-1-4648-0160-0 (alk. paper) — ISBN 978-1-4648-0161-7 (electronic)
1. Education, Elementary—South Asia. 2. Education and state—South Asia. 3. Academic achievement—South Asia. I. Title.
LB1556.7.S65D86 2014
372.95—dc23 2013048722

Contents

Boxes

Figures

Tables

Foreword

For the past decade, South Asian governments have been investing heavily to achieve the education Millennium Development Goals (MDGs). As a result, net enrollment in South Asia's primary schools rose from 75.0 percent in 2000 to 89.0 percent in 2010, bringing it closer to that of the Latin America and the Caribbean (94.0 percent) and East Asia and the Pacific (94.8 percent) regions. Between 1999 and 2010, the number of out-of-school children ages 8–14 years fell from 35 million to 13 million, and the number of out-of-school girls in the region dropped by 59 percent.

Despite these significant gains, this report documents that learning outcomes and the average level of skill acquisition in the region are low in both absolute and relative terms. Hence, schooling does not translate into what it could and what it should: better life chances, including the rise out of poverty for many. In parallel, schooling also does not contribute to productivity increases and economic growth; it represents, as such, a major constraint to the acceleration of economic and social development.

Throughout the 2000s, most South Asian countries have invested in school inputs and directed their efforts toward achieving universal access to primary education. While these investments have led to more children retained in school, they have not translated into better learning outcomes. As governments in the region have increasingly come to realize, they now need to direct their attention to improving quality—schooling is successful when it enables students to lead fuller lives, both as individuals and as labor market participants. To achieve this, merely spending time in school is not enough; there has to be a significant gain in skills, noncognitive as well as cognitive, if countries in the region are to reap the full expected returns on their investments and generate gains in employment, including job creation, and productivity.

Stressing the importance of a focus on education quality, this study explores not only what kinds of interventions hold promise for improving learning outcomes in South Asia but also whether incentive structures in the system are aligned with countries' learning goals. It attempts to answer three questions:

- **How well do education systems in South Asia perform?** How much are students learning and what are they learning? How do disparities in student learning outcomes vary by country, socioeconomic group, gender, and location?

- **What determines student learning outcomes?** How important are school resources and inputs? How important is socioeconomic background? At an even more basic level, how important, for instance, are the health and nutritional status of children entering school?
- **What policy options are effective in improving learning outcomes, especially given increasing demand and competition for public resources?**

This report covers education from primary through upper secondary school. Given its importance for school readiness, this report also reviews early childhood development even though that is outside formal education systems in the region.

This study is the first to comprehensively analyze the performance of South Asian educational systems in terms of student learning. To examine what types of policies hold promise for improving student learning, it reviews data from large-scale national learning assessments and the findings of a small but increasing number of impact evaluations being conducted in the region. Finally, based on evidence from South Asia and other regions, it identifies strategic options and priorities to improve learning outcomes in South Asia.

The findings make it clear that to be successful, policies to ensure lasting improvements in student learning outcomes need to be integrated into a larger agenda of inclusive economic growth and governance reform.

This report makes an important contribution to our understanding of the performance of education systems in South Asia and the causes and correlates of student learning outcomes. Further, drawing on successful initiatives both in the region and elsewhere in the world, it offers an insightful approach to setting priorities for enhancing the quality of school education despite growing competition for public resources.

Martin Rama
Chief Economist
South Asia Region
The World Bank

Jesko Hentschel
Director, Human Development
South Asia Region
The World Bank

Acknowledgments

Student Learning in South Asia: Challenges, Opportunities, and Policy Priorities is the first comprehensive review of how education is performing and the causes and correlates of education quality in South Asia. The study was prepared by a team led by Halil Dundar, under the general direction of Amit Dar, education sector manager; Michal Rutkowski and his successor, Jesko Hentschel, sector directors; and Kalpana Kochhar and her successor, Martin Rama, chief economists of the South Asia Region. The core team comprised Tara Béteille, Michelle Riboud, and Anil Deolalikar. The team also benefited from the contributions of Reema Nayar, who was the co-task team leader during the initial phase of the study, and from significant contributions made by Karthik Muralidharan, Shinsaku Nomura, and Yevgeniya Savchenko to specific chapters.

Many people provided written inputs and contributions on a variety of subjects. The report draws on specific contributions or background papers by Monazza Aslam, Geeta Kingdon, and Shenila Rawal (teacher quality); Geeta Kingdon, Monazza Aslam, and Paul Alterton (education finance); Harold Alderman, Aisha Yousafzai, Jena Derakhshani Hamadani, and Pia Rebello Britto (early childhood development); Marguerite Clarke (student assessment); Emiliana Vegas (teacher quality and education finance); Hasaan Khawar (education decentralization in Pakistan); Wilfred Perera (education decentralization in Sri Lanka); Priyanka Pandey (education decentralization in South Asia); Dhir Jhingran (pedagogy and classroom practices); Quynh T. Nguyen and Mahesh Dahal (private education); and Olga Shemyakina and Christine Valente (education quality in conflict-affected areas).

The team also benefited from the advice and comments from many individuals at critical points in the report's preparation, notably Pablo Gottret, Robert Chase, Umbreen Arif, Benoit Millot, Dhushyanth Raju, Jacob Bregman, Harsha Aturupane, Toby Linden, Dilip Parajuli, Leopold Sarr, Ayesha Vawda, Helen Craig, Kurt Larsen, Priyam Saraf, Indhira Santos, Joel Reyes, Sangeeta Goyal, Mokhlesur Rahman, Nicole Goldstein, Shabnam Sinha, and Deepa Sankar.

Elizabeth King, Helen Craig, Venkatesh Sundadaraman, and Dhir Jhingran were peer reviewers of the report. The team also benefited from advice and comments at the concept stage from Emmanuel Jimenez, sector director, the World Bank; Christopher Colclough, professor of education, Cambridge University;

Richard Murnane, professor of economics, Harvard University; and Marshall S. Smith, visiting scholar, Carnegie Foundation for the Advancement of Teaching.

None of the aforementioned individuals bear any responsibility for the analyses and findings of this report. The authors alone assume full responsibility for its conclusions.

The team gratefully acknowledges financial support from the Bank Netherlands Partnership Program Trust Fund and the Australian Trust Fund for Policy Facility for Decentralization and Service Delivery in South Asia.

Kalpana Kaul assisted with editing of the report's background papers. Anne Grant has been responsible for editing and preparing the manuscript for publication. We are grateful to Julie-Anne Graitge for her assistance on administrative issues. We also thank the World Bank's Publishing and Knowledge Division for efficient management of the publication process, in particular Rumit Pancholi, who supported the publication process.

About the Authors

Halil Dundar is a lead education specialist at the World Bank. He is currently leading the Bank's operational and analytical work on tertiary education in Pakistan and skills development in Sri Lanka. Previously, he managed the Bank's operational and analytical work on education in Azerbaijan, Ethiopia, and Nigeria. Before joining the Bank, he worked as a research associate in the Office of Planning and Analysis at the University of Minnesota and subsequently held the position of assistant professor of education policy at the Middle East Technical University in Ankara, Turkey, and served as a policy advisor to the Turkish Ministry of Education. He has published numerous journal articles and book chapters on education finance, productivity, and quality improvement issues. Mr. Dundar obtained a PhD from the University of Minnesota in education, with a concentration in the economics of higher education.

Tara Béteille is an economist at the World Bank, where she has been working on the Bank's India and Sri Lanka education programs. She obtained her PhD from Stanford University in the economics of education, focusing on the political economy of teacher labor markets. She has published a number of journal articles and book chapters on the economics of education. Previously, she led ICICI Bank's nonprofit education initiatives in India.

Michelle Riboud is an economist who started her professional career working in academia. In late 1988, she joined the World Bank, working in various capacities and regions, combining analytical work with the management of investment operations and policy loans. In her last assignment, she was education sector manager in the South Asia region. Since she retired, she has been consulting with various units of the World Bank. Ms. Riboud has published numerous articles on human capital, household economics, and labor market issues in developed and developing countries. She holds doctorates in economics from both the University of Paris 1 and the University of Chicago.

Anil Deolalikar is a professor of economics and founding dean of the School of Public Policy at the University of California, Riverside. In 2002–03, he served as a lead human development economist in the World Bank's New Delhi office.

He is a development economist who has published five books and more than 75 journal articles on the economics of child schooling, nutrition, health, and poverty in developing countries. He is also an elected Fellow of the American Association for the Advancement of Science. He obtained a PhD in economics from Stanford University.

Abbreviations

ABL	activity-based learning
ACER	Australian Council for Educational Research
ADB	Asian Development Bank
ALM	Active Learning Methodologies
ASER	Annual State of Education Report
ASSL	annual status of student learning
BLQS	Bhutan Learning Quality Survey
BPEP	Basic Primary Education Project
BRAC	Bangladesh Rural Advancement Committee
BRICS	Brazil, Russia, India, China, and South Africa
CAMaL	Combined Activities for Maximized Learning
CARE	Cooperation for Advancement, Rehabilitation, and Education
CBSE	Central Board of Secondary Education
CCE	continuous and comprehensive evaluation
CCT	conditional cash transfer
C-in-Ed	certificate in education
CISCE	Council for the Indian School Certificate Examinations
CLAPS	Children's Learning Acceleration Programme for Sustainability
CSP	Community Support Program
CSSP	Community School Support Program
CTEVT	Council for Technical Education and Vocational Training
DEO	district or divisional education officer
DFID	Department for International Development, United Kingdom
DHS	Demographic and Health Survey
DISE	District Information System for Education
DPE	Directorate of Primary Education
DSHE	Directorate of Secondary and Higher Education
ECD	early childhood development
EDSC	Educational and Developmental Services Centre

EFA	Education for All
EI	Educational Initiatives
ESDFP	Education Sector Development Framework and Program
EVS	environmental studies
FAS	Foundation-Assisted Schools
FATA	Federally Administered Tribal Areas
FCI	family care indicators
FMRP	Financial Management Reform Programme
FSSAP	Female Secondary School Assistance Project
GCE	General Certificate of Education
GCE (A-level)	General Certificate of Education, Advanced Level
GCE (O-level)	General Certificate of Education, Ordinary Level
GDP	gross domestic product
GPS	government primary schools
GTZ	German Agency for Technical Cooperation
HIES	Household and Income Expenditure Survey
HOME	home observations for measurement of the environment
HSC	Higher Secondary Certificate
HSEB	Higher Secondary Education Board
HSLC	Higher Secondary-Level Certification
IALS	International Adult Literacy Survey
ICDDRB	International Centre for Diarrhoeal Disease Research, Bangladesh
ICDS	Integrated Child Development Services
IGCSE	International General Certificate of Secondary Education
IHDS	Indian Human Development Survey
ILIP	Integrated Learning Improvement Programme
INGO	international nongovernmental organization
IQ	intelligence quotient
IRT	item response theory
KIPP	Knowledge Is Power Program
KSQE	Karnataka Schools towards Quality Education
LEAPS	Learning and Educational Achievement in Punjab Schools
LFSs	Labor Force Surveys
LHW	Lady Health Worker
LOCs	learning outcomes categories
M&E	monitoring and evaluating
MDGs	Millennium Development Goals
MDMS	Midday Meal Scheme
MHRD	Ministry of Human Resource Development

MICS	Multi-Indicator Cluster Survey
MNCH	maternal, neonatal, and child health
MOE	Ministry of Education
MOES	Ministry of Education and Sports
MoPME	Ministry of Primary and Mass Education
NAPE	National Academy for Primary Education
NASA	National Assessment of Student Achievement
NCERT	National Council for Educational Research and Training
NCME	National Council on Measurement in Education
NEAS	National Education Assessment System (Pakistan)
NER	net enrollment rate
NEREC	National Education Research and Evaluation Center
NGO	nongovernmental organization
NRSP	National Rural Support Programme
NSA	National Student Assessment
NSP	New School Program
NSS	National Sample Survey
NTRCA	National Teacher Registration and Certification Authority
OECD	Organisation for Economic Co-operation and Development
OLPC	one laptop per child
OLS	ordinary least squares
OTL	opportunity to learn
PACE-A	Partnership for Advancing Community Education in Afghanistan
PEACE	Provincial Education Assessment Center
PEAS	Punjab Education Assessment System
PEDP	Primary Education Development Program
PEF	Punjab Educational Foundation
PIRLS	Progress in International Reading Literacy Study
PISA	Programme for International Student Assessment
PMT	proxy means-testing
PPP	public-private partnership
PPRS	Promoting Private Schooling in Rural Sindh
PRP	performance-related pay
PSU	population sampling unit
PTA	parent teacher association
PTR	pupil-teacher ratio
QAT	quality assurance test
RCC	Releasing Creativity and Confidence
RCT	realistic conflict theory

RECURSO	*Rendicion de Cuentas para la Reforma Social,* or Accountability for Social Reform
REO	regional education officer
RMSA	*Rashtriya Madhyamik Shiksha Abhiyan*
RNGPS	registered nongovernment primary schools
ROSC	Reaching Out-of-School Children
Rs	rupees
RTE	Right to Education
SABER	Systems Approach for Better Education Results
SACMEQ	Southern and Eastern Africa Consortium for Monitoring Educational Quality
SAFED	South Asian Forum for Education Development
SBA	school-based assessment
SBM	school-based management
SCERT	State Council of Educational Research and Training
SEQAEP	Secondary Education Quality and Access Enhancement Project
SESP	Secondary Education Support Program
SIMCE	*Sistema de Medicion de la Calidad de la Educacion* (System for Measuring Education Quality)
SLC	school leaving certificate
SLS	student learning study
SMC	school management committee
SSA	*Sarva Shiksha Abhiyan* (Education for All)
SSC	Senior Secondary Certificate
SSRP	School Sector Reform Program
TED	teacher education development
TET	teacher eligibility test
TETP	Third Education and Training Program
TIMSS	Trends in Mathematics and Science Study
Tk	taka
TQISEP	Teaching Quality Improvement in Secondary Education Project
UNESCO	United Nations Educational, Scientific, and Cultural Organization
UNICEF	United Nations International Children's Emergency Fund
USAID	United States Agency for International Development
WHO	World Health Organization

Overview*

Introduction

For the past decade, South Asian governments[1] have been investing heavily to achieve the education Millennium Development Goals (MDGs). As a result, South Asia's primary net enrollment rate (NER) rose from 75.0 percent in 2000 to 89.0 percent in 2010, closer to that of regions such as Latin America and the Caribbean (94.0 percent) and East Asia and the Pacific (94.8 percent).[2] Between 1999 and 2010, the number of out-of-school children ages 8–14 years fell from 35 million to 13 million—an impressive achievement in a decade. The region has also made great progress in enrolling girls in both primary and secondary school. The number of out-of-school girls in the region has dropped 59 percent over the past decade.

Yet, much remains to be done. The rapid gains in enrollment have not been accompanied by commensurate improvements in learning levels, with the average level of skill acquisition in South Asia being low by both national and international standards. A major reason for this is that throughout the 2000s, most South Asian countries focused on (a) achieving universal access to primary education and (b) sustained investment in better-quality school inputs to improve the quality of primary and secondary education.[3] The focus was not explicitly on learning outcomes; the implicit assumption was that more inputs would translate into better learning outcomes.

While school systems face an initial trade-off between increasing access and improving quality, this initial phase has passed in South Asia, except for Afghanistan. As governments in the region have increasingly recognized, they now need to shift their focus to learning outcomes to determine what types of inputs and system-level reforms are worth investing in. A focus on learning is also a key part of the World Bank Group's Education Strategy 2020 (box O.2). Schooling is successful when it enables students to lead fuller lives—as individuals and as labor market participants. For this to happen, merely spending time in school is not enough; there has to be a

*See box O.1 for a summary of the study's key messages.

Box O.1 Key Messages

Message 1: South Asia has made considerable progress in improving access to education but faces a major quality challenge in primary and secondary education.

- The regional primary net enrollment rate (NER) rose from 75 percent in 2001 to about 89 percent in 2010—closer to that of regions such as Latin America and the Caribbean. At the secondary level, the regional gross enrollment rate rose from about 44 percent in 2000 to 58 percent in 2010. Between 1999 and 2009, the number of out-of-school children ages 8–14 years fell from 35 million to 13 million—an impressive achievement in a decade, especially given high population growth.
- Progress is still uneven and the region needs to continue its efforts to provide better services to socioeconomic and culturally marginalized groups. Afghanistan and Pakistan still lag significantly behind the other countries in the region. There are also wide disparities in enrollment rates between countries and between groups within each country (such as gender, income, caste, and geographic location). Girls, especially in Pakistan and Afghanistan, and children of low socioeconomic status or from rural and lagging regions continue to have less access to primary education. Finally, South Asia's secondary enrollment rate is still below the world average by nearly 12 percentage points.
- Especially worrisome is the fact that learning outcomes are very low at every level of education in comparison to international standards. To some extent, this is understandable; the large increase in access to schooling in recent years has meant the entry into schools of millions of children from disadvantaged backgrounds, with low levels of learning, into the educational systems. While gaps in enrollment between disadvantaged groups and population averages have narrowed over time, gaps in learning remain large. The gaps exist at the point of entry into the school system and grow over time. Thus, bridging gaps in learning in early grades is essential for meeting efficiency and equity goals.

Message 2: The poor quality of education, as measured by learning outcomes, undermines the region's competitiveness, economic growth, and efforts to alleviate poverty.

- A better educated and skilled labor force is critical to sustaining long periods of growth in a world of rapid technological change and increasing global competitiveness and complexity. The fact that—in addition to 13 million children who never attend school—one-quarter to one-third of those who graduate from primary school lack basic numeracy and literacy skills that would enable them to further their education, undermines the growth potential and social cohesiveness of the region. Limited access to (mostly poor-quality) secondary education further exacerbates the damage to the region's growth potential. Employer surveys confirm that inferior education systems and the shortage of skills are constraining private-sector investment. Consequently, improving learning outcomes at all levels of education, while providing education opportunities to a wider range of children, is critical for building a broad base for growth and modernization of the region. Improving learning outcomes should therefore be one of the key priorities of education policy in the region.

box continues next page

Box O.1 Key Messages *(continued)*

Message 3: Although low learning achievement can be partly explained by factors outside the control of education policy makers, effective public policy geared to improving school quality and learning outcomes could make a major difference.

- In South Asia, as in other parts of the world, student and household characteristics are strong predictors of student achievement. A child's gender and nutritional status, the language spoken at home, parental schooling, household income, and social status all influence student achievement. These variables, which are not directly under the control of education policy makers, affect achievement through such factors as school choice, financial resources, nutrition and study facilities at home, and parental ability to help children with school work.
- However, student background only explains a portion of the variation in student achievement. In many South Asian countries, about one-half to two-thirds of the variation in student achievement can be attributed to school-specific factors (e.g., teachers, school resources)—more than is typical in other regions of the world. This provides considerable scope for improving learning outcomes with an effective education policy directed at school quality.

Message 4: To improve quality, the education reform agenda needs to prioritize interventions that focus on outcomes rather than on inputs.

- *Early childhood nutrition is a crucial policy priority for improving learning outcomes, and a multisectoral approach is necessary to ensure that disadvantaged children come to school well nourished and ready to learn.* South Asia has the world's highest prevalence of child malnutrition, which has been shown to affect children's brain development and cognition. A large number of South Asian children enter primary school with huge learning disadvantages, which get compounded over time. Investing in early-life nutrition, with appropriate coverage and age targeting, is critical to offset those disadvantages and can be a highly cost-effective investment in the quality and efficiency of education. Since early childhood nutrition has traditionally been outside the realm of education ministry activities in the region, a multisectoral approach is central to ensuring children receive such inputs.
- *Teachers need to be more effective and accountable.* There is robust evidence that what matters most for student learning is teachers' knowledge, how much effort they expend on instruction in the classroom, how motivated they are, and how they teach. A large percentage of teachers cannot explain basic concepts or address student queries and thus cannot satisfactorily transmit knowledge to their pupils. In addition, teacher absenteeism rates of 15–25 percent are pervasive in South Asia. Even when teachers are in school, they are often unable to tailor learning to children's needs. To address these issues, clear and transparent standards are necessary from the time of recruitment on through deployment and transfers. Rampant politicization of teacher appointments and postings has led to non-merit-based decisions, undermining efforts to build a quality teaching force. Preservice and in-service training should equip teachers with relevant, up-to-date knowledge and approaches to teaching. For teachers to be effective, they also need to know from the start that acquiring new skills and

box continues next page

Box O.1 Key Messages *(continued)*

performing well will be rewarded. A career progression structure with performance-related pay and other rewards is likely to foster greater accountability and teacher effort.

- *Financing could help as a tool to improve quality.* Countries have tended to use additional resources for infrastructure improvements, reducing class size, or raising teacher salaries to improve school performance. Although some of these inputs may help attract and retain children in school, there is little evidence that they bring significant gains in student learning by themselves. Thus, business as usual is unlikely to do much to enhance quality, and countries should consider using promising financing tools that focus on outcomes rather than inputs. These include changes in the incentive structure for teachers and in the incentive structure for schools through changes in funding formulas and, for districts and states, by linking funding to a combination of need and performance.
- *South Asia should leverage the contribution of the private sector, comprising not-for-profit and for-profit players, both to expand access to schooling for disadvantaged populations and to improve learning outcomes.* The region has severe resource constraints and cannot improve access and quality without the combined effort of governments, households, and the private sector (which includes for-profit and not-for-profit schools). There is a long history of nongovernmental presence in the educational sector in South Asia, and available evidence suggests that private schools can, on average, offer access at a lower social cost and with comparable , and sometimes better, outcomes than government schools. Thus, South Asian countries will gain by easing barriers to private entry and through well-designed public-private partnerships. The government and the private sector have different strengths and weaknesses in the provision of education. Optimal education policy should therefore aim to set up financing and accountability structures that leverage the strengths of both sectors and provide greater choice and autonomy to parents and students in their schooling options.
- *Decentralization reforms hold promise for improving the governance of education systems in the region because of wide spatial disparities within countries.* Many countries in the region have already been implementing decentralization policies in education, but for these reforms to be effective in improving schooling outcomes, they will need to be implemented systematically and consistently. Decentralization reforms in the region will benefit from greater political support and from providing lower levels of government with greater fiscal authority. Importantly, such reforms will need to build local capacity so that communities can contribute effectively to education governance, accountability and improved learning outcomes.
- *Building and improving systems to assess progress in student learning outcomes over time in both government and private schools will be important going forward.* Although most countries in the region have begun to move in this direction, additional progress is needed in (a) ensuring the quality and reliability of public examinations, (b) creating more balanced systems that emphasize classroom and large-scale assessments, and (c) benchmarking national learning outcomes against regional and international standards through participation in international test initiatives. While there has been a move to limit high-stakes testing in early grades, there is good reason to have high-quality, low-stakes testing annually to

box continues next page

Box O.1 Key Messages *(continued)*

provide regular and reliable feedback about how the education system is performing. This will enhance accountability for national education outcomes and enable policy makers to use the assessment results to adjust their strategic planning for quality improvement.

Message 5: To be successful, policies to improve student learning outcomes should be embedded within a larger agenda of inclusive growth and governance reform.

- Technical solutions to improving school quality, such as more teachers, better teacher training, and more accountability, will work only if larger issues of accountability and governance in the education sector are addressed. As in other parts of the world, teacher unions in many South Asian countries are powerful but do not lobby for improving educational outcomes. In many cases, there is a strong nexus among teachers, politicians, and government officials that weakens teacher accountability and contributes to poor student learning outcomes. To sustain improvements in student learning, governments in South Asia will need to build coalitions with communities, teachers unions, civil servants, private schools, and civil-society groups to obtain their buy-in for educational reforms. There are already examples of countries elsewhere in the world—as well as countries and states within the region—where governments have partnered with nongovernmental actors and used these groups as agents of change. Technical solutions need to go hand in hand with such broader efforts to achieve lasting improvements in learning outcomes.

Box O.2 World Bank Education Strategy 2020: Invest Early, Invest Smartly, Invest for All

The World Bank's Education Strategy 2020 sets the goal of achieving learning for all. The emphasis on learning, not merely putting students in school, is important, because it is the knowledge and skills individuals acquire that are associated with growth, development, and poverty reduction. With this in mind, the strategy emphasizes the need to invest early, invest smartly, and invest for all. It is important to invest early, because foundational skills acquired early in childhood make possible a lifetime of learning. Next, it is important to make investments that have proven to contribute to learning, with quality being the focus of education investments and learning gains being a key metric of quality. Finally, learning for all means ensuring that *all* students, not just the privileged or gifted, acquire the knowledge and skills they need. To achieve learning for all, the World Bank Group is channeling its efforts in education in two strategic directions: reforming education systems at the country level and building a high-quality knowledge base for education reforms at the global level. The education system approach will focus on increasing accountability and results as a complement to providing inputs. Simultaneously, at the regional and global levels, the Bank will help develop a high-quality knowledge base on education reform. Toward this end, the Bank is developing new knowledge approaches to guide education reform, such as the Systems Approach for Better Education Results (SABER). Better knowledge of the strengths and weaknesses of particular education systems will allow the Bank to respond more effectively to the needs of its partner countries.

Box O.3 The Importance of Investing in Education Quality

Recent literature provides ample evidence that it is the quality, not quantity, of schooling that explains variation in labor market outcomes between individuals and differences in economic growth rates between countries. Cognitive skills, measured through test scores, explain a substantial part of the variation in income levels across individuals. Studies from developing countries on the relationship between test scores and labor market outcome come mainly from Pakistan and countries in Africa, such as Ghana, Kenya, Morocco, South Africa, and Tanzania. In Pakistan, for instance, Behrman, Ross, and Sabot (2008) estimated that a 1 standard deviation increase in cognitive achievement is associated with a 25 percent increase in earnings.

If schooling and cognitive skills influence individual income, then how cognitive skills are distributed across different population groups is likely to influence the distribution of income between these groups. Using International Adult Literacy Survey data, one study found that a large part of the variation in earnings inequalities can be explained by skills dispersions. Indeed, one reason governments finance education is to reduce social and income inequalities between groups.

There is also a significant body of work that establishes a positive relationship between measures of schooling and economic growth. From a theoretical perspective, there are at least three ways in which education may affect economic growth: (a) education may increase the productivity of the existing labor force, which may lead to a higher level of equilibrium output; (b) by increasing the innovative capacity of the economy, education may lead to the creation of new technologies, products, and processes, all of which promote growth; and (c) education may help in the assimilation and diffusion of the knowledge needed to effectively use technology devised by others.

At the macro level, student learning outcomes, especially in mathematics and science, have been found to have a significant effect on economic growth. For example, Hanushek and Woessman (2008) estimated that an increase of 1 standard deviation in student test scores on international assessments of literacy and mathematics is associated with a 2 percent increase in annual growth of per capita gross domestic product (GDP). More recently, an Organisation for Economic Co-operation and Development (OECD) study noted that increases in student PISA (Programme for International Student Assessment) test scores may have very large impacts on the future well-being of countries by dramatically improving national labor force skills; it estimated that bringing all OECD countries up to the average performance of Finland, the top performer on PISA tests, would boost aggregate OECD GDP by US$260 trillion—six times the current GDP of OECD countries (OECD 2010). The study emphasizes that the quality of learning outcomes, not the length of schooling, makes the difference (OECD 2010). In South Asia, employer surveys increasingly suggest that inferior education systems and a shortage of skills are barriers to private sector investment and growth (World Bank 2012a). For example, Sri Lankan employers see an inadequately educated labor force as a severe constraint on company growth. Studies have also found that the availability of skills has a powerful positive correlation with firm productivity.

significant gain in cognitive and noncognitive skills. It is improvements in these skills (box O.3) that generate gains in terms of employment and productivity (Hanushek and Woessmann 2008). Unfortunately, South Asia's record here is poor; inadequately prepared graduates of government and private schools (both for-profit and not-for-profit) constrain not only the growth and competitiveness of the economy but also deter creation of more and better jobs (World Bank 2012a). Unless the focus is explicitly shifted to improving student learning, the investments governments have made over the past decade will be wasted.

The focus on learning outcomes is also important for another reason. As access to schools has expanded and socioeconomic disparities in school enrollment have narrowed, gaps in school quality and learning outcomes have started widening. Students from poor backgrounds start with large learning disadvantages, which grow over time because of low-quality schools and poorly performing teachers. Figure O.1, which shows the Lorenz curves of inequality for enrollment as well as cognition for children ages 8–11 years in India, suggests that student learning outcomes are more unequally distributed than school enrollment.[4] So policies to promote equity in education need to focus on reducing the large and growing learning gaps between poor and better-off children.

Improving student learning in the region is a complicated policy endeavor, with no "magic bullet," for several reasons. First, there is very little systematic

Figure O.1 Lorenz Curves for School Enrollment and Ability to Write and Divide, India, 2004–05

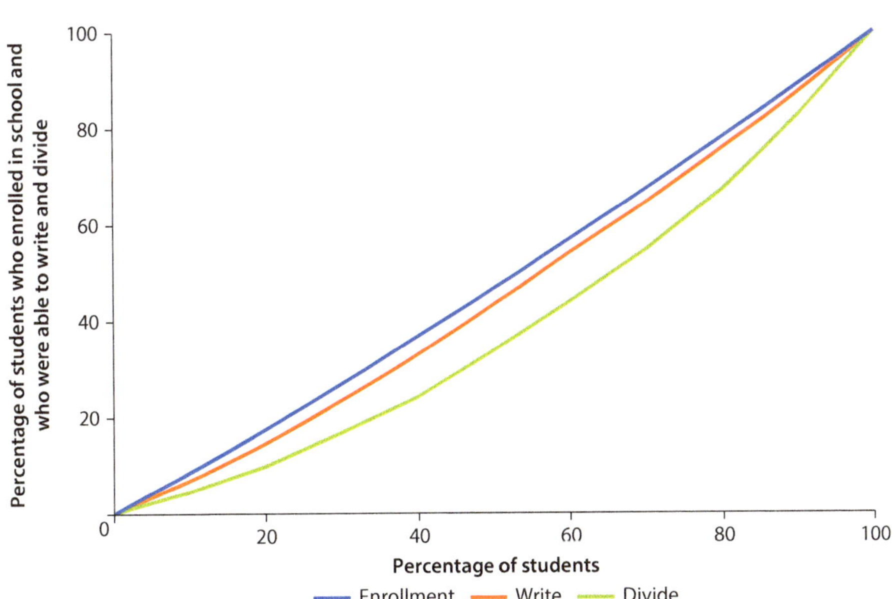

Source: Data from the India Human Development Survey, 2005.

evidence on what policy-amenable interventions will improve student learning in the South Asian context. Next, the region has the largest number of school-age children relative to any other world region, many of whom are first-generation schoolgoers. There is also much greater heterogeneity among population subgroups in terms of socioeconomic and linguistic background than in other parts of the world. The variation in linguistic background is especially important because it constrains the effectiveness of teachers who teach in the dominant language and of textbooks written in that language. Most countries in the region have conflict-affected areas, where the learning challenge is especially high.[5] Finally, the multiple parallel initiatives in the region, such as the practice of private tuition, offer education of variable quality.

Given these challenges, it is important to understand what kinds of interventions hold promise for improving learning outcomes in South Asia. This makes it important to closely examine which inputs translate into improved learning and whether incentive structures in the system are aligned with countries' learning goals. The main objective of this study is to review what is known about the quality of primary and secondary education in South Asia, examine factors influencing education quality, and identify practices and policy options that could improve and sustain learning outcomes. It thus aims to answer three questions:

- *How well do education systems in South Asia perform?* How much are students learning and what are they learning? How do disparities in student learning outcomes vary by country, socioeconomic group, gender, and location?
- *What determines student learning outcomes?* How important are school resources and inputs, and how important is socioeconomic background?
- *What policy options are effective in improving learning outcomes, especially given increasing demand and competition for public resources?*

The study covers education from primary through upper secondary school, excluding vocational and technical education. Given its importance for school readiness, it also reviews early childhood development (ECD) even though that is outside the formal education system in the countries in the region. It is the first study to comprehensively analyze the performance of South Asian educational systems in terms of student learning.[6] To examine what types of policies hold promise for improving student learning, it reviews data from large-scale national learning assessments and the findings of a small but increasing number of impact evaluations being conducted in the region. Finally, based on evidence from South Asia and other regions, it identifies strategic options and priorities to improve learning outcomes in South Asia.

The study draws upon numerous sources of data, among them key government data (such as Bangladesh's Directorate of Primary Education; India's National Sample Survey, District Information System of Education, and National Council of Education Research and Training Assessment; and Pakistan's National Education Assessment System); data from nongovernmental entities (such as Pakistan's Annual Status of Education Report, India's Student Learning

Study, and its Annual Status of Education Report); international agencies (such as the Organisation for Economic Co-operation and Development [OECD] Programme for International Student Assessment [PISA] 2009+ for India; the World Bank Secondary Education Quality and Access Enhancement Project in Bangladesh); and qualitative studies undertaken for the report (such as examining decentralization reforms in Sri Lanka and Pakistan). The study also uses the World Bank Systems Approach for Better Education Results (SABER) framework to examine issues related to ECD, education finance, assessment systems, and teacher policies. Despite these many sources of data, however, the region lacks high-quality cross-sectional and longitudinal educational data, which limits the ability to make causal assessments of what types of interventions work and what types do not.

The remainder of this overview is organized into three sections. The next section summarizes South Asia's education performance as measured by participation and completion rates, as well as increases in inputs. The section notes that the increase in inputs has not been accompanied by a corresponding improvement in learning outcomes. The following section examines why an increase in inputs has not been successful in increasing learning outcomes commensurately and the factors underlying the current levels of student learning in the region. The final section identifies promising strategic priorities for improving primary and secondary education.

The Quality Challenge

Progress in School Participation

Trends in Enrollment

In the past decade, South Asia has made impressive strides in expanding access to basic education. The regional primary NER rose from 75.0 percent in 2001 to about 89.0 percent in 2010, moving South Asia's NER closer to that of other regions, such as Latin America and the Caribbean (94.0 percent), and East Asia and the Pacific (94.8 percent). At the secondary level, gross enrollment rates also increased by 14 percentage points, from about 44 percent in 2000 to 58 percent in 2010—substantial, though still below the world average by nearly 12 percentage points, and below developing countries in Latin America and the Caribbean by 16 percentage points and in East Asia and the Pacific by 14 percentage points.

All countries have made progress, although with different starting points and at different speeds (figure O.2). Sri Lanka is the outlier in the region, having achieved practically universal primary education long ago. In Maldives, 96 percent of all primary school–age children are now enrolled. All other countries had a much lower starting point. The most significant change among these countries took place in Bhutan, where the primary NER increased by 30 percentage points to 88 percent over the decade. This was followed by Pakistan, where the NER jumped from 58 percent to 74 percent between 2000 and 2011, although still below the regional average. Bangladesh, India, and

Figure O.2 Primary and Secondary Enrollment Rates, South Asia, 2000–11

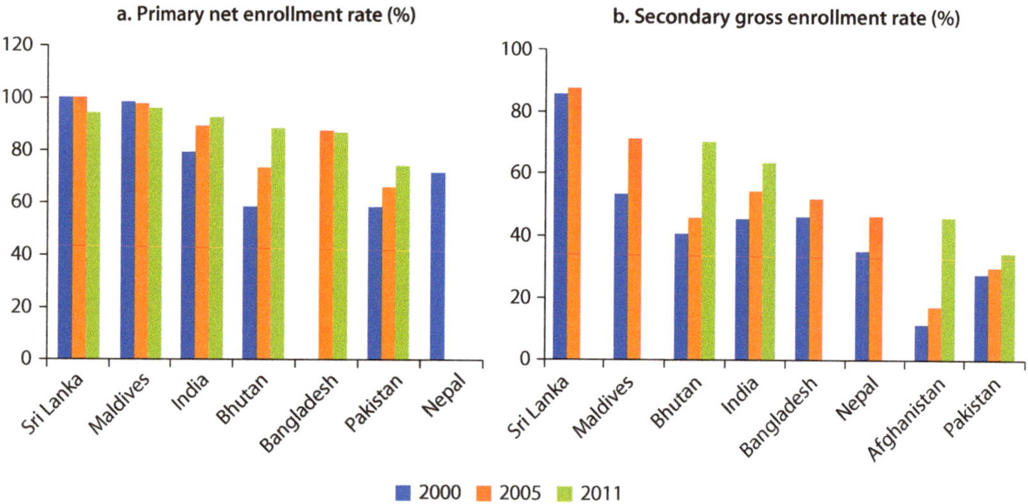

Source: UNESCO Institute for Statistics in EdStats, August 2012.

Nepal have made significant progress, increasing enrollment to about 90 percent. Although modest, Afghanistan has also registered an increase in primary school enrollment over the last decade. At the secondary level, Sri Lanka again stands out with an NER of 87 percent and with 80 percent of young people ages 20–29 years having achieved at least 10 years of schooling. India, Maldives, Nepal, and Pakistan have made the most progress.

The region has also made great progress in educating girls. In fact, in Bangladesh and Sri Lanka more girls than boys are now in secondary school (grades 6–12). In India, the percentage of girls in secondary education went from 60 percent in 1990 to 74 percent in 2010. Since 1999, the number of out-of-school girls in the region has dropped 59 percent, from 23 million to 9.5 million.

Despite impressive enrollment increases in the region, improving learning outcomes will not be easy. First, low attendance—driven by factors on the demand side (such as children engaged in household chores) and supply side (such as teacher absenteeism)—undermines efforts to improve learning outcomes, especially for students from disadvantaged backgrounds. In India, for example, while the NER rate for children ages 6–14 years is about 92 percent, average attendance in government schools is about 75 percent, varying by state and urban or rural residence. It ranges from less than 60 percent in Bihar to 92 percent in Kerala. In all other states, attendance rates are 15–30 percent lower than enrollment rates. Thus, children are registered but do not come to school regularly, lowering learning outcomes.

Second, in 2010, 13 million South Asian children from disadvantaged backgrounds and hard-to-reach areas were not attending school. Income, gender, and rural residence are the main reasons for disparities in access. For example, in

India, a child in the highest income quintile averages four more years of schooling than one from the lowest income quintile. There are also large gender disparities, especially in Afghanistan and Pakistan. Progress among all groups continues to be uneven geographically as well. In India, for instance, enrollment rates are significantly lower in the poorer northern and eastern regions, including the populous states of Bihar and Uttar Pradesh, than in southern and western states such as Tamil Nadu and Gujarat. As children from these backgrounds enter school, many of whom are first-generation schoolgoers, it is likely that they will push down average learning levels.

Third, South Asian school retention rates remain low. Although the proportion of children starting school who reach the final year of a given level has risen markedly through the 2000s, retention rates at higher levels remain low in an absolute sense. The primary completion rate rose from 65.0 percent in 1999 to 85.0 percent in 2009 but it still trails the world average of 88.5 percent. Afghanistan, Bangladesh, Pakistan, and Nepal are unlikely to meet the education MDGs by 2015 (figure O.3).

The Growth of School Inputs

To increase school participation, most South Asian governments have given high priority to increasing education inputs in the past decade. Most countries in the region have devoted a large proportion of their budget to education—close to that observed in East Asia and in line with what is done in developed countries. Yet public spending as a percentage of gross domestic product (GDP) versus as a percentage of budget remains below the OECD average. For instance, in Bangladesh, Pakistan, and Sri Lanka, approximately 2 percent of GDP is spent

Figure O.3 Primary Completion Rates in South Asia
Percent

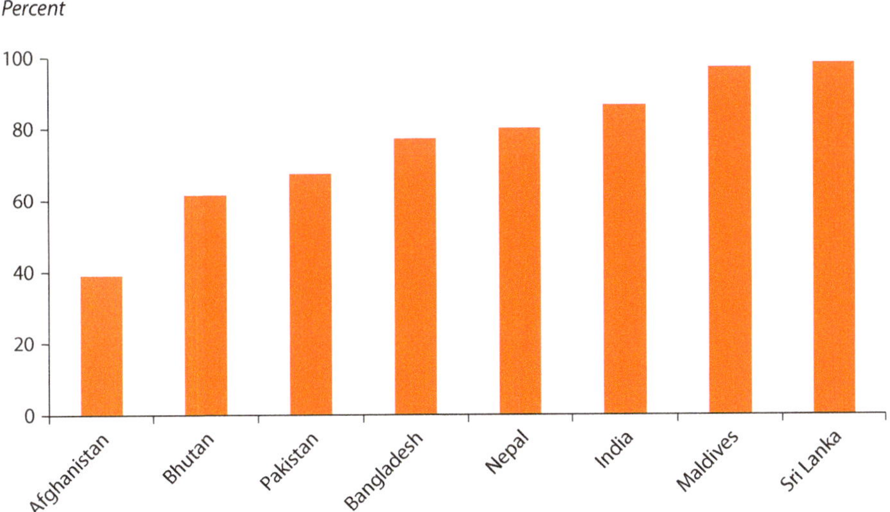

Source: UNESCO Institute for Statistics data as of 2012.

on education. Public financial constraints have been eased by increases in household spending and a rapid expansion of the private sector. In India, private spending on education increased from 5 percent of total spending in 2000 to 27 percent by 2005. Indeed, it is the combined efforts of the government and the private sector that has led to the recent impressive progress in access to education observed in the region.

Most South Asian countries have made demonstrable progress on providing two important educational inputs: school infrastructure and teachers. Because the primary concern of education policy in most of these countries has typically been to ensure access to schooling, investments in infrastructure and teachers have represented a high share of their education budgets for the past decade (see box O.4 for India). However, the quality of the learning environment in most countries is still poor by developed country standards and varies noticeably both between and within countries, with inadequate school infrastructure and poor conditions of facilities often reported. In 2011, the Bangladesh government reported that half the primary schools, government and nongovernment, had more than 56 students per class and lacked drinking water, toilets, and furniture.

The number of primary school teachers in South Asia has grown by more than 2 percent annually for the last decade. Yet it has barely kept pace with the growth in the number of students. The primary school pupil-teacher ratio (PTR) has held steady at about 40—nearly 1.5 times the global average of 24 pupils per teacher. The PTR varies from 12.7 in Maldives to 43.0 in Bangladesh, although it has declined in most countries over the decade. At the secondary level, the average regional PTR has declined from 34 in 2000 to 26 in 2010 but again shows wide variance within each country. Indeed, it is this wide variance that is cause for concern. Because deployment of teachers between schools varies

---

Box O.4 India's *Sarva Shiksha Abhiyan*: A Decade of Progress

In 2001, the Government of India launched the *Sarva Shiksha Abhiyan* (SSA, or education for all) to achieve universal elementary education. In 2009, the Indian Parliament passed the Right to Education (RTE) Act, guaranteeing free and compulsory education to all children ages 6–14 years. The RTE sets minimum school infrastructure standards (e.g., building, library, toilets, kitchen), pupil-teacher ratios, and teacher hours, in all of which there has been notable progress.

Both SSA and RTE have led to impressive increases in enrollment, in part because of significant increases in public spending for education. On average, 77 percent of the education budget is spent on teachers and management costs, and school infrastructure accounts for another 15 percent. In 2011–12, over 3.4 million teachers were trained and over 82.8 million children received free textbooks. As a result, the government has largely met its objective of ensuring access to elementary schools even in rural areas where, the government estimates, 99 percent of the population lives within one kilometer of a school. However, neither SSA nor RTE sets clear standards for learning.

---

widely, some schools, mainly in rural areas and low-income regions, have only one teacher, while urban schools and schools in better-off regions have many.

Several countries have also invested in other school inputs (e.g., textbooks and teaching materials, instructional technology, remedial education), as well as student-related inputs (e.g., midday meals, school health programs), often on the belief that they will improve the quality of education and the drawing power of schools. However, there are few data to examine trends in public spending on such inputs across the region.

These are considerable achievements in a short span of time, especially considering the scale and diversity of the education systems in the region. Nevertheless, while technical inputs are needed as enablers, the quality of learning outcomes depends largely on how they are used, how (and how regularly) classroom instruction is transacted, and whether learning outcomes are continually monitored to improve efficiency and modify processes. The overarching system of governance and accountability in the educational sector is also key; additional technical inputs can improve learning outcomes on a sustained basis only if educational authorities, schools, and teachers are accountable—and responsive—to student needs. For instance, no amount of textbooks and teaching materials will improve learning outcomes if teachers are frequently absent or disengaged.

Level of Learning Achievement and Trajectories

While much is known about patterns and trends in participation and completion, information on student learning is scarce. National learning assessments, in contrast to mass examinations, are relatively new in the region, and administration of tests, procedures, and practices is still evolving. Within the region, national assessments are not comparable,[7] and no South Asian country has participated in any major international achievement test, although two Indian states did participate on a pilot basis in OECD's PISA 2009+ test. The following is a summary of the main findings of the available assessments.

Student Achievement is Low

Student achievement levels are generally low throughout the region, except for Sri Lanka. A significant proportion of school leavers do not achieve minimum mastery of mathematics, reading, and language as defined by national governments. For example, in India, on a test of reading comprehension administered to grade 5 students across the country, only 46 percent of students were correctly able to identify the cause of an event (NCERT 2011). Only a third of students could compute the difference between two decimal numbers (NCERT 2011). Another recent study found that about 43 percent of grade 8 students could not solve a simple division problem. Even recognition of two-digit numbers, supposed to be taught in grade 2, tends to be achieved only by grade 4 or 5 (ASER-India 2011).

In Pakistan, the ASER 2011 assessment also found that arithmetic competence was very low in absolute terms (figure O.4). For instance, only 37 percent of grade 5 students in rural Pakistan could divide a three-digit by a single-digit number. By grade 8, only 72 percent could perform simple division.

Figure O.4 Proficiency in Arithmetic, Rural Pakistan, by Grade, 2011

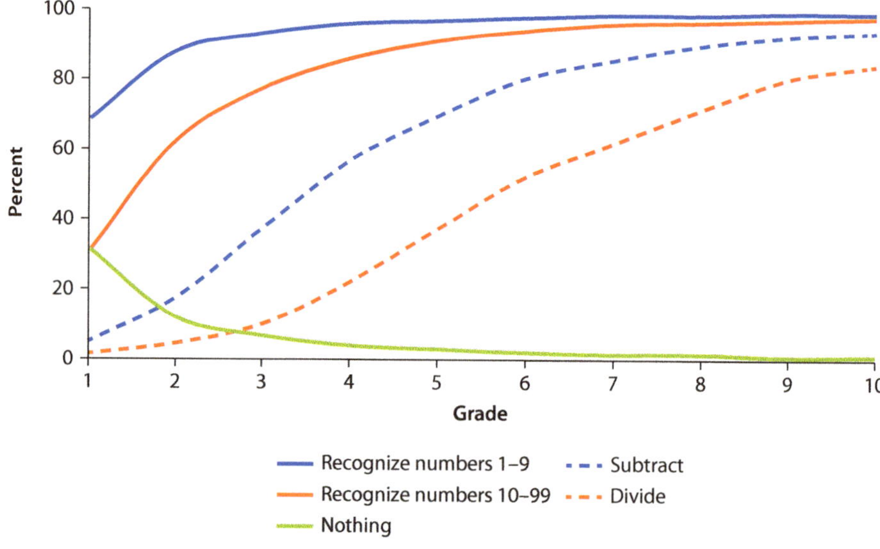

Source: ASER-India 2011.

As for reading, many students are three to four grades behind in grade-appropriate competencies. Understandably, comprehension and reading achievement are lower in English than in the mother tongue. Even in Sri Lanka, where achievement tends to be higher, fourth-grade students had a 14–18 percentage point deficit in English compared to first-language competence.

International Comparisons of Student Achievement Are Difficult

International comparisons of student achievement are difficult due to the lack of participation in international assessments. With the exception of two Indian states, Tamil Nadu and Himachal Pradesh, none of the South Asian countries have to date participated in any of the major international or regional assessments (Trends in Mathematics and Science Study [TIMSS], Progress in International Reading Literacy Study [PIRLS], or PISA), making it difficult to benchmark the intra- and interregional performance of South Asian countries. Most of the national learning assessments in South Asia do not permit comparison of achievement levels in the region against those in other countries because they are benchmarked to national curricular standards that vary from country to country.

However, recent efforts to pilot international tests and administer selected questions from those tests (e.g., a survey in Bangladesh and in two states in India) suggest that the region would probably rank in the bottom decile of participating countries. For example, Das and Zajonc (2010) compiled data from tests of grade 9 students from Odisha and Rajasthan in India using TIMSS mathematics questions. Students from both states ranked toward the bottom of a sample of 51 countries, and the states showed a high dispersion of test scores. Goyal and Pandey (2009) had similar results for student learning in India (albeit only in two states).

Likewise, Himachal Pradesh and Tamil Nadu, the two Indian states that participated in the PISA 2009+ test, had lower mean scores than any participating country in mathematics, reading, and scientific literacy, with the exception of the Kyrgyz Republic, doing worse than would be expected given their relatively high level of development.[8]

Learning Outcomes Tend to Be Unequal

Learning outcomes tend to be much more unequally distributed than school access or enrollment.[9] While enrollment gaps between disadvantaged groups and population averages have narrowed, learning gaps remain large. Learning gaps exist at the point of entry into the school system and grow over time. Large and growing learning gaps threaten the equity gains from wider enrollment because children who learn less are more likely to drop out.

Disparities in learning outcomes are especially pronounced depending on urban-rural residence and geographic location. In all South Asian countries, as would be expected, achievement in urban areas is typically higher than in rural areas, with the divide being wider in reading and languages than in mathematics. In some countries (e.g., India), the gap narrows with grade, but that could be explained by the selection of better-performing students into higher levels of schooling in both urban and rural areas. In general, there are also geographic disparities in achievement within each country, and these are frequently worse than rural-urban disparities. In India, for instance, achievement is higher in Kerala, Maharashtra, and Karnataka and lower in Rajasthan and Madhya Pradesh. In Pakistan, students in Balochistan and Sindh score lower on achievement than in Islamabad and Khyber Pakhtunkhwa. In Bangladesh, Barisal and Khulna divisions generally have the highest achievement and Sylhet the lowest. In Nepal, students in the Central Region typically learn more than those in the Far-Western Region. In Sri Lanka, the Western and North Western provinces generally have the highest student achievement and the Eastern Province the lowest. In general, geographical locations with lower income levels tend to have lower student achievement.

Student Achievement Varies

Student achievement varies considerably within countries in South Asia; only a few students can meet international standards. Although mean student achievement levels are low, variance is high within countries, with a number of students either meeting or surpassing international standards. This inconsistency in achievement appears greater in South Asia than in other regions. Evidence from India suggests two different views of the learning distribution: On the one hand, the top pupils in South Asia are able to perform as well as the best students worldwide despite the low mean achievement in the region. For instance, Das and Zajonc (2010) found that 9 percent of students in Odisha state met the "high" learning mathematics benchmark established by the TIMSS (more than in South Africa, Indonesia, the Philippines, and Chile). Because of its large population, if India were added to the TIMSS sample (and if the performance of students in Rajasthan and Odisha were representative of the country), India would have the fifth-largest cohort of grade 9 students passing the advanced benchmark set by TIMSS (after Japan; the United States; the Republic of Korea; and Taiwan, China). On the other hand, South Asia has a much larger number of 14-year-old students who cannot meet the lowest international benchmarks. Das and Zajonc (2010) estimated that this is true of 50 percent of the students in Odisha. Thus, if India were part of the TIMSS sample, it would have more than 18 million 14-year-old children who would not be enrolled or would fail to meet international math benchmarks.

One explanation for student achievement being relatively low over the last five years is the expansion in schooling access that took place during this period. Much of this growth occurred because of the entry into schools of disadvantaged and previously out-of-school children, who typically have far lower levels of achievement than those from mainstream groups. It is likely that their increased participation might have pulled down the average student achievement rate. Indeed, in India, while enrollment rates of all children ages 6–10 years rose by 4.7 percentage points between 2005 and 2010, enrollment rates of children from scheduled castes and scheduled tribes rose by 6.6 percentage points (household survey data).

In summary, most South Asian countries have made significant progress in achieving their quantitative enrollment goals, especially in primary education, but the quality of education as measured by learning outcomes remains low in absolute terms (measured by the competencies children demonstrate in school) and relative to other regions—not only OECD countries, but also emerging economies in East Asia, such as Shanghai, China.

A Closer Look at Student Learning in South Asia

The conceptual framework for analyzing learning outcomes used in this report is summarized in figure O.5. Educational systems use a set of policy inputs that include early-childhood interventions (e.g., preschool and early nutrition programs); school inputs (e.g., teacher quantity and quality, curriculum, classroom

Figure O.5 Conceptual Framework for Improving Learning Outcomes

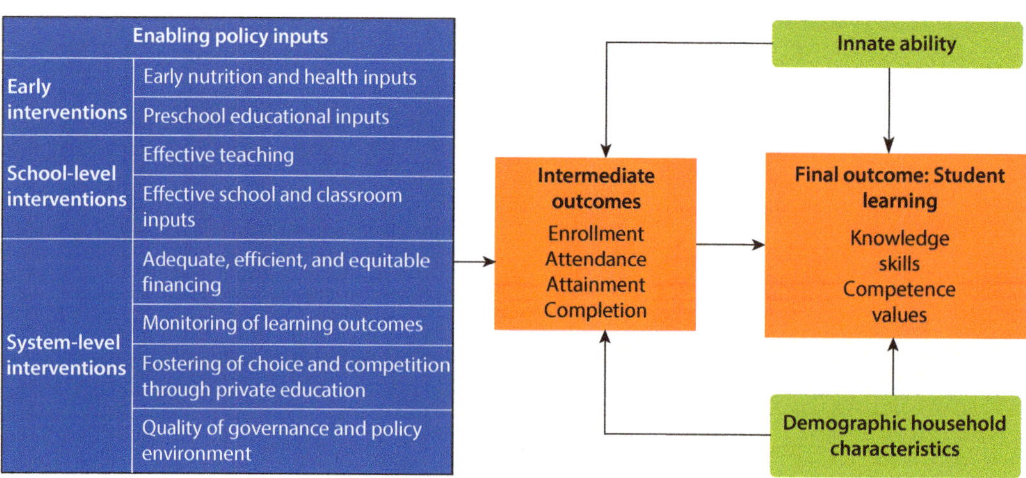

practices, etc.); and system-level reforms (e.g., standards, finance, learning assessments, and governance) to produce intermediate outcomes, typically measured by school enrollment, attendance, attainment, and completion rates. The policy inputs, along with individual and household factors (such as gender, income, and parental education) and innate student ability, "produce" student outcomes, such as knowledge, skills, and values. (Household factors and innate ability also influence the intermediate outcomes.) The combination of inputs produces longer-term individual outcomes (not shown in figure O.5), measured by productivity, labor market performance, social behavior, and civic participation. The relationship between inputs, outputs, and outcomes is complex; it is often confounded by factors that can interact in complex ways, sometimes reinforcing and sometimes offsetting each other. Treating any single input as synonymous with quality is erroneous and can be misleading.

The Role of Demographic and Household Characteristics

As elsewhere, in South Asia parental schooling is a strong predictor of student achievement. Well-educated parents reflect the value placed on schooling and knowledge in a family, which is likely to be transmitted to children. They also offer their children advantages in terms of motivation, encouragement, and assistance with studies and homework.

With few exceptions, family income heavily influences student achievement. Poverty is a pervasive barrier to both attendance and learning, and children from the poorest families tend to drop out early. Moreover, achievement of the richest quintile of students is three to four times higher than for the poorest (figure O.6). Children from affluent households have a more supportive home

Figure O.6 Ability to Divide, Children Ages 8–11 Years, by Age and Per Capita Consumption Expenditure Quintile, India, 2005

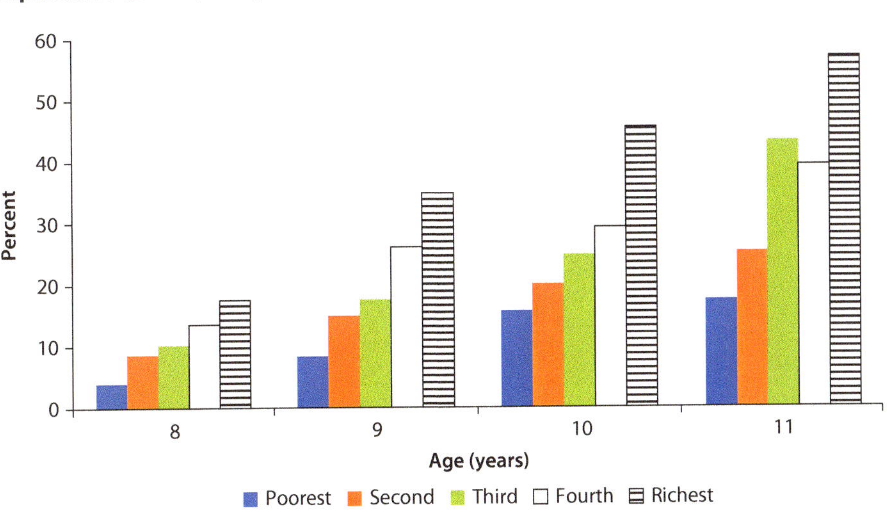

Source: Data from the India Human Development Survey 2005.

learning environment; they have easier access to achievement-enhancing inputs, such as textbooks and private tuition; and they typically have access to better-quality schools.

Gender constrains not only school participation but also learning, causing substandard learning outcomes for girls, especially those from rural areas, low socioeconomic backgrounds, or conflict areas. For example, girls are more likely to enroll in, and more likely to drop out from, poor-quality schools (Lewis and Lockheed 2007). Indeed, South Asia is unlike much of the rest of the world, where girls typically outperform boys. Although it is difficult to generalize because of the heterogeneity of experience, achievement tends to be higher among male than female students, particularly in mathematics and science but also often in reading and languages (Bangladesh and Sri Lanka being exceptions). It is likely that the resources and home study environment for girls is less conducive to academic achievement; for instance, girls may be responsible for household chores and not able to allocate as much time to studies and homework (Aslam 2009).

School Environment Is More Important

In South Asia, compared to other regions, school environment is more important than socioeconomic background in explaining student achievement. International evidence shows that with economic growth, the quality of a nation's schools typically becomes more homogenous (perhaps because governments become better at enforcing minimum learning standards), which in turn implies that in more developed economies, learning variations are mostly the result of differences in student and household backgrounds. In South Asia, as elsewhere, variables such as parental schooling, household income, and social status influence student achievement. Nevertheless, there is evidence that a larger share of the variation in student test scores (about one-half to two-thirds) in the region can be attributed to between-school variations arising from the presence and performance of teachers, school resources, and other school-specific factors. This share is considerably higher than is typical in other regions. It also suggests that improving school quality can have large effects on student learning. Much of the rest of this overview summarizes ways in which public policy can improve school quality.

Addressing Disadvantages before School: Early Childhood Development

ECD interventions promote school readiness, higher completion rates, and better school attainment (Heckman 2000).[10] ECD interventions range from nutrition and health care to cognitive stimulation through parental interaction and preschool programs. International evidence suggests that ECD is a cost-effective investment to improve the quality and efficiency of elementary education, help students progress at the secondary level, and promote the student's ultimate success in the labor market. A five-country study, including a birth cohort of Indians tracked since 1969, estimated that an increase of 1 standard deviation in weight gain in the first two years of life was associated with 0.43 more years of schooling, but weight gain between ages two and four years had no such association

(Martorell et al. 2010). Another longitudinal study of a large group of Filipino children found that a 0.6 standard deviation increase in height resulted in almost 12 additional months of schooling (Glewwe 2002). Economic returns from effective ECD programs could also include cost savings due to lower drop-out and repetition rates; less need for remedial programs in primary school and beyond; and possible long-term effects, such as reduced inequality and delinquency. Additionally, because ECD interventions start early, they have the potential to play an important equity-enhancing role (Cunha and Heckman 2007).

ECD programs in South Asia vary greatly, from informal day care to formal preschools. From a survey of preschools in South Asia, certain patterns emerge:

- Enrollment in preschool is low (only about 15 percent in Bangladesh and India).
- The income or wealth disparity in preschool is greater than in primary school.
- There is almost no consensus among policy makers on what constitutes a quality preschool program.
- There are more gaps in data on preschool enrollment than on primary school enrollment, partly because private and informal preschools are not always tracked in national systems, and there is no consensus on what constitutes a preschool.

Although the educational component in ECD programs can play a significant role in a student's later life development, given the paucity of data designing an effective and scalable preschool education program in South Asia is a considerably complex task. In contrast, evidence on the effectiveness of nutritional supplements in the region is more robust, and interventions focused on this aspect are easier to design and deliver.

In South Asia, early childhood nutrition programs can play an important role in determining a child's cognitive development and school readiness. The incidence of infants weighing less than 2,500 grams at birth is higher in South Asia than even in considerably poorer sub-Saharan Africa. South Asia has the highest rates in the world of low birth weight, infant and child malnutrition, and micronutrient deficiencies. Each year, there are about 18 million low-birthweight newborns in the world; more than half are in South Asia, and India alone accounts for 40 percent of all low-birthweight newborns worldwide. Moreover, a large proportion of children ages 0–5 years are underweight or stunted in South Asia (see figure O.7). India, Bangladesh, Nepal, and Pakistan have the largest proportion of children who are underweight. A larger number of children in the region, therefore, start schooling with a disadvantage. There is wide consensus in the literature on best-practices investments in child health and nutrition that governments in South Asia need to make.

Rather than immediately expanding preprimary schooling and early childhood education, what is needed is to target early nutrition to children from disadvantaged backgrounds and to make such programs more efficient. Nepal's recent Community Action for Nutrition Project (*Sunaula Hazar Din*) is based on

Figure O.7 Low-Birthweight Infants, by Region, 2006–10
Percent

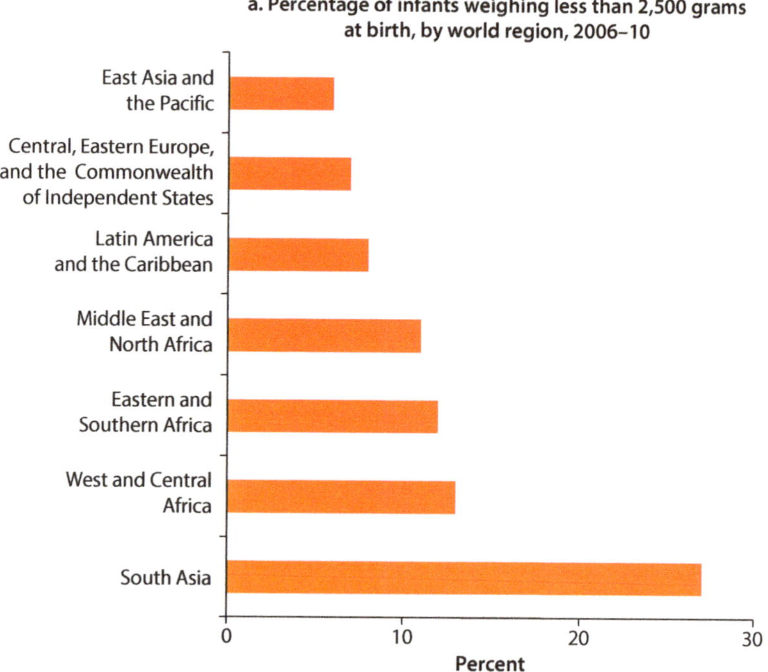

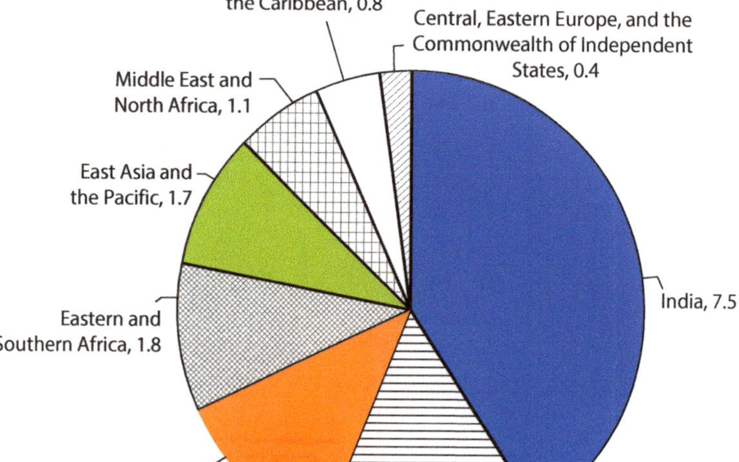

Source: UNICEF data, as reported in http://www.childinfo.org/low_birthweight_status_trends.html.

a holistic life-cycle approach, targeting specific age groups, so that children are born healthy and receive key nutritional supplements in the first 1,000 days of life. The project not only targets children ages 0–24 months and their caregivers but also girls and young women, pregnant women, and those who may want to become pregnant in the next six months. It also includes community-wide nutrition-related interventions, such as hygiene, safe drinking water, and sanitation. Holistic approaches such as this, targeting children before they are born and before they are in school, are likely to enhance the effectiveness of public expenditure on school education.

School-Level Interventions

Effective teachers have consistently been shown to be the most important factor in student learning (Hanushek and Rivkin 2010). While the quality of education is likely affected by other school-related factors as well (facilities, textbooks, and so forth), improving teaching has repeatedly been shown to be the most effective way to raise school quality (Glewwe and Kremer 2006). Improving teacher effectiveness has traditionally been addressed by hiring more teachers in proportion to the number of students so as to reduce class size, thereby allowing teachers to devote more time per student. It has also been achieved by targeting interventions aimed at raising the quality of the teaching force, whether through better training or through incentives.

Numbers of Teachers

Policy makers often view the lack of teachers as one of the main causes of bad teaching.[11] Hiring more teachers per student or, equivalently, reducing class size is believed to improve learning outcomes in two ways: (a) smaller classes may allow teachers to give each student more individual attention and (b) smaller classes can reduce the probability of disruptive students inhibiting learning. In South Asia, the average primary school PTR of about 40 to 1 is still fairly high compared to the international average[12] and has remained stagnant for the past decade. Despite robust teacher recruitment, staffing has barely kept pace with growth in the student population, and many governments have plans to further reduce the PTR. For example, the Indian Right to Education (RTE) Act stipulates a maximum PTR ratio of 30 to 1 in primary schools.

Given the cost implications of hiring more teachers, measuring the impact of the PTR on student learning has been the subject of intense debate in both developed and developing countries. International evidence points to a weak negative correlation between class size and student achievement. In a meta-analysis of school resources and outcomes in developing countries, Glewwe et al. (2011) found that reducing class size frequently leads to an improvement in student learning (as would be expected), but the gain tends to be statistically insignificant. They also found evidence of a reduction in class size worsening student achievement.

In South Asia, the issue of class size differs from that in most countries by an order of magnitude. In this region, the debate is not about reducing class size from 25 students to 20 but from 100 students to less than 40. Two experimental evaluations provide indirect evidence, albeit in opposite directions, about the impact of class size on learning outcomes at the primary level. In the first experiment, children with low test scores were taken outside the regular classroom for remedial instruction by a volunteer. The experiment (Banerjee et al. 2007) showed that, while the test scores of these children went up significantly, there was no impact on the test scores of the students who remained in the original classroom, although the class size was now smaller. In another experiment in Andhra Pradesh, Muralidharan and Sundararaman (2013) found that students in schools that had an extra contract teacher scored 0.16 standard deviations higher in math and 0.15 standard deviations higher in language tests at the end of the two-year experiment. They also estimated that reducing school-level PTR by half with an extra contract teacher would improve average test scores by 0.27 standard deviations. Their findings suggest, however, that the effect of class size declines as the grade level rises. Small classes may mainly matter in the initial years of schooling.

Focusing on reducing the average class size hides the fact that there are enormous disparities in the PTR between schools: some schools (especially in urban areas and in better-off regions) have many more teachers than needed and others (particularly in rural areas and in poor regions) have only a single teacher for several classes. Research suggests that teachers, who prefer schools with better working conditions and in more habitable locations, will attempt to transfer to such schools using informal means and circumventing procedure (Béteille 2009; Sharma and Ramachandran 2009). This creates vacancies in the schools teachers want to leave, most of which are located in remote and poor areas. Policy should therefore focus on ensuring that teacher redeployment policies are designed and implemented in a manner that ensures each individual school has the teachers it needs.

Teacher Quality

Raising teacher quality is perhaps the single most significant way to improve learning outcomes, and its benefits are expected to translate into national economic gains. Estimating the economic value of higher teacher quality in the United States, Hanushek (2011) found that a teacher who is 1 standard deviation above mean teacher effectiveness would generate annual marginal gains of US$400,000 in terms of the present value of future student earnings—and potentially more when other conditions change. He also suggests that replacing the bottom 5–8 percent of teachers with "average-quality" teachers could move the United States to near the top in international rankings in mathematics and science achievement. While no such calculations exist for South Asia, the economic value of better teacher quality is bound to be large because the role of teachers is magnified when children are first-generation schoolgoers and home inputs are limited.

In South Asia, much of the concern about poor learning outcomes has centered on the corrosion of teacher quality, yet measuring it is difficult. The common thinking in education policy in South Asia and elsewhere is that teacher quality is reflected in their qualifications, training, and experience. Most policy discussions about improving teacher quality, therefore, focus on hiring more qualified teachers and improving the amount of training. Salary scales are also based on these characteristics. Although it seems reasonable to think that qualifications and experience are good indicators of quality, the consensus in international research and research in South Asia is that these characteristics seldom predict teacher effectiveness in raising student achievement (see Pandey, Goyal, and Sundararaman 2008; Kingdon and Teal 2010 for India; Aslam and Kingdon 2011 for Pakistan; Aturupane, Glewwe, and Wisniewski 2013 for Sri Lanka).

If standard "resume characteristics" are not good predictors of student learning, what is it about a teacher that matters most for student learning? Why are teachers with more human capital (measured by education, training, and experience) not necessarily more effective? One possible explanation is that teacher training is of poor quality and does not transmit the knowledge and skills teachers need. A related reason may be that teachers lack interest and motivation in being actively engaged in ensuring that their students learn. In turn, this lack of motivation and interest may arise from the weak accountability structure in the public education sector and limited opportunities for career progression. Evidence from South Asia gives validity to both possibilities.

Teacher subject knowledge and pedagogical skills need substantial improvement. Research has highlighted the criticality of a teacher's mastery of the subject being taught. This need not be reflected through teachers' formal qualifications. For example, Metzler and Woessmann (2012) have shown that a 1 standard deviation increase in teacher achievement increases student achievement by one-tenth of a standard deviation. Aslam and Kingdon (2011) also found that in Pakistan, government school teachers with higher scores on achievement tests are better at imparting learning to students.

Evidence from South Asia suggests that teacher subject knowledge is low and needs substantial improvement (box O.5). Many South Asian teachers barely know more than their students. For example, surveys from India and Pakistan show that teachers performed poorly in math and language tests based on the primary curriculum they are supposed to teach. Similarly, a survey of government primary schools in Bangladesh found that only about 54 percent of teachers answered a short math test correctly. Low teacher competencies translate into low student learning. Plotting average student performance by class against teacher performance in Bangladesh shows that students taught by teachers with less subject knowledge perform worse than students taught by teachers with more subject knowledge (World Bank 2013). Students often sense when teachers do not know the subject well. One study shows that students think roughly 30 percent of their teachers are not knowledgeable because they cannot give specific examples to explain the topic or answer students' questions (CAMPE 2007).

In addition to subject knowledge, strong pedagogical skills are crucial for effective student-teacher transactions. Studies from South Asia show that teachers employ poor pedagogical practices, focusing on teacher-centric activities rather

Box O.5 Teacher Competency in Language and Mathematics, India and Pakistan

In India, teachers in both Bihar and Uttar Pradesh on average scored only 47.2 percent correctly on math tests and 64.9 percent correctly on language tests based on the primary curriculum they are supposed to teach (Banerji and Kingdon 2010). Figure BO.5.1 shows average scores by teacher type in the two states. Teacher competency was further examined by the total score from three parts: content knowledge, ability to explain topics simply, and ability to spot children's mistakes in written work. In both language and math, teachers were quite capable of spotting student mistakes but had less content knowledge and were also less able to explain content to students.

In Pakistan, many of the same questions were posed to both students and teachers, and while 82 percent of the teachers could explain long division correctly, only 33 percent of the students could do so. Similarly, while 64 percent of the teachers could explain the meanings of difficult words, only 11 percent of the children could do so. In a significant proportion of cases, teachers themselves are not competent to teach the curriculum. For example, only 36 percent of the teachers were able to explain two-digit addition.

In secondary education in Bangladesh, students and teachers were tested using common test items as part of the Secondary Education Quality and Access Enhancement Project baseline study. Although teachers generally performed better than students on the same questions, a number of teachers did not (Figure BO.5.2). On 16 mathematical test items that were the same for grade 8 students and their teachers, the teachers scored an average of 66.8 percent and students 33.4 percent. While 15 percent of the students scored more than 50 percent, 21 percent of teachers scored less than 50 percent on exactly the same test items.

Figure BO.5.1 Teacher Scores in Bihar and Uttar Pradesh

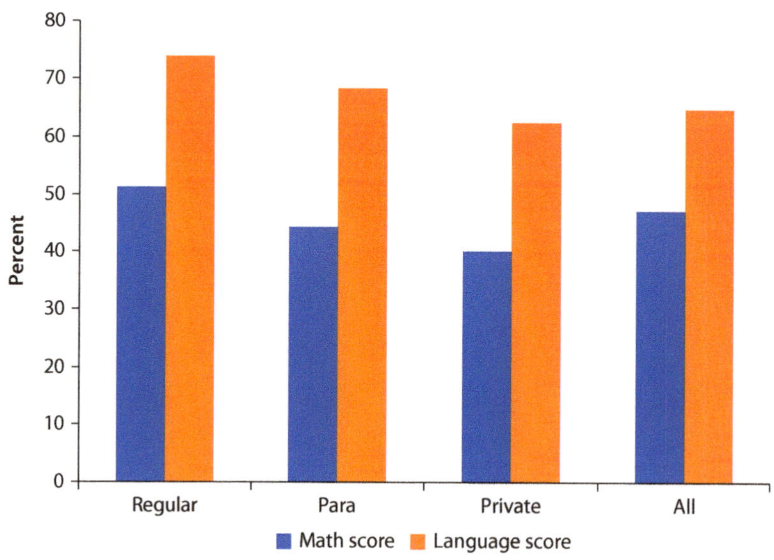

Source: Data from India SchoolTELLS Survey.

box continues next page

Box O.5 Teacher Competency in Language and Mathematics, India and Pakistan *(continued)*

Figure BO.5.2 Bangladeshi Teacher and Student Scores on a Common Test
Percent

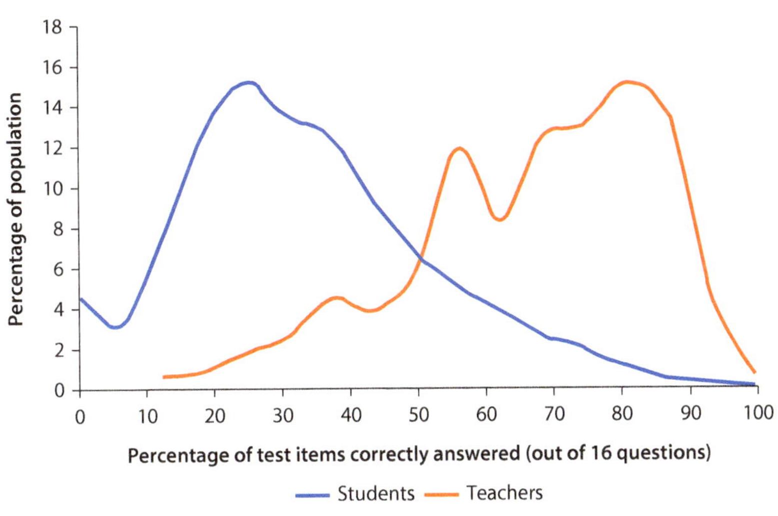

Source: World Bank 2013.

than dialoguing with students and undertaking student-centric activities (Sankar 2009; Jhingran 2012).

Careful attention to teacher development through well-designed preservice and in-service training programs is crucial. The average quality of preservice teacher training in South Asia is poor. The curriculum taught to teachers in South Asia is often outdated and delivered through lectures, an approach that teachers replicate in their own classrooms. Even when the teacher training curriculum is not outdated, trainers often lack innovation and fail to pass on key messages. Universal standards and competencies are not at the core of the process. Ultimately, this translates into poor classroom practices.

Training programs in many South Asian countries also tend to be short, and opportunities for practice teaching before acquiring a teaching degree are virtually nonexistent. For instance, in Pakistan, until recently it used to take only a year (with frequent holidays) to qualify to teach primary school. Similarly, in Bangladesh, primary school teachers were required only to have completed grade 10 or 12 and the one-year certificate in education. In Nepal, a one-year teacher preparation course is required in addition to the minimum academic qualification, which is a higher secondary degree to teach in primary school and a master's in education to teach in secondary school. In-service training programs in the region are also brief, as short as seven days a year in some instances in Pakistan. Since it is usually not considered mandatory and participation in training does not affect promotion or career development, teachers attach little value to it.

Box O.6 Teacher Development through Peer Support in Shanghai, China

In Shanghai, China, the quality of teaching rests on government policies aimed to attract the best into teaching, policies that match teacher skills to student needs, and mentoring of new teachers. The government attracts the best into the profession through targeted scholarship programs, with an assignment system whereby teachers and principals are assigned to those schools where they are most needed. This is combined with a school accountability mechanism focusing on low-performing schools. Professional communities play an important role in supporting teachers to improve instruction, monitoring teaching and learning, and motivating teachers to perform well. Teaching study groups bring together teachers in the same subject and level so that they can jointly plan their lessons. Workloads are structured so that teachers can regularly observe their peers during actual lessons. Novice teachers are supported by master teachers during their first year of classroom experience and can observe more seasoned instructors to learn from them through apprenticeships. The underlying theory of action in Shanghai is that no individual teacher is perfect, but that capable teachers can help each other improve. In this way, the government creates the mechanisms for teachers to support their peers and holds them accountable, but rarely intervenes directly.

Source: World Bank 2012b.

New teachers in the region receive very little support on the job. This is in stark contrast to well-performing systems such as that in Shanghai, China (box O.6). According to a USAID assessment of teacher training in Pakistan, there is hardly any supervision or guidance of novice teachers, and "practical teaching" is not accorded importance. Moreover, supervisors and others with guidance roles are often appointed from among a cadre of teachers with little if any management training or experience. Sometimes, supervisory duties are assigned along with other work, leading to overburdening and inefficiencies. Although head teachers are meant to monitor and supervise school teachers, across the region they have virtually no power to recruit, transfer, hire, and fire them. Such decisions are centralized for regular government school teachers, provincially or at the district rather than the school level.

Improving the quality of preservice and in-service training will require more focus on student-centric methods and greater coordination across programs. The inferior quality of teacher training across the region cannot be attributed to an absence of the requisite infrastructure. South Asian countries have well-established teacher training institutions and systems, ranging from purpose-built institutes and colleges to university departments offering education diplomas and degrees. In Bangladesh, for instance, there is a training system that runs all the way from university down to a cluster of schools in the village. For most South Asian countries, the problem lies more in a lack of coordination in developing a coherent teacher training program that meets minimum standards for the country as a whole. Programs have arisen piecemeal, leading to overlaps, duplication, and gaps.

In addition to poor preparation and mentoring, lack of motivation and effort, as demonstrated by the high rates of teacher absenteeism in the region, also affect teacher effectiveness.[13] Surveys in India found teacher absenteeism rates of 26.3 percent in rural India in 2003. These rates had fallen only slightly by 2.7 percentage points in 2010, although states vary, with some (Himachal Pradesh and Madhya Pradesh) registering sharp increases and others (Chhattisgarh and Punjab) registering sharp falls (Muralidharan and Sundararaman 2013). Surveys in Pakistan found that 11 percent of the teachers in rural Punjab, were absent on any given day (Banerji and Kingdon 2010). Most nonattendance was unexplained, and illness accounted for the majority of absences that were explained.

Such high rates of teacher absenteeism present a fundamental barrier to student learning by increasing unplanned multigrade teaching and by reducing the stability of the teacher-student relationship. They also engender inequity in educational access and outcomes, since schools with more low-income and poorly performing students also tend to suffer from higher rates of teacher absenteeism (Clotfelter, Ladd, and Vigdor 2006; Miller, Murnane, and Willett 2007). Implications for learning are severe: Das et al. 2007 found that, in Pakistan, a 5 percent increase in teacher absences reduced student learning achievement by 4–8 percent. Other studies in India (Kremer et al. 2005; Kingdon and Sipahimalani-Rao 2010; Duflo, Hanna, and Ryan 2012) report similar results. Even when they are in school, teachers spend much of their time on activities other than active teaching.

Effective policy options to address teacher motivation and effort include

- *Transparent, merit-based procedures for appointment of teachers:* Several countries are experimenting with recruitment based on rigorous testing and safeguards against patronage-based recruitment in order to improve the quality of their teaching force (box O.7).

- *Clear and transparent policies for deployment, transfers, and postings of teachers:* Given the importance of working conditions for teachers, countries need to design redeployment policies that balance the amount of time teachers spend in postings with superior working conditions and those with inferior working conditions.

- *Career progression structures:* Career progression in South Asia is based upon years of service and provides individual teachers with little opportunity to move into administrative or leadership roles. The absence of opportunities for teachers to develop as professionals in South Asia stymies the potential of talented teachers and demotivates them. Countries that perform well in student learning, such as Singapore, pay special attention to providing teachers with multiple options for rising in the profession (box O.8).

- *Rewards for good performance and penalties for poor performance:* Emerging evidence from the region suggests that rewards for good performance can be effective in generating greater accountability and teacher effort. However, the

Box O.7 Preventing Patronage-Based Recruitment in Bangladesh and Pakistan

In Bangladesh, school management committees (SMCs) recruited secondary school teachers from recognized nongovernment schools, but lack of monitoring capacity and inadequate parental and community participation in SMCs led to frequent violation of hiring practices. Because schools need funds for operating costs, poor but well-qualified applicants were often overlooked in favor of candidates who could help finance the school. Schools were also pressured to appoint relatives of SMC members or powerful members of the community. In 2005, Bangladesh established an independent National Teacher Registration and Certification Authority (NTRCA) that uses a standardized and transparent procedure to accredit potential teachers; candidates for teaching positions must be accredited.

Patronage-based recruitment was also a longstanding problem in Sindh, Pakistan, where the academic and professional credentials of prospective teachers were often questionable because of skepticism about the quality and integrity of Sindh's certifying institutions. To improve the quality of new hires and reduce political interference, in 2009 the province introduced a policy of recruitment based on transparent and merit-based criteria, including a written examination administered by a third party. Since then, 13,000 new teachers have been placed on fixed-term, school-specific contracts. An independent survey suggests that the new teachers have less absenteeism on average than older teachers.

design of the incentive or reward system is critical (Bruns, Filmer, and Patrinos 2011). A four-year experiment in Andhra Pradesh, India (box O.9), and policies adopted in Brazil, Chile, and Mexico could provide guidance for designing effective incentive and promotion structures.

School and Student Inputs and Classroom Practices

An implicit assumption in most educational policy discussions is that school resources matter for student achievement and can to some extent offset socioeconomic disadvantages. As a result, most South Asian countries have substantially increased their spending on construction and rehabilitation of school facilities and on school and student inputs.

School facilities and infrastructure. Though investment in school facilities is likely to attract and retain children, there is little evidence that, by itself, such investment improves learning. Because the primary concern of education policy in developing countries has typically been to ensure access, investments in infrastructure have taken up a high share of education budgets in recent decades.[14] Access remains an issue in some parts of South Asia, and the pressure of rising enrollment and insufficient quality control and attention to maintenance have left significant needs unmet. For example, in 2011 the Bangladesh government reported that half of primary schools, government and nongovernment, had more than 56 students per class and lacked drinking water, toilets, and furniture.

Box O.8 Impact of Performance Pay on Student Outcomes in South Asia

Kingdon and Teal (2010) and Muralidharan and Sundararaman (2009) provide evidence of the impact of teacher performance on student outcomes in India. The former study, in Uttar Pradesh, found that private schools relate pay to teacher performance as measured by student achievement and that achievement is improved by increasing teacher salaries. Interpreting this as evidence of an efficiency-wage pay structure in Indian private schooling, the authors suggest that linking performance to pay may be an effective way to elicit greater teacher effort and thus better student outcomes.

The study by Muralidharan and Sundararaman (2009, 2011) is based on an experiment conducted in 500 rural government schools in Andhra Pradesh with a student population of 50,000 in grades 1–5. Four different approaches to improving learning were tried: two incentive schemes (an individual teacher bonus and a group teacher bonus) and two input schemes (provision of an additional contract teacher and of a block grant to the school). The experiment also included a comparison group of 100 schools. Two years after the experiment began, all four schemes had improved student learning. However, students in schools with performance incentives for teachers performed significantly better than those without, by 0.28 standard deviations in math and 0.16 in language tests. Incentive schools also showed better performance in subjects for which there were no bonuses, suggesting positive spillover effects. In the first year, the team-incentive and individual-incentive schools performed equally well but, in the second year, the latter schools outperformed the former. Incentive schools also performed better than schools that received additional schooling inputs of the same value. It was also found that combining incentives with training and improved inputs also increases teacher effectiveness.

Box O.9 Career Progression for Teachers: The Case of Singapore

Singapore's Education Service Professional Development and Career Plan (Edu-Pac) is designed to help teachers develop their potential to the maximum. It has three parts: a career path, recognition through monetary rewards, and an evaluation system. The program provides for teachers with different aspirations by promoting three tracks. The Teaching Track allows teachers to continue in the classroom while advancing to the new level of Master Teacher. The Leadership Track gives teachers opportunities to take on leadership positions in schools and at ministry headquarters. The Senior Specialist Track allows teachers to move to ministry headquarters to become part of a "strong core of specialists with deep knowledge and skills in specific areas in education that will break new ground and keep Singapore at the leading edge." Each teacher's performance is monitored through the Enhanced Performance Management System, which incorporates planning (for teaching goals, innovations instruction, school improvements, and personal and professional development); regular support and coaching; and an intensive performance evaluation. The evaluation leads to a performance grade, which is linked directly to the annual bonus of the teacher and to promotion decisions.

Source: OECD 2013.

In the Sindh province of Pakistan, the government introduced a new mechanism to prioritize the rehabilitation of schools in 2009 and ensure that all new construction follows quality and functionality standards. In coming years, substantial resources are again likely to be spent on facilitating access to school and on infrastructure.

While such investments may be required to make schools more attractive, it is uncertain whether they will improve learning outcomes on their own. A number of cross-sectional studies (Glewwe and Kremer 2006; Dreze and Kingdon 2001; Aturupane Glewwe, and Wisniewski 2013) have found that indicators of the quality of physical facilities are associated with higher enrollment and higher test scores, but the results may be confounded by omitted variables. Other studies (Borkum, He, and Linden 2012; Muralidharan and Zieleniak 2012)[15] have found no evidence of impact on learning outcomes, even though the quality of infrastructure improved significantly during the period under study.

There may be several reasons for the lack of solid evidence that school infrastructure matters to learning outcomes: infrastructure (for example, toilets) may be built but not always used (Accountability Initiative 2012). Availability of better-quality infrastructure may make the school more appealing but leave teaching and learning processes unchanged. Importantly, impact may take a while to show. Thus, the evidence should not be interpreted as suggesting that investments in infrastructure and its maintenance should not be made. Such investments are likely to be important for attracting and retaining children in schools, although they seem unlikely to have a significant impact on improving learning levels on their own.

Textbooks, teaching materials, and other student inputs. What is learned in South Asian schools is not usually relevant. A great deal of the knowledge imparted to students is "procedural"—rote based—and because students do not understand what they are being taught, they cannot answer questions that deviate even slightly from what was presented in class. Students are also not prepared in practical competencies, such as measurement, problem solving, and writing meaningful and grammatically correct sentences, all of which are important in the real world. Even in Sri Lanka, where achievement levels are relatively high, students have difficulty expressing their thoughts in writing.

Textbooks are the main instructional materials in South Asia but do not meet learning needs. Although many countries have made progress toward timely delivery of textbooks, they often arrive in bad condition and are poorly designed in terms of the scope of subject matter to be taught and the sequence of instruction. In Bangladesh, India, and Pakistan, for instance, textbooks lack substance to reinforce development of problem-solving skills and critical thinking (Banu 2009; Jhingran 2012). Textbooks tend to be targeted toward the needs of well-performing students, leaving the needs of other students unmet. Further, most textbooks require little more than memorization of problem solutions (as in mathematics) and little engagement with real-life problems. Instead of discouraging a culture of rote learning, textbooks in South Asia reinforce that culture.

Teaching materials, such as textbooks, can have a positive impact on student learning, subject to certain conditions (Moulin, Kremer, and Glewwe 2009). The first is that books and learning materials reach intended beneficiaries by the beginning of the school year. Most South Asian countries now meet this condition. Sri Lanka has a long-standing multibook policy that ensures that all students have textbooks, and it relies on private publication of competing textbooks to increase quality and reduce costs. Bangladesh and Pakistan have recently addressed administrative inefficiencies and are improving monitoring to ensure timely distribution. In Afghanistan, however, although the distribution of textbooks has improved significantly, poor storage conditions and discrepancies between books needed and received remain problems.

A second condition is that households do not react to an increase in public spending on textbooks and learning materials by reducing their own spending on education and diverting their resources to other household needs. Recent research has shown that the impact of increased public provision can be offset by a reduction in family spending, leaving the net effect close to zero (see box O.10). Accounting for household re-optimization in response to public spending programs is thus important when considering this type of expenditure.

A third factor that can reduce the impact of additional learning materials is how well students read. If their reading level is too low, children may not be able to use textbooks effectively (Moulin, Kremer, and Glewwe 2009). Indeed, what this often means is that increasing textbook availability improves learning only among higher-income students, because these students are more likely to have

---

Box O.10 Public Student Inputs, Household Expenditures, and Learning Outcomes

Das et al. (2013) present evidence of the impact of a school grant that stipulated that funds be spent on inputs for direct student use. In the two-year program in the Indian state of Andhra Pradesh, the spending categories were books, stationery, and writing materials (~50 percent); workbooks and practice books (~20 percent); and classroom materials (~25 percent). They found that the program had a significant positive impact on student test scores at the end of the first year but virtually none in the second year; the cumulative two-year effect was positive but not significant. Households had sharply reduced their own spending on the education of their children in the second year.

Thus, when the program was unanticipated, there was a net increase in materials, which translated into significant improvements in test scores, but when parents became aware of the program, they reduced their own spending, and learning levels plateaued.

Sankar (2012), in an analysis of out-of-pocket household spending on education in India (using National Sample Survey 52nd- and 74th-round data), found that expenditures on children who attend government primary schools declined in real terms between 1995–96 and 2007–08, especially spending on transportation, textbooks, and stationery. This corresponded to a period of increased government spending on textbooks and ease of access to schools.

---

literate parents who can support their learning at home. Textbooks, therefore, need to be at a level where they can be pitched effectively to all students, especially those with illiterate parents.

School feeding programs are popular with South Asian policy makers but mostly function as social protection programs that improve school attendance. Large-scale school feeding programs have been implemented in both India (the Midday Meal Scheme [MDMS]) and Bangladesh (the Food for Education Program) over the past 10 years. Bangladesh, which had shifted to a cash transfer program, is now considering reintroducing school feeding. Such programs can, in principle, jointly serve nutrition, education, and social protection objectives. However, Alderman and Bundy (2012) conclude that in developing countries such programs are not especially effective as nutrition or education programs but are effective as a means to enhance demand for schooling.

In India, the MDMS is a major initiative to improve nutrition and raise school enrollment and attendance. It provides cooked lunches to pupils in elementary government schools; in some states it replaced an earlier scheme that provided take-home food rations once a month. In 2008–09, the scheme reached almost 112 million students. Jayaraman, Simroth, and De Vericourt (2010) found that the program increased enrollment in the first grade by about 17 percent and by a smaller but still significant margin in higher grades. However, no increase in test scores was found.

Afridi (2010) found that switching the delivery mode from a take-home ration to a cooked meal at school improved the attendance of first-grade girls by more than 12 percentage points. In Bangladesh, Ahmed (2004) found large and significant positive effects on nutrition, enrollment, attendance, and test scores. Overall, evidence to date on the impact of school feeding programs on learning outcomes is mixed.[16]

Some health interventions have been cost-effective in reducing the incidence of illness, raising attendance, and indirectly improving learning. The health status of South Asian children is typically poor, which adversely affects their enrollment and learning. In India, poor child health status has been inversely associated with long-term learning (Kingdon and Monk 2010). Kingdon and Banerji (2009) report that illness is likely to have a significant adverse impact on school attendance. Health interventions, such as deworming, have been found to be cost-effective in lifting student attendance as well as improving general health (Miguel and Kremer 2004; Bobonis, Miguel, and Puri-Sharma 2006). Targeted programs to reduce the incidence of preventable illnesses should therefore be considered as complements to school feeding programs such as the MDMS (OECD 2011).

Pedagogy and classroom processes. Primary and secondary curricula in South Asian countries are visionary but are typically not well implemented. Even though countries like India and Sri Lanka design their curricula with a strong constructivist element, poor field-testing of the curricula and training of teachers, among other problems, undermine the effectiveness of the curricula in improving student learning. In addition, curricula are often "overcrowded" relative to the quality of available teachers.

In primary classrooms, students are exposed to fewer instructional hours than planned. Sankar (2009) found that in India, depending on the state, 12.5–16.5 percent of a school's functional day is lost from academic activity, and even when teaching takes place, it tends to be didactic, primarily emphasizing teacher-centric activities and repetitive learning. Very little class time is devoted to such activities as engaging pupils in discussion and listening to them.

Poor pedagogic practices are especially obvious in early-grade reading classes. Ensuring that students learn to read early on, and read well, is the most significant route to ensuring that every child gets an equal opportunity to learn across the entire curriculum. A child who struggles to read will find it very difficult to catch up in later years unless there is intensive and individualized remedial support, which is rare. In a detailed analysis of the reading patterns of Indian students in grades 1 and 2 in the states of Rajasthan and Assam, Jhingran (2012) found that achievement in reading-related tasks was characterized by low means and high variances. Students did not acquire mastery or automaticity in recognizing letters by the end of grade 1. Word reading skills were poor, and oral reading fluency for connected text was low. Most students could not answer questions that required an inference to be made or an opinion to be expressed. Less than 5 percent of students in Assam and 1 percent in Rajasthan had achieved the reading fluency considered essential for reasonable comprehension. Jhingran (2012) attributes poor reading achievement to poor teaching practices that focus primarily on drill-type activities, with little attention paid to understanding content. He argues that teaching strategies can be effective only when they balance drill-type activities with understanding content.

System-Level Interventions

Financing as a Tool for Quality Improvement

School finance systems must provide the resources necessary for all students, regardless of background, to learn. While governments are ultimately tasked with ensuring access to schooling, both as a fundamental right (see India's RTE) and to garner the social benefits of education for society as a whole, they are also the foremost providers of education, with government schools the primary vehicle through which the aims of universal quality education are realized.

Financing systems in South Asia vary tremendously and are extremely complex. Because countries in the region differ noticeably not only in size but also economically, ethnically, and politically, they also differ in how much they spend on education, where they direct the spending, the degree of decentralization, the extent of private provision, and the modalities of financing—all of which affect the efficiency of the state in education provision and make intraregion comparability difficult. However, one consistency across the region is the recent rapid rate of economic growth, with average annual growth rates ranging from 3.9 percent to 7.2 percent over the last decade. The increased demand for schooling that is stimulated by economic growth is putting immense stress on education systems throughout the region.

Although all governments demonstrate high commitment to education, public spending as a proportion of GDP and per-pupil public expenditures in most countries of the region are significantly lower than in developed countries. While there have been increases in the absolute amount of public funding of education in the region, made possible in large part by rapid economic growth, these increases have been absorbed by the large increases in student enrollment, leaving per-pupil expenditures roughly constant and far below the averages for OECD and East Asian countries. The public resource limitation has been partly compensated for by a surge in household spending on education and the rapid expansion of the private education sector in the last two decades. However, the surge in private spending could have unfavorable distributional implications, given that low-income parents may not be able to afford the costs. Improving quality in the public sector requires not only additional public spending on education but also more efficient and effective use of current resources.

With continued growth, one would expect more resources to be spent on education, leading to more and better inputs being made available. The implicit assumption is that increasing inputs, such as numbers of schools, toilets, and textbooks, will translate into improved learning. However, the evidence available so far (discussed previously) suggests that more inputs will not necessarily lead to significant improvements in learning outcomes. Most of the impact of these inputs will likely be on enrollment. To achieve significant learning gains, the objective of a country's financing strategy should be to induce behavioral changes through incentive structures and accountability mechanisms. This report suggests three promising financing options:

- *Financing tools that change the incentive structure of teachers appear promising for significant improvements in quality.* Though the evidence is still limited, it strongly suggests that accountability systems based on performance-related pay and promotions, with teacher performance measured by student learning gains, could modify teacher behavior, eliciting more effort in the classroom, improved pedagogical processes, and more effective use of the inputs and training they receive. However, the design of incentive and reward systems is critical to achieving learning impacts.

- *Similarly, changes in school funding mechanisms could create incentives for quality improvement.* A shift from block grants to per-pupil funding would help make schools more accountable. A system of funding that ties increases in allocations to performance indicators could also have large learning benefits for children. The policy objective is to forge a closer link between funding and outcomes, rather than between funding and inputs as is currently the case.

- *More extensive use of public-private partnerships (PPPs) could also increase resources for education and maximize efficiency, as long as efficiency and equity incentives are built into the agreements.* The cost-efficiency of the private sector makes it attractive as a means to relax resource constraints and make school financing more efficient. However, given the wide variance in the performance of private providers, financing arrangements need to be carefully designed. Public financing of private schools through block grants has not produced significant learning gains. Per capita funding, conditional on performance, is more promising, as shown by the experience of Bangladesh with the Reaching Out-of-School Children (ROSC) schools and of Pakistan with the Foundation Assisted Schools (FAS). In ROSC schools, a combination of supply-side financing (per-student grants to cover stationery, uniforms, and so on) and demand-side financing (a block grant to the center to cover teacher salary, maintenance, and training costs, and a per-student allowance paid to the child's mother) led to an improvement in enrollment and greater transparency in the utilization of funds. In the FAS program, funding given to private schools on a per-student basis and conditional on student achievement, led to an improvement in student learning outcomes.

Monitoring Learning Outcomes: Assessments and Quality Improvement

Student assessment systems provide key information about what students learn and the skills they acquire in terms of curriculum objectives. A focus on measuring student learning is crucial, since it is student test score gains, and not inputs or time spent in school, that correlate with later life opportunities for individuals and with the competitiveness and growth of national economies (Hanushek and Woessmann 2008). Thus, assessment provides essential information about whether an education system is producing the desired outcomes for students, the economy, and society, and is increasingly recognized as a means to monitor and evaluate student learning levels (box O.11). Typically, an effective assessment system has three components: classroom assessment; public examinations; and large-scale, system-level assessments.[17] This section briefly reviews the status of these three types of assessments in South Asia and identifies recommendations for a more effective use of assessment results for policy making.

Most South Asian countries carry out classroom assessments. However, they are not effective in improving student learning and there is a critical need for system-wide guidelines, resources, and training for teachers in the use of such assessments and for a formal mechanism to systematically monitor the quality of classroom assessments.

Although South Asian countries have established examination systems, challenges remain: (a) There needs to be better alignment of curriculum objectives with how examinations measure student performance. Because examinations in the region have extremely high stakes, there is a tendency for lessons to be examination focused; students study only to pass, without acquiring real-world competence. (b) Little is done with classroom assessments; most important, they do not feed back to teacher training. This limits their usefulness as a means of improving student learning. (c) Examinations based on rote memorization do not promote critical thinking and problem-solving skills. (d) Despite government

Box O.11 Using National Learning Assessment Results: Lessons from Chile, Uruguay, and Uganda

Chile's *Sistema de Medicion de la Calidad de la Educacion* (SIMCE, or System for Measuring Education Quality) is implemented annually for all students in the country in grades 4 and 8. All schools receive a ranking in comparison with other schools in the same socioeconomic category and a national ranking. SIMCE identifies the 900 schools that score in the lowest 10 percent in the mathematics and language tests within their provincial regions, for which special resources are provided. The program uses an intensive public relations campaign that includes brochures for parents and schools, posters for schools, videos for workshops, TV programs, and press releases. Parents receive an individualized report for their school so that they know which schools in their neighborhood perform well.

Uruguay implements national assessments in grade 6 in mathematics and reading comprehension on a sample basis. Results are used mainly by teachers, principals, and school inspectors to identify schools needing special support and for large-scale, in-service teacher training programs. Participating schools receive a confidential report with aggregate school results presented item by item. The unit responsible for the assessments produces (a) teaching guides to help address weaknesses and organize in-service training programs for disadvantaged schools, (b) reports for supervisory personnel, and (c) workshops for inspectors that draw on the test results.

Uganda implements sample-based assessments in grades 3 and 6 in English literacy and numeracy. The National Examination Board, the agency that implements the assessment, prints a poster for each grade 3 and 6 classroom listing curriculum areas where national-level student performance is considered adequate (for example, "We can count numbers") and less than adequate (for example, "Help us to carry out dividing numbers correctly"). The results and implications of results are shared with teachers, head teachers, supervisors or inspectors, teacher educators, and policy makers.

Source: Greaney and Kellaghan 2008.

efforts over decades, in many countries malpractices such as cheating continue unabated. (e) Finally, improving the validity and reliability of public examinations is important for fully assessing student achievement and producing graduates whose knowledge and skills are adequate and comparable over time.

Countries in South Asia have carried out national large-scale assessment programs in the past decade, but most are not committed to regular assessment. Sri Lanka administered its National Assessment of Achievement exercise in 2003, 2007, and 2009 to a representative sample of grade 4 students. In Bangladesh, the National Student Assessment was conducted on grades 3 and 5 in 2006, 2008, and 2011 in literacy (Bangla) and numeracy (math). In India, the National Council for Educational Research and Training carried out a national survey of grade 5 students in 2010. The Nepal Department of Education commissioned a national assessment of the performance of students in grades 5 and 8 in 2008. In Pakistan, large-scale assessments are mainly conducted at the provincial level (such as the Punjab Education Assessment System). Since the early 2000s, in South Asia, especially India, nongovernmental organizations (NGOs) have also been carrying out large-scale, systemwide assessments.

International assessments can motivate countries to make their education systems more competitive with better-performing economies. One of the main trends over the last decade or so is the rise of large-scale international assessment exercises, such as TIMSS, PIRLS, and PISA. Mexico and Brazil, among other middle-income countries, have significantly benefited from such assessments to improve learning outcomes (box O.12). Assessments can also generate political support for reforming national education systems. Although South Asian countries have been slow to adopt international assessments, this may be changing. Two states in India—Himachal Pradesh and Tamil Nadu—participated in the international PISA 2009+ assessment.

Box O.12 How PISA Promoted Educational Quality in Mexico

Mexico demonstrates that participation in international assessments can positively affect learning relatively quickly when the initiative gets strong government support. In mathematics, the performance of Mexico on the OECD Programme for International Student Assessment (PISA), as measured by mean scores, rose from 385 in 2003 to 406 in 2006 and to 419 in 2009, making it the country with the biggest increase (33 score points) over this period. Although the proportion of Mexican students below level 2 on the PISA mathematics scale (levels range from 1 to 6) is still very high at 50.8 percent—the OECD countries average 20.8 percent, G-20 countries 32.6 percent, and countries with similar per capita gross domestic product to Mexico 38.8 percent—Mexico has been able to considerably reduce its proportion of poor performers, which was 65.9 percent in 2003.

Mexico achieved these performance gains because Mexico's President Felipe Calderón set the main strategies, objectives, and PISA performance targets. In 2008, the Mexican government and the National Union of Educational Workers, the largest trade union in Latin America, together launched the Alliance for Educational Quality to promote innovative policies and to mobilize human, material, and institutional resources to improve student learning outcomes. The OECD advised the Mexican government on this process. Because of the nationwide commitment to improving learning outcomes, according to the OECD, Mexico was on the right trajectory to reach a score of 435 on the PISA in reading and mathematics for 2012.

Despite the potential benefits of international assessments, a word of caution is in order, especially where there are large discrepancies between the national curriculum and what the assessments test for. Test items are developed not only to measure average achievement but also to capture variances in learning. In developing countries where average achievement is low, accurate capture of the complete range of achievements of students may not be possible. Political pressures as a result of relatively unfavorable performance could also be a risk for policy makers, although the risk needs to be measured against the opportunities that participation in international assessments opens up for effective policy reforms.

Source: OECD 2011.

Student Learning through Private Education

In South Asia, the private sector is emerging as a major provider of education services. Today, around one-third of primary and secondary students in South Asia attend such schools: 27 percent of those ages 6–10 years, 31 percent ages 11–15 years, and 39 percent ages 16–18 years (figure O.8). The only countries where private education is minimal are Bhutan and Afghanistan, where the private provision of education is incipient, and Sri Lanka, where legal restrictions constrain its expansion.

The expansion of private education is fairly recent, dating back only to the 1980s, and although predominant in urban areas it has also reached rural areas. In the last five years, expansion in private education has been faster than in the public sector. Private tutoring is also increasingly common, even in rural areas and among children from the poorest families. Approximately 50 percent of schoolchildren ages 11–15 years in slums in Dhaka have private tutoring, regardless of whether they go to government or private schools (Cameron 2011). Private tutoring has even grown in Sri Lanka, where private schools are banned. A recent study found that 75 percent of primary-school children took some form of private tutoring.

There are a variety of management and financing arrangements for private education. Besides privately financed and managed schools, there are different types of PPPs. The most common PPP category is privately managed schools that receive full or partial financial support from the government, mainly to pay teacher salaries. Some governments in the region have already embraced this model; for instance, India's Eleventh Five-Year Plan proposed to set up enough PPP schools by 2014 to be able to educate 6.5 million students, of whom 2.5 million are to be from disadvantaged social groups. In Bangladesh, some primary schools and over 97 percent of all secondary schools operate under this type of arrangement.

The private sector in its broadest sense includes communities, NGOs, faith-based organizations, trade unions, private companies, small-scale informal classes, and individual tutoring. Our discussion of private sector schools includes both for-profit and NGO-run schools. It is important to be aware that NGOs and

Figure O.8 Private School Enrollment, by Gender, in South Asia

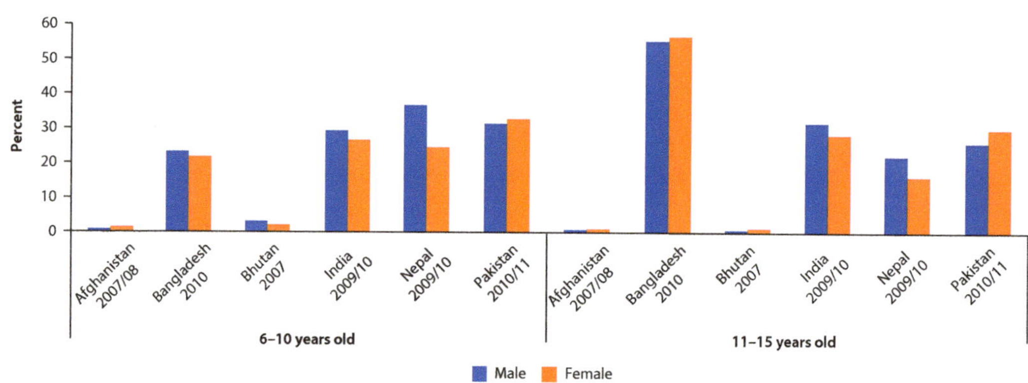

Source: Household surveys.

civil-society organizations play an important role in education in many countries in the region. South Asia has a long and established history of such groups being involved in the delivery of social services. Often, the reach of the NGO-run schools is more extensive than that of government-run schools, especially in remote, poor, and minority-dominated regions. The nongovernment schools thus improve access to schooling among disadvantaged groups.

There is often debate about the relative effectiveness of private schools relative to public schools. Based on data from India, Nepal, and Pakistan, three facts stand out. First, on average, unadjusted test scores are higher in private schools than in public schools, both urban and rural. Second, even in private schools, average learning levels are low, with a large number of primary-school children mastering little more than basic literacy and numeracy. Further, there is significant variance in test scores within schools of both types, with good and bad scores in both.

Part of the learning premium of private schools can be explained by the fact that children in urban and richer areas and from more affluent households are more likely to attend private schools. Indeed, controlling for social background, the learning differential narrows. Still, in most cases, it remains. Other differences between public and private schools, such as in infrastructure or school characteristics (class size, availability of textbooks, and teacher qualifications or experience), do not seem to explain the remaining gap. Recent research is now looking at less easily observable variables, such as teacher behavior or effort, as possible contributing factors. Overall, once observable student and school characteristics are taken into account, private schools appear no worse, and often better, than public schools.

One particular type of PPP arrangement shows promise (box O.13). In a number of PPPs targeted at low-income children in the region, public support to nongovernment schools is conditioned on some measure of performance. There is growing evidence that such mechanisms could raise learning outcomes for disadvantaged groups. These findings also provide solid support to the hypothesis that learning improves when teachers are motivated. Well-designed PPPs with efficiency and equity incentives built in, when scaled up, could help achieve the objective of quality education for all.

In summary, in most of South Asia private schools have come to account for a significant share of enrollment at all levels. Given its resource constraints, South Asia cannot both increase the educational attainment of the population and improve the quality of learning without the combined effort of governments, households, and the private sector. Leveraging the contribution of the private sector is critical to increasing the human capital of the next generations. Since the private sector has already demonstrated that it can offer access at lower cost, with outcomes comparable to the public sector, countries will gain by facilitating its expansion, easing barriers to entry, monitoring outcomes, and designing efficient PPPs.

Has Decentralization Improved School Quality in South Asia?

How effectively inputs translate into educational outcomes depends on governance. In any country, the governance framework—the system of laws, regulations,

Box O.13 The Promise of Public-Private Partnerships for Improving Education Quality

Several public-private partnership (PPP) programs recently introduced in Pakistan have proved to generate cost-effective gains in participation and achievement.

Introduced in 2005, the Foundation-Assisted School (FAS) program administered by the Punjab Education Foundation provides conditional cash subsidies to low-cost private schools to open up private schooling opportunities for children from low-income households and raise the level of learning in the schools. Per-student cash subsidies are provided monthly, with essentially no conditions on how they are to be used. The amount is purposely set low (half the estimated per-student cost in the public school system) to ensure that only low-cost private schools self-select into the program. In return for the subsidy, the program school has to waive tuition and other fees for all students and ensure that the school achieves a minimum student pass rate in the quality assurance test (QAT). The QAT is a curriculum-based, multisubject test designed by subject specialists and administered by independent testing agencies. Program schools are also eligible for group bonuses for teachers whose students achieve high QAT pass rates and for competitive bonuses for schools that rank highest in the QAT. Schools that do not achieve a minimum pass rate twice in succession are dropped from the program.

As of June 2010, the FAS program had proceeded through six phases of expansion and supported about 800,000 students in 1,800 schools in 29 of the 36 districts in the province. A rigorous evaluation (Barrera-Osorio and Raju 2010, 2011) found that within two years the program generated major gains in enrollment and school inputs (roughly 40 percent) and student achievement (a gain of 0.3–0.5 standard deviation).

The Punjab Education Foundation also runs a sister program, the New School Program (NSP), which supports the opening of new schools in underserved communities. The program provides per-student subsidies to new private schools in underserved areas, conditional on a school's achievement in standardized, competency-based test scores. The program currently covers over 20,000 students in 230 schools in 16 districts

Another program, similar to the NSP, called Promoting Private Schooling in Rural Sindh (PPRS) is run by the Government of Sindh, Pakistan. It also attempts to give the private sector incentives to deliver schooling to underserved rural communities. Program schools get grants for construction and other support and per-student subsidies conditional on maintaining minimum student achievement levels. A rigorous evaluation found that the program produced substantial gains in participation and achievement (Barrera-Osorio et al. 2011).

and procedures within which decisions pertaining to policy, financing, implementation, and accountability are made—is pivotal in institutionalizing change. These formal rules of the game coexist with informal norms, customs, and beliefs; the interplay of the two determines outcomes. An ideal governance framework should not only improve student learning but also minimize inefficiencies, waste, and leaks in the system.

Decentralization has been a popular policy for modifying the governance of educational programs worldwide. Decentralization involves the transfer or reallocation of responsibility for public functions from the central government to subordinate levels of government, government organizations (such as schools), or the private sector. By explicitly bringing government and governance closer to the people served, decentralization aims to improve the quality of education by increasing policy responsiveness and enhancing accountability (Bardhan and Mookerjee 2006). As policy making has moved from access to issues of quality, relevance, and equity, centralized systems have gradually given way to the greater involvement of subnational levels of government and schools.

Internationally, decentralization has been associated with increases in school enrollment, attendance, retention, and teacher presence and effort, but the link with student learning has not been conclusively established. The link between decentralization and improvement in student learning has been difficult to establish partly because decentralization programs tend to be accompanied by an increase in enrollment, with that enrollment coming from the left tail of the test score distribution, thereby lowering the average test score (Rodriguez 2006; Madeira 2007; Galiani, Gertler, and Schargrodsky 2008). Learning also takes time. Bruns, Filmer, and Patrinos (2011) provide evidence from developed countries that suggests that it can take up to eight years before any impact of decentralization reforms in education on student learning outcomes can be observed.

Evidence from Nepal and India suggests that decentralization reforms may hold promise for improving student learning. An evaluation of a program in Nepal where school management powers, including teacher hiring and firing, were transferred to the community found that after two years the program led to increased grade promotion, a reduction in dropouts, and fewer out-of-school children. There was as yet no impact on learning (Chaudhury and Parajuli, 2010). Pandey et al. (2011) provided information to communities in three states in India regarding their oversight roles and responsibilities in school management and the services they were entitled to from schools. After two and a half years, Pandey, Goyal, and Sundararaman (2011) reported a consistent and significant increase in learning outcomes, although mainly in mathematics.

Although they hold promise, decentralization reforms in the region face a number of implementation challenges that need to be addressed if they are to be effective. If they are to improve learning, the following issues need to be addressed:

- *Political support and consistency in implementation of reforms:* Decentralization reforms in the region have been uncertain and inconsistent, frequently oscillating between greater and lesser centralization. Such inconsistency has not only reduced commitment and ownership of decentralization reforms, it has also led to duplication of roles, responsibilities, and structures and to confusion about accountability.

- *Adequate resources and fiscal authority at lower levels of government:* For a system to function efficiently, decision makers at all levels must have access to the resources they need to implement decisions. In countries across the region, financial decentralization has yet to allow lower levels of governments to make effective decisions. In India, for instance, although the *Sarva Shiksha Abhiyan*

(SSA), or Education for All) and the RTE set out a bottom-up planning structure for schools, SMCs have spending power only over about 5 percent of SSA funds, and even these need to be spent based on central government norms (Dongre, Chowdhury, and Aiyar 2012). This limits the ability of SMCs to undertake important functions related to improving learning outcomes.

- *Systematically building up local capacity so that communities can contribute effectively to decision making:* In most parts of the region, local capacity is minimal, with low-income communities having little ability to contribute effectively to decision making in education. As an example, most Indian states list "ensuring children are learning at grade-appropriate levels" as one responsibility of SMCs. However, committees and parents often have little idea of what grade-appropriate learning levels are. Programs to assist parents in understanding what learning means have proved useful in improving student outcomes in other countries (box O.14). Due to their limited capacity, community-based

---

Box O.14 RECURSO: Creating High Expectations among Parents

Peru's RECURSO (*Rendicion de Cuentas para la Reforma Social*—Accountability for Social Reform) program is aimed at breaking the low-quality equilibrium that characterized school performance in the mid-2000s. Low performance expectations were seen as the fundamental barrier to quality improvement efforts; while various stakeholders were actively engaged in expanding coverage, they were not focusing on improving quality. Analyses suggested that one reason stakeholders were not pressing for improved quality was because it was difficult for them to see or measure quality. While coverage is concrete and therefore easy to see and measure, the quality of education is an abstract concept. Parents who have not been to schools themselves do not always know what to expect from them. Since there are no benchmarks on how to measure their child's achievement, parents believe their children are doing well as long as they get passing grades and show some improvement. If they were to know that their child was taking five years to learn to read at a level that should have been achieved after one to two years, they might demand change.

RECURSO aimed to provide parents with information and methods to track whether their children had the skills expected at their age. The program produced a number of instruments for the general public, many directed specifically to the parents of poor children. These included three videos, a radio theater series, and numerous brochures and posters produced in multiple languages. The videos have been especially effective in building public opinion. They demonstrate poor education quality by showing children who cannot read or struggle to read. These dramatic scenes are followed by images of high-quality education, with poor rural children of the same age reading fluently, sometimes in multiple languages. The video then defines a standard: children finishing the second grade should be able to read 60 words per minute; and the video gives clear, simple instructions on how parents can measure this with any watch. The video challenges parents to find out how well their children are reading and tells them they have the right to demand a good education.

Source: Cotlear 2008.

---

groups tend to be to accorded responsibility only over low-stakes tasks. The typical SMC in India is not empowered to hire and fire teachers; instead, SMCs tend to be involved in enrollment drives and managing civil work (Béteille and Muralidharan 2011). For SMCs to make meaningful contributions, they need to be assigned roles and responsibilities they have been trained to undertake.

Priorities for Quality Improvement in South Asia

Priority 1. Make Learning Outcomes the Central Goal of Education Policy

Student achievement in South Asia is very low. Student learning in South Asia falls short not only of international but also of local standards. Many students do not acquire basic literacy and numeracy skills even after several years of schooling. Available student assessments suggest that up to one-third of primary school students lack the numeracy and literacy skills that would enable them to further their education. It is no wonder that the region's primary and secondary school completion rates are among the lowest in the world. Such students, when they drop out of school, have few options in the rapidly changing labor markets of the region. They either remain unemployed or get only low-productivity jobs, which keeps them persistently in poverty. There is thus a vicious cycle in which poverty, among other things, inhibits learning, and too little learning prevents the poor from escaping poverty.

Not only is the lack of basic numeracy and literacy skills an enormous waste of human resources, it is increasingly a major constraint on the growth and competitiveness of the countries in South Asia. Employers cite shortages of skilled workers as a constraint on private-sector investments (World Bank 2012a). A Goldman Sachs report found that India scored poorly relative to BRICS (Brazil, Russia, India, China, and South Africa) and even below the average for all emerging economies in terms of school quality and that its growth and productivity were affected by low educational standards across the board (O'Neill and Poddar 2008).

Operationally, what would making learning outcomes an explicit and central goal of education policy imply? It would mean defining and tracking student learning outcome measures consistently, and then using those measures to guide all aspects of education policy, including both teacher deployment and training and allocation of public spending on education.

Priority 2. Invest in Early Childhood Nutrition

Some of the most important interventions to raise student learning outcomes lie outside the education sector. Early childhood nutrition programs are highly cost-effective investments to improve the quality and efficiency of education, especially in South Asia, which has the highest prevalence of child malnutrition in the world, even higher than much poorer Sub-Saharan Africa. Because early-life malnutrition has large negative and permanent effects on brain development and cognition, millions of South Asian children, particularly from poor households, who start primary school with huge cognitive disadvantages either drop out of school or fall farther and farther behind as they progress through school.

Following Nepal's lead, countries in the region need to design and expand cost-effective interventions targeting the first 1,000 days of life and addressing the pervasive problems of low birth weight, infant and child malnutrition, and deficiencies in micronutrients if they are to improve learning outcomes and make public spending on education more effective.

The fact that nutritional and health interventions do not usually fall under the purview of education ministries means that there is an urgent need for much better coordination between educational agencies and other government ministries in charge of maternal and child health. A multisectoral, cross-departmental approach will be central to ensuring that all children have the opportunity to come prepared for school.

Priority 3. Improve Teacher Effectiveness and Accountability

Teachers are among the most important determinants of educational quality, yet policies have not always focused on which aspects of teacher quality matter most. The evidence is robust: what matters more for student learning than degrees or seniority is teachers' knowledge, how motivated they are, and how they teach. On all aspects, too many teachers in South Asia are found lacking. In countries across the region, a large percentage of teachers cannot explain basic concepts or address student questions and thus cannot satisfactorily transmit knowledge to their pupils. Teacher absenteeism is also pervasive across the region, and even when they are present, teachers are often not able to tailor learning to children's needs.

Countries would do well to reorient their recruitment and management policies to raise the level of teachers' subject knowledge, encourage them to adopt effective pedagogical methods, and motivate them to enhance the level of learning of their students. Evidence from the region suggests that there are three important policies that could engender greater accountability and teacher effort and would also incentivize teachers to use their training and other school inputs more effectively: (a) clear standards are needed for recruitment, deployment, transfers, and postings, with strong safeguards against non-merit-based decisions—and the administrative capacity to implement those standards; (b) preservice and in-service training need to equip teachers with up-to-date approaches to teaching; and (c) teachers need to have clear prospects that acquisition of new skills and performance will be rewarded. While there is limited evidence on performance-related pay, there is a need for more experimentation in the region on different types of teacher incentives.

Priority 4. Give Disadvantaged Children Additional Instructional Resources in Early Grades

The learning trajectories of students over time are substantially flatter than curricula envisage. Not only is there significant variation in what students have learned at the end of grade 1, but the variance grows over time. Since teachers consider the textbook the default mode of instruction and define their goals in terms of completing the curriculum over the course of the year, it is not surprising that they effectively teach to the upper end of the distribution and that a large number of children in the class do not learn because they find the lessons too advanced.

The fact that poorly performing children do not learn much owing to both their initial disadvantages and the pedagogical practices inside the classroom is a systemic issue that needs to be addressed by a comprehensive set of public policies, including streamlining and simplifying the curriculum and providing support to poor populations, children from minority ethnolinguistic groups, and children with disabilities. While teacher training programs will need to equip regular teachers to address the needs of poorly performing students, supplemental remedial instruction can be effective in improving learning among disadvantaged groups. There is evidence to suggest that considerable quality gains are possible by targeting pedagogy at the appropriate level and giving additional instruction to children who are not keeping up. Supplemental instruction programs would improve both equity (by helping children catch up) and efficiency (because the regular teacher would be more effective in school if there were less variance in student learning levels).

Priority 5. Use Financing Tools to Improve Quality

Although better infrastructure and more schooling inputs may attract and retain children in school, there is little evidence that in themselves they will raise the quality of learning. Nor is there much evidence that on average, without accountability, more teachers or higher teacher salaries will improve quality.

Thus, business as usual is not likely to have much impact on quality, and countries should consider other financing tools that have shown promise, among them changes in the incentive structure for both teachers and schools. Introducing accountability systems (e.g., performance-related pay and promotions) based on student learning achievements could be effective in modifying teacher behavior and stimulating more effort in the classroom. Similarly, modifications of school funding formulas could create incentives for quality improvement. Block grants that do not demand any accountability from schools could be replaced by grants that carry a range of incentives for efficiency and equity. Another avenue for quality improvement would be partnerships with the private sector that condition funding on results. As noted earlier, changing accountability systems through financing will likely face serious administrative and political challenges, because political patronage is deeply embedded within the public education system. But the potential rewards from increased accountability in terms of improved student learning are likely to be huge.

Priority 6. Leverage the Contribution of the Private Sector

Leveraging the contribution of the private sector, both for-profit and NGO-run schools, is crucial for meeting the double challenge of improved access and quality in the face of capacity and resource constraints. The South Asia region has a long history of active civil-society groups and NGOs involved in education delivery.

These groups operate learning centers for first-generation schoolgoers and for students who have dropped out. They also provide technical support to governments in the design of teacher training programs, curricula, and textbooks.

Countries will gain by facilitating expansion of this sector, easing barriers to entry, and carefully designing PPPs. Many nongovernment schools have more extensive reach than government schools in poor and remote regions. Expanding the role of this sector, with appropriate mechanisms for accountability, could provide increased access to more and better education services for disadvantaged groups. Innovative and cost-effective programs in Bangladesh and Pakistan could be replicated.

Priority 7. Improve Quality through Enhanced Learning Assessment Systems

Enhanced assessment systems are necessary to monitor progress in learning outcomes and improvements in schooling quality over time. These comprehensive assessments need to cover students in both public and nongovernment schools, and should be designed in a manner that does not pressure students unduly.

Unlike data on school enrollment and attendance, administrative data on student achievement are not typically collected. It is only recently that some countries have conducted regular and systematic large-scale learning assessments. National capacities to monitor student learning and assure quality outcomes are generally weak, and examinations are the only indicator of student achievement. Without knowing how students are performing, it is difficult to tell which policies are working or when new ones are needed. There is an urgent need for an enabling environment for assessment, to align assessment activities with other aspects of the education system, to improve the technical quality of the instruments being employed, and to use assessment results in making education policy decisions to improve quality.

South Asian countries need to create more balanced assessment systems that emphasize both classroom testing and large-scale assessments to build up the quality of educational outcomes. Classroom assessments are useful for monitoring a child's progress and taking corrective measures; system-wide assessments provide an overview of how an education system is performing and evolving. Important considerations for improving the former include giving teachers more resources, materials, and training to assess students appropriately and building in provision of regular feedback to students and their parents.

National learning outcomes also need to be benchmarked against regional and international learning standards to identify specific areas of weakness in countries in the region relative to each other and to other regions and to create the political imperative for school quality reform. Thus, it is important that South Asian countries consider participating regularly in international assessments to benchmark the quality of their education systems.

Looking Ahead

In South Asia, the quality of schooling as measured by traditional notions of school inputs has been improving steadily because governments have been spending more over the past decade. Yet learning outcomes are very low in both absolute and relative terms. This represents an enormous waste of resources and a major constraint on growth in the region.

There is an urgent need for South Asia to raise learning outcomes for all students while affirming the continuing importance of access. The study has identified seven strategic directions for quality improvement that governments in the region might consider. Clearly, given the very different conditions of each country, there is no single best approach. Each country needs to design policies consistent with its national development objectives, taking into account financial and political constraints and opportunities. Although in Afghanistan and Pakistan access issues are still pressing, all countries in South Asia need to make learning outcomes an explicit and overriding goal of education policy. Improving learning outcomes for all will help reduce poverty and income inequality and make the region more competitive globally.

The political economy of reforms means that changing educational systems and reorienting them toward quality will not be easy. As in other parts of the world, teacher unions in many countries in South Asia are powerful and often resistant to change and reform if they do not see the benefits clearly. In many parts of the region, there are strong vested interests that weaken teacher accountability and contribute to poor student learning outcomes. But these challenges are not insurmountable; they have been addressed successfully in other parts of the world (see box O.15) as well as in Bangladesh and Pakistan (box O.7).

Box O.15 Overcoming Opposition to Education Reform: The Role of Effective Leadership in Latin America

In countries across the world, developed and developing, the path to education reform can be a politically daunting task. Powerful antireform interest groups, most often teachers unions, complicate efforts to address pressing reform issues, such as greater teacher accountability and superior teacher deployment policies. Nevertheless, there are instances of successful reform, even when the political odds do not appear to favor reform.

Based upon case studies in 16 countries in Latin America and the Caribbean, Grindle (2004) argued that countries where reform efforts succeeded were those where reformers seized the moment, systematically weakened and marginalized antireform groups, and organized political patrons and networks to carry forward key elements of their reform agenda. For instance, Mexico's President Salinas timed his 1992 education reforms carefully. He waited three years to strengthen his authority and shape how much change the union and the ministry would accept. This involved not only altering the powers of the union and the ministry, but also waiting until the midterm election gave him the constitutional majority needed to legislate important changes.

Successful reformers also make use of their powers of appointment to promote their initiatives. In Brazil's Minas Gerais, the governor spearheading the education reforms of the 1990s

box continues next page

Box O.15 Overcoming Opposition to Education Reform: The Role of Effective Leadership in Latin America *(continued)*

chose a minister who then chose allies he trusted to lead the initiative in the ministry. Equally important is the ability to weaken and marginalize interest groups opposed to reforms. In Minas Gerais, school directors posed a threat to reforms, while the union was in favor of many aspects of the reforms. Here, the minister mobilized those supporting the reforms, asking them to testify in the public debate about the benefits of reform, and the governor provided visible support to offset the resistance of the directors association.

Finally, successful reformers find opportunities to set the terms of the debate about reform. In Bolivia and Mexico, presidents emphasized the importance of reforms for modernizing their economies, implicitly suggesting that entities opposing reform were opposed to modernization, growth, and the alleviation of poverty.

Source: Grindle 2004.

Notes

1. In the World Bank's regional grouping, South Asia comprises eight countries: Afghanistan, Bangladesh, Bhutan, India, Maldives, Nepal, Pakistan, and Sri Lanka.
2. The data refer to only the developing countries in each region and are for 2010.
3. Primary education usually covers grades 1–8, lower secondary grades 9–10, and senior secondary grades 11–12. However, there are variations within and between countries in what constitutes primary and secondary education. In some countries, secondary starts with grade 6, in others with grade 7. The distinction between primary and secondary is further blurred by a proliferation of middle, lower secondary, and other divisions. Some countries also distinguish between secondary education (generally grades 9–10) and higher or senior secondary (generally grades 11–12).
4. Of course, equitable distribution of school enrollment reflects the fact that there has already been significant expansion of access in the region, especially at the primary level.
5. Many countries in South Asia have experienced some degree of violence and conflict, ranging from recent civil wars in Nepal and Sri Lanka to the violence in Afghanistan and Pakistan and low-level insurgency in parts of India. Schools are often targeted, although evidence of the impact of civil conflict on learning outcomes is scant.
6. Education systems can be evaluated in terms of internal efficiency (as measured by the relationship between inputs and outputs), effectiveness (the degree to which goals or objectives are achieved), and external efficiency or relevance (as measured by the relationship between inputs and outcomes). Quality often refers to effectiveness, the degree to which students have acquired knowledge and skills through schools (Heneveld 1994). Thus, in this study, quality improvement refers to a qualitative change in the knowledge and skills a student population acquires. Although not a perfect proxy, the gain in skills is measured through achievement tests at school and at subnational, national, regional, and international levels.

7. However, several studies in India Bangladesh, and Sri Lanka piloted international tests (e.g., Trends in Mathematics and Science Study [TIMSS]), or incorporated questions from these tests in their own assessments. Additionally, a growing number of impact evaluations provide insights into both outcomes and their possible causes and correlates.
8. The OECD PISA is an international comparison of the skills of 15-year-old students in reading, mathematics, and scientific literacy. The data from the PISA 2009+ project are directly comparable to the original PISA 2009 database, so that the PISA 2009 and 2009+ databases contain information on almost a half-million students tested in 74 countries, representing a total population of about 24 million. The mean reading score for Himachal Pradesh was 315 and for Tamil Nadu 335; only the Kyrgyz Republic at 314 had a lower score. In mathematics and science, as well, both Indian states had the lowest mean scores of all countries participating in PISA 2009 and PISA 2009+.
9. Of course, equitable distribution of school enrollment reflects the fact that there has already been significant expansion of access in the region, especially at the primary level.
10. This report views ECD as the period from point of conception to when the child is 6 years old (0–6 years).
11. In South Asia, the rapid expansion of enrollment has meant a large increase in the size of the teaching force. However, this discussion focuses on hiring of more teachers for existing schools, not on new hiring for new schools.
12. Exceptions are in Bhutan and Sri Lanka where the average PTR is about 24–26.
13. Teachers' salaries in South Asia, especially for regular teachers, are comparable to counterparts with similar credentials. In 2008 in Sri Lanka, for instance, teachers earned 51 percent more than nonteacher professionals and in Pakistan 22 percent more.
14. For example, India's RTE sets minimum school infrastructure standards (e.g., building, library, toilets), student-teacher ratios, and teacher hours, in all of which there has been notable progress, but it does not set standards for learning outcomes. It is expected that the RTE will further increase public spending for education to meet minimum school standards.
15. Muralidharan and Zielenik (2012) used village-level panel data from a nationally representative sample of more than 1,250 villages in 19 Indian states. They found substantial improvements in school infrastructure for 2003–10. For instance, the proportion of schools with toilets and electricity more than doubled.
16. Note that these programs are distinct from early-childhood nutritional interventions, which have generally been found to be very effective in raising learning outcomes.
17. Classroom assessments are carried out on a day-to-day basis by teachers to provide real-time information to support teaching and learning in a classroom. Public examinations provide information for high-stakes decision making about individual students—whether they should be assigned to a particular type of school or academic program, graduate from high school, or be admitted to a university. Mainly about assessment of learning, it is summative in nature. Large-scale assessments primarily provide policy makers and practitioners with information on the overall performance of the system, changes in performance, and related or contributing factors. Large-scale assessments may be national, subnational, regional, and international. They are not high stakes for the individual student.

Bibliography

Accountability Initiative. 2012. *PAISA Report*. New Delhi: Accountability Initiative.

Afridi, F. 2010. "Child Welfare Programmes and Child Nutrition: Evidence from a Mandated School Meal Programme in India." *Journal of Development Economics* 92 (2): 152–65.

Ahmed, A. U. 2004. *Impact of Feeding Children in School: Evidence from Bangladesh*. Washington, DC: International Food Policy Research Institute.

Alderman, H., and D. Bundy. 2012. "School Feeding Programs and Development: Are We Framing the Question Correctly?" *World Bank Research Observer* 27 (2): 204–21.

ASER-India. 2011. *Annual Status of Education Report (Rural) 2011*. New Delhi: Pratham Resource Center.

———. 2012. *Annual Status of Education Report (Rural) 2012*. New Delhi: Pratham Resource Center.

Aslam, M. 2009. "The Relative Effectiveness of Government and Private Schools in Pakistan: Are Girls Worse Off?" *Education Economics* 17 (3): 329–54.

Aslam, M., and G. Kingdon. 2011. "What Can Teachers Do to Raise Student Achievement?" *Economics of Education Review* 30 (3): 559–74.

Aturupane, H., P. Glewwe, and S. Wisniewski. 2013. "The Impact of School Quality, Socio-Economic Factors and Child Health on Students' Academic Performance: Evidence from Sri Lankan Primary Schools." *Education Economics* 21 (1): 2–37.

Banerjee, A., S. Cole, E. Duflo, and L. Linden. 2007. "Remedying Education: Evidence from Two Randomized Experiments in India." *Quarterly Journal of Economics* 122 (3): 1235–64.

Banerji, R., and G. Kingdon. 2010. "How Sound Are Our Mathematics Teachers? Insights from the SchoolTELLS Survey." In *Learning Curve*. Banglore, India: Azim Premji Foundation.

Banu, L. F. 2009. "Problems and Misconceptions Facing the Primary Language Education in Bangladesh: An Analysis of Curricula and Pedagogic Practices." *BRAC University Journal* 6 (1).

Bardhan, P., and D. Mookherjee, eds. 2006. *Decentralization and Governance in Developing Countries*. Cambridge, MA: MIT Press.

Barrera-Osorio, F., and D. Raju. 2010. "Short-Run Learning Dynamics under a Test-Based Accountability System: Evidence from Pakistan." Policy Research Working Paper 5465, World Bank, Washington, DC.

———. 2011. "Evaluating Public Per-Student Subsidies to Low-Cost Private Schools: Regression-Discontinuity Evidence from Pakistan." Policy Research Working Paper 5638, World Bank, Washington, DC.

Barrera-Osorio, F., D. S. Blakeslee, M. Hoover, L. L. Linden, and D. Raju. 2011. "Expanding Educational Opportunities in Remote Parts of the World: Evidence from a RCT of a Public Private Partnership in Pakistan." Paper presented at the Third Institute for the Study of Labor (IZA) Workshop, "Child Labor in Developing Countries," Mexico City. http://www.iza.org/conference_files/childl2011/blakeslee_d6783.

Behrman, J. R. 1999. "Labor Markets in Developing Countries." In *Handbook of Labor Economics*, edited by O. Ashenfelter, and D. E. Card. Amsterdam: Elsevier Science B.V.

Behrman, J. R., D. Ross, and R. Sabot. 2008. "Improving the Quality Versus Increasing the Quantity of Schooling: Evidence for Rural Pakistan." *Journal of Development Economics* 85: 94–104.

Béteille, T. 2009. "Absenteeism, Transfers and Patronage: The Political Economy of Teacher Labour Markets in India." PhD thesis, Stanford University, Palo Alto, CA.

Béteille, T., and K. Muralidharan. 2011. "School Governance in Rural India." Working Draft Paper, Department of Economics, University of California, San Diego, CA.

Bobonis, G. J., E. Miguel, and C. Puri-Sharma. 2006. "Anemia and School Participation." *Journal of Human Resources* 41 (4): 692–721.

Boissiere, M. 2004a. "Determinants of Primary Education Outcomes in Developing Countries." Background paper for the Evaluation of the World Bank's Support to Primary Education, Operations Evaluation Department, World Bank, Washington, DC.

———. 2004b. "Rationale for Public Investment in Primary Education in Developing Countries." Background paper for the Evaluation of World Bank Support to Primary Education, Operations Evaluation Department, World Bank, Washington, DC.

Borkum, E., F. He, and L. L. Linden. 2012. "School Libraries and Language Skills in Indian Primary Schools: A Randomized Evaluation of the Akshara Library Program." NBER Working Paper 18183, National Bureau of Economic Research, Cambridge, MA.

Bruns, B., D. Filmer, and H. A. Patrinos. 2011. *Making Schools Work: New Evidence on Accountability Reforms*. Washington, DC: World Bank.

Cameron, S. 2011. "Whether and Where to Enroll: Choosing a Primary School in the Slums of Urban Dhaka, Bangladesh." *International Journal of Educational Development* 31 (4): 357–66.

CAMPE (Campaign for Popular Education Bangladesh). 2007. *Education Watch Report 2006. Financing Primary and Secondary Education in Bangladesh*. Dhaka.

Chaudhury, N., and D. Parajuli. 2010. Nepal Community School Impact Evaluation. Manuscript, South Asia Region, Human Development Unit, World Bank, Washington, DC.

Clotfelter, C. T., H. F. Ladd, and J. L. Vigdor. 2006. "Teacher-Student Matching and the Assessment of Teacher Effectiveness." *Journal of Human Resources* 41 (4): 778–820.

Cotlear, D. 2008. "Making Accountability Work: Lessons from RECURSO. En breve No 135." Operations Services Department, Latin America and the Caribbean Region, World Bank, Washington, DC.

Cunha, F., and J. Heckman. 2007. "The Technology of Skills Formation." *American Economic Review* 97 (2): 31–47.

Das, J., S. Dercon, J. Habyarimana, and P. Krishnan. 2007. "Teacher Shocks and Student Learning: Evidence from Zambia." *Journal of Human Resources* 42 (4): 820–62.

Das, J., S. Dercon, J. Habyarimana, P. Krishnan, K. Muralidharan, and V. Sundararaman. 2013. "School Inputs, Household Substitution, and Test Scores." *American Economic Journal: Applied Economics* 5 (2): 29–57.

Das, J., and T. Zajonc. 2010. "India Shining and Bharat Drowning: Comparing Two Indian States to the Worldwide Distribution in Mathematics Achievement." *Journal of Development Economics* 92 (2): 175–87.

Dongre, A., A. Chowdhury, and Y. Aiyar. 2012. "Unpacking School Finances." Background Note, Human Development Unit, South Asia Region, World Bank, Washington, DC.

Dreze, J., and G. Kingdon. 2001. "School Participation in Rural India." *Review of Development Economics* 5 (1): 1–24.

Duflo, E., R. Hanna, and S. P. Ryan. 2012. "Incentives Work: Getting Teachers to Come to School." *American Economic Review* 102 (4): 1241–78.

Galiani, S., P. Gertler, and E. Schargrodsky. 2008. "School Decentralization: Helping the Good Get Better, but Leaving the Poor Behind." *Journal of Public Economics* 92 (10): 2106–20.

Glewwe, P. 2002. "Schools and Skills in Developing Countries: Education Policies and Socioeconomic Outcomes." *Journal of Economic Literature* 40 (2): 436–82.

Glewwe, P., E. A. Hanushek, S. D. Humpage, and R. Ravina. 2011. "School Resources and Educational Outcomes in Developing Countries: A Review of the Literature from 1990 to 2010." Working Paper 17554, National Bureau of Economic Research, Cambridge, MA.

Glewwe, P., and M. Kremer. 2006. "Schools, Teachers, and Education Outcomes in Developing Countries." In *Handbook of the Economics of Education*, Vol. 2, edited by E. Hanushek and F. Welch. New York: Elsevier.

Goyal, S., and P. Pandey. 2009. *How Do Government and Private Schools Differ? Findings from Two Large Indian States*. Report No. 30, South Asia Human Development Unit, Washington, DC: World Bank.

Greaney, V., and T. Kellaghan. 2008. *Assessing National Achievement Levels in Education*. Vol. 1 of *National Assessments of Educational Attainment*. Washington, DC: World Bank.

Grindle, M. 2004. *Despite the Odds: The Contentious Politics of Education Reform*. Princeton, NJ: Princeton University Press.

Hanushek, E. A. 2010. "How Much Do Educational Outcomes Matter in OECD Countries?" Working Paper 16515, National Bureau of Economic Research, Cambridge, MA.

———. 2011. "The Economic Value of Higher Teacher Quality." *Economics of Education Review* 30: 466–79.

Hanushek, E. A., and S. G. Rivkin. 2010. "Constrained Job Matching: Does Teacher Job Search Harm Disadvantaged Urban Schools?" Working Paper 5816, National Bureau of Economic Research, Cambridge, MA.

Hanushek, E. A., and L. Woessmann. 2008. "The Role of Cognitive Skills in Economic Development." *Journal of Economic Literature* 46 (3): 607–68.

Heckman, J. J. 2000. "Policies to Foster Human Capital." *Research in Economics* 54 (1): 3–56.

Heckman, J. J., L. J. Lochner, and P. E. Todd. 2006. "Earning Functions, Rates of Return and Treatment Effects: The Mincer Equation and Beyond." In *Handbook of the Economics of Education*, edited by E. Hanushek and F. Welch, 310–458. Oxford, U.K.: North-Holland; Amsterdam: Elsevier.

Heneveld, W. 1994. "Planning and Monitoring the Quality of Primary Education in Sub-Saharan Africa." Technical Note 14, Human Resources and Poverty Division Technical Department, Africa Region, World Bank, Washington, DC.

Jayaraman, R., D. Simroth, and F. De Vericourt. 2010. *The Impact of School Lunches on Primary School Enrollment: Evidence from India's Mid-Day Meal Scheme*. Kolkata: Indian Statistical Institute.

Jhingran, D. 2012. "A Study of the School-Based Academic Factors Affecting Reading Achievement of Students in Primary Grades." Dissertation, Jamia Millia Islamia University, New Delhi.

Kingdon, G., and R. Banerji. 2009. "Addressing School Quality: Some Policy Pointers from Rural North India." RECOUP Policy Brief 5, Faculty of Education, University of Cambridge, Cambridge, U.K.

Kingdon, G., and C. Monk. 2010. "Health, Nutrition and Academic Achievement: New Evidence from India." Manuscript, Institute of Education, University of London, London.

Kingdon, G., and V. Sipahimalani-Rao. 2010. "Para Teachers in India: Status and Impact." *Economic and Political Weekly* 45 (12): 20–26.

Kingdon, G., and F. Teal. 2010. "Teacher Unions, Teacher Pay and Student Performance in India: A Pupil Fixed Effects Approach." *Journal of Development Economics* 91 (2): 278–88.

Kremer, M., N. Chaudhury, F. H. Rogers, K. Muralidharan, and J. Hammer. 2005. "Teacher Absence in India: A Snapshot." *Journal of the European Economic Association* 3 (2–3): 658–67.

Lange, F., and R. Topel. 2006. "The Social Value of Education and Human Capital." In *Handbook of the Economics of Education*, edited by E. Hanushek and F. Welch, 460–509. Oxford, U.K.: North-Holland; Amsterdam: Elsevier.

Lewis, M. A., and M. E. Lockheed, eds. 2007. *Exclusion, Gender and Education: Case Studies from the Developing World*. Washington, DC: Center for Global Development.

Madeira, R. 2007. "The Effects of Decentralization on Schooling: Evidence from the Sao Paulo State's Education Reform." Manuscript University of São Paulo, São Paulo. http://www.cid.harvard.edu/neudc07/docs/neudc07_s1_p12_madeira.pdf.

Martorell, R., B. Horta, L. Adair, A. Stein, L. Richter, C. Fall, S. Bhargava, S. Dey Biswas, L. Perez, F. Barros, and C. Victora. 2010. "Weight Gain in the First Two Years of Life Is an Important Predictor of Schooling Outcomes in Pooled Analyses from Five Birth Cohorts from Low- and Middle-Income Countries." *Journal of Nutrition* 40: 348–54.

Metzler, J., and L. Woessmann. 2012. "The Impact of Teacher Subject Knowledge on Student Achievement: Evidence from Within-Teacher Within-Student Variation." *Journal of Development Economics* 99: 486–96.

Miguel, E., and M. Kremer. 2004. "Worms: Identifying Impacts on Education and Health in the Presence of Treatment Externalities." *Econometrica* 72 (1): 159–217.

Miller, R., R. Murnane, and J. Willett. 2007. "Do Teacher Absences Impact on Student Achievement?" NBER Working Paper 13356, National Bureau of Economic Research, Cambridge, MA.

Moulin, S., M. Kremer, and P. Glewwe 2009. "Many Children Left Behind? Textbooks and Test Scores in Kenya." *American Economic Journal: Applied Economics* 1 (1): 112–35.

Muralidharan, K., and V. Sundararaman. 2009. "Teacher Performance Pay: Experimental Evidence from India." NBER Working Paper 15323, National Bureau of Economic Research, Cambridge, MA.

———. 2011. "Teacher Performance Pay: Experimental Evidence from India." *Journal of Political Economy* 119 (1): 39–77.

———. 2013. "Contract Teachers: Experimental Evidence from India." NBER Working Paper 19440, National Bureau of Economic Research, Cambridge, MA.

Muralidharan, K., and Y. Zieleniak. 2012. *Measuring Learning Trajectories in Developing Countries with Longitudinal Data and Item Response Theory*. Manuscript, University of California, San Diego, CA.

NCERT (National Council of Educational Research and Training). 2011. *What Do They Know? A Summary of India's National Achievement Survey, Class V, Cycle 3 2010/11*. New Delhi: NCERT.

OECD (Organisation for Economic Co-operation and Development). 2010. *Education at a Glance 2010: OECD Indicators*. Paris: OECD.

———. 2011. *Lessons from PISA for Mexico, Strong Performers and Successful Reformers in Education*. Paris: OECD.

———. 2013. *Teachers for the 21st Century: Using Evaluation to Improve Teaching*. Paris: OECD.

O'Neill, J., and T. Poddar. 2008. "Ten Things for India to Achieve its 2050 Potential." Global Economics Paper 169, Goldman Sachs, Washington, DC. https://portal.gs.com.

Pandey, P., S. Goyal, and V. Sundararaman. 2008. "Public Participation, Teacher Accountability and School Outcomes: Findings from Baseline Surveys in Three Indian States." Policy Research Working Paper 4777, South Asia Human Development Department, World Bank, Washington, DC.

———. 2011. "Does Information Improve School Accountability? Results of a Large Randomized Trial." Discussion Paper Series Report 39, South Asia Human Development Unit, World Bank, Washington, DC.

Pritchett, L. 2001. "Where Has All the Education Gone?" *World Bank Economic Review* 15 (3): 367–91.

Psacharopoulos, G., and H. A. Patrinos. 2002. "Returns to Investment in Education: A Further Update." Policy Research Working Paper 2881, Education Sector Unit, Latin America and the Caribbean Region, World Bank, Washington, DC.

Rodriguez, C. 2006. "Households' Schooling Behavior and Political Economy Trade-Offs after Decentralization." Working Paper, Universidad de los Andes, Colombia.

Sankar, D. 2009. "Teachers' Time on Task and Nature of Tasks: Evidence from Three Indian States." Human Development Department, South Asia Region, World Bank, Washington, DC.

———. 2012. "India's Right to Education Act: Opportunities and Challenges." Background paper prepared for India Economic Update, South Asia Poverty Reduction and Economic Management Unit, World Bank, Washington, DC.

Sharma, R., and V. Ramachandran. 2009. *The Elementary Education System in India*. New Delhi: Routledge.

World Bank. 2012a. More and Better Jobs in South Asia. Washington, DC: World Bank.

———. 2012b. What Matters Most in Teacher Policies. Washington, DC: World Bank.

———. 2013. "Education Sector Review in Bangladesh". Quality Policy Note, World Bank, Washington, DC.

PART 1

Introduction

Although education quality is recognized as both a major determinant of economic growth and social development and an effective vehicle for reducing poverty, this study is the first comprehensive assessment of the status and trends of learning outcomes in South Asia. It identifies causes and correlates of education quality and recommends policy priorities to improve learning outcomes.

Chapter 1 sets out the conceptual framework for examining the quality of education in South Asia, gives a working definition of it, and discusses issues related to measuring student learning. It then summarizes the evidence for the impact of education quality on economic growth, labor market outcomes, and the welfare of individuals. Poor-quality education is a major barrier to economic growth and poverty alleviation in South Asia.

Chapter 2 summarizes the evidence on the status of learning outcomes across the region based on student achievement tests and national assessments. Most South Asian countries are just beginning to measure education outcomes and have not yet participated in major international assessments (e.g., the Programme for International Student Assessment [PISA], the Trends in Mathematics and Science Study [TIMSS], or the Progress in International Reading Literacy Study [PIRLS]), except for two states in India that participated in the PISA+ in 2009. The chapter concludes that

- All countries in South Asia have made notable progress in increasing participation in primary education and improving gender parity, although access is still a major challenge, particularly for disadvantaged groups.
- Except in Sri Lanka, learning outcomes in the region are very low and there are major disparities by gender, location, and socioeconomic background.
- The shortage of cognitive skills in South Asia is undermining growth and making it harder to reduce poverty.

CHAPTER 1

Why Look at Student Learning Outcomes in South Asia?

Introduction

The primary objective of any educational system is for students to learn in terms of not only cognitive skills but also personal, socioemotional, and professional behavior. Schooling is successful when it helps students to lead fuller lives, become better individuals and citizens, and acquire skills and competencies that can lead to productivity in the labor market—which translates into national economic growth and competitiveness and better social outcomes (see box 1.1). Student learning outcomes—as measured not just by years of schooling but also by cognitive skill formation—have been found to be powerfully related to an individual's potential to earn, to the distribution of income in society, and to the growth of the national economy (Hanushek and Woessmann 2007, 2008).

Recognizing the importance of education for economic and social development, South Asian governments[1] have been investing heavily to meet the education Millennium Development Goals (MDGs). Net primary enrollment in the region rose from 75 percent in 2000 to 88 percent in 2010, and thus the number of children not in school declined from 36 million to 13 million. Though achievement in the region was uneven, especially for girls and other disadvantaged groups, it is still significant, especially since the region accounts for nearly 25 percent of the world's primary school–age population. Gross enrollment in lower secondary schools also rose, from 45 percent in 2001 to 51 percent in 2006. Most South Asian countries have also been successful in reducing disparities in access—indeed, Bangladesh and Sri Lanka both now have more girls than boys in secondary schools.

Unfortunately, although more children are in school, the region still has a major learning challenge in that the children are not acquiring basic skills. For example, only 50 percent of grade 3 students in Punjab, Pakistan, have a complete grasp of grade 1 mathematics (Andrabi et al. 2007). In India, on a test of reading comprehension administered to grade 5 students across the country, only 46 percent were able to correctly identify the cause of an event, and only a third of the

Box 1.1 The Importance of Investing in Education Quality

Recent studies provide ample evidence that it is the quality, not the quantity, of schooling that explains variation in labor market outcomes between individuals and differences in economic growth rates between countries. Cognitive skills, measured through test scores, explain a substantial part of variations in income between individuals (Mulligan 1999; Lazear 2003; Murnane, Willett, and Cardenas 2006; Hanushek and Woessmann 2008, 2010). The literature from developing countries on the relationship between test scores and labor market outcomes comes mainly from Pakistan (Alderman et al. 1996; Behrman, Ross, and Sabot 2008) and countries in Africa: Ghana (Glewwe 1996; Jolliffe 1998; Vijverberg 1999), Kenya (Boissiere, Knight, and Sabot 1985; Knight and Sabot 1990), Morocco (Angrist and Lavy 1997), South Africa (Moll 1998), and Tanzania (Boissiere, Knight, and Sabot 1985; Knight and Sabot 1990). In Pakistan, for instance, Behrman, Ross, and Sabot (2008) found that a 1 standard deviation increase in cognitive achievement is associated with a 25 percent increase in earnings.

If schooling and cognitive skills influence individual incomes, then the manner in which cognitive skills are distributed across different population groups is likely to influence the distribution of income between these groups. Using International Adult Literacy Survey data, Nickell (2004) found that a large part of the variation in earnings inequalities can be explained by skills dispersion. Indeed, one reason governments finance education is to reduce social and income inequalities between different groups.

There is also a significant body of work that establishes a positive relationship between measures of schooling and economic growth (Topel 1999; Krueger and Lindahl 2001; Sala-I-Martin, Doppelhofer, and Miller 2004; Temple and Woessmann 2006). At the macro level, student learning outcomes, especially in mathematics and science, have been found to have a significant effect on economic growth. For example, Hanushek and Woessman (2008) estimated that an increase of 1 standard deviation in student test scores on international assessments of literacy and mathematics is associated with a 2 percent increase in annual growth of gross domestic product (GDP) per capita. More recently, an Organisation for Economic Co-operation and Development (OECD) study (2010) noted that increases in PISA student test scores could have very large impacts on the future well-being of countries by dramatically improving national labor-force skills; it estimated that bringing all OECD countries up to the average performance of Finland—the top performer on Programme for International Student Assessment tests—would boost aggregate OECD GDP by US$260 trillion, six times the current GDP of OECD countries. The study emphasizes that the quality of learning outcomes, not the length of schooling, makes the difference. In South Asia, employer surveys in South Asia increasingly suggest that inferior education systems and a shortage of skills are a bar to private sector investment and growth (World Bank 2012). For example, Sri Lankan employers see an inadequately educated labor force as a severe constraint on company growth. Studies have also found that the availability of skills has a powerful positive correlation with firm productivity (Dutz and O'Connell 2012).

students could compute the difference between two decimal numbers (NCERT 2011). Another recent study found that about 43 percent of grade 8 students could not solve a simple division problem. Even recognition of two-digit numbers, supposed to be taught in grade 2, is often not achieved until grade 4 or 5 (Pratham 2011). In Bangladesh, only 25 percent of fifth-grade students have mastered Bangla and 33 percent have mastered the mathematics competencies specified in the national curriculum (World Bank 2013). In the current environment, there is little evidence that learning outcomes will improve by simply increasing school inputs in a business-as-usual manner (Muralidharan and Zieleniak 2012).

Poorly prepared graduates of both government and private schools in South Asia constrain not only the growth and competitiveness of the private sector but also deter creation of more and better jobs (World Bank 2012). Recognizing the risk, governments in South Asia have generated ambitious agendas of reform across the entire education spectrum. Initially, most focused on expanding basic education and improving the quality of school inputs. Today, while universal primary education is still the goal, virtually every country in the region is giving high priority to better student learning outcomes.

Learning outcomes tend to be much more unequally distributed than school access or enrollment. For one thing, in the last two decades expansion of access has created wide gaps in learning between historically disadvantaged children and better-off children who have access to supportive parental and other resources. These gaps start at the point of entry into the school system and widen over time to threaten enrollment equity gains, because children who learn less are more likely to drop out. Thus, bridging learning gaps at an early stage is essential.

Although interest in better learning has increased, there is too little understanding of what can be done to ensure improvement in learning outcomes (Kingdon and Riboud 2009). Although proposals to reform teacher training, decentralize, reform the curriculum, use contract teachers, and provide midday meals are widely debated, there is often little application of lessons learned in other parts of the world (Kingdon and Muzammil 2009).[2]

The main objective of this study is to review learning outcomes for both primary and secondary students in the region and identify good practices and policy options for sustainably improving those outcomes. The study responds to three questions:

- **How are educational systems in South Asia performing?** How much and what are students learning? How do learning outcomes vary by country, socioeconomic group, gender, and locations within countries?
- **What determines student learning outcomes?** How important are school resources and inputs compared to disparities in social background in terms of raising student learning in South Asia?
- **What policy options have proved effective in improving learning outcomes in South Asia?** What policies should be considered, especially now that demand is increasing while public resources are tight?

As far as can be ascertained, this is the first study of the region that goes beyond reviewing years of schooling and the inputs normally associated with quality education; it is concerned with the *comparative performance of educational systems in the region in terms of student learning outcomes*. While there have been comparative studies of progress within the region in expanding schooling access and participation (see Riboud, Savchenko, and Tan 2007), none has looked explicitly at what children are actually learning. This study is also one of the first to identify *determinants of student learning outcomes* in different South Asian countries. It does so by reviewing evidence from both recent large-scale national learning assessments and from the burgeoning literature on impact evaluations conducted in many South Asian countries. Finally, and again uniquely, this study identifies *core strategic options and priorities to improve learning outcomes* in the region.

The rest of this chapter deals with South Asia's education performance as measured by participation and completion rates, why the region needs to focus on school quality and learning outcomes, the methodology and data sources used in the study, and what to expect in the rest of the report.

Progress in School Participation

Trends in Enrollment Rates

To increase access to quality schooling, most South Asian countries have taken a number of initiatives (box 1.2). As a result, South Asia has been making significant progress in accumulating human capital stock in terms of school completion rates. Figure 1.1 shows the proportion of individuals in different age cohorts in the region who have completed at least grade 5 (primary) and grade 10 (lower secondary). Note that younger cohorts in all countries are far more likely to have completed both than older cohorts.

Box 1.2 South Asia: National and Regional Reforms in Primary and Secondary Education

Afghanistan: In 2002, through the Emergency Education Rehabilitation and Development Project, Afghanistan sought to increase access to formal and nonformal education for underserved groups, especially girls. In 2004, the Afghanistan Education Quality Improvement Program was launched in 10 provinces to improve infrastructure, teacher training programs, school principal development, and the capacity of provincial and district agencies to strengthen governance and accountability.

Bangladesh: Bangladesh launched the Third Primary Education Development Program (PEDP III) in 2011 as part of its National Education Policy (2010) to improve enrollments, primary school completion, and measurement of student learning. Between 2005 and 2012, a series of reforms targeted teacher training, equity, quality, and access (Teaching Quality Improvement

box continues next page

Box 1.2 South Asia: National and Regional Reforms in Primary and Secondary Education *(continued)*

in Secondary Education Project [TQISEP 2005]; Secondary Education Quality and Access Enhancement Project [SEQAEP 2008]; Higher Secondary Female Stipend Project [Phase-4 2009]).

Bhutan: As part of its 9th Five-Year Plan (2002–07) and its Vision 20/20 goals, Bhutan launched a plan to increase access to primary and secondary education and improve educational quality at all levels. In 2003, the Bhutan Education Development Project was launched to increase enrollment of children through Grade 10, improve teaching and learning, and enhance the capacity of all educational planning and monitoring agencies.

India: India launched the *Sarva Shiksha Abhiyan* (SSA or Education for All) central government program in 2001 to achieve universal elementary enrollment and retention by 2010. In 2009, the government launched the *Rashtriya Madhyamik Shiksha Abhiyan* (RMSA or Program for Universalization of Secondary Education) to expand the number of secondary schools in order to achieve universal lower secondary enrollment (grades 9–10) by 2018. In 2009, the Indian Parliament passed the Right to Education (RTE) Act, mandating free and compulsory education for all children ages 6–14 years. The RTE sets minimum school infrastructure standards (e.g., building, library, toilets), pupil-teacher ratios, and teacher hours, in all of which there has been notable progress. It does not set standards or goals for learning outcomes.

Maldives: To support the Education Master Plan and the 5th National Development Plan (1997–2001), the government launched the Third Education and Training Program (TETP) in 2000 to expand lower and upper secondary enrollment, enhance the quality and internal efficiency of primary and secondary education, increase the number of secondary school teachers nationwide, and strengthen institutional capacity.

Nepal: In 2009, Nepal launched the School Sector Reform Program (SSRP) to increase access and improve the quality of education for children in grades 1–8, focusing on marginalized groups and with decentralization goals. The SSRP was the last in a series of national programs, consisting of the Basic Primary Education Projects (BPEP I 1992–98; BPEP II 1999–2004), Community School Support Program (CSSP 2003–08), Secondary Education Support Program (SESP 2003–09), and Education for All Program (EFA 2004–09).

Pakistan: The World Bank supports major, multifaceted federal and provincial reforms to improve basic administrative systems and functioning as well as sector governance and accountability on all levels and in vocational education and training. These reforms are viewed as critical for improving service delivery and thus school participation, academic achievement, and skills acquisition. World Bank–financed projects that presently support these government initiatives include the Sindh and Punjab Education Sector Projects.

Sri Lanka: The Sri Lanka Ministry of Education put in place the Education Sector Development Framework and Program (ESDFP) for 2006–10 to promote equitable access to basic education (grades 1–9) and secondary education (grades 10–13), improve the quality of education, enhance the efficiency and equity of resource allocation, and strengthen education governance and service delivery.

Figure 1.1 Proportion of Population Who Have Completed at Least Grades 5 and 10, South Asia, 2010

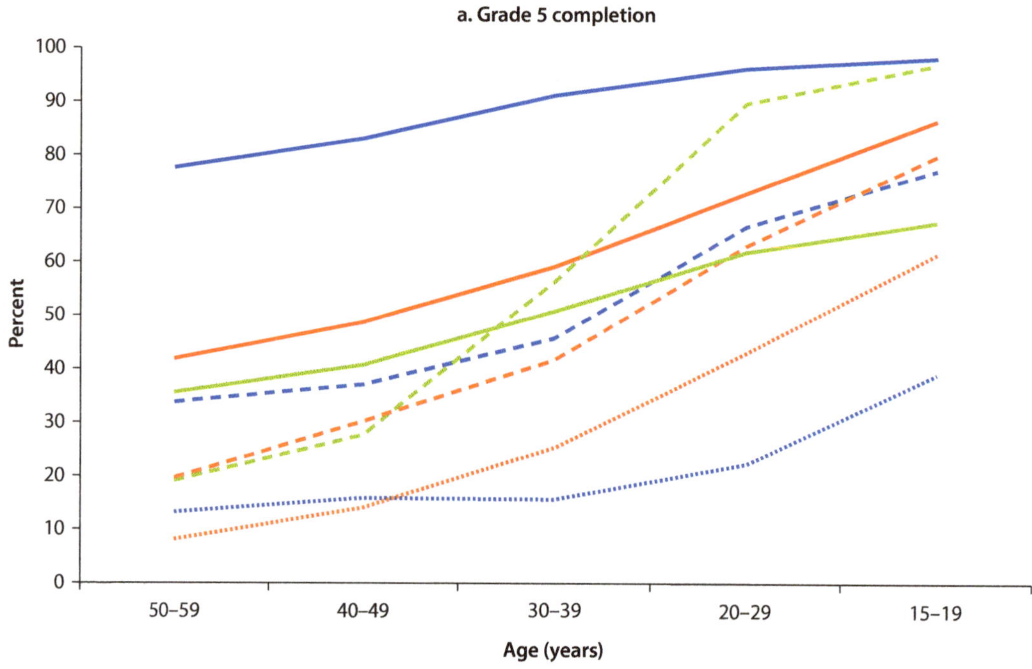

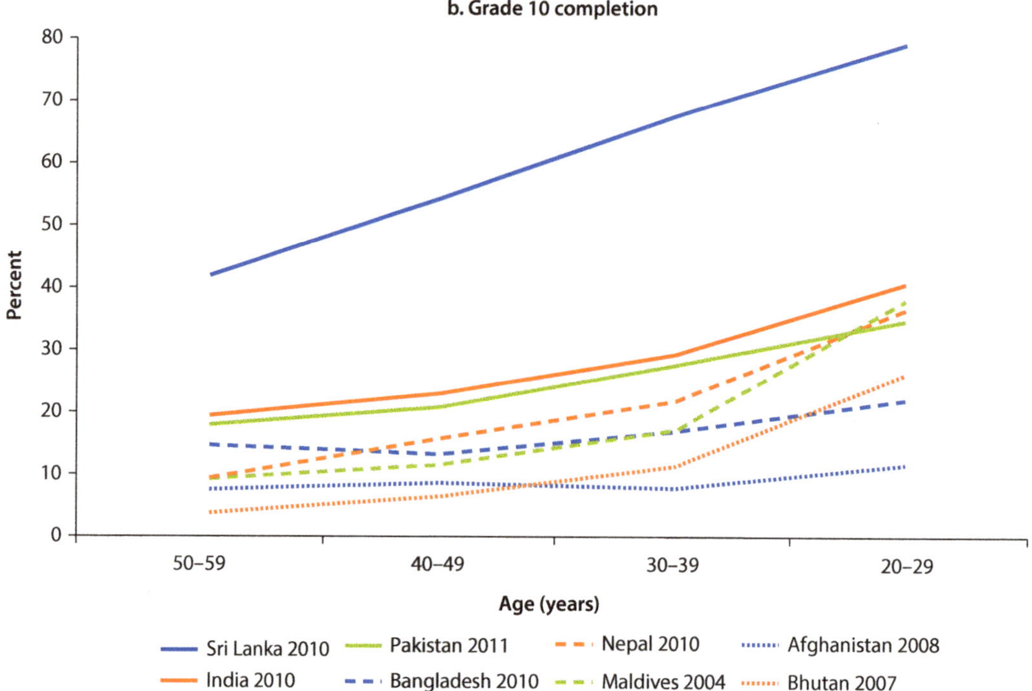

Source: Data from household surveys.

Several points stand out:

- Many more people in the region are completing primary school. Less than 40 percent of people ages 50–59 years in the region had completed grade 5 in 2010, except in Sri Lanka, where the completion rate for this cohort is close to 80 percent. However, more than 60 percent of people ages 15–19 years had finished primary school in all South Asian countries except Afghanistan, where the grade 5 completion rate was only 39 percent.
- Countries that started lowest, such as Maldives, Bhutan, and Nepal, have made the most progress.
- However, accumulation of human capital stock with secondary education has been very slow. With Sri Lanka again an outlier, less than 20 percent of those who were born in the 1950s have completed at least grade 10. Even though India, Bhutan, and Maldives were able to double the proportion of those ages 20–29 years who have completed at least grade 10, still less than 40 percent of South Asians born in the 1980s have completed secondary education. And in the youngest cohort, grade 10 completion rates are still abysmal in Bhutan, at 26 percent; Bangladesh, at 22 percent; and Afghanistan, at 12 percent.

The South Asian primary net enrollment rate (NER) rose from 75 percent in 2001 to about 88 percent in 2010, moving South Asia's NER closer to that of other regions. However, there are wide variations by country in schooling access. Sri Lanka and Maldives have consistently enrolled almost all their children in primary schools. Bhutan and India, on the other hand, have only recently made significant progress, increasing enrollment rates steadily to about 90 percent of children ages 6–14 years. In Pakistan, the NER jumped from 58 percent to 74 percent between 2000 and 2011, although that is still lower than the regional average (see figure 1.2).

Between 2000 and 2010, lower secondary enrollment rates increased from about 44 percent to 58 percent—impressive growth, though still below the world average by nearly 12 percentage points. In all South Asian countries the achievements in primary education, gradual improvements in retention and transition rates (particularly for more disadvantaged groups), and the rising rates of return on education have stimulated demand for postprimary education.

The region has made great progress in the last decade in educating girls. Bangladesh and Sri Lanka both now have more girls than boys in grades 6–12. In India, too, the percentage of girls in secondary school went up from 60 percent in 1990 to 74 percent in 2010. Since 1999, the region has decreased the total number of out-of-school girls from 23 million to 9.5 million (59 percent).

Despite the obvious progress, several major challenges still affect access to schooling as well as education outcomes. For instance:

- Attendance rates are relatively low. In India, for example, while the NER for children ages 6–14 years is about 96 percent, average attendance at all

Figure 1.2 Enrollment Rates in Primary and Secondary Education in South Asia, 2000–10

a. Primary net enrollment rate

b. Secondary gross enrollment rate

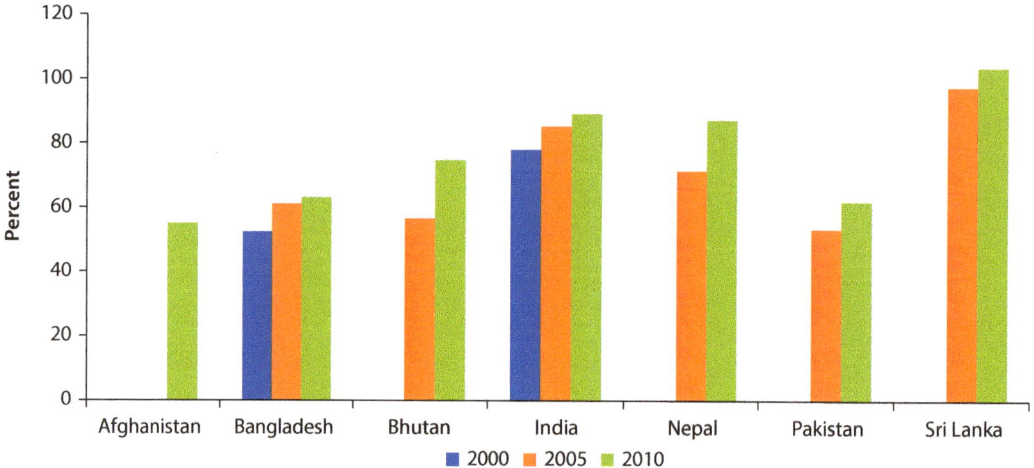

Source: EdStats 2012.

government schools is about 75 percent, though it ranges from less than 60 percent in Bihar to 92 percent in Kerala. In all other states attendance rates are about 15–30 percent lower than enrollment rates (Pratham 2009).

- Not all problems of access have been resolved. For example, the primary NER in Pakistan is 68 percent and in Afghanistan 39 percent—close to the rates in low-income countries in Sub-Saharan Africa. Primary participation rates in most of South Asia are particularly low for girls, children from poor families, rural children, and children who are members of caste, ethnic, and religious minorities. The estimated 13 million South Asian children still not enrolled in primary school in 2010 accounted for about one-fourth of all out-of-school children worldwide. As for lower secondary schools, in 2010 just over 58 percent of the relevant school-age population in the region was enrolled. While Bhutan, Maldives, Sri Lanka, Bangladesh, and India have shown impressive achievement in expanding secondary school enrollment, Afghanistan and Pakistan have not.

Completion rate is usually a proxy for both schooling quality and internal efficiency, and South Asian completion rates for primary education are among the lowest in the world, though its retention rates are improving; the proportion of children starting school who reach the final year of a given level has risen markedly through the 2000s. The primary completion rate rose from 65 percent in 1999 to 85 percent in 2009, approaching—though still behind—the world average of 88.5 percent. Nevertheless, in absolute terms, rates are low. Afghanistan, Bangladesh, and Pakistan are unlikely to meet the education MDGs by 2015 (figure 1.3). In India, on average only 75 percent of children who started grade 1 in 2003–04 reached grade 5 by 2007–08, and the proportion of children from minority groups who made the cut was even smaller. Retention rates drop off markedly as schooling advances, with just over half of those who started school in 2000–01 reaching grade 8 in 2007–08 (Hill and Chalaux 2011).

School inputs have been growing. To achieve their access goals, most countries in South Asia have demonstrated progress on two important educational inputs—school infrastructure and number of teachers. Investments in infrastructure have represented a high share of education budgets in recent decades. However, the quality is low by developed country standards and varies noticeably

Figure 1.3 Primary Completion Rates in South Asia

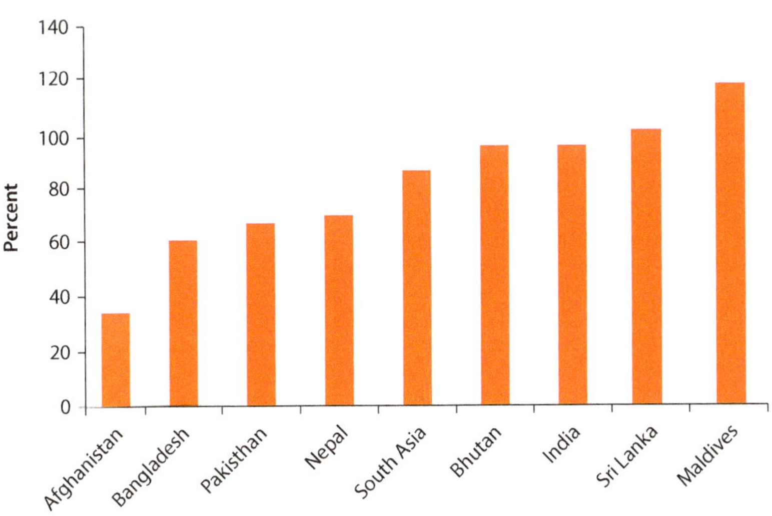

Source: UNESCO Institute for Statistics 2012.

within as well as between countries. For example, in 2011 the Bangladesh government reported that classrooms in half the primary schools, government and nongovernment, were overcrowded (more than 56 students each) and lacked drinking water, toilets, and furniture. Poor and nonexistent education facilities are also often reported in other countries in the region.

Although the number of primary school teachers in South Asia has grown more than 2 percent annually for the last decade, the increase has barely kept pace with the growth in enrollments. The pupil-teacher ratio (PTR) in primary education remained at about 40—the global average is 24. Figure 1.4 shows primary and secondary PTRs in South Asia in selected years. The primary PTR varies from

Figure 1.4 Primary and Secondary Pupil-Teacher Ratios in South Asia, by Country, Selected Years

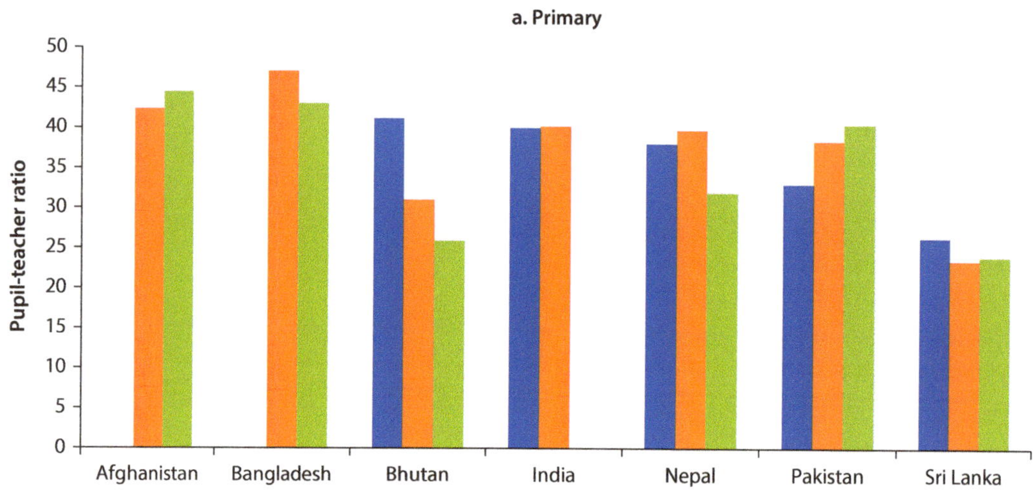

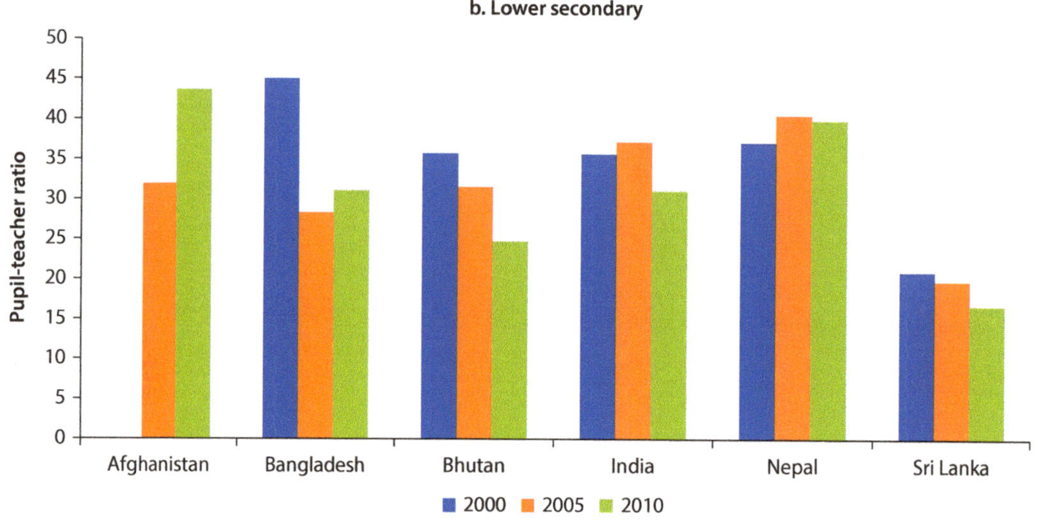

Source: EdStats 2012.

12.7 in Maldives to 43.0 in Bangladesh. Except in Afghanistan and Pakistan, PTRs have declined in most South Asian countries. Several intend to decrease PTRs further. The Indian RTE Act, for example, stipulates a maximum primary PTR ratio of 30 to 1. Except in Afghanistan and Nepal, the South Asian lower secondary PTR dropped in most countries from 34 in 2000 to 26 in 2010, again with wide variations.

Several South Asian countries have also invested in non-teacher-related inputs, such as textbooks and instructional technology, remedial education, mid-day meal programs, and school health programs. However, there is often too little information to assess trends in input provision across the region and their relative impact on student access and learning outcomes (see chapter 7 for a review of the evidence).

In summary, despite the rapid expansion of enrollments, improvements in the quality of school inputs have not translated into better learning outcomes. As will be shown, while inputs are needed as enablers, the quality of learning outcomes depends largely on how they are used, how classroom instruction is transacted, and whether education systems continuously monitor learning outcomes to improve efficiency and modify processes.

Why Focus on the Quality of Education?

The four main priorities for Education for All policies are access, equity, quality, and governance. These priorities are also articulated in the World Bank Group's Education Strategy 2020 (box 1.3). This report assumes that studying student learning at the system level will yield the greatest returns because doing so will help to address all four priorities.

Box 1.3 World Bank Education Strategy 2020: Invest Early, Invest Smartly, Invest for All

The World Bank's Education Strategy 2020 sets the goal of achieving learning for all. The emphasis on learning, not merely putting students in school, is important, because the knowledge and skills individuals acquire are associated with growth, development, and poverty reduction. With this in mind, the strategy emphasizes the need to invest early, invest smartly, and invest for all. It is important to invest early, because foundational skills acquired early in childhood make possible a lifetime of learning. Next, it is important to make investments that have proven to contribute to learning, with quality being the focus of education investments and learning gains being a key metric of quality. Finally, learning for all means ensuring that *all* students, not just the privileged or gifted, acquire the knowledge and skills they need. To achieve learning for all, the World Bank Group is channeling its efforts in education in two strategic directions: reforming education systems at the country level and building a high-quality knowledge base for education reforms at the global level. The education system approach will focus on

box continues next page

Box 1.3 World Bank Education Strategy 2020: Invest Early, Invest Smartly, Invest for All *(continued)*

increasing accountability and results as a complement to providing inputs. Simultaneously, at the regional and global level, the Bank will help develop a high-quality knowledge base on education reform. Toward this end, the Bank is developing new knowledge approaches to guide education reform, such as the Systems Approach for Better Education Results (SABER). Better knowledge of the strengths and weaknesses of particular education systems will allow the Bank to respond more effectively to the needs of its partner countries.

Access

In South Asia, primary school enrollment is no longer a major challenge except in Afghanistan and Pakistan; what is a challenge is reducing dropouts and increasing secondary enrollments. The latter is not just a matter of building school infrastructure. To increase secondary enrollment, it is necessary to ensure that students are better prepared to benefit from it without being so discouraged they drop out. Improving primary learning outcomes is thus critical for improving enrollment in, and effective access to, secondary schools.

Equity

While gaps in enrollment between disadvantaged groups, such as religious minorities and girls, and the population averages have narrowed significantly, there is a considerably wider gap in learning levels: historically disadvantaged and poorer children do significantly less well. Large and growing learning gaps threaten the enrollment equity gains because children who learn less are more likely to drop out.

Quality

Although in practical policy terms, improving education quality has typically been interpreted as improving the quality of schooling inputs, a decade of research finds few if any correlations in South Asia between input-based measures of school quality and student learning outcomes. A direct focus on learning outcomes as a goal of the education system may therefore be necessary to convert inputs into learning for children.

Governance

Several studies have reported challenges in education governance, exemplified by teacher absence and delayed flows of funds to schools. Other studies have found that better measurement and management of teacher performance has a significant positive impact on student learning. Specific and targeted measures of student learning and measures to hold teachers, schools, and school systems accountable for learning may help improve governance by orienting the education system toward outcomes.

Addressing the problem of the quality of student learning will simultaneously address many of the other challenges. Inputs and resources do matter, but a focus on learning outcomes will help to ensure that these inputs and resources are used effectively where they have the greatest impact.

The Economic and Social Impact of Learning Outcomes

At the macro level, student learning outcomes, especially in mathematics and science, have much more effect on economic growth than number of schooling years. For example, Hanushek and Woessman (2008) estimate that an increase of 1 standard deviation in student test scores on international assessments of literacy and mathematics is associated with a 2 percent increase in annual growth of GDP per capita. More recently, an OECD study found that increases in PISA student test scores could have very large impacts on future well-being by dramatically improving national labor force skills; it estimated that bringing all OECD countries up to average performance in Finland—the top performer on PISA tests—would boost aggregate OECD GDP by US$260 trillion, six times the current GDP of OECD countries, over the lifetime of the generation of students born in 2010 (OECD 2010). The study also found that the quality of learning outcomes, not the length of schooling, makes the difference (OECD 2010).

Employer surveys in South Asia increasingly suggest that inferior education systems and a shortage of skills are a bar to private sector investment and growth (World Bank 2012). For example, Sri Lankan employers see an inadequately educated labor force as a severe constraint on firm growth (figure 1.5). Dutz and O'Connell (2012) also found that the availability of skills has a powerful positive correlation with firm productivity.

Figure 1.5 Sri Lanka: Firm Ranking of Investment Climate Constraints

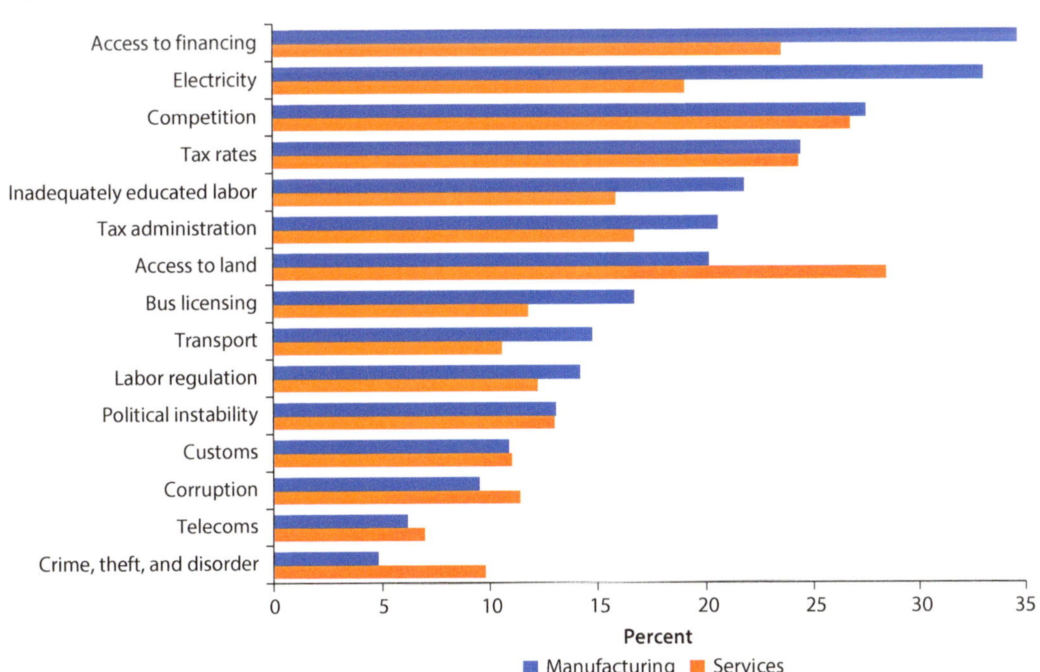

Source: Dutz and O'Connell 2012.
Note: Averages weighted by 2003 industry and size sampling.

Rising rates of return on secondary and senior secondary education in countries like India suggest that demand for what is learned at these levels has increased faster than supply (World Bank 2009). By raising student learning outcomes rather than merely average years of schooling, countries in South Asia may be able to stimulate innovation, promote diversification of products and services, and develop a more skill-intensive route to development.

Better-quality education is associated with higher future earnings. At the micro level, a number of studies in developed countries (summarized in Hanushek and Woessmann 2008) and developing countries (Boissiere, Knight, and Sabot 1985; Alderman et al. 1996; Moll 1998; Blunch 2009) have found that student learning outcomes, as measured by test scores, have a positive impact on earnings even after controlling for number of years in school, worker experience, and other factors that might influence income.

However, studies of links between the quality of education and labor market outcomes in South Asia are very scarce. Box 1.4 summarizes the evidence on rates of return to education in selected South Asian countries. Findings of a few studies suggest that not only do years of schooling matter to labor market outcomes but so do the cognitive skills that workers possess. For example, Behrman, Ross, and Sabot (2008), using household data from 1989 in rural Pakistan, found that a 1 standard deviation increase in cognitive achievement is associated with a 25 percent increase in earnings. They also estimated that, given the environment in Pakistan in the early 1990s, the "social" rate of return on improving the quality of primary schooling is substantially greater than the rate of return on increasing access to middle school.

Even after controlling for education of the individuals, a recent study on skills supply in Sri Lanka (Savchenko 2012) found a statistically significant positive relationship between noncognitive and technical skills and earnings. A study in India also found that, relative to numeracy and literacy skills, the largest increase in individual earnings of wage workers is generated by knowledge of the English language, which suggests that the Indian labor market values credentials, but the same study found that among Pakistani wage workers the largest earnings rewards come from literacy skills (Aslam et al. 2012).

In Bangladesh basic reading, writing, and numeracy tests were administered to adults as part of the World Bank-financed Secondary Education Quality and Access Enhancement Project (SEQAEP). Figure 1.6 presents the means of normalized test scores by type of employment. The simple averages suggest that test performance is closely correlated with the occupations individuals select. Nonagricultural workers have significantly higher test scores than agricultural workers, and in the nonagricultural category, salaried workers score higher on the basic tests than the self-employed and daily labor. Simple analysis shows a positive correlation between quality of employment and quality of education, and regression analysis finds a statistically significant positive relationship between performance on basic cognitive tests and earnings in rural Bangladesh even after controlling for education outcomes; an increase of 1 standard deviation in basic math scores is associated with 15 percent higher earnings, and a similar increase in basic reading scores brought a 20 percent earnings premium.

Box 1.4 Wage Premiums in Selected South Asian Countries, by Level of Education

Several notable trends in the estimated returns on education over the last 10–15 years are evident in India, Nepal, Pakistan, and Sri Lanka (see figure B1.4.1):

- Returns to lower secondary and below have held steady or declined. For example, the returns to incomplete primary education relative to no education at all fell in all countries. The returns to primary relative to incomplete primary education declined in India and Sri Lanka but were relatively stable and low in Nepal and Pakistan.
- Returns to higher secondary and tertiary education have been increasing. For instance, in Sri Lanka the wage premium to higher secondary relative to lower increased from 33 percent in 2000 to 50 percent in 2008. In India, estimated returns to tertiary education more than tripled from 1994 to 2010, suggesting higher demand for skilled labor.

These changes suggest that the supply of South Asian workers with less education is increasing faster than demand, and demand for workers with higher secondary and tertiary

Figure B1.4.1 Wage Premiums in Selected South Asian Countries, by Level of Education

a. India and Sri Lanka

Percent
60
40
20
0
1994
2000
2005
2010
India
2000
2008
Sri Lanka

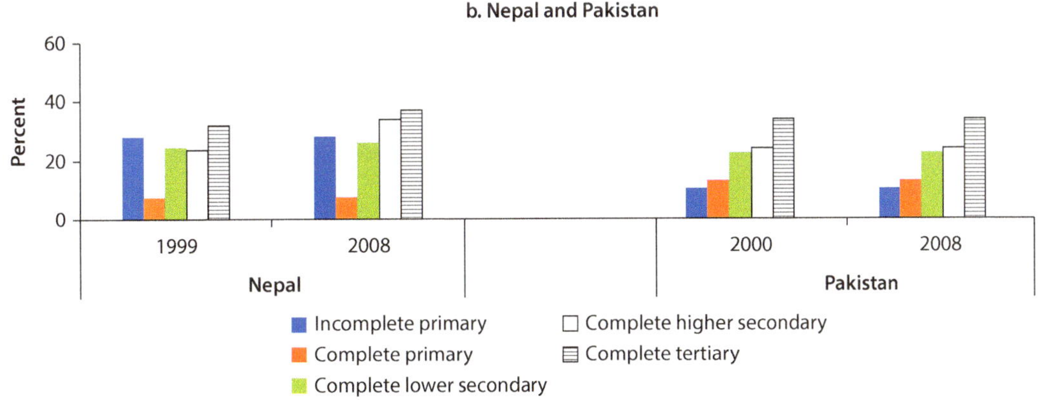

Source: World Bank 2012.
Note: The first bar for each country-year pair reflects the wage premium for primary relative to no education; the last reflects the wage premium for completing tertiary relative to completing upper secondary education. The wage premiums represent the differences in the coefficients of a regression of log hourly wage on basic controls (the highest level of education completed, experience, and experience squared). The qualitative results are robust to other specifications with additional controls.

box continues next page

Box 1.4 Wage Premiums in Selected South Asian Countries by Level of Education *(continued)*

education is growing faster than supply. Poor-quality primary and lower secondary education at lower levels may become a barrier to accessing tertiary education and ultimately limit worker labor market opportunities. It may also exacerbate inequalities. There are substantial differences in learning outcomes by income (see chapter 3). Ensuring adequate primary and secondary education for all of the population is crucial for reaping the benefits of higher education.

Figure 1.6 Average Normalized Test Scores, by Employment Type, Rural Bangladesh, 2008

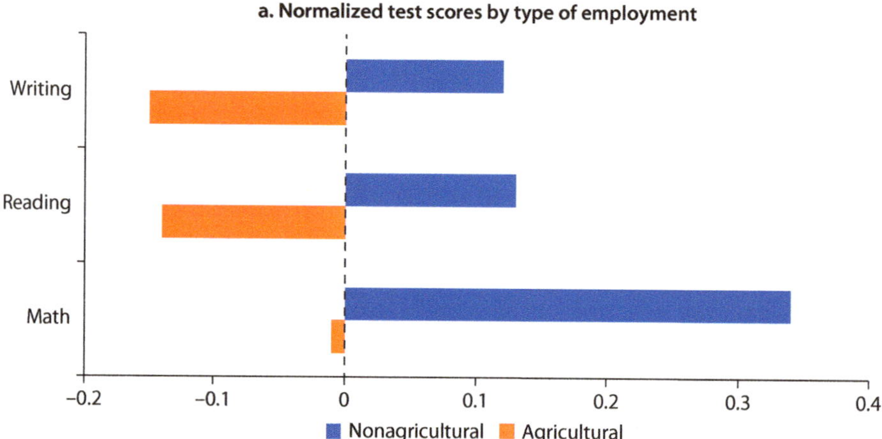

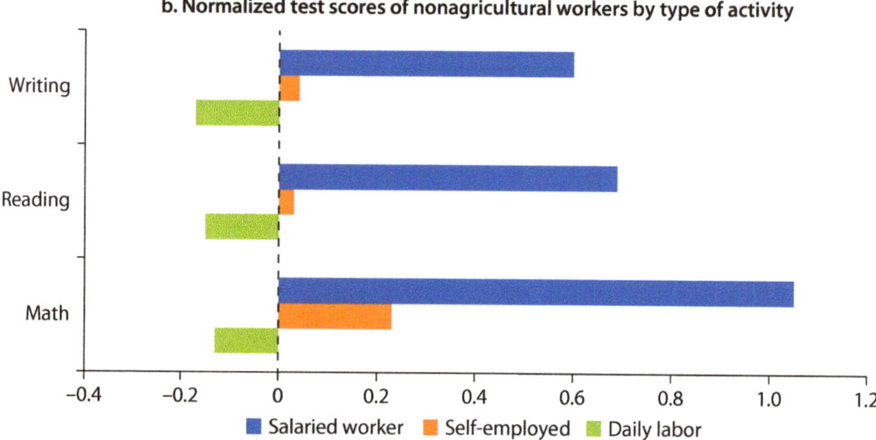

Source: Based on data from the Bangladesh SEQAEP baseline survey.

Better learning outcomes could translate into better labor market outcomes, especially in countries undergoing rapid technical and economic change, because education can make it possible for workers to continue learning throughout life and to adapt to new technology. For example, Mittal and Tripathi (2009) found that farmers who had higher-level skills were better able to process codified and complex information and thus benefit from a program that used mobile phones to communicate current market, production, transport, and meteorological data.

Better-quality education helps to improve social outcomes, such as better health, lower infant mortality, and a narrowing of income inequality. The quality of education has been positively linked to health, healthy behaviors, and more use of preventive health services (OECD 2005). Jones, Rice, and Dias (2011) found that in the United Kingdom, while educational attainment was associated positively with healthier behaviors (less smoking, less smoking in pregnancy, and consumption of healthy foods) and negatively with mental ill health in adulthood, the positive association was strengthened by the quality of schooling—as proxied by attendance at an academically intensive grammar school. Cutler and Lleras-Muney (2010) also suggested that peer effects (a broad proxy for schooling quality) are likely to magnify the positive effects of education on health.

Improved student test scores have been found to accelerate the decline in infant mortality, an effect that is stronger in open than in closed economies (Jamison, Jamison, and Hanushek 2007). The International Adults Literacy Survey (IALS) showed that dispersion in student learning outcomes has an impact on income inequality (Nickell 2004). Thus, better learning outcomes not only yield economic returns but also seem to improve general well-being.

Inferior education disproportionately affects poor and disadvantaged groups. Students from poor backgrounds have difficulty accessing education, and those who do enter tend to drop out early. More important, while gaps in enrollment between disadvantaged groups and population averages have narrowed, historically disadvantaged and economically weaker children still have significantly lower learning outcomes (Assadullah et al. 2009). Figure 1.7 shows that learning outcomes tend to be much more unequally distributed than school access or enrollment.[3] Large and growing learning gaps threaten the equity gains in enrollment because children who learn less are more likely to drop out. School-age children who miss out on educational opportunities rarely have many opportunities to remedy this loss later in life. Poor-quality primary education also hinders access to, and performance in, higher education. Thus, an early focus on learning outcomes and bridging gaps in learning levels are essential to meet the equity and efficiency goals of education policy in South Asia.

Poor education system performance increases educational costs. For instance, to combat high illiteracy, governments spend significant amounts on adult literacy programs. Students repeating grades, as is common in South Asia, further burden an education system. Finally, inadequate worker skills create a need for training and retraining, the costs of which may be borne by employers, public or private, or by the individuals themselves (OECD 2005; Dutz 2007).

How Student Learning Outcomes Are Analyzed

This section describes the conceptual framework for analyzing learning outcomes and discusses data issues and limitations. At the heart of it is an educational production function that converts school and nonschool inputs into learning outcomes (figure 1.8). Educational systems use a variety of inputs to produce short- and long-term outcomes. Typically, short-term outcomes are the knowledge, skills, and values gained during schooling, measured by achievement tests (box 1.5). Intermediate outputs are measured by enrollment, attendance, attainment, and completion rates. Long-term outcomes are, among others, employment, occupation, and earnings; improved health; and civic participation.

Figure 1.7 Lorenz Curves for School Enrollment and Ability to Write and Divide, India, 2004–05

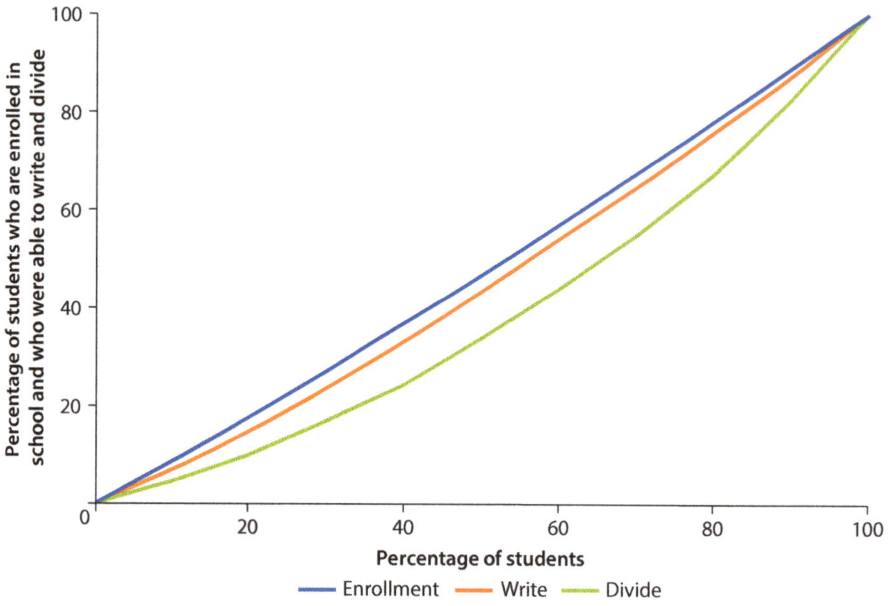

Source: Data from the India Human Development Survey.

Figure 1.8 Conceptual Framework for Improving Learning Outcomes

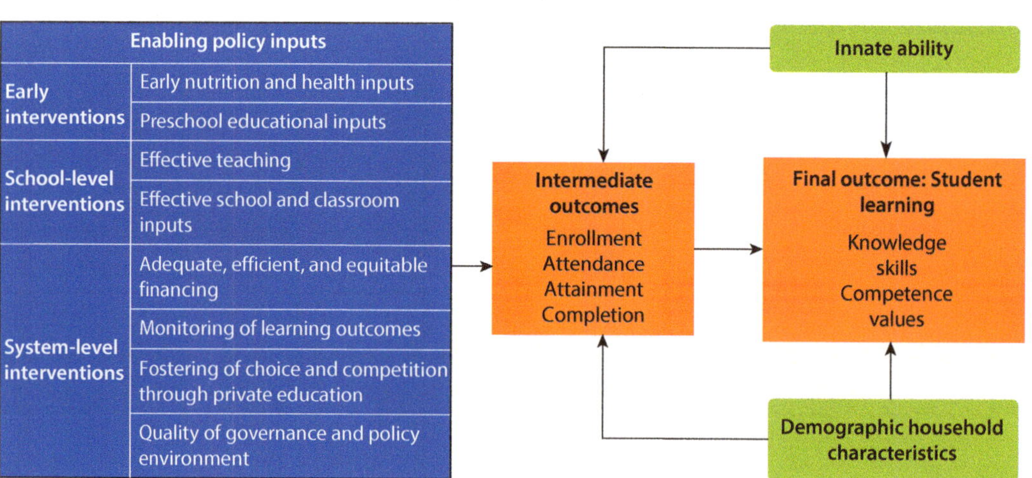

Box 1.5 Types of Skills Defined

Cognitive skills are defined as the "ability to understand complex ideas, to adapt effectively to the environment, to learn from experience, to engage in various forms of reasoning, [and] to overcome obstacles by taking thought." They include (a) verbal ability, numeracy, problem-solving, memory, and mental speed; (b) raw problem-solving ability versus knowledge to solve problems; and (c) use of logical, intuitive, and creative thinking.

Noncognitive skills are domains not directly associated with intelligence (cognition). These skills, which may have multiple dimensions, have been referred to as soft skills, personality traits, or socioemotional skills. They include (a) social and life skills and personality traits; (b) openness to experience, conscientiousness, extraversion, agreeability, and emotional stability; and (c) self-regulation, perseverance, decision making, and interpersonal skills.

Technical skills are specialized skills relevant to performing specific tasks. They include (a) skills related to a specific occupation; (b) skills developed though vocational schooling or acquired on the job; and (c) manual dexterity and use of methods, materials, tools, and instruments.

Source: World Bank 2010.

Education quality encompasses the cognitive, noncognitive, and technical skills a student is expected to exhibit after a period of study—usually cognitive skills as measured by test scores. The importance of test scores in shaping later-life outcomes has been well-documented (box 1.6).

Education systems can be evaluated in terms of internal efficiency (as measured by the relationship between inputs and outputs); effectiveness (the degree to which goals or objectives are achieved); and external efficiency or relevance (again as measured by the relationship between inputs and outcomes). Quality often refers to effectiveness—the degree to which students have acquired knowledge and skills in school (Heneveld 1994). Thus, quality improvement refers to a qualitative change in the knowledge and skills a student population acquires, as measured through achievement tests at school and in subnational, national, regional, and international tests.

The relationship between inputs and outcomes is complex. It is confounded by contemporaneous factors that can interact in complex ways, some reinforcing each other and others offsetting each other. Treating any single input as synonymous with quality can be misleading. For instance, despite general agreement on the importance of noncognitive skills, achievement tests typically only measure the skills and knowledge acquired by students in a few areas, such as reading, writing, and numeracy.

Where comparative learning outcome indicators are lacking, educational quality is often assessed by either proxy indicators (e.g., enrollment, repetition, transition, or completion rates) or input-based indicators. In fact, poor conditions in schools (such as dilapidated buildings, overcrowded classrooms, inadequate or outdated learning materials, and poorly educated and unmotivated

Box 1.6 Student Test Scores and Later-Life Outcomes

One potential limitation of directing education policy to student learning outcomes (as measured by scores on standardized assessment tools) is that for many dimensions of human capital that matter for the long-term success of students, test scores may be a very imperfect measure. However, an extensive body of research suggests that interventions that improve learning as measured by test scores also contribute to positive long-term outcomes, such as school completion, college attendance, and even wages. Deming (2009) showed that students who attend Head Start (a U.S. early childhood program) have both better test scores in the short run and superior long-term outcomes, even though test score gains fade after a few years. More recently, Chetty, Friedman, and Rockoff (2011) conducted a long-term follow-up of 2.5 million U.S. children and linked their adult outcomes to measures of teacher quality in grades 3–8. They found that teacher quality (measured by the extent to which teachers improve learning outcomes) is highly predictive of both such adult outcomes as college attendance, quality of college attended, and wages and such social outcomes as reduced teenage pregnancy and living in a better neighborhood.

Without data on long-term outcomes, such as wages, the metrics of education system performance necessarily rely on short-term proxies. It appears that though learning outcomes as measured by student scores on standardized assessments may be an incomplete measure of human capital, they are useful enough to be considered a meaningful proxy for creation of skills and human capital.

teachers) influence both student achievement and parental demand for schooling. Consequently, attempts to raise learning outcomes often rely on better inputs. Yet the extent to which such reforms actually improve student achievement has often been disappointing.

Numerous studies have reviewed the determinants of student learning outcomes. (For a review of the literature, see Lockheed and Verspoor 1991; Heneveld 1994; Heneveld and Craig 1996; UNESCO 2004; Vegas and Petrow 2008; Glewwe et al. 2011). Student learning outcomes are determined by individual and household characteristics and three categories of related policy interventions—early, school level, and system level—plus a variety of contextual factors:

- Factors relate to *individual and household characteristics,* such as student endowments (e.g., innate ability), gender, household income, and parental education.
- *Health, nutrition, and early childhood interventions* before children begin primary education are factors that must be considered. Because these contribute to a child's cognitive and noncognitive development, they affect school readiness and ultimately achievement of learning outcomes.
- Whether the *school environment* promotes teaching and learning through, for example, well-trained and motivated teachers and good textbooks, teaching materials, equipment and technology, infrastructure, and facilities is another

important factor. Often, too, demand for schooling or increased completion and retention rates and learning outcomes relate to enhancements for students that are not directly related to education, such as midday meal and school health programs, conditional cash transfers, school grants, and information campaigns. A component of this factor is the process of translating inputs into learning outcomes, which is affected by (a) curriculum, pedagogy, classroom structure, and other teaching and learning arrangements; (b) management and leadership within a school; and (c) school governance and autonomy.

- Finally, *institutional, economic, political, and social factors* have a direct bearing on student learning. For example, ministries of education affect how the education system functions through policies covering education governance, financing, student assessment, and quality assurance. Similarly, political and economic conditions affect how the education system operates. These exogenous factors are beyond the control of the education system (Heneveld 1994).

Studies analyzing what determines learning measure the relationship between education inputs and learning outcomes based on achievement scores. Most studies do not examine contextual factors or process factors like leadership, curriculum, pedagogy, and the content of training programs (Glewwe et al. 2011). One contextual factor is civil conflict. Many South Asian countries have had long-standing civil conflicts that may well have disrupted both schooling access and student learning outcomes. However, the evidence of their effects on learning is weak to nonexistent (Shemyakina and Valente 2012).

Methodology and Data Sources

To make this study as comprehensive as possible in covering South Asia, it was necessary to use several approaches to overcome data limitations. First, to the extent possible the review and conclusions are based on quantitative data. In addition to country-specific analytical work, the study benefited from the World Bank's recent regional flagship study, *More and Better Jobs in South Asia* (2012), and its continuing study on *Equity and Development*. The study also drew on such other World Bank work as the recent analysis of education and skill requirements carried out in Europe and Central Asia, Latin America, and East Asia and regional and global analyses of secondary and tertiary education.

Where evidence was not available, the issues were addressed through country-specific studies using national assessment and examination results, household and labor force surveys, and secondary education data and the results of the recent PISA 2009+ in two Indian states.

Although this report covers both, it emphasizes primary rather than secondary education, partly because there are simply more data available for the former and partly because, for secondary education, countries in the region other than Sri Lanka are still very heavily focused on access issues. Since schooling quality and learning outcomes are often perceived as a second-order problem to be addressed after access issues have mostly been resolved, there has naturally been less focus on secondary school quality.

There are also wide variations in what constitutes secondary education. In some South Asian countries, secondary school starts at grade 6, in others grade 7. The distinction between primary and secondary schools is further blurred by the proliferation of middle schools, lower secondary schools, and other divisions (box 1.7).

Box 1.7 Some Primary and Secondary Education Systems in South Asia

Bangladesh: Primary education spans grades 1–5, lower secondary grades 6–8, secondary grades 9–10, and higher secondary grades 11–12. Bangladesh has a centralized system administered by the Ministry of Education (MOE) and the Ministry of Primary and Mass Education (MoPME). The MOE Directorate of Secondary and Higher Education (DSHE) is responsible for planning and management of postprimary and higher education, including *madrassas*. Administration of lower secondary and secondary schools is more decentralized than for grades 11 and 12.

India: Primary education covers grades 1–5, middle-stage education grades 6–8, secondary grades 9 and 10, and higher secondary grades 11 and 12. Responsibility for education is shared between central and state governments in India, but there is significant variation by state in the degree of decentralization. Students who have completed grade 10 can take either the national examination conducted by the Central Board of Secondary Education (CBSE) or the Council for the Indian School Certificate Examinations (CISCE). West Bengal, Maharashtra, and other states have their own alternatives to the national examinations. Tertiary institutions accept state test scores,

Nepal: Primary education spans grades 1–5, lower secondary grades 6–8, secondary grades 9–10, and higher secondary grades 11–12. Administration of primary and secondary education has three levels: the central level is managed by the Ministry of Education and Sports (MOES), the regional level by Regional Education Directorates and District Education Offices, and grades 11–12 by the Higher Secondary Education Board. Secondary technical and vocational education is managed by the Council for Technical Education and Vocational Training (CTEVT) under MOES.

Pakistan: Primary education covers grades 1–5, middle-stage education grades 6–8, secondary education grades 9 and 10, and higher secondary or intermediate education grades 11 and 12. Education is a provincial responsibility; however, under the Local Government Ordinance 2000–01, district governments are given more administrative authority and control over grades 1–10. The efficacy of decentralization varies significantly by province. According to the 18th Amendment to the Constitution, the federal government has no role in education.

Sri Lanka: Primary education consists of grades 1–5, junior secondary grades 6–9, and senior secondary grades 10–13. Students take national General Certificate of Education (GCE) O-level tests at the end of grade 11 and GCE A-level tests at the end of grade 13; pre-employment training is possible after taking either. The center and the provinces share the education function. The Ministry of Education is responsible for national policies and Provincial Councils of Education manage primary and secondary education.

For this report, thematic background studies were prepared that drew on research on such regional issues as (a) early childhood development; (b) school resources, including the impact of curriculum, textbooks, and other school inputs; (c) teacher quality; (d) student assessment systems; (e) costs and financing of education; (f) education and labor market outcomes; (g) education decentralization; (h) private education; and (i) education in conflict-affected areas.

This study also examines the effectiveness of interventions to improve the quality and relevance of education in Bank-financed operations through a review of the portfolio of recent operations. Finally, it identifies significant issues that warrant further research because they cannot be addressed satisfactorily with the information currently available.

Scope and Limitations

This report focuses on learning outcomes for primary and secondary students; it does not consider outcomes of vocational and technical or tertiary education. It is also limited to mainstream education and only tangentially examines outcomes for children with special needs to the extent that the question enters into discussions on teacher standards and financing. The report also does not fully address some issues, such as management, governance, quality assurance mechanisms, and non-teaching-staff-related school resources, that may also help to shape student learning.

The fact that educational systems have multiple goals that have multiple outcomes makes it difficult to measure their "success" or lack thereof based on a single indicator like student learning outcomes. That limitation is inherent in all studies in this area.

Structure of the Report

The first of four parts discusses the context, rationale, and framework for looking at education quality in South Asia (chapter 1) and profiles learning outcomes there (chapter 2). Part 2 looks at school readiness and the extent to which household and individual endowments, such as nutrition and early childhood development, lay a foundation for scholastic success (chapters 3 and 4). Part 3 looks at specific school-related factors that affect learning outcomes: number of teachers and their quality (chapter 5) and the roles of pedagogy and classroom procedures (chapter 6). Part 4 then analyzes specific system-level factors, such as financing of education (chapter 7), the role of student assessment systems (chapter 8), private education (chapter 9), and governance and education decentralization (chapter 10).

Two cross-cutting issues that are central to quality learning are addressed:

1. **Equity in opportunity in terms of income, gender, location, and caste.** For example, Part 1 looks at the extent to which different groups are disadvantaged at the point of entry. Parts 3 and 4 look at which schools can respond to the specific learning needs of different groups of students.

2. **How poor governance and inadequate accountability mechanisms constrain educational quality.** Parts 3 and 4 look at the extent to which specific interventions promote accountability and performance.

Notes

1. Throughout this report, following the World Bank standard definition, South Asia refers to Afghanistan, Bangladesh, Bhutan, India, Maldives, Nepal, Pakistan, and Sri Lanka.
2. For the past decade, as the world has made significant achievements in expanding primary education, education quality has been studied extensively (see, for example, Chapman and Adams 2002; UNESCO 2004; OECD 2005; Vegas and Petrow 2008; Sondergaard and Murthi 2011). However, in South Asia, there is limited systematic comprehensive review and analysis of progress, major issues, and policy options for quality improvement in education systems. A regional conference, "Quality Education for All," was organized by the World Bank and the United Kingdom's Department for International Development in 2007 in New Delhi, India. Selected papers were published in 2009 *Education Economics* 17 (3).
3. Of course, equitable distribution of school enrollment reflects the fact that there has already been significant expansion of access in the region, especially at the primary level.

Bibliography

Alderman, H., J. Behrman, D. Ross, and R. Sabot. 1996. "Decomposing the Gender Gap in Cognitive Skills in a Poor Rural Economy." *Journal of Human Resources* 31 (1): 229–54.

Andrabi, T., J. Das, A. Khwaja, T. Vishwanath, and T. Zajonc. 2007. *Pakistan: Learning and Educational Achievements in Punjab Schools (LEAPS): Insights to Inform the Educational Policy Debate.* http://www.leapsproject.org/assets/publications/LEAPS_Report_ExecSummary.pdf.

Angrist, J. D., and V. Lavy. 1997. "The Effect of a Change in Language of Instruction on the Returns to Schooling in Morocco." *Journal of Labor Economics* 15 (1): S48–76.

Asadullah, M., N. Chaudhury, D. Prajuli, L. R. Sarr, Y. Savchenko, and S. R. Al-Zayed. 2009. "Secondary Education Quality and Access Enhancement Project (SEQAEP) Baseline Report." Human Development Department, South Asia Region, World Bank, Washington, DC.

Aslam, M., D. Anuradha, G. Kingdon, and R. Kumar. 2012. "Economic Returns to Schooling and Cognitive Skills." In *Education Outcomes and Poverty: A Reassessment*, edited by C. Colclough. New York: Routledge.

Behrman, J. R., D. Ross, and R. Sabot. 2008. "Improving the Quality Versus Increasing the Quantity of Schooling: Evidence for Rural Pakistan." *Journal of Development Economics* 85: 94–104.

Blunch, N.-H. 2009. "Multidimensional Human Capital, Wages and Endogenous Employment Status in Ghana." In *Labor Markets and Economic Development*, edited by R. Kanbur and J. Svejnar. New York: Routledge.

Boissiere, M., J. Knight, and R. Sabot. 1985. "Earnings, Schooling, Ability and Cognitive Skills." *American Economic Review* 73 (5): 926–46.

Chapman, D. W., and D. Adams. 2002. "The Quality of Education: Dimensions and Strategies." In *Education in Developing Asia Series*, Vol. 5. Manila: Asian Development Bank; Hong Kong: University of Hong Kong, Comparative Education Research Centre.

Chetty, R., J. N. Friedman, and J. E. Rockoff. 2011. "The Long-Term Impacts of Teachers: Teacher Value-Added and Student Outcomes in Adulthood." Working Paper 17699, National Bureau of Economic Research, Cambridge, MA.

Cutler, D., and A. Lleras-Muney. 2010. "Understanding Differences in Health Behaviors by Education." *Journal of Health Economics* 29: 1–28.

Deming, D. 2009. "Early Childhood Intervention and Life-cycle Skill Development: Evidence from Head Start." *American Economic Journal: Applied Economics* 1 (3): 111–34.

Dutz, M. 2007. *Unleashing India's Innovation: Toward Sustainable and Inclusive Growth.* Washington, DC: World Bank.

Dutz, M., and S. O'Connell. 2012. "Productivity, Innovation and Growth in Sri Lanka: Empirical Investigation." Draft Working Paper, World Bank, Washington, DC.

EdStats. 2012. http://web.worldbank.org/WBSITE/EXTERNAL/TOPICS/EXTEDUCATION/EXTDATASTATISTICS/EXTEDSTATS/0,,menuPK:3232818~pagePK:64168427~piPK:64168435~theSitePK:3232764,00.html.

Glewwe, P. 1996. "The Relevance of Standard Estimates of Rates of Return to Schooling for Education Policy: A Critical Assessment." *Journal of Development Economics* 51 (2): 267–90.

Glewwe, P. W., E. A. Hanushek, S. D. Humpage, and R. Ravina. 2011. "School Resources and Educational Outcomes in Developing Countries: A Review of the Literature from 1990 to 2010." Working Paper 17554, National Bureau of Economic Research, Cambridge, MA.

Hanushek, E. A., and L. Woessmann. 2007. "The Role of Education Quality for Economic Growth." Policy Research Working Paper 4122, World Bank, Washington, DC, Cambridge, MA.

———. 2008. "The Role of Cognitive Skills in Economic Development." *Journal of Economic Literature* 46 (3): 607–68.

———. 2010. "How Much Do Educational Outcomes Matter in OECD Countries?" Working Paper 16515, National Bureau of Economic Research, Cambridge, MA.

Heneveld, W. 1994. "Planning and Monitoring the Quality of Primary Education in Sub-Saharan Africa." Technical Note 14, Human Resources and Poverty Division Technical Department, Africa Region, World Bank, Washington, DC.

Heneveld, W., and H. Craig. 1996. "Schools Count: World Bank Project Designs and the Quality of Primary Education in Sub-Saharan Africa." Technical Paper 303, Africa Technical Departmental Series. World Bank, Washington DC.

Hill, S., and T. Chalaux. 2011. "Improving Access and Quality in the Indian Education System." OECD Economics Department Working Paper 885, Organisation for Economic Co-operation and Development, Paris. http://dx.doi.org/10.1787/5kg83k687ng7-en.

Jamison, E. A., D. T. Jamison, and E. Hanushek. 2007. "The Effects of Education Quality on Mortality Decline and Income Growth." *Economics of Education Review* 26 (2): 772–89.

Jolliffe, D. 1998. "Skills, Schooling, and Household Income in Ghana." *World Bank Economic Review* 12 (1): 81–104.

Jones, A. M., N. Rice, and P. R. Dias. 2011. "Long-Term Effects of School Quality on Health and Lifestyle: Evidence from Comprehensive Schooling Reforms in England." *Journal of Human Capital* 5 (3): 342–76.

Kingdon, G., and M. Muzammil. 2009. "A Political Economy of Education in India: The Case of Uttar Pradesh." *Oxford Development Studies* 37 (2): 123–44.

Kingdon, G., and M. Riboud. 2009. "Special Issue on Quality Education for All in South Asia." *Education Economics* 17 (3): 287–89.

Knight, J., and R. Sabot. 1990. *Education, Productivity, and Inequality.* New York: Oxford University Press.

Krueger, A., and M. Lindahl. 2001. "Education and Growth: Why and for Whom?" *Journal of Economic Literature* 39 (4): 1101–36.

Lazear, E. P. 2003. "Firm-Specific Human Capital: A Skill-Weights Approach." Working Paper 9679, National Bureau of Economic Research, Cambridge, MA.

Lockheed, M. E., and A. M. Verspoor. 1991. *Improving Primary Education in Developing Countries*. Oxford, UK: Oxford University Press for World Bank.

Mittal, S., and G. Tripathi. 2009. "Role of Mobile Phone Technology in Improving Small Farm Productivity." *Agricultural Economics Research Review* 22: 451–59.

Moll, P. G. 1998. "Primary Schooling, Cognitive Skills and Wages in South Africa." *Economica* 65: 263–84.

Mulligan, C. B. 1999. "Galton versus the Human Capital Approach to Inheritance." *Journal of Political Economy* 107 (S6): S184–224.

Muralidharan, K., and Y. Zieleniak. 2012. "Measuring Learning Trajectories in Developing Countries with Longitudinal Data and Item Response Theory." Unpublished manuscript, University of California, San Diego, CA.

Murnane, R. J., J. B. Willet, and S. Cardenas. 2006. "Did the Participation of Schools in *Programa Escuelas De Calidad* Influence Student Outcomes?" Working Paper, Harvard University Graduate School of Education, Cambridge, MA.

NCERT (National Council of Educational Research and Training). 2011. *What Do They Know? A Summary of India's National Achievement Survey, Class V, Cycle 3 2010/11.* New Delhi: NCERT.

Nickell, S. 2004. "Poverty and Worklessness in Britain." *Economic Journal* 114: C1–25.

OECD (Organisation for Economic Co-operation and Development). 2005. *School Factors Related to Quality and Equity: Results from PISA 2000.* Paris: OECD.

———. 2010. *The High Cost of Low Educational Performance.* Paris: OECD.

Pratham. 2009. *Annual Status of Education Report (Rural) 2009 (ASER).* New Delhi: Pratham Resource Center. http://www.pratham.org/aser08/Aser_2009_Report.pdf.

———. 2011. *Annual Status of Education Report (Rural) (ASER) 2011.* New Delhi: Pratham Resource Center. http://pratham.org/images/Aser-2011-report.pdf.

Riboud, M., Y. Savchenko, and H. Tan. 2007. *The Knowledge Economy and Education and Training in South Asia.* Washington, DC: World Bank.

Sala-I-Martin, X., G. Doppelhofer, and R. Miller. 2004. "Determinants of Long-Term Growth: A Bayesian Averaging of Classical Estimates (BACE) Approach." *American Economic Review* 94 (4): 813–35.

Savchenko, Y. 2012. "Skills Development in Sri Lanka: Skills Supply, Education and Labor Market Outcomes." Background study prepared for this report, World Bank, Washington, DC.

Shemyakina, O., and C. Valente. 2012. "Education Quality and Conflict in South Asia." Background study prepared for this report.

Sondergaard, L., and M. Murthi. 2011. *Skills, Not Just Diplomas*. Washington, DC: World Bank.

Temple, J., and L. Woessmann. 2006. "Dualism and Cross-Country Growth Regressions." *Journal of Economic Growth* 11: 187–228.

Topel, R. 1999. "Labor Markets and Economic Growth." In *Handbook of Labor Economics*, edited by O. Ashenfelter and D. Card. Amsterdam: Elsevier Science B.V.

UNESCO (United Nations Educational, Scientific and Cultural Organization). 2004. *Education for All: The Quality Imperative.* EFA Global Monitoring Report. Paris: UNESCO Publishing.

Vegas, E., and J. Petrow. 2008. *Raising Student Learning in Latin America: The Challenge for the 21st Century*. Washington, DC: World Bank.

Vijverberg, W. P. M. 1999. "The Impact of Schooling and Cognitive Skills on Income from Non-Farm Self-Employment." In *The Economics of School Quality Investments in Developing Countries: An Empirical Study of Ghana*, edited by P. Glewwe. London: Macmillan.

World Bank. 2009. "Teacher Support Networks and Continuous Professional Development (CPD)." World Bank Policy Brief 7, World Bank, Washington, DC.

———. 2010. *Stepping Up Skills: For More Jobs and Higher Productivity.* Washington, DC: World Bank.

———. 2012. *More and Better Jobs in South Asia*. Washington, DC: World Bank.

———. 2013. *Bangladesh Education Sector Review.* Human Development Sector, South Asia Region, Report 80613-BD. Washington, DC: World Bank.

CHAPTER 2

What and How Much Are Students Learning?*

Introduction

The primary objective of an educational system is to enable students to address and solve real-world problems and become productive workers and better-informed citizens. In a low-income country, an educational system focused on student-centered learning can be a powerful force for reducing poverty and inequality, increasing competitiveness, and generally promoting economic and social development.

As summarized in chapter 1, over the past decade South Asia has made impressive strides in expanding access to primary and lower secondary education. What is not well documented, however, is whether expanded access has been accompanied by commensurate improvements in student learning. Instead, anecdotal evidence suggests that schooling may have expanded at the expense of educational quality and student learning. Unfortunately, although most administrative units routinely collect data on enrollment and attendance, only recently have systematic, large, survey-based national learning assessments been conducted regularly, and test design and administrative practices are still evolving. Furthermore, while they shed valuable light on regional, gender, and economic disparities in student learning, the assessments, which are based on national curricular standards, vary from country to country. No South Asian country as yet participates in any of the major international tests, such as the Programme for International Student Assessment (PISA), the Trends in Mathematics and Science Study (TIMSS), or the Progress in International Reading Literacy Study (PIRLS).

This chapter reviews the evidence on student achievement in South Asian countries, makes international and intraregional comparisons where possible, and looks at changes over time, variance in achievement, and geographical disparities between rural and urban areas and between administrative units. Given data limitations because of a shortage of learning assessments and the variance in

*See box 2.1 for a summary of the chapter's key questions and findings.

Box 2.1 Questions and Findings

Questions

- What does the evidence show about learning achievements in South Asia? How do levels of learning differ within and between countries? How do South Asian countries compare with the rest of the world?
- Has expanded access to schooling been accompanied by improvements in student learning?

Findings

- While much is known about participation rates in primary and secondary schooling in the region, much less is known about actual learning. Large-scale learning assessments are relatively recent in the region, and test administration procedures and practices are still evolving.
- Mean student achievements in mathematics, reading, and language are very low throughout the region, except for Sri Lanka; it appears that a very large number of children do not master basic primary-school skills even by grade 5.
- Much of the knowledge taught to students is procedural and rote based. Questions that require understanding, inference, and extrapolation confuse students, who are poorly prepared in such practical competencies as measurement, problem solving, or writing meaningful sentences. This is a major reason for the low test scores.
- Because South Asian countries do not participate in the major international achievement tests, comparison of learning in South Asia with that in other regions is difficult. However, recent pilots of international tests in India and Bangladesh suggest that as a region, South Asia would probably rank relatively low among countries where such testing is administered.
- Within countries mean levels of achievement are low, but variance is high; a small proportion of students can meet international benchmarks while the rest perform very poorly. Inequality in achievement seems to be worse in South Asia than in other regions. Yet given the population of South Asia, the small percentage of students able to perform as well as the top students worldwide could still be a very significant cohort.
- Achievement is higher in urban than in rural areas. The gap, however, is not very large and tends to narrow at the highest grades, and whenever it is present, the gap tends to be in reading and language rather than numeracy. Provincial and regional disparities in achievement are larger than rural-urban disparities.
- Although comparing test results over time must be approached cautiously, evidence for Bangladesh, India, and Pakistan suggests that the rapid expansion in access to schooling in recent years has not been accompanied by more learning at each grade level, possibly because of the recent entry of large cohorts of disadvantaged children and those who had not previously attended school. Only in Sri Lanka, which for decades has had high levels of participation, have there been improvements in test scores over time. However, in all countries, gains in student achievement can be seen through progression across grades and higher completion rates.

quality across the region, country coverage of these issues will of necessity be uneven. Annex 2A briefly describes major learning assessments undertaken in each South Asian country.

Levels of Student Achievement

South Asian student achievement in arithmetic is very low. For example, in India, on a test of reading comprehension administered to grade 5 students across the country, only 46 percent of the students were able to correctly identify the cause of an event (NCERT 2011). Only one-third of students could compute the difference between two decimal numbers. Another recent study found that about 43 percent of grade 8 students could not solve a simple division problem. Even recognition of two-digit numbers, supposed to be taught in grade 2, tends to be achieved only by grade 4 or 5 (Pratham 2011). In the Student Learning Study (SLS) conducted by Educational Initiatives (EI) in 2010—a national assessment of about 100,000 Indian children in grades 4, 6, and 8—when given four numbers (4, 7, 9, and 2), fewer than half of the sixth-grade students could correctly identify a number that was greater than 5 but less than 8.

In rural Pakistan, the Annual State of Education Report (ASER) 2011 assessment suggests, arithmetic competency is very low in absolute terms (figure 2.1). For instance, only 37 percent of grade 5 students can divide three-digit numbers by a single-digit number (and only 27 percent in India); and 28 percent of grade 8 students cannot perform simple division. Unlike in rural India, however, in rural Pakistan recognition of two-digit numbers is widespread by grade 3 (SAFED 2012).

The Learning and Educational Achievement in Punjab Schools (LEAPS) survey—a 2003 assessment of 12,000 children in grade 3 in the province—also found that children were performing significantly below curricular standards (Andrabi et al. 2007). Most could not answer simple math questions, and many children finished grade 3 unable to perform mathematical operations covered in the grade 1 curriculum (figure 2.2). A 2009 assessment of 40,000 grade 4 students in the province of Sindh similarly found that while 74 percent of students could add two numbers, only 49 percent could subtract two numbers (PEACE 2010).[1]

In rural Bangladesh (figure 2.3), after completing grade 9 only 80–90 percent of students attain basic grade 5 competencies in oral and written mathematics (Asadullah et al. 2009).[2] The fact that written math competency is significantly lower than oral points to the difficulties children have in reading, understanding, and writing. A 2011 National Student Assessment (NSA) also showed that more than a third of fifth-grade students did not even have grade 3 competencies (World Bank 2013).

In Afghanistan, a rapid test of numeracy was administered in 2008–09 to 1,000 students in grades 1–4 in 15 provinces, but the sample was not representative of the entire country (PACE-A 2009). Students were tested on counting and matching numbers, reading numbers, understanding the value of numbers

Figure 2.1 Student Arithmetic Achievement, by Grade, 2011
Percent

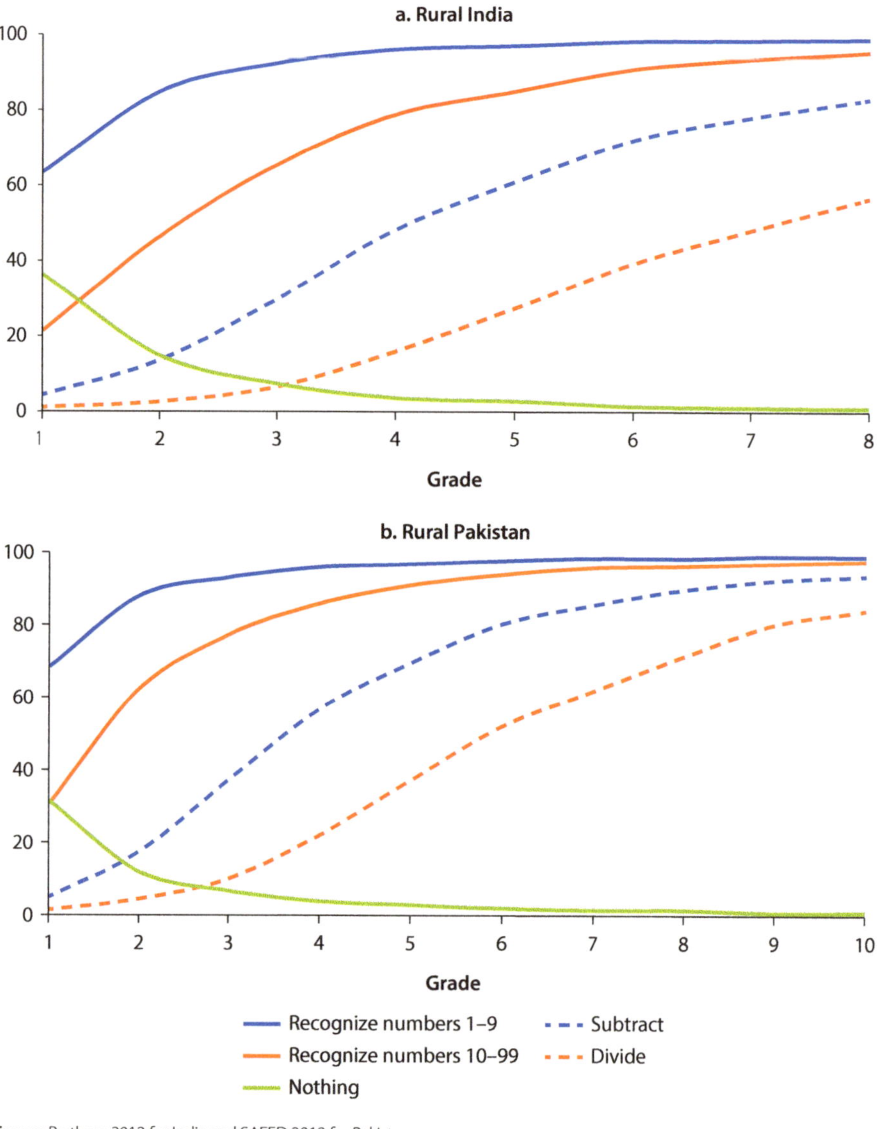

Source: Pratham 2012 for India and SAFED 2012 for Pakistan.

(e.g., identifying the lowest and highest values in a string), and performing simple mental arithmetic. The survey found that 87 percent of students were acquiring numeracy skills at a level appropriate for their grade—a much larger proportion than those who did well in reading (57 percent). However, since the assessment does not report the proportion of students who could successfully complete specific arithmetic operations (e.g., recognize one- or two-digit numbers or perform subtraction or division), student achievement in Afghanistan cannot be compared with that of neighboring countries.

Figure 2.2 Grade 3 Arithmetic Competence, Punjab, Pakistan, 2003

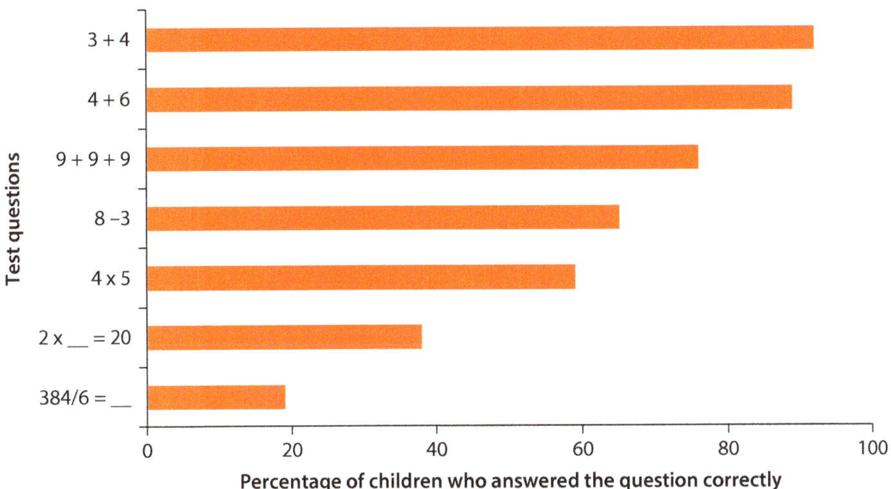

Source: Andrabi et al. 2007.

Figure 2.3 Students Minimally Competent in Mathematics, by Grade Completed, Bangladesh, 2007

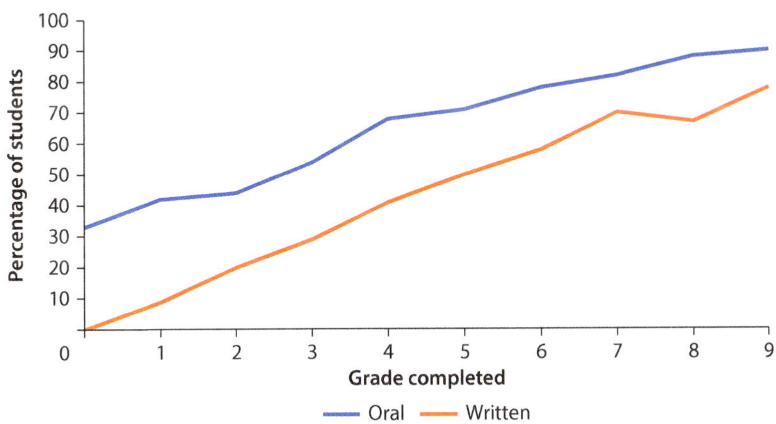

Source: Asadullah et al. 2009.

Nepal undertook a national assessment of students in grades 5 and 8 in 2008.[3] The tests were based on learning outcomes as defined in the local curriculum.[4] However, the assessment notes that achievement of this level of competence does not indicate a satisfactory or desirable level of competence. Scores in mathematics were very low, especially for grade 8 pupils (see figure 2.4).

Similarly, in a 2008 Maldives assessment of learning outcomes at grades 4 and 7, the mean grade 4 score for mathematics was just 39 percent; by grade 7, the mean score was down to 30 percent (World Bank 2012). Conversely, in

Figure 2.4 Mean Student Test Scores, by Subject and Grade, Nepal, 2008
Percent

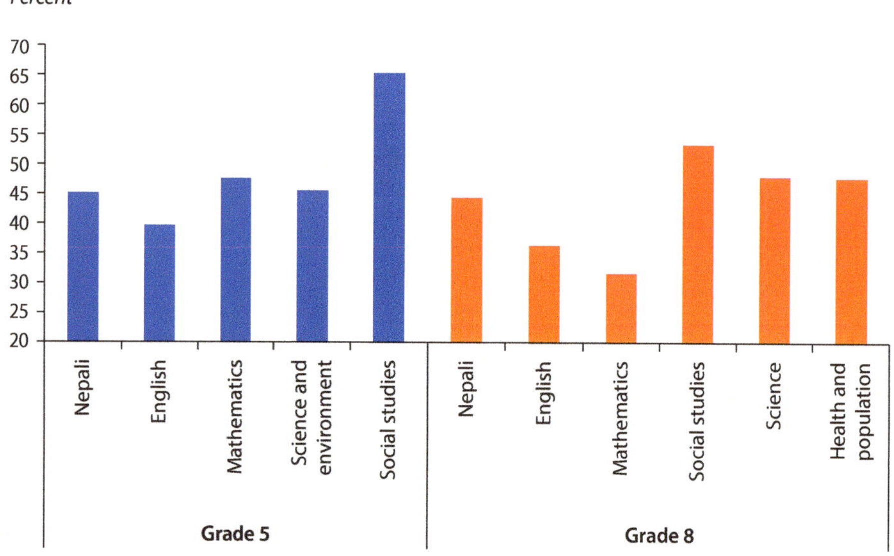

Sources: Government of Nepal 2008a, 2008b.

Sri Lanka a 2009 national assessment of grade 4 students conducted by the National Education Research and Evaluation Center (NEREC) of the University of Colombo found that a relatively large proportion of grade 4 students were able to master the essential learning competencies the national curriculum expected. The mean achievement score in mathematics was 77 percent in Sinhala medium schools and 62 percent in Tamil-medium schools (NEREC 2009).

Student achievement in reading and language is low in most South Asian countries. In rural India, for instance, about a third of grade 3 students could not read words (figure 2.5), and less than half of the fifth-grade students were able to read grade 2 text in their native language, which meant they were already three years behind in grade-appropriate competency. Even by grade 7, more than a quarter of the students were unable to read grade 2 text.

In rural Pakistan, the situation is not much better. Only 41 percent of grade 3 students were able to read a sentence in Urdu or Sindhi (figure 2.6). More than 50 percent of the fifth-grade students and a full 25 percent of eighth-grade students were unable to read a short story. Only 31 percent of third-grade students could write a grammatically coherent sentence in Urdu using the word "school," although second-grade students should be able to do so (Andrabi et al. 2007).

A recent national assessment of both rural and urban learning competencies in Bangladesh also showed that only 25 percent of fifth-grade students had attained the reading achievement expected of their grade (World Bank 2013). Not surprisingly, competency in English is significantly lower than in native languages. In Bangladesh, students who have completed primary schooling are able to answer 86 percent of questions correctly in Bengali

Figure 2.5 Student Reading Level in the Local Language, Rural India, 2011
Percent

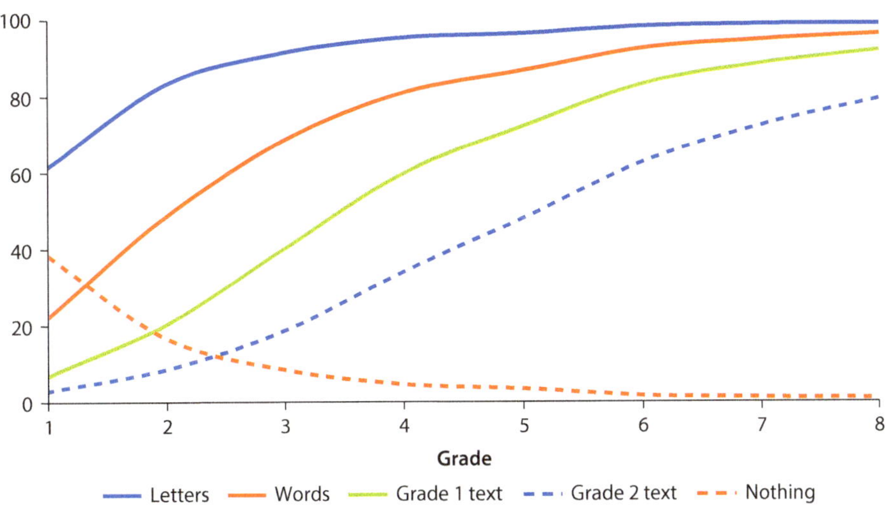

Source: Pratham 2012.

Figure 2.6 Student Reading Ability in Urdu or Sindhi, Rural Pakistan, 2011
Percent

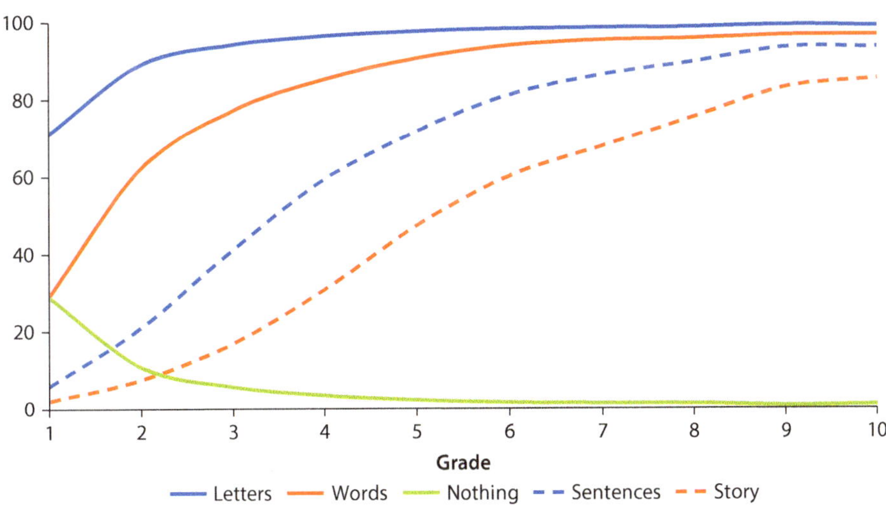

Source: SAFED 2012.

(figure 2.7).[5] As would be expected, reading comprehension improves with grade, so that students who completed secondary school were able to answer virtually all the questions in Bengali. However, English comprehension is relatively low. Even students who have completed secondary school were able to answer only half the questions in English.

Figure 2.7 Questions Answered Correctly in Bengali, by Schooling Level, Ages 12–20, Bangladesh, 2007
Percent

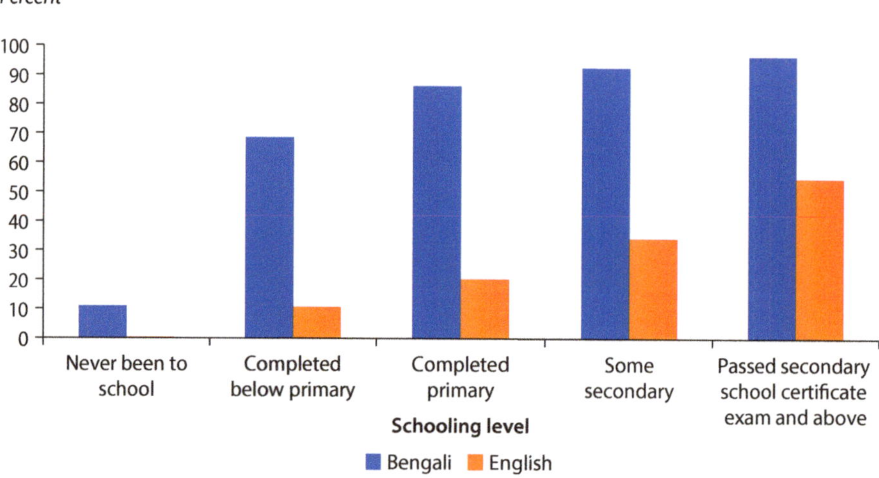

Source: Asadullah et al. 2009.
Note: SSC = Senior Secondary Certificate.

Figure 2.8 Ability to Read Words and Sentences in Urdu or Sindhi and English, by Grade, Rural Pakistan, 2011
Percent

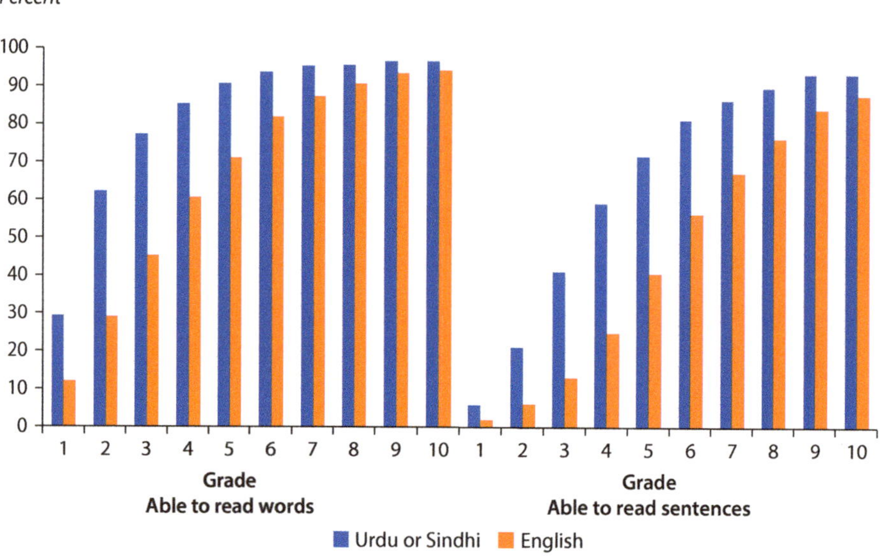

Source: SAFED 2012.

In rural Pakistan, there is a similar marked difference in ability to read in Urdu or Sindhi and in English. By grade 5, nearly 91 percent of students can read words in Urdu or Sindhi, but only 71 percent can do so in English (figure 2.8). As reading level increases, as demonstrated by the ability to read sentences versus words, the gap becomes even larger. The proportion of grade 5 students who can

Figure 2.9 Mean Grade 4 Test Scores, by Subject and Language of Instruction, Sri Lanka, 2009
Percent

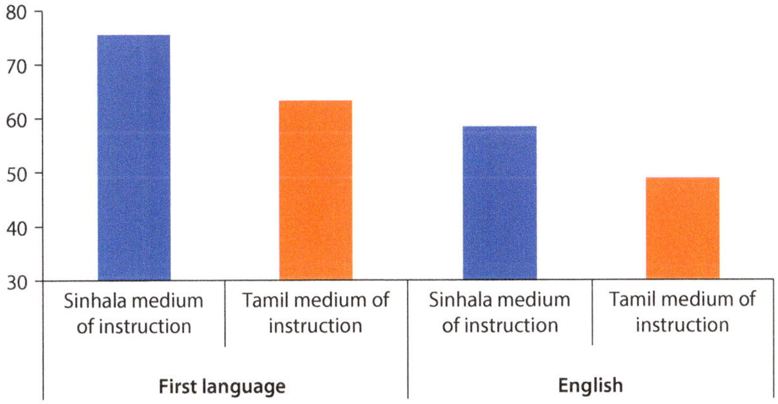

Source: NEREC 2009.

read a sentence, rather than just a word, is 72 percent in Urdu or Sindhi and 41 percent in English. Almost a quarter of students cannot read a sentence in English even by grade 8.

The 2008 Maldives learning assessment found that the mean score in English for grade 4 students was just 32 percent (39 percent for mathematics). In grade 7, the mean score in English was even lower, 29 percent, suggesting that student achievement in English is low at both the primary and lower secondary levels.

Even in outlier Sri Lanka, data for 2009 show a 14–18 percentage point deficit in English versus first-language competency among grade 4 students, depending on the medium of instruction. Interestingly, the data show higher achievement—in both the first language and English—for students in Sinhala-medium than for those in Tamil-medium schools (figure 2.9).[6] This may suggest that the quality of Tamil-medium schools is poorer than that of Sinhala-medium, but it could also reflect the socioeconomic disadvantages faced by Tamil students.

In Bhutan, too, competency is generally lower in English than in Dzongkha among second- and fourth-grade students, although there are variations depending on the type of question asked.[7] For instance, while 82 percent of second-grade students in 2007 were able to look at a picture and circle the missing letter in a Dzongkha word (grade 2 competency), the proportion was only 68 percent in English (annex 2B). But the proportion of grade 2 students who could circle the missing word in a sequence was almost the same in the two languages (31–33 percent) (World Bank 2009).

International Comparisons

The recent efforts to pilot international tests in India and Bangladesh suggest that student achievement in South Asia is very low relative to international standards. NEREC, which has undertaken national learning assessments in Sri Lanka since

2003, fielded a TIMSS module in 2009 in addition to local tests of competency in English, mathematics, and Sinhala or Tamil, but the TIMSS module data have not yet been analyzed.

In 2005, as part of a World Bank project, Wu et al. (2009) surveyed 3,418 grade 9 students in the Indian state of Rajasthan and 2,856 in Odisha (formerly Orissa).[8] The mathematics assessment test included 36 items from the 1999 TIMSS for grade 8 students, which allowed for international benchmarking (though to students one grade behind) on common items. Compared with the international mean, the Indian students were much less likely to correctly answer any of the individual items (figure 2.10). Using the same data, Das and Zajonc (2008) reported that among the 51 countries in the TIMSS 2003 test, Odisha would have ranked 42nd and Rajasthan 46th. The mean score for Indian students was 0.7—1.0 standard deviation below the mean for all 51 countries tested. Given the very unequal distribution of their scores, this meant that a very large proportion of ninth-grade students in the two Indian states—58 percent in Rajasthan and 50 percent in Odisha—could not even pass the lowest international benchmark (described as "some basic mathematical knowledge").

More recently, 4,850 15-year-olds from two other Indian states, Himachal Pradesh and Tamil Nadu, participated in the PISA 2009+ study. PISA 2009+ tested about 46,000 students in nine countries or economies, representing about 1,377,000 15-year-olds in these countries. The PISA 2009 and 2009+ databases,

Figure 2.10 Grade 9 Student Achievement, Rajasthan, Odisha, and International Average
Percentage answered correctly

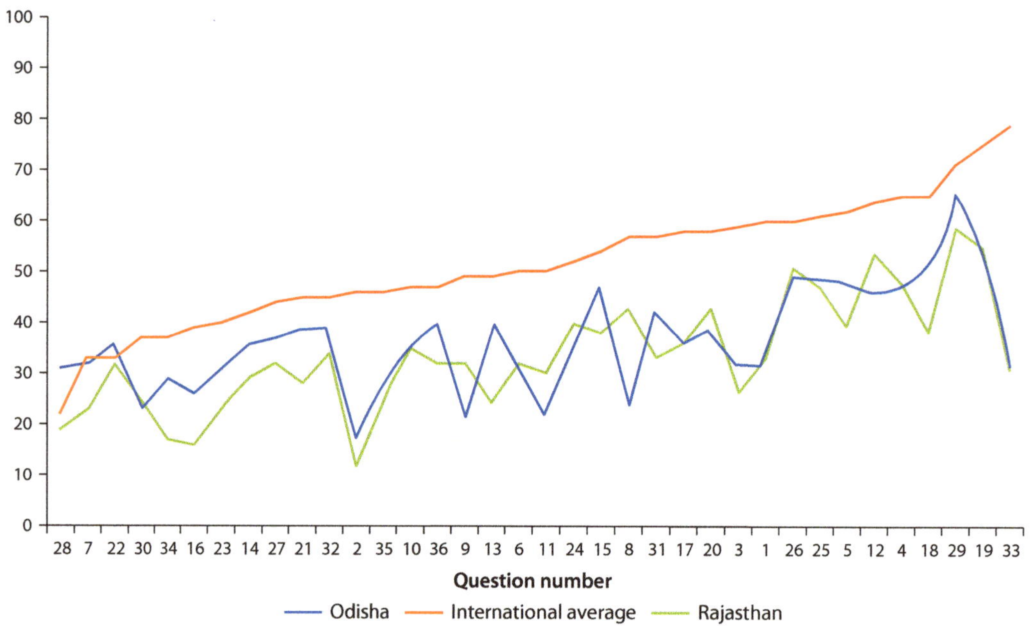

Source: Wu et al. 2009.
Note: No. = number.

which are directly comparable, contain information on almost half a million students tested in 74 countries, representing about 24 million 15-year-olds. The mean reading score was 315 for Himachal Pradesh and 335 for Tamil Nadu, putting them virtually at the bottom of the rankings. In comparison, the mean reading score was 556 for Shanghai, China, 464 for Turkey, 421 for Thailand, 402 for Indonesia, and 370 for Peru. Only the Kyrgyz Republic had a lower score (314) than the two Indian states. In mathematics and science, the Indian states also had the lowest mean scores of all countries participating in PISA 2009 and PISA 2009+.

Not surprisingly, there is a close association between mean student performance in PISA and country per capita income (figure 2.11). Yet the two Indian states have low reading scores even relative to their per capita incomes.

To benchmark student learning against international standards, another Indian learning assessment conducted in 2009, the SLS for grades 4, 6, and 8, included 5–7 TIMSS questions for grades 4 and 8 and a few items from the PIRLS (which tests the language and literacy skills of grade 4 students) (EI 2010).[9]

Apparently, poor student achievement is not limited to Himachal Pradesh and Tamil Nadu. Figure 2.12 shows that Indian fourth- and eighth-grade students performed significantly worse—in some cases by 50 percent or more—on the TIMSS questions than peers elsewhere. Nor is there evidence of later catch-up; Indian eighth-grade students also did badly in mathematics relative to international students.

The results are similar for language and literacy skills, as tested by the few PIRLS questions that were included in the SLS. Indian fourth-grade students

Figure 2.11 Mean Reading Scores and Gross National Income Per Capita (Purchasing Power Parity, 2009)

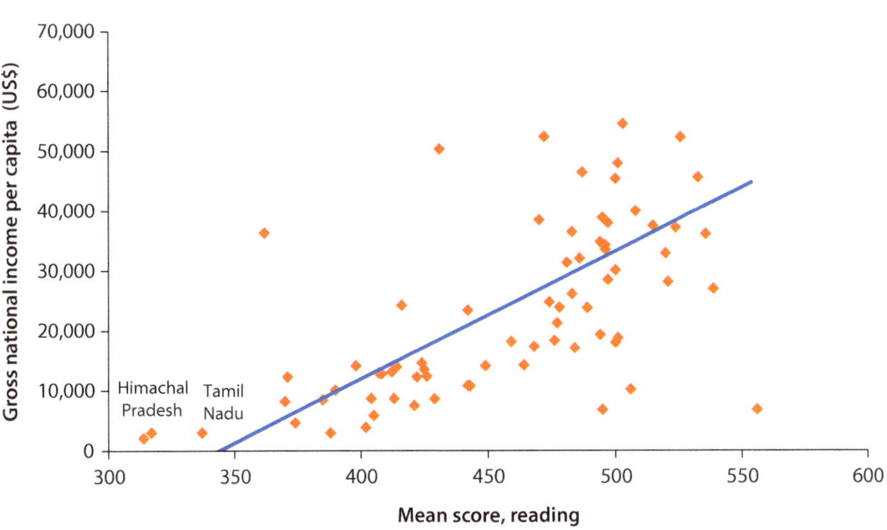

Source: OECD 2010.

Figure 2.12 Achievement of International Students and Indian Students in Government Schools, Grades 4 and 8, 2009
Percent

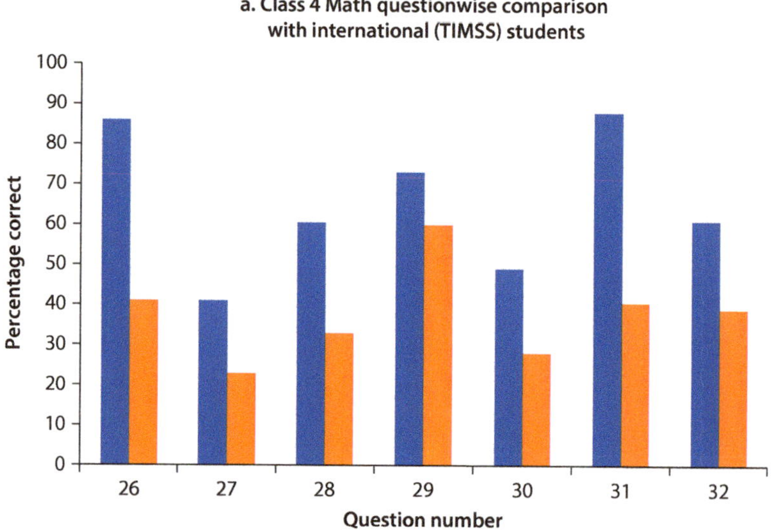

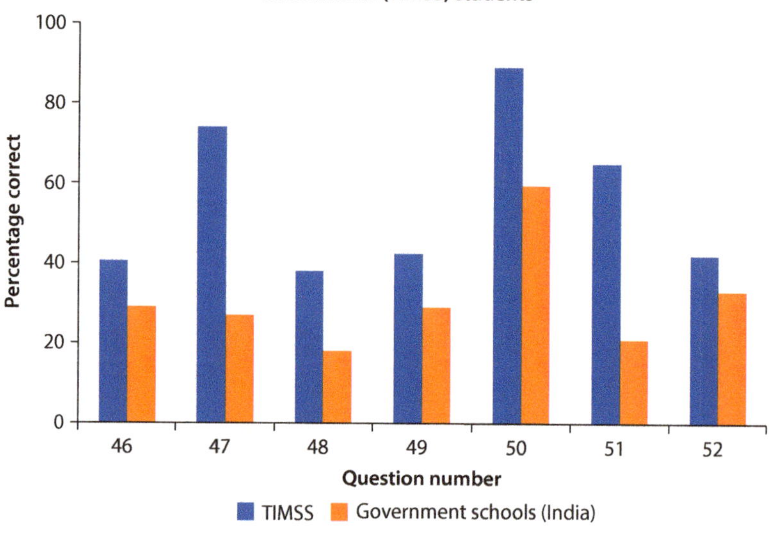

Source: EI 2010.
Note: TIMSS = Trend in Mathematics and Science Study.

performed significantly worse—nearly two-thirds worse in some cases—than fourth-grade students elsewhere in the world on the five PIRLS questions borrowed by the SLS (figure 2.13).

Figure 2.14 compares the achievement of fourth-grade students in India and in 37 other countries on one of the PIRLS questions. Indian students placed

Figure 2.13 Language Achievement, International Students and Indian Students in Government Schools, Grade 4, 2009
Percent

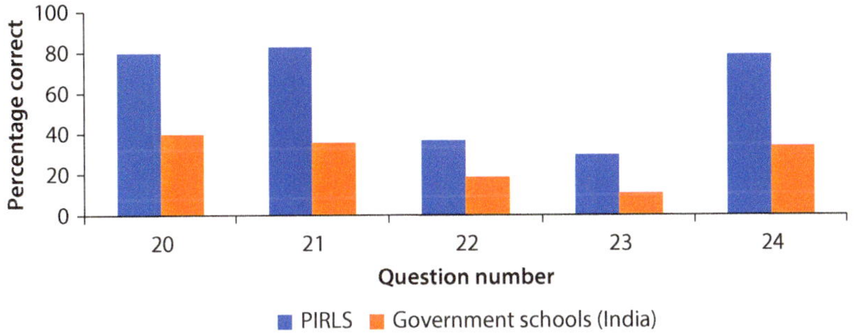

Question number	PIRLS	Government schools (India)
20	80	40
21	83	36
22	38	20
23	31	12
24	80	36

Source: EI 2010.
Note: PIRLS = Progress in International Reading Literacy Study.

second last—just ahead of Kuwait, equivalent to the Islamic Republic of Iran, but below Belize.

When the SLS included the PIRLS grade 4 questions in the grades 6 and 8 tests, even grade 8 students in Indian public schools performed significantly worse than international fourth-grade students on all the PIRLS questions (figure 2.14). As would be expected, however, the eighth-grade students did do better than the sixth-grade students.

In 2007, an evaluation of a World Bank secondary education project in Bangladesh included a baseline (random) survey of 6,542 children in grade 6 and 6,304 students in grade 8 (Asadullah et al. 2009). Sixth-grade students were given a subset of math questions from the TIMSS grade 4 math test and eighth-grade students a subset from the TIMSS grade 8 math test. On average, only 40 percent of the sixth-grade students and 37 percent of the eighth-grade students could correctly answer the questions (figure 2.15 and table 2.1). Grade 6 scores were higher than grade 8 scores because they were being tested on grade 4-level TIMSS questions; the grade 8 students were tested on their own grade level.

Some intraregional comparisons are possible. Some questions in an EI assessment of students in Bhutan in 2008 were used in its 2010 assessment in India. The language achievement of Indian grade 4 students in government schools is slightly better than that of comparable Bhutanese students (figure 2.16), though this may have been because the Indian students (covered in the SLS study) were tested in their mother tongue while the Bhutanese students, for whom English is the medium of instruction from grade 1, were tested in English.

However, any learning advantage that Indian students have due to learning in their mother tongue appears to be lost as they progress to higher grades. Bhutanese students perform better than Indian in both language and mathematics in grades 6 and 8. It is also possible to compare student achievement in India

Figure 2.14 Grade 4 Students Obtaining Full Credit on a Sample Question, PIRLS 2001, by Economy
Percent

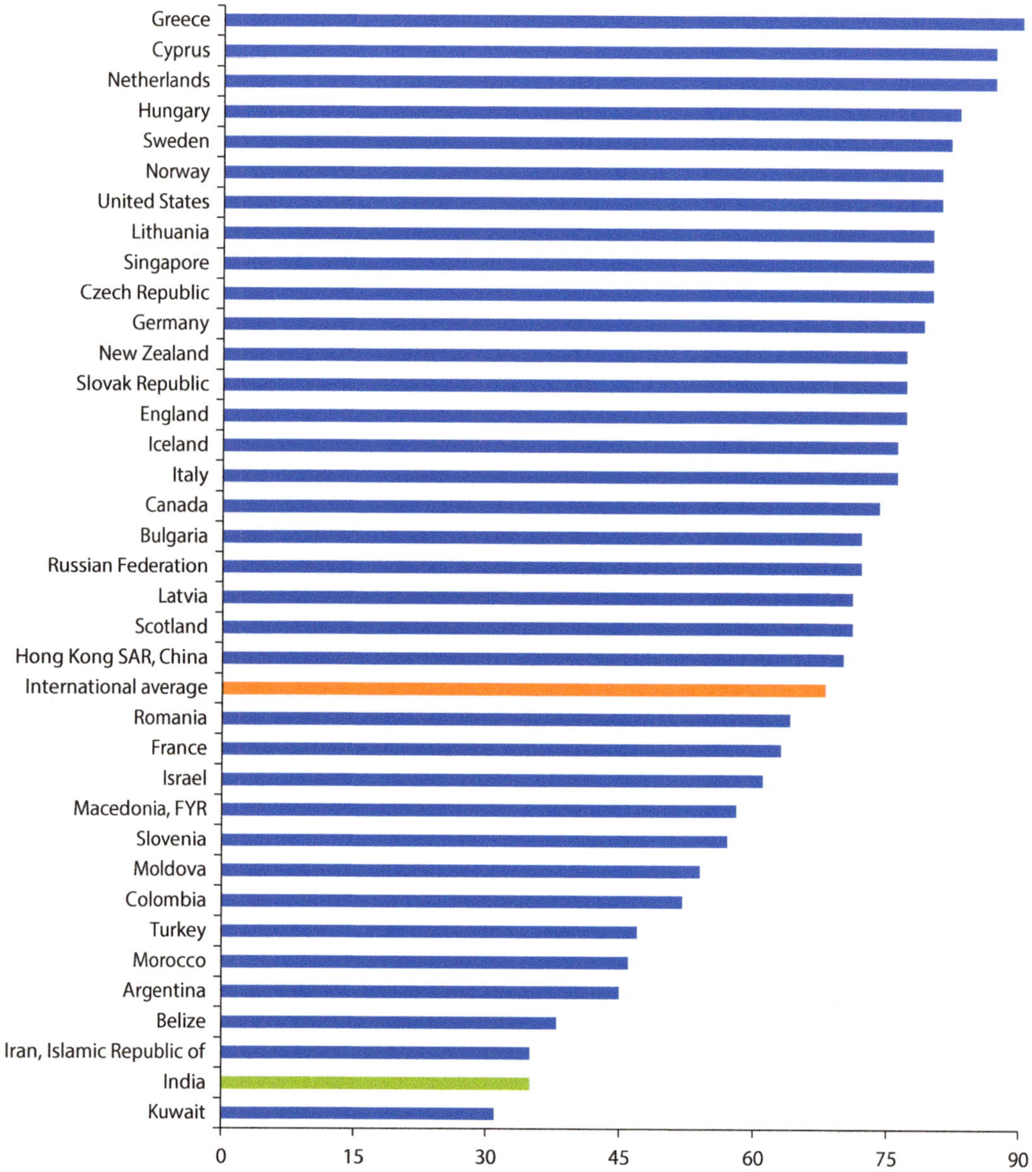

Source: EI 2010.
Note: PIRLS = Progress in International Reading Literacy Study.

and in Pakistan, since the ASER assessments used a similar methodology in both. Figure 2.17 suggests that the proportion of students who can read at least a letter (a competency that should be acquired in grade 1) is higher in rural Pakistan than in rural India until about grade 5, when it reaches close to 90 percent in both. After that, there are virtually no differences in achievement.

Figure 2.15 Indian Students in Grades 6 and 8, Correct Responses to PIRLS Questions and International Grade 4 Averages
Percent

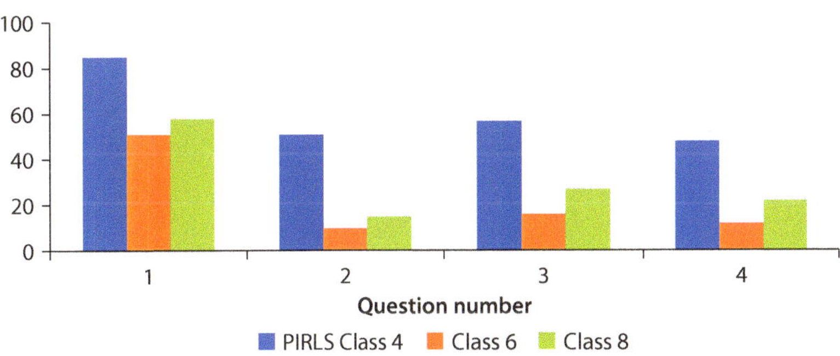

Source: EI 2010.
Note: PIRLS = Progress in International Reading Literacy Study.

Table 2.1 Average Correct Mathematics Scores, TIMSS-Based Items, Bangladesh
Percent

	Grade 6			*Grade 8*		
	Girls	*Boys*	*Total*	*Girls*	*Boys*	*Total*
Mean	37.99	43.64	40.41	33.99	40.54	36.76
Standard deviation	16.28	14.99	15.98	15.10	16.64	16.10
Number of observations	3,749	2,807	6,556	3,650	2,667	6,317

Source: Asadullah et al. 2009.
Note: TIMSS = Trends in Mathematics and Science Study.

Figure 2.16 Correct Answers to Common Language and Mathematics Questions, Grades 4, 6, and 8, Bhutan 2008 and India 2010
Percent

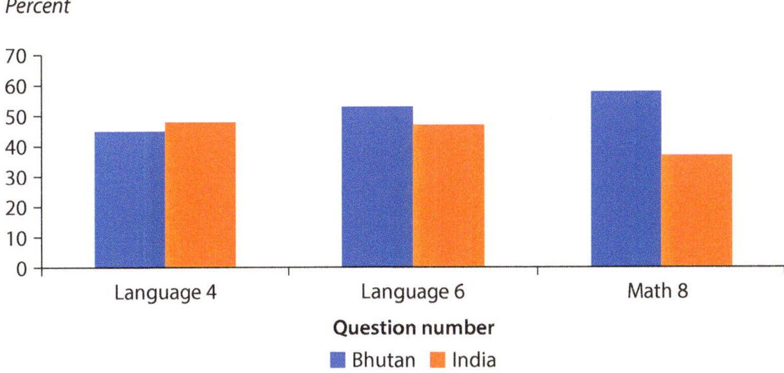

Source: EI 2010.

Figure 2.17 Rural Students Who Can Read at Least a Letter in Local Language, by Grade, India and Pakistan, 2011
Percent

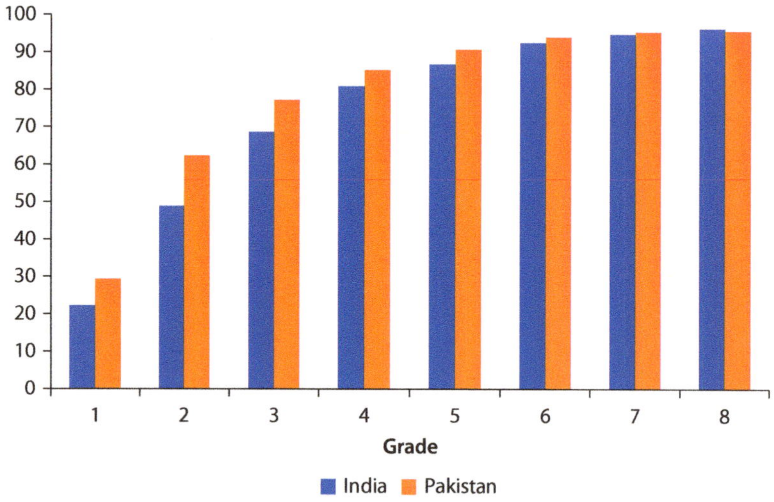

Sources: Pratham 2012; SAFED 2012.

Variance in Student Achievement

Although the discussion has focused on mean levels of student achievement, there is a large variance, with some students performing very poorly and others very well. Using the 2005 grade 9 assessment data from Rajasthan and Odisha that included some TIMSS-based items, Das and Zajonc (2008) showed that while the average child performed very poorly in comparison to students from other countries, inequality in India was so large (more significant than in any country participating in the TIMSS 2003 survey except South Africa) that the top 1 percent of students in Rajasthan and Odisha actually passed the advanced international benchmark established by TIMSS 2003 (annex 2C).[10] In Odisha, as many as 9 percent of students cleared the high benchmark—more than in the Philippines, South Africa, Chile, Indonesia, the Arab Republic of Egypt, and Lebanon, and almost the same as in Norway (10 percent).[11]

On the assumption that students in Rajasthan and Odisha are representative of India, Das and Zajonc (2008) calculated the absolute number of Indian students that would reach the advanced international benchmark. The result—100,000 children—would be the fifth-largest cohort of ninth-grade students in the world to meet that benchmark, after only Japan; the United States; the Republic of Korea; and Taiwan, China. Indeed, if India were added to the TIMSS sample, 1 out of 14 children who pass the advanced benchmark would be Indian. Nevertheless, in the two Indian states the *average* student score was very low, and more than half of grade 9 students could not even pass the lowest international benchmark ("some basic mathematical knowledge").

The 2010 SLS also underscores the wide variance in Indian student achievement. It ranked different states by the mean composite performance of their students and by the proportion of tested students who scored zero on the assessment. Although Andhra Pradesh, Assam, Chhattisgarh, and Jharkhand ranked below the national average, fewer of their students scored zero than those of better-performing states, such as Haryana and Karnataka (EI 2010). One possible explanation for this is that the former states direct their efforts toward the lowest-ability students, which comes at the cost of improving the quality of education for the average or most able children.

The 2010 NCERT[12] grade 5 assessment also found that the variance in student reading comprehension test scores is more unequal in some Indian states than in others (NCERT 2011). For example, the interquartile range (between the 25th and the 75th percentile) was only 39 in Pondicherry but 93 in Uttar Pradesh, which suggests that grade 5 students in Pondicherry are far more homogenous than in Uttar Pradesh. The wide variance means that students in the 90th percentile in a low-achievement state like Bihar scored above the median (50th percentile) student in a high-achievement state like Tamil Nadu.

The 2011 National Student Assessment in Bangladesh also found significant inequality in learning outcomes, with the bottom 20 percent of grade 5 performing worse in Bangla than the top 20 percent of grade 3 despite having had two more years of schooling. Figure 2.18 shows that in both Bangla and mathematics, many grade 5 students have lower test scores than do the top performers in grade 3.

Figure 2.18 Comparison of the Distribution of Bangla and Mathematics Test Scores between Grade 3 and 5 Students, Bangladesh

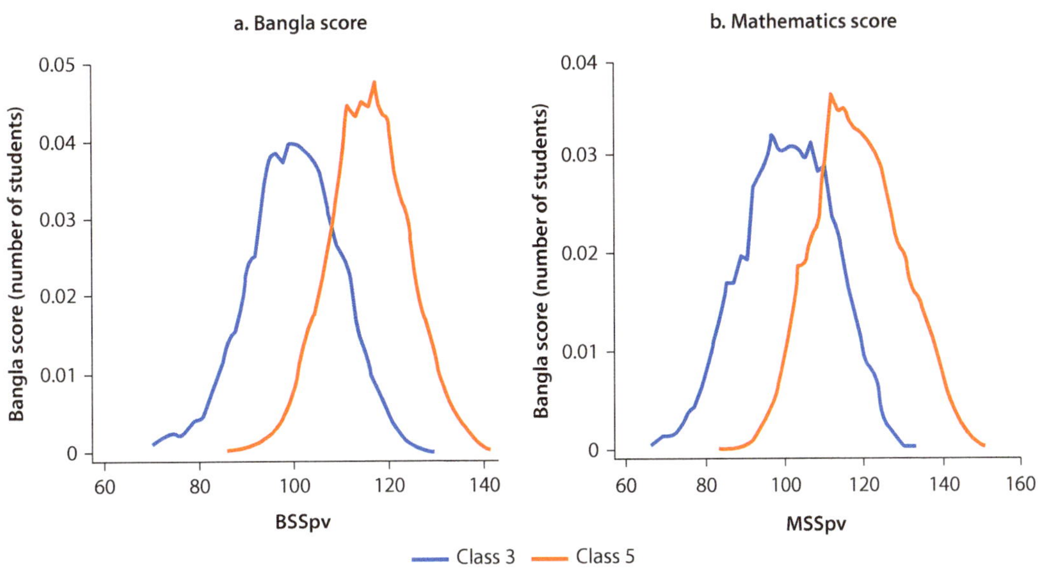

Source: World Bank 2013, 61.

Changes in Achievement over Time

Although few national learning assessments in the region allow comparisons over time, in India ASER assessments have been conducted annually since 2005 without a significant change in methodology. The findings from them are troubling (figure 2.19). For instance, between 2006 and 2011 the proportion of third-grade students who can read at first-grade level fell from 48 percent to 40 percent, and the proportion of fifth-grade students who can read at third-grade level fell from

Figure 2.19 Student Achievement, Reading and Arithmetic, Rural India, 2006–11

a. Reading comprehension

Percent
60
55
50
45
40
35
30
2006 2008 2010 2011
Percentage of third-grade students who can read grade 1 text
2006 2008 2010 2011
Percentage of fifth-grade students who can read grade 2 text

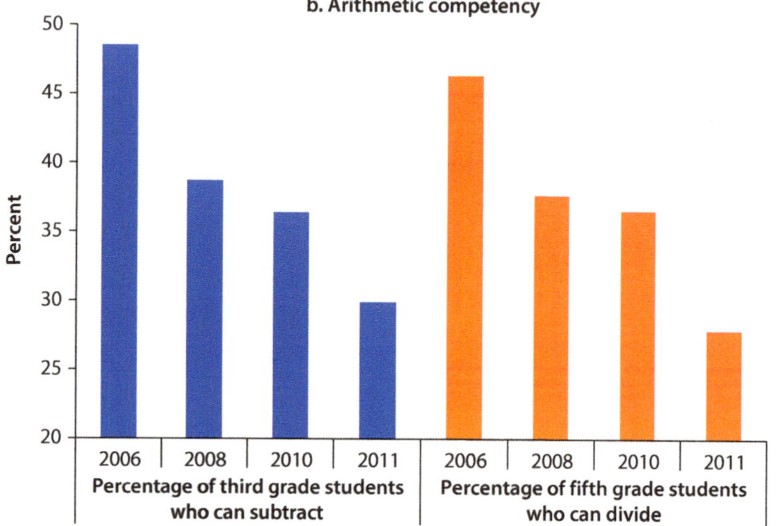

Sources: Pratham 2007, 2009, 2011, 2012.

53 percent to 48 percent. In arithmetic, student achievement seems to have plunged even further: the percent of third-grade students able to perform subtraction fell from 45 percent to 28 percent and of fifth-grade students able to perform division from 49 percent to 30 percent (figure 2.19).

Why has student achievement fallen so steeply in five years? One likely explanation is the expansion in schooling access that took place during this period. Much of the enrollment growth came from the entry of disadvantaged children and those who had not previously been in school, who typically achieve far less than those from mainstream groups. Their increased participation may well have pulled down average student achievement. Indeed, in India, while enrollment of all children ages 6–10 years rose by 4.7 percentage points between 2005 and 2010, enrollment of children from scheduled castes and scheduled tribes rose by 6.6 percentage points, according to household survey data.

As would be expected, gains in student achievement can be seen across grades. In other words, by the time students reach higher grades, they gain the knowledge they were supposed to acquire earlier, and by staying in school achieve higher learning levels. To test learning gains across grades, the SLS included a few of the same questions in tests administered to students from all three grades. As students moved from grade 4 to 6 to 8, their performance in both language and mathematics increased in the common questions, though the improvement was small and incremental (figure 2.20).

Asadullah et al. (2009) compared mathematics data from two national assessments in Bangladesh conducted 15 years apart, the first in 1992, the second in 2007. They both used the same four oral and four written math questions, and there seems to have been some improvement in math achievement in grades 1–5, but in grades 6–9 achievement was either flat or fell (figure 2.21). As in India, the decline in average achievement may be explained by the enrollment of disadvantaged children, but why would this result in falling levels of achievement only in the higher grades?

Figure 2.20 Student Performance on Common Questions, by Grade, India, 2009

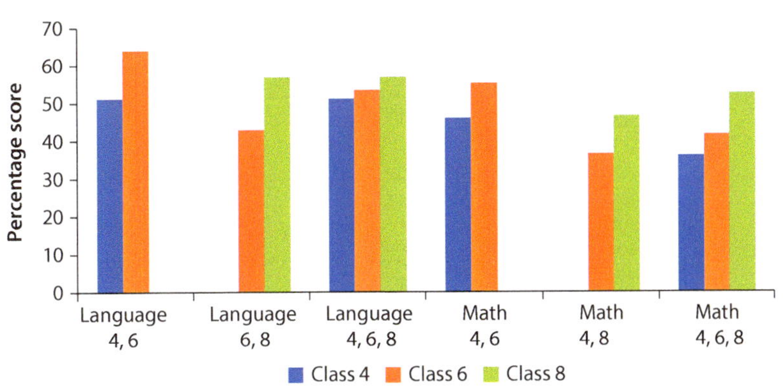

Source: EI 2010.

Figure 2.21 Bangladesh: Students Achieving Minimal Competency in Mathematics, by Grade Completed, 1992 and 2007

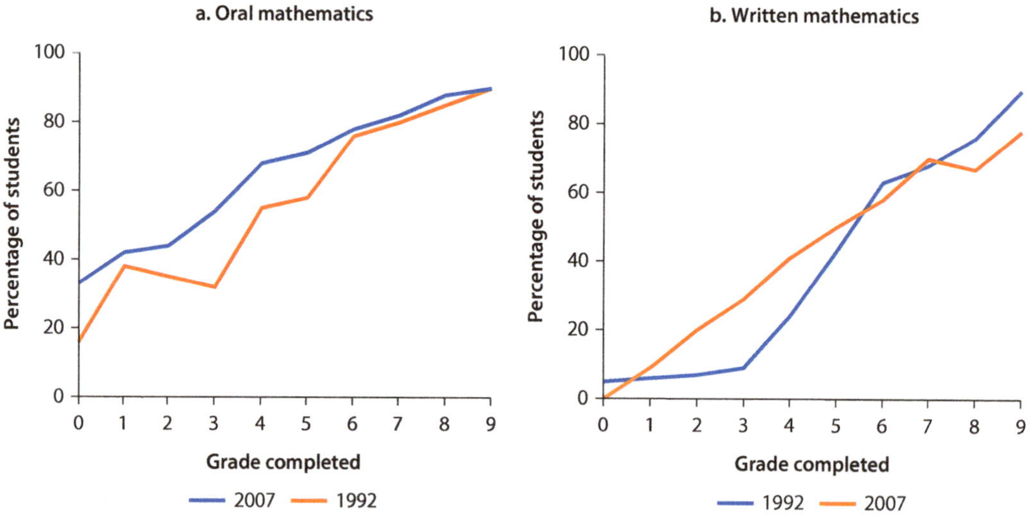

Source: Asadullah et al. 2009.

Figure 2.22 Reading and Arithmetic Achievement, Rural Pakistan, 2008–11

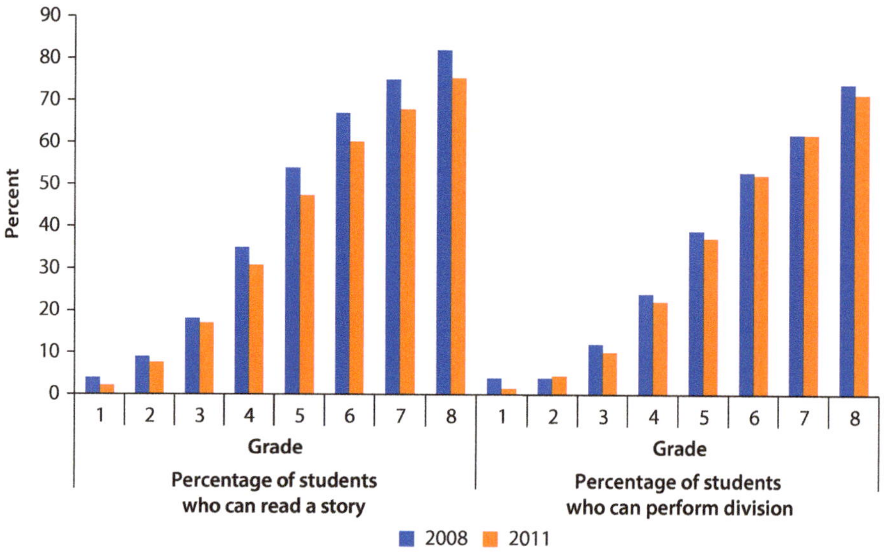

Source: SAFED 2012.

A comparison of the 2008 and 2011 ASER surveys suggests a similar conclusion for Pakistan: at every grade, there is a small decline in the percentage of students who can read a story or perform division (figure 2.22). Another study (Asim and Raju 2013) that examines student achievement in Punjab public education analyzed standardized tests for grades 5 and 8 in 2009 and 2010 as part of a government-administered large-scale student assessment. It, too, found that student performance was worse in 2010 than in 2009 in the majority of core subjects. However, the study points out that tightening of test administration procedures over time may help explain changes in test scores.

The only country where average achievement does not appear to have fallen over time is Sri Lanka. The NEREC national assessments of fourth-grade students in 2003, 2007, and 2009 show appreciable improvement. In the six years between 2003 and 2009, average test scores in all subjects went up by at least 12 percent. In some subjects, such as English, the improvement was as high as 28–30 percent (figure 2.23).

The fact that mean achievement has increased over time in Sri Lanka but may have declined in Bangladesh, India, and Pakistan underlines the effect in the latter of opening up access to students from disadvantaged backgrounds. Sri Lanka has enjoyed uniformly high rates of school enrollment for several decades.

However, the improvement in Sri Lankan fourth-grader achievement is not corroborated by the results of the General Certificate of Education (GCE) O-level examinations (figure 2.24) taken after grade 10, where failure rates can go as high as 70 percent, especially for the English language examination. Figure 2.25 shows that in Bangladesh, except for mathematics, the failure rate did not change appreciably between 2003 and 2009. Of course, if student achievement improved at the primary level (grade 4) only after 2003, performance rates would be unlikely to improve until after 2009, when the primary cohort took the GCE O-levels.

Figure 2.23 Test Scores, by Subject and Medium of Instruction, Sri Lanka, 2003–09
Percent

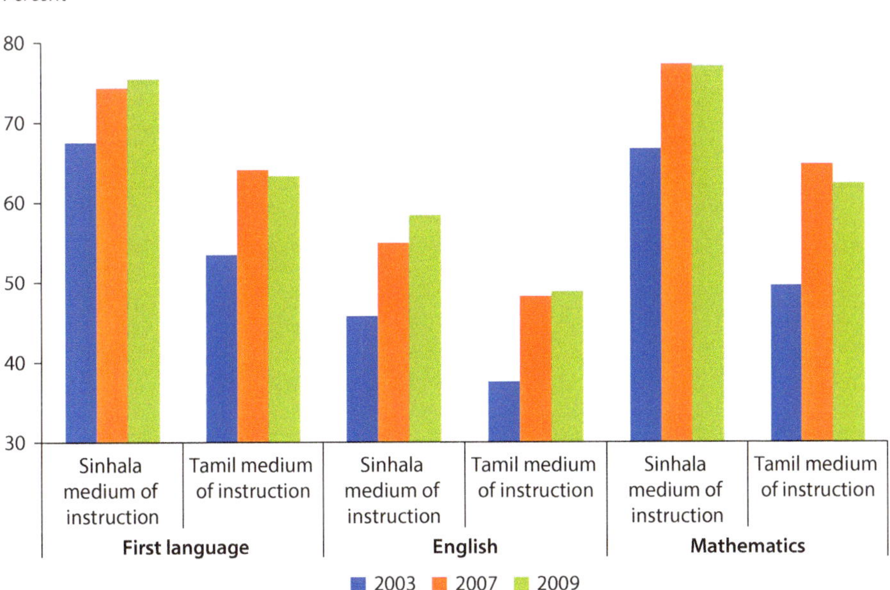

Source: NEREC 2009.

Figure 2.24 Students Failing GCE O-Levels, by Subject, Sri Lanka, 2005–09
Percent

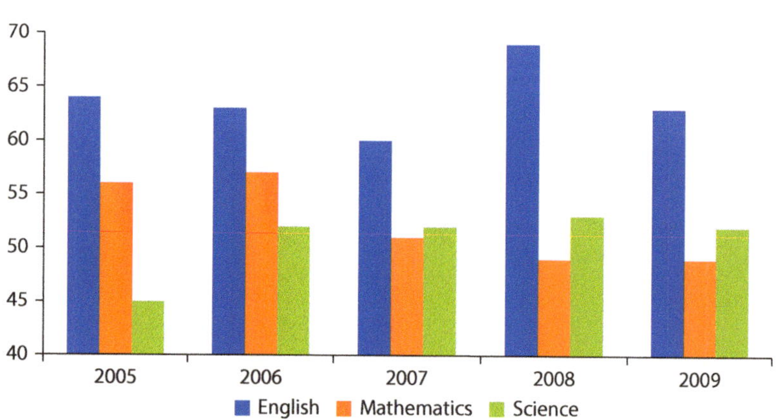

Source: Aturupane 2009.
Note: GCE = General Certificate of Education.

Figure 2.25 Bangladesh: Percentage of Grade 3 Students Attaining Mastery in Learning Outcome Categories, by Subject, 2008
Percent

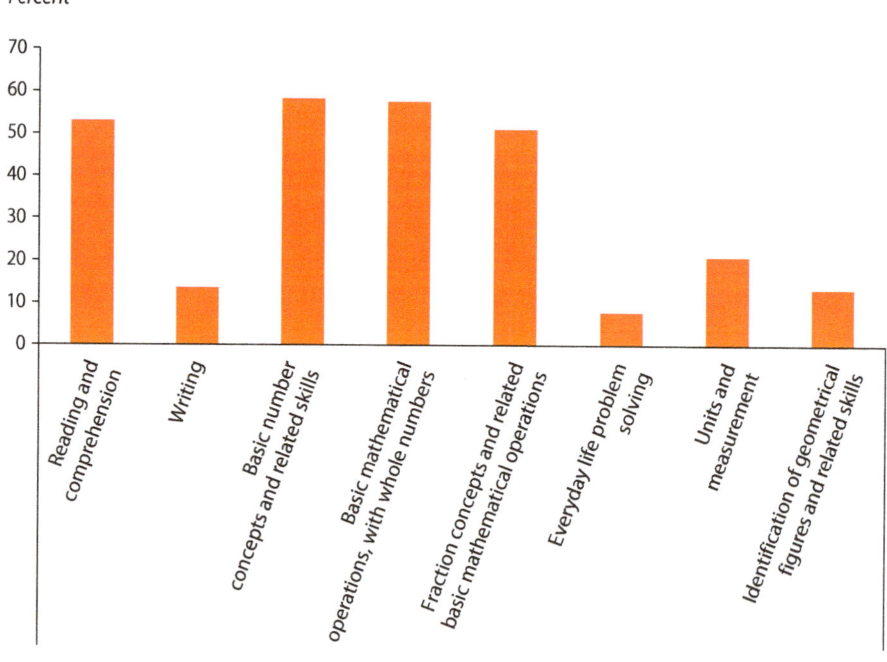

Source: DPE 2009.

Quality of Learning

A great deal of what South Asian students are taught is "procedural," or rote based. This means that most pupils cannot answer questions that deviate even slightly from the textbook or what was presented to them in class. The national SLS found that Indian students in the lower grades generally performed well in very basic numeracy skills, such as recognition of numbers, number sequencing, reading clock time, and understanding currency. In the higher grades, however, they lost the advantage of procedural learning. Thus, for example, half of those in grade 4 were unable to handle multidigit subtraction that involved regrouping, though this is a grade 2 concept (box 2.2). Similarly, students displayed basic vocabulary skills and could match pictures with simple sentences but faltered when asked to make sense of atypical sentences that used simple interrogative words like "what" or "where."

In the Bhutan learning assessment, 91 percent of fourth-grade students were able to look at a clock and tell the time correctly, but only 68 percent, when shown a picture of a circle with a quarter of it shaded, were able to identify correctly the proportion that was shaded. Questions that involve understanding, inference, and extrapolation usually confuse pupils used to rote learning (World Bank 2009).

Clearly, most students in South Asia do not, in fact, understand what they are being taught and thus do not acquire problem-solving skills. There is very little

---

Box 2.2 Procedural Learning, India

The first question, which is asked of fourth-grade students, is a straightforward procedural question checking whether students are able to read clock time; 71.5 percent answered this correctly.

What time is this clock showing?

However, the subtraction question is not a straightforward procedural question because there is a zero in the minuend. Only 49.4 percent of students answered it correctly, which involves multidigit subtraction with regrouping. These are grade 4 students, and subtraction with regrouping is typically taught in grade 2.

Write the answer.

$$\begin{array}{r} 70 \\ -\,43 \\ \hline \\ \hline \end{array}$$

Source: EI 2010.

---

comprehension of concepts—especially how and when to use them. Students can recall facts but cannot apply what is learned in a different context, restate what they learned in their own words, or integrate learning from different sources or subjects. For instance, the SLS found that only 30.4 percent of Indian fourth-grade students understood the concept of multiplication as repeated addition (e.g., $3 \times 4 = 3 + 3 + 3 + 3$). Similarly, 33 percent of fourth-grade students could not correctly say that half of a 10-kilogram watermelon would weigh 5 kilograms. In language, students could answer a question if it was verbatim from a passage they had just read, but if the question required making inferences from the text, they were at a loss.

The Pakistani Sindh Student Assessment 2009, which tested fourth-grade students in mathematics, found that students scored highest on procedural knowledge items (57.7 percent), less well on conceptual understanding items (52.7 percent), and lowest on problem-solving items (43.8 percent). Table 2.2 shows that while 74 percent of students could add two numbers, only 24 percent could demonstrate understanding of the concept of a number line and how it is constructed. The LEAPS assessment found similar results in the province of Punjab (box 2.3).

Students are poorly prepared in such practical competencies as measurement, problem solving, and writing of meaningful and grammatically correct sentences, all of which, though important in the work world, are not in the school curriculum. In the India SLS, for instance, only 20 percent of grade 6 students were able to correctly infer the length of a pencil 5-cm long placed against a ruler starting at the 1-cm mark and ending at the 6-cm mark. As many as 40 percent of students

Table 2.2 Number Competence of Grade 4 Students in Sindh Province, Pakistan

Type of number competence	*Students (%)*
Student is able to read natural and Roman numbers and convert natural to Roman numbers, and vice versa.	43.23
Student is able to demonstrate an understanding of prime, even, and odd numbers.	55.55
Student is able to demonstrate an understanding of the concept of a number line and how it is constructed.	23.86
Student is able to identify smallest and largest numbers.	45.09
Student is able to sequence numbers from smaller to larger, and larger to smaller.	28.30
Student is able to identify the place value of numbers within a figure (units, tens, hundreds, thousands; tenths, hundredths).	41.16
Student is able to translate written numbers into digital form and digital numbers into written form.	49.82
Student is able to add together two numbers of three, four, or five digits.	74.07
Student is able to subtract two numbers of three, four, or five digits.	49.44
Student is able to multiply one-, two-, and three-digit numbers by a single-digit number.	48.68
Student is able to divide two numbers of three, four, or five digits.	59.97
Student will be able to estimate products and quotients.	31.45
Student will be able to solve simple word problems involving addition, subtraction, multiplication, and division.	35.74

Source: PEACE 2010.

Box 2.3 Rote Learning, Punjab Province, Pakistan

"We encountered rote learning first-hand during the test development phase of the LEAPS assessment tool in a small private school in a village about 100 miles from Lahore. The children in the school struggled with a simple reading comprehension exercise conducted informally by the LEAPS team. We were puzzled because the same children had done quite well in a much more advanced English reading comprehension passage used in the school in their last internal examination. The puzzle was solved when we found out that the passage on the internal test was taken verbatim from the textbook used in the class. Each child had practiced and mostly memorized all the main passages.

"Testing children using template questions not only leads to official exams overstating children's subject mastery, it also results in them forgetting the important skill of decoding instructions. When administering the English exam in a second school in Rawalpindi, we found that students were completely stumped when the format of the question was changed slightly. The question was on understanding the difference in usage of a masculine vs. a feminine gender noun—a standard third grade question in Urdu. In Pakistani exams, the question is typically asked by having students convert a masculine noun into a feminine one and vice versa. Our question asked students whether a given noun was masculine or feminine. Most of the students could not answer that question even though the content was well below grade level.

"Other examples abound. An essay on 'your last actual holiday trip' led to a majority of students in a school in central Punjab answering in very similar tone about the beauties of Murree. In math, a free response question showed the picture of a parallelogram and a rectangle drawn on graph paper and asked 'How are these shapes different and how are they similar?' It drew a complete blank, even among fourth graders at an 'elite' English-medium school. Upon prompting, the students confided that they had never been exposed to that type of question. We eventually dropped that question in our actual test because of low discriminatory power vis-à-vis student ability. In plain English, nobody came even close to giving a satisfactory answer" (Andrabi et al. 2007, 23).

thought it was 6 cm because they only read the value at the end point. Similarly, very few students were able to reorganize a jumbled sentence correctly or complete a miniature short story by adding two sentences from word clues provided.

Data from a national assessment of learning achievement undertaken by the Bangladesh Directorate of Primary Education (DPE) in 2008 are instructive about the types of learning that children are and are not good at.[13] The assessment analyzed both mean scores on each subject test and the percentage of students achieving mastery of "learning outcomes categories" (LOCs). The assessment was based on 45 terminal competencies specified by the National Curriculum and Textbook Board of Bangladesh that children should ideally achieve at the end of five years of primary education. There are 4 competencies each in the Bangla language, English, and religious studies; 5 in mathematics; and 28 in environmental studies (EVS). The DPE identified grade-specific learning outcomes for each ("competency-based learning outcomes") and tested students on those. The outcomes were aggregated into 21 LOCs. Students scoring 80 percent or more of the marks allocated to a given LOC were considered to have mastered that LOC.

Figure 2.26—which shows the proportion of fifth-grade students who attained mastery in the two Bangla LOCs and six mathematics LOCs—shows wide variation: in Bangla, for instance, while 53 percent had mastered reading and comprehension, only 14 percent had mastered writing. In mathematics, while nearly half had mastered basic operations, including basic number and fraction concepts, far fewer were competent in everyday problem solving, including units and measurements. This reinforces the observation that learning in South Asia is procedural; while they are able to read and comprehend written material, students have trouble expressing thoughts in their own words. Likewise, while they can recognize numbers and carry out the mathematical operations that are

Figure 2.26 Bangladesh: Percentage of Grade 5 Students Attaining Mastery in Learning Outcomes Categories, by Subject, 2008

Source: DPE 2009.
Note: EVS = environmental studies; UN = United Nations.

Figure 2.27 Sri Lanka: Mean Student Test Scores, by Subject and Subskill within Subject, 2008
Percent

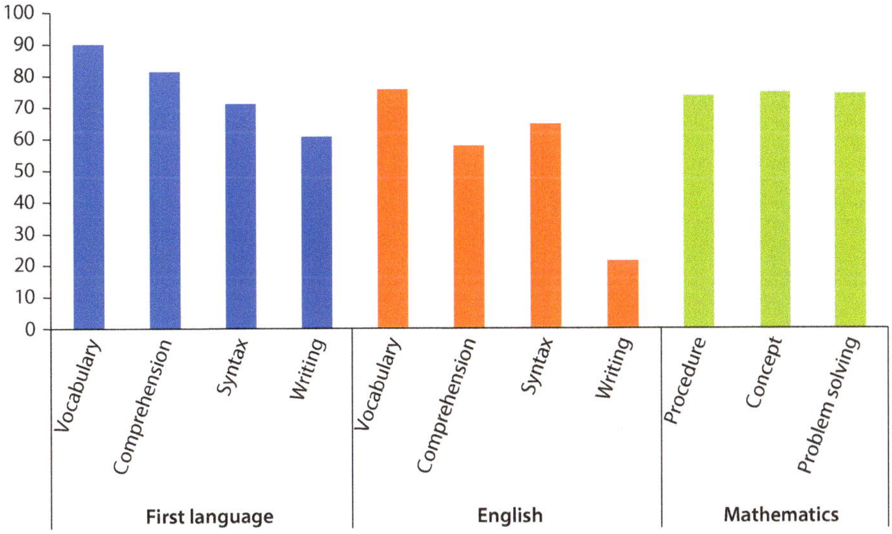

Source: NEREC 2009.

in their textbooks, they are unable to relate mathematical concepts to life in the real world.

For fifth-grade students, although there is a marked difference in competencies between reading comprehension and writing in English (although, surprisingly, not in Bangla), competency in everyday science is high at 58 percent and in units and measurements it is 63 percent (figure 2.26). Thus, as students progress from the third to the fifth grade, they increasingly acquire competencies related to everyday life.

The 2009 NEREC learning assessment in Sri Lanka also highlights the difficulties students have in expressing their thoughts in writing (figure 2.27). In English, for instance, while students perform well in vocabulary and syntax, they do less well in comprehension and very badly in writing. Even in their first language, students are much better at vocabulary than at writing.

Geographical Variations

Student achievement in urban areas is generally higher than in rural areas. In India, for instance, the SLS shows higher student achievement in both mathematics and language in urban than in rural areas (figure 2.28). Interestingly, the rural-urban disparity is greater in language than in mathematics. It is also smallest at the higher grades, with virtually no difference observable in grade 8 mathematics scores. This may be affected by selection bias: because of high rural dropout rates (primarily because staying in school has a high opportunity cost for students

Figure 2.28 Rural versus Urban Student Achievement, India, Bangladesh, Sri Lanka, and Pakistan, 2008 and 2009
Percent

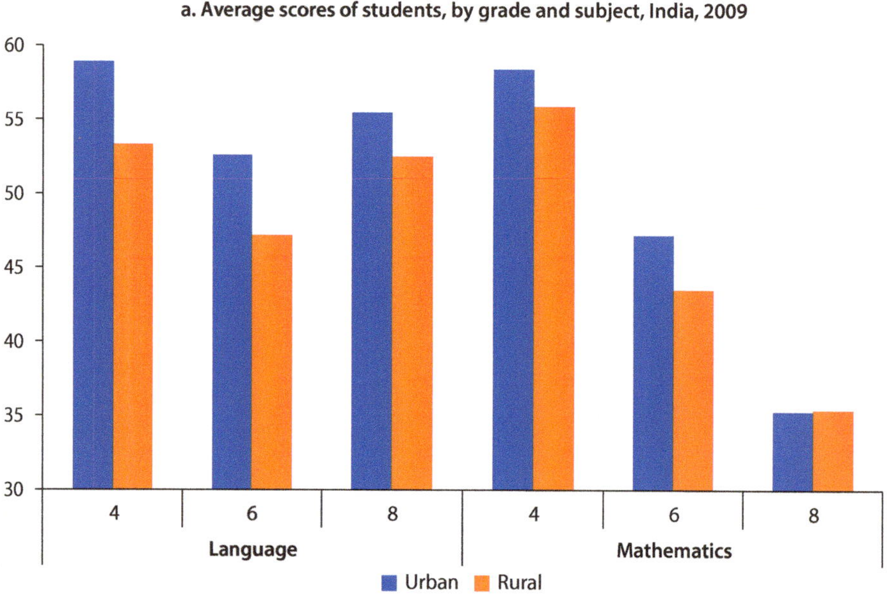

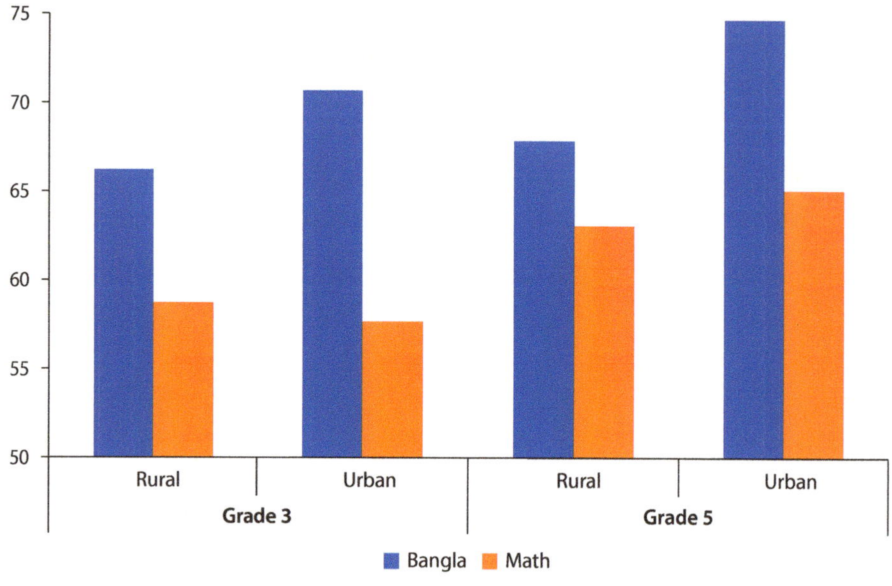

figure continues next page

Figure 2.28 Rural versus Urban Student Achievement, India, Bangladesh, Sri Lanka, and Pakistan, 2008 and 2009 *(continued)*
Percent

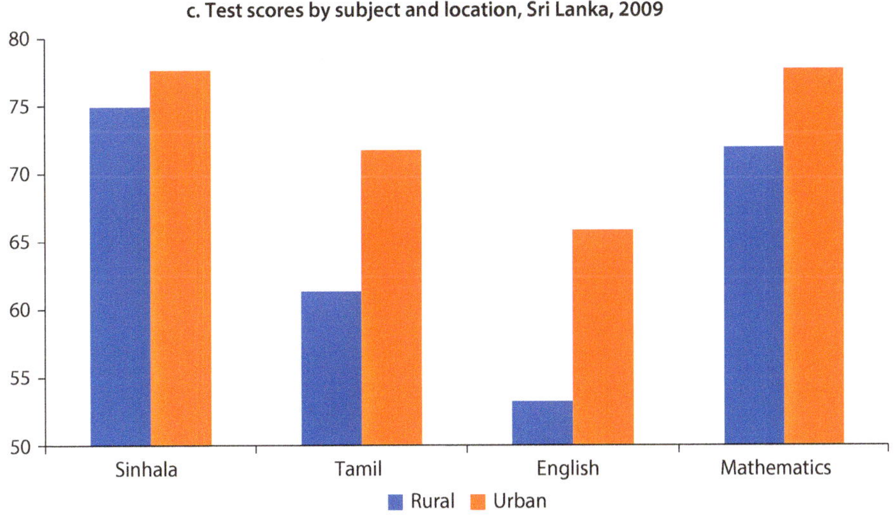

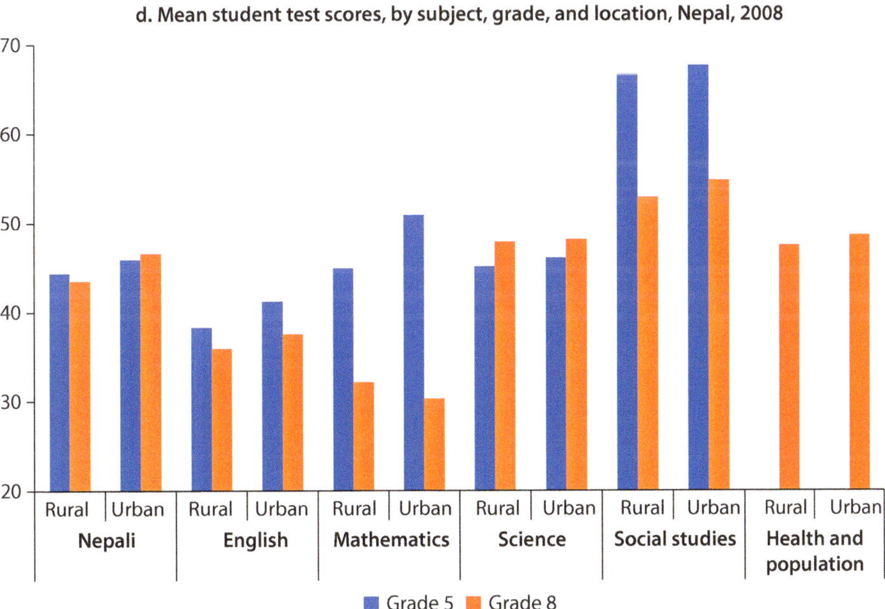

Sources: EI 2010; DPE 2009; NEREC 2009; Government of Nepal 2008a, 2008b.

from farm families), rural students who make it to grade 8 are likely be academically strong and motivated.

In Bangladesh, there is a significant rural-urban difference in student achievement, especially in language. Depending on the grade, mean scores for students in urban areas are 7–10 percent higher than in rural areas. However, math achievement is fairly similar in both. In Sri Lanka, the disparity between urban and rural achievement is widest in Tamil and in English but relatively small in Sinhala and mathematics. Finally, in Nepal, urban and rural differences in student achievement are relatively modest—mostly under 7 percent (figure 2.28). Only in grade 5 mathematics is the urban test score more than 10 percent higher than the rural (13.3 percent). But in grade 8, the results turn around, and urban students have 6 percent lower math scores than rural students. It is not clear, however, that these differences are statistically significant.

Pakistan's National Education Assessment System (NEAS) also found that urban students in grades 4 and 8 performed somewhat better on language and social studies tests than their rural counterparts (MOE 2007). However, mathematics and general science scores did not appear to differ significantly. Thus, in much of South Asia the rural-urban gap in achievement does not seem to be particularly large, and the gaps that exist are mainly in reading and language proficiency scores, not in mathematics.

There are wide variations in student achievement across administrative units in all South Asian countries. In India, as measured by a composite performance index (averaged over grades 4, 6, and 8, and across mathematics and language) developed by the SLS (EI 2010; figure 2.29), student achievement is highest in Kerala, followed by Maharashtra, Odisha, and Karnataka. It is lowest in Chhattisgarh, Rajasthan, Madhya Pradesh, and Jammu and Kashmir.

Figure 2.29 shows the relationship, as calculated by the SLS, between state GDP and composite student learning performance across all grades and all subjects. There appears to be a positive, although not perfect, association between the two, suggesting that states with higher per capita income generally have

Figure 2.29 Indian State Composite Student Performance Index, by State Per Capita GDP, 2010

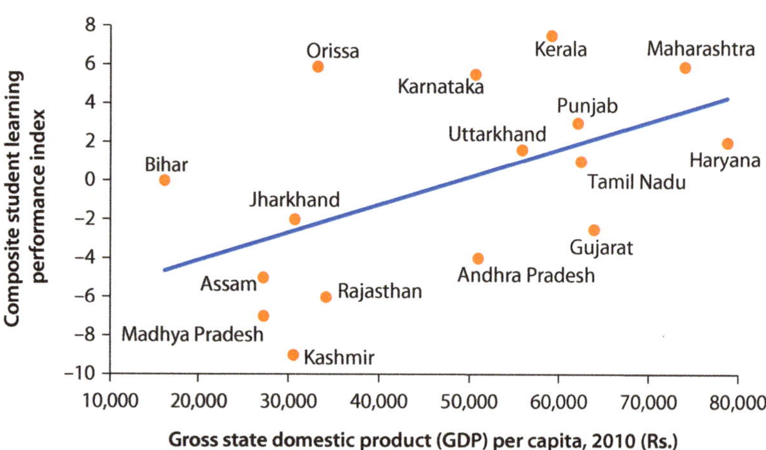

Sources: EI 2010; http://www.indiastat.com.
Note: A.P. = Andhra Pradesh; M.P. = Madhya Pradesh.

higher student achievement than poorer states. Bihar, Odisha, Karnataka, and Kerala are positive outliers in the sense that the achievement of their students is considerably higher than would be predicted by income; Madhya Pradesh, Rajasthan, Jammu and Kashmir, Andhra Pradesh, and Gujarat are negative outliers.

Figure 2.30 shows changes in reading and arithmetic achievement by state between the ASER 2007 and ASER 2011 assessments.[14] It is somewhat disconcerting that achievement declined in the vast majority of states; only Punjab and Karnataka showed modest gains in achievement (3–5 percentage points) in both reading and arithmetic. Achievement declined most (>15 percent) in Bihar, West Bengal, Jharkhand, and Assam.

The large decline in mean achievement in Bihar, Jharkhand, and West Bengal may be because so many children who were previously out-of-school children, especially from disadvantaged backgrounds, enrolled.[15] Bihar and Jharkhand experienced the largest increases in school enrollment. The decline in achievement

Figure 2.30 Changes in Percentage of Children in Grades 3–5 Who Can Read Grade 1 Text or Subtract, Rural India, 2007–11

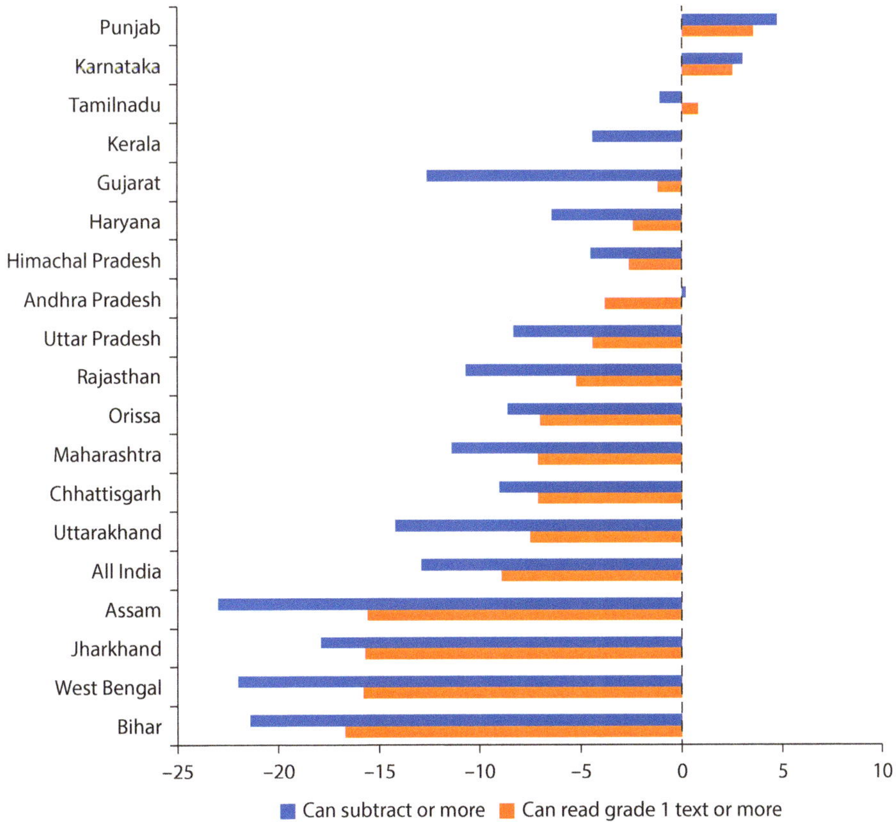

Sources: Pratham 2008, 2012.

in Assam is more difficult to understand, since enrollment there rose by only 3.3 percentage points, below the national average.

Bangladesh, too, has large divisional differences in student achievement. Barisal and Khulna divisions have generally the highest achievement in grades 3 and 5 and Sylhet the lowest in both language and mathematics (figure 2.31). Surprisingly, Dhaka, the most affluent division in the country, has a very low mean level of mathematics achievement, although its mean in language is about average.

In Pakistan, the NEAS reported (rescaled) test scores by language spoken in a student's home. Urdu is the language of instruction in all government schools, but only 9 percent of students report that it is spoken at home. The most common language is Punjabi, followed by Sindhi and Pashto. Surprisingly, Sindhi-speaking students performed better in Urdu than even speakers of Urdu and other home languages. In general, Pashto-speaking students scored the lowest in most subjects (except for math, where they tied with Urdu-speaking students). However, except for Urdu reading comprehension, test score differences by home language are relatively small (figure 2.32).

In Pakistan, students in Balochistan and Sindh underperform students in other provinces in reading in both their own language and English and in arithmetic (annex 2D). Though true at all grade levels, the differences are largest in the middle grades, 5 and 7. The provincial differences in achievement are not large, and there is some evidence that by grade 10 pupils in laggard provinces catch up, at least in arithmetic, so interprovincial variations in arithmetic achievement are relatively small.

In Nepal, provincial differences in student achievement are largest in English, followed by mathematics and Nepali (figure 2.33). Interprovincial disparities are

Figure 2.31 Bangladesh: Average Student Achievement, by Subject, Grade, and Division, 2008
Percent

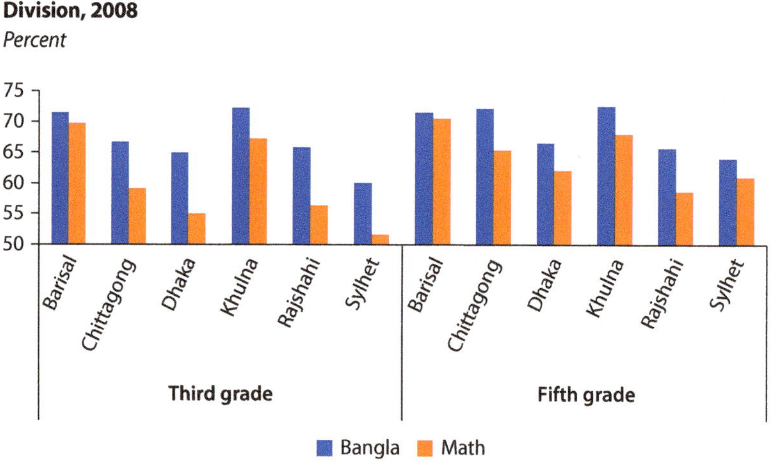

Source: DPE 2009.

Figure 2.32 Pakistan: Student Achievement, by Subject and Language Spoken at Home, Grade 4, 2006

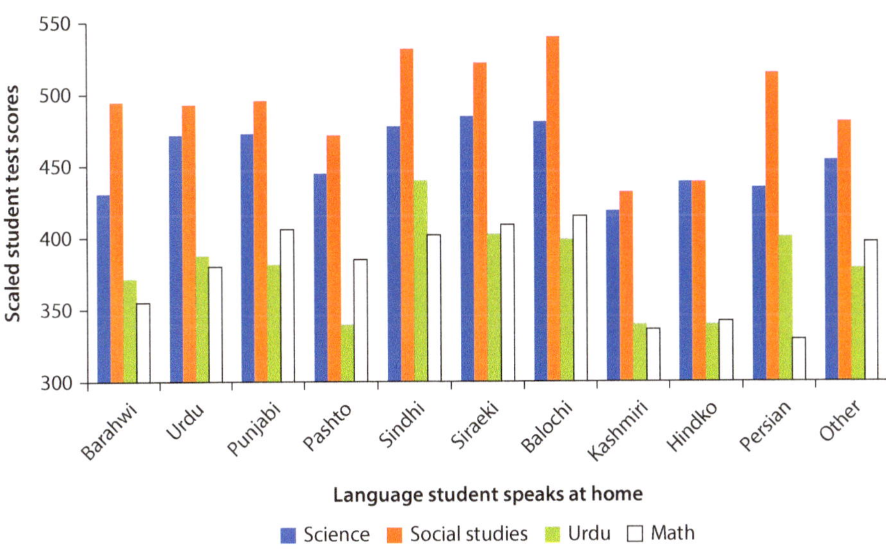

Source: MOE 2007.

Figure 2.33 Nepal: Mean Student Achievement, by Subject, Grade, and Region, 2008
Percent

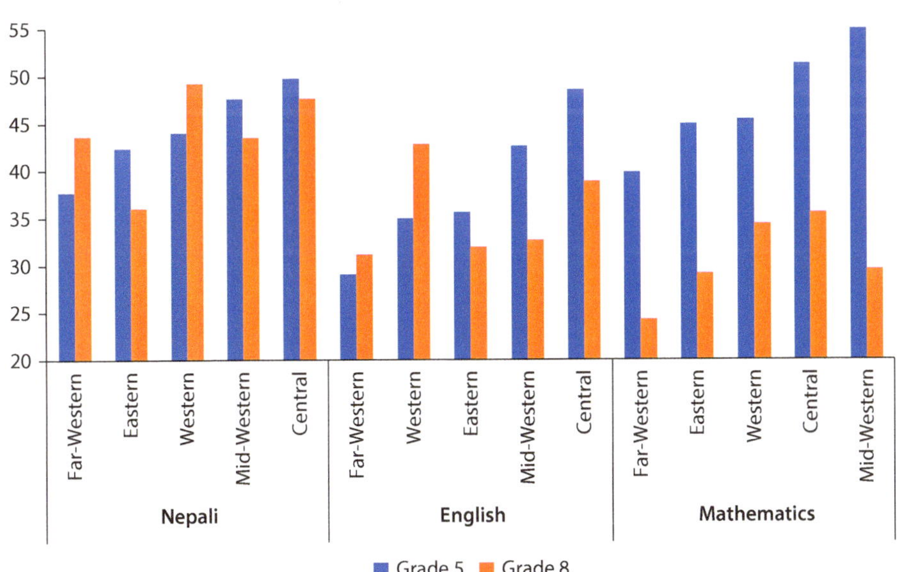

Sources: Government of Nepal 2008a, 2008b.

Figure 2.34 Sri Lanka: Student Achievement in Grade 4, by Subject and Province, 2009
Percent

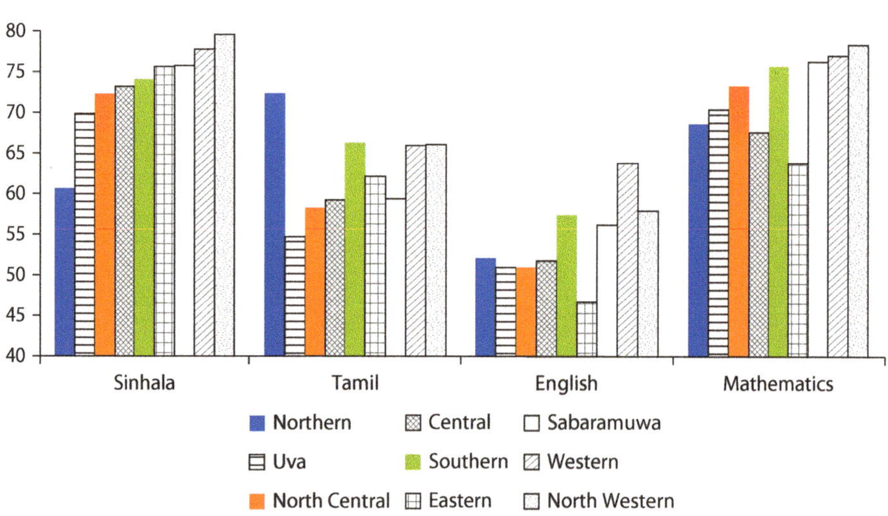

Source: NEREC 2009.

larger in grade 5 than in grade 8. For fifth-grade students, achievement is highest in the central and midwestern regions and lowest in the far west. For eighth-grade students, the central and western regions generally fare best and the far west the worst.

In Sri Lanka in general, the northern and eastern provinces have the lowest student achievement, except for Tamil language competency, where the Northern province (which is predominantly Tamil) has the highest (figure 2.34). Students in the Western and North Western provinces generally perform best in most subjects. Interprovincial disparity is greatest in English and smallest in mathematics.

In the mathematics and science portions of the 2009 GCE O-level examinations, failure rates were typically high (figure 2.35). Interestingly, although the Western province, which has the highest rate of student achievement in grade 4, has the smallest GCE O-level failure rates, the Northern and Eastern provinces, which have the lowest grade 4 achievement, do not have the highest failure rates. Indeed, the Northern province has the second-lowest rate of failure on the mathematics test. Uva and Central provinces do worse in both subjects; the Western province does best.

Maldives, too, has large disparities in learning outcomes across its atolls. Student achievement in both grades 4 and 7 is considerably higher in the Male atoll than elsewhere. In English, there is more than a two-fold difference in average test scores between students from the atolls that perform best (Male) and worst (Raa).

Figure 2.35 Sri Lanka: Students Failing the GCE O-Level Examinations, by Subject and Province, 2009
Percent

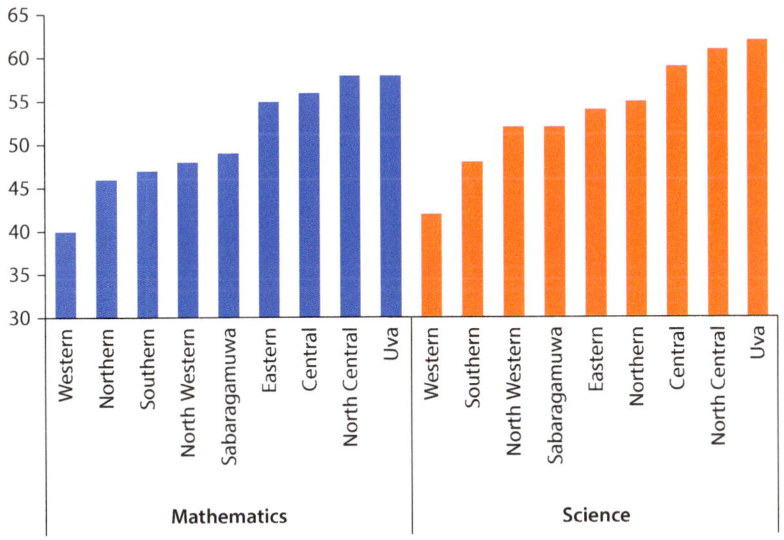

Source: World Bank 2011.
Note: GCE = General Certificate of Education.

Annex 2A: National Learning Assessments in South Asia

Afghanistan

Afghanistan Rapid Reading and Numeracy Test 2008

Afghanistan used this test to assess students graduating from grades 1–4. The sample, although not representative of the entire country, consisted of more than 1,000 students in 15 provinces. The objective of the USAID-funded assessment, part of the Partnership for Advancing Community Education in Afghanistan (PACE-A), was to find out whether students were becoming literate and numerate. The results were measured against norms that would indicate whether there was need for any intervention or change in the strategies that the PACE-A was currently using to support teachers and communities.

Bangladesh

DPE Assessment 2008

The Directorate of Primary Education (DPE) in Bangladesh conducted a national assessment, the second in a series, to measure learning achievement at two points in schooling. The sample consisted of 16,910 third-grade students and 12,745 fifth-grade students from 720 schools that covered 64 *upazillas* from 32 districts in 6 administrative divisions. For third-grade students, Bangla and mathematics were assessed. For fifth-grade students, Bangla, mathematics, English, EVS: Science, and EVS: Social were assessed.

SEQAEP Baseline Study 2007

As part of an evaluation of the World Bank Secondary Education Quality and Access Enhancement Project (SEQAEP), a random baseline survey of 6,542 sixth-grade students and 6,304 eighth-grade students was conducted (Asadullah et al. 2009). The sixth-grade students were given a subset of math questions from the TIMSS grade 4 math test and the eighth-grade students a subset from the TIMSS grade 8 math test. The survey covered 373 secondary schools, mostly aided private schools (194), and aided *madrassas* (102).

Bhutan

Bhutan ASSL 2008

In 2008, the NGO Educational Initiatives (EI) conducted a national Annual Status of Student Learning (ASSL) to test 34,000 students in grades 4, 6, and 8 for learning in English, mathematics, and science. Anchor questions from Indian benchmarking studies and international tests were included for comparison, and background information was collected from students, teachers, and schools to identify factors associated with learning.

Bhutan Learning Quality Survey 2007

The Learning Quality Survey was a nationally representative World Bank survey of second- and fourth-grade students in public and private schools in Bhutan. The report identified learning levels for various types of school, and correlated teacher- and child-related characteristics with test scores as an indicator of learning achievement. About 2,400 students were tested in Dzongkha (the national language), English, and mathematics. Both grades were given the same test.

India

ASER 2005–11

The Annual State of Education Report (ASER) is a national rural survey that collects information about basic learning in reading and arithmetic for children ages 3–16 years. Facilitated by Pratham, an Indian nonprofit organization, the survey annually measures changes in basic learning and school statistics for every rural district in India. The sample size is 600 households per district, reached by randomly selecting 30 villages per district and 20 households per village. To enable comparisons, core questions on school status and basic learning stay the same, but every year new questions are added to explore different dimensions of elementary schooling and learning.

NCERT Assessment 2010

The NCERT Assessment was a national survey that collected data from 117,653 fifth-grade students in 6,411 schools in 274 Indian districts. In addition to testing student achievement in different subjects, the 2010 assessment looked into student backgrounds, resources available at home, resources available at school, and student activities outside of school that may affect learning.

Student Learning Study (SLS) 2010

The SLS was a benchmarking study of student learning in mathematics and language conducted by EI, an independent consulting firm in 48 districts in 18 states (Uttar Pradesh, West Bengal, and Himachal Pradesh did not agree to participate) and one Union territory. A total of 101,643 students in grades 4, 6, and 8 at 2,399 government schools took the test. In an attempt to benchmark achievement of Indian students against those from other countries, some items from international studies such as the TIMSS and PIRLS were used as anchor items for comparison; items used were from question banks for grades 4 and 8 (TIMSS) and grade 4 (PIRLS). Test papers for each grade were translated into 13 languages.

World Bank Study as a comparison to TIMMS 2008

"India Shining and Bharat Drowning: Comparing Two Indian States to the Worldwide Distribution in Mathematics Achievement" is a two-state study that used questions released from the TIMSS 1999 grade 8 mathematics test to rank Indian students on an international achievement scale. The test, which consisted of 36 items from the full TIMSS item bank, was administered to 6,000 students in public and private schools in Rajasthan and Odisha. A distribution of scores for those tested was constructed to be directly comparable to the worldwide distribution and allow for comparison to the international average.

Nepal

EDSC National Assessment of Grade 8 Students 2008

Commissioned by the Department of Education, the National Assessment of eighth-grade students in Nepal was conducted by the Educational and Developmental Services Centre (EDSC) to identify performance in the core subjects of Nepali, English, mathematics, social studies, science, health and physical education, and population and environment education. The study, which tested 2,640 students from 132 schools, was designed to establish national norms of performance and explore factors, such as home resources and teacher competence, that contribute to achievement in lower secondary school.

National Assessment of Grade 5 Students 2008

The Department of Education also commissioned a national assessment of the performance of fifth-grade students in Nepali, mathematics, social studies, English, and science and environment. Besides measuring learning outcomes, another objective was to compare 2008 data with 1999 baseline information and monitor whether policy recommendations made in 1999 were adopted. The study examined factors, such as home resources and teacher competence, that contributed to grade 5 student achievements. The main analyses assessed 16,117 students.

Pakistan

Pakistan ASER 2008–11

The Annual Status of Education Report 2011 (ASER) is a national survey facilitated by the South Asian Forum for Education Development (SAFED) for children ages 3–16 years. It was conducted in 3,642 public and private schools in 84 rural and 3 urban districts. In rural Pakistan, ASER collected information on enrollment, achievement, and learning quality for 143,826 children (59 percent male, 41 percent female) from 48,646 households in 2,502 villages. ASER 2011 also collected data on mother literacy from 50,473 of their mothers.

LEAPS 2003

The Learning and Educational Achievements in Punjab Schools (LEAPS) Report surveyed public and private schools offering primary education in 112 villages in the Punjab province (Andrabi et al. 2007). It studied learning outcomes for 12,000 third-grade students in Urdu, English, and mathematics and gathered information on the beliefs and behavior of schools, teachers, and parents. The assessment was first conducted in 2003 in collaboration with the World Bank, and four rounds were conducted between 2003 and 2007.

NEAS Assessment 2006

The National Education Assessment System (NEAS) studied what Pakistani students in grades 4 and 8 learned in language, mathematics, social studies, and general studies. It tested 11,954 students in 127 of the 137 districts and federal regions. NEAS was a priority program of the Ministry of Education as part of the Education Sector Reform Action Plan and was intended to inform policy makers of the extent to which geography and gender are linked to performance and inequality in Pakistan.

Sindh Students Assessment Math (Grade 4) 2009

The 2009 assessment was a provincially representative assessment of how much math Sindh province students knew and could do. It was conducted by the Provincial Education Assessment Centre (PEACE) in all the districts of Sindh in 4,333 schools (Primary Sample Units) where 28,684 students took 106,716 tests. The intent was to use the findings about student attitudes to mathematics and teaching to improve the quality of education and learning outcomes, and to use information from teachers to improve teacher training and classroom practices.

Sri Lanka

NEREC Sri Lanka 2009

In 2009, NEREC conducted the National Assessment of Achievement of Grade 4 Pupils in Sri Lanka as a follow-up to similar studies in 2003 and 2007. The objective was to assess the achievement of students completing grade 4 in 2008 in their first language, English, and mathematics in order to identify patterns of learning achievement. In 2009, NEREC fielded a TIMSS module in addition to locally developed competency tests.

Annex 2B: Bhutan: Grade 2 and 4 Students Who Attained Competency in Dzongkha and English, 2007

Competency	Grade 2	Grade 4	Corresponding grade of curriculum
		Dzongkha	
Circle the name of the picture (picture of a hen).	91	99	Grade 2
Circle the name of the picture (picture of scissors).	88	94	Grade 2
Look at the picture and circle the missing letter (picture of a rabbit).	82	88	Grade 2
Look at the picture and circle the missing letter (picture of a book).	76	80	Grade 2
Circle the missing word (apple *orange* banana).	45	82	Grade 2
Circle the missing word (bear *lion* tiger).	31	56	Grade 2
Look at the picture and circle the missing word (picture of a flute).	77	84	Grade 2
Look at the picture and circle the missing word (picture of a star).	49	85	Grade 2
Look at the picture and circle the correct word (picture of a boy *digging* with a hoe).	63	92	Grade 2
Look at the picture and circle the correct word (picture of a girl *boiling* tea).	31	34	Grade 2
Circle the correct verb tense ("goes" from "go").	81	94	Grade 4
Circle the correct verb tense ("teaches" from "teach").	64	84	Grade 4
Circle the correct name of the letter (whether prefix, suffix, or root letter).	36	87	Grade 4
Circle the correct missing word (the cat eats *oranges).*	13	40	Grade 4
Read the passage and answer questions.	30	60	Grade 4
Look at the picture and circle the correct sentence (picture of a hen on a chair).	26	58	Grade 4
		English	
Circle the name of the picture (picture of a cube).	68	90	Grade 2
Circle the name of the picture (picture of an egg yolk).	29	37	Grade 2
Look at the picture and circle the missing letter in a word (picture of a snake).	67	93	Grade 2
Look at the picture and circle the missing letter in a word (picture of number 17).	68	87	Grade 2
Circle the missing word in a sequence (mother father *son*).	36	70	Grade 2
Circle the missing word in a sequence (wrist *knee* ankle).	33	43	Grade 2
Look at the picture and circle the correct word in a sentence (picture of a frog *jumping*).	28	40	Grade 4
Look at the picture and circle the correct word in a sentence (picture of an elephant with big ears).	46	79	Grade 4
Circle the correct sentence (variations of "I wash my hands").	37	75	Grade 4
Circle the correct missing word (I *weigh* 40 kilograms).	20	38	Grade 4
Read the passage and answer questions.	38	59	Grade 4

Source: World Bank 2009.

Annex 2C: Grade 9 Students Meeting TIMSS International Mathematics Benchmarks, 2003

Percent

	TIMSS International Mathematics Benchmark			
Economy or state	*Low (>400)*	*Intermediate (>475)*	*High (>550)*	*Advanced (>625)*
Singapore	99	93	77	44
Korea, Rep.	98	90	70	35

table continues next page

Economy or state	TIMSS International Mathematics Benchmark			
	Low (>400)	Intermediate (>475)	High (>550)	Advanced (>625)
Hong Kong SAR, China	98	93	73	31
Japan	98	88	62	24
Netherlands	97	80	44	10
Estonia	97	79	39	9
Taiwan, China	96	85	66	38
Hungary	95	75	41	11
Belgium	95	82	47	9
Malaysia	93	66	30	6
Latvia	93	68	29	5
Russian Federation	92	66	30	6
Sweden	91	64	24	3
Slovak Republic	90	66	31	8
Australia	90	65	29	7
United States	90	64	29	7
Lithuania	90	63	28	5
Scotland	90	63	25	4
Slovenia	90	60	21	3
New Zealand	88	59	24	5
Israel	86	60	27	6
Italy	86	56	19	3
Bulgaria	82	51	19	3
Armenia	82	54	21	2
Norway	81	44	10	0
Serbia	80	52	21	4
Romania	79	52	21	4
Cyprus	77	45	13	1
Moldova	77	45	13	1
Lebanon	68	27	4	0
Macedonia, FYR	66	34	9	1
Jordan	60	30	8	1
Indonesia	55	24	6	1
Iran, Islamic Rep.	55	20	3	0
Tunisia	55	15	1	0
Egypt, Arab Rep.	52	24	6	1
Bahrain	51	17	2	0
Odisha	50	27	9	1
Palestine	46	19	4	0
Rajasthan	42	17	4	1
Morocco	42	10	1	0
Chile	41	15	3	0
Philippines	39	14	3	0
Botswana	32	7	1	0
Saudi Arabia	19	3	0	0
South Africa	10	6	2	0
Ghana	9	2	0	0

Source: Das and Zajonc 2008.

Annex 2D: Rural Pakistan: Student Reading and Arithmetic Achievement, by Province, 2010

Percent

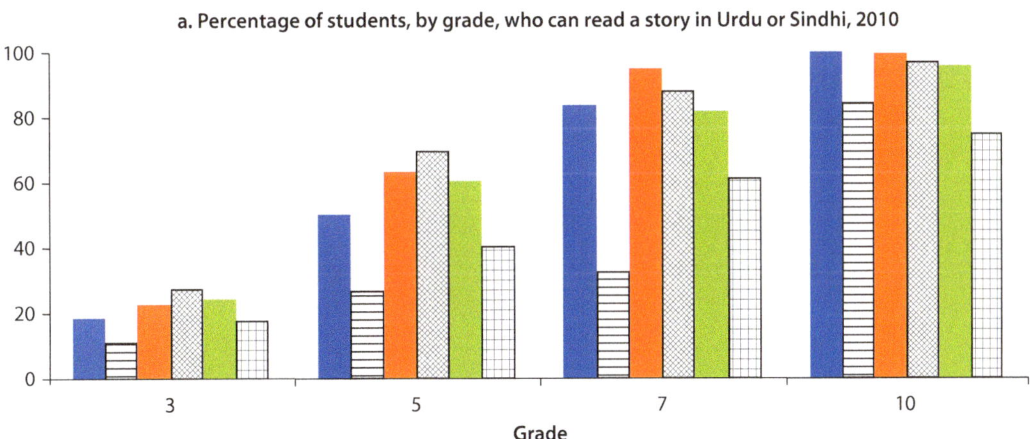

a. Percentage of students, by grade, who can read a story in Urdu or Sindhi, 2010

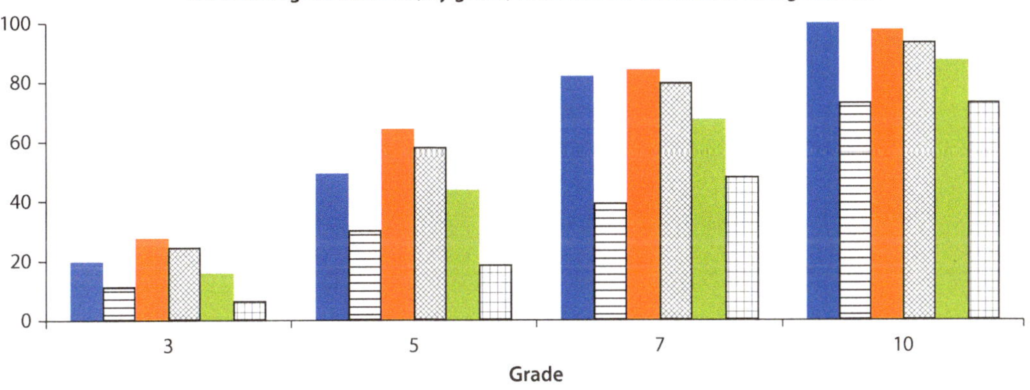

b. Percentage of students, by grade, who can read a sentence in English, 2010

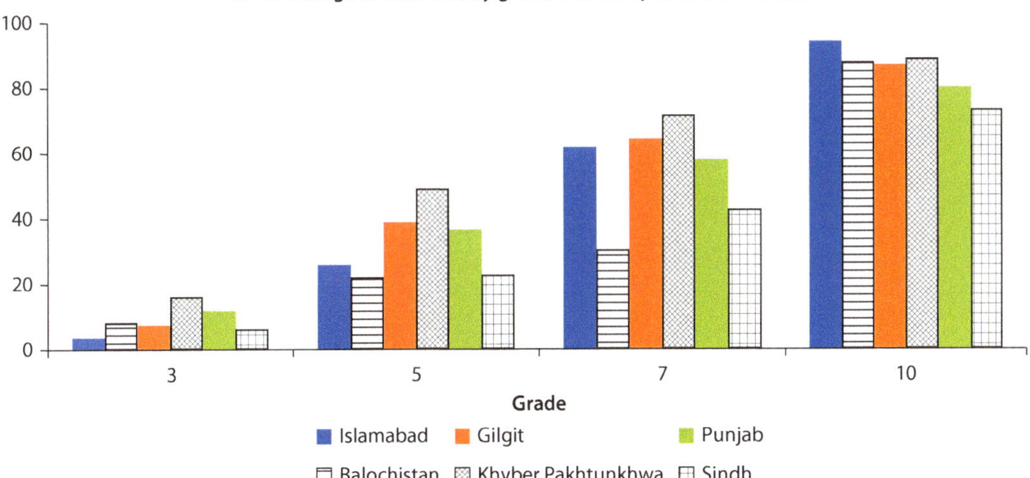

c. Percentage of students, by grade, who can perform division, 2010

Source: SAFED 2012.

Notes

1. Interestingly, even though the LEAPS assessment was only for Punjab, the 49 percent of students who were unable to subtract is similar to the proportion of grade 4 students that the ASER national assessment found could not subtract.
2. Two of the four oral math questions were: (a) Suppose you went to market taking two Tk. 100 notes and ten Tk. 5 notes. What amount of money did you take in total to the market? (b) You save Tk. 20 every month. How much money will be saved in six months? Two of the written math questions were: (a) There are 365 days in a year. It has rained for 123 days. How many days did it not rain this year? (b) Rahima has 32 mangoes. She gave the mangoes to her four children by dividing equally. How many mangoes will each child get? (Asadullah et al. 2009).
3. An assessment of students in the same grades was also conducted in 1999, but because of differing methodologies the results of the two assessments are not comparable.
4. The assessment reported mean test scores, but it is not clear how the mean scores can be interpreted, since Nepal has not established basic competence in some skills and abilities for particular grades. The assessment set an arbitrary score of 30 percent as the cutoff for passing a grade.
5. The household-based survey of children and youth ages 12–20 years contained five questions relating to Bengali reading comprehension and 10 questions on English reading and writing (Asadullah et al. 2009). Unfortunately, no details are available about what these questions were, or their source.
6. In 2009, the NEREC (2009) assessment used the same questions for English and Tamil as had been used in the 2003 and 2007 assessments. They were based on identified grade 4 learning competencies.
7. A total of 2,359 students in grades 2 and 4 in 120 schools across the country were surveyed in 2007. The Dzongkha and English questions were based on the grades 2 and 4 national curricula.
8. The school survey was stratified by rural and urban and by school type (government, private aided, and private unaided). In each of the 253 schools selected, a maximum of 30 students was selected randomly from the ninth grade.
9. The SLS was based on a stratified random survey of 160,000 students in grades 4, 6, and 8 in 2,399 government schools in 48 districts in 18 states and one union territory. These students were tested in language and arithmetic through common test papers in 13 languages.
10. TIMSS describes the advanced benchmark this way: "students can organize information, make generalizations, solve non routine problems, and draw and justify conclusions from data. They can compute percent change and apply their knowledge of numeric and algebraic concepts and relationships to solve problems. Students can solve simultaneous linear equations and model simple situations algebraically. They can apply their knowledge of measurement and geometry in complex problem situations. They can interpret data from a variety of tables and graphs, including interpolation and extrapolation."
11. The TIMSS high benchmark includes "students [who] can apply their understanding and knowledge in a wide variety of relatively complex situations. They can order, relate, and compute with fractions and decimals to solve word problems, operate with negative integers, and solve multi-step word problems involving proportions with whole numbers. Students can solve simple algebraic problems including evaluating

expressions, solving simultaneous linear equations, and using a formula to determine the value of a variable. Students can find areas and volumes of simple geometric shapes and use knowledge of geometric properties to solve problems. They can solve probability problems and interpret data in a variety of graphs and tables."

12. The National Council for Educational Research and Training is a Government of India body that advises on school-related issues and also publishes textbooks for schools that follow Central Board of Secondary Education curricula.
13. In 2008, the national assessment tested 16,910 grade 3 students, and 12,745 grade 5 students from 720 schools in 64 *upazilas* in 32 districts of 6 administrative divisions.
14. Data for smaller states and union territories are not shown because of small sample size.
15. Between 2005 and 2010 enrollment of children ages 6–10 rose by 9.8 percentage points in Jharkhand, 11.5 percentage points in Bihar, and 5.6 percentage points in West Bengal, well above the all-India average of 4.7 percentage points.

Bibliography

Andrabi, T., J. Das, A. Khwaja, T. Vishwanath, and T. Zajonc. 2007. *Pakistan: Learning and Educational Achievements in Punjab Schools (LEAPS): Insights to Inform the Educational Policy Debate*. http://www.leapsproject.org/assets/publications/LEAPS_Report_ExecSummary.pdf.

Asadullah, M., N. Chaudhury, D. Prajuli, L. R. Sarr, Y. Savchenko, and S. R. Al-Zayed. 2009. *Secondary Education Quality and Access Enhancement Project (SEQAEP): Baseline Report*. Washington, DC: World Bank.

Asim, S., and D. Raju. 2013. "Achievement in Government Schools in Punjab, Pakistan: Evidence from Large Scale Administrative Data." South Asia Human Development Unit, World Bank, Washington, DC.

Aturupane, D. H. 2009. *The Pearl of Great Price: Achieving Equitable Access to Primary and Secondary Education and Enhancing Learning in Sri Lanka*. CREATE Monograph 29. London: Institute of Education, University of London.

Das, J., and T. Zajonc. 2008. "India Shining and Bharat Drowning: Comparing Two Indian States to the Worldwide Distribution in Mathematics Achievement." Policy Research Working Paper Series 4644, World Bank, Washington DC.

DPE (Directorate of Primary Education). 2009. "National Assessment of Pupils of Grades 3 and 5, 2008." Ministry of Primary and Mass Education (prepared by Associates for Development Services Ltd.), Dhaka.

EI (Educational Initiatives). 2010. *Student Learning Study. Status of Learning across 18 Sites of India in Urban and Rural Schools*. Ahmedabad, India: EI. http://www.ei-india.com/wp-content/uploads/2012/01/Main_Report_StudentLearningStudy_2010_by_Educational_Initiatives1.pdf.

Government of Nepal. 2008a. "Final Report—National Assessment of Grade V Students." Department of Education, Ministry of Education and Sports, Kathmandu.

———. 2008b. "Final Report—National Assessment of Grade VIII Students." Department of Education, Ministry of Education and Sports, Kathmandu.

MOE (Ministry of Education). 2007. *National Assessment 2006—Technical Report*. National Education Assessment System, Government of Pakistan, Islamabad.

NCERT (National Council of Educational Research and Training). 2011. *What Do They Know? A Summary of India's National Achievement Survey, Class V, Cycle 3 2010/11.* New Delhi: NCERT.

NEREC (National Education Research and Evaluation Center). 2009. *National Assessment of Achievement of Grade 4 Pupils.* Colombo, Sri Lanka: NEREC.

OECD (Organisation for Economic Co-operation and Development). 2010. *PISA 2009 Results: Overcoming Social Background—Equity in Learning Opportunities and Outcomes.* Vol 2. http://dx.doi.org/10.1787/9789264091504-en.

PACE-A (Partnership for Advancing Community Education in Afghanistan). 2009. *Rapid Reading and Numeracy Test Report 2008.* https://www.eddataglobal.org/countries/index.cfm?fuseaction=pubDetail&ID=247.

PEACE (Provincial Education Assessment Centre). 2010. "Sindh Students Assessment Math (Grade 4) 2009." PEACE, Sindh.

Pratham. 2007. *Annual Status of Education Report (Rural) 2007.* New Delhi: Pratham Resource Center.

———. 2008. *Annual Status of Education Report (Rural) 2008.* New Delhi: Pratham Resource Center.

———. 2009. *Annual Status of Education Report (Rural) 2009.* New Delhi: Pratham Resource Center.

———. 2011. *Annual Status of Education Report (Rural) 2011.* New Delhi: Pratham Resource Center.

———. 2012. *Annual Status of Education Report (Rural) 2012.* New Delhi: Pratham Resource Center.

SAFED (South Asia Forum for Economic Development). 2012. *Annual Status of Education Report (Rural), ASER-Pakistan 2011.* Islamabad: SAFED.

World Bank. 2009. "Findings from the Bhutan Learning Quality Survey." Report 21, Human Development Unit, South Asia Region, World Bank, Washington, DC.

———. 2011. *Transforming School Education in Sri Lanka: From Cut Stones to Polished Jewels.* Washington, DC: World Bank.

———. 2012. *Human Capital for a Modern Society. General Education in the Maldives. An Evolving Seascape.* Washington, DC: World Bank.

———. 2013. "Bangladesh Education Sector Review." Report 80613-BD, Human Development Sector, South Asia Region, World Bank, Washington, DC.

Wu, K. B., P. Goldschmidt, C. K. Boscardin, and D. Sankar. 2009. "International Benchmarking and Determinants of Mathematics Achievement in two Indian States." *Education Economics* 17 (3): 395–411.

PART 2

Foundations for Learning: School Readiness

Whereas education systems in South Asia have made considerable progress in providing more school-age children with educational opportunities, they have fallen short in several areas:

1. The region is still home to about 13 million children not enrolled in school.
2. It is estimated that 80 million to 100 million South Asian children who have completed grade 5 still lack basic numeracy and literacy skills.
3. South Asia is far behind other regions—such as East Asia and Latin America and the Caribbean—in centering education policy on learning outcomes, partly because the region lacks the national, regional, and international data that are needed to shape outcomes-centered policies.

What factors contribute to low learning outcomes in the region? While poor outcomes are often attributed to flaws in school systems, it may also be that individual and household factors contribute (see chapter 3), and that interventions such as nutrition and preschool programs could lay the foundation for academic success (see chapter 4). It appears that a child's gender and parental background (e.g., education and household income) contribute to disparities not only in access to education but also in learning outcomes. Moreover, the region has the highest rates of infant and child malnutrition and micronutrient deficiencies in the world, which means that many children are at a big disadvantage when they enter school.

CHAPTER 3

Learning Outcomes and Individual and Household Characteristics*

Introduction

In terms of influences on student achievement, there has been much scholarly debate about the relative roles of student characteristics and household socioeconomic background (see, for example, Sirin 2005, for a meta-analysis of the effect of socioeconomic status in the United States) and of school-level variables like student-teacher ratios, how well trained teachers are, and the availability of textbooks (see, e.g., Hedges and Greenwald 1996; Krueger 1999).[1]

Variations in test scores can be statistically decomposed into variations arising due to differences between schools and variations within schools. The latter are generally attributed to differences in student family backgrounds. Analysis of cross-country data from the 2009 Programme for International Student Assessment (PISA) assessments suggests that the between-school variation typically declines as national per capita income rises (figure 3.1): with economic growth and development, schools within a country typically become more homogenous in quality, perhaps due to better enforcement of learning standards, so that interstudent variations in learning outcomes are mostly the result of differences in student family backgrounds.[2]

Among demographic and socioeconomic variables that typically influence student achievement are a child's sex and birth order, the language spoken at home, parental schooling, household income, social status, and family size and composition. In a developing country, lack of good nutrition in early childhood can have a serious negative effect.

This chapter reviews the evidence from South Asia on what individual and household characteristics may influence student achievement. Among questions it explores are: How does achievement vary by gender? How does parental schooling influence a child's academic achievement? What is the relationship between household living standards and student achievement? Even though data

*See box 3.1 for a summary of the chapter's key questions and findings.

Box 3.1 Questions and Findings

Questions

- How do children's characteristics, such as gender, age, birth order, and motivation, affect achievement? Is there any evidence that gender disparities in achievement have narrowed?
- How much of the variation in student achievement can be explained by household rather than school characteristics?
- What is the association between household variables—ethnicity, parental education, parental occupation and income, etc.—and student achievement?

Findings

- The evidence on gender differences in student achievement is mixed, making it difficult to generalize, but in most South Asian countries achievement tends to be higher among male than female students—mainly, as in other parts of the world, in mathematics and science but sometimes in reading and language. Sri Lanka is a notable exception, as are some states in India. It may be that for girls the resources and study environment at home may be less conducive to academic achievement—girls may be responsible for household chores and not able to allocate as much time to studies as boys.
- Although the evidence for this in South Asia comes only from Sri Lanka, at the top of the distribution of test scores girls apparently outperform boys.
- The data on sex differences in outcome improvement over time are very limited, but evidence from Sri Lanka suggests there are no major gender differences. Both boys and girls there appear to have enhanced their achievement between 2003 and 2007.
- In most countries of the region, about half, and in some cases as much as 70 percent, of the variation in student achievement can be attributed to variations in school quality—considerably more than is typical in other parts of the world. One implication of this is that while some variation in student learning outcomes is inevitable, due to differences in innate student ability and family background, improving the quality of schools can have major effects on learning. The rest of this report identifies ways the quality of schools can be improved.
- As elsewhere, parental schooling is a strong predictor of student achievement. This may simply reflect the importance of unobserved heterogeneity—for instance, well-educated parents may be reflecting the value the family places on education, which is likely to be transmitted to their children. Educated parents are also likely to offer their children more motivation, encouragement, and assistance with studies. In South Asia, parental schooling seems to matter more for achievement in reading and English than in mathematics.
- With few exceptions, living standards heavily influence student achievement. In some cases, achievement is three to four times higher for the richest quintile of students than for the poorest. More affluent students have a more supportive learning environment at home; better access to achievement-enhancing inputs, such as private tuition; and access to better-quality schools. The large economic differences in achievement highlight the importance of enhancing school quality for students from low-income backgrounds.

Figure 3.1 Between-School Variation (Percent) and Per Capita Income, 2009

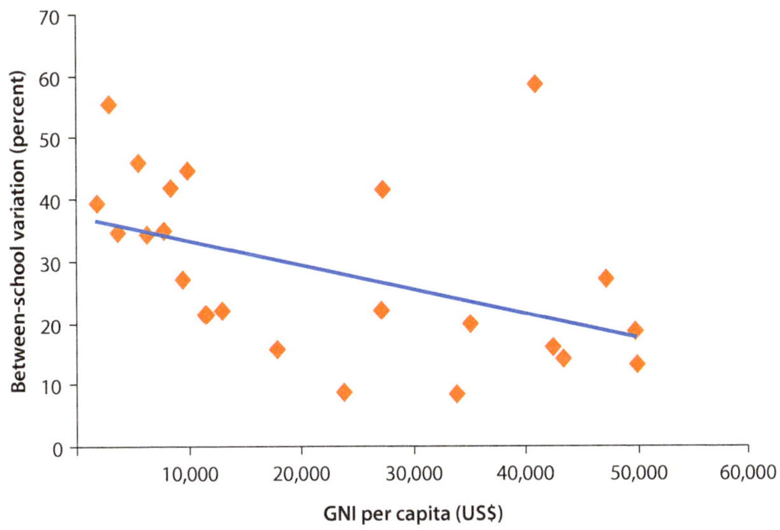

Sources: OECD 2010; World Bank 2012b.
Note: GNI = gross national income.

on student learning in South Asia are difficult to come by, understanding these relationships will help clarify demand-side constraints on raising school quality for students from different backgrounds.

As this chapter will demonstrate, even where national assessments are available, evidence of the socioeconomic correlates of student achievement is generally sparse, although most assessments have analyzed the roles of gender and parental education.

Gender

In much of South Asia, girls typically have lower secondary enrollment rates than boys (although not in primary school and not for Bangladesh). However, the evidence on their academic performance relative to boys is mixed. It might be expected that because there are fewer girls than boys in secondary school, the girls who are there would be self-selected in terms of motivation and academic performance, so that on average their achievement should exceed that of boys. Conversely, adolescent girls are likely to have more household responsibilities and so less time to study than their brothers. What does the empirical evidence suggest?

India

In India, the Pratham (2010) and the NCERT 2010 (NCERT 2011) national assessments did not report student achievement by gender, but the 2009 Student Learning Study (SLS)—which assessed 160,000 students in grades 4, 6, and 8—did. It found no significant difference between average test scores of boys and girls in language achievement, but boys scored significantly higher (46 percent) than girls (42.7 percent) in mathematics achievement—a result consistent with many studies elsewhere.

In the PISA 2009+ study in India,[3] with one exception (see table 3.1) boys outperformed girls in reading, which was contrary to the general experience in PISA 2009+ countries, where girls outperformed boys by an average of 39 points—more than half a proficiency level, or one year of schooling (NCERT 2011). Further, in Tamil Nadu, boys also outperformed girls in math and science, particularly in the upper quartile of test scores.

In Himachal Pradesh, however, in all quartiles girls outperformed boys in math and science by an average of 20–30. Thus, even the evidence from the PISA 2009+ itself is mixed, with the two Indian states showing different results for girls and boys.

Rather than explicitly looking at mean achievement differences by gender, a study by Wu et al. (2009) for two other Indian states, Rajasthan and Odisha, instead assessed how having an "opportunity to learn" (OTL)[4] through more effective teaching raised achievement in mathematics differently for boys and girls. Using internationally comparable items on math achievement drawn from the 1999 TIMSS, secondary-school students were asked about how lessons were introduced, how lessons were taught, and how teachers assigned and used homework.[5] They found that in Rajasthan, a good introduction to new concepts was closely associated with improved test scores for girls, reducing the gender gap and to some extent compensating for a lack of home resources.

Bangladesh

The evidence of gender differences from Bangladesh is also mixed. Asadullah et al. (2009), who tested 12,879 students in grades 6 and 8 in Bangladesh, gave sixth-grade students a subset of questions from the TIMSS grade 4 mathematics test and eighth-grade students a subset from the TIMSS grade 8 math test. For intertemporal comparisons, students in both grades were also asked five questions drawn from a 1992 test of Bangladeshi students by Greaney, Khandker, and Alam (1998). Four of these related to written competency and one to oral.

On average, sixth-grade students could correctly answer only 40 percent of the questions and eighth-grade students 37 percent (table 3.2). Boys scored significantly higher on math than girls, by 15–19 percent, in all types of schools, including aided and non-aided *madrassas*[6] (figure 3.2).[7] The gender differences persisted when Asadullah et al. used the test scores from Greaney's 1997 written math competency test.

Asadullah et al. (2009) also tested sixth- and eighth-grade students in English. Sixth-grade students were asked 18 questions that tested spelling, ability to translate simple sentences from English to Bengali and Bengali to English, knowledge of nouns and verbs, and reading comprehension. Eighth-grade students were tested on the same 14 core questions but were also asked to form sentences from suggested words and were tested on advanced reading

Table 3.1 Scores of 15-Year-Old Students, Himachal Pradesh and Tamil Nadu, India, 2009

		Test score quartile			
State	*Gender*	*0–25th*	*25th–50th*	*50th–75th*	*75th–100th*
Reading					
Himachal Pradesh	Boys	280	281	327	373
	Girls	267	268	315	362
Tamil Nadu	Boys	205	306	352	404
	Girls	275	275	321	366
Mathematics					
Himachal Pradesh	Boys	278	279	323	365
	Girls	310	311	353	395
Tamil Nadu	Boys	304	305	349	398
	Girls	301	302	345	389
Science					
Himachal Pradesh	Boys	267	268	312	358
	Girls	288	289	334	379
Tamil Nadu	Boys	305	306	345	390
	Girls	300	301	338	377

Source: OECD 2010.

Table 3.2 Bangladesh: Student Performance on Mathematics Questions, Grades 6 and 8, 2008
Percent

		Grade 6			*Grade 8*		
Type of test		*Girls*	*Boys*	*Difference*	*Girls*	*Boys*	*Difference*
TIMMS items test	Mean	37.99	43.64	14.9	33.99	40.54	19.3
	SD	16.28	14.99		15.10	16.64	
Greaney written math test	Mean	71.45	80.93	13.3	79.99	87.93	9.9
	SD	29.91	25.05		25.70	19.97	
Number of observations		3,749	2,807		3,650	2,667	

Source: Asadullah et al. 2009; questions based mainly on TIMSS.

comprehension. The results, which revealed very poor English achievement in rural Bangladeshi schools, again found that boys outperformed girls by about 8–9 percent—a somewhat smaller difference than in mathematics (table 3.3).[8]

Are the gender differences more pronounced in certain skills than in others? The 2008 Directorate of Primary Education (DPE) national assessment of the learning achievement of 16,910 pupils in grade 3 and 12,745 pupils in grade 5 addressed this question (DPE 2009).[9] Students who scored 80 percent or more of the score allocated to a given learning outcome were considered to have mastered that outcome. Annex 3A shows virtually no gender differences in Bangla, English, and social studies competencies but modest differences in mathematics and science: Boys did better than girls in basic number concepts, fraction concepts (fifth-grade students), everyday problem solving (fifth-grade students), everyday science, and knowledge of technology.

Figure 3.2 Bangladesh: Student Performance on Mathematics Questions, by Gender and Type of School, Grades 6 and 8, 2008
Percent

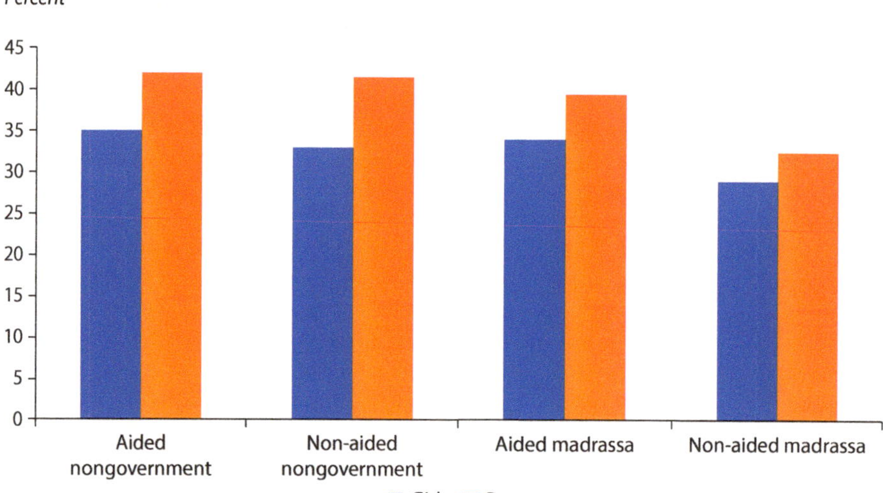

Source: Asadullah et al. 2009.

Table 3.3 Bangladesh: Student Performance on English Questions, Grades 6 and 8, 2008
Percent

	Grade 6			*Grade 8*		
English	*Girls*	*Boys*	*Difference*	*Girls*	*Boys*	*Difference*
Mean	24.50	26.60	8.6	33.58	36.15	7.7
SD	19.75	19.92		23.44	23.04	
N	3,742	2,800		3,648	2,656	

Source: Asadullah et al. 2009.

With data from their 2008 sample of 12,879 students in sixth and eighth grades, Asadullah et al. (2009) examined the correlates of student achievement in mathematics and English through multivariate regression analysis. The explanatory variables were various child characteristics (age, education, height, mother's and father's education, availability of tutor, and teacher standard); household wealth; and village-level fixed effects. The analysis found that after controlling for other socioeconomic factors, girls underperformed boys in mathematics but not in English.

Nepal

The 2008 national learning assessment of Nepalese fifth- and eighth-grade students shows very small gender differences in achievement in most subjects except for mathematics in grade 8, where boys outperform girls by 10 percent (figure 3.3). In Nepali and in health and population, girls outperform boys but not significantly.[10]

Figure 3.3 Nepal: Mean Student Test Scores, by Gender and Subject, Grades 5 and 8, 2008

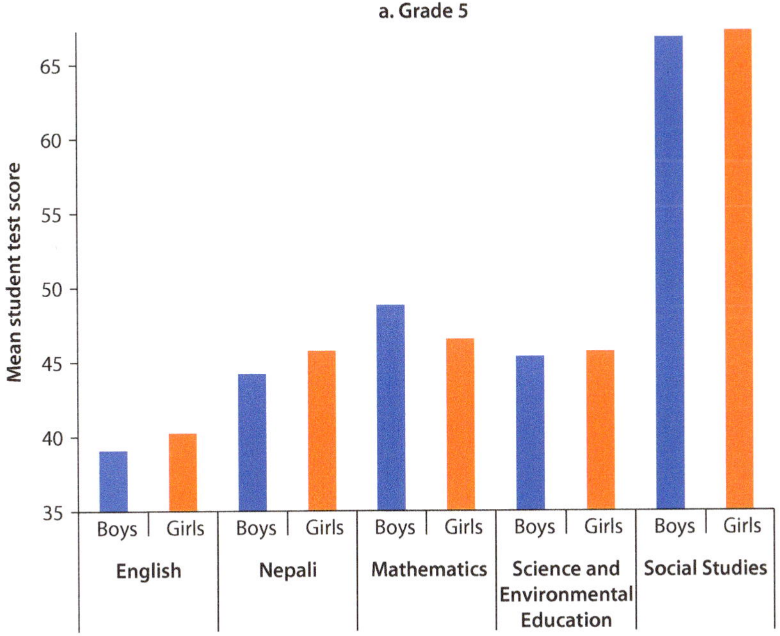

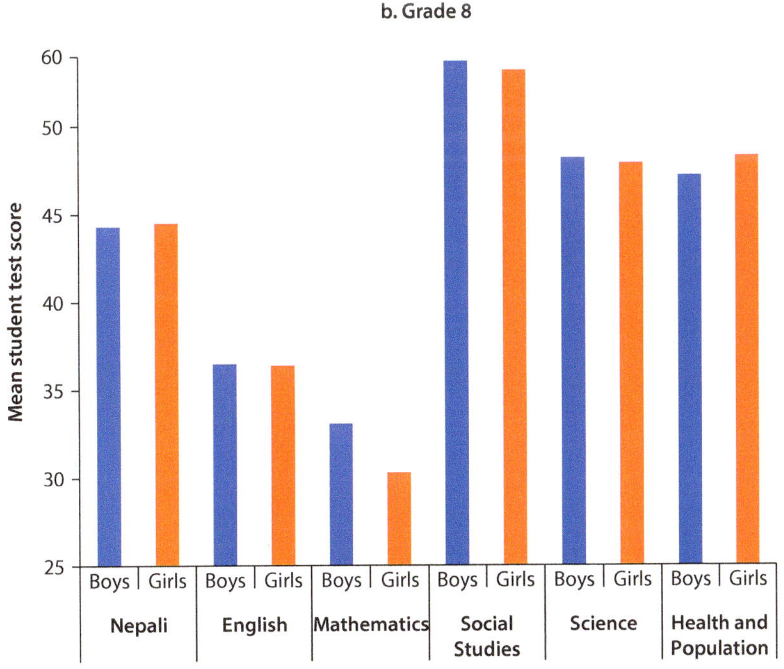

Sources: Department of Education 2008a, 2008b.

Sri Lanka

The gender achievement picture is different in Sri Lanka. National assessments of students completing grade 4 show girls consistently outperforming boys in every subject, with mean test scores 11–17 percent higher (figure 3.4).[11] The largest disparity is in the Tamil language, the smallest in mathematics.[12]

The Sri Lanka data allow us to examine gender differences in improvements in achievement over time because the NEREC learning assessment was conducted in 2003, 2007, and 2009. In Sinhala and English, there were large improvements in mean test scores, particularly between 2003 and 2007, for both boys and girls (figure 3.5). In mathematics, there were somewhat smaller improvements for both sexes. However, in Tamil, while there were improvements in mean test scores of both sexes between 2003 and 2007, between 2007 and 2009 mean scores fell. This may be the result of changes in sample coverage of the Tamil test in 2007; it is doubtful that achievement of both boys and girls in Tamil actually declined.

Aturupane, Glewwe, and Wisniewski (2013) investigated the determinants of school achievement in Sri Lanka using data collected in 2003 by NEREC from a random sample of 20,000 fourth-grade students in government schools who were tested in mathematics, English, and the student's first language (Sinhala or Tamil). The standardized aggregated test scores are shown in figure 3.6. The gender differences observed from the NEREC 2009 data can also be seen in 2003, with girls having somewhat higher test scores than boys.

Figure 3.4 Sri Lanka: Student Achievement, by Gender and Subject, Grade 4, 2009
Percent

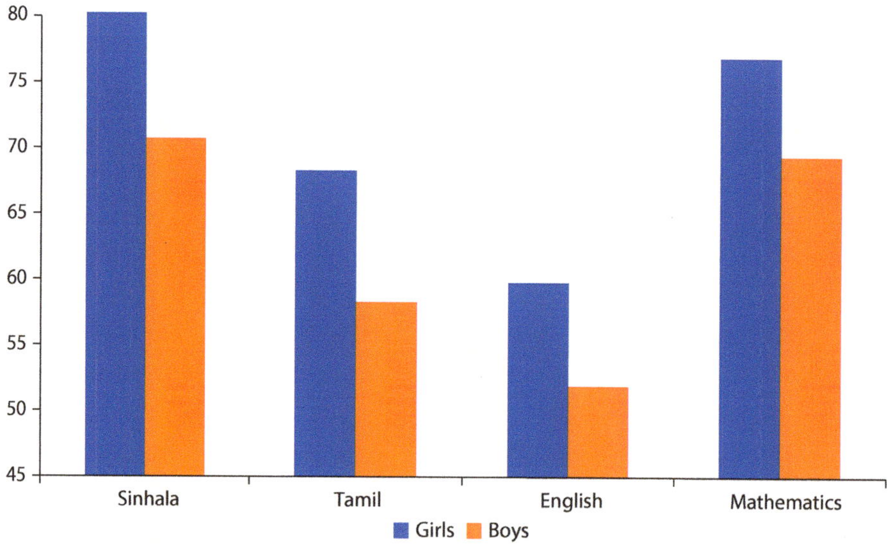

Source: NEREC 2009.

Figure 3.5 Student Achievement, by Subject and Sex, Grade 4, Sri Lanka, 2003–09
Percent

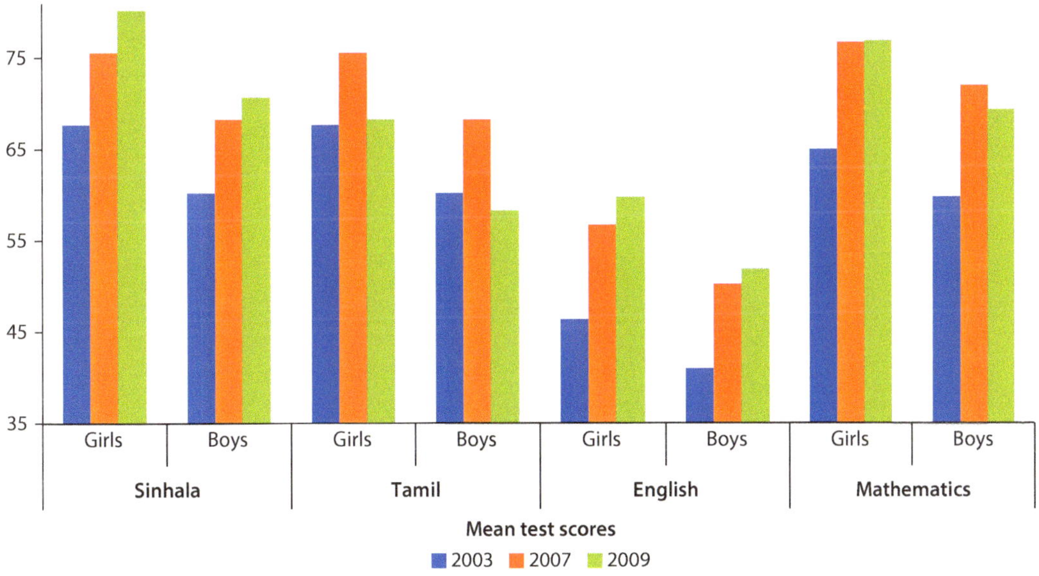

Source: NEREC 2009.

Figure 3.6 Sri Lanka: Standardized Student Test Scores, Grade 4 Students, 2003

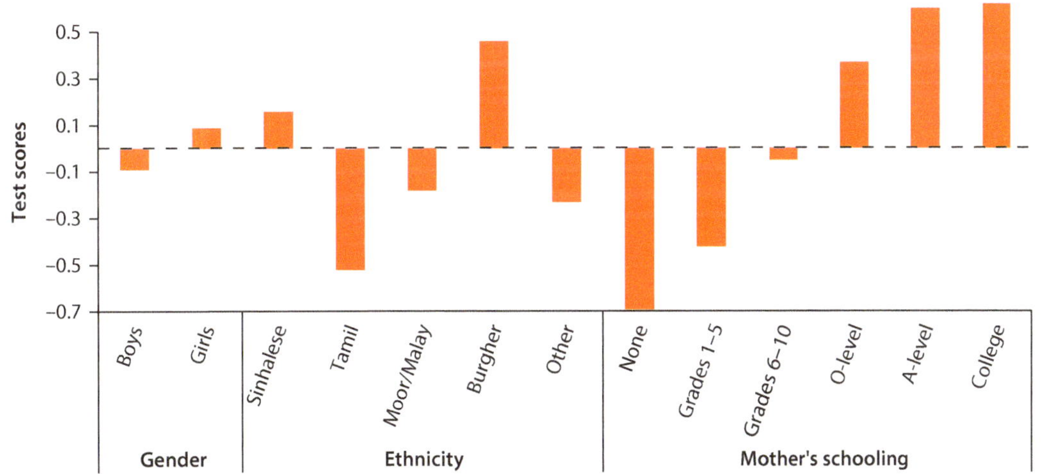

Source: Aturupane, Glewwe, and Wisniewski 2013.

Pakistan

The mathematics assessment of 28,866 grade 4 students that the Sindh government conducted in 2009 for the entire province found that boys outperformed girls in both urban and rural areas and in all content domains: numbers, fractions, measurement, and geometry (figure 3.7). All students found test items written in context to be most difficult, but especially girls.

Figure 3.7 Pakistan, Sindh Province: Mean Test Scores of Grade 4 Students, by Gender, Residence, Content Domain, and Test Item, 2009

Percent

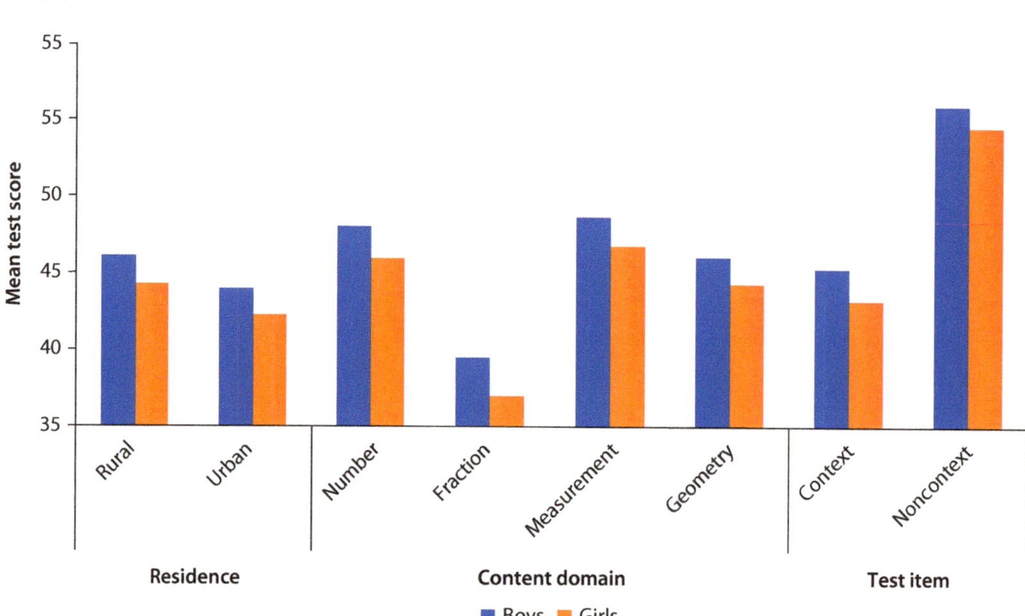

Source: Government of Sindh 2010.

The 2003 LEAPS assessment of 13,735 third-grade students in both public and private schools in 112 villages in Punjab (Andrabi et al. 2007) found that in general boys had significantly higher scores in mathematics than girls, but where wealth and literacy were both high, the gender gap narrowed significantly or even reversed itself (figure 3.8). Thus the context within which children go to school—proxied here by average village wealth and literacy—influences how well girls learn.

Using panel data from the LEAPS survey for 2003–07, Andrabi et al. (2007) used regression analysis to identify correlates of student achievement in English, Urdu, and mathematics for about 4,000 third-grade students. After controlling for parental education, household assets, and child height and weight, they found that girls significantly outperformed boys in English and Urdu, although not in mathematics, but the gender difference was statistically not significant.

One of the few studies to control for the innate ability of a child in analyzing gender differences in performance was carried out by Aslam (2009a), who analyzed correlates of student test scores in numeracy and literacy using data from a school-based survey of 1,887 eighth-grade students in 65 schools (25 government, 40 private) in the Lahore district of the Punjab in 2002–03.[13] Student scores on the Raven's Standard Progressive Matrices test were used as an explanatory variable in the regression analysis of student

Figure 3.8 Mean Mathematics Scores, by Village Literacy and Wealth, Grade 3, Pakistan, 2003

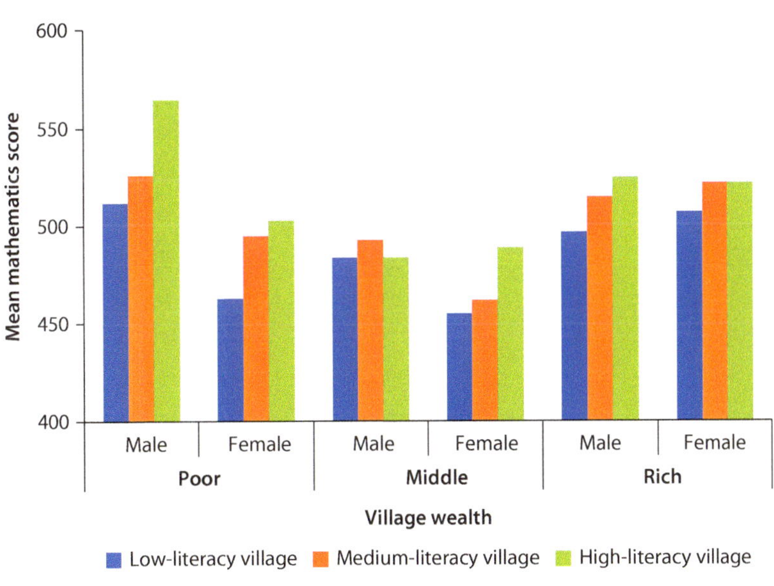

Source: Andrabi et al. 2007.

achievement. The study estimated private and public school student achievement separately.

Controlling for other factors, including innate intelligence, Aslam found that boys outperform girls in mathematics in both public and private schools but girls outperform boys in reading only in government schools. The Raven score proved to be a strong predictor of achievement in both reading and mathematics in both types of schools, which suggests that ability is positively associated with student achievement.

Bhutan

In Bhutan, gender disparities in student achievement are modest. The Bhutan Learning Quality Survey (BLQS), a 2007 nationally representative school-based survey that studied 2,359 second- and fourth-grade students showed girls outperforming boys in Dzonghka and English but not in mathematics (figure 3.9). However, the relatively small differences are likely not significant.

Maldives

The pass rates for the General Certificate of Education (GCE) O- and GCE A-level examinations (see figure 3.10) show girls outperforming boys at both levels but more so on the GCE A-levels, perhaps because of self-selection (the most able girls continue on to the GCE A-levels). Unfortunately, pass rate data are not available by subject, so it is not possible to know whether the female advantage occurs in all subjects.

Figure 3.9 Bhutan: Student Test Scores, by Gender, Grades 2 and 4, 2007

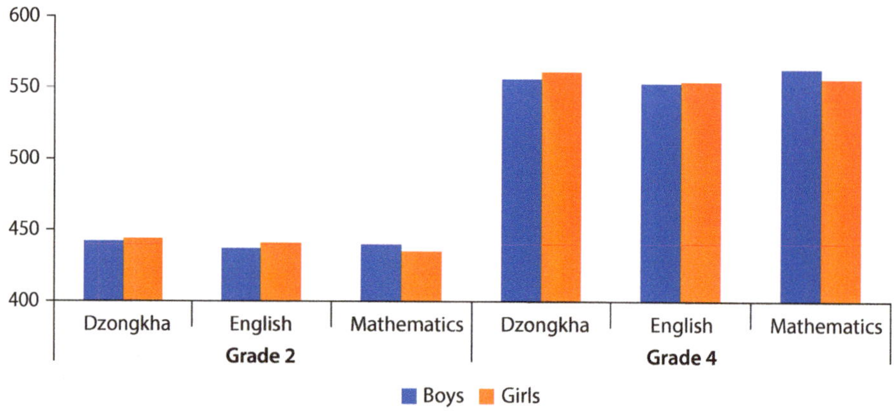

Source: World Bank 2009.

Figure 3.10 Maldives: GCE O-Level and GCE A-Level Pass Rates, by Gender, 2007–10
Percent

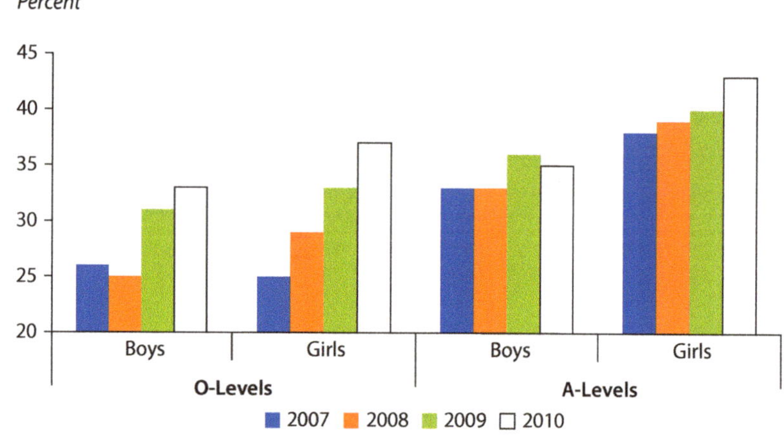

Source: World Bank 2012a.
Note: GCE = General Certificate of Education.

The country findings on gender are so heterogeneous that it is difficult to generalize from them. However, in South Asian countries except Sri Lanka, boys tend to outperform girls in mathematics (not uncommon globally). The picture in reading is more complex, with some studies showing boys perform better than girls in reading and language and others the reverse. For Sri Lanka, too, simple gender comparisons of test scores can be misleading because there is no control for other characteristics affecting performance that might be correlated with gender.

Other Child-Specific Factors

Age, birth order, and number of siblings

A child's age bears on student performance. For India, the 2009 SLS found a negative correlation between age and mathematics scores for students in grades 4, 6, and 8. This probably is because over-age students in a class are those who have not progressed beyond with their age cohort because of poor performance or who have joined school later than their age cohort.

The NEAS data on Pakistani fourth-grade students does not suggest that age is a significant determinant of achievement. In Pakistan, students typically begin school at 6 years of age, which means that most fourth-grade students are 10 years old, but in the NEAS sample the age range was wide. In Urdu and social studies, the oldest students generally did best (figure 3.11), but achievement differences were minor, and in mathematics and science there was almost no age pattern.

Among fourth-grade students in Sri Lanka (using NEREC 2003 data), Aturupane, Glewwe, and Wisniewski (2013) found birth order to be significant. First-born children had test scores 0.2–0.3 of a standard deviation higher than later-born children, even after controlling for sex and age. The researchers suggested this could be because later-born children have lower innate abilities due to biological factors, such as maternal nutrient depletion, or because first-born children receive more attention from parents in their early years than younger siblings.

Some studies have looked at the number of siblings a child has. Using the LEAPS data from Pakistan, Andrabi et al. (2007) found that student achievement is lower when there are numerous older brothers but not when there are numerous older sisters. Although they offered no explanation, it could be that older brothers compete for parental resources and attention and older sisters do not.

Figure 3.11 Pakistan: Scaled Test Scores, Grade 4 Students, by Student Age, 2006

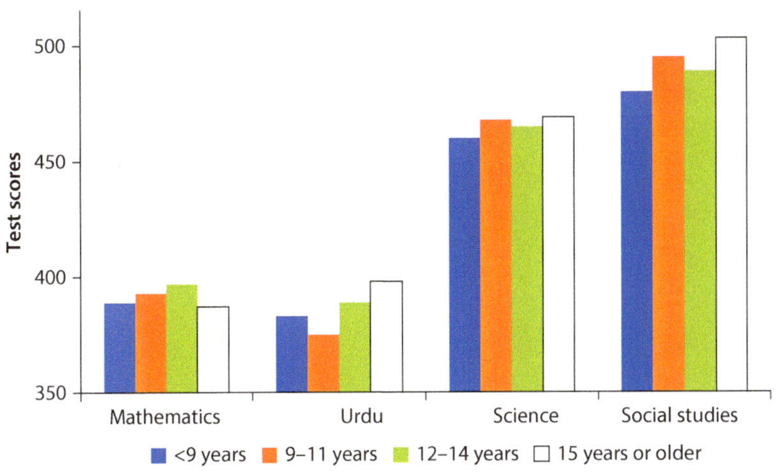

Source: MoE (Pakistan) 2007.

It could also be that sisters are more likely than brothers to help younger siblings with schoolwork.

Student attitudes, aspirations, and intelligence

In India, the 2009 SLS analyzed the association between student achievement and a range of indicators of student attitudes. For instance, students who thought school was not relevant had lower scores in language and mathematics than those who considered it fun and useful. Students who saw themselves as doing badly in their studies showed the lowest average scores for language and mathematics; those who reported not liking *any* subject also reported significantly lower scores in both. However, these associations tell us little about the causes of low achievement. It is not necessarily that pupils with negative attitudes perform poorly; it is just as likely that the unfavorable attitudes of students who are not doing well are a result of their lack of success.

On the basis of a sample of 1,887 eighth-grade students in 65 government and private schools in Pakistan's Lahore district, Aslam (2009a) found that in both types of school children's aspirations about how much education they wanted were closely associated with achievement. Again, it is not clear how much to make of these results; it is unlikely that educational goals are set independently of performance in school, but the causation could go in either direction.

Another interesting LEAPS finding was the association between a mother's assessment of her child's intelligence and the child's actual test score (figure 3.12). Children considered less intelligent by their mothers had test scores that were

Figure 3.12 Pakistan: Mother's Perception of Intelligence and Child Test Scores, Grade 3, 2003

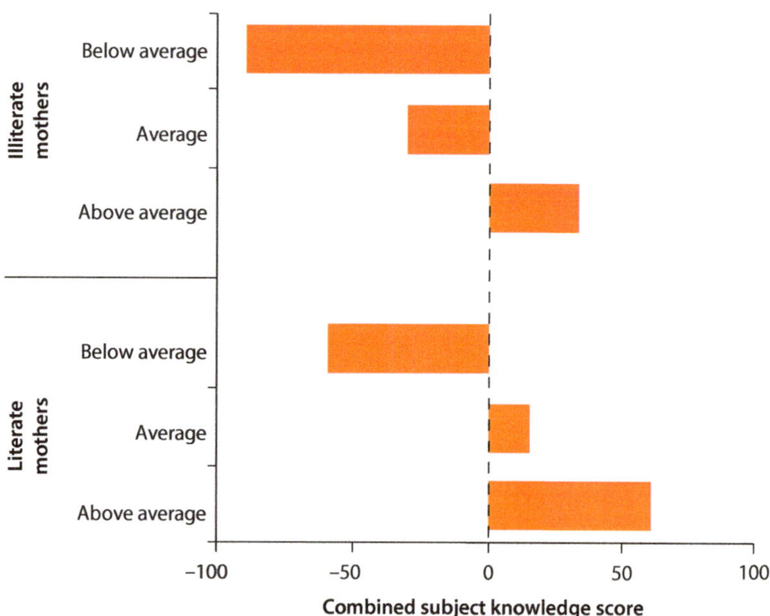

Source: Andrabi et al. 2007.

Figure 3.13 Pakistan: Scaled Test Scores of Grade 4 Students, by Home Language, 2006

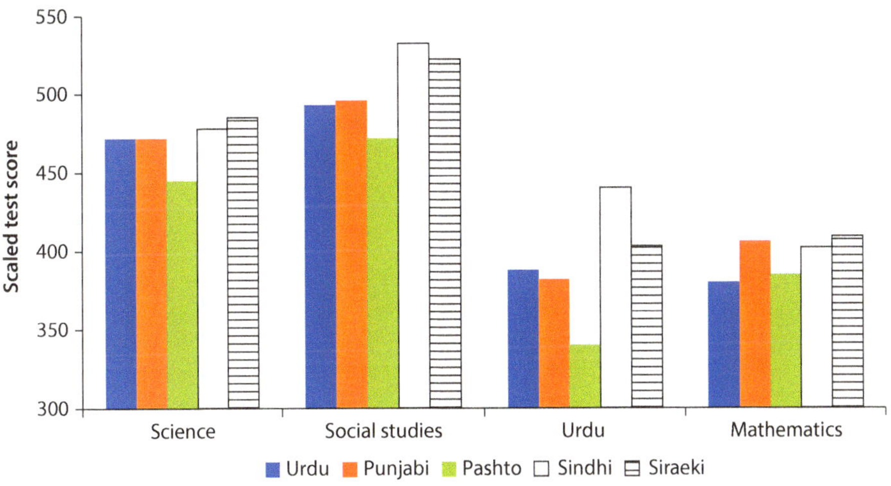

Source: MOE (Pakistan) 2007.

lower by a 0.7 standard deviation than children considered more intelligent. This was true whether or not the mothers were literate. Andrabi et al. (2007) did find that factors other than learning, such as age and gender, were not significantly associated with parental assessments of child intelligence, which suggests that in assessing intelligence mothers do not discriminate against younger children or against girls.

Language

In their sample of Sri Lankan fourth-grade students, Aturupane, Glewwe, and Wisniewski (2013) observed that children who spoke English at home tended to have higher English test scores than children who did not. Similarly, children who spoke Sinhala or Tamil at home performed better in their first-language tests than those who did not speak the language of instruction at home.

The NEAS data on Pakistani fourth-grade students also show that the language spoken at home affects student achievement, especially in Urdu (figure 3.13). Surprisingly, Sindhi-speaking students performed better on the Urdu test (as well as in most other subjects) than Urdu-speaking students. Students who spoke Pashto at home had the lowest test scores not only in Urdu but also in other subjects.

Parental Background

Parental education, occupation, and income heavily influence student achievement in most countries. These background variables mediate their way to achievement through such factors as school choice, student motivation, financial resources, study facilities at home, and parental ability to help children with school work.

India

Using a school-based sample of students in 12 districts in Madhya Pradesh and Uttar Pradesh, Goyal and Pandey (2009) decomposed the total variation in test scores into variation between and within schools. Between-school variation seems to account for 30–56 percent of the total variation, depending on the state, grade, and subject (figure 3.14). While this indicates that household- and child-level factors do matter a great deal (within-school variation is mostly attributable to child and household factors), the results make it clear that school-level factors also matter for student achievement. Although in developed countries most of the variation in student achievement is attributable to within-school differences, in Madhya Pradesh and Uttar Pradesh variations in school quality account for one-third to one-half of the inequality in student achievement.

The 2010 NCERT assessment found disparities in student achievement by amount of parental schooling, but they were relatively modest (figure 3.15): on average, students with college-educated parents scored 8 percent higher in language and 4 percent higher in mathematics than students with illiterate parents. These differences are much smaller than have been observed even in developed countries like the United States.[14] However, the association between parental education and student achievement varied considerably by state; in Odisha and Kerala, for instance, the difference in language achievement between students whose parents had the most education and those

Figure 3.14 Test Score Variations within and between Schools, Madhya Pradesh and Uttar Pradesh, India, 2006–07

Percent

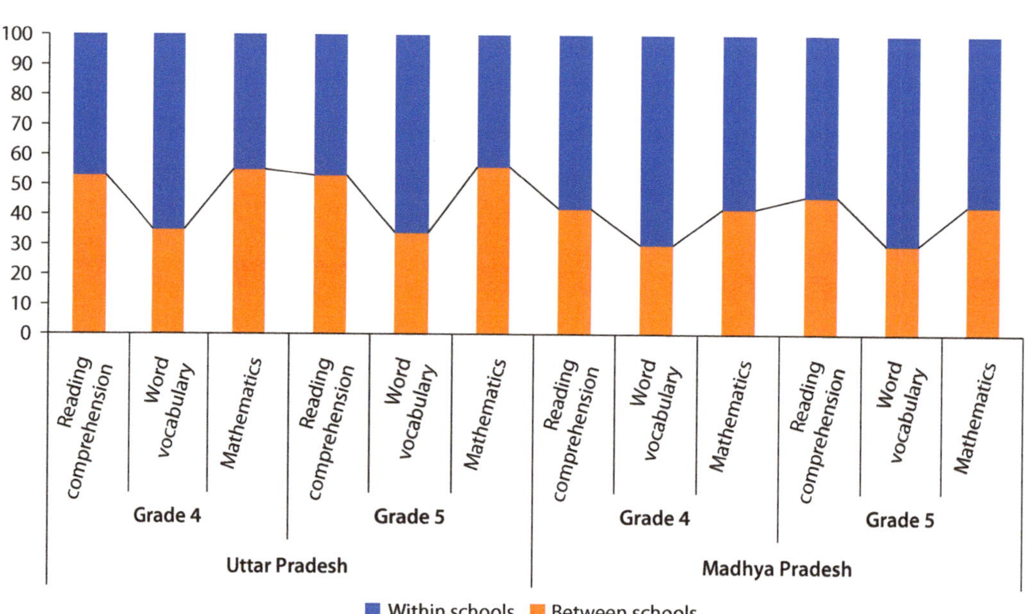

Source: Goyal and Pandey 2009.

Figure 3.15 Mean Language Achievement Difference between Students with College-Educated Parents and Those with Illiterate Parents, Grade 5, India, 2010
Percent

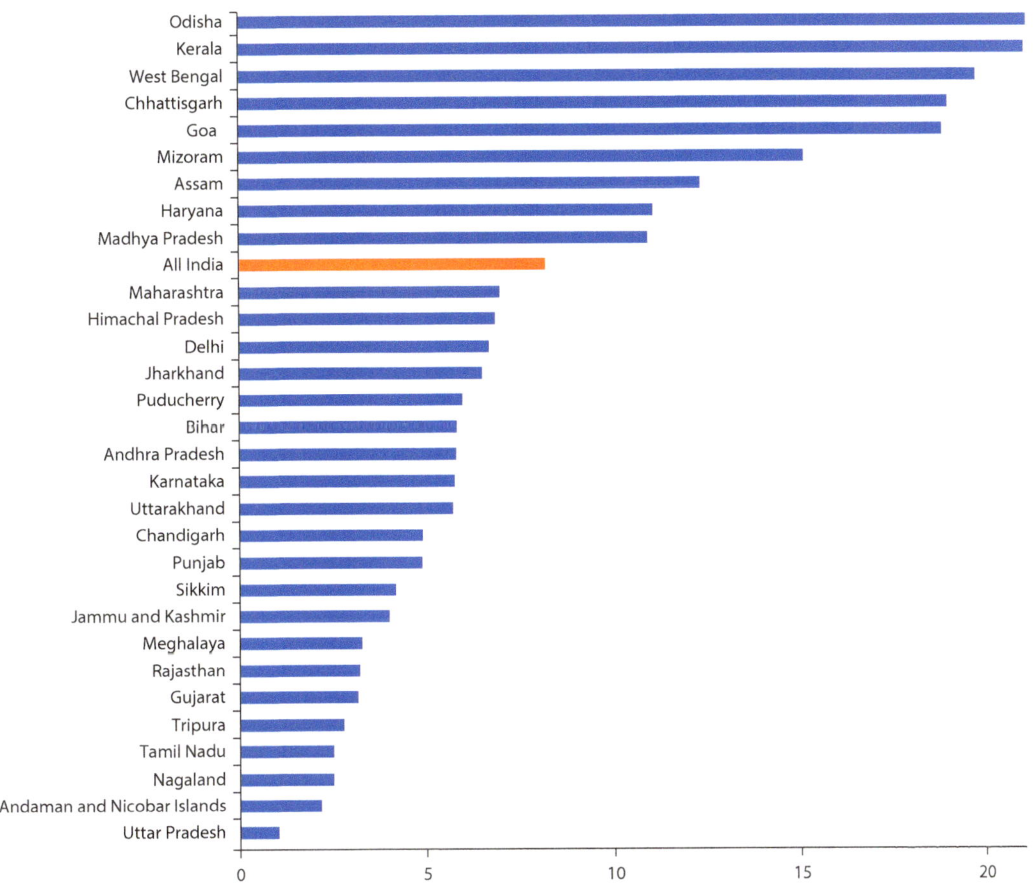

Source: NCERT 2011.

whose parents had the least was more than 20.0 percent, but in Uttar Pradesh and Tamil Nadu the difference was only about 2.5 percent. There appears to be no systematic pattern for state differences; disparities are large in both high-performing Kerala and Goa and low-performing Odisha and Chhattisgarh.

The SLS found that parental occupation was closely associated with student achievement. Students whose parents were in private business performed better in both language (55 percent versus 52 percent) and mathematics (47 percent versus 45 percent) than children of civil servants, but the latter did significantly better than children of farmers (figure 3.16). However, the differences are again relatively modest. The results of the PISA 2009+ in Himachal Pradesh and Tamil Nadu also confirmed the importance of parental education: children of parents with eight or more years of schooling performed significantly better

Figure 3.16 India: Scaled Student Test Scores, by Subject and Parental Occupation, Grades 4, 6, and 8, 2009
Percent

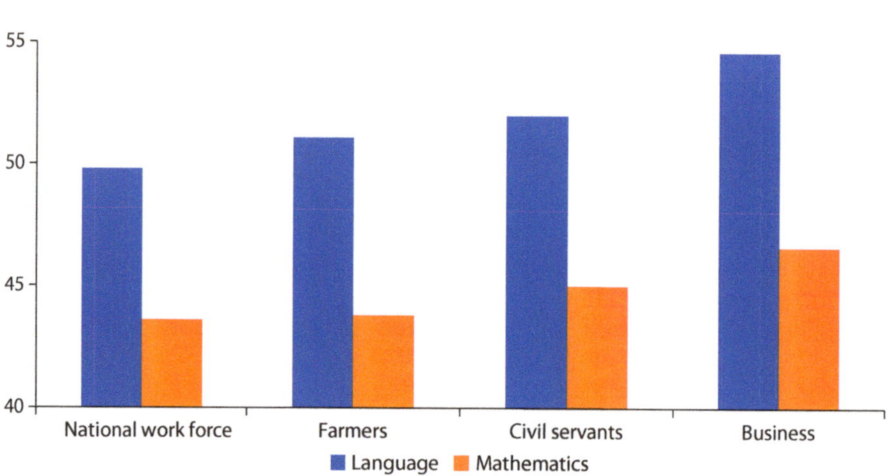

Source: EI 2010.

Figure 3.17 India: PISA Test Scores, by Parental Schooling, 15-Year-Old Students in Himachal Pradesh and Tamil Nadu

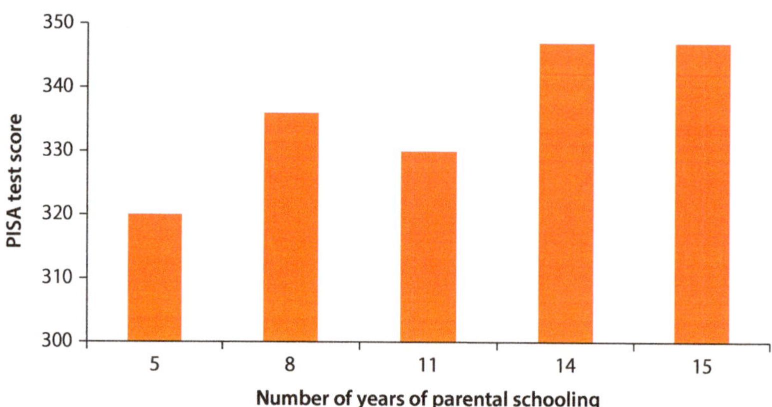

Source: OECD 2010 (PISA+ data).

than those whose parents had five or fewer years (figure 3.17). For instance, the mean reading score of students whose parents had 15 years of schooling was 7.8 percent higher than that of students whose parents had five years. The results were similar in mathematics and science.

Relatively little is known about the relationship between student achievement and household income. The PISA data suggest that, in 2010 Indian fifth-grade students who reported that their family possessed a below-poverty-line card

Figure 3.18 India: Student Achievement and Socioeconomic Background, Grades 4, 6, and 8, 2009
Percent

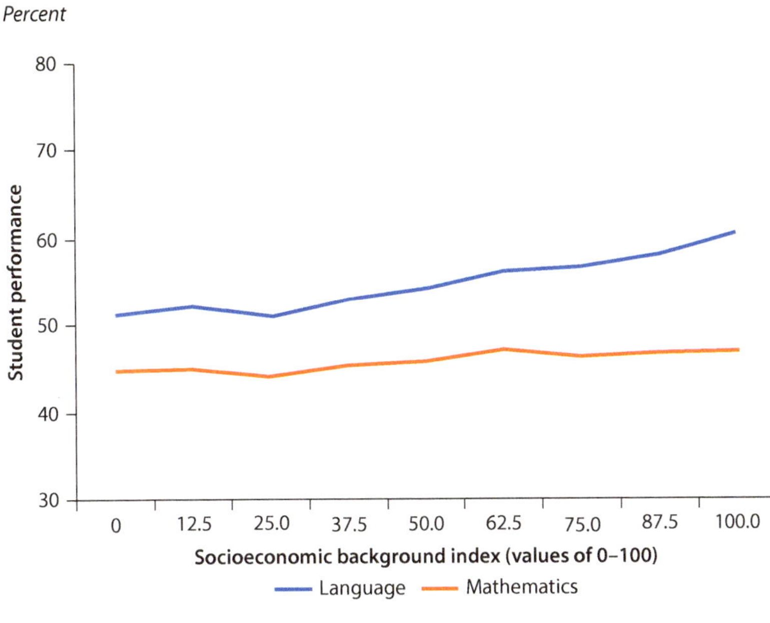

Source: EI 2010.

scored 7 points lower in both language and mathematics—a difference of only about 2.5 percent.

Figure 3.18 highlights the relationship found in the SLS 2009 data between student achievement and household socioeconomic background. To measure socioeconomic background, the SLS used an additive scale of variables based on possession of belongings, such as a bicycle, scooter, radio, television, and cooking stove. The relationship between student achievement—especially in mathematics—and socioeconomic background seems to be weak.

The Indian Human Development Survey (IHDS)—a rich, nationally representative socioeconomic survey of 41,500 rural and urban households—is one of the few studies that has gathered data on both student achievement and per capita household consumption expenditure, which is often used as a proxy for permanent income.[15] The IHDS administered simple tests of reading comprehension, writing ability, and mathematics to a subsample of children ages 8–11 years in the language the children were most comfortable using, typically their mother tongue. The reading tests were scored from 0 to 4 in ascending order of performance, the mathematics tests from 0 to 3, and writing ability on a binary scale (can write/cannot write).[16]

Figures 3.19–3.21 show the percentages by per capita consumption quintile of children who were able to read a story, perform division, and write a sentence. The differences are large. For instance, while only 9 percent of 8-year-olds in the poorest quintile could read a story, 32 percent of those in the richest could do

Figure 3.19 India: Ability to Read a Story, Children Ages 8–11 Years, by Age and Consumption Quintile, 2005
Percent

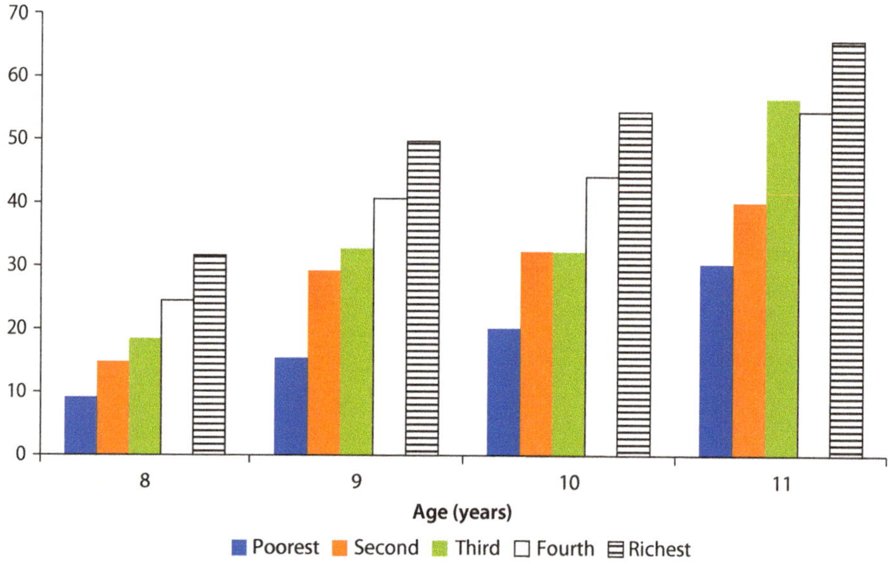

Source: IHDS 2005 data.

so (figure 3.19). At older ages, the relative gap across quintiles is somewhat smaller but still large in absolute terms. At age 11, for instance, 30 percent of children in the poorest quintile but 65 percent of children in the richest could read a story.

The quintile differences in arithmetic achievement are even larger (figure 3.20). For instance, only 4 percent of the poorest 8-year-olds were able to do division but 18 percent in the richest quintile could. Among 11-year-olds, 18 percent in the poorest quintile could do division and 57 percent in the richest quintile. In other words, after three years the 11-year-olds in the poorest quintile had just caught up with the 8-year-olds in the richest.

A larger proportion of children showed competence in writing than in reading a story, probably because the threshold for the writing test was lower; students only had to write a sentence with two or fewer mistakes (figure 3.21). Even so, only 39 percent of the poorest 8-year-olds passed the test, while 72 percent of the richest did. As with reading and arithmetic, a powerful income gradient is thus observable.

Bangladesh

For their 2008 sample of 12,879 students in grades 6 and 8 in Bangladesh, Asadullah et al. (2009) decomposed the total variation in student achievement in math and English into differences between and within schools. They found that in both grades 40 percent of the difference was attributable to

Figure 3.20 India: Ability to Do Division, Children Ages 8–11 Years, by Age and Consumption Quintile, 2005
Percent

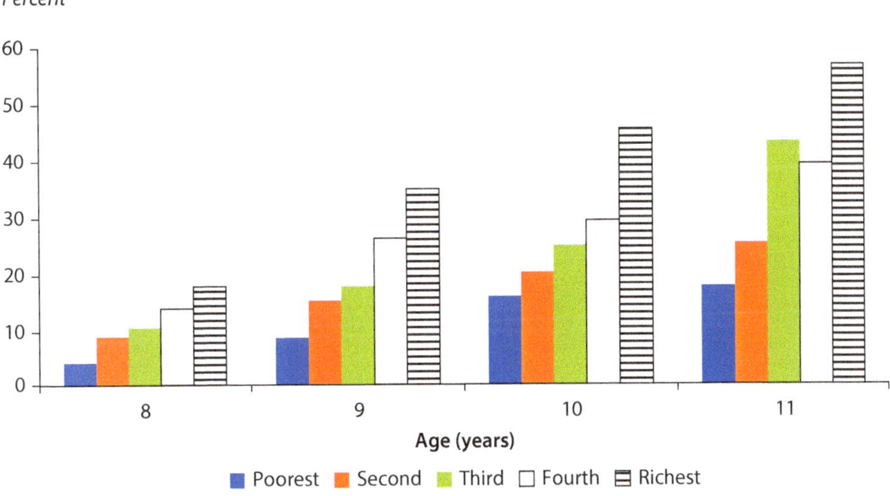

Source: IHDS 2005 data.

Figure 3.21 India: Ability to Write a Sentence, Children Ages 8–11 Years, by Age and Consumption Quintile, 2005
Percent

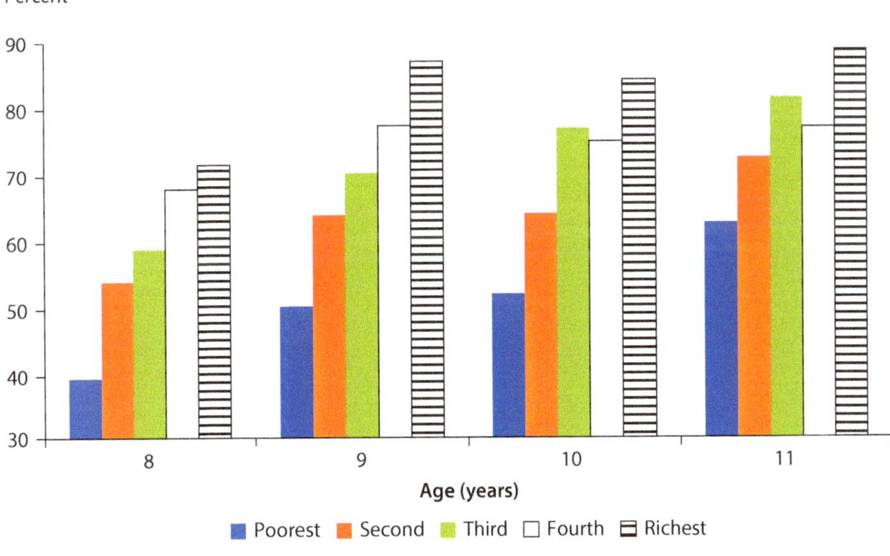

Source: IHDS 2005 data.

within-school variations, such as differences in student background and home learning environments, and 60 percent to differences between schools. The National Student Assessment (NSA) 2011 estimated that the between-school variation in Bangla grade 5 test scores accounted for 55 percent of the total variation (World Bank 2013).

Figure 3.22 Bangladesh: Scores of Children Ages 11 Years and Older, by Subject and Consumption Quintile, 2008

Percent

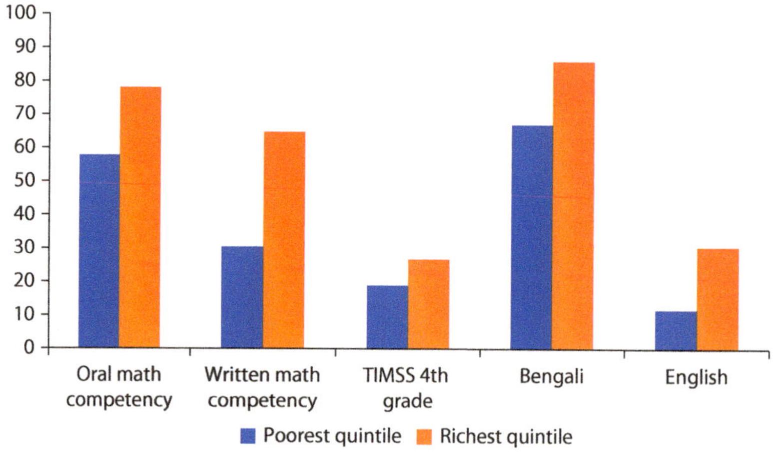

Oral math competency | Written math competency | TIMSS 4th grade | Bengali | English

■ Poorest quintile ■ Richest quintile

Source: Asadullah et al. 2009.

In a separate exercise, Asadullah et al. (2009) administered the same competency tests to children 11 and older drawn from a national survey of 2,400 households. This allowed the researchers to examine the association between student achievement and household economic status. They found very large differences in student performance between the richest and the poorest students (figure 3.22). For instance, student achievement in English was 250 percent higher among the richest quintile than among the poorest. In written math competency, the difference was more than 100 percent.

The 2011 NSA in Bangladesh also shows a steep wealth gradient in test scores (figure 3.23). Students from poor families are at least three-quarters of a school year behind their wealthier counterparts in Bangla and half a year behind in mathematics (World Bank 2013).

Nepal

Two observations about the relationship between student achievement and parental ethnicity can be drawn from the 2008 Nepal National Learning Assessment data (figure 3.24): (a) differences in student achievement by ethnic group are large, with Madhesis and Dalits scoring much lower than other ethnic groups, particularly Janjatis and "Others" and (b) the ethnic differences are smallest in English, science, and mathematics, and largest in Nepali, social studies, and health and population.

Sri Lanka

In their analysis of the 2003 NEREC data on 20,000 fourth-grade students in Sri Lanka, Aturupane, Glewwe, and Wisniewski (2013) also found ethnicity to be a strong predictor of student achievement. Burgher children score highest

Figure 3.23 Bangladesh: Mean Student Test Scores, by Wealth Groups, Grade 5

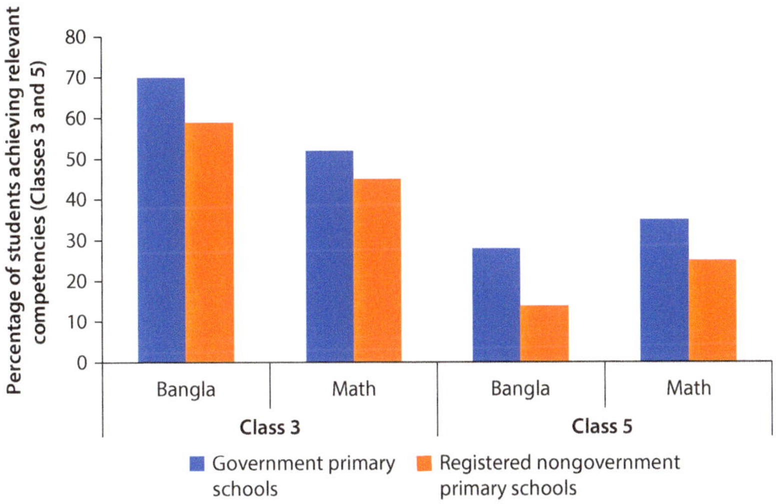

Source: World Bank 2013.

Figure 3.24 Nepal: Mean Student Test Scores, by Ethnicity and Subject, Grade 8, 2008
Percent

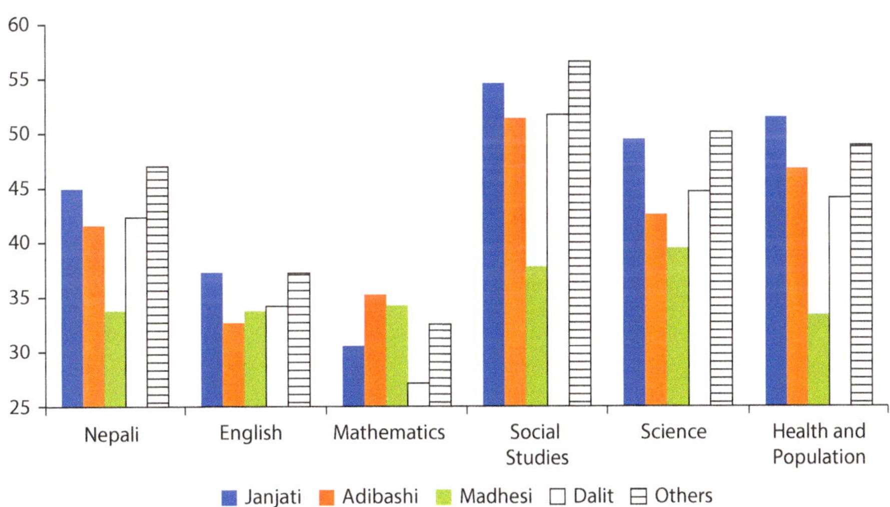

Source: Department of Education (Nepal) 2008b.

on standardized tests and Tamil children score lowest. There is also a close association between student achievement and schooling of the mother; for instance, the test scores of children whose mothers are college-educated are more than 1 standard deviation higher than the scores of those whose mothers have had no schooling.

Aturupane, Glewwe, and Wisniewski (2013) also found a close association between student performance and household living standards. The test scores of

Figure 3.25 Sri Lanka: Test Scores, by Expenditure Quintile, Grade 4, 2003

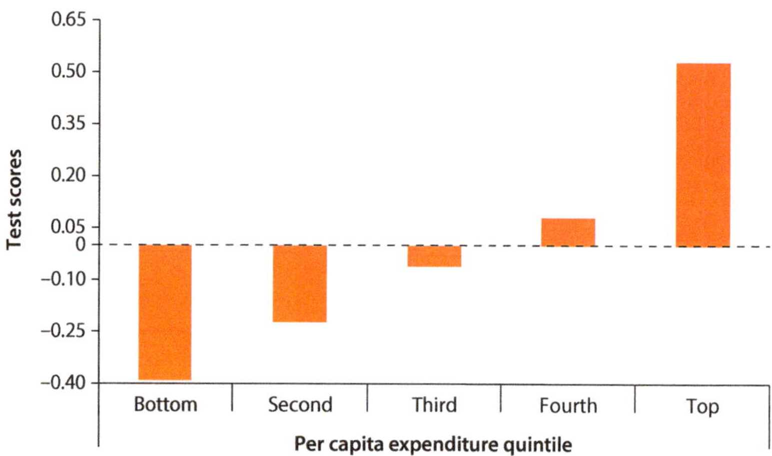

Source: Aturupane, Glewwe, and Wisniewski 2013.

students from the richest quintile are a full standard deviation higher than those of the poorest students (figure 3.25).

When Aturupane, Glewwe, and Wisniewski (2013) ran multivariate regressions of the standardized test scores on a number of individual and household variables and school fixed effects to account for unobserved heterogeneity between schools, many of the associations continued to hold. For instance, they found strong positive effects on student achievement from parental schooling and household per capita consumption. In almost all cases, too, the father's education seems to have had more effect on a child's test scores than the mother's. Household access to electricity is also consistently associated with higher test scores in all subjects.

An interesting variable in the Aturupane model is the educational aspirations of parents for their child. This variable consistently has significant positive effects on student achievement, with higher parental aspirations (e.g., expectation that the child will complete college or postgraduate education) associated with higher student performance. Such a result is to be expected, since parents who have high expectations are likely to provide the proper home environment, resources, support, and encouragement for the child to succeed in school. Of course, the causality might well go in the other direction; parents may keep adjusting their aspirations for a child upward as the child performs better and better in school.

Pakistan

In 2006, the Ministry of Education's NEAS tested nearly 12,000 fourth-grade students in language, mathematics, general science, and social studies and found variations in student achievement related to household characteristics (figure 3.26). The schooling of fathers is positively associated with student test scores in all subjects, but the gradient is not as steep as might be expected.

Figure 3.26 Pakistan: Fourth-Grade Test Scores, by Family Characteristics, 2006

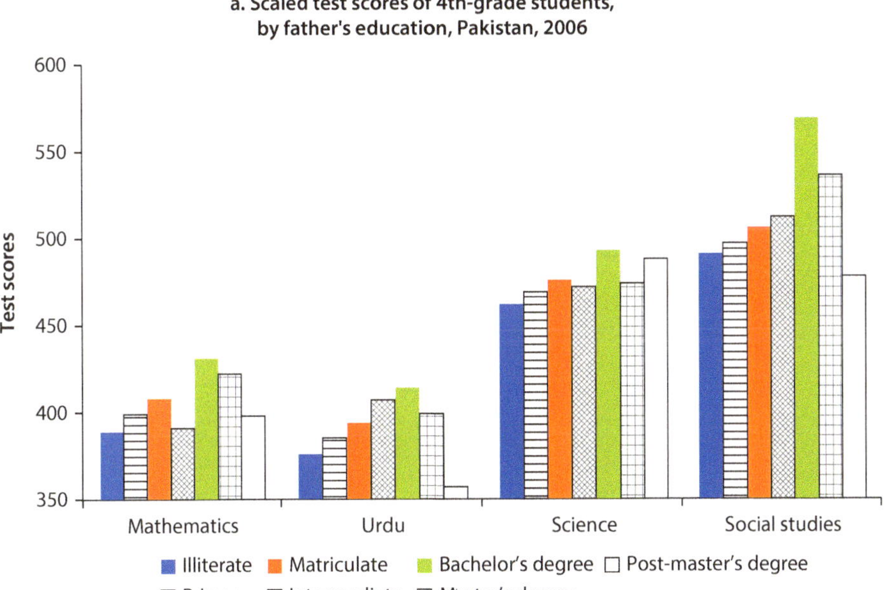

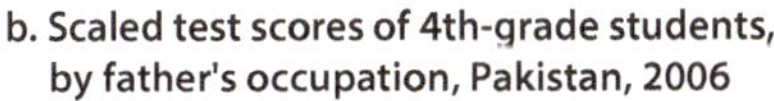

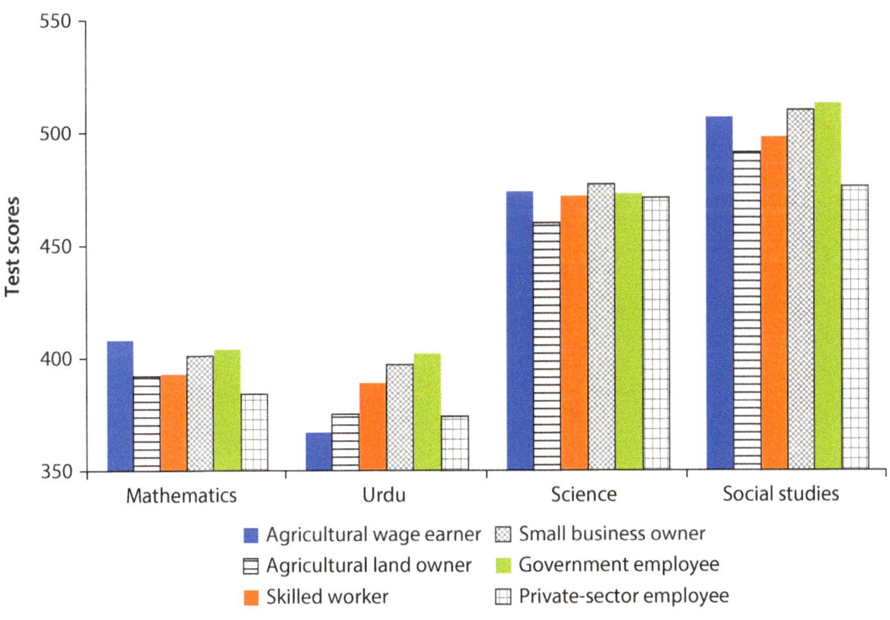

Source: MOE 2007.

For instance, test scores of students whose fathers had completed college were only 7–16 percent higher than those of students whose fathers were illiterate.[17]

There seems to be no clear association between father's occupation and student achievement in most subjects except Urdu. In Urdu, children of government employees have the highest test scores, followed by children of small business owners and skilled workers, and, at the bottom, children of agricultural wage earners.

Aslam (2009b) found that, after controlling for the innate ability of a child (proxied by the Raven's score), the home learning environment (proxied by the number of hours of help with school work provided by any relatives and whether a child was tutored privately at home), has a negative association with student achievement in government but not in private schools. A possible explanation is that students performing poorly in school are the ones who seek private home tuition and help from parents.

Bhutan

The 2007 BLQS data (figure 3.27) indicated that 35–74 percent of the variation in student test scores is attributable to within-school factors (diversity of children and households within a school) and 26–45 percent to between-school factors (typically, school quality). Household factors were most important in grade 4 Dzonghka and least important in grade 4 English.[18] These findings contrast with India and Pakistan, where between-school differences accounted for more than

Figure 3.27 Bhutan: Between- and Within-School Variation in Student Test Scores, Grades 2 and 4, 2007

Percent

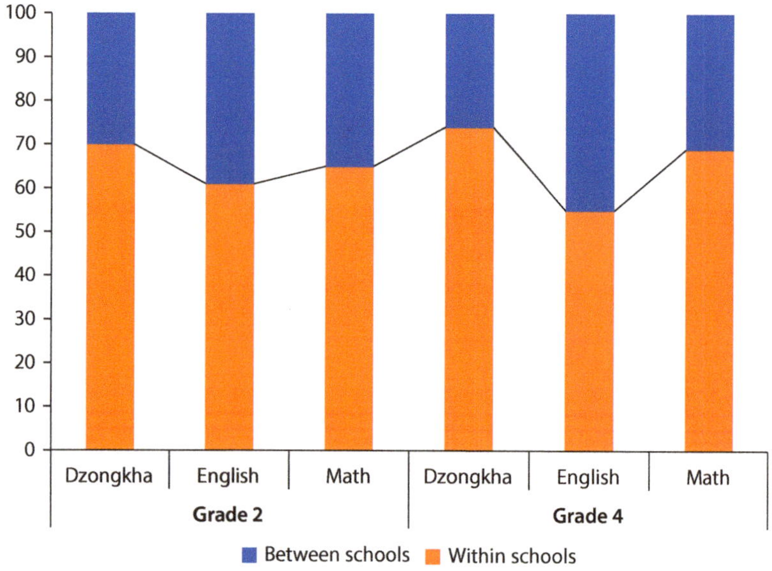

Source: World Bank 2009.

60–70 percent of test score variation (Goyal 2006a, 2006b; Andrabi et al. 2007; Siaens 2008).

The Bhutan data also demonstrate that children of literate mothers and fathers have significantly higher achievement than children of illiterate mothers, and poor children perform far worse than richer children (figure 3.28), though the differences are less pronounced in Dzongkha than in English and mathematics.

Figure 3.28 Bhutan: Test Scores, by Certain Student and Household Characteristics, 2007

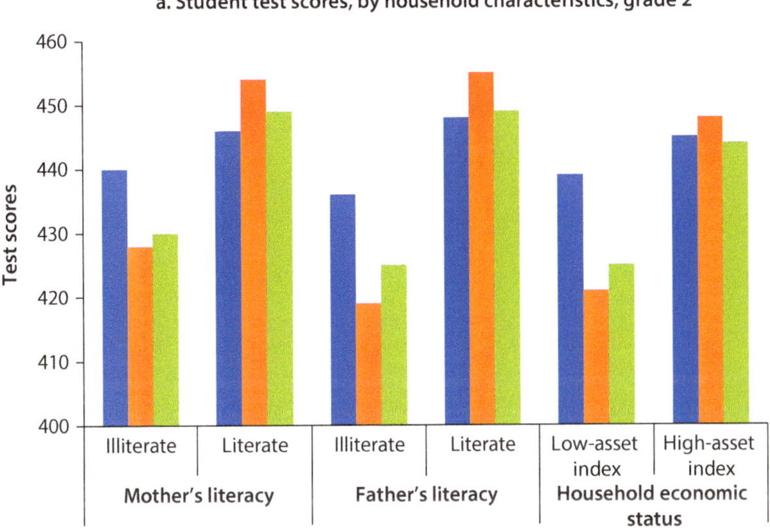

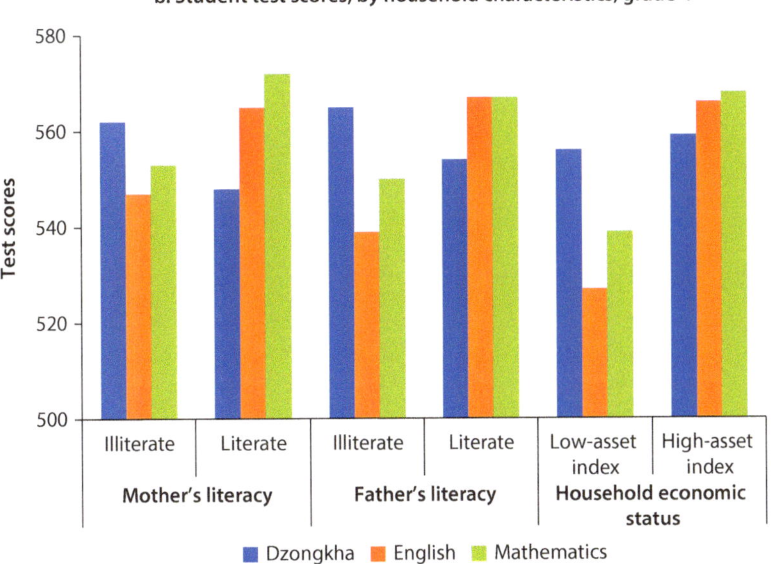

Source: World Bank 2009.

Annex 3A: Bangladesh: Mastery of Learning Outcomes, by Subject and Sex, Grades 3 and 5, 2008

Percent

		Grade 3		*Grade 5*	
Subject	*Learning outcome category*	*Boys*	*Girls*	*Boys*	*Girls*
Bangla	Reading and comprehension	52.2	53.8	27.3	25.8
	Writing	13.2	14.0	27.1	26.6
Mathematics	Basic number concepts and related skills	60.0	56.9	50.7	47.4
	Basic mathematical operations with whole numbers	59.0	56.4	n.a.	n.a.
	Fraction concepts and related basic mathematical operations	50.9	51.4	28.2	24.2
	Everyday-life problem solving	8.0	7.9	35.4	30.7
	Units and measurement	22.0	20.2	63.2	62.3
	Identification of geometrical figures and related skills	13.2	13.5	4.3	3.7
English	Reading and comprehension	n.a.	n.a.	67.8	66.1
	Writing	n.a.	n.a.	3.4	3.5
Environmental science	Environmental phenomena	n.a.	n.a.	55.8	51.2
	Properties of substances	n.a.	n.a.	48.5	45.2
	Basic facts about living things	n.a.	n.a.	82.3	79.9
	Everyday science	n.a.	n.a.	60.1	56.3
	Knowledge of technology	n.a.	n.a.	80.5	74.3
	Health and nutrition	n.a.	n.a.	2.9	2.8
Social studies	Environment and health	n.a.	n.a.	10.0	9.8
	Country-related social, cultural, historical, and geographical factors	n.a.	n.a.	16.9	15.9
	Duties, responsibilities, human rights, and leadership qualities	n.a.	n.a.	49.2	48.9
	National industries, resources, and economy	n.a.	n.a.	57.4	53.6
	Countries in Europe and Africa and functions of UN organizations	n.a.	n.a.	48.6	48.2

Source: DPE 2009.
Note: n.a. = not applicable; UN = United Nations.

Notes

1. Houtenville and Conway (2008) have argued that parental effort, independent of family background, has a considerable positive effect on achievement that is larger than the effect of school resources.
2. Of course, to the extent that socioeconomic background influences school choice and thereby school characteristics, family background and socioeconomic status will affect student achievement both directly (independent of school choice) and indirectly (through the choice of school).
3. In the 2009+ PISA study, 4,850 15-year-olds from two Indian states—Himachal Pradesh and Tamil Nadu—participated. PISA 2009+ tested about 46,000 students in nine countries where 15-year-olds totaled about 1,377,000. Data from the PISA 2009+ project is directly comparable to the original PISA 2009 data, so that together the PISA 2009 and 2009+ databases contain information on almost half a million students, tested across 74 countries, representing a total population of about 24 million 15-year-olds.

4. OTL is a term widely used in educational research.
5. Time-on-task studies in India suggest that on average fewer than 60 percent of primary students are engaged in learning activities at any given time (Sankar 2009).
6. Educational institutions for Islamic instruction.
7. Grade 8 students scored lower than grade 6 students because their mathematics questions were harder.
8. This table is based on the 14 core questions posed to both grades.
9. As noted in chapter 2, the DPE assessment is based on 50 competencies specified by the National Curriculum and Textbook Board of Bangladesh that children should achieve on completion of five years of primary education.
10. The grade 5 assessment was based on a random stratified sample of 16,117 students, the grade 8 assessment on a random sample of 2,640 students.
11. The assessment covered 12,690 students who had completed grade 4 in 2008, drawn from 458 government schools.
12. The frequency distribution of the scores reveals an interesting pattern: in Sinhala language, for instance, girls greatly outperformed boys at the top end of the distribution. For example, while 22 percent of boys and 27 percent of girls scored 90 (of 100), the proportions for those obtaining a test score of 100 were 23 percent of boys and 35 percent of girls. The trend in Tamil language and mathematics was similar, but in English the difference in scores between boys and girls narrowed considerably at the top of the score distribution (85–100). English is also the only subject that showed a bimodal distribution: a large number of students (mostly boys) were clustered around a score of 35 and a large number (mostly girls) around 85, but few students of either sex were clustered around 60.
13. The literacy and numeracy tests were those used by Boissiere, Knight, and Sabot (1985) and Knight and Sabot (1990) but adapted to the Pakistani context.
14. The differences observed in the NCERT data are also much smaller than those observed in the India Human Development Survey data. See the discussion below.
15. The IHDS administered a special questionnaire to students ages 8–11 years in each household surveyed that gathered anthropometric data (height and weight).
16. For a detailed description of the tests and survey instruments, see Desai et al. (2009).
17. The anomalous results with respect to master's and post-master's degrees are probably due to the very small number of students sampled whose fathers had earned those degrees.
18. The survey was a nationally representative school-based survey of 2,359 children in grades 2 and 4 in three subjects: Dzongkha (the national language), English, and mathematics.

Bibliography

Andrabi, T., J. Das, A. Khwaja, T. Vishwanath, and T. Zajonc. 2007. *Pakistan: Learning and Educational Achievements in Punjab Schools (LEAPS): Insights to Inform the Educational Policy Debate.* http://www.leapsproject.org/assets/publications/LEAPS_Report_ExecSummary.pdf.

Asadullah, M., N. Chaudhury, D. Prajuli, L. R. Sarr, Y. Savchenko, and S. R. Al-Zayed. 2009. *Secondary Education Quality and Access Enhancement Project (SEQAEP): Baseline Report.* Washington, DC: World Bank.

Aslam, M. 2009a. "The Relative Effectiveness of Government and Private Schools in Pakistan: Are Girls Worse Off?" *Education Economics* 17 (3): 329–54.

———. 2009b. "Education Gender Gaps in Pakistan: Is the Labour Market to Blame?" *Economic Development and Cultural Change* 57 (4): 747–87.

Aturupane, D. H., P. Glewwe, and S. Wisniewski. 2013. "The Impact of School Quality, Socio-Economic Factors and Child Health on Students' Academic Performance: Evidence from Sri Lankan Primary Schools." *Education Economics* 21 (1): 2–37.

Boissiere, M., J. B. Knight, and R. H. Sabot. 1985. "Earnings, Schooling, Ability, and Cognitive Skills." *American Economic Review* 75 (5): 1016–30.

Department of Education. 2008a. *Final Report—National Assessment of Grade V Students.* Kathmandu: Ministry of Education and Sports, Nepal.

———. 2008b. *Final Report—National Assessment of Grade VIII Students.* Kathmandu: Ministry of Education and Sports, Nepal.

Desai, S., A. Dubey, R. Vanneman, and R. Banerji. 2009. "Private Schooling in India: A New Educational Landscape." *India Policy Forum* 5 (1): 1–38.

DPE (Directorate of Primary Education). 2009. "National Assessment of Pupils of Grades 3 and 5, 2008." Ministry of Primary and Mass Education (prepared by Associates for Development Services Ltd.), Dhaka, Bangladesh.

EI (Educational Initiatives). 2010. *Student Learning Study. Status of Learning across 18 Sites of India in Urban and Rural Schools.* Ahmedabad, India: EI. http://www.ei-india.com/wp-content/uploads/2012/01/Main_Report_StudentLearningStudy_2010_by_Educational_Initiatives1.pdf.

Government of Sindh. 2010. "Sindh Students Assessment Technical Report 2009—Mathematics Grade 4." Bureau of Curriculum and Extension Wing Sindh, Jamshoro, Pakistan.

Goyal, S. 2006a. "Learning Achievement in India: A Case Study of Primary Education in Orissa." World Bank, New Delhi.

———. 2006b. "Learning Achievement in India: A Case Study of Primary Education in Rajasthan." World Bank, New Delhi.

Goyal, S., and P. Pandey. 2009. *How Do Government and Private Schools Differ? Findings from Two Large Indian States.* Report 30, South Asia Human Development Unit. Washington, DC: World Bank.

Greaney, V., S. R. Khandker, and M. Alam. 1998. *Bangladesh: Assessing Basic Learning Skills.* Washington, DC: World Bank.

Hedges, L., and R. Greenwald. 1996. "Have Times Changed? The Relationship between School Resources and Student Performance." In *Does Money Matter? The Effect of School Resources on Student Achievement and Adult Success,* edited by G. T. Burtless. Washington, DC: Brookings Institution Press.

Houtenville, A. J., and K. S. Conway. 2008. "Parental Effort, School Resources, and Student Achievement." *Journal of Human Resources* 43 (2): 437–53.

Knight, J., and R. Sabot. 1990. *Education, Productivity, and Inequality.* New York: Oxford University Press.

Krueger, A. 1999. "Experimental Estimates of Education Production Functions." *Quarterly Journal of Economics* 64 (2): 497–532.

MOE (Ministry of Education). 2007. "National Assessment 2006—Technical Report." National Education Assessment System, Government of Pakistan, Islamabad.

NCERT (National Council of Educational Research and Training). 2011. *What Do They Know? A Summary of India's National Achievement Survey, Class V, Cycle 3 2010/11*. New Delhi: NCERT.

NEREC (National Education Research and Evaluation Center). 2009. *National Assessment of Achievement of Grade 4 Pupils*. Colombo: NEREC, Sri Lanka.

OECD (Organisation for Economic Co-operation and Development). 2010. *PISA 2009 Results: Overcoming Social Background—Equity in Learning Opportunities and Outcomes*. Vol. 2. Paris: OECD. http://dx.doi.org/10.1787/9789264091504-en.

Pratham. 2010. *The Annual Status of Education Report (ASER)—India*. New Delhi: Pratham Resource Center.

Sankar, D. 2009. "Teachers' Time on Task and Nature of Tasks: Evidence from Three Indian States." Human Development Unit, South Asia Region, World Bank, Washington, DC.

Siaens, C. 2008. "Challenges for the Education Sector in Sindh, Pakistan." World Bank, Islamabad.

Sirin, S. R. 2005. "Socioeconomic Status and Academic Achievement: A Meta-Analytic Review of Research." *Review of Educational Research* 75 (3): 417–53.

World Bank. 2009. "Findings from the Bhutan Learning Quality Survey." Report 21, Human Development Unit, South Asia Region, World Bank, Washington, DC.

———. 2012a. *Human Capital for a Modern Society. General Education in the Maldives. An Evolving Seascape*. Washington, DC: World Bank.

———. 2012b. *World Development Indicators 2012*. Washington, DC: World Bank.

———. 2013. *Bangladesh Education Sector Review*. Report 80613-BD, Human Development Sector, South Asia Region, Washington, DC: World Bank.

Wu, K. B., P. Goldschmidt, C. K. Boscardin, and D. Sankar. 2009. "International Benchmarking and Determinants of Mathematics Achievement in two Indian States." *Education Economics* 17 (3): 395–411.

CHAPTER 4

Early Childhood Development and the Role of Preschool*

Introduction

The large gap between schooling (attendance) and learning (achievement) in South Asia (see, for example, chapter 2 of this report and Hanushek and Woessmann 2008) is often attributed to flaws in school systems, limited incentives to motivate teachers to prepare students with the skills needed to succeed, and sometimes inadequately trained teachers who cannot transmit curriculum content effectively. While schools and teachers play a crucial role in student learning, however, it may also be the case that some students come to school with huge disadvantages that make them unable to learn effectively but that could be offset through interventions in early childhood.

Resources wasted when children fail to attain basic literacy and drop out in part reflect wasted opportunities before schooling begins. A child's first years—long before formal schooling begins—are the foundation for building human capital. As children grow beyond the first few years of life, although their mortality risk recedes, the risk of malnutrition and illness continues to be a major determinant of their future because health has a significant impact on how they fare in school.

Beyond the general importance of childhood as the foundation of human capital formation, there are short critical periods within it that may undermine subsequent development if certain inputs are missing. For example, the number of neurons devoted to language peaks before a child is 1 and then declines. This implies that children lose plasticity even before they can engage in rudimentary conversations. Neuroscience is increasingly tracking these processes (Shonkoff and Phillips 2000; Nelson, de Haan, and Thomas 2006). While the biology is universal, the context in which children develop and are either stimulated or shocked has a huge influence on how much of their potential is realized.

This chapter looks at the literature on how child health, nutrition, and care and stimulation in the years before children enroll in school influence their

*See box 4.1 for a summary of the chapter's key questions and findings.

Box 4.1 Questions and Findings

Questions

- What is the status of early childhood development (ECD) in South Asia?
- What are the most important policy priorities in South Asia with regard to early childhood education and development?

Findings

- In South Asia, the gap between schooling and learning—enrollment and achievement—is large: a significant proportion of children in lower primary school lack even the most rudimentary numeracy or literacy skills. While poor learning outcomes are often attributed to flaws in school systems, it is also possible that a large number of South Asian students enter primary school with huge disadvantages, notably malnutrition, that could be offset through interventions in early childhood. South Asia has the highest rates in the world of low birth weight, infant and child malnutrition, and micronutrient deficiencies.
- India, Nepal, and Sri Lanka have ECD policies that cover the period from birth to grade school, but early childhood policies in the region are generally focused only on preventing malnutrition. Many of these programs suffer from problems like poor coverage and incorrect methods of age targeting. Where there is no national policy on early childhood stimulation, a range of programs serve this role, many of which are pilot programs or modest nongovernmental organization (NGO) activities—again with minimal population coverage.
- Since the evidence demonstrating the educational benefits of preschool education in the region is inconclusive, it does not seem advisable to recommend that countries divert scarce educational resources to preschool programs. The most pressing early-life challenge is nutrition, which is a formidable factor in learning throughout the school years. The main policy recommendation of this chapter is that early childhood policies be directed to reducing the incidence of low birth weight and providing food supplements to reduce protein-energy malnutrition and deficiencies in micronutrients, such as iron and vitamin A, especially for children age 2 and under.
- A secondary recommendation is that ECD programs to improve school readiness through stimulation and emotional development be targeted primarily to disadvantaged and poor children, who start primary school with enormous learning disadvantages. Investing in their social and emotional development as well as their nutrition will help ready them for school and make public expenditure on primary education more efficient.

school experience, applying region-specific examples. Before reviewing some of this evidence, it is useful to summarize a few relevant academic perspectives on child development.

Early childhood development (ECD) as used here is the period from conception until a child is age 6. Many carry the period through age 8, but this report is concerned with what happens to children before they enter primary education.

Three aspects of these early years are critical for children's future development: physical growth and well-being, cognitive development, and socio-emotional development. Though these are primarily the result of home activities and investments, they can be enhanced by community and preschool health and education programs (table 4.1).

Increasingly, both education specialists and economists are recognizing how investments in ECD enhance equity and efficiency (Cunha and Heckman 2007). The efficiency perspective is obvious: resources spent on students who drop out without acquiring basic literacy or numeracy are largely wasted. Similarly, grade repetition increases classroom sizes and implies delayed entry into the labor force.

In terms of equity, learning in school increases the higher the initial human capital, so that skill gaps widen over time. Moderate shocks to a child's health or emotional development can lead to major and widening differences in primary and secondary school outcomes. This concerns what is called *self-productivity*. While the evidence for self-productivity comes mainly from developed countries, it has been confirmed in longitudinal studies in South Asia (Helmers and Patnam 2011).

Table 4.1 Issues, Interventions, and Expected Outcomes of Early Childhood Development Programs

Main issues	*Early childhood development interventions*	*Expected outcomes*
Inadequate nutrition and health care (0–3 years)	Community growth promotion	
Malnutrition Stunting Anemia Iodine deficiency Zinc deficiency	• Iron fortification or supplementation • Iodine fortification or supplementation • Zinc supplementation	Physical well-being and improved health Preschool readiness
Infectious diseases and parasites	Deworming	Improved development, cognitive and noncognitive
Lack of cognitive stimulation and parental interaction (0–3 years)	Parental support and enrichment training Home visits in high-risk cases (Ideally these interventions are combined with the health interventions)	Improved development, cognitive and noncognitive
Insufficient age-appropriate stimulation and development of social skills (4–5 years)	Preschool and community-based programs with appropriate curricula and continuing parental enrichment	School readiness Improved development, cognitive and noncognitive Fewer dropouts

A related issue is whether an investment in school has more impact for more able students. Quite plausibly, investments in school inputs lead to better outcomes for students who entered school with more ability and better health than for those without those advantages. This concept—*dynamic complementarity*—raises the empirical question of whether such complementarity magnifies inequality in earlier health investments. Conceptually, there may also be schooling inputs that can compensate for earlier limited investment in children's well-being.

Since economic efficiency implies investing more where the returns are higher, complementarity implies allocating more resources to higher-performing students, who are often those from households that were able to invest more in their health. However, if in investments before schooling there is no income gradient at entry to school, or if there is no complementarity in school-level investments, there may be no trade-off between investment efficiency and equity.

South Asia: Situational Analysis

The incidence of low-birthweight infants (weighing less than 2,500 grams at birth) is even higher in South Asia than in Sub-Saharan Africa (figure 4.1). Of about 18 million low-weight babies born globally each year, more than half are in South Asia; India alone accounts for 40 percent.

Moreover, more children ages 0–5 years are underweight or stunted in South Asia than in Sub-Saharan Africa (figure 4.1), even though economically the latter is more disadvantaged. India, Bangladesh, Nepal, and Pakistan rank at the top in terms of the proportion of children who are underweight.

Table 4.2 presents data by wealth quintile on children in the three largest South Asian countries who are underweight. Underweight is being tracked as part of the Millennium Development Goals (MDGs).[1] The United Nations Children's Fund (UNICEF) reports that in the region only Afghanistan, Bhutan, and Maldives are on track to meet the MDG weight target.[2] MDG progress, however, is only part of the picture; Sri Lanka has evidenced steady, if rather slow, improvement from a comparatively low base of malnutrition, while Afghanistan's progress is based on a high level of malnutrition. And while Afghanistan has made progress in reducing the number of underweight children, it has the highest rate of stunting (figure 4.2).

Malnutrition rates are inversely related to wealth (table 4.2), although only modestly—nutrition poverty is more pervasive than income poverty. This is consistent with global evidence that historic patterns of income growth, even when evenly distributed, do not eliminate the problem of underweight children (see, for example, Haddad et al. 2003). This pattern suggests that a nutrition program would have far wider benefits than would an initiative to reduce income poverty. In other words, malnutrition cuts across wealth class lines. The pattern also implies that income growth is a blunt instrument for addressing malnutrition. To illustrate, based on the data in table 4.2, if Pakistan were to provide transfers or income growth to bring the poorest 40 percent of the population up to the

Figure 4.1 Low-Birthweight Infants, by Region, 2006–10
Percent

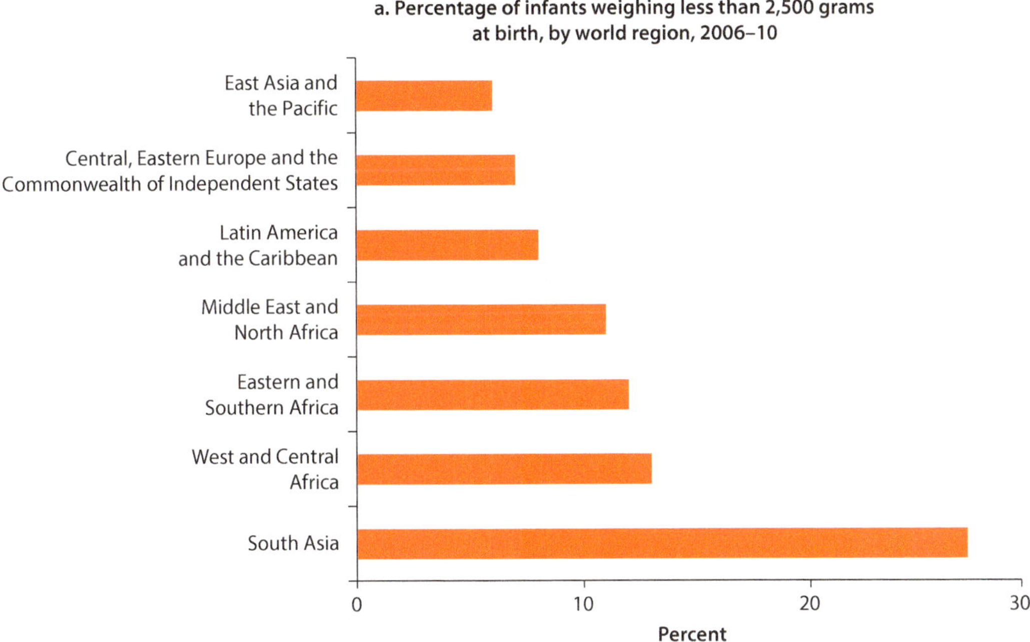

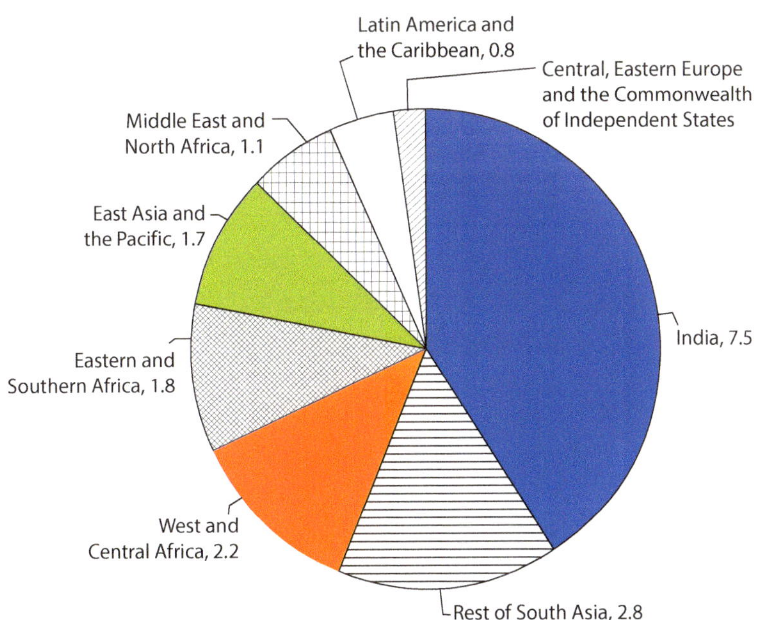

Source: UNICEF data, as reported in http://www.childinfo.org/low_birthweight_status_trends.html.

Table 4.2 Child Underweight, by Wealth Quintiles, Selected Countries (Percent)

		Wealth Quintile				
Region	*Country*	*Lowest*	*2nd*	*3rd*	*4th*	*Highest*
South Asia						
	Bangladesh	59	53	45	43	30
	India	61	54	49	39	26
	Pakistan	54	47	43	37	26
Africa						
	Benin	29	30	23	20	10
	Burkina Faso	42	40	41	39	22
	Ethiopia	49	51	51	45	37
	Mozambique	31	28	26	19	9
	Rwanda	27	30	28	24	14
	Tanzania	25	26	22	20	12
	Uganda	27	26	25	19	12

Source: Gwatkin et al. 2007.
Note: Data for children <5 years. Underweight refers to children whose weight falls 2 or more standard deviations below the World Health Organization median standard.

Figure 4.2 Under-5 Children Moderately or Severely Underweight, Selected Asian Countries, Circa 2005

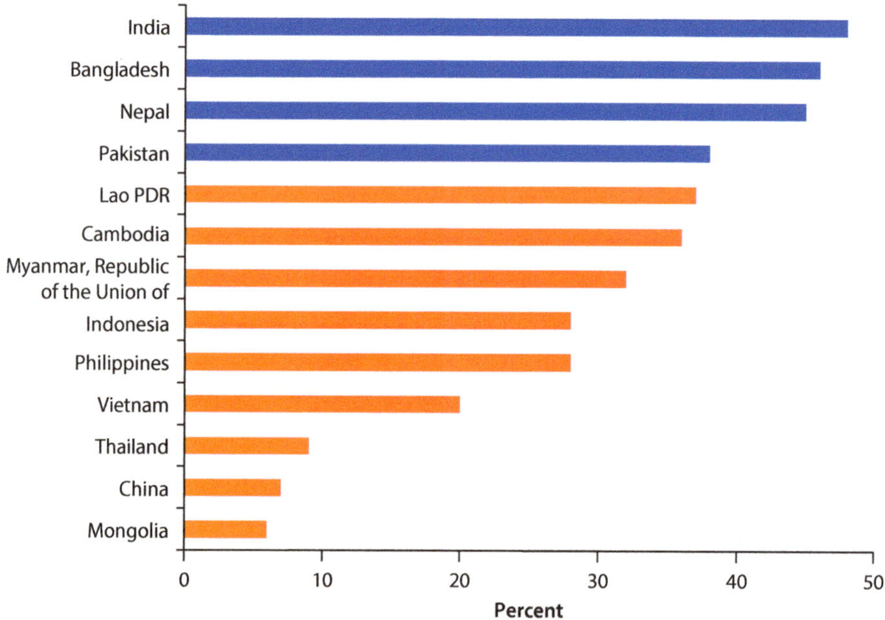

Source: UNICEF 2006.

median, it would virtually eliminate poverty—but over 38 percent of all the children would still be malnourished.

To make matters worse, the region has high levels of anemia and iodine deficiency. By one estimate, nearly 70 percent of Indian children under age 5 suffer from anemia (National Family Health Survey 2005–06). A survey in rural Bangladesh conducted by the Helen Keller Institute and the Institute of Public Health Nutrition in 2004 found that 68 percent of children under age 5—and 92 percent of children ages 6–11 months—were anemic (Helen Keller Institute 2006). Also, following global patterns, the poor are more likely to have these nutritional deficiencies, although the risks are by no means confined to the poor (Alderman and Linnemayr 2009).

Both conceptual and logistical measurement issues make it difficult to assemble indicators of cognitive and noncognitive skills for preschool children for use in tracking populations over time or comparing them by country. However, UNICEF has devised an index of inputs and resources, the family care indicators (FCI), based on more comprehensive—and time-intensive—home observations for measurement of the environment (HOME) that can be adapted to household surveys. The FCI have been validated as predictive of cognitive development in a variety of settings. For example, in Bangladesh, controlling for wealth and parental education, the FCI subscales on play activities and variety of play materials have a close relationship with development indicators (Black et al. 2007).

Using the FCI indicators, researchers in the Sindh province of Pakistan found that only 13 percent of a sample of 240 mothers correctly reported that children start to learn about the world around them from birth and 38 percent correctly reported that children respond to communication before they are six months old. However, mothers otherwise appeared to have a good grasp of their children's abilities at different ages. This sample, however, had relatively low levels of the HOME-scale indicators: Responsivity, Learning Materials, and Involvement. Similar results have been reported for Bangladesh, with an additional observation that from infancy parents are more interactive with sons than with daughters—surprising in a country where schooling patterns favor girls.

Another global risk for child development is postnatal depression, which has been found to increase when a household experiences economic difficulties or marital disharmony (Field 2011). The risk appears to be higher when the newborn is female. South Asia offers strong evidence of this. Maternal depression has been associated with increased risk of malnutrition and developmental delays (Black et al. 2009; Wachs, Black, and Engle 2009).

Skills Important for Schooling Success

Economists have begun to recognize that in determining an individual's future, noncognitive skills may be as important as cognitive, if not more so. Noncognitive skills consist of such behavioral factors as emotional regulation, motivation, persistence, teamwork, approaches to utilization, and attitudes to risk. The numerous issues related to measuring both cognitive and noncognitive skills are largely beyond the scope of this chapter (see, for example, Borghans et al. 2008), but one issue for both sets of skills that is germane here is the degree of plasticity: Are there critical periods during which these skills are formed, after which there is little or no malleability? Similarly, are there periods when an investment or activity is far more efficient for forming skills? If so, that period is considered sensitive. Early childhood is at least sensitive—and probably critical—for many of the skills that determine success in school and beyond (Heckman 2011; Reardon 2011). Further, as is implied in the concept of dynamic complementarity, if simple skills are not learned early, it is more difficult to acquire more complex ones. The evidence reviewed in the next section documents the sensitivity of investment in human capital in the first few years of a child's life.

Nutrition, Preschool Readiness, and School Outcomes

The contribution of good nutrition to child survival is beyond reasonable doubt (Bhutta et al. 2008). Moreover, there is a large body of evidence that demonstrates the positive effects of good child nutrition on lifetime learning and productivity (see, for example, Behrman, Alderman, and Hoddinott 2004) and how both birth weight and growth in the first two years of a child's life are linked to later schooling outcomes. A recent review of ECD risk factors acknowledges that stunting is a well-known risk and notes that addressing restrictions on intrauterine growth has recently been documented as a priority (Walker, Wachs, et al. 2011). This is clearly relevant for South Asia.

While it is a challenge to separate factors that directly affect nutrition from socioeconomic and behavioral conditions that affect schooling, a variety of approaches have been applied to discern the causal role of nutrition. Using one approach—tracking large cohorts from birth to adulthood, with a panel pooled from five countries, including a birth cohort of Indians tracked since 1969—researchers estimated that a 1 standard deviation increase in weight gain in the first two years of life was associated with 0.43 more years of schooling, but weight gain between ages 2 to 4 had no association (Martorell et al. 2010). Another longitudinal study of a large dataset of Filipino children found that a 0.6 standard deviation increase in height resulted in almost 12 additional months of schooling (Glewwe, Jacoby, and King 2001). To identify the consequences of malnutrition for children affected by drought in Zimbabwe, another study followed the children for two decades afterward; it concluded that had the median preschool child in the sample had the stature of a median child in a developed country, by adolescence she or he would have completed an additional 0.85 grades of schooling and would have had 14 percent higher earnings (Alderman, Hoddinott, and Kinsey 2006). A study of the effect of price changes on nutritional insult found that malnourished Pakistani girls—but not boys—were less likely to enter school. Thus, a 0.5 improvement in height for age Z-scores would lead to a 19 percent increase in girls' schooling and close half of the gender gap (Alderman et al. 2001).

For both ethical and logistical reasons, it is difficult to design experimental studies that track improved nutrition interventions from childhood through the school years. One project in Guatemala, however, managed to follow for four decades a group that had received nutritional supplements as children. They also followed a randomized control group. When both groups were between 25 and 42 years old, women who had received the supplements before age 3 were found to have had 1.2 years additional years of schooling, and both men and women scored higher on cognitive tests. Moreover, the earnings of men in the treatment group were more than 40 percent higher than in the control group (Hoddinott et al. 2008; Maluccio et al. 2009). Regardless of methodology or, to a significant degree, setting, these and other studies have tended to find that early malnutrition has significant economic consequences. From a different perspective, they show that economic returns to preventing malnutrition are as high as, or often higher than, the returns on investment in such growth sectors as infrastructure and trade policy.

Experimental evidence from South Asia is consistent with this global review. Preschool children who received iron supplements and deworming medicine in a randomized trial in New Delhi had less absenteeism than a randomized control group, and children who were anemic at baseline responded particularly well (Bobonis, Miguel, and Puri-Sharma 2006). The experiment, however, was not able to track the children long enough to measure their performance in primary school. Yet the evidence of the impact of iron supplements for infants on cognitive development at school age is mixed; in general, most interventions in infancy seem to have had little impact (Christian 2012). However, prenatal supplementation for mothers seems to have had lasting impact on the children. One experiment provided both iron and zinc to Nepali mothers during pregnancy (Christian et al. 2010). Cohort follow-up of children when they were ages 7–9 years indicated higher performance on both cognitive and noncognitive measures. In particular, the treated children had higher scores on tests of working memory, inhibitory control, and fine motor functioning. The zinc, however, had no additional impact over iron supplementation alone.

Iodine deficiency, which can set in prenatally, is a well-known cause of reduced mental capacity in a child, though it generally does not manifest itself in physical stature. Meta analyses using different samples have been consistent in their findings that iodine deficiency can depress brain development to the point that iodine-deficient individuals have an intelligence quotient (IQ) lower on average by 13.5 points than comparison groups (Zimmermann 2009). Similarly, a decade and a half after pregnant women in Tanzania received iodine supplements, their children had on average 0.35–0.56 more years of schooling than their peers, with the impact greater for girls (Field, Robles, and Torero 2009).

Iron deficiency anemia clearly affects a child's cognitive and motor development but is not necessarily associated with stunting. A review of ECD in *The Lancet* claimed that "the short-term improvements seen in iron supplemented infants suggest that adverse effects [of deficiency] can be prevented, reversed, or both with iron earlier in development or before iron deficiency becomes severe or chronic" (Walker et al. 2007, 148). The review, however, also notes that there is less evidence that later supplementation will fully mitigate the consequences of early deficiency, which include more grade repetition and lower IQ measures.

Finally, it should be noted that the association between poor nutrition and poor schooling outcomes can be seen among older as well as preschool children. One of the few data sets from South Asia with information on the nutritional status and learning outcomes of older children is the Indian Human Development Survey (IHDS), which administered a special questionnaire to school children ages 8–11 years. Besides collecting anthropometric information, about 72 percent of the children surveyed were also given one simple test each of reading comprehension, writing ability, or mathematics. All the tests were translated into several Indian languages, and children were tested in the language in which they were most comfortable.

Figures 4.3 and 4.4 show the mean heights and weights and the academic achievement of the children surveyed. Without exception, children who were able to read a story, perform division, and write a sentence were consistently taller and heavier than less-skilled peers; the difference in height was typically 2–4 centimeters and in weight 1–2 kilograms. While obviously no causality can be inferred, the evidence is highly suggestive that poor nutrition has a deleterious effect on a child's cognitive skills.

Asadullah et al. (2009) also examined the correlates of student achievement in mathematics and English using a household survey of 2,400 secondary school children in Bangladesh. The students were given an English and math test with questions from the TIMSS grade 6 test. The explanatory variables included

Figure 4.3 Average Height of Children Ages 8–11 Years, by Age and Level of Achievement, India, 2005

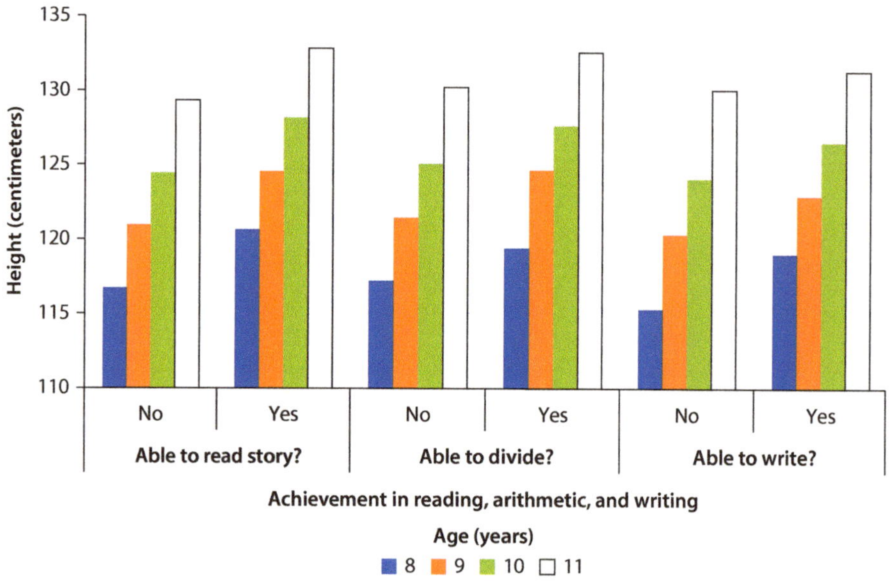

Source: IHDS 2005 data.

Figure 4.4 Average Weight of Children Ages 8–11 Years, by Age and Level of Achievement, India, 2005

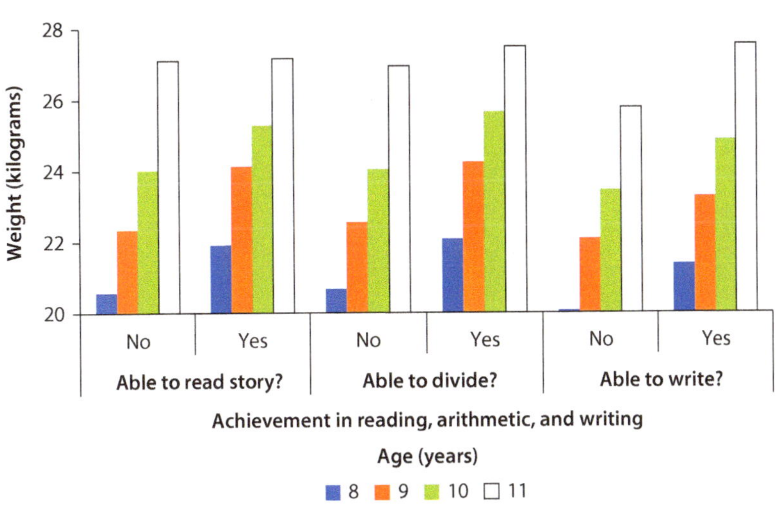

Source: 2005 IHDS data.

child characteristics, household wealth, and village-level fixed effects. Regression analysis found that a child's height was positively and significantly associated with the test scores, even though the magnitudes of the coefficients were small.

Another study, by Aturupane, Glewwe, and Wisniewski (2013), investigated the association between school achievement and child malnutrition in Sri Lanka. The analysis incorporated standardized height-for-age that reflected slow physical growth owing to poor nutrition or diarrheal and other infections during preschool years. Standardized weight-for-height was also included as an indicator of recent (short-term) malnutrition or recent infections. The results showed that stunted children (height-for-age Z-score < –2) performed about 0.33 of a standard deviation below the average student. Children with modest stunting (Z-score from –2 to –1) scored slightly below average, and children who were not stunted (Z-score > –1) performed above average by 0.20 of a standard deviation. But weight-for-height (wasting) showed a weak association with academic performance. This suggests that for academic achievement long-term (cumulative) nutrition matters more than current or short-term nutrition.

Three observations relevant for policy can be derived from these studies:

- Even older children show the negative effects on learning outcomes of stunting caused by nutritional insults in early childhood.
- While severe nutritional deficiencies—goiter, iodine deficiency, and severe anemia—warrant clinical response, there is also a measurable degree of cognitive impairment for individuals with subclinical deficiencies. Because of the large number of children in this category, the consequences for learning are also large.

- There is debate about the degree to which early deficiencies are later reversible. For example, new evidence for iodine suggests it has potential to offset moderate early deficiencies. Still, to a large degree second-chance interventions are motivated by a sense of fairness rather than a first best use of resources; from an economic perspective, it is far more efficient to prevent micronutrient deficiencies long before school begins, especially prenatally.

Many programs to increase nutrient consumption also promote cognitive development, as do programs to increase stature or weight, either with supplements or changes in child care and health-seeking behavior. This is particularly apparent in the prevention of early malnutrition, for which the economic returns are highly favorable. However, just what the most effective interventions are to offset the development consequences of malnutrition is less clear.

Parenting, Stimulation, and Early Learning Opportunities

Low cognitive development in early childhood correlates closely with low socioeconomic status as measured by wealth and parental education as well as with malnutrition. Moreover, throughout the world developmental delays that begin early in life accumulate quickly over time for the poorest children. In countries as diverse as Cambodia, Ecuador, Nicaragua, Madagascar, and Mozambique, from about 36 months children from poorer households began to fall behind more prosperous neighbors on measures of cognitive development (Naudeau, Premand, and Filmer 2011). This pattern of children from households with fewer assets falling behind their peers occurs not just in language development but also in such noncognitive abilities as sustained attention (Fernald et al. 2011).

Early developmental shortfalls clearly contribute substantially to the intergenerational transmission of poverty through reduced schooling and subsequent low productivity. While the consequences of skill gaps are apparent, the factors behind them are still being defined (see Walker et al. 2011 for a recent review). In addition to nutrition and infectious diseases, early learning opportunities and caregiver-child interactions influence the rate at which a child develops, and caregiving is influenced by time available and maternal depression.

For young children, stimulation occurs through responsive and increasingly complex and developmentally appropriate interactions between them and their caregivers (see, for example, Young 2002; Landry, Smith, and Swank 2006). These interactions promote the growth of cognitive and socio emotional skills, which later influence academic and employment outcomes (see Heckman 2006; Grantham-McGregor et al. 2007). Affectionate relationships in which children receive encouragement, support, and appropriate instruction from their mothers are correlated with smoother schooling transitions, better academic grades, and fewer behavior problems (Pianta and Harbers 1996; Pianta, Nimetz, and Bennet 1997). Efforts to promote positive parenting practices in the home have demonstrated a positive impact on cognitive skills, social adjustment, and academic performance in a range of settings (see, for example, Kagitcibasi, Sunar, and Bekman 2001; Meeks-Gardner et al. 2003). Home activities that provide learning opportunities show positive effects at age 5 on children's literacy and numeracy (Sylva et al. 2008).

Studies of interventions in Jamaica and Vietnam that provided both stimulation and supplementation to malnourished children 18 months or older found that stimulation does more than supplementation to close the gap in cognitive skills (Walker et al. 2005; Watanabe et al. 2005). A study from Peru suggests that some preschool catch-up in nutrition is possible and is associated with improvements in cognitive development (Crookston et al. 2010). More generally, there is a growing body of evidence demonstrating that it is possible to shape the development of children at a very early age through stimulation—promoted through home visits, counseling of caregivers at clinics, and specialized training programs (box 4.2; Walker et al. 2007; Walker 2011). While only a handful of studies have been able to track the effects of early stimulation on adult outcomes, there is evidence that it favorably influences noncognitive skills (Walker, Chang, et al. 2011).

Box 4.2 Scaling Up: The Challenge of Reaching the Youngest Children

While it is clear that child development can stall at very young ages, it is less clear how to reach the youngest children with cost-effective interventions to increase stimulation. Evaluations of day care for children younger than age 3 regularly reveal a contribution to the entry of former caregivers into the labor market, but the impact on children is less consistent. For example, a comparison of day care and home visits in Ecuador using a sample from a program that covered 300,000 children found no impact of day care on cognitive outcomes, but home visits led to significant improvements in measures of memory, language, and fine and gross motor skills. Conversely, mothers with children in day care increased their labor supply compared to mothers in the home visit program or in no program, but the cognitive skills of the children did not improve. Moreover, the center-based program cost nearly US$500 per child, almost five times the cost of home visits. Note, however, that while the regression discontinuity design used for this analysis is valid for comparing each treatment with its controls, it can only suggest comparisons between programs because it selects into the preferred intervention.

Other center-based programs, such as Bolivia's PIDE, have been more successful in improving outcomes, but PIDE proved too costly to be sustainable. The mixed results on center-based programs have motivated efforts to verify whether home-based programs are effective alternatives in a range of environments. A noteworthy study has recently been completed in Colombia. The program was based on the often-studied small-scale program in Jamaica. It compared stimulation alone, a nutrition intervention (micronutrient supplementation) alone, and the combination of these two; it also used a control group. While the results are preliminary, child stimulation had a significant effect on a range of cognitive outcomes, with the effect larger for children who were ages 19–24 months at baseline than for those ages 12–18 months. The micronutrient supplementation added nothing to the

box continues next page

Box 4.2 Scaling Up: The Challenge of Reaching the Youngest Children *(continued)*

outcomes of stimulation and had a significant impact only in the stand-alone intervention for the 19–24-month subgroup.

As weekly visits for 18 months are still costly—US$500 in this trial, although this would likely fall if the program were to go to a full-scale, long-run intervention—the results encourage investigation into means to achieve similar results with parental training. One such model for parental enrichment in Turkey has revealed a favorable cost-benefit ratio (Kagitcibasi, Sunar, and Bekman 2001); other pilots of this concept are in the field, but the results are not yet available.

Sources: For Ecuador, see Rosero and Oosterbeek 2011. The preliminary results of the Colombian trial reflect communication with Costas Meghir.

The International Centre for Diarrhoeal Disease Research, Bangladesh (ICDDRB) in Dhaka has studied nutrition and child development in longitudinal studies on the growth of children in Matlab subdistrict. One report from a study tracking 1,439 children from birth has confirmed that as early as 18 months, controlling for household wealth, language development is associated with household food security and the HOME score (Saha et al. 2010). Clinical studies in the ICDDRB nutritional rehabilitation unit have confirmed that severely malnourished children benefit from psychosocial stimulation as part of their treatment, followed by home visits. Larger trials have turned the question around, asking whether stimulation added to food supplementation can promote weight gain, and other trials have found that information sessions that support and strengthen parenting practices, such as enhanced stimulation, can improve responsiveness. Grameen Shikkha, a Bangladeshi education NGO, also assessed the effectiveness of adding to its regular 12-session community-based parenting program a five-session training program that emphasized two-way stimulation (interaction with a child) and peer education of parents of children ages 18–40 months. The results were promising in terms of parental care giving but the assessment was too short to measure impact on cognitive measures (Opel et al. 2009). There are as yet no large-scale programs that promote stimulation at home to improve child development up to age 3.

Investments in ECD have been shown to promote school readiness and better education outcomes (Lynch 2005). Participation in quality ECD programs has been linked to higher levels of attention, learning outcomes, completion rates, and school attainment (Kagitcibasi, Sunar, and Bekman 2001; Schweinhart et al. 2005; Aboud 2006; Vegas and Petrow 2008; Berlinski, Galiani, and Gertler 2009). School systems that have a 10 percentage point advantage in the proportion of students who had attended preschool scored an average of 12 points higher in the Programme for Student Assessment (PISA) reading assessment (OECD 2011). When children come to school underprepared, not only are their own chances of success limited but they can have a detrimental influence on classroom dynamics and the experiences of all their classmates (Wentzel and Wigfield 1998; Reynolds et al. 2001).

Relative to developed countries, surprisingly little is known about the impact of broad-based preschool programs in middle- and low-income settings. In part this reflects difficulty in separating the impact of program specifics from the influence of self-selection. For example, many early comparisons of school achievement for those who went to preschool and those who did not often merely show that if a family values education—reflecting unobserved household characteristics—school performance is generally better. However, recent studies (Kagitcibasi, Sunar, and Bekman 2001; Berlinski, Galiani, and Manacorda 2008). in middle-income settings in Argentina and Turkey show that, as in the United States, preschool programs have impact into the adult years, affecting labor market outcomes and in some cases other interactions with family and community. Gains in several studies were predominantly among households with relatively few assets. For example, in Argentina an expansion of preschool classrooms in areas where enrollments were lowest led to higher test scores in mathematics and Spanish by the third grade, comparable to the reported impact of a decrease of 10 students per primary classroom (Berlinski, Galiani, and Gertler 2009). Similar results (box 4.3) were found in Uruguay (Berlinski, Galiani, and Manacorda 2008).

A few other global patterns are relevant to South Asia. First, in preschool enrollment the income or wealth disparity is greater than in primary school. Second, and perhaps related, the share of preschool students in private schools is generally greater than the share of the private sector in primary schooling. Finally, there is

Box 4.3 Going to Scale: Preschool

Since it cannot be assumed that results from a full-scale program covering the poorest members of the population will be comparable to findings from small-scale trials, the experience of Uruguay is encouraging. Uruguay has both the highest rates in Latin America of preschool participation and the smallest gap between participation from the poorest and wealthiest quintiles. In 1995, Uruguay embarked on a program to increase the number of preschool classrooms and teachers to provide children with basic foundations before the start of primary school and to socialize students and their parents to school early. Using the expansion to identify difference in participation of siblings and employing extensive retrospective data on schooling, researchers were able to estimate that by the time children reached age 15, those who had attended preschool had accumulated 0.8 year more of education, and the impact of preschool was largest for children from households with less education. There was no significant difference in the impact of one year of preschool or more years. For every US$1 spent on preschool education—construction as well as staffing—there was an estimated increase in the stream of future earnings of at least US$3 even using a high discount rate of 10 percent to account for the lag between the investments and the increase in earnings. When the discount of future earnings is lower, the cost-benefit ratio was estimated at 19.1.

Source: Berlinski, Galiani, and Manacorda 2008.

virtually no consensus on what constitutes a quality program (Alderman and Vegas 2011; Britto, Yoshikawa, and Boller 2011).

Preschool enrollment data contain more gaps than data on primary schooling, partly because private and non formal schools are not always tracked in national information systems but also because there are huge variations in the definitions of what constitutes a preschool and in the age brackets used to define preschool, which further complicates cross-country comparisons. Moreover, most household surveys ask about primary schooling but few ask about preschool. Finally, in surveys that do ask, it is not easy to distinguish day care and preschool programs that have age-specific pedagogy.

Early Childhood Development Policies and Interventions in South Asia

India and Sri Lanka have fully articulated ECD policies spanning the period from birth through grade school. Other countries in the region have a national nutrition policy, but it is not always linked explicitly to child stimulation, and many programs are pilots or of modest scale. This section therefore presents only the main ECD policy and service features and describes a few programs that either show promise or raise questions.

Bangladesh

As of December 2011, Bangladesh had no official ECD policy, although the Bangladesh Shishu Academy is preparing a document for cabinet approval. As in most countries, nutrition tends to be viewed as a separate issue, and although the impact of nutrition programs on cognitive development is recognized, there is no structural health-education coordination.

Although it is unlikely to meet the MDG target, Bangladesh has evidenced steady improvement in its nutritional standards since the 1990s, thanks to a combination of vitamin A and deworming programs and a community-based nutrition project that is currently integrated into the government's health program. Progress on girls' education also probably contributes to better nutrition.

Bangladesh has the relatively unique problem of arsenic in drinking water, although this is also a problem in some parts of India. Arsenic has been found to affect growth and cognitive performance in older children. A recent study in Bangladesh, however, did not show an independent risk of arsenic exposure for children ages 18 months (Hamadani et al. 2010).

Data on preschool enrollment in Bangladesh from a 2005 Multi-Indicator Cluster Survey (MICS) indicate that only 15 percent of children ages 3–4 years are in preschool[3]—12 percent of those in the poorest quintile and 17 percent of those in the wealthiest. The range for the 27 countries covered in the 2005 MICS was an average of 12 percent for the poor (as in Bangladesh) to 38 percent for the wealthiest, with a mean of 21 percent for all children. Bangladesh's very active NGO sector is highly active in preschool programs: reported figures vary by source, but it appears that the number of children attending preschools run by the Bangladesh Rural Advancement Committee (BRAC) is about equal to the number in programs administered by the Ministry of Women and Children Affairs, which is responsible for national ECD policy. Curricula for preschool education are designed at the BRAC University Early Childhood Development Resource Center.

Nor is BRAC the only large NGO providing preschool education. Indeed, recognizing that 30 percent of children who start primary school drop out by the third grade, a consortium of five NGOs has initiated a joint program, Succeed, to improve school readiness. Succeed set up both home- and school-based preschools for 5-year-olds and transition activities in communities and schools for 6- to 8-year-olds. These rely on volunteer teachers, parental management, and monthly meetings for parents. An evaluation (although without controls for selective participation, as is common with many preschool assessments) showed that children who attended Succeed preschools performed better in four of five competencies relating to reading, writing, and oral math than children in neighboring communities with no preschool experience (Aboud, Hossain, and O'Gara 2008).

Since 2005, Bangladesh has been running *Sisimpur,* a version of Sesame Street, that was designed to take into account local concerns, such as health and the need to encourage parental interaction with young children (Kibria and Jain 2009). *Sisimpur* reaches rural populations who have limited access to electricity and television via a road show.[4]

India

The enabling environment for ECD in India is based on article 15(3) of the Constitution and the Directive Principles of State Policy (guidelines for government framing of the law). Article 15[3] empowers the state to discriminate in favor of economically and educationally weaker groups. This is particularly important given that a majority of Indian children face economic and social disadvantages. Even the Convention on the Rights of the Child, a touchstone for ECD in many countries including India, does not provide explicitly for positive discrimination. Article 47 of the Directive Principles is particularly relevant; it stipulates that the state must endeavor to improve public health by raising the level of nutrition and the standard of living of its citizens.

A 2002 amendment to the constitution converted a directive principle for education into a right to free and compulsory education for children ages 6–14 years, but it failed to mention children under 6, who had been covered by an earlier directive principle. However, children of all ages have historically been prominently featured in national development plans. For example, the Fourth Five-Year Plan (1969–74) culminated in adoption of the National Policy for Children (1974), which defined the state's roles and responsibilities, and in 2005 the National Plan of Action for Children was formulated. The Fifth Five-Year Plan (1974–79) set the tone for every successive national plan in terms of ECD by shifting the perspective from welfare to development and emphasizing integration and convergence of sectors. This plan translated into Integrated Child Development Services (ICDS), the principal ECD policy implementer in India.

Since the program falls under the Ministry of Women and Child Development, some of the tension between the health and education departments, a common problem for integrated approaches, may have been resolved.

The ICDS is the world's largest comprehensive program of nutrition and child development, having expanded from a pilot serving 33 development blocks in 1975 to serving more than 6,500 development blocks in 2007. In 2007, it served over 60 million children, about 40 percent of the age-eligible population (children ages 0–6 years), and 13 million mothers. Having begun in poorer areas, the ICDS thus to some degree targeted poverty, although the tendency to place centers in the core of villages made the services less accessible to lower castes. As coverage expanded, coverage of the highest wealth quintiles expanded more rapidly than among the poorest, which suggests that the program has not concentrated on those least able to obtain food and services (Gragnolati et al. 2006).

The near-universal coverage of ICDS may be more fictional than real. A recent study using nationally representative household survey data found that although 92 percent of Indian villages have an ICDS center, only 7 percent of children ages 0–2 years and 15 percent of those ages 3–5 years were receiving daily ICDS supplementary feeding (Jain 2012). Another problem is the expansion of ICDS scope (see table 4.3). With only two workers per center, one of them considered a helper, the program aims to provide services from counseling on antenatal care and referral services for young children to distribution of hot meals and nonformal preschooling. The tight structure allows hardly any opportunity for counseling and child stimulation. The little time available for early education is largely devoted to 4- and 5-year-olds, and even then much of the time is spent on food distribution rather than age-appropriate education. In rupee terms, half the ICDS budget is allocated to food, although the amount of supplementation for children is still meager and sporadic.

There are wide variations by state in ICDS administration, even in number of staff and their remuneration. For example, Bihar and Jharkhand added an additional worker through Dulal, a UNICEF-sponsored program. Throughout India, there are similar localized innovations, which are evaluated with varying degrees of rigor. Any assessment of ICDS impact therefore needs to be contextualized.[5] Nevertheless, there is convergence on the findings of detailed evaluations conducted by both the government and the World Bank: (a) food supplementation has been overemphasized relative to other critical aspects of an effective nutrition package; (b) program delivery has been inadequate, stewardship weak, and funding—although large and growing—insufficient, particularly as there are no measures to promote cost-effectiveness; and (c) community response mechanisms are underdeveloped, meaning that targeting has not been fully successful and stakeholder participation has been suboptimal.

The Department of Women and Child Development is also responsible for another flagship ECD program, the Rajiv Gandhi National Crèche Scheme.[6] Established in 2001, this program gives grants to NGOs to establish crèches for children of working mothers and to train *anganwadi*[7] workers to integrate health care, nutrition, immunization, and preschool education for the children.

Table 4.3 ICDS Services to Children and Women

Services	*Children under 6 years of age*	*Pregnant women*	*Lactating women*
Health checkups and treatment	Health checkups Treatment of diarrhea Deworming Basic treatment of minor ailments Referral for more severe illness	Antenatal checkups	Postnatal checkups
Growth monitoring	Monthly weighing of children under 3 years of age Quarterly weighing of those ages 3–6 years Weight recorded on growth cards		
Immunization	Immunization against poliomyelitis, diphtheria, tetanus, tuberculosis, and measles	Tetanus toxoid immunization	
Micronutrient supplementation	Iron, folate, and vitamin A supplementation for malnourished children	Iron and folate supplementation	
Health and nutrition education		Advice on infant feeding practices, child care and development, utilization of health services, family planning, and sanitation	Advice on infant feeding practices, child care and development, utilization of health services, family planning, and sanitation
Supplementary nutrition	Hot meal or ready-to-eat snack providing 300 calories and 8–10 grams protein Double ration for malnourished children	Hot meal or ready-to-eat snack providing 500 calories and 2–25 grams protein	Hot meal or ready-to-eat snack providing 500 calories and 2–23 grams protein
Preschool education	Early childhood care and preschool education consisting or "early stimulation" of children under 3 years old and education "through the medium of play" for children 3–6 years old.		

Source: Gragnolati et al. 2006, 39.
Note: ICDS = Integrated Child Development Services.

The ICDS plays a similar central role in preschool education for 4- and 5-year-olds as it does for the nutrition and overall care of younger children, particularly in rural areas. However, although the government is aiming for an integrated approach, the most common recommendation for improving services is that one staff member should be dedicated to early education, which would allow *anganwadi* workers to focus on nutrition for younger children. The early education workers may receive specialized training in preparing children for primary education.[8]

Private centers and other NGO activities have a significant role in Indian preschool programs. The *Annual Status of Education Report* (Pratham 2010) found that over 60 percent of rural children ages 3 and 4 years attend the ICDS program, nearly 15 percent attend some form of kindergarten, and only

25 percent are not enrolled in a center-based program. By age 5, many of these students shift to formal schooling. By age 6, 62.5 percent of children are in government schools, 23.6 percent in private schools, and most of the rest in other centers (including *anganwadis*). Only 5 percent of children were not in any kind of school. While the total enrollment rates reported are surprisingly high for any age group, the relative roles of the different school types are consistent with other reports. Specific data are not available for urban areas but most estimates suggest that the overwhelming majority of preschool children in urban areas attend private centers.[9] While private schools generally charge fees, they are not necessarily high. Rural private school participation statistics and other localized studies suggest that many low-income Indian families opt to pay for private preschools (Tooley and Dixon 2007).

As in Bangladesh, in India a wide array of NGOs are active in preprimary education. Some, such as Plan International, adapt global models to the country. Others, such as Bodh Shiksa Samiti, originate in India—in this case, Rajasthan—but partner with international NGOs to expand coverage. Some larger NGO projects, like the *balwadi* program of Pratham, began with primary education but have expanded to preschool as well. Although the range of programs provides a dynamic laboratory to explore approaches, as yet there are few robust evaluations of NGO ECD programs.

Pakistan

Pakistan has no formal federal policy on ECD, no federal entity or institutional anchor for ECD policy, and no ECD line items within sectoral budgets. The 18th amendment to the constitution in April 2010 created some ambiguity about implementation of ECD policy, since it devolved the functions of the Ministry of Education (MOE), Ministry of Health, and Ministry of Social Welfare and Special Education to provincial governments. Implementation, planning, and monitoring for ECD budget allocations are all done in the provinces. At the local level, the district education officer and the district health officer are responsible for ECD services.

Punjab and Sindh have set ECD goals in all four essential sectors (education, health, nutrition, and child protection), although they are not termed ECD goals. Data are routinely collected to measure progress against subnational and local goals.

While Pakistan has made gains in some aspects of public health related to nutrition, such as vitamin A supplementation and inoculation, there are no national nutrition programs, and in 2010 the constitution was amended to transfer the bulk of responsibility for health to the provinces, sharply reducing the role of the federal government. There is no national policy to mandate iodization of salt to prevent iodine deficiency, for instance, or to promote fortification of staples with iron to prevent anemia.

One initiative that has promise is the National Program for Family Planning and Primary Health Care, commonly known as the Lady Health Worker (LHW) program. Initiated in 1994, this provides community-based preventive care by over 100,000 LHWs who have at least an eighth-grade education and who have had 3 months of structured classroom training and 12 months of supervised field work (see http://www.phc.gov.pk/site/). The target catchment for each LHW is 1,000 individuals, and the planned supervision ratio is 1 to 25.

A recent pilot project in Sindh showed that trained LHWs can significantly reduce neonatal mortality (Bhutta et al. 2011). Project tie-ups with traditional birth attendants likely accounted for the drop in both stillbirths (20 percent) and neonatal deaths (15 percent). However, promotion of adequate maternal nutrition and early breastfeeding was deemed most likely to make a long-term contribution to education (the trial did not include food supplements or income transfers). Reduced neonatal mortality has similarly been reported for programs in Bangladesh, India, and Nepal, but the Sindh project was the first in the region to use government staff rather than staff hired by the research team.

Since many of the most successful ECD initiatives have relied on regular interaction between young children and highly trained staff, can the LHW program also promote other aspects of child care? Parental support and enrichment or parent-based interventions have been proposed as a cost-effective ECD approach where resources are short. The idea was piloted in a randomized trial in the Punjab (Rahman, Iqbal, et al. 2008) in which LHWs integrated into their regular work education on child care; the knowledge of mothers was found to have improved significantly, although changes in practices or outcomes were not measured. A similar trial is underway in Sindh.

LHWs were also part of a pilot intervention to reduce maternal depression (Rahman, Malik, et al. 2008). While it did not have a significant effect on child growth, it did reduce diarrheal disease and influence indicators of depression and parental interactions with children; it seems to be a viable vehicle for the health and cognitive development of children. To date, however, no studies have assessed the number of tasks that LHWs can be assigned before the quality of their work is reduced. Of 22 tasks formally assigned to LHWs, four are related to nutrition: provision of iron and folate to pregnant women, nutrition education, growth monitoring, and promotion of exclusive breastfeeding and complementary feeding, though it is generally acknowledged that the last is not thoroughly delivered. A recent external evaluation of the LHW program found favorable trends in health services, particularly for antenatal health, but viewed the program as lagging in improving health knowledge and sanitation behavior (Oxford Policy Management 2009). An expansion of the LHW mission to counseling and parental support for stimulation of children would thus challenge the generally effective program at its weakest point.

Punjab is presently drawing up a strategy for early childhood education. Data on child mortality, growth monitoring, immunization of children under age 5, maternal mortality, and maternal immunization are being collected to measure progress against goals, benchmarks for which are set out in the draft National Health Policy (2009). For nutrition, the integrated PC1[10] being planned for nutrition; maternal, neonatal, and child health; and the LHW programs all have clear goals, and there is a plan to collect data to measure progress.

The National Education Policy (1998–2010) formally reintroduced *katchi* classes for children ages 3–5 years as a preparatory year before entry into grade 1. In 2007, the Teacher Resource Centre, an NGO based in Karachi, helped the government to draft curricula and guidelines. However, fewer than half the children ages 3–5 years attend *katchi* classes; older and younger children are often seen in overcrowded multigrade *katchi* classrooms; and teachers, who are generally not trained in ECD, lack child-centered teaching and learning resources.

One of the largest initiatives to address preschool program design is Releasing Creativity and Confidence (RCC), coordinated by the Aga Khan Foundation. The RCC is a network of academic institutions and NGOs working with the government and community-based and private schools in Sindh, Balochistan, and Gilgit-Baltistan to improve *katchi* access and quality and to support ECD policy dialog and advocacy. The impact of the initiative is being evaluated.

The Rafi Peer Theatre Workshop launched a Pakistani version of Sesame Street in 2011. The female characters are expected to challenge the gender bias prevailing in Pakistani society, and in time the show may be able to address some of the many issues of intolerance and violence.[11] Given the importance of mother-tongue instruction in the early years, the show will be aired in Urdu but will also feature episodes in the major languages of each province.

Nepal

Nepal is likely to meet the MDG goals of reducing both child and maternal mortality; the country has made significant nutrition gains in recent years (World Bank 2011). It has strong laws and regulations that promote prenatal and early nutrition. One of the more dramatic improvements was in 1998, when Act 2055 mandated salt iodization, thus reducing the risk of cognitive impairment. In August 2011, an order under the Food Act made fortification of staples like wheat, maize, and rice compulsory. There has also been progress in providing iron and folates to pregnant women. The Substitute of Breast Milk (Sale, Distribution and Control) Act 2049 enshrines the guidelines set forth in the International Code of Marketing of Breast Milk Substitutes to promote evidence-based infant feeding practices. Vitamin A supplementation has also been a success, manifested mainly in reduced mortality rather than physical or cognitive growth. Nepal's recent *Sunaula Hazar Din* (Community Action for Nutrition) project is based on a holistic life-cycle approach, targeting population age groups so that children are born healthy as well as receive nutritional supplements in the first 1,000 days of life. The project not only targets children ages 0–24 months and their caregivers, but also girls and young women, pregnant women, and those who may want to become pregnant within six months, as well as such community-wide nutrition-related interventions as hygiene, safe drinking water, and sanitation.

Infrastructure standards for health facilities in Nepal are monitored immediately after construction via site visits and facility reports. Facilities serving young children must be evaluated at least annually for compliance with service delivery standards. Currently, all 4,087 public and private health centers in Nepal meet the standards.

Children in Nepal are entitled to two free years of preschool (usually at ages 4 and 5). The Education for All (EFA) National Plan of Action states that providing early childhood care and education are the responsibility of village development committees and municipalities. Preprimary education in Nepal is mainly school- and community-based. The main distinction is that while both target children ages 36–59 months, community-based schools are also open to even younger children. Both types are subject to the ECD Curriculum 2062, which requires that preprimary classes last at least five hours a day. In total, the Ministry of Education reports, there are 26,773 preschools that reach 1,028,543 children, 48 percent of whom are girls; the average student-teacher ratio is 28:1.

UNICEF (2011) reported a fivefold increase in preschools in Nepal between 2004 and 2009, with 62 percent of the age-eligible population attending. It is hard to imagine that such a rapid expansion would not reduce the massive wealth gap in enrollment noted in the 2004 Demographic and Health Survey (DHS); data from the 2011 DHS have not yet been analyzed. However, as with most rapid expansions, staff training and operational budgets still have to catch up. It is too soon for an impact evaluation, and any future evaluation will have to accommodate the nonexperimental design (see the studies cited by Berlinski, Galiani, and Manacorda 2008; Berlinski, Galiani, and Gertler 2009).

Nepal's learning standards for preprimary schools are mainly concerned with literacy and linguistic development; there are none pertaining to motor skills or cognitive and sociopsychological development. According to the Education Act of 2002–03, preschools must be inspected no less than monthly to ensure that registration and compliance standards are observed. Health facilities must be inspected at least annually.

Sri Lanka

Sri Lanka has a long history of investing in health, although only in recent years have improvements in nutritional indicators matched its well-documented extension of life expectancy. Pursuant to the National Food and Nutrition Policy the Ministry of Healthcare and Nutrition addresses the problems of child under-nutrition, regional disparities in nutritional indicators, and emerging nutrition problems using a combination of direct food assistance and an integrated package of maternal health and nutrition services. Though Sri Lanka's food assistance programs since independence have focused more on cash transfers to vulnerable households than on child-specific services, the government does distribute supplementary food to pregnant and lactating mothers and children ages 6–60 months. The effectiveness of food assistance has been questioned, however, because of ineffective targeting and lapses in the supply of food supplements.

The National Policy for Early Childhood Care and Development, approved by the cabinet in 2004, explicitly links nutrition with opportunities for stimulation and suggests that the constitution mandates that the state ensure the full physical, mental, and social development of children. The policy recognizes the need to integrate programs and sets standards for both home-based and center-based care and capacity-building programs. However, little in the national nutrition policy reflects an integrated ECD approach.

In keeping with its virtually universal primary completion, the majority of children in Sri Lanka attend preschools. Once again, the private and NGO sectors have a larger role in preschool education than at other levels.

Equity in Access to ECD Services in South Asia

Inequalities in child development begin even before birth and increase over time. These disparities widen when children experience multiple risks. In the most recent *Lancet* series on child development, Engle et al. (2011) presented data showing that children in the highest income quintile are more likely to receive quality stimulation in the home, are more than twice as likely to attend preschool, and score better on language performance than children in the lowest income quintiles. It thus appears that the most effective and cost-efficient time to address inequality is early in life.

Disadvantaged children benefit most from investments in the early years. Poor children who participate in quality ECD programs do better in school and have higher completion rates (Kagitcibasi, Sunar, and Bekman 2001; Vegas and Petrow 2008; Berlinski, Galiani, and Gertler 2009). It appears from the 2009 results that those school systems that perform the best and provide equitable learning opportunities to all students also provide more inclusive access to preprimary education. Widening access to preprimary education can improve performance and equity by reducing student socioeconomic disparities; it is important to ensure, however, that extending coverage does not compromise quality.

The benefits of improved access to ECD can extend beyond young children to yield results for other at-risk groups. A study in Kenya, for example, showed that making childcare more available pushed up primary and secondary school enrollment rates for older girls who would otherwise be caring for younger siblings (Lokshin, Glinskaya, and Garcia 2000). ECD programs can also reach marginalized populations, such as immigrant families, and promote gender equality from an early age.

Data related to regional or wealth inequalities in preschool enrollment, like other data, are not available for many countries in South Asia. Using MICS3 data, however, wealth and regional inequality can be examined using several ECD-related health and nutrition indicators.

ECD Policies and Outcomes

Laws and policies are not necessarily correlated with desired ECD outcomes. Many countries have well-defined policies but poor outcomes because of resource constraints, flawed service delivery, or a lack of quality assurance mechanisms. However, salt iodization, fortification of foods with iron, and laws about marketing of breast milk substitutes are examples of how the law can be used to promote better nutrition for young children.

Ensuring that the diets of young children have adequate iodine impacts cognition and behavior substantially and positively (Walker et al. 2007). Universal salt iodization is the most cost-effective way to deliver iodine, costing as little as $.05 per beneficiary (World Bank 1996). Iron supplements not only prevent anemia but also have positive effects on children's motor, socio-emotional and language development (Walker et al. 2007). A six-month trial in South Africa reported better motor development for infants who received iron-fortified porridge than infants who received nonfortified porridge (Faber et al. 2005). In the *Lancet* series, Black et al. (2008) asserted that increasing the rate of exclusive breastfeeding to 90 percent for children up to 6 months old could prevent up to 13 percent of all young children's deaths annually. A trial in Honduras showed improved motor development for children who were exclusively breastfed (Dewey et al. 2001). The International Code of Marketing of Breast-Milk Substitutes provides clear guidance on how to structure policies and regulation to encourage breast-feeding and infant feeding in accordance with the World Health Organization guidelines.

Policy Implications

Three policy implications follow from the discussion in this chapter:

- Since there is no conclusive evidence about the impact of broad-based preschool programs in middle- and low-income settings, it is difficult to recommend a design that can be effectively rolled out at a large scale. What is needed instead is to reinforce existing programs by improving their scope, implementation capacity, and efficiency.

- Poor nutrition is a major barrier to learning in South Asia. The evidence is very clear—from the region and around the world—that low birth weight, poor early-life nutrition, and micronutrient deficiencies have profoundly adverse effects on not only student cognition and learning but also later-life outcomes, such as employment and labor productivity (Behrman, Alderman, and Hoddinott 2004). With the highest rates of child malnutrition and low birth weight in the world, countries in the region need to invest heavily in child health and nutrition programs; there is full consensus on best-practice investments (Darmstadt et al. 2005; Bhutta et al. 2008).

- Even though it may not be practical for South Asian countries to provide universal ECD services, there is a case for targeting preprimary school and nutrition supplement services to disadvantaged and poor children, who start primary school with enormous learning disadvantages, fall ever further behind as they move through schooling, and often drop out. Investing in both their nutrition and health and their social and emotional stimulation and development will help get them ready for school and make public spending on primary education more efficient.

What kind of preschool programs make sense for disadvantaged children? Because those that merely bring primary-school curricula to younger children are unlikely to be cost-effective. Programs specifically centered on the young child are imperative, these programs often have to compensate for limited stimulation at home.

Notes

1. Height for age is another common indicator of nutrition. Low height for age is termed stunting or chronic malnutrition. Underweight and stunting trends tend to move together, but underweight has a somewhat higher risk of mortality. See Black et al. (2008).
2. See http://www.childinfo.org/undernutrition_mdgprogress.php. The data, however, are spotty. For example, the latest data for Bhutan are from 1999 and for Pakistan are from 2001–02.
3. See http://www.childinfo.org.
4. The Indian counterpart, *Galli Galli Sim Sim*, uses this approach plus an outreach component that uses DVDs and radio programs.
5. Micronutrient Initiative. 2007. *Review of "Best Practices" in ICDS*. Processed.
6. The ministry also conducts a pilot conditional cash transfer (CCT) scheme for pregnant/nursing mothers in 52 districts (the Indira Gandhi Matritva Sahyog Yojana), which promotes care of pregnant women and early and exclusive breast feeding. To the degree that this improves nutrition it will affect cognitive development. It is, however, less directly aimed at ECD than ICDS or the crèche program.
7. An Anganwadi Center is a child and mother-care center catering to children ages 0–6 years.
8. An example, but by no means the sole report to call for such a policy, is the review of ICDS best practices by the Micronutrient Initiative, published in 2007.
9. For example, see the Social and Rural Research Institute (nd), "The Extent of Coverage and Utilization of Early Childhood Education Provision in the Public and the Private Sector," which estimates that 90 percent of children enrolled in preschools are in private centers, aided or unaided.
10. PC1 stands for Planning Commission form 1, which is prepared for development projects approved by the Planning Commission.
11. See http://www.usaid.gov/pk.

Bibliography

Aboud, F. 2006. "Evaluation of an Early Childhood Preschool Program in Rural Bangladesh." *Early Childhood Research Quarterly* 21 (1): 46–60.

Aboud, F., K. Hossain, and C. O'Gara. 2008. "The Succeed Project: Challenging Early School Failure in Bangladesh." *Research in Comparative and International Education* 3 (3): 295–307.

Alderman, H., J. Behrman, V. Lavy, and R. Menon. 2001. "Child Health and School Enrollment: A Longitudinal Analysis." *Journal of Human Resources* 36 (1): 185–205.

Alderman, H., J. Hoddinott, and W. Kinsey. 2006. "Long Term Consequences of Early Childhood Malnutrition." *Oxford Economic Papers* 58 (3): 450–74.

Alderman, H., and S. Linnemayr. 2009. "Anemia in Low-Income Countries Is Unlikely to Be Addressed by Economic Development without Additional Programs." *Food and Nutrition Bulletin* 30 (3): 265–70.

Alderman, H., and E. Vegas. 2011. "The Convergence of Equity and Efficiency in ECD Programs." In *No Small Matter: The Interaction of Poverty, Shocks, and Human Capital Investments in Early Childhood Development*, edited by H. Alderman. Washington, DC: World Bank.

Asadullah, M., N. Chaudhury, D. Prajuli, L. R. Sarr, Y. Savchenko, and S. R. Al-Zayed. 2009. *Secondary Education Quality and Access Enhancement Project (SEQAEP): Baseline Report*. Washington, DC: World Bank.

Aturupane, D. H., P. Glewwe, and S. Wisniewski. 2013. "The Impact of School Quality, Socio-Economic Factors and Child Health on Students' Academic Performance: Evidence from Sri Lankan Primary Schools." *Education Economics* 21 (1): 2–37.

Behrman, J., H. Alderman, and J. Hoddinott. 2004. "Hunger and Malnutrition." In *Global Crises, Global Solutions*, edited by B. Lomborg. Cambridge, UK.: Cambridge University Press.

Berlinski, S., S. Galiani, and P. J. Gertler. 2009. "The Effect of Pre-Primary Education on Primary School Performance." *Journal of Public Economics* 93: 219–34.

Berlinski, S., S. Galiani, and M. Manacorda. 2008. "Giving Children a Better Start: Preschool Attendance and School-Age Profiles." *Journal of Public Economics* 92: 1416–40.

Bhutta, Z. A., T. Ahmed, R. E. Black, S. Cousens, K. Dewey, E. Giugliani, B. A. Haider, B. Kirkwood, S. S. Morris, H. P. S. Sachdev, M. Shekar. 2008. "Maternal and Child Undernutrition 3: What Works? Interventions for Maternal and Child Undernutrition and Survival." *Lancet* 371: 417–40.

Bhutta, Z. A., S. Soofi, S. Cousens, S. Mohammad, Z. Memon, I. Ali, A. Feroze, F. Raza, A. Khan, S. Wall, and J. Martines. 2011. "Improvement of Perinatal and Newborn Care in Rural Pakistan through Community-Based Strategies: A Cluster-Randomised Effectiveness Trial." *Lancet* 377: 403–12.

Black, M. M., A. H. Baqui, K. Zaman, S. El Arifeen, and R. E. Black. 2009. "Maternal Depressive Symptoms and Infant Growth in Rural Bangladesh." *American Journal of Clinical Nutrition* 89 (3): 951S–57S.

Black, M. M., A. H. Baqui, K. Zaman, S. W. McNary, K. Le, S. El Arifeen, J. D. Hamadani, M. Parveen, M. Yunus, and R. E. Black. 2007. "Depressive Symptoms among Rural Bangladeshi Mothers: Implications for Infant Development." *Journal of Child Psychology and Psychiatry* 48 (8): 764–72.

Black, R. E., L. H. Allen, Z. A. Bhutta, L. E. Caulfield, M. De Onis, M. Ezzati, C. Mathers, and J. Rivera. 2008. "Maternal and Child Under-nutrition Global and Regional Exposures and Health Consequences." *Lancet* 371: 243–60.

Bobonis, G. J., E. Miguel, and C. Puri-Sharma. 2006. "Anemia and School Participation." *Journal of Human Resources* 41 (4): 692–721.

Borghans, L., A. L. Duckworth, J. J. Heckman, and B. ter Weel. 2008. "The Economics and Psychology of Personality Traits." *Journal of Human Resources* 43 (4): 972–1059.

Britto, P., H. Yoshikawa, and K. Boller. 2011. "Quality of Early Childhood Development Programs in Global Contexts." *Social Policy Report* 25 (2): 3–23.

Christian, P. 2012. "Iron in Infancy and Long-term Development." *Archives of Pediatrics & Adolescent Medicine* 166 (3): 285–88.

Christian, P., L. E. Murray-Kolb, S. K. Khatry, J. Katz, B. A. Schaefer, P. M. Cole, S. C. LeClerq, and J. M. Tielsch. 2010. "Prenatal Micronutrient Supplementation and Intellectual and Motor Function in Early School-Aged Children in Nepal." *The Journal of the American Medical Association* 304 (24): 2716–23.

Crookston, B. T., M. E. Penny, S. C. Alder, T. T. Dickerson, R. M. Merrill, J. B. Stanford, C. A. Porucznik, and K. A. Dearden. 2010. "Children Who Recover from Early Stunting and Children Who Are Not Stunted Demonstrate Similar Levels of Cognition." *The Journal of Nutrition* 140 (11): 1996–2001.

Cunha, F., and J. Heckman. 2007. "The Technology of Skills Formation." *American Economic Review* 97 (2): 31–47.

Darmstadt, G. L., Z. Bhutta, S. Cousens, T. Adam, N. Walker, and L. de Bernis. 2005. "Evidence-based, Cost-Effective Interventions: How Many Newborn Babies Can We Save?" *Lancet* 365: 977–88.

Dewey, K. G., R. J. Cohen, K. H. Brown, and L. L. Rivera. 2001. "Effects of Exclusive Breastfeeding for Four versus Six Months on Maternal Nutritional Status and Infant Motor Development: Results of Two Randomized Trials in Honduras." *The Journal of Nutrition* 131 (2): 262–7.

Engle, P. L., L. C. H. Fernald, H. Alderman, J. Behrman, C. O'Gara, A. Yousafzai, M. C. de Mello, M. Hidrobo, N. Ulkuer, I. Ertem, S. Iltus, and the Global Child Development Steering Group. 2011. "Strategies for Reducing Inequalities and Improving Developmental Outcomes for Young Children in Low-Income and Middle-Income Countries." *Lancet* 378 (9799): 1339–53.

Faber, M., J. D. Kvalsvig, C. J. Lombard, and A. S. Benadé. 2005. "Effect of a Fortified Maize-Meal Porridge on Anemia, Micronutrient Status, and Motor Development of Infants." *The American Journal of Clinical Nutrition* 82 (5): 1032–39.

Fernald, L. C. H., A. Weber, E. Galasso, and L. Ratsifandrihamanana. 2011. "Socioeconomic Gradients and Child Development in a Very Low Income Population: Evidence from Madagascar." *Developmental Science* 14 (4): 832–47.

Field, E., O. Robles, and M. Torero. 2009. "Iodine Deficiency and Schooling Attainment in Tanzania." *American Economic Journal: Applied Economics* 1 (4): 140–69.

Field, T. 2011. "Postpartum Depression Effects on Early Interactions, Parenting, and Safety Practices: A Review." *Infant Behavior & Development* 33 (1): 1–6.

Glewwe, P., H. G. Jacoby, and E. M. King. 2001. "Early Childhood Nutrition and Academic Achievement: A Longitudinal Analysis." *Journal of Public Economics* 81(3): 345–68.

Gragnolati, M., C. Bredenkamp, M. Shekar, M. Das Gupta, and Y. Lee. 2006. *India's Undernourished Children: A Call for Reform and Action*. Washington, DC: World Bank.

Grantham-McGregor, S., Y. Cheung, S. Cueto, P. Glewwe, L. Richter, and B. Strupp. 2007. "Developmental Potential in the First 5 Years for Children in Developing Countries." *Lancet* 369 (9555): 60–70.

Gwatkin, D. R., S. Rutstein, K. Johnson, E. Suliman, A. Wagstaff, and A. Amouzou. 2007. *Socio-Economic Differences in Health, Nutrition, and Population. An Overview.* Washington, DC: World Bank.

Haddad, L., H. Alderman, S. Appleton, L. Song, and Y. Yohannes. 2003. "Reducing Child Malnutrition: How Far Does Income Growth Take Us?" *World Bank Economic Review* 17 (1): 107–31.

Hamadani, J. D., S. M. Grantham-McGregor, F. Tofail, B. Nermell, B. Fängström, S. N. Huda, S. Yesmin, M. Rahman, M. Vera-Hernández, S. E. Arifeen, and M. Vahter. 2010. "Pre-and Postnatal Arsenic Exposure and Child Development at 18 Months of Age: A Cohort Study in Rural Bangladesh." *International Journal of Epidemiology* 39 (5): 1206–16.

Hanushek, E. A., and L. Woessmann. 2008. "The Role of Cognitive Skills in Economic Development." *Journal of Economic Literature* 46 (3): 607–68.

Heckman, J. J. 2006. "Skill Formation and the Economics of Investing in Disadvantaged Children." *Science* 312 (5782): 1900–2.

———. 2011. "The American Family in Black and White: A Post-Racial Strategy for Improving Skills to Promote Equality." *Daedalus* 140 (2): 70–89.

Helen Keller Institute. 2006. "The Burden of Anemia in Rural Bangladesh: The Need for Urgent Action." *Bulletin No. 16, April,* Nutritional Surveillance Project. http://www.hki.org/research/NSP%20Bulletin%2016.pdf.

Helmers, C., and M. Patnam. 2011. "The Formation and Evolution of Childhood Skill Acquisition: Evidence from India." *Journal of Development Economics* 95 (2): 252–66.

Hoddinott, J., J. Maluccio, J. Behrman, R. Flores, and R. Martorell. 2008. "Effect of a Nutrition Intervention During Early Childhood on Economic Productivity in Guatemalan Adults." *Lancet* 371 (9610): 411–16.

Jain, M. 2012. "Evaluating the Benefits of an Integrated Child Development Program in Rural India." Unpublished doctoral dissertation submitted to the University of California, Riverside.

Kagitcibasi, C., D. Sunar, and S. Bekman. 2001. "Long-Term Effects of Early Intervention: Turkish Low-Income Mothers and Children." *Journal of Applied Developmental Psychology* 22 (4): 333–61.

Kibria, N., and S. Jain. 2009. "Cultural Impact of Sisimpur, Sesame Street, in Rural Bangladesh: Views of Family Members and Teachers." *Journal of Comparative Family Studies* 40 (1): 57–75.

Landry, S. H., K. E. Smith, and P. R. Swank. 2006. "Responsive Parenting: Establishing Early Foundations for Social, Communication, and Independent Problem-Solving Skills." *Developmental Psychology* 42 (4): 627.

Lokshin, M., E. E. Glinskaya, and M. Garcia. 2000. "The Effect of Early Childhood Development Programs on Women's Labor Force Participation and Older Children's Schooling in Kenya." Policy Research Paper 2376, World Bank, Washington, DC.

Lynch, R. G. 2005. "Early Childhood Investments Yield Big Payoff." Policy Perspectives, WestEd, San Francisco, CA.

Maluccio, J., J. Hoddinott, J. Behrman, R. Martorell, A. Quisumbing, and A. Stein. 2009. "The Impact of Improving Nutrition During Early Childhood on Education Among Guatemalan Adults." *Economic Journal* 119 (537): 734–63.

Martorell, R., B. Horta, L. Adair, A. Stein, L. Richter, C. Fall, S. Bhargava, S. Dey Biswas, L. Perez, F. Barros, and C. Victora. 2010. "Weight Gain in the First Two Years of Life Is an Important Predictor of Schooling Outcomes in Pooled Analyses from Five Birth Cohorts from Low- and Middle-Income Countries." *Journal of Nutrition* 40: 348–54.

Meeks-Gardner, J., S. P. Walker, C. A. Powell, and S. Grantham-McGregor. 2003. "A Randomized Controlled Trial of a Home-visiting Intervention on Cognition and Behavior in Term Low Birth Weight Infants." *Journal of Pediatrics* 143 (5): 634–9.

Naudeau, S. S. M., P. Premand, and D. Filmer. 2011. "Cognitive Development among Young Children in Low-Income Countries." In *No Small Matter: The Interaction of Poverty, Shocks, and Human Capital Investments in Early Childhood Development*, edited by H. Alderman. Washington, DC: World Bank.

Nelson, C. A., M. de Haan, and K. M. Thomas. 2006. *Neuroscience and Cognitive Development: The Role of Experience and the Developing Brain*. New York: John Wiley.

OECD (Organisation for Economic Co-operation and Development). 2011. *Lessons from PISA for Mexico, Strong Performers and Successful Reformers in Education*. Paris: OECD.

Opel, A., S. S. Zaman, F. Khanom, and F. Aboud. 2009. "Effectiveness of a Community-Based Child Stimulation Program in Rural Bangladesh." BRAC University, Bangladesh. http://www.bracuniversity.net/ied/apanel/admin_content/research/rp1186829.pdf.

Oxford Policy Management. 2009. *Lady Health Worker Programme: External Evaluation of the National Programme for Family Planning and Primary Health Care: Final Report*. Oxford, U.K.: Oxford Policy Management.

Pianta, R. C., and K. L. Harbers. 1996. "Observing Mother and Child Behavior in a Problem-Solving Situation at School Entry: Relations with Academic Achievement." *Journal of School Psychology* 34 (3): 307–22.

Pianta, R. C., S. L. Nimetz, and E. Bennett. 1997. "Mother-Child Relationships, Teacher-Child Relationships, and School Outcomes in Preschool and Kindergarten." *Early Childhood Research Quarterly* 12 (3): 263–80.

Rahman, A., Z. Iqbal, C. Roberts, and N. Husain. 2008. "Cluster Randomized Trial of a Parent-Based Intervention to Support Early Development of Children in a Low-Income Country." *Child: Care, Health and Development* 35: 56–62.

Rahman, A., A. Malik, S. Sikander, C. Roberts, and F. Creed. 2008. "Cognitive Behaviour Therapy–Based Intervention by Community Health Workers for Mothers with Depression and Their Infants in Rural Pakistan: A Cluster-Randomised Controlled Trial." *Lancet* 372: 902–9.

Reardon, S. F. 2011. "The Widening Academic Achievement Gap between Rich and Poor: New Evidence and Possible Explanations." In *Whither Opportunity? Rising Inequality, Schools, and Children's Life Chances*, edited by G. J. Duncan and R. J. Murnane, 91–115. New York: Russell Sage Foundation.

Reynolds, A. J., J. A. Temple, D. L. Robertson, and E. A. Mann. 2001. "Long Term Effects of an Early Childhood Intervention on Educational Achievement and Juvenile Arrest—a 15-Year Follow-Up of Low-Income Children in Public Schools." *Journal of the American Medical Association* 285 (18): 2339–46.

Rosero, J., and H. Oosterbeek. 2011. "Trade-Offs between Different Early Childhood Interventions: Evidence from Ecuador." Tinbergen Institute Discussion Paper 11-102/3, Tinbergen Institute, Amsterdam, the Netherlands.

Saha, K. K., F. Tofail, E. A. Frongillo, K. M. Rasmussen, S. E. Afreen, L. A. Persson, S. N. Huda, and J. D. Hamadani. 2010. "Household Food Security is Associated with Early Childhood Language Development: Results from a Longitudinal Study in Rural Bangladesh." *Child Care Health and Development* 36 (3): 309–16.

Schweinhart, L., J. Montie, Z. Xiang, W. S. Barnett, C. R. Belfield, and M. Nores. 2005. *Lifetime Effects: The High/Scope Perry Preschool Study Through Age 40*. Ypsilanti, MI: High/Scope Press.

Shonkoff, J. P., and D. A. Phillips. 2000. *From Neurons to Neighborhoods: The Science of Early Childhood Development*. Washington, DC: National Academy Press.

Sylva, K., E. C. Melhuish, P. Sammons, I. Siraj-Blatchford, and B. Taggart. 2008. "Effective Preschool and Primary Education 3–11 Project: Final Report from the Primary Phase: Preschool School and 57 Family Influence on Children's Development during Key Stage 2 (Age 7–11)." Research Report DCSF-RR061, Institute of Education, University of London.

Tooley, J., and P. Dixon. 2007. "Private Schooling for Low-Income Families: A Census and Comparative Survey in East Delhi, India." *International Journal of Educational Development* 27 (2): 205–19.

UNICEF (United Nations Children's Fund). 2006. *Progress for Children: A Report Card for Nutrition*. New York: UNICEF Publication. http://www.childinfo.org/files/PFC4_EN_8X11.pdf.

———. 2011. *Nepal: Evaluation of UNICEF's Early Childhood Development Programme with Focus on Government of Netherlands Funding (2008–10)—Nepal Country Case Study Report*. Kathmandu: UNICEF.

Vegas, E., and J. Petrow. 2008. *Raising Student Learning in Latin America: The Challenge for the 21st Century*. Washington, DC: World Bank.

Wachs, T., M. Black, and P. Engle. 2009. "Maternal Depression: A Global Threat to Children's Health, Development, and Behavior and to Human Rights." *Child Development Perspectives* 3: 51–9.

Walker, S. 2011. "Promoting Equity through Early Child Development Interventions for Children Zero to Three Years." In *No Small Matter: The Interaction of Poverty, Shocks, and Human Capital Investments in Early Childhood Development*, edited by H. Alderman. Washington, DC: World Bank.

Walker, S., S. Chang, C. Powell, and S. Grantham-McGregor. 2005. "Effects of Early Childhood Stimulation and Nutritional Supplementation on Cognition and Education in Growth-Stunted Jamaican Children: Prospective Cohort Study." *Lancet* 366: 1804–7.

Walker, S., S. Chang, M. Vera-Hernandez, and S. Grantham-McGregor. 2011. "Early Childhood Stimulation Benefits Adult Competence and Reduces Violent Behavior." *Pediatrics* 127 (5): 849–57.

Walker, S., T. Wachs, J. Meeks-Gardner, B. Lozoff, G. Wasserman, E. Pollitt, J. Carter, and the International Child Development Steering Group. 2007. "Child Development: Risk Factors for Adverse Outcomes in Developing Countries." *Lancet* 369: 145–57.

Walker, S., T. Wachs, S. Grantham-McGregor, M. Black, C. Nelson, S. Huffman, H. Baker-Henningham, S. Chang, J. Hamadani, B. Lozoff, J. Meeks-Gardner, C. Powell, A. Rahman, L. Richter. 2011. "Inequality in Early Childhood: Risk and Protective Factors for Early Child Development." *Lancet* 378: 1325–38.

Watanabe, K., R. Flores, J. Funiwara, and L. Tran. 2005. "Early Childhood Development Interventions and Cognitive Development of Young Children in Rural Vietnam." *Journal of Nutrition* 135: 1918–25.

Wentzel, K. R., and A. Wigfield. 1998. "Academic and Social Motivational Influences on Students' Academic Performance." *Educational Psychology Review* 10 (2): 155–75.

World Bank. 1996. *Repositioning Nutrition as Central to Development A Strategy for Large-Scale Action.* Washington, DC: World Bank.

———. 2011. *Accelerating Progress in Reducing Maternal and Child Undernutrition in Nepal: A Review of Global Evidence of Essential Nutrition Interventions for the Nepal Health Sector Plan II and Multi-Sectoral Plan for Nutrition.* Washington, DC: World Bank.

Young, M. E., ed. 2002. *From Early Child Development to Human Development: Investing in Our Children's Future.* Washington, DC: World Bank.

Zimmermann, M. 2009. "Iodine Deficiency in Pregnancy and the Effects of Maternal Iodine Supplementation on the Offspring: A Review." *American Journal of Clinical Nutrition* 89 (2): 668S–72S.

PART 3

Determinants of Learning Outcomes: School-Level Factors

At least to some extent schools can overcome disadvantages arising from socioeconomic background. In South Asia, as in most countries, teacher salaries and other schooling inputs take up the major share of education budgets. Implicitly assuming that better school inputs will translate into better learning outcomes, most South Asian countries have substantially increased their spending on education. Yet, student learning has not improved meaningfully. Part 3 examines how school inputs and processes affect student learning: chapter 5 examines the impact of teacher quality, and chapter 6 looks at other classroom inputs, such as pedagogy and classroom procedures, teaching methods, and technology.

This study provides clear evidence that teacher subject knowledge and teacher management and accountability mechanisms affect learning outcomes in South Asia. But even when teachers are available, South Asian countries face major challenges in presenting curricula due to inadequate teacher training, use of rote learning and too little time allocated to classroom activities. Addressing these challenges for the long term is a priority. Considering the poor learning environment in the region and the economic and social urgency of improving student learning, effective short- and medium-term teaching strategies include remedial and supplemental instruction, activity-based learning, and technology-assisted instruction.

CHAPTER 5

Teacher Quality in South Asia*

Introduction

South Asia has recently made significant strides in increasing educational access and average years of education completed. However, while years of schooling are important to worker productivity and labor market and life outcomes, what matters just as much, if not more, is what students learn in school. The quality of schooling—measured by the cognitive skills of the population—has sizable economic effects on individual earnings and national growth (see Hanushek 2005 for a summary of the literature).

Educational leaders and policy makers acknowledge that while some schools in South Asia perform well, most are of poor quality, and student achievement is generally low (see chapter 2). In arithmetic, nearly half of grade 3 and 4 students cannot subtract one number from another. In reading, many students are as much as three or four grades behind the competency level for their grade.

While many factors contribute to the low quality of education, *substandard teaching* is cited as the foremost factor in the developing world generally. Improving teaching may thus be the most effective way to raise school quality (Glewwe and Kremer 2006), and its benefits can translate into economic gains for the entire country. In estimating the economic value of teacher quality in the United States, Hanushek (2011) stated that for a class of 20 students a teacher who is 1 standard deviation above mean effectiveness would generate annual marginal gains of US$400,000 in terms of the present value of future student earnings—and perhaps more when other conditions change. He also suggested that replacing the bottom 5–8 percent of teachers with "average" teachers could very likely move the United States closer to the top in international rankings in math and science achievement. The present value of such an upward movement is estimated to be worth up to US$112 trillion.

While there are no such calculations for South Asia, the economic value of better teacher quality is bound to be immense, not only because so many of the world's children study in this region, but also because teacher betterment will

*See box 5.1 for a summary of the chapter's key questions and findings.

Box 5.1 Questions and Findings

Questions

- What is the quality of teachers in South Asia?
- What must be done to improve teacher quality and to enable teachers to provide meaningful education to children in South Asia?

Findings

Subject knowledge is central to teacher quality, and it appears that in South Asia subject knowledge needs substantial improvement.

- Evidence from India, Pakistan, and Bangladesh demonstrates that teachers do not know their subjects thoroughly. Because student learning depends to a great extent on teacher competence, this clearly must be remedied.
- Recruitment needs to be directed to hiring teachers with the requisite knowledge and teaching skills, with safeguards put in place to prevent decisions about appointments, transfers, and promotions that are not based on merit.
- Preservice training needs to equip teachers with relevant, up-to-date knowledge and practice in dynamic approaches to teaching. Wherever teachers lack skills and content knowledge, carefully designed in-service training is essential if they are to be effective.
- In South Asia, the performance of both students and teachers is pitiably low, especially in math. Most countries in the region do not provide for teachers who specialize in math up to grade 8. Recruitment of subject-specialist teachers or better deployment of current teachers could help alleviate this problem.

Well-designed career progression structures and remuneration schemes can motivate teachers.

- In South Asia, teachers seem on average to be well paid relative to nonteachers with similar credentials. Nevertheless, the lack of career progression structures or rewards for good performance undermines teachers' professionalism and motivation. This has an adverse effect on quality.
- Evidence from the region, although limited, suggests that a career progression structure and performance-related pay (PRP) could engender more accountability, elicit greater teacher effort, and incentivize use of better inputs and training.
- Yet implementing an effective remuneration scheme has proved elusive, partly due to opposition from teacher organizations and partly due to the complexity of designing transparent and acceptable ways of judging teacher performance. A four-year experiment in Andhra Pradesh and policies adopted in countries like Mexico or Chile could provide guidance on shaping remuneration and career promotion strategies. Incentives need to be carefully designed and their impact evaluated before programs are scaled up.

Better teacher deployment, management, and accountability systems can reduce teacher absences.

- Low teacher effort and high teacher absenteeism are major problems in South Asia. Adequate monitoring, coupled with rewards for presence and negative consequences for absence and with mechanisms to promote active participation in the classroom, is likely to produce more gains in quality than any other school input.
- There is an obvious need in the region for clear and transparent policies about deployment, transfers, and postings. In many cases, redeployment of current teachers would help alleviate absenteeism, both by addressing teacher shortages in remote rural areas and by reducing distance to school.
- The politicization of teachers could be leveraged to improve educational outcomes if teacher and student interests are brought into alignment.

start from a lower level than in the developed world. That is why it is important from an equity perspective to assess teaching quality in South Asia.

Many people believe that the rapid expansion of schooling in South Asia has been achieved at enormous cost in educational quality. Expansion has been accompanied by a demand for teachers that has been met by relaxing recruitment standards. For example, Sri Lanka's colossal expansion in the late 1970s and into the 1980s was accomplished by recruiting teachers with little or no training, which produced a huge pool of poorly qualified teachers.

This chapter starts by assessing the significance and effectiveness of teachers worldwide, but especially within South Asia. It summarizes international evidence to demonstrate the role of teachers in student learning outcomes and how various interventions and policy changes contribute to learning. In examining the quality of current South Asian teachers, the chapter probes such components of teacher quality as subject knowledge, the efficacy of training, imbalances in teacher allocation, and the credentials of recruits. It also examines such policies as salary, recruitment, and teacher management systems. Finally, it studies what the governance environment in which teachers work implies for teacher quality and student outcomes.

The review of evidence and the analysis of data in this chapter identify the region's main problems but also show that many could be addressed through effective policy. For example, salaries in South Asia do not reflect teacher effort or improvement in student learning, and the general lack of teacher accountability needs to be addressed. Moreover, contrary to the belief that teacher shortages are a major concern, effective redeployment could address many of the shortfalls that plague rural schools and could help to diminish regional and gender inequalities.

Improving Learning by Enhancing Teacher Skills and Knowledge

Teacher quality, which encompasses a range of competencies and skills, is not easy to measure. Narrowly, it can be defined as a "teacher's ability to produce growth in student achievement" (Eide, Goldhaber, and Brewer 2004), although a more accurate reflection of teacher effectiveness would include a comprehensive array of student outcomes. Despite early research to the contrary, it is now recognized that schools do make a difference in determining student outcomes, and it is acknowledged that teacher quality is probably the most important institutional influence (Goldhaber 1999). However, studies of whether traditional observable teacher characteristics explain differences in teacher effectiveness have had mixed results; thus research continues on more nuanced hypotheses about what makes teachers differentially effective.

Defining Teacher Quality

The international literature probing teacher quality reflects two approaches. One defines a good teacher as someone who consistently produces high achievement gains for pupils. This approach measures total teacher quality by its output and does not require identification of specific characteristics that generate student learning (Aaronson, Barrow, and Sander 2003; Rockoff 2004; Hanushek et al. 2005; Rivkin,

Hanushek, and Kain 2005). This approach has not been applied in South Asia, largely due to the lack of data linking teachers to what their own students learn.

The second approach links measurable teacher characteristics to pupil achievement, controlling for student characteristics. The methodologies used vary from instrumental variable approaches (Hoxby 1996; Sprietsma and Waltenberg 2005; Kingdon and Teal 2007) to panel data studies (Hanushek 2005; Clotfelter, Ladd, and Vigdor 2006) and randomized experiment studies (Lavy 2002; Glewwe and Kremer 2006). The consensus is that many easily measurable characteristics—such as certification, degree held, training, and experience (at least in the first two years)—that might reasonably be thought to encompass teacher quality seldom predict a teacher's effectiveness in raising student achievement (Fuller 1987; Hanushek and Rivkin 2006; Burgess, Davies, and Slater 2009). This is also the consensus of research from countries in South Asia (Pandey, Goyal, and Sundararaman 2008a and Kingdon and Teal 2010, for India; Aslam and Kingdon 2011, for Pakistan; Aturupane, Glewwe, and Wisnieski 2013, for Sri Lanka). Yet policy makers have tended to simply use résumé qualifications as a basis for teacher recruitment and salaries.

Among the characteristics of teachers that seem to matter, gender is one of the most critical for student enrollment and learning. Teacher gender and ethnicity have been found to be significant for learning outcomes (Rawal and Kingdon 2010, for India; Dee 2005, for the United States) in that students taught by a teacher of the same gender fare better than those taught by one of the opposite gender. Warwick and Jatoi (1994) found that in Pakistan, teacher gender had much more influence on math outcomes than the student's own gender. Aslam and Kingdon (2011) reported that female students in Pakistan benefit more from being taught by female teachers. They offer a variety of explanations, such as entrenched stereotypes that influence the process through which knowledge is disseminated in the classroom. They also propose a "role models" explanation: students of the same gender as teachers may perform better because they view them as role models. This hypothesis is especially convincing for Pakistan given cultural norms that restrict the mobility of females after adolescence.

Since South Asia studies echo the international finding that résumé characteristics of teachers are not good predictors of student learning, the crucial question from a policy perspective is: What about the teacher *does* matter for student learning? Why is it that teachers with more education, training, and experience are not more effective?

There are two possible explanations. One is that teacher training, both preservice and in-service, does not build the knowledge and skills a teacher needs to be effective. The second is that teachers are not motivated to be actively engaged in helping their students learn. The evidence that follows lends some validity to both hypotheses, which are not mutually exclusive.

The Importance of Behavioral Skills

While social science has not made enough progress to accurately measure all types of personality or behavior traits, the more effective teachers are probably those who have superior pedagogical standards (teaching style), good communication, empathy, and interpersonal skills and who set high standards, have the ability to elicit student cooperation, and display concern for student learning (see chapter 6, Inside the Classroom). A study by Aslam and Kingdon (2011) found evidence that the teacher's chosen teaching process and working style—such as lesson planning and interactive teaching—matter substantially for student learning in Pakistan. Thus, current criteria for recruitment and remuneration in South Asia are too narrow to be effective in identifying and rewarding the most effective teachers.

The Importance of Teacher Competence

Although teacher skills, competence, ability to teach, and content and subject knowledge are believed to matter more to student learning than their experience, there is not much data on these less tangible measures of teacher quality. The tacit assumption has been that content knowledge and skills are ensured if teachers complete a minimum threshold of academic qualifications, which makes them "good" teachers. This view is now being questioned.

A teacher's subject-specific achievement has been shown to increase pupil achievement significantly (Park and Hannum 2001). Metzler and Woessmann (2012) showed that a 1 standard deviation increase in teacher achievement increases student achievement by 10 percent of a standard deviation. This highlights how critical it is for a teacher to master a subject—something better measured by testing than by mere reliance on degree completion.

Aslam and Kingdon (2011) found that in Pakistan, students learn more from government teachers with higher scores in achievement tests. While there is anecdotal evidence that many teachers in South Asia barely know more than their students, only recently have data been generated to quantify the extent of the problem.

A survey in Bangladesh (FMRP 2006) tested more than 800 teachers in 150 government primary schools (GPS) and registered nongovernment primary schools (RNGPS). The test consisted of 14 questions (7 math, 3 Bangla, and 4 nonverbal reasoning). Teachers averaged only about 53 percent correct answers—"surprising given the relatively straightforward nature of the questions" (FMRP 2006, 107). GPS teachers performed somewhat better, and the highest-scoring teachers gave correct answers to 71 percent of questions compared to the abysmal 29 percent scored by the worst performers. Less experienced GPS teachers who are likely to have obtained their qualifications more recently were found to perform somewhat better than their more experienced colleagues. The survey also assessed teacher knowledge on the four terminal competencies students are expected to acquire by the end of grade 5. Worryingly, only 4 percent of GPS teachers and 1 percent of RNGPS Bangla teachers could list all four competencies. Math teachers fared even worse: only 1 percent was aware of all five terminal math competencies.

In India and Pakistan, SchoolTELLS surveys measured (a) teacher competence in relation to curriculum knowledge, (b) teacher ability to spot common mistakes by children, and (c) teacher proficiency in explaining concepts in math and language. Identical in many respects, these surveys tested the extent to which teachers in rural India and Pakistan were capable of teaching primary school curricula (see box 5.2 for sample questions). Using SchoolTELLS data, Kingdon and Banerji (2009) found that in rural India at the grade 5 level of difficulty only 28 percent of the teachers could solve an area problem and only 25 percent could work out a percentage (table 5.1). About 60 percent of the teachers made spelling mistakes in their two-sentence summaries of a section from the textbook. As many as 80 percent admitted to having difficulty in responding to student math queries. About 66 percent of Pakistani teachers made similar reports.

Table 5.2 presents the striking results of further analysis of teacher competency data from SchoolTELLS-India. Of particular concern in both Bihar and Uttar Pradesh, two of the most educationally and economically disadvantaged states, is the limited teaching ability of math teachers (Banerji and Kingdon 2010). The best-scoring of the regular teachers scored only 55 percent in Bihar and 51 percent in Uttar Pradesh on a test based on the primary math curriculum they are supposed to teach, in which the authors tested not only teacher content knowledge but also their ability to explain topics in simple terms and spot mistakes in written student work.[1]

Box 5.2 Questions That Test Teacher Knowledge

Percentage

A class has 55 children. Of these, 32 children have books. What percentage of children do not have books?

Sums involving area

To plant a litchi tree you need 25 square meters. Ramesh has a field that is 80 meters long and 70 meters wide. What is the maximum number of trees that he can plant in his field?

Such questions are found in grade 5 textbooks in schools in Uttar Pradesh and Bihar state in India.

Table 5.1 Teacher Content Knowledge of Grades 4 and 5 Math Material, India

	Bihar		*Uttar Pradesh*		*Both states*	
	Area	*Percent*	*Area*	*Percent*	*Area*	*Percent*
Teacher performance	*Sum*	*Sum*	*Sum*	*Sum*	*Sum*	*Sum*
Not attempted or incomplete	56.5	60.9	61.4	63.2	59.0	62.0
Wrong steps, wrong answer	3.7	7.2	4.6	5.7	4.2	6.5
Correct steps, wrong answer	4.0	4.3	3.8	4.6	3.9	4.5
Correct answer only, no steps	3.4	1.2	7.5	2.1	5.4	1.7
Solved correctly	32.6	26.4	22.7	24.5	28.4	25.3

Source: Banerji and Kingdon 2010.

Table 5.2 Teacher Language and Math Scores, by State and Teacher Type, India, 2008

	Bihar				*Uttar Pradesh*			
	Regular	*Para 05*[a]	*Para 06*[a]	*Private*	*Regular*	*Para*	*Private*	*All*
Math score (total)[b]	54.8	49.2	40.3	48.6	51.3	44.4	40.2	47.2
Knowledge	14.5	10.6	7.3	10.6	10.8	8.2	5.1	9.7
Explain	13.2	12.1	9.5	12.1	12.9	10.0	8.6	11.2
Spot mistake	26.8	26.5	23.6	25.8	27.6	26.2	26.7	26.2
Language score (total)[b]	64.1	62.3	57.9	65.2	74.0	68.3	62.5	64.9
Knowledge	20.3	19.7	17.6	18.7	22.6	21.3	19.0	20.1
Explain	19.6	18.9	16.7	19.4	22.5	20.1	18.9	19.4
Spot mistake	23.5	23.2	22.4	25.3	27.6	26.3	24.9	24.7

Sources: SchoolTELLS; Banerji and Kingdon 2010.
Note: Para-teachers are called "contract teachers."
a. Para05 and Para06 denote the years, 2005 and 2006, in which the teacher became a contract teacher.
b. The maximum total math and total language scores are 100 each. Each of the three components is given equal weight (one-third) in calculating the total competency mark for a teacher.

Table 5.3 Teacher Scores in Language and Math, by Teacher Type, Punjab, Pakistan, 2011

	Pakistan, Punjab Province		
	Government	*Private*	*All*
Language Score (total)[a]	**69.5**	**70.9**	**69.5**
Knowledge	23.5	24.3	23.6
Spot mistake	20.8	21.3	21.0
Ability to explain	25.2	25.3	24.9
Math Score (total)[a]	**63.9**	**77.8**	**73.9**
Knowledge	21.7	28.1	22.6
Spot mistake	22.2	24.8	22.7
Ability to explain	20.0	24.9	28.6

Source: Data from SchoolTELLS (Pakistan).
a. The maximum total math and language scores are each 100. Each component of each subject has been given equal weight (one-third) in calculating the total competency score.

When the total score in ability to teach math (out of 100) is broken up into its three constituent parts (scored at 33.3 each), the picture becomes clearer. In both language and math, teachers are more capable of spotting student mistakes but have less content knowledge (obtaining on average 9.7 out of 33.3 in math) and are also less able to explain content to students (11.2 out of 33.3).

SchoolTELLS data from Pakistan (table 5.3) tell a similar story. Even in the most prosperous province, Punjab, teachers in rural areas perform relatively poorly in both math and language.

Low teacher competencies translate into even worse scores for students, underlining the importance of not only knowing a subject but also of being able to satisfactorily transmit it. In the SchoolTELLS-Pakistan data, many of the same questions were posed to both students and teachers (see table 5.4). For example, 82 percent of the teachers could explain long division correctly but only

Table 5.4 Competencies of Teachers and Students on Identical Tests, Pakistan, 2011

Competency	*Getting answer*	*Student (%)*	*Teacher(%)*
Math			
Division (927 ÷ 9)	Completely right	34	82
	Completely wrong	46	13
Complex multiplication	Completely right	5	36
	Completely wrong	81	32
Fractions and problem solving	Completely right	6	56
	Completely wrong	83	24
Language			
Definitions	Completely right	11	49
	Completely wrong	51	17
Summarizing paragraph	Completely right	8	54
	Completely wrong	81	21
Explaining difficult words	Completely right	11	64
	Completely wrong	58	7

Source: Data from SchoolTELLS-Pakistan.

34 percent of the students could answer the question accurately. Similarly, for language, while 64 percent of the teachers could explain the meanings of difficult words, only 11 percent of the children could. In a significant proportion of cases, teachers themselves are not competent to teach the curriculum. For example, only 36 percent of the teachers were able to correctly explain a question relating to two-digit addition.

Several factors may explain low teacher skills and competence: the poor quality of their own education, inadequate preservice training that does not fill skill gaps before teachers are deployed, in-service training that fails to build missing skills, low teacher salaries that attract only those near the bottom of the ability distribution, and corruption in appointments so that the most meritorious are not selected if they cannot pay the required bribes. There is supportive evidence for these reasons in South Asia. For example, preservice training courses tend to be theoretical rather than practical and skill based. There is also evidence that applicants commonly pay Rs 100,000 to Rs 200,000 to be selected to teach in India's aided schools (Tilak 2008).

Ensuring Merit-Based Recruitment

Until recently, there was little formal testing of teachers for merit-based hiring in the region; teachers were recruited based purely on minimum qualifications and training rules. The exception was Nepal, where teachers underwent rigorous testing and interviews. Recently, other countries have also experimented with merit-based recruitment (box 5.3). For example, 13,000 new teachers were recently hired in Sindh province in Pakistan based on a test administered by a third party. In 2005, Bangladesh set up a Teachers Registration and Certification Authority to reduce rent-seeking and collusion in the hiring of secondary school teachers. India has introduced the Teacher Eligibility Test (TET) for merit-based appointments.

Box 5.3 Preventing Patronage-Based Recruitment: Examples from Bangladesh and Sindh, Pakistan

In Bangladesh, secondary school teachers from recognized nongovernment schools used to be recruited by School Management Committees (SMCs). Lack of monitoring capacity and inadequate parental and community participation in the SMCs led to frequent violation of hiring practices. Because schools need funds for running costs, poor but well-qualified applicants were often overlooked in favor of candidates who could contribute to the school financially. Schools were also pressured to appoint relatives of SMC members or those in powerful positions within the community. To overcome this problem, a nongovernment Teacher Registration and Certification Authority (NTRCA) was established in 2005. It uses a standardized and transparent procedure to accredit potential teachers. To be eligible for a teaching position, candidates must be registered as qualified under NTRCA.

Recruitment of teachers in Sindh has historically been patronage based, often without due consideration of whether the new hire was appropriately qualified or whether the school where the new hire was placed had a genuine need. In addition, academic and professional qualifications used to screen and select candidates are generally viewed in the country as a poor signal of candidate knowledge and ability in part because of concerns about the quality and integrity of the institutions that confer diplomas and certificates. This state of affairs potentially compromises teacher quality at entry and the alignment of teacher interest and efforts with the desired duties and responsibilities.

The new recruitment policy under the Sindh Education Sector Project delineated merit-based, objective, transparent, and standardized criteria for recruiting new teachers and set school-specific, three-year contracts. Under the new policy, (a) the candidate is required to pass a standardized, written knowledge test designed and administered by an independent testing agency; (b) female candidates are given additional marks in the objective scoring of the candidates; (c) the candidate is not subject to a selection interview (reducing the possibility for bias by eliminating discretion); (d) candidates are ranked using a composite score that sums up the test score and points for other attributes, and jobs are offered first to the top-ranked candidate and then moving down the list; (e) qualifying candidates are to be placed at a school under a nontransferable, school-specific contract, which implies that the teacher cannot be transferred between schools; and (f) to the extent possible, a qualifying candidate for primary-school teaching service is placed locally (i.e., within the union council where the candidate resides).

Two rounds of recruitment and placement of about 13,000 teachers have been completed under SERP. In the second round, needs-based placement was also introduced: a candidate qualified for primary-school teaching would only be hired if an understaffed school was identified (the school has a pupil-teacher ratio [PTR] higher than the PTR floor) in the candidate's union council of residence. Descriptive evidence from a school sample survey conducted by a third-party firm indicates that the teachers recruited in Round 1 were less likely to be absent than older co-teachers in the same schools.

However, most countries still do not have requirements for specialist teachers or teachers with the knowledge needed to impart quality learning. Even where tests have been introduced, there are problems. For example, less than 10 percent of teachers pass India's TET; in Gujarat state in 2012, only 3.2 percent passed[2] (*Newsknol* June 23, 2012), and in the Central TET for India, taken by nearly 800,000 aspiring teachers, only 7 percent passed (*Times of India* March 11, 2012). The scale of India's teacher competence problem is clear.

Teacher Training

Preparing teachers for the challenges of a changing world involves equipping them with subject-specific expertise, effective teaching practices, an understanding of technology, and the ability to work collaboratively with other teachers, parents, and community members (UNESCO 2004). How effective training is, however, depends on the quality of both the candidates and the training program. Trainees in preservice training courses are often believed to be from the lower part of the ability distribution. Those who fail admission into desired professional degree courses or cannot afford them are believed to turn to teaching. As for quality, preservice training falls short in many South Asian countries and there are virtually no opportunities for practice teaching before acquiring teaching degrees. For instance, in Pakistan, until recently and often still, it used to take only a year (with frequent holidays) to qualify to teach primary school. Similarly, in Bangladesh, primary school teachers were required only to have completed grade 10 or 12 and the one-year certificate in education (C-in-Ed). In Nepal, a one-year teacher preparation course is required in addition to the minimum academic qualification of a higher secondary degree to teach in primary school or a master's in education to teach in secondary school.

When available, in-service training is also very brief, sometimes as short as seven days in Pakistan. Since it is usually not considered mandatory and participation in training does not affect promotion or career development, teachers do not value it. Often the same teachers are repeatedly sent for training and others do not receive any for years. In any case, both pre- and in-service training courses are considered to be of poor quality.

While many South Asian countries have teacher training institutions and systems, ranging from purpose-built institutes and colleges to university departments offering education diplomas and degrees, most of these are of poor quality, understaffed, or staffed with people who do not have the necessary skills. An additional problem for most South Asian countries is the lack of coordination in developing a coherent teacher training program that meets minimum standards for the country as a whole. Programs have arisen piecemeal, leading to overlaps, duplication, and gaps.

The World Bank (2012) argued that throughout the world, teacher training programs too often stifle creativity, rely on memorization of abstract theories, and seldom model in their own programs valuable teacher characteristics. In South Asia, curricula are often outdated and delivered through lectures, an approach that teachers replicate in their own classrooms. Even when the teacher training curricula are not outdated, the trainers lack innovation and fail to pass on key messages. Universal standards and competencies are not at the core of the process. Ultimately, this translates into poor classroom practices (see chapter 6).

New teachers in the region receive very little on-the-job support. This is in stark contrast to such well-performing systems as Shanghai's (box 5.4). According to a United States Agency for International Development (USAID) assessment of teacher training in Pakistan, there is hardly any guidance of novice teachers and "practical teaching" is not considered important (USAID nd). Moreover, supervisors and others with guidance roles are often appointed from among a cadre of teachers who have little if any management training or experience. Sometimes, supervisory duties are assigned along with other work, leading to overburdening and inefficiencies. Almost without exception across the region, although head teachers are meant to monitor and supervise school teachers, they have virtually no power to recruit, transfer, hire, or fire—decisions that for regular government school teachers are centralized, provincially or at the district rather than the school level.

To summarize, evidence from India, Pakistan, and Bangladesh demonstrates that teachers do not know their subject matter well, especially in math. Since teacher competence is related to student learning, improving their subject knowledge is clearly crucial. Preservice training needs to equip them with dynamic knowledge and approaches to teaching, and recruitment policies need to be directed to individuals with knowledge and teaching skills. Where there

Box 5.4 Teacher Development through Peer Support in Shanghai, China

In Shanghai, the quality of teaching rests upon government policies aimed to attract the best into teaching, policies that match teacher skills to student needs and mentoring of new teachers. The government attracts the best into the profession through targeted scholarship programs, with an assignment system that appoints teachers and principals to those schools where they are most needed. This is combined with a school accountability mechanism focusing on low-performing schools. Professional communities play an important role in supporting teachers to improve instruction, monitoring teaching and learning, and motivating teachers to perform well. Teaching Study Groups bring together teachers in the same subject and level so that they can jointly plan their lessons. Teacher workloads are structured so that teachers can regularly observe their peers during actual lessons. Novice teachers are supported by master teachers during their first year of classroom experience, and can observe more seasoned instructors to learn from them through apprenticeships. The underlying theory of action in Shanghai is that no individual teacher is perfect, but that capable teachers can help each other improve. In this way, the government creates the mechanisms for teachers to support their peers and hold them accountable, but rarely intervenes directly.

Source: World Bank 2012.

are gaps in skills and content knowledge, carefully designed in-service training is necessary.

Many South Asian governments are introducing new teacher standards and competencies, lengthening preservice training, and providing continuing teacher support (box 5.5). How successful those reforms will be in improving teachers' knowledge and teaching methods is not yet known.

Box 5.5 Reforms in Teacher Training and Professional Development in Bangladesh, Pakistan, Nepal, and Sri Lanka

In Bangladesh, primary school teachers were hired after having completed grade 10 for female teachers or grade 12 for males. Once recruited, they were required to take one year of training to get a certificate in education (C-in-Ed). Eighty percent of teachers met the criteria. In 2011, the government decided to better prepare teachers by introducing a new diploma in education to replace the C-in-Ed that will require 18 months of training. Once piloted, it will be rolled out in all primary teacher training institutions. Orientation for new teachers will also be introduced, and subcluster training and teacher training networks will be strengthened to provide peer support.

Punjab, Pakistan, now has a continuous professional development program that includes mentoring and on-site support for teachers. Initially implemented in 12 of Punjab's 36 districts, it was later expanded to 24. On-site advisory support to teachers operates through a network of field-based district teacher educators and teacher educators located in high schools and teacher education colleges. It is a new and promising conduit for customizing teacher support and potentially improving teaching. Also, the Provincial Institute of Teacher Education has been regenerated and district and grassroots training structures created, expanding the number of trainings held and teachers trained.

Similarly, in Sindh, Pakistan, a comprehensive teacher education development policy was designed as part of reforms launched in 2007–08. It envisions a coherent system for preservice and systematic in-service training to be implemented over several years. The first steps are (a) adoption of universal standards and competencies to be used for appointment, professional development, and certification and (b) design of a new continuous professional development program based on the new standards; and (c) introduction of an accreditation and quality assurance system for training providers.

Nepal has recently raised the minimum qualification of teachers for basic education from a school leaving certificate (SLC) degree to a grade 12 degree and has made preservice training and a teaching license mandatory. Teachers with lower qualifications can teach only grades 1–3; they must upgrade their qualifications within five years or retire. Every five years teachers must take a refresher course.

Sri Lanka raised the bar early for teacher training. Potential teachers must be university graduates or complete a three-year preservice education program and be certified. Sri Lanka is also advanced in having on-site academic support in schools. Nevertheless, even there the policies for teacher professional development require constant reevaluation.

The Role of Remuneration in Motivating Teachers

Incentives affect teacher attitudes and effectiveness. The structure of teacher pay—how teaching is rewarded—can powerfully affect teacher effort and student outcomes. This is particularly important in South Asia, where teacher salaries and benefits account for a very significant proportion of government education budgets, often crowding out funding for other areas of the system (see chapter 7). Ensuring effective use of teachers is therefore essential for enhancing the cost-effectiveness of spending on education (Pritchett and Filmer 1997).

This section will first examine whether teaching is economically attractive, and then whether reforms modifying the pay structure could improve teacher effectiveness. Teacher salaries also affect retention, especially of able and motivated individuals who might have opportunities for other employment.

Salary and Nonpecuniary Job Factors

The following inquires how well teachers in a given country are paid relative to the "average" person and to individuals in other occupations, and whether their salaries have deteriorated over time in real terms.

Teacher Salaries and Per Capita Income

One way to benchmark teacher wages is to compute the ratio of teacher salaries as a proportion of a country's per capita gross domestic product (GDP or income) and compare it within the region and with countries at different levels of development. This ratio tells us how affluent the teacher is with respect to the average person in the country. It is also a measure of the economic and social distance between teacher and taught—a vast economic distance can be a barrier to effective teaching and learning. The ratios are disaggregated by state, province, and division.

Tables 5.5 and 5.6 show the ratio of teacher salary to per capita incomes for Bangladesh and Pakistan. There is evidence of heterogeneity in teacher salaries as a multiple of per capita incomes, both between countries and between provinces within countries. The ratio is higher, for instance, in Pakistan (5.2 to 1) and low in Bangladesh (2 to1). These compare with ratios of 3 to 1 for Asian countries generally and 2 to 1 for Organisation for Economic Co-operation and Development countries (Mingat 2002). Within countries, too, there is variation. For instance, in 2008 the national ratio in India was 4.2 to 1 (taking regular and contract teachers together), but state ratios ranged between 2.0 to 1 and 11.7 to 1. As might be expected, the ratio tends to be higher in poorer states where per capita incomes are lower (annex 5A). Ratios can also change dramatically over time: for example, after implementation of the Sixth Pay Commission's recommendations in India in 2009, regular state teacher salaries roughly doubled immediately.

Table 5.5 Ratio of Teacher Salary to Per Capita Income (Taka), by Division, Bangladesh

Division	1999–2000 per capita GDP at constant (1995–96) prices (Tk) (a)	Inflated 1999–2000 per capita GDP to 2002 prices[a] (Tk) (b)	Annual teacher salaries in 2002[b] (Tk) (c)	Teacher salary as multiple of per capita GDP in 2002 (d)
Barisal	13,343	17,381	40,745	2.3
Chittagong	15,715	20,470	39,001	1.9
Dhaka	19,308	25,151	38,672	1.5
Khulna	15,464	20,143	39,665	2.0
Rajshahi	13,091	17,052	43,437	2.5
Sylhet	12,591	16,401	39,460	2.4
Bangladesh	15,791	20,569	40,163	2.0

Source: Statistical Yearbook of Bangladesh 2005.
Note: GDP = gross domestic product.
a. Column (b) shows column (a) figures inflated to 2002 prices using the Consumer Price Index (General), Statistical Yearbook of Bangladesh (2008). Teachers were identified from the 2002 Bangladesh Labour Force Survey (LFS 2002) using the 3-digit occupation codes.
b. The reported salaries are for all teachers at all levels in government and private school jobs.

Table 5.6 Ratio of Teacher Salary to Per Capita Income, by Province, Pakistan

Province	Average monthly household income (2004–05), (PRe)/ month (a)	Average household size (1998 census)[a] (b)	Estimated monthly per capita income (PRe) (c)	Annual per capita income (d)	Annual teacher salaries in 2008[b] (PRe) (e)	Annual per capita income in 2008 prices[c] (PRe) (f)	Teacher salary as multiple of per capita income in 2008 (g)
Punjab	9,488	7.0	1,355	16,265	115,172	22,283	5.2
Sindh	10,413	6.1	1,707	20,485	128,624	28,064	4.6
NWFP	9,395	8.0	1,174	14,093	106,572	19307	5.5
Balochistan	8,849	6.8	1,301	15,616	127,070	21,394	5.9
Pakistan	9,685	6.9	1,404	16,844	119,480	23,076	5.2

Source: Pakistan Statistical Yearbook 2007.
Note: Teachers were identified using the occupation codes in Pakistan Labour Force Survey (2008). NWFP = North-West Frontier Province.
a. Pakistan Statistical Yearbook (2007).
b. The reported salaries are for all teachers in government and private school jobs teaching at all levels.
c. Column (f) shows column (d) figures inflated to 2008 prices using the Wholesale Price Index reported in Pakistan Statistical Yearbook (2007).

Teacher Salaries and Salaries in Other Occupations

Teachers in some countries of South Asia are on average substantially more affluent than the average person in that state or country (table 5.7). In Bangladesh, the difference is similar to what is observed in the rest of the world but it is significantly higher in India and Pakistan. It is sometimes argued that a large social distance between teacher and taught in South Asia may partly explain

Table 5.7 Teacher Pay Relative to Other Occupations, India

	1998/99			
	Monthly salary (in 2005 PPP US$)		Ratio of teacher salary/salary in other occupation	
Occupation	*Mean*	*Median*	*Mean*	*Median*
Teachers	535.7	426.6	1.0	1.0
Legislators	485.1	387.3	1.1	1.1
Professionals	503.9	373.7	1.1	1.1
Associate professionals	505.7	396.1	1.1	1.1
Clerks	484.0	423.0	1.1	1.0
Service workers/shops	264.9	183.9	2.0	2.3
Skilled agriculture	157.7	131.8	3.4	3.2
Crafts	215.1	170.6	2.5	2.5
Plant/machine operators	273.3	213.8	2.0	2.0
Elementary occupations	147.6	132.1	3.6	3.2
All nonteachers	213.0	152.8	2.5	2.8

Source: Calculations from National Sample Survey Employment Unemployment Schedule 2009/10.
Note: Teachers include pre-primary, primary, and secondary teachers. Persons identified as teachers were separately coded as "Teachers" and were excluded from "Professionals" and "Associate professionals" categories to prevent double counting. Salary estimates are for all individuals 18 years of age and older, working as wage/salaried workers and reporting higher secondary education or above. PPP = purchasing power parity.

a high teacher absentee rate if well-paid teachers feel it "beneath them" to teach poor children, or if it causes them to not take the education of these children seriously. As discussed in chapter 10, such social distance also represents highly unequal relations between teachers and villagers and may explain, at least in part, why community participation in monitoring education has apparently not been effective: "Citizens face substantial constraints in participating to improve the public education system, even when they care about education and are willing to do something to improve it" (Banerjee et al. 2010).

Tables 5.8 and 5.9 use data from Labour Force Surveys (LFSs) for Pakistan and Sri Lanka to look at the issue of relative teacher pay.[3] Teachers were identified using 2- or 3-digit occupation codes. It was not possible to differentiate teachers in primary, secondary, and higher education or those teaching in public and private schools or colleges, although salaries in public schools are far higher than in private schools. All persons who identify as teachers have been included even if they teach in early childhood care centers, which pay only a small monthly honorarium. The data are rendered comparable by restricting the sample to wage earners ages 18 years and above with at least 10 years of schooling. The availability of two years of data in each country permits temporal analysis. Finally, rendering monthly salaries in U.S. dollars and deflating them to 2005 purchasing power parity allows for quick comparison of how teachers fare across South Asia. The overriding conclusion is that teachers in the region are not worse off monetarily than workers in other occupations and, contrary to popular perception, their relative pay has not deteriorated in recent years.

Table 5.8 Teacher Pay Relative to Other Occupations, Pakistan, 2005

	2000		2008	
Pakistan	*Mean monthly salary (US$)*	*Ratio of teacher salary to other salaries*	*Mean monthly salary (in 2005 PPP US$)*	*Ratio of teacher salary to other salaries*
Teachers	230	—	303	—
Legislators	351	0.7	384	0.8
Professionals	314	0.7	360	0.8
Associate professionals	253	0.9	303	1.0
Clerks	239	1.0	300	1.0
Service workers/shops	221	1.0	239	1.3
Skilled agriculture	170	1.4	234	1.3
Crafts	215	1.1	242	1.3
Plant/machine operators	251	0.9	227	1.3
Elementary	172	1.3	179	1.7
All nonteachers (weighted average)	257	0.9	277	1.1

Source: Data from Pakistan Labour Force Survey 2000 and 2008.
Note: Teachers were identified using occupation codes. Although they are often classified within the broader "Professionals" and "Associate Professionals" categories in survey data, 2- and 3-digit occupation codes within these categories help identify teachers, who were separately coded as "Teachers" by generating a new occupation code and excluding them from "Professionals" and "Associate Professionals" to prevent double counting. Salary estimates are for all individuals ages 18 years or above working as wage earners and reporting at least 10 years of schooling. Total income (deflated to 2005 purchasing power parity [PPP} dollars) reportedly earned from all jobs in the past month is used for the salary estimate. — = not available.

Table 5.9 Teacher Pay Relative to Other Occupations, Sri Lanka, 2005

	2000		2008	
Sri Lanka	*Mean monthly salary (US$)*	*Ratio of teacher salary to other salaries*	*Mean monthly salary, 2005 (US$ PPP)*	*Ratio of teacher salary to other salaries*
Teachers	242	—	280	—
Legislators	257	0.9	249	1.1
Professionals	258	0.9	281	1.0
Associate professionals	238	1.0	250	1.1
Clerks	219	1.1	212	1.3
Service workers/shops	211	1.1	187	1.5
Skilled agriculture	121	2.0	117	2.4
Crafts	163	1.5	156	1.8
Plant/machine operators	180	1.3	178	1.6
Elementary	158	1.5	133	2.0
Armed forces	296	0.8	315	0.9
Other	151	1.6	170	1.6
All nonteachers (weighted average)	216	1.1	191	1.5

Source: Data from the Sri Lanka Labour Force Survey 2000 and 2008.
Note: See note under table 5.8. — = not available; PPP = purchasing power parity.

Nonpecuniary benefits, such as working conditions, help make teaching a desirable occupation. One reason why women in particular seem to prefer teaching is that they can achieve a more attractive work-life balance by taking advantage of school holidays and the flexibility in working hours that teaching allows—teachers in South Asia work significantly fewer hours than nonteachers (table 5.10).

Given the fewer hours of work, a more stringent salary comparison would look at hourly pay; doing so confirms the relatively advantageous position of teachers (table 5.11).

Table 5.10 Hours Worked Per Month by Teachers and Nonteachers

Hours worked	*Teachers (a)*	*Nonteachers (b)*	*Gap (c) = (a)–(b)*
2000			
Bangladesh[a]	164	194	−30***
India	219	219	0
Nepal	163	195	−32***
Pakistan	149	190	−41***
Sri Lanka	115	194	−79***
2008			
Bangladesh[a]	193	220	−27***
India	241	234	7***
Nepal	175	205	−30***
Pakistan	163	210	−47***
Sri Lanka	112	198	−86***

Source: Labour Force Surveys and National Sample Survey data (India) for a sample of wage earners ages 18 years or over with at least 10 years of education.
Note: Hours worked per month in *main* reported occupation.
a. Estimates for Bangladesh are for 2002 and 2005.
Significance level: *** = 1 percent.

Table 5.11 Hourly Salary for Teachers and Nonteachers

	2000				*2008*			
Country	*Hourly teacher (T) salary (a)*	*Hourly nonteacher (NT) Salary (b)*	*T-NT Gap (c)*	*t-test (d) = (a)–(b)*	*Hourly T salary (e)*	*Hourly NT salary (f)*	*T-NT gap (%) (g)*	*t-test (h) = (e)–(f)*
Bangladesh[a] (*taka*)	22.7	17.8	21.6	8.6***	26.0	20.1	22.7	5.9***
India (*Indian rupees*)	22.5	18.6	17.3	3.9***	38.7	33.2	14.2	5.5***
Nepal (*Nepalese rupees*)	17.5	18.8	−7.4	1.3*	41.1	36.8	10.5	4.3**
Pakistan (*Pakistani rupees*)	27.6	22.2	19.6	5.4***	67.0	48.2	28.0	18.8***
Sri Lanka (*Sri Lankan rupees*)	46.8	29.1	37.8	17.7***	139.1	63.6	54.3	75.5***

Source: Labour Force and National Sample Surveys (India) on a sample of wage earners ages 18 years or above and with at least 10 years of education.
Note: Hours worked per month and salary in *main* reported occupation (except in Bangladesh, where total salary in all jobs has been used). Hourly salary = monthly salary/hours worked per month.
a. Estimates for Bangladesh are for 2002 and 2005.
Significance level: * = 10 percent, ** = 5 percent, *** = 1 percent.

An even more nuanced comparison of salaries is achieved by estimating an ordinary least squares (OLS) earnings function and including a "teacher" dummy variable while controlling for gender, years of education and work experience, and other individual characteristics. The coefficient on the teacher dummy variable measures the salary premium earned or deficit borne by teachers. The sample includes only wage workers ages at least 18 years with at least 10 years of schooling. The dependent variable is hourly earnings (monthly earnings divided by hours worked per month).[4] Table 5.12 reports the results.

In 2008, teachers in Sri Lanka earned more than 50 percent more than nonteachers, in Pakistan 24 percent more, and in Bangladesh 6 percent more. The wage differential seems to have increased since 2000. There also seems to be a wage premium for male relative to female teachers. However, in Nepal, there is no longer any statistically significant wage difference between teachers and nonteachers, and in India, a positive premium observed in 2000 had become nonsignificant by 2008. Given the evidence showing that on average teachers in India earn more than nonteachers, this most likely reflects an older teaching force with more years of experience than the nonteaching wage earners in the sample.

What do these findings imply for teacher quality? Whatever the past salary levels of teachers were, the fact that in much of South Asia they are now paid as much or more than nonteachers with similar credentials augurs well for attracting good-quality teachers.

Are Teachers in South Asia Worse Off in Real Terms in Recent Years?

The World Bank (2005) suggested that teacher salaries in Sri Lanka in the early 2000s had declined from their 1978 values. In South Asian countries, this might harm the quality of schooling by attracting less-qualified entrants, reduce the prestige of the teaching profession, and negatively impact the morale of teachers in service. Table 5.12 shows instead that in Bangladesh, Pakistan, and Sri Lanka, teacher salary premiums have been rising. Another way of looking at this is to compute the real value of past teacher salaries and the corresponding change in salaries in real terms over that time period, as is done for table 5.13.

Contrary to common perception, on average for five South Asian countries, between 2000 and 2008 teacher salaries rose by about 40 percent, compared to 20 percent for nonteachers. In Nepal, salaries rose in real terms by as much as 61 percent. In India, the Sixth Pay Commission's recommendations led to teacher salaries about doubling in 2009 (the raise was retroactive to 2006). Some improvements in teacher pay are probably the result of government policies pushing up civil service pay scales. Even if real teacher salaries had previously been declining, in the last decade they have improved throughout South Asia.

Table 5.12 OLS Estimates of Earnings Functions (Pooled Wage Regressions), South Asia

Log hourly earnings	*Bangladesh*		*India*		*Nepal*		*Pakistan*		*Sri Lanka*	
(local currency)	*2002*	*2005*	*2000*	*2008*	*2000*	*2008*	*2000*	*2008*	*2000*	*2008*
Teacher	0.038	0.064	0.116	−0.048	−0.077	−0.012	0.144	0.218	0.367	0.509
	(1.78)*	(2.82)***	(7.35)***	(−1.09)	(−2.55)**	(−0.40)	(5.22)***	(10.50)***	(6.71)***	(10.36)***
Experience	0.060	0.062	0.057	0.063	0.034	0.038	0.044	0.045	0.050	0.041
	(19.96)***	(16.70)***	(32.10)***	(4.80)***	(7.41)***	(9.53)***	(11.37)***	(16.59)***	(9.08)***	(8.10)***
Exp2*100	−0.056	−0.062	−0.082	−0.091	−0.048	−0.040	−0.072	−0.067	−0.074	−0.065
	(−15.90)***	(−13.44)***	(−20.25)***	(−2.74)**	(−4.56)***	(−4.32)***	(−7.00)***	(−10.29)***	(−6.30)***	(−5.92)***
Male	0.044	0.082	0.088	0.165	0.046	0.137	0.034	0.206	0.036	0.176
	(1.99)**	(2.84)***	(5.72)***	(5.55)***	(1.54)	(4.95)***	(0.84)	(6.59)***	(1.04)	(6.27)***
Years of education	—	—	0.066	0.140	0.100	0.120	0.076	0.084	0.070	0.112
			(25.48)***	(23.22)***	(19.95)***	(22.76)***	(16.31)***	(26.31)***	(10.57)***	(14.38)***
N	8,202	7,519	25,709	27,971	2,242	3,059	2,348	7,547	3,918	7,819
R^2	0.22	0.24	0.19	0.38	0.26	0.27	0.19	0.24	0.11	0.10

Sources: Labour Force Surveys and National Sample Survey data (India).

Note: Earnings are reported deflated hourly earnings from an individual's main job (the one on which the person devoted most time in the survey reference period). They include both cash and in-kind payments from wages, tips, bonuses, etc. The earnings are deflated using a regional price deflator (see World Bank 2010). Robust t–statistics clustered at the population sampling unit (PSU) level are in parentheses. TEACHER is a dummy equaling 1 if the person reports being a teacher as primary occupation, 0 otherwise. EXPERIENCE is calculated as age-completed schooling-6 (except in Bangladesh, where it is proxied by age). All regressions have the following controls: state/province dummies, regional dummy, gender dummy, education (in years for all countries except Bangladesh where it is controlled for as a dummy equaling 1 if a person has completed 10 years of education or more), religion dummies (for all countries except Bangladesh and Pakistan), and caste dummies for India. All regressions are estimated on a sample of wage workers ages 18 years or more with at least 10 years of schooling. — = not available; N = number; OLS = ordinary least squares.

Significance level: * = 10 percent, ** = 5 percent, *** = 1 percent.

Table 5.13 Changes in Real Value of Teacher and Nonteacher Salaries, South Asia

Teachers	*Teacher salary, 2000 (a)*	*Teacher salary, 2008 (b)*	*CPI inflator (2008/2000) (c)*	*2000 salary, 2008 prices (d) = (a)*(c)*	*Change in real terms (e) = (b)–(d)*	*Change in real terms (%) (f)*
Bangladesh[a] (*takas*)	40,213	58,573	1.20	48,254	10,319	+21
India (*I. Rupees*)	60,470	111,946	1.57	94,938	17,008	+18
Nepal (*N. Rupees*)	34,300	86,890	1.57	53,851	33,039	+61
Pakistan (*P. Rupees*)	44,442	119,480	1.70	75,551	43,929	+58
Sri Lanka (*SL. Rupees*)	73,138	211,925	2.00	146,276	65,649	+45
Nonteachers	*Nonteacher salary, 2000 (a)*	*Nonteacher salary, 2008 (b)*	*CPI inflator (2008/2000) (c)*	*2000 salary, 2008 prices (d) = (a)*(c)*	*Change in real terms (e) = (b)–(d)*	*Change in real terms (%) (f)*
Bangladesh+ (*takas*)	37,306	50,859	1.20	44,767	6,092	+14
India (*I. Rupees*)	49,474	95,026	1.57	77,674	17,352	+22
Nepal (*N. Rupees*)	42,807	84,086	1.57	67,207	16,879	+25
Pakistan (*P. Rupees*)	48,025	109,332	1.70	81,643	27,689	+34
Sri Lanka (*SL. Rupees*)	63,370	144,766	2.00	126,740	18,026	+14

Source: Labour Force Surveys and National Sample Survey data (India), sample of wage earners ages 18 years or more with 10 years of education or more.

Note: CPI = consumer price index. All teachers (government and private, regular and contract) are included in the sample. Nepal CPI figures are from http://www.nationsonline.org/oneworld/Country-Stats/Nepal-statistics.htm, downloaded on May 17, 2011, and Sri Lanka figures from http://www.nationsonline.org/oneworld/Country-Stats/Sri-Lanka-statistics.htm, downloaded on May 17, 2011; CPI = Consumer Price Index.

a. Estimates for Bangladesh are for 2002 and 2005.

Uniform Pay Structure versus Performance-Related Pay and Career Promotion Schemes

Paying teachers well, it is hoped, will not only attract superior candidates but also raise teacher effort since well-paid teachers face a higher cost if they lose their jobs because they made too little effort. However, this only works when the threat of disciplinary action or dismissal is credible. In South Asia, private schools and community schools can dismiss nonperforming teachers, but government schools rarely do. For example, Muralidharan and Kremer (2008) found only one public school head teacher, of nearly 3,000, who reported dismissing a teacher for repeated absences. In private schools, on the other hand, of about 600 head teachers, 35 reported doing so. Shirking teachers in the private sector were thus about 175 times more likely to attract disciplinary action. Thus, while higher pay may raise teacher effort in private schools, it is much less likely to do so in government schools.

Proposals to link teacher pay to student performance have been discussed in many countries, and some have moved away from a uniform pay structure that rewards qualifications and experience (inputs) toward different models of performance-related pay (PRP), effectively basing elements of teacher pay on student outcomes. The evidence on the impact of PRP on student outcomes is mixed. For the United States and the United Kingdom, some studies have shown improvements in student achievement (Atkinson et al. 2004, 2009; Figlio and Kenny 2007) and others have not (Goodman and Turner 2010).

Experimental evidence from Israel (Lavy 2002) found positive effects, and a review of PRP in Latin American countries has shown that its effectiveness depends on how carefully incentives are designed and the program is implemented (Lopez-Acevedo 2004; Vegas and Umansky 2005; see box 5.6).

There is a dearth of data, and therefore evidence, on the impact of PRP on student outcomes in South Asia. Studies of Uttar Pradesh by Kingdon and

---

Box 5.6 Incentive Reforms in Mexico and Chile: Design Matters

In the 1990s as incentive for reform Mexico and Chile linked teacher compensation to student performance. Although both share the objective of raising education quality, the designs are different (Vegas and Umansky 2005).

The Mexican program grants individual teachers permanent promotions and thus higher compensation based on a number of factors—including their education and years of professional experience and their students' performance—that are evaluated using a point system. The total number of possible points is 100, of which 20 relate to student performance. Rewards are earned starting at 70 points. The purposes of the reform were to give teachers incentives to improve both their qualifications and their classroom effectiveness and to create opportunities for promotion without teachers having to move into administrative positions. Participation is voluntary but most have enrolled. The size of the bonus is substantial, ranging from 25 to 200 percent of the base wage.

The Chilean initiative is a school-level performance-based program that awards a bonus to teachers in schools that outperform other schools on a national student exam. Schools are divided into groups that serve students with similar demographics in similar settings. The bonus is awarded every two years. As much as 90 percent of it is divided between the teachers (the school director determines use of the remaining 10 percent), and the size of the incentive is 5–7 percent of annual salaries.

The reforms have several differences: (a) the Mexican initiative rewards individual teachers and the Chilean program all the teachers in a winning school; (b) the Mexican reform offers a permanent salary increase and the Chilean bonus is temporary; (c) the Chilean reform groups schools according to type of population served and the Mexican program does not distinguish between teachers serving different types of students; and (d) the incentive is much larger in Mexico.

Evaluation Results. Using data from a national assessment survey covering over 3,600 Mexican schools and about 50,000 students, Lopez-Acevedo (2004) found that enrollment in *Carrera Magisterial* positively impacts learning achievement, particularly in rural areas. Some preliminary evidence on the impact of the Chilean program also suggests that the program has had a cumulative positive impact on student performance in schools with relatively good chances of winning the award (Vegas and Umansky 2005).

The evidence thus supports the view that incentives can improve quality. However, an analysis of the data also show that results are sensitive to design features and that changes in design could make the programs more effective. Three points are worth taking into

box continues next page

Box 5.6 Incentive Reforms in Mexico and Chile: Design Matters *(continued)*

consideration: The larger the proportion of teachers and schools that are offered incentives, the greater the impact. For example, in Mexico, because of the weight of personal characteristics vs. student performance in the point system, a large proportion of good teachers are still not likely to be promoted. Also, in Mexico absolute rather than comparative test scores are used, which makes it much harder for teachers of poorer students to succeed; in Chile, 51 percent of schools that ranked poorly in their homogeneous group never got a bonus. Secondly, the reward should be large enough to make it worth trying to improve student performance. And finally, there is a question whether the incentive rewards sustained improvements. In Mexico, teachers who are awarded a promotion in a given year will receive higher pay for the rest of their careers, which reduces motivation to continuously improve thereafter.

Teal (2010) and Andhra Pradesh by Muralidharan and Sundararaman (2013) are exceptions. The former found that private schools relate pay to teacher performance as measured by student achievement and that student achievement is improved by increasing teacher salaries; Kingdom and Teal (2010) believe that this is because higher wages motivate enhanced teacher effort, rather than being a proxy for better-quality teachers, and thus better student outcomes. However, teacher salaries operate as effort-motivating devices only when there is a credible punishment for shirking.

The second study by Muralidharan and Sundararaman (2011, 2013) reports a learning improvement experiment conducted in 500 rural government schools in Andhra Pradesh state in India on a student population of 50,000 in grades 1–5. Four approaches were tried: two incentive schemes (an individual teacher bonus and a group teacher bonus) and two input schemes (provision of an additional contract teacher and of a block grant to the school). There was also a comparison group of 100 schools. Two years after the experiment began, all four schemes had improved learning but students in schools with performance incentives for teachers performed significantly better, by 0.28 standard deviation in math tests and 0.16 standard deviation in language tests. Incentivized schools also performed better in subjects for which there were no bonuses, suggesting positive spillover effects. Over the course of the first year, team-incentive and individual-incentive schools performed equally well but in the second year, the latter outperformed the former. The incentive schools also performed better than randomly chosen schools receiving additional schooling inputs of the same value. The study also found that combining incentives with training and improved inputs further increases teacher effectiveness (box 5.7).

The evidence from South Asia, although limited, thus suggests that linking teacher pay to student outcomes can make teachers more accountable, elicit better teacher effort, and improve the quality of both teaching and learning (box 5.7). It may also be more cost-effective than alternative uses of funds, such as cash grants for supplies.

Another problem for South Asian nations is nonexistent or minimal career progression structures and lack of incentives for teacher professional development. Career progression in South Asia is based upon years of service and gives individual teachers little opportunity to move into administrative or leadership roles. The absence of opportunities for teachers to develop as professionals in South Asia stymies the potential of talented teachers and demotivates them. Countries that perform well in student learning, such as Singapore, pay special attention to providing teachers with multiple options for rising in the profession (box 5.8). Pritchett and Pande (2006) argue that the current government teacher

Box 5.7 Incentives to Make Use of Improved Inputs and Training

Results from the program providing performance-linked bonuses in the state of Andhra Pradesh in India showed that teachers with more training were significantly more effective in schools eligible for the performance-pay program but were no more effective in nonprogram (control) schools. Similarly, student performance improved when teachers were given detailed diagnostic feedback on the performance of their students in schools that received both reports and performance pay, but there was no correlation with the scores in schools that only received the reports.

These results strongly suggest that improved inputs and training give teachers the capacity to do better, but the capacity is only utilized effectively when there is an incentive to do so.

Source: Muralidharan and Sundararaman 2011, 2013.

Box 5.8 Career Progression for Teachers: The Case of Singapore

Singapore's Education Service Professional Development and Career Plan is designed to help teachers develop their potential to the maximum. It comprises three parts: a career path, recognition through monetary rewards, and an evaluation system. The program provides for teachers with different aspirations by promoting three tracks: Teaching, Leadership, and Senior Specialist. The Teaching Track allows teachers to continue in the classroom and advance to the new role of master teacher. The Leadership Track provides teachers opportunities to take on leadership positions in schools and the Ministry of Education's headquarters. The Senior Specialist Track allows teachers to join the ministry's headquarters and become a "strong core of specialists with deep knowledge and skills in specific areas in education that will break new ground and keep Singapore at the leading edge." Each teacher's performance is monitored through the Enhanced Performance Management System, involving planning (for teaching goals, innovations instruction, school improvements, and personal and professional development), regular support and coaching to the teacher, and an intensive performance evaluation. The evaluation leads to a performance grade, which is linked directly to the annual performance bonus of the teacher as well as promotion decisions.

Source: OECD 2013.

Box 5.9 A Framework for Career Progression for Teachers

Pritchett and Pande (2006) proposed a professional career path for all new teachers in government schools in India. Pay scales and service conditions for current civil service teachers would continue until they retire. This would ensure their cooperation and minimize teacher union opposition because it would be fair to the current cadre. All new teachers would start out on pay and terms similar to those enjoyed by most current contract teachers. The authors refer to the teacher in this phase as a *Shiksha Karmi* (SK), using the terminology used in some states. SKs would be hired locally and assigned to a school on a fixed-term contract, the renewal of which would depend on performance. "After the probationary/learning period of five to seven years, the SK can apply to become an 'associate' (*Adhyapak*) teacher and enter Phase 2. This decision will depend on an evaluation of the teacher's performance as an SK" (Pritchett and Pande 2006, 65). *Adhyapaks* would receive higher salaries and benefits. Finally, "in Phase 3, outstanding *Adhyapaks* can be promoted to *Maha-Adhyapaks* or Masters, which would carry another step jump in salary [and] more perks and prestige.... The jump to Phase 3 would be controlled and limited, with most teachers expecting to spend their career as *Adhyapaks*" (Pritchett and Pande 2006, 65).

compensation system in India is unprofessional and anti-teacher because it does not reward performance with career progress. Box 5.9 sets out their career progression recommendations.

Teacher Accountability, Management, and Deployment

In South Asia, the problem often is not low-quality teaching but no teaching at all (World Bank 2004). Low teacher effort, as measured by high absenteeism, is a fundamental barrier to student learning. Teacher absence has immediate consequences for learning: it increases unplanned multigrade teaching and reduces the stability of the teacher-taught match, which can deeply depress child learning levels (Kingdon and Banerji 2009). It also appears to engender inequity in educational access and outcomes (Clotfelter, Ladd, and Vigdor 2006; Miller, Murnane, and Willett 2007). Each additional increase of 5 percent in teacher absence has the effect of lowering student learning outcomes by a remarkable 4–8 percent over an academic year (Das et al. 2007; for similar results, see also Kremer et al. 2005; Duflo, Hanna, and Ryan 2007; Kingdon and Sipahimalani-Rao 2010).

In the early 2000s, the World Bank National Absence Survey of teaching and health personnel in seven developing countries (Bangladesh, India, Indonesia, Ethiopia, Uganda, Ecuador, and Peru) found that median teacher absence was as high as 25 percent in India, with some teachers reportedly absent 40 percent of the time (table 5.14). Rather than being caused by a small minority of teachers, absenteeism appears to be a system-wide problem (Chaudhury et al. 2006). Regional variations are apparent from table 5.15, which shows that on average reported leave taken by teachers in Sri Lanka varied from 23 days in the

Table 5.14 Annual Primary School Teacher Absence, Selected Countries
Percent

Country	*Mean*
Bangladesh	16
India	25
Indonesia	19
Ecuador	14
Peru	11
Uganda	27

Source: Chaudhury et al. 2006.

Table 5.15 Leave Taken by Teachers, Sri Lanka, 2007

Province	*Leave days*	*Total teachers*	*Leave days/teacher*
Western	1,239,022	41,891	30
Central	944,188	31,495	30
Southern	927,963	29,106	32
North-Western	775,435	26,787	29
Northern	273,768	12,144	23
Eastern	484,907	17,116	28
North-Central	409,219	12,465	33
Uva	506,302	16,442	31
Sabaragamuwa	650,116	21,751	30
Sri Lanka	6,210,920	209,197	30

Source: Aturupane 2009.

Northern region to 33 days in the North-Central province. Government teachers were found to be absent 20 percent of the time in Pakistan and 16 percent in Bangladesh. (FMRP 2006; Andrabi et al. 2007). More recent estimates are available from the SchoolTELLS–India and Pakistan surveys, which actually counted the number of teachers present on the (random) day of each visit (four visits in India) rather than relying on reports by school heads. It found that on any given day 11 percent of the teachers in rural Punjab, Pakistan, were absent, mostly "unexplained" and with illness accounting for most of the absences that were "explained." In India, teachers were absent more than one in five days in Bihar and Uttar Pradesh. Much of the absence was for "personal leave," not official nonteaching duties or in-service training.

Teacher absence is believed to stem from low morale, low pay, and systemwide failures in imposing accountability (Rogers and Vegas 2009), though in South Asia teacher salaries, especially those of regular teachers, are not low in comparison with nonteachers with similar levels of education. Furthermore, in India, absence rates are significantly higher among civil-service than among low-paid contract teachers, who earn about one-quarter the salaries of regular teachers (see Kingdon and Sipahimalani-Rao 2010, for a review of Indian studies on this issue). It thus appears that absenteeism results mostly from lack of monitoring and low accountability (absenteeism is higher among senior teachers entrenched in their jobs and in areas remote from government offices).

Teacher absenteeism can be reduced with adequate monitoring. In Uganda, for example, teacher absenteeism fell from 27 percent in 2004 to 19 percent in 2006 after measures to monitor attendance were intensified (Kingdon and Sipahimalani-Rao 2010). In India, Muralidharan and Zieleniak (2012) found that an increase in the probability that a school would be inspected in the previous three months from 0 to 1 was correlated with a 7 percentage point reduction in teacher absence (30 percent of the observed absence rates). Using conservative estimates, they calculated that increased monitoring would be more than 10 times more cost-effective in raising teacher-student contact time than hiring additional teachers. Evaluating an intervention that paid teacher salaries as a function of the number of valid days of attendance, Duflo, Hanna, and Ryan (2012) found the program reduced absences by half. In that case, the mechanism may not have been monitoring alone but monitoring coupled with positive consequences for presence and negative consequences for absence.

Even when they are on site, teachers in South Asia often do not make much effort. As the PROBE report (1999) on rural north India noted, among teachers who were in school when the survey team visited, about half were sitting idle or engaged in such pastimes as knitting, sipping tea, or reading comics. More recent research (Pandey 2005; Pandey, Goyal, and Sundararaman 2008a; Sankar 2009) also found that in India teachers spend a significant amount of time in activities other than teaching (see chapter 6 for a detailed discussion). The studies also provide evidence that raising teacher effort can have a significant and positive impact on both test scores and whether students show up for school (box 5.10).

Box 5.10 Teacher Effort and Educational Achievement

Policies that provide better work incentives and can foster teacher presence in school—as well as their active participation in teaching—are likely to produce larger gains in the quality of education than other inputs.

Pandey (2005) has shown that teacher effort has a significant and positive effect both on test scores and on whether students show up for school. A more active teacher makes school more attractive to students and raises their interest in learning. A 1 standard deviation increase in the share of teachers actively teaching increases test scores by 0.5 standard deviation. Moreover, worker effort has more impact on the quality of teaching than other school inputs.

In a study of three Indian states (Madhya Pradesh, Uttar Pradesh, and Karnataka), Pandey, Goyal, and Sundararaman (2008b) showed that state differences in test scores are mirrored by differences in teacher attendance and in teachers observed who were actually teaching. Karnataka teachers were much more engaged in teaching than those in Madhya Pradesh and Uttar Pradesh, where only 25–35 percent of teachers were found to be actively engaged—a very low effort.

Contract Teachers and Accountability

One consequence of the rapid growth of schools and enrollment has been an expansion of the use of locally hired contract para-teachers to cost-effectively meet both teacher shortages (especially in remote regions) and the demand from rising numbers of students. India has experimented with introducing this type of teacher on a relatively large scale. In Sri Lanka and Nepal, local bodies hire temporary teachers to overcome deployment problems and improve local accountability. Contract and temporary teachers usually have less education (though significant youth unemployment in countries like India often means they are no less qualified than regular teachers), are paid a fraction of what regular teachers are paid, and are generally on fixed-term contracts with varied renewability terms.[5]

Many argue that using contract teachers is a practical way to handle the surge in students that has outpaced the supply of regular teachers. The relatively higher salaries of regular teachers impose a huge burden on the public system; hiring cheaper teachers is one way to relieve that stress. Proponents even argue that contract teachers may be superior because they tend to be from the community they serve, which means there is less social distance between teacher and student, and attendance and community involvement are thus more likely. Furthermore, the contract basis may heighten quality incentives—unlike regular teachers, these teachers risk not having their contracts renewed by the local education committee. Opponents of the use of contract teachers, however, fear that the lower training and education requirements will lead to lower-quality teachers. If contract teachers are more likely to be hired in areas that already suffer from a lack of resources, a reduction in quality would exacerbate equity issues. They might also feel they have to seek secondary employment to supplement their meager incomes—which in turn could lead to greater absenteeism, low morale, and poor performance (UNESCO-IUS 2006). Many also point out that in the long run it could be unsustainable to have a parallel system in which some are paid substantially less for doing the same job.

In this debate, the most crucial policy question for South Asian governments is the extent to which these teachers help provide quality education. Globally, evidence of the effect of contract teachers on student learning is mixed. Only a handful of studies have investigated the relationship in South Asia. Analyzing data from a survey of government schools in Madhya Pradesh and Uttar Pradesh, Goyal and Pandey (2009) found that contract teachers made more effort than regular teachers, and that after controlling for other variables, greater teacher effort was associated with better student performance. A study by Muralidharan and Sundararaman (2013) in Andhra Pradesh similarly found that students in schools that had an extra contract teacher performed significantly better than students in schools without one. However, this effect could also be due to class sizes being smaller because there was an extra teacher. Even after controlling for class size Atherton and Kingdon (2010) found contract teachers in rural India to be no less effective

Table 5.16 Teacher Effort, by Teacher Type, Bihar and Uttar Pradesh, India

	Uttar Pradesh			*Bihar*			*Both states*		
Measure of teacher effort	*Regular*	*Contract*	*t-test of difference*	*Regular*	*Contract*	*t-test of difference*	*All government*	*Private*	*t-test of difference*
Absence rate	0.23	0.11	−3.07***	0.21	0.12	1.70*	0.16	0.13	7.19***
Proportion of the working day spent in teaching	0.75	0.84	2.82***	0.76	0.84	−2.41***	0.81	0.89	−8.087***
Supports weak students	0.08	0.15	1.14	0.16	0.32	2.30**	0.20	0.27	−8.182***

Source: Atherton and Kingdon 2010.
Significance level: * = 10 percent, ** = 5 percent, *** = 1 percent.

than regular teachers. It may well be that the incentive to ensure their contract is renewed motivates teachers to apply more effort.

Table 5.16 presents measures of teacher effort from the SchoolTELLS-India data that offer further insight into whether accountability and tenure can affect teacher effort. In Uttar Pradesh regular teachers are more often absent and spend proportionally less time during the school day on teaching-related activities than contract teacher colleagues. In Bihar, although there is no difference in absence rates, when they are in school, contract teachers are likely to spend more time than regular teachers on teaching and on supporting poorer students. Effort in private schools is higher in that teachers are less often absent and also spend more time during the working day teaching. Interestingly, they also dedicate more time to supporting poorer students than their government counterparts. This implies that teachers who have to be more accountable display more effort.

While current research suggests increasing use of contract teachers, the political economy of teachers being publicly hired could make that difficult. It is also unclear how this policy would manifest itself in the long run. It is quite possible that contract teachers are attracted to the position because there is the possibility of becoming a better-paid tenured regular teacher in the future. If this career option disappeared, it is not clear how candidates and the effort of contract teachers might change.

Teacher Management and Deployment

The highly centralized management of teaching is a principal weakness of South Asian education systems (Aturupane 2009). Because they belong to a national and provincial cadre, on paper teachers can be transferred as needed to any part of the country. In reality, teachers use political connections to prevent transfers to unfavorable locations and to transfer to more popular schools and destinations, causing an oversupply of teachers in popular areas and an undersupply in remote rural regions. Flawed deployment has contributed to rural-urban disparities, differences in PTRs, and a shortage of female teachers in cultures where they are especially important to attracting girls to school and may be critical to their learning.

Figure 5.1 Suboptimal Use of Teachers in India

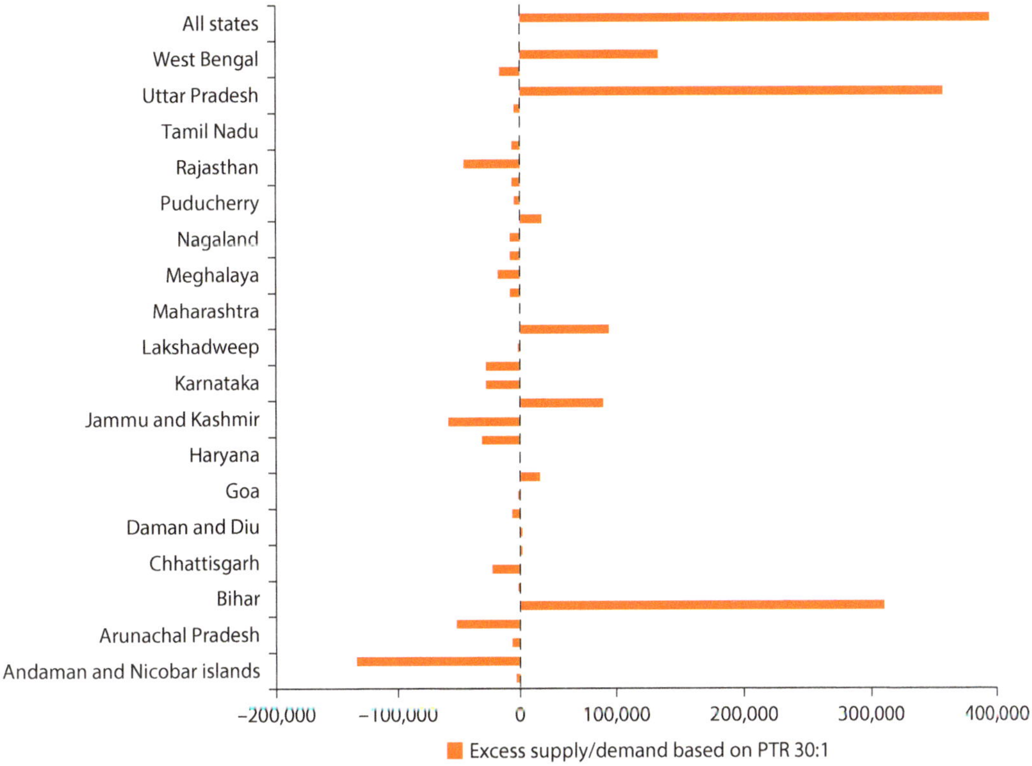

Source: District Information System for Education data 2009/10.
Note: PTR = pupil-teacher ratio.

Suboptimal use of teacher resources is illustrated in figure 5.1, which shows how redeployment of teachers in India might alleviate disparities in teacher supply by state. These estimates are based on pupil enrollment and teacher employment data for 2009/10. On the basis of an ideal PTR of 30 to 1, for all the states together there is demand for an additional 387,778 teachers. However, for individual states, the picture is dramatically different—there is a shortfall of teachers in some states (Uttar Pradesh needs 348,945 more teachers) and a surplus in others (Andhra Pradesh has 133,818 more than it needs). More effective deployment of teachers could result in a more effectively managed system. However, the practical problem of state regulations and of language differences may complicate effective redeployment. For instance, the language in Andhra Pradesh is primarily Telugu and in Uttar Pradesh Hindi.

Teacher Politicization

In government schools, most regular teachers in the region work in fairly lax environments, with accountability low and absenteeism high. Is there a conflict of interest that impels teacher organizations to oppose reforms aimed at improving teacher quality and hence South Asian educational systems?

Because there is no link between effort and performance on the one hand and salary and promotions on the other and because they have permanent tenure, regular teachers in South Asia have an incentive to retain the current state of governance and (lack) of accountability. The lax attitudes of some teachers toward their schools and students are in part a result of the strength and influence of their unions (Kingdon and Muzammil 2009).

Anecdotal evidence from newspaper reports of strike actions and political lobbying in South Asian countries suggests significant political penetration by teachers, but robust evidence on the extent of teacher politicization is hard to come by. The Punjab Teachers Union in Pakistan claims to have as members almost 350,000 government teachers in 63,000 schools in 38 districts[6]—equivalent to almost 100 percent union membership. When asked what percentage of Indian teachers were members of a union, the SchoolTELLS-India data show 54 percent reported that all teachers in the school were and 15 percent that no teacher was. In Pakistan, however, 5 percent reported all teachers to be union members while as many as 85 percent stated that not one teacher was. This indicates a reluctance to reveal union membership, which may be linked to the motives for joining unions discussed below.

Teacher unions are often structured to fulfill their demands through political action. Indeed, there is evidence from the SchoolTELLS-Pakistan survey that while teachers are reluctant to reveal union membership, up to 53 percent say that it is helpful to consult the union on transfers and postings, 63 percent believe it is important to build pressure through the union to either remain where they are or to transfer, and 64 percent believe that paying a bribe is helpful for transfers.

Excessive politicization of public education has had a profound impact on teacher accountability in South Asia (Bennell 2004). For example, the Indian Constitution stipulates that secondary school and higher education teachers shall select one-twelfth of the members of the state legislative councils. Where those councils are in place, teacher representatives can use their political power to advance their self-interest and lobby for legislation that benefits them. Teacher unions have used their immense political strength to raise salaries to inefficient levels.

The deleterious effect of teacher politicization on school functioning and performance arises in part because their political activities keep them away from actual teaching (Kingdon and Muzammil 2009). Kingdon (2006) and Kingdon and Teal (2010) also found that union membership has a powerful negative effect on student outcomes. A test score in a subject taught by a teacher who is a union member is about 0.25 standard deviations lower than a score in a subject taught by a nonunion teacher. Union membership increases pay and high-scoring schools are more likely to have unionized teachers, but within schools unionization suppresses achievement across the whole range of student ability.

Table 5.17 What Teachers Think Their Unions Should Argue For

Agenda item that trade union should undertake	*Teachers (%)*
Salary increments	24.7
Timely payment of salary	14.9
Insufficient number of teachers	8.3
Noncooperation from parents and guardians	8.2
Deployment of an extra teacher	7.8
School infrastructure	6.7
Facilities	6.1
Training	5.4
Work environment (pension, holidays, etc.)	4.9
Transfer and promotion	4.9
Nonteaching activities	4.8
Teaching and learning materials	2.2
Noncooperation from pupils	0.9
Other	0.1
Total	100.0

Source: SchoolTELLS-India data.

In South Asia, the high politicization of teachers is not aligned with student interests. The issues on which Indian teachers have lobbied have almost invariably had to do with salaries and job security and rarely, if ever, with improvements in schooling or the promotion of education in general (Kingdon and Muzammil 2009). The SchoolTELLS-India data confirm these observations. Asked which three main agenda items they would like the union to undertake (table 5.17), teachers gave the highest priority to salary increments and timely payment of salaries. Improved teaching materials accounted for only about 2 percent of the responses, even though the respondents were from rural schools in two of the most educationally and economically disadvantaged states in India. This certainly suggests that the motivation for union membership in India is rent-seeking. While it would be implausible to attribute the poor functioning of the school system only to teacher politicization, the fact that improvements in physical facilities in recent years in much of South Asia have not been matched by corresponding increases in teacher effort or student learning suggest that politicization may be contributing heavily to the poor quality of teaching in the region.

Such politicization manifests itself in a close nexus between teachers, politicians, and government officials—often for personal gain and power—which weakens teacher accountability and contributes to poor student learning outcomes (Béteille 2009). But these challenges are not insurmountable; they have been addressed successfully in other parts of the world (see box 5.11).

Box 5.11 Overcoming Opposition to Education Reform: The Role of Effective Leadership in Latin America

In countries across the world—developed and developing—the path to education reform can be politically daunting. Powerful anti-reform interest groups, most frequently teachers unions, complicate efforts to address pressing reforms issues, such as greater teacher accountability and superior teacher deployment policies. Nevertheless, there are instances of successful reform, even when the political odds do not appear to favor reform.

Based upon case studies in 16 countries in Latin America and the Caribbean, Grindle (2004) argued that countries where reform efforts succeeded were those where reformers seized the moment, systematically weakened and marginalized anti-reform groups, and organized political patrons and networks to carry forward key elements of their reform agenda. For instance, Mexico's President Carlos Salinas timed his 1992 education reforms carefully. He waited three years to strengthen his authority and shape how much change the union and the ministry would accept. This involved not only altering the powers of the union and the ministry but also waiting until the midterm election gave him the constitutional majority needed to legislate important changes.

Successful reformers also make use of their powers of appointment to promote their initiatives. In Brazil's Minas Gerais, the governor spearheading the education reforms of the 1990s chose a minister who then chose allies he trusted to lead the initiative in the ministry. Equally important is the ability to weaken and marginalize interest groups opposed to reforms. In Minas Gerais, school directors posed a threat to reforms, although the union was in favor of many aspects of the reforms. Here, the minister mobilized those supporting the reforms, asking them to testify in the public debate about the benefits of reform, and the governor provided visible support to offset the resistance of the directors association.

Finally, successful reformers find opportunities to set the terms of debate about reform. In Mexico and Bolivia, presidents emphasized the importance of reforms for modernizing the economies of the countries, implicitly suggesting that entities opposing reform were opposed to modernization, economic growth, and alleviation of poverty.

Source: Grindle 2004.

Low Teacher Morale

High politicization of the teaching cadre in large parts of South Asia coexists with low teacher morale. One reason, again, could be that the average motivated teacher finds it difficult to progress through a system where there is little reward for merit. Another reason, paradoxically, is the limited political power of individual teachers, who are frequently harassed by politicians and their middlemen. In a survey of 2,350 teachers in three large states in India—Rajasthan, Madhya Pradesh, and Karnataka—depending on the state, 12 percent to 25 percent of teachers reported being harassed often, directly and indirectly, by politicians for reasons unrelated to teaching (Béteille 2009). Harassment included threat of transfer to a remote area, demand for bribes to avoid transfer, and the expectation that school administrators would cooperate with local politicians in hiring contractors for school construction projects and issue no-objection certificates even if the construction was visibly substandard. Harassment did not end with politicians and their middlemen. It also included having to cultivate connections with government clerks in order to be reimbursed for claims owed to the teacher (Béteille 2009). No wonder otherwise motivated teachers who are expected to educate large classrooms of first-generation learners may feel considerably demotivated.

Policy Implications

The quality of education a child receives closely reflects teacher quality, but what makes teachers differentially effective is debatable. Yet some countries have been successful in raising the quality of teaching (see box 5.12).

Box 5.12 Teacher Recruitment, Management, and Governance Policies That Promote Performance

The Programme for International Student Assessment 2010 results are based on tests of about half a million high school students in over 70 economies that account for about nine-tenths of the world economy. Shanghai, China, and the Republic of Korea; Hong Kong SAR, China; Singapore; Finland; Canada; Japan; and New Zealand consistently have the highest student achievement. In mathematics, more than a quarter of Shanghai's 15-year-olds can conceptualize, generalize, and creatively use information. Finland shows consistently high performance regardless of where its children go to school. In 2000, Korea's average performance was already high, but it was believed this was only because a small elite minority of students achieved excellence in reading literacy. In less than a decade, however, the country doubled its share of students demonstrating reading excellence. What sets Korea apart from the rest of the world? For one thing, Korea's exceptional certification curriculum—which covers subject study, subject teaching, general education, and a teaching practicum—provides a versatile foundation for teachers.

The Finnish education system has attracted substantial interest from policy makers and educational experts alike. One major reason Finnish education stands out from others is that its teachers have high qualifications, moderate salaries, and high commitment to their profession. Teaching is a very popular career in Finland, but only 10 percent of the most talented applicants are selected through a rigorous recruitment process, and training is based on pedagogical research.

Singapore, like Korea, is an excellent example of a country that has used powerful and comprehensive policies to stop the vicious cycle of political activism and consequent decline in education quality. The positive effects of top executive modeling on lower civil service echelons have been noted in both countries. As a result, corruption has gone down and public servants seem more motivated. This in turn ensures that teaching is given the respect it needs to attract the most capable applicants.

Source: http://www.oecd.org/document/7/0,3746,en_21571361_44315115_46635719_1_1_1_1,00.html.

Recruitment and Deployment

A striking characteristic common to higher-performing education systems is their sustained attention to recruiting the right people. Across South Asia there is evidence of systematic abuse and non-merit-based decisions in the appointment, transfer, and promotion of teachers. To halt this vicious cycle—and the decline in educational quality—comprehensive policies are required. Bangladesh and Sindh in Pakistan have recently shown that this can be done.

There is also a need for clear regulations governing recruitment and deployment of teachers in each country. This is of particular concern in rural areas where teachers typically deal with poorer health care, lower rent allowances, and isolation. Policy makers thus need to address a range of factors when crafting policies to encourage teacher redeployment to remote rural areas. While ambitious targets for recruiting female teachers, particularly to rural posts, must be established, quotas and scholarships alone may not be enough. In many countries, support and encouragement are essential to enable women to break powerful social norms in order to teach.

The analysis of intracountry differences in the supply and quality of teachers across South Asia illustrates two points: (a) by looking beyond national averages (e.g., PTRs), effective redeployment policies could address many of the shortages that plague rural schools without the need for elaborate recruitment drives; and (b) redeployment of current staff may help to alleviate inequities in teacher quantity and quality.

Teacher Training

In most South Asian countries, effort spent on expanding teacher numbers might be better spent on redeploying current teachers and better training of both regular and contract teachers, particularly given the positive effects incentive-based schemes have been found to have on learning outcomes (Atherton and Kingdon 2010). In much of the region, teacher training problems are mainly rooted in a lack of good management and governance practices.

There is also a need for more specialized training that updates teacher content knowledge and helps them learn techniques for successfully transferring their expertise to students. Recent data from Pakistan demonstrate that even when teachers have facts and other information, their students do not gain much from it. Chingos and Peterson (2011) claim that it is easier to recruit a good teacher than to train one. Thus, policies need to ensure appropriate recruitment as well as careful training of teachers thereafter. In-service training that provides a continuum of professional development and support to teachers fosters creativity in teaching, as Singapore has shown (box 5.8).

Teacher Salaries and Accountability

Most teacher pay schemes in South Asia are characterized by some combination of guaranteed appointment after training, lifetime tenure, automatic annual salary increases, absence of performance-related rewards or sanctions, pay that is not received regularly, and salaries unrelated to working conditions.

These poor incentives have all been instrumental in reducing teacher motivation and job satisfaction (Zymelman and DeStefano 1993; Bennell 2004). Coupled with poor management and ineffective deployment, it is not surprising that teacher attrition and turnover are high, with a resultant negative effect on student learning.

Teachers tend not to be paid according to either their performance or that of their students. In fact, not even the most basic of indicators of employee performance—attendance—is at an acceptable level. Absence and "time on task" investigations highlight the need for policies that set clear expectations of teachers and give them the tools (through training, for instance), sanctions, and compensation (based on both regular and decentralized appraisals) to motivate them to meet the targets.

Not only are teachers in South Asia relatively well compensated but in some cases, such as India, the economic distance created between students and teachers is so large that it may have a negative impact on student outcomes. Yet despite good salaries, teachers display low self-esteem, which underscores the need to look beyond financial motivations to such aspects as responsibility, transparency of governance, and autonomy. Teachers need to think of themselves not as secure government employees but as members of a respected and significant profession.

Annex 5A: Ratio of Teacher Salary to Per Capita Income (Rupees), by State, India, 2008

State	*Per capita net domestic product at factor cost (base = 1999–2000)* *(a)*	*Per capita net domestic product in 2008 prices*[a] *(b)*	*Annual teacher salaries in 2008*[b] *(c)*	*Teacher salary as multiple of per capita income* *(d)*
Andhra Pradesh	27,362	42,958	89,876	2.1
Assam	16,272	25,547	127,853	5.0
Bihar	10,206	16,023	187,685	11.7
Jharkhand	16,294	25,582	124,290	4.9
Gujarat	—	—	123,862	—
Haryana	41,896	65,777	148,944	2.3
Himachal Pradesh	32,343	50,779	124,982	2.5
Jammu and Kashmir	—	—	103,415	—
Karnataka	27,385	42,994	110,681	2.6
Kerala	35,475	55,696	126,593	2.3
Madhya Pradesh	—	—	157,147	—
Chhattisgarh	19,521	30,648	124,383	4.1
Maharashtra	—	—	107,886	—
Odisha	18,212	28,593	207,023	7.2
Punjab	33,198	52,121	149,073	2.9
Rajasthan	19,708	30,942	166,609	5.4
Tamil Nadu	30,652	48,124	96,034	2.0
Uttar Pradesh	12,481	19,595	103,396	5.3
Uttarakhand	25,114	39,429	170,831	4.3
West Bengal	24,720	38,810	108,534	2.8
Simple means for states	23,642	37,119	11,9540	4.2

Source: Reserve Bank of India: Handbook of Statistics on Indian Economy, http://www.rbi.org.in/scripts/AnnualPublications .aspx?head=Handbook%20 of% 20Statistics%20on%20Indian%20Economy.
Note: — = not available.
a. Column (b) shows column (a) figures inflated to 2008 prices using the All India Consumer Price Index (General) for industrial workers.
b. Teachers were identified using the National Sample Survey (NSS) 2008 3-digit occupation codes. It is not possible to sort regular from para-teachers in NSS data because occupation codes do not distinguish between the two teacher types. The reported salaries are for regular and para-teachers in government and private school jobs.

Notes

1. As judged by senior teachers in the Bihar State Council of Educational Research and Training (SCERT).
2. To pass, a teacher needed to score at least 90 out of 150, but this was relaxed to 82 for backward-caste takers.
3. Similar tables were created using data from Bangladesh, India, and Nepal, which are also discussed in this section.
4. Salaries are observed only for labor market participants and wage earners. This subsample of wage earners may not be random due to self-selection of individuals into wage work because of unobserved characteristics, such as ability, which may also determine wages. OLS estimates may therefore be biased. While Heckman (1979) selection-corrected models can be estimated, they make little difference so are not reported.

5. In Bangladesh, however, the same recruitment criteria are applied to teachers in government and in recognized nongovernment schools. The starting salary for both is similar, but allowances and benefits throughout working life are much lower for nongovernment teachers.
6. http://punjabteachersunion.com/, accessed on November 6, 2013.

Bibliography

Aaronson, D., L. Barrow, and W. Sander. 2003. "Teachers and Student Achievement in the Chicago Public High Schools." Working Paper WP-2002-08, Federal Reserve Bank of Chicago, Chicago, IL.

Andrabi, T., J. Das, A. Khwaja, T. Vishwanath, and T. Zajonc. 2007. *Pakistan: Learning and Educational Achievements in Punjab Schools (LEAPS): Insights to Inform the Educational Policy Debate*. http://www.leapsproject.org/assets/publications/LEAPS_Report_ExecSummary.pdf.

Aslam, M., and G. Kingdon. 2011. "What Can Teachers Do to Raise Student Achievement?" *Economics of Education Review* 30 (3): 559–74.

Atherton, P., and G. Kingdon. 2010. "The Relative Effectiveness and Costs of Contract and Regular Teachers in India." CSAE Working Paper Series WPS/2010–15, Centre for the Study of African Economies, University of Oxford, Oxford, U.K.

Atkinson, A., S. Burgess, B. Croxson, P. Gregg, C. H. Propper, and D. Wilson. 2004. "Evaluating the Impact of Performance-Related Pay for Teachers in England." Working Paper Series 04/113, Centre for Market and Public Organisation, University of Bristol, Bristol, U.K.

Atkinson, A., S. Burgess, B. Croxson, P. Gregg, C. H. Propper, H. Slater, and D. Wilson. 2009. "Evaluating the Impact of Performance-Related Pay for Teachers in England." *Labour Economics* 16 (3): 251–61.

Aturupane, H. 2009. *The Pearl of Great Price: Achieving Equitable Access to Primary and Secondary Education and Enhancing Learning in Sri Lanka*. CREATE Monograph 29. London: Institute of Education, University of London.

Aturupane, D. H., P. Glewwe, and S. Wisniewski. 2013. "The Impact of School Quality, Socio-Economic Factors and Child Health on Students' Academic Performance: Evidence from Sri Lankan Primary Schools." *Education Economics* 21 (1): 2–37.

Banerjee, A., S. Cole, E. Duflo, and L. Linden. 2006. "Remedying Education: Evidence from Two Randomized Experiments in India." *Quarterly Journal of Economics* 122 (3): 1235–64.

Banerjee, A. V., R. Banerji, E. Duflo, R. Glennerster, and S. Khemani. 2010. "Pitfalls of Participatory Programs: Evidence from a Randomized Evaluation in Education in India." *American Economic Journal: Economic Policy* 2 (1): 1–30.

Banerji, R., and G. Kingdon. 2010. "How Sound Are Our Mathematics Teachers? Insights from the SchoolTELLS Survey." *Learning Curve*, Azim Premji Foundation, Bangalore.

Bennell, P. 2004. "Teacher Motivation and Incentives in Sub-Saharan Africa and Asia." Knowledge and Skills for Development Program, Brighton, U.K. http://www.eldis.org/vfile/upload/1/document/0708/doc15160.pdf.

Béteille, T. 2009. "Absenteeism, Transfers and Patronage: The Political Economy of Teacher Labour Markets in India." PhD thesis, Stanford University, Stanford, CA.

Burgess, S., N. Davies, and H. Slater. 2009. "Do Teachers Matter? Measuring Teacher Effectiveness in England." CMPO Working Paper 09/212, Bristol Institute of Public Affairs, University of Bristol, Bristol, U.K.

Chaudhury, N., J. Hammer, M. Kremer, K. Muralidharan, and F. H. Rogers. 2006. "Missing in Action: Teacher and Health Worker Absence in Developing Countries." *Journal of Economic Perspectives* 20 (1): 91–116.

Chingos, M. M., and P. E. Peterson. 2011. "It's Easier to Pick a Good Teacher than to Train One: Familiar and New Results on the Correlates of Teacher Effectiveness." *Economics of Education Review* 30: 449–65.

Clotfelter, C. T., H. F. Ladd, and J. L. Vigdor. 2006. "Teacher-Student Matching and the Assessment of Teacher Effectiveness." *Journal of Human Resources* 41 (4): 778–820.

Das, J., S. Dercon, J. Habyarimana, and P. Krishnan. 2007. "Teacher Shocks and Student Learning Evidence from Zambia." *Journal of Human Resources* 42 (4): 820–62.

Dee, T. 2005. "A Teacher Like Me: Does Race, Ethnicity or Gender Matter?" *American Economic Review* 95 (2): 158–65.

Desai, S., A. Dubey, R. Vanneman, and R. Banerji. 2009. "Private Schooling in India: A New Educational Landscape." *India Policy Forum* 5 (1): 1–38.

Duflo, E., R. Hanna, and S. P. Ryan. 2007. *Monitoring Works: Getting Teachers to Come to School*. Cambridge, MA: Massachusetts Institute of Technology.

———. 2012. "Incentives Work: Getting Teachers to Come to School." *American Economic Review* 102 (4): 1241–78.

Eide, E., D. Goldhaber, and D. Brewer. 2004. "The Teacher Labour Market and Teacher Quality." *Oxford Review of Economic Policy* 20 (2): 230–43.

Figlio, D., and L. Kenny. 2007. "Individual Teacher Incentives and Student Performance." *Journal of Public Economics* 91 (5–6): 901–14.

FMRP (Financial Management Reform Programme). 2006. *Primary Education in Bangladesh: Assessing Service Delivery*. Final Report of Social Sector Performance Survey. Bangladesh: FMRP.

French, R., and G. Kingdon. 2010. "The Relative Effectiveness of Private and Government Schools in Rural India: Evidence from ASER Data." Department of Quantitative Social Science Working Paper10-03, Institute of Education, University of London, London, UK.

Fuller, B. 1987. What School Factors Raise Achievement in the Third World? *Review of Educational Research* 57 (3): 255–92.

Glewwe, P., and M. Kremer. 2006. "Schools, Teachers, and Education Outcomes in Developing Countries." In *Handbook of the Economics of Education, Vol. 2*, edited by E. Hanushek and F. Welch. New York: Elsevier.

Goldhaber, D. 1999. "School Choice: An Examination of the Empirical Evidence on Achievement, Parental Decision Making and Equity." *Educational Researcher* 28 (9): 16–25.

Goodman, S., and L. Turner. 2010. "Teacher Incentive Pay and Educational Outcomes: Evidence from the New York City Bonus Program." Unpublished manuscript, Columbia University, New York. http://www.columbia.edu/~ljt2110/Goodman_Turner_Nov10.pdf.

Goyal, S., and P. Pandey. 2009. *How Do Government and Private Schools Differ? Findings from Two Large Indian States*. Report No. 30, South Asia Human Development Unit. Washington, DC: World Bank.

Grindle, M. 2004. *Despite the Odds: The Contentious Politics of Education Reform*. Princeton, NJ: Princeton University Press.

Hanushek, E. A. 2005. "The Economics of School Quality." *German Economic Review* 6 (3): 269–86.

———. 2011. "The Economic Value of Higher Teacher Quality." *Economics of Education Review* 30: 466–79.

Hanushek, E. A., J. Kain, D. O'Brien, and S. Rivkin. 2005. "The Market for Teacher Quality." Working Paper 11154, National Bureau of Economic Research, Cambridge, MA.

Hanushek, E. A., and S. G. Rivkin. 2006. "Teacher Quality." In *Handbook of the Economics of Education, Vol. 2*, edited by E. Hanushek and F. Welch. New York, NY: Elsevier.

Heckman, J. J. 1979. "Sample Selection Bias as a Specification Error." *Econometrica: Journal of the Econometric Society* 47 (1): 153-161.

Hoxby, C. 1996. "How Teachers' Unions Affect Education Production." *Quarterly Journal of Economics* 111 (4): 671–718.

Kingdon, G. 2006. "Teacher Pay and Student Performance: A Pupil Fixed Effects Approach." Working Paper Series GPRG-WPS-059, University of Oxford, Oxford, U.K.

Kingdon, G., and R. Banerji. 2009. "Addressing School Quality: Some Policy Pointers from Rural North India." RECOUP Policy Brief No. 5, Faculty of Education, University of Cambridge, Cambridge, U.K.

Kingdon, G., and M. Muzammil. 2009. "A Political Economy of Education in India: The Case of Uttar Pradesh." *Oxford Development Studies* 37 (2): 123–44.

Kingdon, G., and V. Sipahimalani-Rao. 2010. "Para Teachers in India: Status and Impact," *Economic and Political Weekly* 45 (12), March 20–26.

Kingdon, G., and F. Teal. 2007. "Does Performance-Related Pay for Teachers Improve Student Achievement? Some Evidence from India." *Economics of Education Review* 26 (4): 473–86.

———. 2010. "Teacher Unions, Teacher Pay and Student Performance in India: A Pupil Fixed Effects Approach." *Journal of Development Economics* 91 (2): 278–88.

Kremer, M., N. Chaudhury, F. H. Rogers, K. Muralidharan, and J. Hammer. 2005. "Teacher Absence in India: A Snapshot." *Journal of the European Economic Association* 3 (2–3): 658–67.

Lavy, V. 2002. "Evaluating the Effects of Teachers' Performance Incentives on Pupil Achievement." *Journal of Political Economy* 110 (6): 1286–317.

Lopez-Acevedo, G. 2004. "Professional Development and Incentives for Teacher Performance in Schools in Mexico." Policy Research Working Paper 3236, World Bank, Washington, DC.

Metzler, J., and L. Woessmann. 2012. "The Impact of Teacher Subject Knowledge on Student Achievement: Evidence from Within-Teacher Within-Student Variation." *Journal of Development Economics* 99: 486–96.

Miller, R., R. Murnane, and J. Willett. 2007. "Do Teacher Absences Impact on Student Achievement?" NBER Working Paper 13356, National Bureau of Economic Research, Cambridge, MA.

Mingat, A. 2002. *Teacher Salary Issues in African Countries.* Processed, Africa Region, Human Development Analysis and Policy Development Support Team, World Bank, Washington, DC.

Muralidharan, K., and M. Kremer. 2008. "Public and Private Schools in Rural India." In *School Choice International*, edited by P. Peterson and R. Chakrabarti. Cambridge, MA: MIT.

Muralidharan, K., and V. Sundararaman. 2009. "Teacher Performance Pay: Experimental Evidence from India." NBER Working Paper 15323, National Bureau of Economic Research, Cambridge, MA.

———. 2011. "Teacher Performance Pay: Experimental Evidence from India." *Journal of Political Economy* 119 (1): 39–77.

———. 2013. "Contract Teachers: Experimental Evidence from India." NBER Working Paper 19440, National Bureau of Economic Research, Cambridge, MA.

Muralidharan, K., and Y. Zieleniak. 2012. "Measuring Learning Trajectories in Developing Countries with Longitudinal Data and Item Response Theory". Manuscript, University of California, San Diego, CA.

NCERT (National Council of Educational Research and Training). 2006. *Position Paper: National Focus Group on Examination Reforms.* New Delhi: NCERT.

———. 2011. *What Do They Know? A Summary of India's National Achievement Survey, Class V, Cycle 3 2010/11.* New Delhi: NCERT.

———. 2012. *National Achievement Survey Class V.* New Delhi: NCERT.

Newsknol. 2012. "Gujarat Teacher Eligibility Test (TET) Results 2012 Declared," June 23. http://www.newsknol.com/2700/gujarat-tet-results-2012.

OECD (Organisation for Economic Co-operation and Development). 2013. *Teachers for the 21st Century: Using Evaluation to Improve Teaching.* http://www.oecd.org/site/eduistp13/TS2013%20Background%20Report.pdf.

Pandey, P. 2005. "How Much Do Resources Matter for Service Delivery? Effects of Teacher Effort and Other School Inputs on Educational Achievement." Draft Working Paper, Human Development Department, South Asia Region, World Bank, Washington, DC.

Pandey, P., S. Goyal, and V. Sundararaman. 2008a. "Public Participation, Teacher Accountability and School Outcomes: Findings from Baseline Surveys in Three Indian States." Policy Research Working Paper 4777, Human Development Department, South Asia Region, World Bank, Washington, DC.

———. 2008b. "Community Participation in Public Schools: The Impact of Information Campaigns in Three Indian States." Policy Research Working Paper Series WPS 4776, Human Development Department, South Asia Region, World Bank, Washington, DC.

Park, A., and E. Hannum. 2001. "Do Teachers Affect Learning in Developing Countries? Evidence from Matched Student-Teacher Data from China." Paper presented at conference "Rethinking Social Science Research in the Developing World," Park City, Utah.

Pratham. 2010. "The Annual Status of Education Report–Pakistan." South Asian Forum for Education Development and ITA, Lahore, Pakistan.

———. 2012. *Annual Status of Education Report (Rural) 2011.* New Delhi: Pratham Resource Center.

Pritchett, L., and D. Filmer. 1997. "What Educational Production Functions Really Show: A Positive Theory of Education Spending." Policy Research Working Paper 1795, World Bank, Washington, DC.

Pritchett, L., and V. Pande. 2006. Making Primary Education Work for India's Rural Poor: A Proposal for Effective Decentralization. Social Development Papers, South Asia Series 95, Human Development Department, South Asia Region, World Bank, Washington, DC.

PROBE. 1999. *Public Report on Basic Education in India*. New Delhi: Oxford University Press.

Rawal, S., and G. Kingdon. 2010. "Akin to My Teacher: Does Caste, Religious or Gender Distance Between Student and Teacher Matter? Some Evidence from India." DoQSS Working Paper 10–18, Institute of Education, University of London, London.

Rivkin, S., E. Hanushek, and J. Kain. 2005. "Teachers, Schools and Academic Achievement." *Econometrica* 73 (2): 417–58.

Rockoff, J. E. 2004. "The Impact of Individual Teachers on Student Achievement: Evidence from Panel Data." *American Economic Review* 94 (2): 247–52.

Rogers, F., and E. Vegas. 2009. "No More Cutting Class? Reducing Teacher Absence and Providing Incentives for Performance." Policy Research Working Paper WPS 4847, Human Development Network, World Bank, Washington, DC.

Sankar, D. 2009. "Teachers' Time on Task and Nature of Tasks: Evidence from Three Indian States." Human Development Department, South Asia Region, World Bank, Washington, DC.

Spríetsma, M., and F. Waltenberg. 2005. "The Impact of Teacher's Wages on Student's Performance in the Presence of Heterogeneity and Endogeneity—Evidence from Brazil." Working Paper 2005008, Université Catholique de Louvain, Département des Sciences Economiques, Louvain-La-Neuve, Belgium.

Tilak, J. B. 2008. *Financing of Secondary Education in India*. New Delhi: National University of Educational Planning and Administration.

Times of India. 2012. "93% Aspirants Fail Teacher's Eligibility Test," March 11. http://timesofindia.indiatimes.com/home/education/news/93-aspirants-fail-teachers-eligibility-test/articleshow/12215862.cms.

UNESCO (United Nations Educational, Scientific and Cultural Organization). 2004. *Education for All: Quality Imperative*. EFA Global Monitoring Report 2005. Paris: UNESCO Publishing.

UNESCO-UIS (UNESCO Institute for Statistics). 2006. *Teachers and Educational Quality: Monitoring Global Needs for 2015*. Montreal, Canada: UNESCO Institute for Statistics.

USAID (United States Agency for International Development). nd. "Performance Gap Analysis and Training Needs Assessments of Teacher Training Institutions." Pakistan Teacher Training and Professional Development Program, USAID contract.

Vegas, E., and I. Umansky. 2005. "Improving Teaching and Learning Through Effective Incentives: What Can We Learn from Education Reforms in Latin America?" World Bank, Washington, DC.

Warwick, D. P., and H. Jatoi. 1994. "Teacher Gender and Student Achievement in Pakistan." *Comparative Education Review* 38 (3): 377–99.

World Bank. 2004. *World Development Report 2004: Making Services Work for the Poor*. Washington, DC: World Bank.

———. 2005. "Treasures of the Education System in Sri Lanka: Restoring Performance, Expanding Opportunities and Enhancing Prospects." Human Development Unit, South Asia Region, World Bank, Washington, DC.

———. 2010. Methodological Report for the Labor Market Micro-Level Database (LM-MD), Version: 04/22/10, World Bank, Washington, DC.

———. 2012. *What Matters Most in Teacher Policies: Framework for Building a More Effective Teaching Profession*. Washington, DC: World Bank.

Zymelman, M., and J. DeStefano. 1993. "Primary School Teacher Salaries in Sub-Saharan Africa." In *Teachers in Developing Countries*, edited by J. B. Oliveira and J. P. Farrell. Washington, DC: World Bank.

CHAPTER 6

Inside the Classroom: Teacher Effort and Practices*

Introduction

Students experience school primarily through what happens inside the classroom—the type of teaching they are exposed to, the instructional materials available, and peer interaction. One look inside the average classroom in a developing country, however, makes clear that conditions there are often not conducive to learning. Children in developed countries have 900 hours a year of learning time, study a curriculum the scope and sequence of which has been carefully structured, and share their teacher with about 20 children, most of whom have good health and are well-nourished. That is not true elsewhere (Lockheed 2011). In developing countries like those in South Asia, students are likely to have 500 hours a year of learning time, study a poorly designed curriculum, and share a classroom with over 40 other children, most of whom are undernourished, parasite ridden, and hungry (Lockheed 2011).

The rapid expansion of schooling in South Asia, coupled with the problem of widespread teacher absenteeism, means that teachers who do come to work often have to deal with large multigrade teaching situations, which preservice and in-service training rarely prepares them for. That makes it considerably more challenging to educate children.

Differences in how teachers engage their students appear to be the single biggest factor determining student learning (Béteille and Loeb 2009; Pianta and Hamre 2009). In South Asia, where schools serve hundreds of millions of low-income students, the importance of teaching practices cannot be overstated (see chapter 5). A critical component of the effort to produce effective teaching, therefore, is to understand what teachers do in the average classroom, the materials available to them, and classroom practices that get in the way of effective teaching and learning.

*See box 6.1 for a summary of the chapter's key questions and findings.

Box 6.1 Questions and Findings

Questions

- To what extent does the curriculum in South Asian countries reflect sophisticated learning paradigms? What types of instructional materials are most common in South Asia?
- How do teachers spend their time in the classroom?
- How can teaching and learning challenges students in the region face be addressed?

Findings

- Curricula in some South Asian countries, such as India and Sri Lanka, reflect learning paradigms similar to those practiced in high-income countries, such as constructivism. But applying them puts brakes on the extent to which students in South Asian classrooms benefit. The primary instructional material throughout the region is textbooks, which tend to perpetuate rote-learning skills rather than encourage higher-order analytical abilities.
- Whether students can learn depends significantly on how much time in the classroom is devoted to actual teaching. A study in three states in India found that teachers spend only 44–58 percent of their time on classroom activities, and most of that time is given to traditional activities, such as recitation, instruction/demonstration, and desk study—in other words, repetitive and teacher-centric activities.
- The poor learning environment in the average South Asian classroom is not just because of poor teaching practices; there is also the challenge of educating large numbers of first-generation schoolgoers, many of whom do not have much family support. While long-term reforms in preservice and in-service teacher training are certainly crucial to address this new and more challenging situation, it is also important that governments consider interim measures to respond to student learning needs. Among interventions that have demonstrated promise are remedial and supplemental instruction, activity-based learning (ABL), and technology-assisted instruction.

This chapter provides insights into what students in South Asia experience in the classrooms. It begins by discussing the type of curriculum and the instructional materials available and then examines the amount of time Indian teachers spend inside classrooms in general and what they do with that time. Concentrating on building reading skills, which as chapter 5 notes form the backbone of learning gains for all subjects, the chapter then looks not only at what teachers of reading typically accomplish but also at how actively pupils are engaged. Schools in South Asia have a long way to go, it is clear, to make the classroom experience more meaningful for students. The chapter concludes with methods for addressing the main problems students in South Asia face, such as too few learning hours.

Curriculum and Instructional Materials

All countries in South Asia have an official curriculum with broad, typically farsighted, guidelines for instruction. The guidelines often emphasize learning paradigms seen in high-income countries, such as constructivism (see box 6.2 for examples from India and Sri Lanka). Depending on the governmental level to which curriculum design is decentralized, the guidelines become the basis for design of a more specific curriculum. As summarized in chapter 10, governments in South Asia tend to keep curriculum decisions fairly centralized.

Whether or not a visionary curriculum achieves its goals depends considerably on how it is designed, developed, and implemented. As Perera (2009) notes, several hurdles in Sri Lanka's 2007 curricular reforms made it difficult to achieve the curriculum's visionary goals, especially these: (a) appropriateness was not properly pre-tested, (b) different subjects were not horizontally integrated, (c) the only learning methodology followed was the 5E model,

---

Box 6.2 National Curricula in India and Sri Lanka

India. The National Curriculum Framework (NCERT 2005) advocates for a constructivist approach to learning where the child is an active learner engaged in constructing knowledge. Among the core principles it identifies for curriculum development are (a) connecting knowledge to life outside the school, (b) ensuring that learning shifts away from rote methods; (c) enriching the curriculum so that it goes beyond textbooks, (d) making examinations more flexible and integrating them with classroom life, and (e) nurturing an overriding identity informed by caring concerns within the democratic polity of the country (NCERT 2006; Jhingran 2012).

Sri Lanka. The New Education Reforms of 2007 emphasized revising the curriculum based on the following principles: (a) a competency-based curriculum with an emphasis on activity-based learning; (b) the 5Es: engagement of the student, exploration, explanation, evaluation, and elaboration and improvement; (c) active planning; and (d) transforming the role of the teacher, with teacher manuals to aid instruction (Perera 2009).

(d) publicizing of ideas relevant to the new curriculum was inadequate, (e) understanding of how teachers would implement the curriculum was unsatisfactory, and (f) there was a lack of systematic monitoring to identify shortcomings (Perera 2009).

The curriculum is ultimately transacted through instructional materials, primarily the textbook in most South Asian countries. Textbooks define the scope of the subject matter to be taught and lay out the sequence for instruction. Scope and sequence are important because if material is too challenging, it can discourage students; if too easy, it may fail to build problem-solving skills. A study conducted by the National Academy for Primary Education (NAPE) in Bangladesh noted that textbooks in the country lacked consideration of students' development stages and learning process. After a close scrutiny of grade 1–5 mathematics textbooks, the study found that the textbooks lacked important properties, including: (a) consideration of students' development stage and learning process; (b) consideration of the relationship with students' daily lives; (c) inclusion of content that is neither described in the curriculum nor helpful to students; and (d) errors and mistakes in the textbook—including insufficient, misleading, or inappropriate expressions and instructions (World Bank 2013).

In South Asia textbooks are notorious for arriving in schools late and being of substandard quality (PAISA 2011). Even if they reach the end user in reasonable shape, in India, Pakistan, and Bangladesh textbooks often lack the educative substance that reinforces higher-order problem-solving skills and critical thinking (Banu 2009; Jhingran 2012). They require little more than memorization of problem solutions (as in mathematics) and little engagement with real-life problems. A study conducted by NAPE and the Japan International Cooperation Agency in Bangladesh points out that learning mathematics there is equivalent to knowing math terms and procedures. Similarly, learning science means accumulating as many pieces of scientific knowledge as possible. As a result, students can answer the same or very similar questions given in the textbooks without understanding what is happening (World Bank 2013). Thus, far from discouraging a culture of rote learning, textbooks in South Asia reinforce it—as does the public examination system in the region (see chapter 8).

Students are often unable to relate to the reality depicted in textbooks. In an analysis of grade 5 English textbooks designed by the National Curriculum and Textbook Board of Bangladesh, Banu (2009) noted that the lesson on ordinal numbers was replete with illustrations of places unfamiliar to the average rural student: bookshops, shopping malls, libraries, and apartments on different floors of a multistory building.

In general, South Asian classrooms make very little use of other supplementary instructional materials, often because schools do not receive funds early enough to purchase them. As figure 6.1 shows, a majority of schools in seven Indian states received grants to purchase teaching materials six months into the school calendar year (Dongre, Chowdhury, and Aiyar 2012).

Figure 6.1 Receipt of School Grants in Academic Year 2011–12

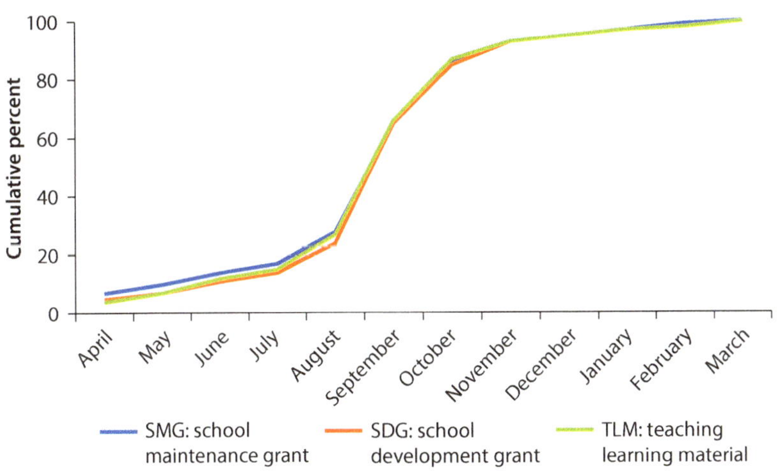

Source: Dongre, Chowdhury, and Aiyar 2012.

Teacher Availability and Instructional Time in Schools

How much time is devoted to actual learning depends on the length of the official school year in hours; the proportion of hours assigned to any given subject; and the amount of time lost through school closings, teacher absences, student absences, and miscellaneous interruptions. Additional time can be made available by after-school study periods and homework assignments. The amount of time teachers spend in school and what they do with that time, therefore, has serious implications for student learning.

Even though the school calendar prescribes the number of school days in a year, hours are lost at numerous points, making the amount of time spent in classroom teaching considerably lower than the number of days for which the school is expected to be functional—900–1,000 hours per year in accordance with international norms (Millot and Lane 2002; Abadzi 2006; Jhingran 2012). In a detailed study of three Indian states, Sankar (2009) found that the estimated number of functioning school days was generally lower than the number of days reported in the school calendar (figure 6.2). In Bangladesh, contact hours in primary school are also much lower than international norms as a result of holidays, double shifts; and other teacher time-consuming responsibilities. According to official directives about school hours, the annual total contact hours in grade 1 is 861 in a single-shift school and 595 hours in a double-shift school, resulting in 30 percent fewer schooling hours for children in double-shift schools, which make up about 90 percent of primary schools (CAMPE 2005). This limited number of official contact hours is further reduced by 19–55 percent (45–130 days out of 238 official days) for various reasons, including elections and teacher training (Rahman, Spaulding, and Tietjen 2004; World Bank 2013).[1]

Figure 6.2 Allocated and Available Time in School, Three Indian States

240
220
200
180
Number of school days
Andhra Pradesh
Madhya Pradesh
Uttar Pradesh
Number of days in school calendar (school reported)
Number of actual days school operated (school reported)
Number of actual functioning school days (estimated)

Source: Jhingran 2012.

Figure 6.3 How Teachers Spend Their Days, Three Indian States

230
220
210
200
190
180
170
160
Number of school days
Uttar Pradesh
Madhya Pradesh
Andhra Pradesh
Number of days on academic activity time in school
Teacher's physical presence time in school
Teacher days for school-related activities
Teacher time within education sector
Available teacher time
School functioning days

Source: Jhingran 2012.

Chapter 5 demonstrated that teacher absenteeism rates in the region were high because of both authorized and unauthorized duty outside of school. Whatever the reason, absenteeism cuts further into the time available for teaching. Ultimately, depending on the state, 12.5–16.5 percent of a school's functioning days are lost (Sankar 2009; see figure 6.3). India is not alone here.

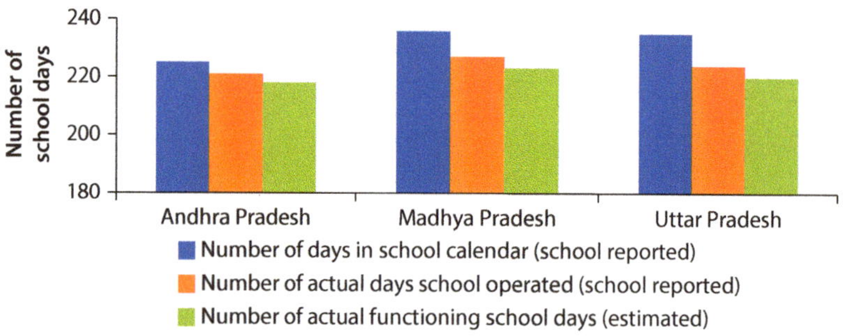

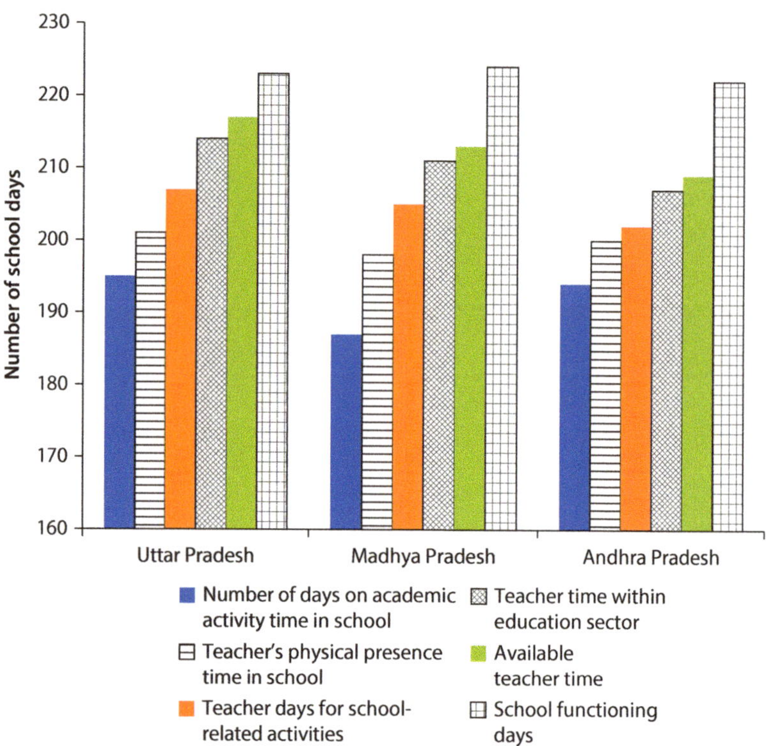

A study of secondary school students in Bangladesh shows that only 82 percent of teachers come to class on time (CAMPE 2007). The situation is worse in primary schools, where approximately 32 percent of government primary school and 29 percent of registered nongovernment primary school teachers are late to school by more than 15 minutes and close to 50 percent of teachers are not in school at the beginning of a school day (FMRP 2006; World Bank 2013).

Teachers reported spending 20–32 hours a week on academic activities, mainly classroom (Sankar 2009): about 26 hours in Andhra Pradesh, 20 in Madhya Pradesh, and 21 in Uttar Pradesh. This means that teaching hours per day were 4 in Andhra Pradesh, 3.2 in Madhya Pradesh, and 3.5 hours in Uttar Pradesh.

Inside the classroom, traditional teaching activities account for a major portion of a teacher's time (figure 6.4). While for lower grades these activities may indeed be important, as children progress toward more senior grades it is important for them to learn higher-order skills, which means instruction should become more student-centric. Yet on average, less than a quarter of classroom time was spent on active learning; classroom discussions, projects, and other creative activity; and remedial teaching. Across the three states, 15 percent of instructional time was spent on rote learning (Sankar 2009).

Studies for Bangladesh also indicate that the most common teaching style is lecturing and reading textbooks (World Bank 2013). As figure 6.5 shows, teachers tend to spend most of their classroom time lecturing or reading textbooks in secondary schools. This pattern is consistent with the findings in primary schools (EI 2010). When there is interaction, it tends to take the form of teachers asking closed questions to check whether students have memorized information in the textbook (Baba 2008).[2] This pedagogical style reflects the pressures from the current examination system, which tests memory recall from the textbooks. Because teachers fear using other approaches may lower performance on examinations, they refrain from using innovative pedagogical practices (Baba 2008).

Figure 6.4 Distribution of Classroom Time, by Activity

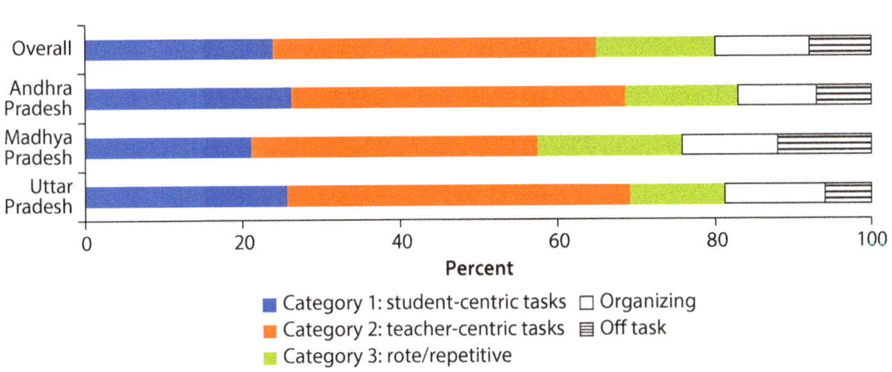

Source: Jhingran 2012.

Figure 6.5 Teachers' Time Allocation in Bangladesh in Grade 9, by Subject

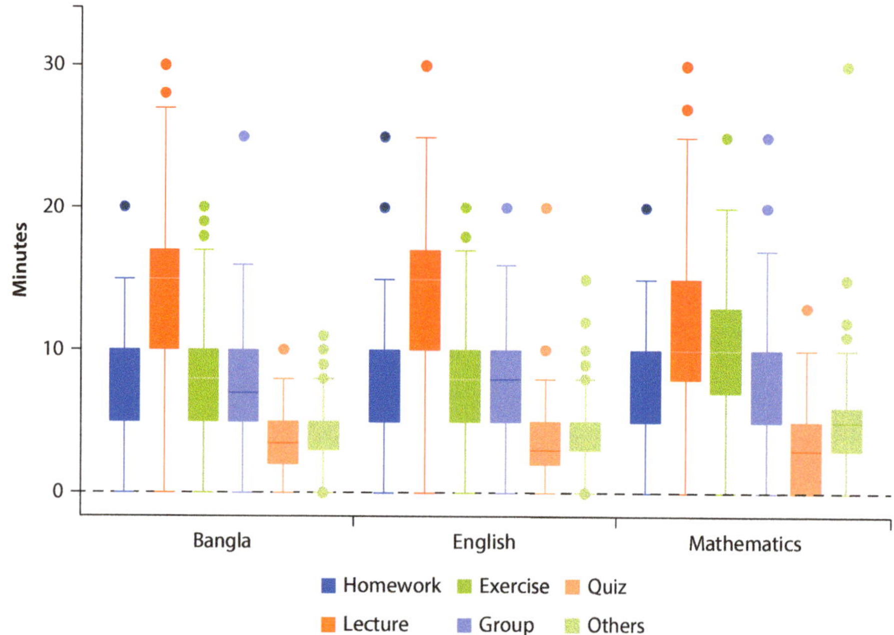

Source: World Bank 2013.
Note: Boxes represent the 75th and 25th percentile, and the line in the middle shows the median.

A Closer Look at Reading

Students in the early grades do particularly badly on reading tests (see chapter 2). In early grades throughout South Asia, a large number of children are taught in a language that differs from their first language, which alienates them from reading and other language-related activities in class. This is especially worrying because reading engenders comprehension, and students need to read with understanding to be able to grasp the entire curriculum, whatever the subject. Ensuring that students learn to read early and well is the most significant way to ensure that every child gets an equal opportunity to learn. It is very difficult for a child who starts falling behind in reading to catch up later without intensive and individualized remedial support, which is rare. "Poor readers read about half as many words as good readers, thus getting half the amount of vocabulary practice and improving their reading skills at a slower rate"(Gove and Cvelich 2010). Deficits early on are difficult to bridge in later grades when textbooks become denser and the language more abstract (Jhingran 2012).

Reading, however, is a complex process that has several constituent subskills (table 6.1). Early grade reading instruction should balance phonics and drill-type activities with meaning-based activities. Decoding must be taught systematically and emphasize revision and practice to ensure the ability to automatically recognize words. In developing countries, language teachers tend to focus on content

Table 6.1 Stages of Reading Development

Stage	*Name*	*The learner*
Stage 0: Birth to grade 1	Emergent literacy	Gains control of oral language; relies heavily on pictures in text; pretends to read; recognizes rhyme
Stage 1: Beginning of grade 1	Decoding	Grows aware of sound and symbol relationships; focuses on printed symbols; attempts to break code of print; uses decoding to figure out words
Stage 2: End of grade 1 through grade 3	Confirmation and fluency	Develops fluency in reading; recognizes patterns in words; checks for meaning and sense; has a stock of words known on sight

Source: Jhingran 2012.

and encourage memorization rather than skills development. South Asia is no exception (Jhingran 2012).

Jhingran (2012) identified school factors that influence learning and reading achievement, particularly number of hours of instruction; strategies for teaching reading; the importance the curriculum and the school place on reading; school resources (e.g., a library); regular assessments; organization of reading activities or events; opportunities for continuing teacher learning; dedicated time for reading; school management; and quality of teachers. Professional development of teachers to respond to early-grade language needs to be prioritized apart from formal training by, for example, mentoring, coaching, and exchange of ideas.

In a detailed analysis of the reading patterns of students in grades 1 and 2 Jhingran (2012) found that student achievement in the Indian states of Rajasthan and Assam had low means and high variances. Students did not acquire mastery/automaticity in recognizing letters by the end of grade 1. Most students were not able to respond to questions that required an inference to be made or an opinion to be expressed. Less than 5 percent of students in Assam and 1 percent in Rajasthan could read with the fluency considered essential for full comprehension. Learning levels in Rajasthan were generally much lower than in Assam (figure 6.6).

As Jhingran (2012) explained the differences in results for the two states

- The existence of a pre-grade 1 class in Assam, though generally neglected, nevertheless offers students a superior foundational experience relative to the largely defunct *anganwadis* in Rajasthan.
- A majority of students in Rajasthan speak Rajasthani and its dialects at home, so in early primary grades their comprehension of standard Hindi is not complete.
- Lower-grade classrooms do not devote time to oral work to help students quickly become competent in the language of instruction.
- Pedagogic practices for teaching reading are inappropriate in both states but in Rajasthan the teaching of letter-sound association (phonics) is done only by

Figure 6.6 Mean Scores for Different Reading Stages, Grades 1 and 2, Assam and Rajasthan, India

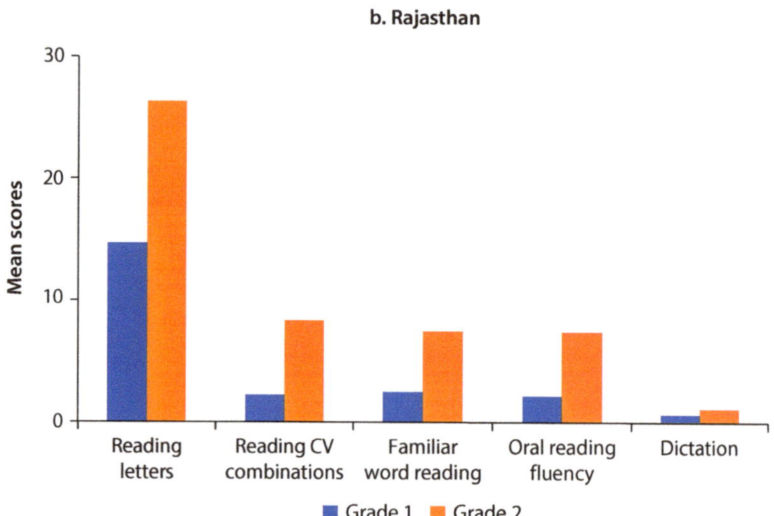

Source: Jhingran 2012.
Note: CV = consonant-vowel.

repeating the alphabet from a chart and copying letters from it. Thus, students do not automatically recognize letters early in grade 1. The same holds true for teaching of vowel signs—a huge barrier to learning to read.

- Teaching of reading/language for early grades is not emphasized in Rajasthan's in-service training programs. Also, the state has no system of regular academic discussion or on-site teacher support. In Assam, although training and academic support are not of high quality, both seem to have had some impact.

Like Sankar (2009), Jhingran found that teachers spend much more of their time on teacher-centric than on student-centric tasks (table 6.2).

In reviewing the time distribution of student activities, Jhingran (2012) noted a disturbing feature: a very high proportion of student time is spent without any meaningful activity or is off task (figure 6.7).[3]

Table 6.2 Teacher Time Spent on Different Activities When Teacher Is On Task, Assam and Rajasthan, India

Percent

Teacher activity	*Assam*	*Rajasthan*
Lecturing/writing on blackboard/explaining	11.5	34.0
Reading from textbook	16.2	11.6
Guiding individual child or group	27.9	24.9
Total for teacher-centric activities	**55.6**	**70.5**
Demonstrating with teaching-learning material	13.5	0
Engaging students in oral activities	8.1	2.8
Engaging students in conversation/discussion	3.4	1.3
Listening to children	1.9	0
Asking/replying to questions	4.1	10.1
Total for student-centric activities	**31.0**	**14.2**
Giving or correcting homework or classwork	4.7	6.9
Giving instructions/forming groups/scolding	8.1	5.4

Source: Jhingran 2012.

Figure 6.7 Distribution of Student Activity, Assam and Rajasthan, India

Percent

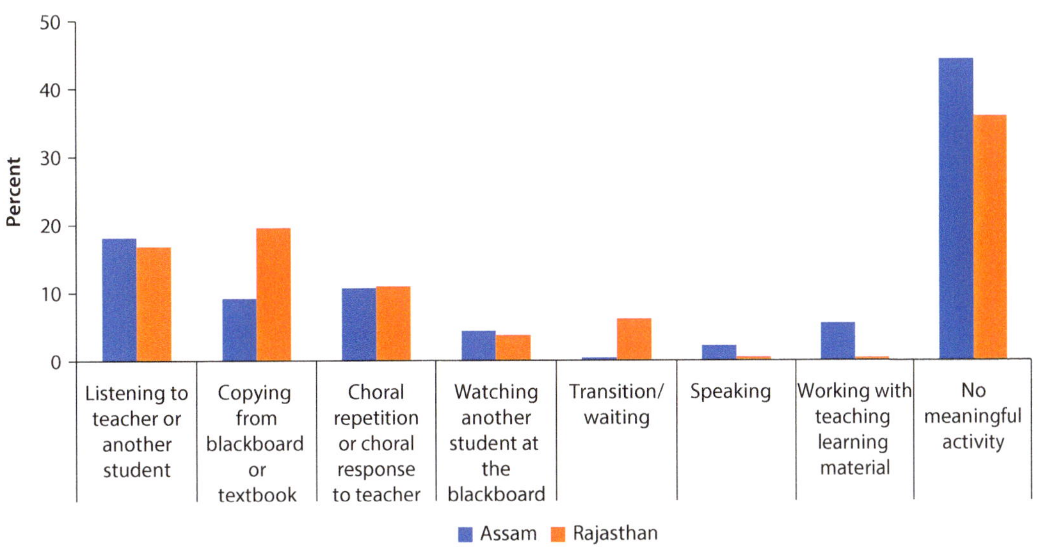

Source: Jhingran 2012.

Addressing Challenges in Pedagogy and Classroom Processes

Getting instruction right is particularly challenging in a context like South Asia, where every year several million first-generation learners enter school, rapidly expanding the scale and scope of the national education system. Many teachers are forced into multigrade teaching or have more than 40 students in a class, and curricula and teaching practices that may have been optimal when fewer were educated may not function well today. Compensatory strategies that Jhingran (2012) identified to support superior reading achievement include enhancing instructional time for language teaching, organizing language learning more effectively, improving teacher understanding and use of effective reading strategies, orienting curriculum and textbooks to real-life situations, supporting active learning pedagogies, promoting within the educational system a better understanding of the importance of reading and language learning in early grades, encouraging professionalization of current teachers, and enhancing quality preprimary education.

While crucial, such reforms take considerable time. In the meantime, several cohorts of students are at risk of gaining very little from schooling. While recognizing the need for substantive reforms in curriculum, textbooks, and teacher training, it is therefore necessary to consider interim strategies to address the immediate challenges. Three strategies that have proved effective in South Asia are remedial and supplemental instruction, ABL, and technology-assisted instruction.

Remedial and Supplemental Instruction

Although meaningful instructional time within classrooms is limited, in any given classroom, certain students lag far behind their peers and the expected curriculum for their grade. Muralidharan and Zieleniak (2012) found that learning trajectories as well as learning levels are low: for most questions of intermediate difficulty, less than 20 percent of students who do not answer a grade N-level question correctly at the end of grade N can answer it correctly at the end of grade N+1 years in school. While no doubt adding some learning, additional years in school do not seem to be very effective in improving learning outcomes, especially considering the economic cost of each additional year. The same authors also found that variance in student ability within a cohort increased over time.

Similarly, Andrabi et al. (2007) found that 50 percent of the variation in learning levels in a representative sample of government-run schools in the Punjab came from students in the same class, taught by the same teacher. Like multigrade schools, such heterogeneous learning raises the analogous question of how a teacher can effectively teach a classroom of students whose academic achievement varies widely. While teacher training programs should equip teachers to help slow learners, remedial education could prove a useful supplement. Remedial programs offer the possibility of teaching pupils who lag behind at a level appropriate to their achievement. Ideally, such intervention increases student advancement and decreases learning heterogeneity in a given grade.

On the other hand, if remedial programs teach at a slower (and lower) level, students who did not need remediation might have achieved more without it.

Banerjee et al. (2007) conducted an experimental evaluation of a remedial program run by Pratham, an Indian nongovernmental organization (NGO), that targeted the lowest-performing children in public schools in Mumbai and Vadodara. The program gave schools an informal teacher hired from the community (a *balsakhi*, "friend of the child") who was directed to focus on third- and fourth-grade students who had not achieved even basic competencies in reading and arithmetic. The children were taken out of the regular classroom for two hours a day and given instruction targeted at their current level of learning. The program improved student test scores by 0.28 standard deviations, with most of the gains coming from students at the lower end of the learning distribution. The effectiveness of the program is particularly remarkable considering that the balsakhis did not have any formal teacher training and were paid less than a fifth of the salary of regular teachers.

Further evidence that remedial instruction can be effective comes from an experimental evaluation in Uttar Pradesh of programs designed to improve community participation in education. Of several interventions tested, the only one found to improve learning outcomes was a remedial program conducted by youth volunteers from the village who were given a week of training and conducted after-school reading camps for two to three months. The effects on learning were substantial: the average child who could not read at baseline and who attended a camp was 60 percentage points more likely to be able to read the alphabet than a similar child in a control village.

A third piece of evidence comes from Lakshminarayana et al. (2013), who studied the impact of a remedial program run by the NGO Naandi Foundation, again working with community volunteers, in randomly selected villages in Andhra Pradesh. The volunteers first worked with parents to elicit commitment to send their children to the after-school program. After this sensitization, the volunteers gave remedial instruction after school two hours every day in the school itself. The subject matter was tailored to class-specific needs and learning levels and reinforced the school curriculum. After two years, student test scores in program villages were 0.74 standard deviation higher than those in the comparison group, suggesting that the remedial instruction had significant impact.

While together these studies present convincing evidence that remedial instruction programs can be effective, to date the evidence all comes from ad hoc programs. Scaling them up will require both careful design to integrate remedial instruction into the regular curriculum and analysis of the impact on students higher up in the learning distribution. A fundamental issue in scaling up is that teachers must modify their pedagogy away from the standard practice of working to complete the textbook-based syllabus. Banerjee et al. (2012) studied the impact of a program implemented by Pratham with the state governments of Uttarakhand and Bihar to scale up remedial instruction in public schools. The program deployed a set of pedagogical materials called CAMaL (Combined Activities for Maximized Learning) that targeted instruction to the learning level of the children and evaluated different models for using the CAMaL materials. The study found that while summer camps conducted by regular teachers trained in the use of the new materials did raise test scores, other models that attempted to incorporate the CAMaL pedagogy into the regular school day had no impact.

While this suggests that the CAMaL pedagogy could be successful, the researchers noted that it was clearly difficult to get teachers to use new curricula during school hours; they appeared to consider the new pedagogy to be a distraction from the regular syllabus they had to cover. But it is important to highlight that the authors were able to fully rule out the possibility that the good results from the summer program reflected the additional instructional time rather than the pedagogy itself. Thus, potential explanations for program success could be students spending more time on the materials, students giving the materials more focused attention, and materials being tailored to lower levels.

Nevertheless, the consistent evidence from four studies that all used a similar model of remedial instruction and were led by community volunteers but in very different settings (urban areas of Gujarat and Maharashtra and rural Uttar Pradesh, Uttarakhand, Bihar, and Andhra Pradesh) is that supplemental instruction can improve learning outcomes. These programs were all highly cost-effective, since local volunteers were paid only modest stipends. It may make sense to scale up remedial instruction as a supplemental program rather than as part of the regular curriculum.

However, to the extent that the bulk of the education budget is allocated to transmission of the regular curriculum, there may be large gains in modifying instructional practices to better tailor teaching to the actual level of the students. More fundamentally, it may be necessary to reconsider the curriculum itself, since it may move too fast for the vast majority of first-generation learners. The issue of curriculum design has been highlighted by Banerjee and Duflo (2011) and by Pritchett and Beatty (2012), who pointed out that curricula in South Asia were designed by highly educated elites at a time when there were no expectations of universal primary education. Indeed, as they note, the historical purpose of education in many developing countries may have been not so much to provide human capital to all students as to screen out gifted students for positions of state and religious responsibility. Since the textbook is the default mode of instruction, and teachers define their yearly goals in terms of completing the curriculum, it is not surprising that they are effectively teaching to the top and that a large number of their pupils are not learning because the lessons are too advanced for them.

While there has been no direct test of this hypothesis in India, it is consistent with the findings of numerous experimental evaluations of education interventions there in the past decade. In particular, the idea that business as usual will enhance learning outcomes is challenged by the positive results of the remedial instruction programs run by lightly trained and modestly paid volunteers, even as heavy investments in teacher qualifications and training, pupil-teacher ratio reductions, and school infrastructure have not raised test scores.

This view is also consistent with evidence from numerous studies in Africa. Glewwe, Kremer, and Moulin (2009) found that a program that provided free textbooks to children in Kenya had no impact on average test scores, but students in the top 20 percent on the baseline test score distribution fared significantly better. This clearly makes sense if only the top 20 percent of students could read well enough to benefit from a textbook. Duflo, Dupas, and Kremer (2009) studied a program in Kenya that compared changes in the test scores of students in the regular classroom with those of students tracked according to initial learning levels and found that students in the tracked classrooms did significantly better whatever their initial level of learning. This suggests that reducing the variance of learning levels in a classroom allows teachers to target instruction much more effectively.

A natural implication of this theory is that there may be high returns when curricula move at different paces for students of different levels (Banerjee and Duflo 2011), or even when the pace of the general curriculum is slower (Pritchett and Beatty 2012). However, since there is as yet no good evidence that such curricular reforms affect learning levels and trajectories, this should be a high priority area for future research. Some governments have made attempts to reform curricula in this way (see the next section), but the changes have been made system wide without careful evaluation, so it is not clear whether the reforms have improved learning outcomes. Considerable further work is needed to design and evaluate optimal models for modifying curricula and pedagogy to raise the quality of education.

Activity-Based Learning

One approach to targeting instruction to student learning levels is Activity-Based Learning (ABL). First developed in the 1990s in the Rishi Valley Rural Education Center in Andhra Pradesh, ABL embraces multigrade and remedial practices along with elements of self-learning so that students can advance at their own pace. The curriculum consists of small units of self-learning materials that are completed sequentially. This means students are not forced to progress with their age cohort and accommodates those who started late, are absent, or learn at different rates.

With ABL converting multigrade environments into a strength rather than a liability, students are encouraged to work together in small groups and even to study with students in different grades. ABL provides structure and materials so that students do not sit idly while the teacher is facilitating the learning of another group. In addition to self-learning techniques and a vertical classroom structure rather than having all students of the same age grouped as a cohort, ABL also provides innovative materials, methods for monitoring and evaluation, and peer teaching (Anandalakshmy 2007).

The most prominent adopter of ABL has been the Indian state of Tamil Nadu. ABL was supported there by the United Nations Children's Fund (UNICEF), piloted by the Chennai Corporation in 2003, and later adopted throughout the state. In 2007–08, the state government conducted a study of ABL in its schools

(SchoolScape 2008). The study selected a representative sample of schools and surveyed—through observations and interviews with teachers and students—how the students were being taught. After a year of training teachers in ABL, the surveyors returned to a subsample of the schools and conducted a similar survey to assess whether any changes could be attributable to the spread of ABL.

Over the course of the year, 88 percent of teachers had attended trainings on ABL and 31 percent had attended more than 10 trainings. There was a decrease in teacher use of blackboards and textbooks and a significant increase in student use of blackboards. They also found displays of student work in classrooms, use of self-learning cards, and multigrade group work. These results suggest that the ABL trainings had changed teacher behavior and classroom processes. Comparing test scores of second- and fourth-grade students in 2007 and 2008, the researchers found on average significant increases in English, Tamil, and math test scores for all baseline test score percentiles. ABL apparently promoted learning at all student levels (SchoolScape 2008). Finally, a decrease in score variances suggests that there was convergence in learning. However, the results are based on simple before-and-after comparisons, and since there would also have been some progress in a non-ABL structure, it is not possible to ascribe causality.

Given the findings reported in Banerjee et al. (2012) about the difficulty of changing pedagogy, the SchoolScape (2008) study of ABL in Tamil Nadu is encouraging. The study found that it is possible to change teacher behavior toward a pedagogy that is substantially different from standard textbook-driven instruction. Of course, the changes were part of a specific decision of state education department leadership to reorient the pedagogy, unlike the pilot projects in Bihar and Uttarakhand studied by Banerjee et al. (2012).

However, while there is evidence that ABL has been adopted throughout Tamil Nadu, there is no rigorous evidence that the change has had an impact on learning. The program was scaled up very quickly, which makes it difficult to construct a valid comparison group even for retrospective studies. The lack of rigorous evidence on outcomes is particularly unfortunate, given (a) the theoretical promise of this technique to address the challenges of multigrade classrooms and heterogeneous learning levels both within and across grades and (b) the keen interest other states in India are showing in replicating it (for instance, the Nalli Kalli program in Karnataka is based on the ABL approach). It should therefore be a priority for researchers and policy makers to rigorously evaluate the effect of ABL on learning outcomes. Perhaps this could be done as the approach is rolled out in other states.

Technology-Assisted Instruction

Greater use of technology in classrooms is commonly thought of as a promising way to rapidly improve education outcomes in developing countries. Posited channels of impact are (a) cost-effective replication and scaling up of high-quality instruction via broadcast technology, such as radio and television; (b) overcoming limitations in teacher knowledge and training, for instance, for teaching more advanced concepts in science and mathematics or a new language like English, for which there is growing demand but a limited supply of competent teachers; (c) providing supplemental instruction at home; (d) engaging children more deeply in the learning process through interactive modules, such as games and puzzles; and (e) customizing learning plans for individual students. Interventions can be quite inexpensive (radio-based instruction, for instance) or very expensive (individual laptops, as envisaged by the One Laptop per Child [OLPC] initiative).

While the promise of technology in instruction is apparent, and there are many advocates for it, there have been few rigorous evaluations of its benefits. Skeptical scholars have even argued that promotion of technology is fueled more by its prestige as a symbol of modernity than by any actual evidence that it is effective. There may be adverse consequences, the simplest of which would be that an ineffective technology would not increase achievement and would take time away from more effective teaching techniques. It is imaginable that if technology were able to cater to different achievement levels, it would be superior in teaching a classroom of heterogeneous students. Yet if technology is effective with those at the higher end of the learning distribution, it might exacerbate the problem of lagging children.

Understanding the efficacy of technology is especially important because it is often far more expensive than other activities, and if it does not lead to superior learning outcomes, other teaching methods would be more cost-effective.

The few studies conducted in South Asia illustrate that while technology can be useful for improving achievement, its success depends on numerous factors, such as the student's initial achievement, its integration with the current teaching structure, and the teacher's knowledge of the subject. The sensitivity of the results to the specifics of the intervention was pointed out by Linden (2008), who found that an after-school computer-assisted learning program contributed to test score gains, but when it replaced regular teacher time average students learned less than they otherwise would. Not all technology is an optimal use of class time. Furthermore, even as the after-school option, it is not clear whether it was the program itself that led to higher gains or the fact that students were spending additional time on the material.

He, Linden, and Macleod (2008) analyzed an intervention for improving English skills that was partly directed by teachers and partly had students using a self-paced machine. While both components led to gains in test scores, stronger students fared better using the machine, but weaker students benefited more from the guidance of a teacher. Therefore, when introducing a technology-based intervention, how much the student already knows needs to be considered. Alternatively, a teacher could perhaps be well equipped to handle weaker students, but more advanced students could use the technology to fill in gaps in the teacher's knowledge. The researchers also found that the achievement gains were most successful when implemented by current teachers rather than an outsider—thus, who implements the program and how may affect achievement. The various studies caution that not all technology-based interventions should be assumed to be successful; it is important to consider how the technology interacts with student and teacher characteristics.

Although set in a different middle-income context, it is worth noting the results of an evaluation of the much-publicized OLPC program in Peru (Cristia et al. 2012). The study found that while the program increased the ratio of computers to students in treatment schools from 0.12 to 1.18, there was no impact on either school enrollment or test scores in math and language, although there were some positive effects on general-purpose measures of intelligence, such as the Raven's Progressive Matrices. Introducing computers into classrooms will not necessarily by itself lead to improvements in learning. These cautionary results are especially relevant where, as in India, it is tempting to scale up interventions like "tablet computers for all" as a short cut to addressing education quality.

In contrast, a recent evaluation of the OLPC program in Sri Lanka found significant gains in student learning and parental involvement (Aturupane and Deolalikar 2012). Despite the fact that the OLPC pilot and the end-line survey were separated by only a year, the experiment noted fairly large impacts of the OLPC intervention on student test scores. On average, for students in grades 2 and 3 (in the baseline period, 2009), the effect of the OLPC pilot was to increase test scores by about 22–23 percent. For students in grade 1 (in 2009), however, the estimated OLPC effect on cognitive scores was not significantly different from zero. The study found considerable heterogeneity in the impact of the OLPC pilot on test scores, with larger effects for boys than girls, older children than children under age 7 years, students with more-educated mothers than students with less-educated mothers, and students from higher-income backgrounds than those from lower-income backgrounds. An implication of these findings is that, along with the distribution of the laptops, the OLPC program also needs to provide mentoring, training, and support services to girls, younger children, and students from poor family education backgrounds so that they can make the most of the laptops they receive.

The study found large increases in parental involvement in their children's studies—in the form of helping children with their homework and attending school functions and parent-teacher association meetings—and in parental aspirations for their children's education both among the treated and the control group of students. It is likely that there was a demonstration effect of the OLPC scheme; in other words, the control group of students and their parents, having heard of the OLPC program in nearby schools, may have thought that their likelihood of being selected into the OLPC scheme in the future could increase if they performed better. Thus, even though it did not touch them directly, the OLPC intervention may have given the parents of the control group the incentive to increase their involvement and participation in their children's academic work and their aspirations for their children's education.

Finally, while technology-based interventions can improve achievement, it is not always clear that they are the most cost-effective means of doing so. Banerjee et al. (2007) found that a computer remedial program increases test scores twice as much as a remedial teacher, but scaling up the teacher-based remedial program would be 5–7 times more cost-effective.

Summary

While inputs are enablers, educating children fundamentally depends on how classroom instruction is transacted. It depends not only upon teachers being present but on how they use the time when they are there. This chapter suggests that the default pattern of instruction has been teachers teaching from a textbook at a uniform pace for all students and spending little time on student-centric activities. This practice, unfortunately, begins early on in primary grades, compromising the ability of a large number of students to read. When students cannot read, they cannot grasp other subjects, such as mathematics and science. Further, reading disadvantages accumulate over time, making it even harder for children to benefit from schooling.

Although research has underscored the urgent need for core reforms in curriculum design, textbooks, and teacher training, reforms take time. What can be done in the interim to ensure that the large numbers of first-generation learners gain from their schooling experience? The evidence is that supplemental instruction programs targeted to the student's own level, ABL, and certain types of technology-assisted learning can have significant positive impacts.

Notes

1. Reasons for school closure include time dedicated for administrative work as the school year begins and ends, training for teachers, health campaigns, elections, school contingencies, and natural disasters (Rahman, Spaulding, and Tietjen 2004).
2. For example, "Yes or No?" questions and "A or B?" questions.
3. Students are considered off task when they are (a) not involved in the instructional activity, (b) engaged in social interaction not related to instruction, or (c) being disciplined. Baker (2007) defines off-task behavior in learning environments as occurring when "a student completely disengages from the learning environment and task to engage in an unrelated behavior."

Bibliography

Abadzi, H. 2006. *Efficient Learning for the Poor: Insights from the Frontier of Cognitive Neuroscience*. Washington, DC: World Bank.

Anandalakshmy, S. 2007. *Activity Based Learning: A Report on an Innovative Method in Tamil Nadu*. Chennai, India: SSA State Project Directorate.

Andrabi, T., J. Das, A. Khwaja, T. Vishwanath, and T. Zajonc. 2007. *Pakistan: Learning and Educational Achievements in Punjab Schools (LEAPS): Insights to Inform the Educational Policy Debate*. http://www.leapsproject.org/assets/publications/LEAPS_Report_ExecSummary.pdf.

Aturupane, D. H., and A. Deolalikar. 2012. "Randomized Evaluation of the One Laptop per Child Program in Sri Lanka, 2009–11." Draft Report, Human Development Unit, South Asia Region, World Bank, Washington, DC.

Baba, T. 2008. "A Study on the Program Approach Framework in International Cooperation and Japanese Style Education Model". Study Report, Hiroshima University, Hiroshima,

Japan. (In Japanese: *Kokusaikyouryoku ni okeru Program Approach no Wakugumi to Nihongata Kyouiku Kyouryoku Model no Kousatu*).

Baker, R. S. J. D. 2007. "Modeling and Understanding Students' Off-Task Behavior in Intelligent Tutoring Systems." *Proceedings of ACM CHI 2007: Computer-Human Interaction*, 1059–68. New York: ACM.

Banerjee, A., R. Banerji, E. Duflo, and M. Walton. 2012. "Effective Pedagogies and a Resistant Education System: Experimental Evidence on Interventions to Improve Basic Skills in Rural India." Unpublished manuscript, Abdul Latif Jameel Poverty Action Lab (JPAL), Massachusetts Institute of Technology, Cambridge, MA.

Banerjee, A. V., S. Cole, E. Duflo, and L. Linden. 2007. "Remedying Education: Evidence from Two Randomized Experiments in India." *The Quarterly Journal of Economics* 122 (3):1235–64.

Banerjee, A., and E. Duflo. 2011. *Poor Economics: A Radical Rethinking of the Way To Fight Global Poverty*. New York: PublicAffairs.

Banu, L. F. 2009. "Problems and Misconceptions Facing the Primary Language Education in Bangladesh: An Analysis of Curricula and Pedagogic Practices." *BRAC University Journal* 1 (2): 1–10.

Béteille, T., and S. Loeb. 2009. "Teacher Quality and Teacher Labor Markets." In *Handbook of Education Policy Research*, edited by G. Sykes, B. Schneider, and D. N. Plank. London: Routledge.

CAMPE (Campaign for Popular Education Bangladesh). 2005. *Education Watch 2003/4. Quality with Equity: The Primary Education Agenda*. Dhaka.

———. 2007. *Education Watch Report 2006. Financing Primary and Secondary Education in Bangladesh*. Dhaka.

Cristia, J., P. Ibarraran, S. Cueto, A. Santiago, and E. Severin. 2012. "Technology and Child Development: Evidence from the One Laptop per Child Program." Discussion Paper 6401, Institute for the Study of Labor, Bonn, Germany.

Desai, S., A. Dubey, R. Vanneman, and R. Banerji. 2009. "Private Schooling in India: A New Educational Landscape." *India Policy Forum* 5 (1): 1–38.

Dongre, A., A. Chowdhury, and Y. Aiyar. 2012. "Unpacking School Finances." Draft Background Note, Human Development Unit, South Asia Region, World Bank, Washington, DC.

Duflo, E., P. Dupas, and M. Kremer. 2009. "Additional Resources Versus Organizational Changes in Education: Experimental Evidence from Kenya." Unpublished manuscript, Abdul Latif Jameel Poverty Action Lab (JPAL), Massachusetts Institute of Technology, Cambridge, MA.

EI (Educational Initiatives). 2010. "Student Learning Study. Status of Learning across 18 Sites of India in Urban and Rural Schools." http://www.ei-india.com/wp-content/uploads/2012/01/Main_Report_StudentLearningStudy_2010_by_Educational_Initiatives1.pdf.

FMRP (Financial Management Reform Programme). 2006. *Primary Education in Bangladesh: Assessing Service Delivery*. Final Report of Social Sector Performance Survey. Bangladesh: FMRP.

Glewwe, P., M. Kremer, and S. Moulin. 2009. "Many Children Left Behind? Textbooks and Test Scores in Kenya." *American Economic Journal: Applied Economics* 1 (1): 112–35.

Gove, A., and P. Cvelich. 2010. *Early Reading: Igniting Education for All.* Report by the Early Grades Learning Community of Practice. Research Triangle Park, NC: Research Triangle Institute.

He, F., L. Linden, and M. MacLeod. 2008. "How to Teach English in India: Testing the Relative Productivity of Instruction Methods within the Pratham English Language Education Program." Unpublished paper, Columbia University, New York.

Jhingran, D. 2012. "A Study of the School Based Academic Factors Affecting Reading Achievement of Students in Primary Grades." Dissertation, Jamia Millia Islamia University, New Delhi.

Lakshminarayana, R., A. Eble, P. Bhakta, C. Frost, and P. Boone. 2013. "The Support to Rural India's Public Education System (STRIPES) Trial: A Cluster Randomised Controlled Trial of Supplementary Teaching, Learning Material and Material Support." *PLoS One* 8 (7): e65775.

Linden, L. L. 2008. *Complement or Substitute? The Effect of Technology on Student Achievement in India.* Boston, MA: Poverty Action Lab, Massachusetts Institute of Technology.

Lockheed, M. 2011. "The Condition of Primary Education in Developing Countries." In *Effective Schools in Developing Countries*, edited by H. Levin and M. Lockheed. New York: Routledge.

Millot, B., and J. Lane. 2002. "The Efficient Use of Time in Education." *Education Economics* 10 (2): 209–28.

Muralidharan, K., and Y. Zieleniak. 2012. *Measuring Learning Trajectories in Developing Countries with Longitudinal Data and Item Response Theory.* Manuscript, University of California, San Diego, CA.

NCERT (National Council of Educational Research and Training). 2005. "National Curriculum Framework." NCERT, New Delhi.

———. 2006. *Position Paper: National Focus Group on Examination Reforms.* New Delhi: NCERT.

PAISA Report. 2011. *Do Schools Get Their Money?* New Delhi: Accountability Initiative. http://www.accountabilityindia.in/article/state-report-cards/2475-paisa-report-2011.

Perera, W. J. 2009. "Programme on School Improvement: A Participatory Approach to Facilitate School Improvement as Opposed to a Bureaucratic Approach." Paper presented at the South Asia Regional Dialogue on Education Quality, Agha Khan University, Karachi, Pakistan.

———. 2012. "Education Decentralization in Sri Lanka." Background note prepared for this report, Human Development Department, South Asia Region, World Bank, Washington, DC.

Pianta, R. C., and B. K. Hamre. 2009. "Conceptualization, Measurement, and Improvement of Classroom Processes: Standardized Observation Can Leverage Capacity." *Educational Researcher* 38 (2): 109–19.

Pritchett, L., and A. Beatty. 2012. "The Negative Consequences of Overambitious Curricula in Developing Countries." Working Paper 293, Center for Global Development, Washington, DC.

Rahman, A., S. Spaulding, and K. Tietjen. 2004. *Bangladesh Educational Assessment Time to Learn: Teachers' and Students' Use of Time in Government Primary Schools in Bangladesh.* Washington, DC: U.S. Agency for International Development.

Sankar, D. 2009. "Teachers' Time on Task and Nature of Tasks: Evidence from Three Indian States." Human Development Unit, South Asia Region, World Bank, Washington, DC.

SchoolScape. 2008. "Activity Based Learning: Effectiveness of ABL under SSA." SchoolScape, Chennai, India. http://www.ashanet.org/siliconvalley/asha20/pdfs/amukta_abl_tn.pdf.

World Bank. 2013. *Bangladesh Education Sector Review*. Human Development Sector, South Asia Region, Report 80613-BD. Washington, DC: World Bank.

PART 4

Determinants of Learning Outcomes: Systems-Level Factors

This report has reached several conclusions about education in South Asian countries:

- Access to education has expanded vastly in the past decade, although several countries in the region are still not likely to achieve the education Millennium Development Goals, especially for girls.
- Average acquisition of basic skills is still very low by both national and international standards.
- Inadequate knowledge and skills among graduates from both government and private school systems are a serious detriment to the growth and competitiveness of the private sector, and therefore to the creation of more and better jobs in the region.
- Poor learning outcomes result not only from disparities in school readiness (e.g., malnutrition) but also from ineffective use of school resources (e.g., teachers), in spite of a significant expansion of resources over the past decade.

Part 4 explores institutional, economic, political, and social factors that have a direct bearing on student learning outcomes in South Asia. Prominent among the institutional factors are ministries of education, which affect how the system functions through the design and application of education policies, such as financing, student assessment, quality assurance, and other regulatory mechanisms. Similarly, political, social and economic conditions affect how the education system operates and the inputs it provides. These exogenous factors are beyond the control of the system itself.

In this part, chapter 7 documents evidence about the use of public finance to improve the quality of learning. Chapter 8 explores the use and effectiveness of student assessments in improving the quality of learning in South Asia.

Chapter 9 reviews trends in the delivery of private education and examines the learning skills private schools engender. Finally, chapter 10 reviews education decentralization as part of broad governance and accountability reforms and examines whether such reforms have improved learning outcomes. It also identifies lessons learned, based on both regional and international experience.

CHAPTER 7

Financing for Quality Education*

Introduction

The push for comprehensive quality education for all carries considerable financial responsibilities. While governments are ultimately tasked with ensuring access—both as a fundamental right (enshrined, for example, in India's Right to Education Act [RTE] of 2009) and in order to garner the social benefits of education for society as a whole—government schools are also the primary vehicle through which the aims of universal quality education are realized.

Financing systems in South Asia not only vary tremendously, they are extremely complex. They differ in level of spending, target of spending, degree of decentralization, extent of private sector provision, and modalities of financing. South Asia is large, diverse, and densely populated, home to about a fifth of the world's population. Countries in the region differ noticeably not just in size[1] but also economically, ethnically, and politically—all of which affect the role and the efficiency of the state in providing education and make it difficult to make comparisons within the region. Nevertheless, one thing that is consistent across the region is the rapid economic growth experienced for the last decade, averaging from 3.9 percent to 7.2 percent. Economic growth has been accompanied by burgeoning growth in demand for schooling: in India, for instance, net primary school enrollment went from 79 percent to 91 percent. The enormous economic changes in the region are placing immense stress on its education systems.

This chapter does not attempt to describe in detail the complex mechanisms for financing education in South Asia, or budgetary processes and the flow of funds. Rather, it considers the financing of primary and secondary education from only one angle—quality—and examines the types of expenditures and financial tools that are more likely to improve it. The starting point is the general assumption that the main barrier to improving education quality is the lack of resources. This is indeed the thrust of educational policy discussions in most developing countries, which talk about the financial and logistical challenges of providing

*See box 7.1 for a summary of the chapter's key questions and findings.

Box 7.1 Questions and Findings

Questions

- Has South Asia been short of resources to invest in education?
- Would more, and more appropriate, inputs improve the quality of education?
- How could financing be used to improve learning outcomes?

Findings

- In South Asia, although public spending on education as a proportion of the budget is in line with that of developed countries—which demonstrates high government commitment—spending per pupil is significantly lower. Increases in the absolute amount of funding, made possible by a long period of growth, have been absorbed by escalations in enrollment, leaving per-pupil expenditures roughly constant. It appears that while countries in the region give the same priority to education as more developed countries, they face financial constraints on providing high-quality education. This resource constraint, although partially alleviated in the past two decades by dramatic increases in household spending on education, means that, to increase quality, use of resources must be highly efficient.

- With continuous growth, presumably more resources could be spent on education so that more and better inputs would be available. The implicit assumption is that this will translate into better learning outcomes. However, the evidence suggests that more inputs do not necessarily improve quality significantly. For instance, upgrading school infrastructure is important to attract and retain children but it has not been found to be correlated with better learning outcomes. That is also true of school feeding programs, which seem effective mostly as a social protection program that stimulates demand for education. For books and other learning materials to have a positive impact on learning, it is necessary to ensure that (a) they reach the intended beneficiaries, (b) they are adapted to children's reading levels, and (c) parents do not offset the impact of higher public spending by reducing their own spending. Households often seem to react to public spending by re-optimizing their own allocations.

- Although (see chapter 5) improvements in teacher quality are likely to have a high payoff, there is mixed evidence internationally about how hiring more teachers and lowering student-teacher ratios affects learning. A number of studies have found that reducing class size has positive impacts, but these are modest. Given its high cost, reducing class size may not be a cost-effective way to improve test scores.

- Raising teacher salaries to a level that can attract and retain the best applicants is another option. This seems to be true for regular government teachers in most of South Asia, but there is no evidence that further increases, unless accompanied by changes in accountability, would bring long-run gains in student learning.

box continues next page

Box 7.1 Questions and Findings *(continued)*

- These findings should not be interpreted as implying that resources and spending on school inputs do not matter; it is just that their impact is likely to be too small to be the source of radical improvements in quality. Internationally, little correlation has been found between spending on schooling and student learning.

- What seems promising to achieve significant improvements in quality are changes in the incentive structure for teachers and schools. The evidence, though limited, implies that accountability systems—based on tests of student learning (performance-related pay [PRP] and promotions)—could induce teachers to put in more effort in the classroom, change pedagogical processes, and use inputs and training received more effectively. Similarly, a shift from block grants to per-pupil funding would help ensure that schools are more accountable, and a system of funding that ties increases in allocations to school performance indicators could have major benefits for children's learning. The point is to forge a closer link between financing and outcomes, rather than inputs. South Asian countries are aware of the importance of incentives and accountability but have barely begun to move in this direction.

- Another approach to quality through more efficient allocation of resources would be to leverage the contribution of the private sector and look for public-private partnership arrangements—with careful attention to their design to ensure that efficiency and equity incentives are built in. Although the evidence on the impact of vouchers is still limited, trial programs accompanied by rigorous evaluation may be worth considering.

- So far educational financing in South Asia has mostly focused on the challenge of improving access, and indeed access to education has increased gradually for all socioeconomic groups, and there is less disparity in educational attainment between the richest and the poorest. There is also greater equality of opportunity for girls. However, inequality in learning across socioeconomic groups is still larger than inequality in access to education.

- In future, countries should consider putting more emphasis on funding mechanisms that can enhance the quality of education, especially in primary schools, which would highly benefit the poor. Also, while continuing to work to reduce the number of out-of-school children generally, it would be beneficial to better target educational subsidies and other interventions directly to the poorest. If these programs were made more efficient, reallocating resources would have a more impressive payoff.

requisite minimum levels as well as better inputs. The implicit assumption is that more and better inputs will automatically enhance learning outcomes.

This chapter first reviews levels of education spending in South Asia and whether South Asia has been able to ensure a minimum threshold of resources to produce certain learning outcomes. It appears that from a share-of-budget point of view, education spending in South Asia is similar to what developed nations spend (implying high government commitment to education), but both as a percentage of gross domestic product (GDP) and per pupil, spending is low in the largest South Asian countries. This short-term resource constraint, although eased by increases in household spending on education, means that to increase quality, use of resources must be highly efficient.

This chapter next examines the impact on quality that could be expected should it be possible to increase spending on school facilities and infrastructure, books and learning materials, school feeding programs, and number and pay of teachers.[2] Finally, the chapter turns its attention to financing tools not yet used extensively in the region that have potential for improving learning outcomes.

One major difficulty in evaluating education financing systems is the lack of data for developing countries. While macro data are available for most countries, micro data are often deficient. This problem is compounded by the fact that even when data are available, they are often contradictory. This makes it hard to draw an accurate picture and discern region-wide patterns, suggesting caution in drawing region-wide inferences.

Has South Asia Been Short of Resources for Education?

To answer this question, we need to examine whether school financing is adequate—whether South Asian school systems have the capacity to ensure that the minimum inputs required for quality basic education are accessible to all learners. Determining how much financing is adequate is not a simple task. Basic education goals and standards, as well as the costs of achieving these standards, may vary by country (Baker and Green 2008). Nevertheless, since some international comparisons may be informative, three types of indicators are discussed here: (a) the percentage of GDP allocated to education, (b) per capita and per-student education expenditure, and (c) the share of government financial outlays allocated to education. All three refer to public financing. Private contributions can add resources to the education sector. This section will also briefly examine the extent to which household contributions have increased the resources invested in basic education.

Education's Share of GDP

Public spending for education as a share of GDP[3] in most of South Asia is well below the Organisation for Economic Co-operation and Development (OECD) average (see table 7.1), particularly in Bangladesh and Pakistan, where for 1999–2009 it seemed to stagnate at an average of just 2.4 percent. These estimates cover all levels of education, from primary to tertiary. In Sri Lanka, education spending as a percentage of GDP seems to have been significantly lower in 2009

Table 7.1 Government Spending on Education[a]
Percentage of GDP

	1999	2000	2001	2002	2003	2004	2005	2006	2007	2008	2009	1999–2009
Afghanistan	—	—	—	—	—	—	—	—	4.6	4.4	—	—
Bangladesh	2.4	2.4	2.5	2.3	2.4	2.3	—	2.5	2.6	2.4	—	2.4
Bhutan[b]	—	5.0	—	—	—	—	—	—	—	—	7.3	—
India	4.5	4.4	—	—	3.7	3.4	3.1	—	3.1	—	—	3.7
Maldives	—	—	—	—	—	—	—	—	—	—	8.4	—
Nepal	2.9	3.0	3.7	3.4	3.1	—	—	—	—	3.8	4.7	3.5
Pakistan	2.6	1.8	—	—	2.0	2.0	2.3	2.6	2.8	2.9	2.7	2.4
Sri Lanka[c]	3.1	2.9	3.1	—	—	—	—	—	—	—	2.1	2.8
OECD average	5.3	5.2	5.3	5.5	5.6	5.6	5.5	5.5	5.3	5.3	5.5	5.4

Sources: a. UNESCO Institute of Statistics except where noted; b. World Bank 2012a; and c. UNESCO Budgeting Report, 2003.
Note: These estimates cover all levels of education, from primary to tertiary. — = not available; GDP = gross domestic product; OECD = Organisation for Economic Co-operation and Development.

Table 7.2 Public Expenditure on Education per Student, All Levels (Purchasing Power Parity)
US dollars

	1999	2000	2001	2002	2003	2004	2005	2006	2007	2008	2009	1999–2009
Bangladesh	—	—	—	—	—	—	—	166.7	187.5	—	—	—
India	365.2	351.1	—	—	317.0	305.2	319.5	351.7	—	—	—	—
Nepal	117.1	123.4	156.9	141.4	135.6	—	—	—	—	—	—	—
Pakistan				—	194.8	197.0	240.8	—	—	—	—	—
Sri Lanka	—	—	—	—	—	—	—	—	—	—	—	—

Sources: UNESCO Institute of Statistics; per-pupil expenditure calculated using Penn World Tables data on PPP-adjusted GDP per capita at current prices.
Note: — = not available; GDP = gross domestic product; PPP = purchasing power parity..

than 10 years earlier. In India, there was also a decline,[4] from 4.5 percent in 1999 to 3.1 percent in 2007, the last year for which data are available. But before drawing conclusions about what is happening to government spending on education as a percentage of GDP, it is necessary to discuss the metric used here. India has experienced tremendous GDP growth over the past decade: GDP rose from 19,520 billion rupees in 1999 to 65,503 billion in 2009.[5] Other countries have also experienced fast growth. A falling share of education spending as a percentage of GDP does not necessarily imply a fall in absolute terms.

In the smallest countries of the region, however, public spending as a percentage of GDP is significantly higher. In Bhutan, after 2000 it rose to reach 7.3 percent of GDP in 2009, and the highest spending is observed in Maldives, 8.4 percent in 2009.

Per Capita and per-Student Public Education Expenditure

Table 7.2 shows government education spending per student, in constant purchasing power parity dollars to control for changes in GDP over the period and differences in national populations. Data are only available for the largest countries. In India, actual per-student spending was relatively stagnant despite rapid economic growth during a period that coincided with the donor-assisted central government program, Education for All (*Sarva Shiksha Abhiyan*), for which the Indian government also raised revenue through a 2 percent education *cess* (tax) on all revenue. In Pakistan, spending increased by nearly 25 percent in purchasing power parity terms from 2003 to 2005, although limited data make it impossible to draw conclusions about a trend. In Nepal, spending increased early in the decade before falling in 2003.

Thus rapid GDP growth in South Asia did not lead to commensurate increases in per-student expenditure, which generally remained constant except in Pakistan, where the limited data suggest that spending rose. Increases in the absolute amount of funding for education made possible by growth were absorbed by surges in school enrollment. Low per-student funding compared to the OECD, and the fact that most countries still report substantial need for additional school construction or repairs and for essential inputs[6] and that enrollment has not yet reached 100 percent, suggest that the largest countries may not be spending enough to provide high-quality learning unless they identify all possible efficiency gains.

Share of Government Expenditure Allocated to Education[7]

While in South Asia education spending was found to be lower than the OECD average as a percentage of GDP, as a percentage of government spending it was much closer to, if not above, OECD levels, except in Sri Lanka (table 7.3), which suggests comparable government concern for investment in education. Indeed, Nepal spent about 19.5 percent of its budget on education in 2009, up from 12.5 percent in 1999. Pakistan, which allocates a very low proportion of its GDP to education, still spends about 11 percent of total government income on it—only slightly below the OECD average.[8]

Tables 7.1–7.3 suggest that per-student financing of basic education in South Asia is too low to provide high-quality education. However, the share of government spending allocated to education is reasonably high, which suggests that per-student spending may be low due to resource, and perhaps also to

Table 7.3 Expenditure on Education in Government Spending[a]
Percent

	1999	*2000*	*2001*	*2002*	*2003*	*2004*	*2005*	*2006*	*2007*	*2008*	*2009*	*1999–2009*
Afghanistan	—	—	—	—	—	—	—	—	12.7	—	—	—
Bangladesh	15.3	15.0	15.7	15.8	15.5	14.8	—	14.2	15.8	14.0	14.0	15.1
Bhutan[b]	—	—	—	—	—	—	—	—	—	—	16.9	—
India	12.7	12.7	—	—	10.7	—	—	—	—	—	—	12.0
Nepal	12.5	13.2	13.0	13.9	14.9	—	—	—	—	19.0	19.5	15.1
Pakistan	—	—	—	—	—	6.4	10.9	12.2	11.2	—	11.2	10.4
Sri Lanka[c]	9.2	7.2	8.0	—	—	—	—	—	—	—	8.1	8.1
OECD average	12.2	12.5	12.4	12.7	12.9	12.5	12.7	12.8	12.4	—	—	12.6

Sources: a. UNESCO Institute of Statistics; b. World Bank 2012a; c. UNESCO Budgeting Report, 2003.
Note: — = not available; OECD = Organisation for Economic Co-operation and Development.

capacity, constraints, which ultimately can only be eased through economic growth and an improvement in government fiscal and human resource capabilities.[9] It should also be noted that foreign assistance makes up a substantial part of government expenditures in Bangladesh and Nepal (table 7.4). Similarly, Bhutan relies heavily on foreign aid and grants: although it spends 7.3 percent of its GDP (one of the highest rates in the region) on education, only 5.7 percent is financed domestically. Now that it is approaching middle-income status, however, developing partners are scaling down their support and Bhutan will have to adjust to a tighter resource constraint.

Governments are thus faced with two broad options on how to improve the quality of education: (a) let nongovernment financing rise and complement public financing, and look for ways to maximize the impact of public spending on quality; (b) increase public financing on education as far as possible with continuous economic growth, and search for efficiencies (see below).

Private Contributions to the Financing of Education

Relying on rising contributions from households and allowing the private sector to play an increasing role in education is to some extent how India, Pakistan, Bangladesh, and Nepal have responded to the growing demand for education. Almost one-third of children enrolled in primary or secondary school in South Asia attend private schools (see chapter 9), and in all countries in the region parents help finance the education of their children, even those who attend public schools. Except for India, there is very little data on the relative shares of public and private spending on education. In India, private spending rose notably between 2000 and 2003 before stabilizing at 27 percent (see table 7.5). This may

Table 7.4 Aid to Education in South Asia, 2000–05
Percent

	GDP	*Education expenditure*
Bangladesh	0.57	23.4
India	0.07	1.2
Nepal	0.96	27.4
Pakistan	0.09	5.0
Sri Lanka	0.25	10.7

Source: Calculations from Dreher, Nunnenkamp, and Thiele 2008.
Note: GDP = gross domestic product.

Table 7.5 India: Public and Private Expenditure on Education as a Percentage of GDP

	1999	*2000*	*2001*	*2002*	*2003*	*2004*	*2005*
Public expenditure	4.47	4.41	—	—	3.67	3.40	3.13
Private expenditure	—	0.24	1.57	—	1.35	1.27	1.15
Share of private expenditure in total		5.00			27.00	27.00	27.00

Source: UNESCO Institute of Statistics.
Note: — = not available; GDP = gross domestic product.

seem surprising at first, since this period coincides with the start of the Education for All program, but it is supported by the surge in private-school enrollments (Kingdon 2007).

In 1993–94, about 10 percent of rural Indian children attended private primary or secondary schools; by 2010 the proportion was about 25 percent. Pakistan among other countries has evidenced a comparable upsurge, and similar growth in the private expenditure share in the region as a whole might be expected (Aslam 2009). In Pakistan, the expansion of the private sector role in education is almost unprecedented. It came about with an increase in the number of private institutions; almost 25 percent of Pakistani schools are private, and up to 60 percent in urban areas.[10]

Private tutoring is also common in the region (see chapter 9). In rural Pakistan, 16 percent of children ages 3–16 years are tutored, at an average cost of US$40 per child per school year (Aslam and Atherton 2012). The extent of private tuition is undoubtedly far greater in urban areas. Bray (2009) in a survey of research found that in Bangladesh in 2005, 31 percent of primary students (51 percent in urban areas) were receiving after-school tutoring, up from 21 percent in 1998. In West Bengal, India, 70 percent of households invested in tutoring for primary school children—a third of household spending on education. Even in Sri Lanka, where the number of private schools is very limited, about 75 percent of primary school students are privately tutored. Clearly, spending on private education is an important component of total education spending in the region.

Would More, and More Appropriate, Inputs Increase Education Quality?

Through continuous economic growth and an improvement in government fiscal and human resource capabilities, a gradual increase in the resources spent on education might be expected. What could those additional resources best be spent on, and what impact would they have on quality?

The major share of education budgets in most countries goes for school facilities and infrastructure, books and learning materials, and teacher salaries, and this is where additional resources are generally deployed. Governments also often direct substantial amounts to programs related to education indirectly, such as school feeding and health programs. This section discusses whether more such inputs will improve quality, and which are likely to be more effective.

This section reviews evidence of the impact on learning outcomes of school facilities and infrastructure, books and learning materials, school feeding programs, and number and salaries of teachers. This section will also discuss the importance of spending on monitoring and evaluation (M&E). Finally, it will summarize the evidence for a link between expenditure and student learning.

Increased Spending on Physical Infrastructure

The primary concern of education policy in developing countries has typically been to ensure access to schools, and then to ensure that the environment in which classes are held is of reasonable quality. Investments in infrastructure have thus taken a high share of education budgets in recent decades. Nevertheless, access is still an issue in some areas, and both the pressure of rising enrollment and insufficient quality control and attention to maintenance have left significant needs unmet. For example, in 2011 the Bangladesh government reported that half of primary schools, government and nongovernment, had more than 56 students per class and lacked drinking water, toilets, and furniture. In Pakistan's Sindh province, the needs were such that in 2009 the government introduced a new mechanism, district terms of partnerships, to push school rehabilitation and ensure that new construction meets quality and functionality standards.

Although in South Asia substantial amounts are still likely to be spent on facilitating access to school and on infrastructure, whether they will improve learning outcomes is uncertain. Some cross-sectional studies (e.g., Drèze and Kingdon 2001; Glewwe and Kremer 2006; Aturupane, Glewwe, and Wisniewski 2013) found basic indicators of the quality of physical facilities associated with higher enrollment and higher test scores, but those results could be confounded by omitted variables. Other studies (Borkum, He, and Linden 2012; Muralidharan and Zieleniak 2012[11]) found no evidence of impact on learning outcomes, even though the quality of infrastructure improved significantly during the period under study.

To save on infrastructure costs, access issues have also been addressed in other ways. The provision of transportation facilities is one. For example, in rural India "all-season" roads were constructed to hamlets that previously only had functional roads in the dry season. Bihar's *Mukhyamantri Balika Cycle Yojna*[12] provides girls who enroll in grade 9 with a bicycle. Both programs were found to have substantial impact on enrollment, but none on test scores (Mukherjee 2011; Muralidharan and Prakash 2013).

Programs are being implemented in Afghanistan, Pakistan, and Bangladesh to support creation of community-led schools. Evaluations of the programs (Burde and Linden 2010 for Afghanistan; Alderman, Kim, and Orazem 2003 for Pakistan; Asadullah et al. 2009 for Bangladesh) show that enrollment has gone up significantly and the gender gap has narrowed. Since community schools generally involve multigrade teaching, quality was a concern, but so far learning outcomes in these schools seem to be similar to those of government schools.

There may be several reasons for the lack of firm evidence on the impact of school infrastructure on learning outcomes. One is that infrastructure (for example, toilets) may be built but not used. Another is that better-quality infrastructure may make the school more appealing but leave teaching and learning processes unchanged. A third is that it takes a long time to detect impact. The conclusion is that the evidence available should not be interpreted as suggesting that infrastructure investments and maintenance of physical capacity should not be made. Such changes are likely to be important for attracting and retaining children, although they seem unlikely to have a significant impact on learning.

More and Better Student Inputs

Since poverty is one of the main constraints on school participation, policy makers seek to decrease the direct costs of schooling and provide immediate and tangible benefits from attending school, such as meals. In thinking about the likely impact of provision of inputs, three questions need to be considered. The first is their effectiveness. Gaps can arise between allocated funds and actual receipts because of administrative inefficiencies (PAISA Report 2011) or corruption (Reinnika and Svensson 2004). The second is the possibility that the inputs provided may not improve learning outcomes. The third is that government provision of inputs may be offset by a diversion of household spending on education to other household needs. With these issues in mind, this section looks at the evidence related to learning materials and school feeding programs (health programs were discussed in chapter 3 in relation to early childhood development).

Textbooks and Learning Materials

South Asian countries have in general succeeded in ensuring timely distribution of textbooks to students. Sri Lanka ensures that all students have textbooks and relies on private publication of competing textbooks to increase quality and reduce costs. Bangladesh and Pakistan have recently addressed administrative inefficiencies and are monitoring to ensure timely distribution. In Afghanistan, however, although the distribution of textbooks is now much better, there are still discrepancies between books needed and received, and storage conditions are often poor.

Textbooks can have a significant impact on learning outcomes (Heyneman, Jamison, and Montenegro 1984; Glewwe, Kremer, and Moulin 2009). Pritchett and Filmer (1999) even found that in India, increasing inputs such as learning materials is 4–14 times more cost-effective than increasing teacher salaries. However, more recent research found that the impact of increased public provision of learning materials may be offset by a reduction in family spending, leaving the net effect close to zero (box 7.2). Accounting for household re-optimization in response to public spending programs is thus important. Another factor that can reduce the impact of learning materials is student reading level. If it is too low, children may not be able to use textbooks effectively (Glewwe, Kremer, and Moulin 2009).

School Feeding Programs

In the past 10 years, large-scale feeding programs have been implemented in both India (Midday Meal Scheme) and Bangladesh. Although Bangladesh had shifted to a cash transfer program, it is considering reintroducing school feeding. Alderman and Bundy (2012) concluded that such initiatives in developing countries are not especially effective as nutrition or education programs but are likely to be effective as a social protection approach that stimulates demand for education.

The evidence from South Asia is limited, although a few studies have examined the impact of the India program on test scores. Jayaraman, Simroth, and

Box 7.2 State Provision of Student Inputs, Household Expenditures, and Learning Outcomes

Das et al. (2013) present evidence of the impact of a school grant that stipulated that the funds should be spent on inputs used directly by students, a two-year program in the state of Andhra Pradesh in India. Categories of spending were books, stationery, and writing materials (~50 percent); workbooks and practice books (~20 percent); and classroom materials (~25 percent). The program had a significant positive impact on student test scores at the end of the first year, but the impact in the second year was close to zero; the cumulative effect was positive but not significant. Measuring household spending in the schools concerned, they found that households sharply reduced their own spending on education in the second year of the program.

Thus, when the program was unanticipated, there was a net increase in materials, which translated into significant improvements in test scores. However, as parents became aware of the program, they reduced their own spending, leaving learning levels unchanged.

Sankar (2012) in an analysis of household out-of-pocket expenditures on education in India (using National Sample Survey 52nd and 64th round data) found that expenditures on children who attend government primary schools declined in real terms between 1995–96 and 2007–08, mostly for transportation, textbooks, and stationery. This was during a period of increased government expenditures for free textbooks and to ease access to schools.

de Véricourt (2011) found that the program pushed up enrollment but not test scores. Muralidharan and Zieleniak (2012) found a negative impact, which they interpret as the result of teacher time being diverted to overseeing the midday meal. In Bangladesh, however, Ahmed (2004) found large and significant effects on nutrition, enrollment, attendance, and test scores. In general, although there is consistent evidence that school feeding programs promote enrollment and attendance, it is uncertain whether learning outcomes improve.

Increased Spending on Monitoring and Evaluation

It is impossible to effectively improve quality without capacity for monitoring outcomes. In South Asia, this area deserves extra attention and resources, technical as well as financial. Although all countries in the region attempt to regularly collect data on school conditions, enrollment, and teacher characteristics and to monitor student achievement, their systems, not yet institutionalized, are somewhat fragile. Monitoring units often lack technical expertise. Financing of M&E systems, which are central to policy decisions and indirectly to quality improvements, is not always secure (see chapter 8).

More Teachers per Student

An expansion of education spending could enable countries to hire more teachers and operate with lower pupil-teacher ratios (PTRs). Smaller class size may allow teachers to pay more individual attention to each student and also decrease the number of disruptions per class period that inhibit learning.

Woessmann (2007) argued that internationally increases in spending on education over time have gone mainly into reducing PTRs; that seems to be true of India. There is a strong negative relationship between per capita education expenditure and PTRs (figure 7.1), which suggests that smaller class size is equated in India with quality—a view not uncommon among policy makers in South Asia and across the world. India's RTE Act (2009) explicitly states that the PTR be no more than 30 to 1 in elementary schools. Although the *Rashtriya Madhyamik Shiksha Abhiyan* program, directed at universalizing secondary schooling, stipulates the same PTR norm in secondary schools, there is active discussion of reducing it to 25 to 1. Since these norms are extremely draining on the exchequer, it is worth examining whether this is the most cost-efficient way to improve schooling outcomes.

In India, states with the highest PTR—conditional on baseline scores—also have higher average performance in the National Council for Educational Research and Training (NCERT)[13] midline tests (figure 7.2). Although this seems to suggest that lower PTRs may not improve learning outcomes, the simple descriptive statistics do not allow us to dismiss PTRs as a possible influence on student performance.

Figure 7.1 Pupil-Teacher Ratios and Per Capita Education Expenditure, India, by State, 2007–08

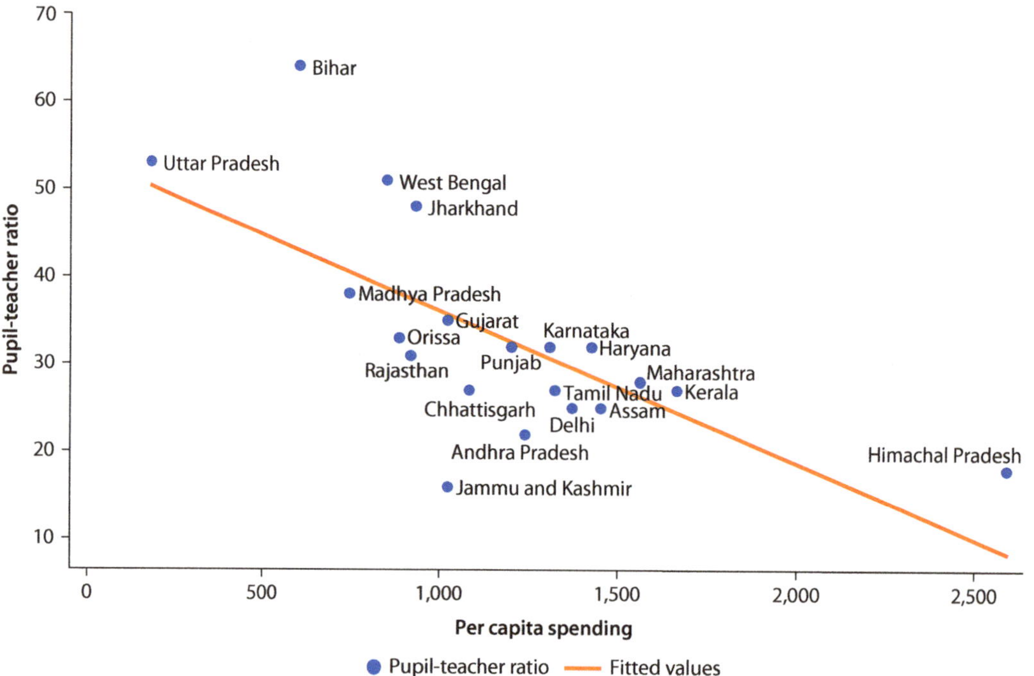

Sources: Data from India Selected Education Statistics (SES) 2007/08; and District Information System for Education (DISE) 2007/08.

Figure 7.2 Pupil-Teacher Ratios and Midline Math Performance, Conditional on Baseline Scores

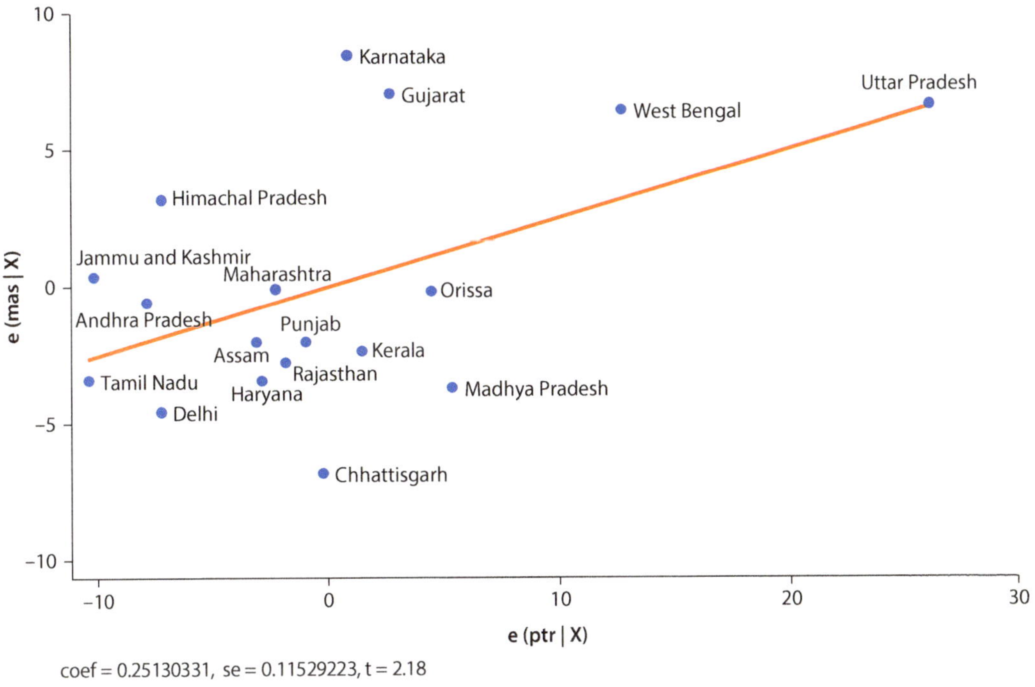

Sources: Data from India Selected Education Statistics (SES) 2007/08; and DISE 2007/08.

With teacher salaries the largest component of education budgets, determining the impact of the PTR on student learning is of critical importance. In South Asia as internationally, the evidence is somewhat mixed. Some studies in which estimation issues (such as nonrandom allocation of pupils to different class sizes) are adequately dealt with have found that reducing PTRs does increase learning (Angrist and Lavy 1999; Krueger 2003), but the beneficial effect is small (Altinok and Kingdon 2012; Muralidharan and Sundararaman 2013). In countries in the region, the issue of class size differs from that in most other countries by an order of magnitude. Here, the debate is about reducing class size not from 25 to 20 students but from 100 students to fewer than 40. Two experimental evaluations provide indirect evidence, in opposite directions, about the impact of class size on learning outcomes at the primary level. In the first experiment, children with low test scores were taken outside the regular classroom for remedial instruction by a volunteer. The experiment (Banerjee et al. 2006) showed that, while the test scores of these children went up significantly, there was no impact on the scores of the students who remained in the original classroom, although the size of their class was now smaller. In the second experiment, in Andhra Pradesh, Muralidharan and Sundararaman (2013) found that students in schools that had an extra contract teacher scored 0.16 standard deviations higher in math and 0.15 standard deviations higher in language tests at the end of the two-year experiment.

Higher Teacher Pay

While salary is important in drawing more able teachers into the profession, evidence on the extent to which teacher pay is correlated with student learning is mixed (Lavy 2002; Kremer, Glewwe, and Ilias 2010). In South Asia (see chapter 5), research has shown that the teaching profession has the potential to attract good candidates.[14] Salaries of regular government teachers are on average higher than those of nonteachers with similar credentials, but there is no evidence that students of government teachers learn more than those of contract teachers who are paid less.

Although higher salaries are thought to enhance performance by triggering more teacher motivation and effort, there is scant evidence of this in the region. In India, it was found that far-higher-paid regular teachers made significantly less effort than contract teachers, which Kingdon and Banerji (2009) attribute to a lack of accountability demanded of regular teachers. Thus, expanding spending on salaries, with no change in accountability, is not likely to bring long-run gains in learning (see chapter 5 for a detailed discussion).

Would Investment in Inputs Improve Education Quality?

At its simplest, putting more resources into schools—more and better infrastructure, more teachers, and so on—is not likely to do much to improve learning. M&E are critical but do not require much funding; spending on books and learning materials holds promise only if certain conditions are met; and there is no firm evidence that better infrastructure, school feeding programs, and lower PTRs improve learning outcomes.

This conclusion is consistent with findings from elsewhere. In summarizing the evidence on cross-national spending differences, Hanushek and Woessmann (2011) concluded that countries with high educational expenditure and countries with low educational expenditure appear to perform at about the same level. This is echoed by data on within-country financing changes, where more spending is not reflected in better educational outcomes. Evaluating expenditure and performance over time in a number of OECD countries, Woessmann (2003) found a slightly negative relationship between changes in expenditure and changes in performance for 1970–95. In the main, it is not that quality is falling; rather, although spending has increased, quality has stagnated.

As previously noted, it is difficult to get comparable cross-country data on quality outcomes for South Asian countries. Within India, however, there are data on state per capita education funding that can be related to outcomes. This study related finance data for the 20 major Indian states from the Ministry of Human Resource Development's Selected Education Statistics for 2007–08 to a number of output- and input-based notions of quality, focusing on the 20 major Indian states.

Figure 7.3 illustrates the relationship between Indian state math scores and per capita education expenditures.[15] As with any statistical relationship, correlation does not imply causation, and conclusions can only be drawn from limited

Figure 7.3 Per Capita Expenditure and Midline Math Achievement, Conditional on Baseline Score

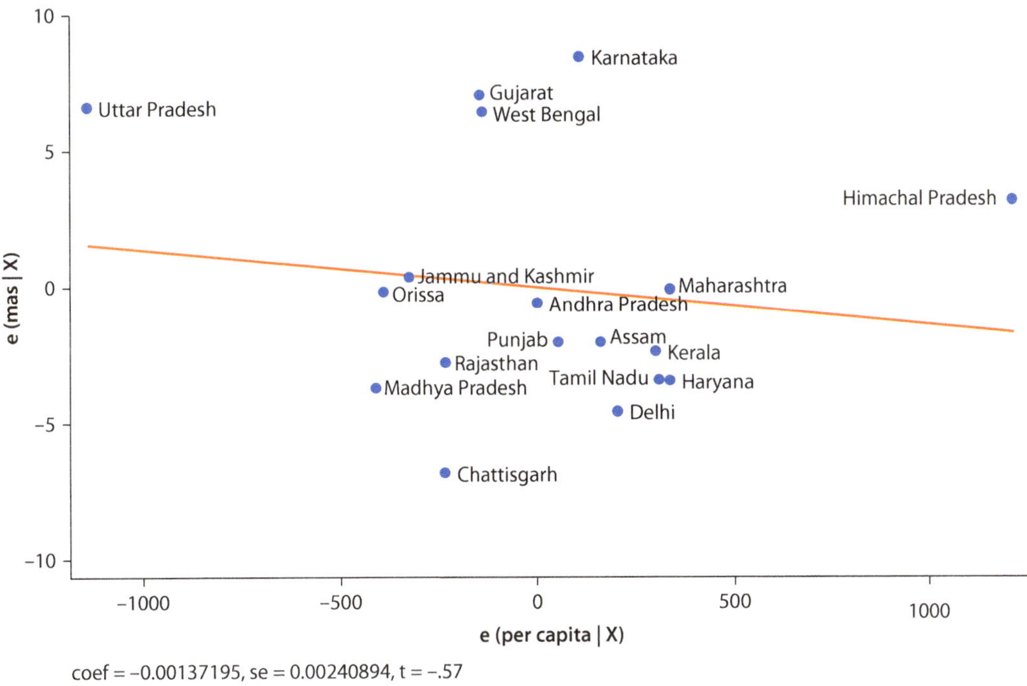

Source: MHRD Selected Education Statistics 2007/08.

data cautiously. The figure shows a negative but insignificant relationship between state per capita expenditure on education and grade 5 math scores in the NCERT midline study of Sarva Shiksha Abhiyan. West Bengal, for example, spends noticeably less than states like Kerala yet has higher learning outcomes.[16]

In India, consistent with cross-country and within-country studies over time, there does not seem to be a statistically significant relationship between per capita spending and school quality as measured by math scores. This raises doubts about whether learning gains can be obtained by relying only on higher spending.

This conclusion should not be misinterpreted to imply that resources and spending on school inputs do not matter. Clearly, for example, infrastructure of reasonable quality is needed in South Asia, but the impact on learning outcomes is likely to be too small to make much difference—unless expenditures were made within a different institutional context and with increased accountability. That possibility is discussed in the next section.

Financing as a Tool to Improve Quality

Financing reform options that hold promise of boosting learning outcomes include (a) modification of the incentive structure for teachers and schools and (b) increased reliance on public-private partnerships (PPPs). These reforms could be implemented with the resources available. It is also possible that financing can be used to improve learning opportunities for the poor.

Improving Incentives for Teachers

Improving teacher quality in South Asia (see chapter 5) could be the most powerful instrument for raising student learning. This implies addressing such issues as poor subject-matter knowledge, absenteeism, inadequate pedagogical skills, low effort, and lack of motivation. While better training may improve subject-matter knowledge, for instance, it will not have much impact unless teachers are motivated to transmit this knowledge to students. One reform option would be to use financing to improve the incentive structure of teachers, increase attendance and time-on-task, and provide inducements for investments in improving pedagogical skills. This could be done by extending contract teacher schemes or by more explicitly relating remuneration[17] to outcomes.

Nowhere in South Asia are teacher salaries linked to performance. Restructuring teacher contracts to minimize absence and maximize professional development could be an option. Evaluations of contract teacher schemes in India, where hires are made locally on annually renewable contracts, without formal teacher certification, at much lower wages, have shown that other things being equal those on contract outperform regular teachers (Atherton and Kingdon 2010, for Uttar Pradesh and Bihar; Goyal and Pandey 2009, for Madhya Pradesh and Uttar Pradesh; Muralidharan and Sundararaman 2013, for Andhra Pradesh). The wage differences are stark: Andhra Pradesh contract teachers earn as little as one-eighth of what regular teachers are paid. Yet their absenteeism is lower—in Uttar Pradesh, contract teachers were absent 11 percent of the time, regular teachers 23 percent—which may be because their contracts are insecure compared to the permanent posts of regular teachers. It may also be that they are hired locally and are more accountable to their communities if they are absent and not teaching.

Contract teacher schemes, however, have often been criticized as inequitable—less-qualified teachers are generally assigned to poorer areas and underprivileged children. Another argument, as the Madhya Pradesh experience suggests, is that once contract teachers constitute a large portion of the teaching force, they could become powerful enough to obtain benefits close to those of permanent staff. There is also uncertainty about the potential long-term effects of a reform that makes all teaching appointments insecure and could ultimately de-professionalize the teaching cadre. All these points need to be balanced against the evidence that contract teachers perform relatively better at substantially lower cost.

An alternative is to retain employment security but tie remuneration and career progression more closely to schooling outcomes. Evidence on the impact of performance-related incentive pay is limited (see chapter 5), but studies in India by Kingdon and Teal (2007) and Muralidharan and Sundararaman (2011) found that performance-related pay elicits better teacher effort and improves the quality of teaching, and consequently the quality of student learning. These authors also measured the relative efficiency of four different approaches to improving learning[18] and demonstrated that providing incentives could be more powerful than providing inputs at equal cost. An additional finding highly relevant for policy is that incentives can reinforce the training and diagnostic feedback given to teachers. Teachers with more training were more effective in schools enrolled in the incentive program and made more use of diagnostic feedback on their students.

These findings suggest that changing the incentive structure for teachers could motivate them to exert more effort, and more effectively use inputs and training. That would not only have a direct impact on student learning but would also raise the return on other types of school investments.

Countries in South Asia are becoming increasingly aware of the importance of accountability and incentives. For example, in 2009, the Punjab government in Pakistan piloted performance-linked incentives for schools based on a mix of indicators for measuring both student learning and school enrollment and retention. Several variants of the incentive structure are being evaluated. In 2008, Bangladesh introduced monetary incentives[19] in secondary schools to encourage rural students, teachers, and institutions to achieve more and to sustain the achievement. Other countries are reforming teacher career paths. However, those reforms are all still small and at a very early stage.

Improving Incentives for Schools

While government funding for public schools always has an incentive structure built into grant formulas, implicitly or explicitly, it is important to understand which funding modalities are most conducive to quality education. For instance, if state support is given as block grants (a flat amount to each school, irrespective of enrollment) rather than per student, schools have less incentive to attract more students.

Government funding to schools in South Asia is currently disbursed mostly as block grants that do not demand accountability from schools in terms of teacher resources. For example, in India, state funding is based on the number of teachers sanctioned for the school and the PTR norm (40 to 1), but the number of teachers appointed is rarely revised when student enrollment changes because (a) the number of students and teachers in a school is not monitored because of a lack of inspection capacity and (b) there is resistance from teachers. Even if student numbers fall, the school still gets its full grant; in consequence, PTRs fall and per-pupil spending rises. In a survey of 10 government-funded schools in Lucknow district, Uttar Pradesh, Kingdon and Muzammil (2010) found that the PTR ratio had fallen to 9.7, but teacher unions and politicians supported teachers who refused to be deployed to local schools with more students.

Properly designed, a revised grant structure could have large cost-efficiency payoffs. Grant formulas could be structured to include incentives for efficiency, equity, parent satisfaction, and so on. How and what incentives can be built into grants is an area that deserves policy attention. For instance, in India, while the formula for government grants to aided schools that India inherited from the British has hardly been revised at all in the past 65 years, in the

United Kingdom it has been reformed many times to make it more efficient and equitable. A desirable incentive structure could relate grants to such indicators as percentage of total non-salary expenses (to encourage quality improvements); percentage of total funds raised from non-fee sources, such as parental donations (to encourage equitable resource generation); percentage of parents satisfied with the school (to encourage accountability); and average PTR (to encourage cost consciousness). Rewarding the most efficient teachers might also be considered. Of course, applying such formulas would require state education departments to have better monitoring, inspection, and accounting capacities. A simple first step could be to partially or totally replace block grants with per-pupil grants. This simple change would itself impose accountability—schools that lose students (due to a fall in quality, for instance) would risk a grant reduction.

Partnerships with the Private Sector

Private provision of educational services in South Asia has been expanding rapidly (see chapter 9). Although South Asian countries have been using a variety of financing modalities, they usually favor supply-side financing for private education (see box 7.3). Private schools have been observed to operate with lower unit costs than public schools (mostly because of lower teacher salaries) while performing at least as well or better (once school and student characteristics are taken into account). This makes them attractive as a means to relax the government resource constraint and make school financing more cost-effective.

As discussed in chapter 9, leveraging the contribution of the private sector, either by facilitating its expansion or through PPPs, should become part of a financing strategy aimed at increasing resources for education and maximizing efficiency. However, given the wide variance in the performance of private schools, that strategy needs to be carefully designed to focus attention on the most cost-effective arrangements. Built-in design and incentives are critical to success.

Three policy questions need to be answered. The first is how best to provide public funds for private education. The two major ways are (a) giving public money directly to private schools as a block or per-student grant, possibly tied to performance (supply side); and (b) giving public money directly to families, such as vouchers for each child (demand side).[20] For private schools these options imply fundamentally different incentives.

Which way of setting up the PPP gives the most incentives to schools and teachers? Evidence for India, although limited, suggests that supply-side funding through block grants, with no incentives built in, led to poor learning outcomes (Kingdon 1996, 2007). Per-student funding provides incentives for increased enrollment (as in Reaching Out-of-School Children [ROSC] schools in Bangladesh), and if grants are also conditioned on some measure of performance, there can be a positive impact on quality, as with the Foundation-Assisted Schools in Punjab and PPRS (Promoting Private Schooling in Rural Sindh) schools in Sindh (see chapter 9).

Box 7.3 Public-Private Partnership Financing in South Asia

Bangladesh. At the primary and secondary levels, block grants are used to finance recognized nongovernment schools based on the number of teachers allocated per school, up to nine. The government also covers some recurrent costs. Recognized nongovernment schools constitute over 90 percent of all secondary schools.

Reaching Out-of-School Children (ROSC) schools, which currently serve about half a million children, are experimenting with two alternative financing schemes. Some of the new schools receive only supply-side financing (per-student grants to cover stationery, uniforms, and so on) and others a combination of supply- and demand-side financing (a block grant to the center to cover teacher salaries, maintenance, and training costs, and a per-student allowance paid to the child's mother). An evaluation that attempted to determine which of the two was more effective could not detect any differential impact on enrollment and learning outcomes but found the combination of supply- and demand-financing superior in terms of governance (transparent utilization of funds).

Demand-side financing is widely used to foster participation. At the primary level, stipends were given to the poorest 40 percent in each school. Since 2010, the scheme has been modified. The proportion of children benefiting from stipends now varies by geographical area and area poverty level. Since 1982, Bangladesh has provided scholarships to encourage girls to attend secondary school. The stipend is conditioned on attendance and on staying single. The majority of beneficiaries attend private aided schools. Recently, proxy means testing was introduced in some districts, and stipends were given to both boys and girls from poor households.

Nepal. Government schools that opt for community management and oversight receive a block incentive grant. Grants are also provided to encourage enrollment. Such schools now enroll about 20 percent of students.

Pakistan. The Punjab Educational Foundation (PEF), created by the Provincial Assembly in 2004, is the main vehicle for PPPs in the province. For both the Foundation Assisted Schools Program (FAS) and the New Schools Program (NSP), funding is given to private schools on a per-student basis (to encourage enrollment) but conditioned on threshold school achievement (to foster accountability). Evaluation suggests that those modalities can lead to significant gains in both participation and learning (Barrera-Osorio and Raju 2010, 2011). Promoting Private Schooling in Rural Sindh, a sister program to NSP, is run in Sindh province with similar funding modalities and outcomes.

PEF is also using demand-side financing. Its Education Vouchers Scheme provides vouchers to children in disadvantaged neighborhoods in the capitals of 36 districts. After several years of piloting, this program was scaled up in 2011, when it distributed 140,000 vouchers. A rigorous evaluation is planned.

Data on the impact of demand-side PPP funding (school vouchers to parents) comes mainly from Chile, Colombia, New Zealand, and the United States. While the evidence is mixed, it appears that voucher funding for private schooling is generally associated with better student outcomes. The most reliable evidence, based on state-of-the-art impact evaluation methodology, comes from Colombia. Not having enough funds for vouchers to all applicants, the Colombian government issued them by lottery. This provided ideal conditions for impact evaluation because lottery winners and losers were from similar backgrounds. Angrist et al. (2002) and Angrist, Bettinger, and Kremer (2006) found that vouchers—which increased parental choice and fostered competition between schools to attract vouchers—had beneficial effects on a range of student outcomes, both in the short term (3 years) and the longer term (7 years).

The second policy question is about the equity effects of demand-side public funding for private education. The expectation is that vouchers would reduce inequality by giving poor children the opportunity to attend private schools they otherwise could not afford. Concerns have been expressed, however, that better-off families may supplement the value of the voucher and send their children to the better private schools, whereas children of poorer families would remain in public schools, some of which would be left with the poorest and least-performing students. In other words, vouchers could be detrimental to students from disadvantaged backgrounds (Ladd 2002). Nechyba (2005) suggested that such equity concerns can be addressed by making the voucher amount inversely proportional to family income, so that the poorest families would receive the highest-value vouchers. Recent initiatives in India, Pakistan, and Bangladesh target vouchers to the most disadvantaged. Even if targeting is effective, however, inequality may never be totally eliminated. For example, private schools could still cream off the best students to maintain high-quality peer groups. In any case, it is hard to argue that public funding of private education would make inequality worse than what it would be without it.

The third question is whether voucher PPP schemes are even feasible in low-income countries. Concerns have been expressed about school choice schemes in developing countries, such as (a) in rural areas there are very few schools and the supply of places is the major constraint, which might make school choice schemes irrelevant; (b) regulatory systems are too weak to ensure that schools comply with standards; (c) uneducated parents will find it difficult to make informed school choices; and (d) the possible scope for monitoring corruption is minimal and verification costs high. While the first concern may occasionally be relevant, the validity of the others is questionable. Successful PPPs that tied funding to performance have shown that they are indeed a possibility for low-income countries. Andrabi et al. (2007; see also Andrabi, Das, and Khwaja 2008) also suggested that even poor parents care about quality and can make informed choices about schools. Furthermore, the potential for corruption and monitoring problems exists in both supply-side-funded PPPs and public school systems. This only highlights the need for poor countries to strengthen administrative capacities to introduce more efficient ways to fund education.

Country specificities and still-limited evidence suggest a need for caution. The most apt policy prescription seems to be that governments considering PPPs should try out different modalities for a few years and rigorously evaluate the achievement and equity impacts of each before scaling up those that are more effective and equitable.

Improving Learning Opportunities for the Poor

Providing learning opportunities to the poor presents a double challenge: first, making school attractive to them, and second, once they are in school, giving them a good-quality education. Access and quality thus need to be achieved concurrently.

All the countries in South Asia have a policy goal of providing free primary education to all children, and primary education receives a substantial share of the education budget, from about 30 percent in Sri Lanka to 60 percent in Nepal, with India, Bhutan, and Bangladesh allocating 35–45 percent. National programs with high political visibility have been launched to promote access and quality, and to remove disparities, namely the *Sarva Shiksha Abhiyan* (SSA) in India; Primary Education Development Program (PEDP) I, II, and III in Bangladesh; Education for All in Nepal; the Education Sector Development Framework and Program (ESDFP) in Sri Lanka; and the Education Sector Reform Program in Punjab and Sindh, Pakistan. Compulsory free education has even been extended beyond primary schooling (up to 14 years in India and 16 years in Pakistan or until grades 8 in Bangladesh and Nepal, 9 in Sri Lanka, and 10 in Bhutan).

In addition to building a school network, appointing teachers, and preparing and distributing textbooks, governments have set aside resources for children with special needs. They have also, to different degrees, invested in early child development (see chapter 3) and used demand-side interventions to stimulate demand and compensate for the costs of private schooling for the poorest and for girls.

Although the magnitude and timing of those efforts have varied by country, a positive trend toward greater equality of opportunities is evident (table 7.6). In all countries, not only has access to education increased over time but the disparity in educational attainment between the richest and poorest has decreased. Younger generations, regardless of their consumption quintile, achieve more education than earlier generations in all countries, and the difference in educational attainment between richest and poorest is narrower among younger generations than among those born 40–50 years ago. Inequality[21] in today's youngest generation appears to be least in India and Nepal (the average number of years of schooling of the richest is 1.6 times that of the poorest in India and 1.85 in Nepal), but it is in Bhutan that the relative change has been the most significant—the ratio of years of schooling of the richest and of the poorest dropped from 11.0 for generations born 40–50 years ago to 3.5 for younger generations).

Table 7.6 Average Years of Schooling, by Age Group and Income Quintiles, South Asia

Age group	*Income quintile*	*Afghanistan 2007/08*	*Bangladesh 2010*	*Bhutan 2007*	*India 2009/10*	*Nepal 2009/10*	*Pakistan 2010/11*
15–19 years	Poorest	2.2	4.2	2.1	5.9	4.9	3.3
	2nd	2.6	5.4	3.3	6.7	6.1	5.3
	3rd	3.4	6.7	4.7	7.8	6.7	6.6
	4th	3.3	7.3	5.8	8.3	8.0	7.4
	Richest	4.6	8.6	7.3	9.5	9.1	8.2
20–29 years	Poorest	1.2	3.1	1.3	4.3	3.1	2.5
	2nd	1.3	4.4	2.3	5.2	4.5	4.4
	3rd	2.5	5.9	4.5	7.2	5.7	6.3
	4th	2.3	6.7	4.3	7.8	7.6	7.8
	Richest	3.7	9.1	6.6	10.6	9.7	9.3
30–39 years	Poorest	0.7	1.7	0.6	3.0	1.5	2.0
	2nd	1.0	2.6	1.0	3.9	2.7	3.5
	3rd	2.0	4.3	2.2	5.4	3.3	5.0
	4th	1.7	5.1	2.4	6.3	5.2	6.5
	Richest	3.0	8.0	4.8	9.5	7.4	8.4
40–49 years	Poorest	0.8	1.2	0.3	2.0	1.1	1.4
	2nd	1.0	1.7	0.4	2.8	1.7	2.5
	3rd	2.0	3.2	1.7	4.3	2.2	3.4
	4th	1.7	3.3	1.4	4.5	3.7	5.1
	Richest	3.0	6.8	3.4	7.8	5.2	7.1

Source: Data from Household Surveys (survey years indicated in each column).
Note: Quintile refers to asset index quintile for Pakistan and consumption quintile for other countries.

The financing of programs targeted at girls has also permitted countries to progress toward greater gender equality in opportunity (table 7.7). Bangladesh has been the most successful in bringing girls to school, but the gender gap is also closing at the primary level in India and Nepal and is likely to close gradually in Pakistan, which has been introducing stipend programs in recent years in its largest provinces.

Nevertheless, the data also show that, despite progress, the equity gap in school enrollment and attendance is still far from closed. Even among children attending school, learning achievements vary depending on socioeconomic background, gender, and caste—learning outcomes tend to be far more unequally distributed in the population than school access. The process of moving toward equality of opportunity is bound to require sustained effort for a long time (see chapter 2). Closing the primary attendance gap will translate into only a gradual narrowing of the gap at the secondary and higher levels, and closing the access gap will most likely precede progress in bridging disparities in student achievement.

To accelerate toward greater equality of opportunity, more could be done through a combination of supply- and demand-side financing mechanisms. In some countries, financing still needs to be deployed so the poor in underserved communities can access education. Programs that reduce distance to

Table 7.7 Enrollment for Children Ages 6–10 Years and 11–15 Years, by Gender, Locality, and Income Quintiles, in Selected South Asian Countries
Percent

		Afghanistan 2007/08		Bangladesh 2010		Bhutan 2007		India 2009/10		Nepal 2009/10		Pakistan 2010/11	
Gender	Income quintile	6–10	11–15	6–10	11–15	6–10	11–15	6–10	11–15	6–10	11–15	6–10	11–15
All	Poorest	40.8	49.1	76.3	63.1	57.8	60.8	85.3	77.9	87.9	83.2	50.5	42.9
	2nd	38.8	50.5	83.4	70.2	74.1	74.3	91.5	84.2	93.3	86.9	68.2	62.9
	3rd	41.5	53.4	88.4	82.4	87.7	83.6	94.2	88.0	96.2	90.3	76.5	73.5
	4th	39.6	55.4	89.3	84.8	89.2	89.2	96.1	90.2	96.8	95.1	80.2	78.0
	Richest	49.5	67.4	93.9	92.7	95.0	95.0	97.8	96.8	99.2	96.7	82.2	84.7
Male	Poorest	46.8	60.3	71.6	54.5	61.6	61.9	86.7	81.0	86.8	86.7	59.2	54.8
	2nd	47.9	63.1	81.7	61.8	77.1	81.8	92.6	86.3	95.1	89.3	73.4	72.1
	3rd	48.5	65.5	86.7	75.7	85.7	86.4	94.9	90.1	95.9	92.5	80.6	80.9
	4th	45.7	66.6	88.5	80.7	90.7	87.0	96.0	92.1	97.7	96.9	81.6	81.5
	Richest	55.5	77.4	92.8	90.7	93.9	95.2	98.1	96.9	98.8	97.5	83.6	86.6
Female	Poorest	34.4	36.1	81.4	71.3	54.2	59.6	83.9	74.6	88.8	80.1	40.5	27.7
	2nd	29.2	36.3	84.9	80.4	71.6	66.8	90.3	82.0	91.8	84.5	62.4	52.6
	3rd	34.0	39.8	90.1	89.6	89.9	80.8	93.4	85.4	96.6	88.0	72.0	65.0
	4th	33.2	42.8	90.2	89.3	87.7	91.5	96.3	87.7	95.8	93.3	78.7	74.2
	Richest	42.9	56.8	95.2	94.9	96.1	94.7	97.5	96.8	99.7	95.9	80.7	82.7

Source: Household surveys (survey years indicated in each column).
Note: Quintile refers to asset index quintile for Pakistan and consumption quintile for other countries.

school can help. Cost-effective programs like the ROSC community schools in Bangladesh or PPPs in Pakistan can also be replicated or adapted to local conditions. These interventions can be complemented by conditional cash transfer programs, which reduce the direct costs of schooling for families.

In countries that already have programs targeted to the poor, careful attention must ensure their efficiency. For example, Bangladesh's cash transfer program for primary education, designed to target the poorest 40 percent, proved to be only partially pro-poor. A significant portion leaked out to children from richer households: about 24 percent of recipients belonged to the richest 40 percent (World Bank 2008). The government is now using geographical poverty mapping to target more children in high-poverty areas. This implies an increase in resources for this program. While the change seems to be in the right direction, it is not clear whether the new design is the most cost-effective. Again, careful evaluation is needed.

In India, about one child in nine receives a scholarship. While ideally such schemes should target the poor, the beneficiaries are actually lower-caste pupils irrespective of wealth. The share of girls who receive a scholarship is 12.7 percent and boys 10.7 percent, which suggests some gender targeting. Table 7.8 shows who receives scholarships, how much, and why, by income quintile and schooling of the recipient. Redeployment of resources might increase equity.

Table 7.8 Scholarships in India

Wealth group	*Percentage of recipients in group*	*Percentage receiving scholarships*	*Scholarship amount in a year (Rs)*	*Why received? (%)*
1	20.0	15.5	551	Caste 96; financially weak 1.5; merit 0.5; others 2.0
2	26.0	14.4	480	Caste 95; financially weak 2.2; merit 0.3; others 2.4
3	23.7	13.2	533	Caste 93; financially weak 1.9; merit 0.8; others 4.5
4	20.4	10.1	760	Caste 92.3; financially weak 2.3; merit 0.8; others 4.6
5	10.0	5.9	1,430	Caste 87.5; financially weak 3.5; merit 2.3; others 6.6

Distribution of scholarships (% of all scholarships)

	Quintiles of monthly consumption					
	1	*2*	*3*	*4*	*5*	*Total allocation*
Primary	9.0	12.4	10.9	8.0	2.9	43.2
Upper primary/middle	6.2	7.6	6.8	5.2	1.8	27.6
Secondary	2.7	3.3	3.0	2.9	1.3	13.2
Higher secondary	1.2	1.7	1.8	2.4	2.0	9.1
Diploma	0.2	0.2	0.2	0.3	0.4	1.3
Graduate diploma	0.1	0.1	0.2	0.2	0.3	1.0
Degree	0.5	0.7	0.7	1.2	1.1	4.1
Postgraduate	0.1	0.0	0.0	0.1	0.3	0.5
Total allocated to wealth quintile	20.0	26.0	23.7	20.4	10.0	100

Source: Aslam, Atherton, and Kingdon 2012.

In Bangladesh, secondary school stipends for girls have led to a situation where enrollment rates of girls from poor backgrounds are now more than 10 percentage points higher than those of boys (box 7.4), and the issue now is to ensure that poor boys also attend school. A targeting mechanism put in place in 2009 in part of the country uses proxy-means testing (PMT) to identify poor beneficiaries (box 7.4). In its first two years, the program has had a significant impact on increasing enrollment for both girls and boys.

However, although interventions that remove constraints on access for the poor are clearly needed, they are not likely to resolve the quality concern. There is a robust finding, for instance, that cash transfer programs can have significant effects on demand for education (enrollment, attendance, and completion of schooling), but not much evidence that they can also improve learning outcomes.

It is thus unlikely that learning outcomes will become more equitable without a policy shift and more emphasis on interventions and funding mechanisms that focus on quality improvements for the poor. The recent Bangladeshi initiative at the secondary level to combine PMT-based stipends with introduction of performance incentives, remedial classes in English and mathematics for lagging groups,

Box 7.4 Improving Access and Learning Opportunities for the Poor in Bangladesh

Bangladesh pioneered the use of conditional cash transfers (CCTs) for girls' education in the early 1990s. Within a decade, female enrollment went up from 35 percent before the program to over 50 percent. The largest gender-differentiated impact was among children from the bottom two income quintiles. Gender ratio (girls to boys) in secondary enrollment was 1.07 overall, but a much larger 1.20 for children from poor households, which suggested that too few boys from poor households had enrolled. In response to a concern about this, in 2009 a new generation CCT was phased in in 122 rural *upazilas*, covering 6,700 schools. Proxy means-testing (PMT) was introduced as a transparent targeting mechanism to identify beneficiaries, both boys and girls. Welfare scores for applicants are calculated based on observable characteristics. Eligible students, male and female, belonging to the poorest 50 percent of households receive stipends and tuition. Per-student stipends range from US$20 to US$40 per month, depending on the grade, and benefits are conditional on students maintaining 75 percent average attendance, receiving a passing grade on final examinations, and remaining unmarried until finishing grade 10. Compliance criteria are confirmed every six months.

In parallel, interventions to improve quality are being introduced. They include performance incentives for students, teachers, and institutions; remedial additional classes in English and mathematics for lagging groups; and a reading habit program.

A rigorous evaluation after two years found that the program has had a significant impact on secondary school enrollment. Boys eligible to receive stipends are 21 percentage points more likely to be enrolled in schools than they would have been without the program. The impact is even more pronounced for boys from the bottom two income quintiles. For girls, the impact is equally strong, and better than in the previous girl-only stipend program. Overall test scores improved by 0.25 standard deviation between the two rounds of the survey but there is no differential effect of the PMT-stipend program. This finding is consistent with evidence from other studies that in the short run CCTs mostly affect enrollment, not student learning. One year is also likely to be too soon to observe an impact of recent quality-enhancing interventions.

Source: World Bank 2012c.

and a reading habit program is an attempt to reach the objective of quality as well as access for the poor (box 7.4). Initial findings show promise but it is too early to measure the full impact.

Policy Implications

Education systems in South Asia find it difficult to provide high-quality education for all. Spending in the region, even after correcting for PPP, is less than US$400 per pupil per year—less than 1/25 of spending in the United States.[22] However, as a share of government budgets, spending on education of countries in the region is similar to that of OECD countries, suggesting that in the short run, spending is being constrained by fiscal capabilities.

Obtaining significant improvements in quality calls for changes in incentives for teachers and schools. Introducing accountability (PRP and promotions) based on student learning could work to modify teacher behavior. Similarly a shift from block to per-pupil grants would help make schools more accountable. A more complex system of funding that ties increases in allocations to school performance indicators could have even bigger learning benefits. In all cases, the policy objective is to forge a closer link between funding and outcomes rather than inputs.

Another avenue for quality improvements would be to leverage the contribution of the private sector and to look for cost-effective PPPs. With careful selection of arrangements that have efficiency and equity incentives built in, benefits from expenditures could be maximized.

Moving forward, countries should consider moving beyond access programs to put more emphasis on funding mechanisms to enhance the quality of education, particularly primary education, which would greatly benefit the poor. And while continuing to reduce the number of out-of-school children, countries would gain by targeting their educational subsidies and other interventions more directly to the poorest income groups. More efficient programs would optimize the payoffs.

Notes

1. This has serious implications for discussions of decentralizing: what is deemed a centralized system in a country as small as Nepal may be considered decentralized in a vast country like India. With just 30 million people, Nepal's population is the size of an administrative division in Uttar Pradesh, India's most populous state.
2. Other types of spending related to the quality of teachers (e.g., training) were discussed in chapter 5.
3. This is the most common indicator of school financing. Its popularity stems from its comparability across nations because it accounts for differences in relative national wealth. However, because it is so broad, it masks the heterogeneity of education spending. Also, it may understate spending in a country where private contributions (through private schools, tuition fees, or tutoring) are large.
4. However, in India (see table 7.6), although public expenditure has been falling as a percentage of GDP, because private expenditure has been rising the overall share has been roughly constant.
5. Based on UNESCO Institute of Statistics data. GDP is evaluated in constant local prices.
6. For example, the Government of Bangladesh reported in 2011 that half of government and recognized nongovernment schools were overcrowded.
7. This indicates the emphasis government places on education relative to other sectors.
8. The share of government revenues and correspondingly expenditure as a percentage of GDP is much lower in the region than in developed countries. Government revenues in India, where tax systems are comparatively further developed, averaged just 18.1 percent of GDP for 1999–2009, compared to 36.6 percent in OECD countries.

9. Although the proportions are much less in India and Pakistan, the absolute amounts are far from insignificant.
10. See http://www.moe.gov.pk/Enrolment%20by%20Stage,%20Gender%20and%20Location%202005-06T5.pdf and http://www.moe.gov.pk/Institutions%20by%20Level,%20Gender%20and%20Location%202005-06T4.pdf.
11. Muralidharan and Zieleniak (2012) used village-panel data from a nationally representative sample of over 1,250 villages in 19 Indian states; they found substantial improvements in school infrastructure between 2003 and 2010. For instance, the proportion of schools with toilets and electricity more than doubled.
12. This is the chief minister's bicycle program for secondary-school girls in Bihar state in India.
13. India's National Council of Educational Research and Training (NCERT) advises and supports the government on academic matters related to school education. It also drafts and publishes textbooks.
14. Except in Maldives, where salaries of teachers have declined relative to those of equivalents in the private sector and in other government services. The most promising school completers and young graduates are now reluctant to enter the profession (World Bank 2012b).
15. One obvious issue is reverse causality, in that the center provides additional grants under the Sarva Shiksha Abhiyan program to states that have the greatest need. To attempt to minimize these concerns, Figure 7.3 shows the conditional effect of per capita funding on achievement in the midline test (in 2008), conditional on scores in the baseline test in 2003. If there was a negative correlation simply because more funds were being distributed to lower-performing states, introduction of baseline scores should reverse the relationship.
16. However, it is possible that these results are subject to a selection bias: West Bengal used to have a board exam at grade 4 that a large proportion of students would fail. Only students who passed would reach grade 5. In contrast, in Kerala almost 100 percent of students reach grade 5.
17. Remuneration does not necessarily have to be financial, although it usually is—it could be through prizes, praise, or any other reward structure.
18. Two incentive schemes (an individual teacher bonus and a group teacher bonus) and two input schemes (provision of an additional teacher and provision of a block grant to the school to purchase school inputs).
19. The best-performing students in the final examinations in grades 6–9 receive an award. Teachers and schools are eligible for awards based on student pass rates.
20. Another form of demand-side financing is cash subsidies to parents conditional on their children attending school. These are often given to help poor parents overcome non-fee costs of schooling and are sometimes targeted at girls' enrollment. Examples are PROGRESA in Mexico and the *Bolsa Escola* in Brazil. While these schemes are intended to address demand deficiency, they could in principle impact school quality by inducing competition between schools just as vouchers do.
21. This measure of inequality is, of course, very crude and is probably an underestimate, since it is based on the number of years of schooling and does not consider quality differences.
22. According to the National Center for Education Statistics, education spending on elementary education in the United States equated to US$10,447 per pupil in 2007/08. See http://nces.ed.gov/fastfacts/display.asp?id=66.

Bibliography

Ahmed, A. U. 2004. "Impact of Feeding Children in School: Evidence from Bangladesh." *International Food Policy Research Institute* http://www.lcgbangladesh.org/fsn/reports/ifpri%20final%20report_school%20feeding%20in%20bangladesh.pdf.

Alderman, H., and D. Bundy. 2012. "School Feeding Programs and Development: Are We Framing the Question Correctly?" *The World Bank Research Observer* 27 (2): 204–21.

Alderman, H., J. Kim, and P. F. Orazem. 2003. "Design, Evaluation, and Sustainability of Private Schools for the Poor: The Pakistan Urban and Rural Fellowship School Experiments." *Economics of Education Review* 22 (3): 265–74.

Altinok, N., and G. Kingdon. 2012. "New Evidence on Class Size Effects: A Pupil Fixed Effects Approach." *Oxford Bulletin of Economics and Statistics* 74 (2): 203–34.

Andrabi, T., J. Das, and A. Khwaja. 2008. "A Dime a Day: The Possibilities and Limits of Private Schooling in Pakistan." *Comparative Education Review* 52 (3): 329–55.

Andrabi, T., J. Das, A. Khwaja, T. Vishwanath, and T. Zajonc. 2007. *Pakistan: Learning and Educational Achievements in Punjab Schools (LEAPS): Insights to Inform the Education Policy Debate.* http://www.leapsproject.org/assets/publications/LEAPS_Report_ExecSummary.pdf.

Angrist, J., E. Bettinger, E. Bloom, E. King, and M. Kremer. 2002. "Vouchers for Private Schooling in Colombia: Evidence from a Randomized Natural Experiment." *American Economic Review* 92 (5): 1535–55.

Angrist, J., E. Bettinger, and M. Kremer. 2006. "Long-Term Educational Consequences of Secondary School Vouchers: Evidence from Administrative Records in Colombia." *American Economics Review* 96 (3): 847–62.

Angrist, J. D., and V. Lavy. 1999. "Using Maimonides' Rule to Estimate the Effect of Class Size on Scholastic Achievement." *The Quarterly Journal of Economics* 114 (2): 533–75.

Asadullah, M., N. Chaudhury, D. Prajuli, L. R. Sarr, Y. Savchenko, and S. R. Al-Zayed. 2009. *Secondary Education Quality and Access Enhancement Project (SEQAEP): Baseline Report.* Washington, DC: World Bank.

Aslam, M. 2009. "Education Gender Gaps in Pakistan: Is the Labour Market to Blame?" *Economic Development and Cultural Change* 57 (4): 747–87.

Aslam, M., and P. Atherton. 2012. "The Shadow Education Sector in India and Pakistan: The Determinants, Benefits, and Equity Effects of Private Tutoring." Education Support Program Working Paper Series 38, Open Society Foundations, New York. http://www.periglobal.org/sites/periglobal.org/files/WP38_Aslam&Atherton.pdf.

Aslam, M., P. Atherton, and G. Kingdon. 2012. "Financing Education in South Asia." Background paper, Human Development Unit, South Asia Region, World Bank, Washington, DC.

Atherton, P., and G. Kingdon. 2010. "The Relative Effectiveness and Costs of Contract and Regular Teachers in India." CSAE Working Paper Series WPS/2010-15, Centre for the Study of African Economies, University of Oxford, Oxford, U.K.

Aturupane, H., P. Glewwe, and S. Wisniewski. 2013. "The Impact of School Quality, Socio-Economic Factors and Child Health on Students' Academic Performance: Evidence from Sri Lankan Primary Schools." *Education Economics* 21 (1): 2–37.

Baker, B., and P. Green. 2008. "Conceptions of Equity and Adequacy in School Finance." In *Handbook of Research in Education Finance and Policy*, edited by H. Ladd and E. Fiske, 203–21. New York, NY: Routledge.

Banerjee, A., S. Cole, E. Duflo, and L. Linden. 2006. "Remedying Education: Evidence from Two Randomized Experiments in India." *Quarterly Journal of Economics* 122 (3): 1235–64.

Barrera-Osorio, F., and D. Raju. 2010. "Short-Run Learning Dynamics under a Test-Based Accountability System: Evidence from Pakistan." Policy Research Working Paper 5465, World Bank, Washington, DC.

———. 2011. "Evaluating Public Per-Student Subsidies to Low-Cost Private Schools: Regression-Discontinuity Evidence from Pakistan." Policy Research Working Paper 5638, World Bank, Washington, DC.

Borkum, E., F. He, and L. L. Linden. 2012. "School Libraries and Language Skills in Indian Primary Schools: A Randomized Evaluation of the Akshara Library Program." NBER Working Paper 18183, National Bureau of Economic Research, Cambridge, MA.

Bray, M. 2009. *Confronting the Shadow Education System: What Government Policies for What Private Tutoring?* Paris: UNESCO-IIEP.

Burde, D., and L. Linden. 2010. "The Effect of Village-Based Schools: Evidence from a Randomized Controlled Trial in Afghanistan." NBER Working Paper 18039, National Bureau of Economic Research, Cambridge, MA.

Das, J., S. Dercon, J. Habyarimana, P. Krishnan, K. Muralidharan, and V. Sundararaman. 2013. "School Inputs, Household Substitution, and Test Scores." *American Economic Journal: Applied Economics* 5 (2): 29–57.

Dreher, A., P. Nunnenkamp, and R. Thiele. 2008. "Does Aid for Education Educate Children? Evidence from Panel Data." *World Bank Economic Review* 22 (2): 291–314.

Drèze, J., and G. Kingdon. 2001. "School Participation in Rural India." *Review of Development Economics* 5 (1): 1–24.

Glewwe, P., and M. Kremer. 2006. "Schools, Teachers, and Education Outcomes in Developing Countries." In *Handbook of the Economics of Education*, Vol. 2, edited by E. Hanushek and F. Welch. New York: Elsevier.

Glewwe, P., M. Kremer, and. S. Moulin. 2009. "Many Children Left Behind? Textbooks and Test Scores in Kenya." *American Economic Journal: Applied Economics* 1 (1): 112–35.

Glewwe, P., N. Ilias, and M. Kremer. 2010. "Teacher Incentives." American Economic Journal: Applied Economics 2(3): 205–27.

Goyal, S., and P. Pandey. 2009. *How Do Government and Private Schools Differ? Findings from Two Large Indian States.* Report 30, South Asia Human Development Unit, Washington, DC: World Bank.

———. 2013. "Contract Teachers in India." *Education Economics* 21 (5): 1–21.

Hanushek, E. A., and L. Woessmann. 2011. "The Economics of International Differences in Educational Achievement." In *Handbook of the Economics of Education*, Vol. 3 edited by E. A. Hanushek, S. J. Machin, and L. Woessmann. New York, NY: Elsevier.

Heyneman, S. P., D. T. Jamison, and X. Montenegro. 1984. "Textbooks in the Philippines: Evaluation of the Pedagogical Impact of a Nationwide Investment." *Educational Evaluation and Policy Analysis* 6 (2): 139–50.

Jayaraman, R., D. Simroth, and F. de Véricourt. 2011. "The Effect of School Lunches on School Enrolment: Evidence from India's Midday Meal Scheme." Working paper, INSEAD, Fontainebleau, France.

Kingdon, G. 1996. "The Quality and Efficiency of Private and Public Education: A Case Study of Urban India." *Oxford Bulletin of Economics and Statistics* 58 (1): 57–82.

———. 2007. "The Progress of School Education in India." *Oxford Review of Economic Policy* 23 (2): 168–95.

Kingdon, G., and R. Banerji. 2009. "Addressing School Quality: Some Policy Pointers from Rural North India." RECOUP Policy Brief 5, Faculty of Education, University of Cambridge, Cambridge, U.K.

Kingdon, G., and M. Muzammil. 2010. "The School Governance Environment in Uttar Pradesh, India: Implications for Teacher Accountability and Effort." RECOUP Working Paper 31, Faculty of Education, University of Cambridge, Cambridge, U.K.

Kingdon, G., and F. Teal. 2007. "Does Performance-Related Pay for Teachers Improve Student Achievement? Some Evidence from India." *Economics of Education Review* 26 (4): 473–86.

Krueger, A. B. 2003. "Economic Considerations and Class Size." *The Economic Journal* 113 (485): F34–63.

Ladd, H. F. 2002. "School Vouchers: A Critical View." *The Journal of Economic Perspectives* 16 (4): 3–24.

Lavy, V. 2002. "Evaluating the Effects of Teachers' Performance Incentives on Pupil Achievement." *Journal of Political Economy* 110 (6): 1286–317.

Mukherjee, M. 2011. "Do Better Roads Increase School Enrollment? Evidence from a Unique Road Policy in India." Manuscript, Department of Economics, Syracuse University, Syracuse, NY. http://www.isid.ac.in/~pu/conference/dec_11_conf/Papers/MuktaMukherjee.pdf.

Muralidharan, K., and V. Sundararaman. 2010. "Contract Teachers: Experimental Evidence from India." Manuscript, Department of Economics, University of California, San Diego.

———. 2011. "Teacher Performance Pay: Experimental Evidence from India." *Journal of Political Economy* 119 (1): 39–77.

———. 2013. "Contract Teachers: Experimental Evidence from India." NBER Working Paper 19440, National Bureau of Economic Research, Cambridge, MA.

Muralidharan, K., and Y. Zieleniak. 2012. "Measuring Learning Trajectories in Developing Countries with Longitudinal Data and Item Response Theory." Manuscript, Department of Economics, University of California, San Diego, CA.

Nechyba, T. 2005. "Mobilizing the Private Sector: A Theoretical Overview." Working Paper PEPG 05-06, Program on Education Policy and Governance, Kennedy School of Government, Harvard University, Cambridge, MA.

PAISA Report. 2011. *Do Schools Get Their Money? Accountability Initiative.* http://www.accountabilityindia.in/article/state-report-cards/2475-paisa-report-2011.

Pritchett, L., and D. Filmer 1999. "What Education Production Functions Really Show: A Positive Theory of Education Expenditures." *Economics of Education Review* 18 (2): 223–39.

Reinnika, R., and J. Svensson. 2004. "Local Capture: Evidence from a Central Government Transfer Program in Uganda." *Quarterly Journal of Economics* 119 (2): 679–705.

Sankar, D. 2012. "India's Right to Education Act: Opportunities and Challenges." Background paper prepared for India Economic Update, South Asia Poverty Reduction and Economic Management Unit, World Bank, Washington, DC.

Woessmann, L. 2003. "Schooling Resources, Educational Institutions and Student Performance: The International Evidence." *Oxford Bulletin of Economics and Statistics* 65 (2): 117–70.

———. 2007. "Fundamental Determinants of School Efficiency and Equity: German States as a Microcosm for OECD Countries." IZA Discussion Paper 2880, Institute for the Study of Labor, Bonn, Germany.

World Bank. 2008. "Education for All in Bangladesh: Where Does Bangladesh Stand in Achieving the EFA Goals by 2015?" Human Development Unit, South Asia Region, World Bank, Washington, DC.

———. 2012a. *Bhutan Human Development Public Expenditure Review.* Washington, DC: World Bank.

———. 2012b. *Human Capital for a Modern Society: General Education in the Maldives—An Evolving Seascape.* Washington, DC: World Bank.

———. 2012c. "Bangladesh SEQAEP, Interim Impact Evaluation Report". Human Development Unit, South Asia Region, World Bank, Washington, DC.

CHAPTER 8

Monitoring Learning Outcomes: Student Assessment Systems*

Introduction

It is widely recognized that a student learning assessment system is a necessary, although not sufficient, condition for sustainable improvement in learning outcomes. It is possible to know whether an intervention has enhanced learning only if learning outcomes can be measured consistently over time.

Traditionally, governments assessed the quality of education primarily by measuring inputs like public spending on education, class size, textbook availability, and teacher credentials. However, much depends on how, if at all, these inputs translate into outcomes (Hanushek, Link, and Woessmann 2013). Outcomes, rather than inputs, are what correlate with both the individual's later life opportunities and the country's economic growth (Hanushek and Woessmann 2008).

Today, governments, international organizations, and education stakeholders increasingly recognize the importance of assessment for monitoring and planning quality interventions and improving student achievement. The main focus of assessment is to monitor what the education system is producing, rather than appraising the achievements of individual students.

This chapter reviews student assessment in South Asia—the process of gathering and evaluating information on how much knowledge students have gained and how much they can apply to other aspects of their lives. Assessment methods can be as simple as oral questioning or as complex as computer-adapted testing models based on multifaceted scoring algorithms and learning progressions (Clarke 2012).

The chapter begins by briefly describing various types of student assessments currently in use. It then analyzes how the three main types are used in South Asian countries and identifies issues and opportunities. It concludes with a discussion of policy actions to strengthen assessment systems in order to enhance the quality of learning.

---

*See box 8.1 for a summary of the chapter's key questions and findings.

Box 8.1 Questions and Findings

Questions

- What is the status of student assessment systems in South Asia?
- What limits the effectiveness of assessment as a tool to improve the quality of teaching and learning in South Asia?
- How can countries better align learning assessment systems with superior learning outcomes?

Findings

- In general, learning assessments in South Asia give priority to high-stakes examinations rather than classroom and large-scale, system-level assessment. The emphasis on public examinations is problematic for student learning as these typically focus on memorization and information recall rather than critical thinking and problem-solving skills.

- To improve the quality of public examinations in South Asia—and their ability to assess student learning—it will be necessary to deal with the limited validity of the questions, the lack of coordination between different examination boards within the same country, the low comparability of test scores across different boards and over time, the high potential for manipulating the results, bad practices such as cheating, and staff members who are poorly trained to carry out examination-related activities.

- To build up educational quality and outcomes, South Asian countries need to create balanced assessment systems that emphasize classroom testing and large-scale assessments. Classroom assessments are useful for monitoring a child's progress and taking corrective measures; system-level assessments provide an overview of how an education system is evolving over time. Important considerations for improving classroom appraisals are giving teachers better resources, materials, and training in assessing students, and building in regular feedback to students.

- As for system-level assessments, except for two Indian states participating in PISA 2009+, no South Asian country has participated in international assessments like Trends in Mathematics and Science Study (TIMSS), Programme for International Student Assessment (PISA), and Progress in International Reading Literacy Study (PIRLS). That makes it difficult to compare student achievement within the region, much less with other parts of the world.

Types and Key Features of Student Assessments

There are three main types of assessment systems (Clarke 2012; see also table 8.1):

- ***Classroom assessments,*** also referred to as continuous or formative assessments, are carried out by teachers and students in the course of the school day (Airasian and Russell 2007). They provide real-time information to support teaching and learning in individual classrooms. This form of testing encompasses such activities as oral questioning and feedback, homework assignments, student presentations, diagnostic tests, and end-of-unit quizzes.

- ***Examinations*** are customized depending on whether they are *public, external,* or *end of cycle*. They provide information for high-stakes decision making on, for example, whether individual students should be assigned to a particular type of school or academic program, graduate from high school, or be admitted to university (Greaney and Kellaghan 1995; Heubert and Hauser 1999).

Table 8.1 Types of Student Assessments

	Classroom assessments	*Public examinations*	*System-level assessments*		
			National	*International*	*Specific purpose*
Type of assessment	Formative (assessment *as* and *for* learning)	Summative (assessment *of* learning)	Summative (assessment of learning)		
Purpose	Provide real-time information to support teaching and learning	Certify and select students	Assess performance against national standards and learning goals, and provide feedback to policy makers	Assess performance against international standards, and provide feedback to policy makers	Assess the impact of particular interventions on learning, or independently assess student learning
Frequency	May be daily, weekly, monthly, quarterly, annually	Annually; more often where the system allows	For individual subjects, offered on a regular schedule	On a regular schedule, usually 3–5 years	Related to a unique stated purpose
Who is assessed	All students in all grades	All students who wish to take this examination at the grade level	Usually, a sample of students at a particular grade or age level		Specific student population in an area, school, grade, category, or community
Format	Oral questioning, homework, student presentations, diagnostic tests, etc.	Usually essay and multiple choice	Usually, multiple choice and short-answer		Designed for a unique stated purpose

Source: Based Greaney and Kellaghan 2008.

- ***Large-scale, system-level assessments*** provide policy makers and practitioners with information on the overall performance of a system, changes in performance, and contributing factors. They may be national, subnational, regional, and international. Examples of international assessments of student achievement are TIMSS, PIRLS, and PISA and of regional assessments are *Programme d' Analyse des Systèmes Éducatifs de la Confemen*[1] (PASEC) in Francophone Africa, the Southern and Eastern Africa Consortium for Monitoring Educational Quality (SACMEQ) in Anglophone Africa, and *el Laboratorio Latinoamericano de Evaluación de la Calidad de la Educación*[2] (LLECE) in South America. *Sistema de Medición de la Calidad de la Educación*[3] (SIMCE) is an example of a national assessment, and tests in U.S. states and Canadian provinces are examples of state assessments. These assessments vary by grades or ages tested, coverage of the target population (sample or census), internal or external focus (national or international benchmarks), subjects or skill areas covered, types of background data gathered, and the frequency with which they are administered.

These three types of assessment are obviously not completely independent of each other; nor are they all-encompassing—some assessment activities do not quite fit within these categories.

Education systems may emphasize different types of assessment. For example, Finland considers classroom assessment as the key source of information on student learning and achievement and draws far less on examinations or large-scale assessments. China has traditionally emphasized examinations and relies less on classroom assessment or large-scale surveys, although this is changing. Factors contributing to the development of different assessment systems can vary from the official vision and goals of the education system to national economic structures and opportunities and the related information needs of stakeholders. Box 8.2 describes a framework for evaluating the policy on learning assessment.

Box 8.2 Learning Assessment

Systems Approach for Better Education Results (SABER) is an initiative that helps countries to systematically examine and build up the performance of their education systems to achieve learning for all. SABER classifies assessments into three main kinds of activities, corresponding to three main information needs or purposes: classroom assessments; examinations; and large-scale, system-level assessments (Clarke 2012). To assess policy development in each area, the key consideration is the individual, but there is also a concern about the quality of assessment activities in terms of the adequacy of the information generated to support decision making (Shepard 2000; Clarke 2012). There are three main drivers of information quality in an assessment system: enabling context, system alignment, and assessment quality (see Clarke 2012 for a review of the literature).

box continues next page

Box 8.2 Learning Assessment *(continued)*

"*The enabling context* refers to the context in which an assessment activity takes place, and the extent to which it is conducive to or supportive of the assessment. It covers such areas as the legislative or policy framework for assessment; leadership of the assessment; public engagement with it; institutional arrangements for designing, carrying out, and using assessment results; availability of sufficient and stable sources of funding; and the presence of competent assessment staff and classroom teachers. … *System alignment* refers to the extent to which the assessment coheres with other components of the education system in terms of system learning goals, standards, and curriculum, and pre- and in-service teacher training opportunities (Fuhrman and Elmore 1994; Smith and O'Day 1991). … *Assessment quality* refers to the psychometric quality of the instruments, processes, and procedures used (AERA, APA, and NCME 1999). It covers such areas as design and conduct of assessment activities, examination questions, or survey items; analysis and interpretation of student responses to assessment activities, questions, or items; and the appropriateness of how results are reported and used (Heubert and Hauser 1999; Shepard 2000)."

Crossing these quality drivers with the different. Assessment types and purposes (Clarke 2012, pp. 9–11) produced the matrix and broad indicator areas diagrammed in table B8.1.1, which provide a starting point for reviewing assessment systems and planning for their improvement.

Table B8.1.1 Framework for Reviewing Student Assessment Systems, with Indicator Areas

	Classroom assessment	*Examinations*	*Large-scale, system-level assessment*
Enabling context	• Policies • Leadership and public engagement • Funding • Institutional arrangements • Human resources		
System alignment	• Learning/quality goals • Curriculum • Pre- and in-service teacher training opportunities		
Assessment quality	• Ensuring quality (design, administration, analysis) • Ensuring effective use		

Source: Clarke 2012.

Public Examinations in South Asia

General Features

In general, assessment systems in countries in South Asia are strong in the area of examinations and weak in classroom and large-scale assessments. This is not surprising, since most of those countries have a long legacy of using examinations for making high-stakes decisions about who gains access to scarce opportunities at the next educational level.

Over the past decade, countries in the region have taken different approaches to examination systems. Bhutan, for example, has reduced the number of examinations by delegating responsibility for primary and lower-secondary examinations to schools. Bangladesh has introduced new primary and lower-secondary public examinations. In India, many states used to conduct annual (board) examinations at the end of primary (grade 5) and upper primary (grade 8) to determine who would be promoted. Based on the National Curriculum Framework of 2005 (NCERT 2005), which highlighted concerns about the negative influence of testing and examinations throughout the school years, the RTE Act advocated continuous and comprehensive evaluations (CCEs) of a child's overall knowledge and development and prohibited board examinations until elementary education is completed (article 30, chapter V). All Indian states have since banned board examinations until grade 10. At present, more than 40 school boards in the country conduct secondary school examinations at the end of grades 10 and 12.

Table 8.2 lists the main public examinations in South Asia. While there are some similarities in the systems, there are also major differences. For example, Bangladeshi students go through four public examinations before completing general education, but students in Bhutan, Maldives, and Sri Lanka go through only two. What is universal to these countries, however, is the high importance accorded to public examinations. In most systems, the most important

Table 8.2 Public Examinations in South Asian Countries

Country	*Grade*	*Name of the examination*
Bangladesh	5	Primary Education Terminal Examination[a]
	8	Junior Secondary Certificate Examination
	10	Secondary School Certificate Examination
	12	Higher Secondary Certificate Examination
Bhutan	10	Bhutan Certificate of Secondary Education (BCSE)
	12	Bhutan Higher Secondary Certificate
India[b]	10	Secondary School Leaving Certificate
	12	Higher Secondary Certificate Examination
Maldives	10	General Certificate of Education Ordinary Level (GCE O/L)[c]
	12	General Certificate of Education Advanced Level (GCE A/L)[d]
Nepal	8	Basic Level Terminal Examination
	10	Secondary Level Certificate (SLC) Examination
	12	Higher Secondary Level Certification (HSLC)
Pakistan[e]	10	Secondary School Certificate Examination
	12	Higher Secondary School Certificate Examination
Sri Lanka	11	General Certificate of Education Ordinary Level (GCE O/L)
	13	General Certificate of Education Advanced Level (GCE A/L)

a. Some states have examinations at grades 5 and 8.
b. Other examinations include the International General Certificate of Secondary Education (IGCSE) and Senior Secondary Certificate (SSC) examinations.
c. Other examinations include Higher Secondary Certificate (HSC).
d. Some states have examinations at grades 5 and 8.
e. For example, teachers in an upper primary school (grades 6–8) in Delhi were aware of changes to the grade 10 high school examination and adjusted their teaching, treating grades 6–8 as preparation for the grade 10 exam (Agrawal 2004).

examination comes at the end of upper secondary school/compulsory education. In Bangladesh, Nepal, and Sri Lanka, this corresponds to the unified examinations held at the end of compulsory education, which determine decisions about high school graduation. In Pakistan, it corresponds to the secondary school certificate examinations administered to students in grades 9 and 10.

Challenges of Public Examinations and Opportunities

The primary function of public examinations in South Asian countries is to assess the competence of student learning relative to the standards for education courses or levels. However, the examination system raises issues such as the quality and standardization of examinations and how they are governed and conducted.

Quality of Examinations

In assessing the quality of examinations, the fundamental issue is their alignment with teaching-learning activities. As international evidence shows, examinations have a significant impact both on what is taught and how, and on what is learned and how (Greaney and Kellaghan 1995). The knowledge teachers impart is circumscribed by what will be asked of their students in examinations. The curriculum is further circumscribed by teachers picking topics that they consider likely to appear in examinations. Teachers are also inclined to emphasize cognitive competence and to neglect practical skills, which tend to be less favored in examinations. Thus, considerable effort and time are invested in building student skills for performing well in examinations, with teachers using past examination papers as a basis for instruction (Greaney and Kellaghan 1995). The influence of examinations on teaching permeates to grades much lower than the ones at which public examinations are taken.[4]

One commonly observed influence of public examinations is rote learning. For instance, in India, because examinations usually call for memorization rather than higher-order skills like reasoning and analysis, classroom practices emphasize rote learning rather than lateral thinking, creativity, and judgment (NCERT 2006). In Bangladesh, a review of all Secondary School Certification examination papers over a five-year period found that more than 80 percent of total marks were for straight recall of facts (Hossain 2009). Pakistan has a similar problem. "Model papers" or "guess paper guides" with ready-made answers based on the last five years of examination papers are readily available in bookshops, and teacher and student reliance on these translates into selective study of exam sections and students committing their content to memory (Greaney and Hasan 1998; Rehmani 2003; Hussain 2009). In some Indian states, students and teachers often give priority to high-scoring subjects and to subjects deemed critical for later studies. Selection of only a few subjects for study instead of embracing and enriching broader knowledge curtails learning.

Two technical issues affecting examination quality relate to the reliability and validity of test questions. *Reliability* refers to whether the assessment produces accurate information. This is particularly important in highstakes testing and for monitoring trends over time. *Validity* refers to whether the test scores represent what they are expected to signify and whether they can be used in the ways intended.[5] In South Asia, specific technical concerns are the repetition of identical or very similar questions from year to year (a further incentive to coach classes); examinations designed to test textbook knowledge rather than competencies and core concepts; inordinately lengthy answers that allow little time for actual thinking; and the overuse of multiple choice rather than open-ended questions, induced by both marking convenience and markers' capacity constraints.

Quality concerns also relate to implementation capacity and financial and human resources. In Pakistan, although examination questions are drafted by academically qualified persons with more than five years of teaching experience, most of them lack training in modern approaches to assessment (Mirza 1999; Rehmani 2003). Also, a shortage of resources often results in overcrowded examination halls and a lack of physical amenities, such as furniture and air conditioners. The quality of proctoring in Pakistan is an additional concern; cheating is prevalent (Hussain 2009). In Bhutan, inadequate staffing of the examination board and insufficient office space for carrying out technical tasks are major constraints in designing good-quality examinations (Rinchen 2009).

Standardizing the Quality of Examinations

Current examination systems in South Asia often lack standardization, which is critical to examination quality. The consequences are a lack of comparability between different years and different examination boards and unreliable marking standards. In Pakistan education boards apply different standards, examination content differs markedly between boards, and there is a large variance in the qualifications of those marking tests. India and Bangladesh have the same problems. There are more than 40 examination boards in India; in Bangladesh each of the eight different secondary examination boards[6] is responsible for setting its own examination questions for every subject, and there is no real attempt to equate standards for examination papers by subject and examination board. The only check on question standards is a group of moderators who read through them and make comments, usually on matters of content (Hossain 2009). In Bhutan, although annual Ministry of Education (MOE) statistical reports provide a historical overview of examination results for grades 10 and 12, the data are not useful for monitoring trends because the questions vary across the years as curricula change. Furthermore, the thresholds set annually for minimum pass marks can also differ, depending on the system's capacity to absorb the students selected (World Bank 2013).

Marker unreliability raises a serious concern about examination reliability. Cases of marker unreliability arise, for instance, when the same questions elicit different scores on two separate occasions, and when different markers award different scores to the same papers. Because in Bangladesh, for instance, marking schemes are not drawn up by either the question setters or the moderators, there are no systematic checks on the weight allocated to each examination question (Hossain 2009). In India, establishing a credible and transparent marking mechanism is also a concern. Students are allowed to request reevaluations of their test scripts, but the processes involved are often kept confidential. Related to this is another common practice in both India and Bangladesh—granting a few "grace" marks to candidates to enable them to pass. This raises yet another question about the credibility of the examination system.

Governance

Many South Asian countries grapple regularly with misconduct and cheating in examination systems before, during, and after an examination. These can take a variety of forms, such as leakage of questions before, external assistance to students during, and substitution of answer papers after the examination.[7] In Pakistan, the Punjab Commission for Evaluation of Examination System and Eradication of Malpractices (1992) reported a high prevalence of misconduct committed by students, teachers, paper setters, proctors, examiners, and the board (Aly 2007). Despite a law to prevent them—the Examination (Prevention of Unfair Means) Act of 1993—and imposition of penalties on misconduct, it persists (Rehmani 2003; Hossain 2009). In India, flying squads have been deployed at examination centers to prevent assistance to student cheating. Nevertheless, post-examination misconduct has largely been reduced, for example in Maharashtra state, through a system of encrypted barcodes for each student and concealing the name of the student and the school from the proctor and examination board staff (NCERT 2006).

Reported manipulation of public examinations is another worrying governance issue. In South Asia, parents, community, and the media often use board examination results to benchmark school quality. There is some anecdotal evidence that pass rates have been manipulated in some countries by putting pressure on weak students to leave school before reaching the public examination stage or to repeat a grade rather than take the examination.

Publishing examination results helps make schools accountable for the quality of education and helps planners to target relatively weak schools (see box 8.2).[8] However, using examinations for such purposes needs to be done carefully in order not to disadvantage weak schools and students. Examinations can provide the stimulus for students to study hard and allow for monitoring of quality standards of educational achievement—but good governance is necessary if examinations are to be effective.

Policy Reforms on Examinations

Examinations have serious consequences not only for the students taking them but also for the societies in which they live. For examinations to produce outcomes that are as fair and equitable as possible for individual students or for those belonging to a particular ethnic, racial, or economic group, certain policies need to be in place system wide:

- Sufficient numbers of trained staff members to carry out examination activities
- Alignment between what should be measured (e.g., student comprehension of the national curriculum) and what the examination actually measures (e.g., textbook knowledge)
- Specific professional development training for teachers, particularly those who actively undertake examination tasks, such as drafting questions or administering and scoring the exam
- Formal mechanisms to ensure the quality of the examination, such as publicly available technical documentation, and transparent and independent security and audit procedures at all stages from design through administration, scoring, and reporting
- Formal mechanisms to monitor the consequences or impact of the examination on learning, education quality, and opportunities for particular student groups, such as a permanent oversight committee or regular surveys of stakeholders
- Alternative options for students who do not perform well on examinations to demonstrate knowledge and skills so they can gain access to opportunities at the next level of the system.

Recognizing both the significance of public examinations for student learning and the persistent quality concerns, countries in South Asia have initiated examination reforms. For example, Bangladesh has begun at both primary and secondary levels to address a disconnect between the goals of the new curricula and the examination system. The grade 5 examination not only provides school leavers with a certificate of primary completion and proficiency, it also identifies pupils eligible for scholarships in grade 6. The aim is to gradually transform the examination into a competency-based test, moving away from rote recall questions to competencies with more applications for solving problems in real-life situations.

The reform will take place over several years. In the 2012 exam, 10 percent of test items were competency based and the percentage is expected to be 25 percent in 2013. The government also intends to analyze successive examination results to guide changes in test-item design, curriculum development, and teacher training, sharpening the focus on curriculum competencies and changing how teachers teach. Skills development for improving the examination, including training markers and test-item developers, will be equally important. The government has also prepared a model Senior Secondary Certificate (SSC) examination with fewer multiple-choice questions and with structured questions replacing narrative questions. The expectation is that the revised examination will test students more effectively across the full range of learning objectives and help to overcome the over-emphasis on recall of textbook facts (ADB 2006).

In its position paper in 2006, the NCERT claimed that in India school board examinations were inappropriate for the 21st century and its need for innovative problem solvers. It also argued that questions focused on rote memorization coupled with the prevalence of cheating eroded examination quality, and that the current style of examinations caused an inordinate amount of traumatic anxiety and stress that could push students to nervous breakdowns and even suicide. Following the spirit of the National Curriculum Framework of 2005 and the Right to Education (RTE) Act of 2009, Indian states have now banned examinations until students complete elementary education. Secondary-level reforms are mainly the domain of examination boards. For instance, the Central Board of Secondary Education (CBSE) introduced a reform in 2009 to exempt grade 10 students from the Secondary School Examination if they were already studying at CBSE-affiliated senior secondary schools and intended to continue there through grade 12. Of course, this does not affect students who intend to leave school after grade 10 or who are in secondary schools. The CBSE also launched reforms of classroom assessments and public examinations in its CCE initiative (CBSE 2009).

System-Level Assessments in South Asian Countries

General Features

In South Asia in the past decade, most countries have launched large-scale assessment programs to assess student performance against curriculum objectives (table 8.3), but no country as yet participates in international assessments, with the recent exception of two Indian states in PISA 2009+.

National assessments normally administer achievement tests either to a sample or to a large population of students across the country. Throughout the world, assessment systems tend to have common features, such as assessing student abilities in language or literacy and mathematics or numeracy. Some systems also assess achievements in a second language, science, or social studies. The results from typically sample-based, low-stakes assessments are used to inform and monitor policies and decision making for improved learning and education quality; box 8.3 shows three examples of countries that have successfully drawn on national assessment results to effect change.

National assessment systems also differ, for example, in their frequency and the agency responsible for them (Greaney and Kellaghan 2008). For example, in India the national assessment initiative—begun as part of the district primary education project and later under Education for All (*Sarva Shiksha Abhiyan*)—was originally meant for one-time tracking of improvement. However, after the success of the first two rounds—the Baseline Achievement Survey (Cycle 1) in 2001–04, and the Midterm Achievement Survey (Cycle 2) in 2005—the initiative was converted to continuous assessment starting with Cycle 3 in 2009–12 (NCERT 2011).[9] As part of the project, a modern item response theory-based system for learning assessment was instituted in order to measure student progress toward agreed system goals. It is expected that these

Table 8.3 National Assessments in South Asian Countries[a]

Country	*Name of the assessment*	*Grades*	*Years*	*Subjects*
Afghanistan[b]	National Student Assessment (NSA)	Planned for Grades 3, 6, 9, and 12	Planned for 2013	Planned for literacy, mathematics
Bangladesh	NSA	Grades 3 and 5	2006, 2008, 2011, 2013	Bangla, mathematics
	Secondary Education Quality and Access Enhancement Project Learning Assessment	Grade 6, 8, and 9	2012, 2013	Bangla, mathematics, English
Bhutan	National Education Assessment (NEA)	Grades 6 and 10	Grade 6 (English and math in 2003, Dzongkha in 2005) Grade 10 (English and math in 2006; Dzongkha in 2007)	Literacy (Dzongkha), English, mathematics
	Bhutan Learning Quality Survey (BLQS)	Grades 2 and 4	2007	Dzongkha, English, mathematics
India	Sarva Shiksha Abhiyan: National Achievement Survey	Grades 3, 5, and 8	Cycle 1 (2001–04), Cycle 2 (2005–08), Cycle 3 (2009–12)	Language, mathematics, environmental studies (G5), science (G8), social studies (G8)
	Assessment Survey Evaluation Research (ASER)	Ages 5–16 (household-based survey in rural areas)	Annually since 2005	Reading (own language), arithmetic (In some years, also critical thinking, English, and daily math skills)
Maldives	National Assessment of Learning Outcomes	Grades 4 and 7	2008	English, mathematics
Nepal	National Assessment of Student Achievement (NASA)	Grade 8 Pilots in grades 5, 8, and 10 (1998–2010)	2012 Grade 5 (1998, 2001, 2008), Grade 8 (2008) Grade10 (2010)	Nepali, mathematics, social studies
Pakistan	National Education Assessment System (NEAS)	Grades 4 and 8	2005, 2006, 2007, 2008	Language (Urdu and Sindhi), mathematics, science, social studies
	Provincial Education Assessment Center (PEACE) Sindh Assessment	Grades 4 and 8 (math only)	2009, 2010, 2011	Mathematics in 2009, 2011; language, 2010; science, 2011
	Punjab Education Assessment System (PEAS)	Grade 5	2010	Mathematics, language, and social studies
Sri Lanka	National Assessment of Achievement	Grades 4, 8, and 10	Grade 4 (2003, 2007, 2009) Grade 8 (2005, 2008) Grade 10 (2005)	First language (Sinhala or Tamil), mathematics, English

a. The list covers major national and some specific-purpose assessments.
b. The Afghani government has been setting the stage for the first National Student Assessment in 2013.

Box 8.3 Using National Learning Assessment Results: Lessons from Chile, Uruguay, and Uganda

Chile

Chile's *Sistema de Medicion de la Calidad de la Educacion* (SIMCE) is implemented annually for all fourth- and eighth-grade students in the country. All schools receive a ranking in comparison with other schools in the same socioeconomic category, as well as a national ranking. SIMCE identifies 900 schools that score in the lowest 10 percent in the mathematics and language tests within their provincial regions and special resources are provided for them. The program uses an intensive public relations campaign that includes brochures for parents and schools, posters for schools, videos for workshops, TV programs, and press releases. Parents receive an individualized report for their school so that they know which schools perform well in their neighborhood.

Uruguay

Uruguay implements national assessments in grade 6 in mathematics and reading comprehension on a sample basis. Results are used mainly by teachers, principals, and school inspectors to identify schools needing special support and for large-scale, in-service teacher training programs. Participating schools receive a confidential report with aggregate school results presented item by item. The unit responsible for the assessments produces (a) teaching guides to help address weaknesses and organize in-service training programs for disadvantaged schools, (b) reports for supervisory personnel, and (c) workshops for inspectors that draw on the test results.

Uganda

Uganda implements sample-based assessments in grades 3 and 6 in English literacy and numeracy. The National Examination Board, an implementing agency of the assessment, prints a poster for each third- and sixth-grade classroom, listing curriculum areas where national-level student performance is considered adequate (for example, "We can count numbers") and less than adequate (for example, "Help us to carry out dividing numbers correctly"). The results and implications of results are shared with teachers, head teachers, supervisors and inspectors, teacher educators, and policy makers.

Source: Greaney and Kellaghan 2008.

assessments will be conducted for the same subject area and grade every five years. The first assessment for grade 5 was completed in 2011.

In South Asia, in addition to national language and mathematics abilities, English, science, social studies, and environmental studies are also assessed. In countries like India, Pakistan, and Sri Lanka that are linguistically diverse, literacy is tested in several languages. Another variance in South Asia relates to what grades are assessed: in Bhutan grade 2 is the lowest grade assessed, and for both Bhutan and Nepal grade 10 is the highest.

Education ministries usually implement and finance system-level assessments, but in India, Assessment Survey Evaluation Research (ASER) was

Box 8.4 Nongovernmental Student Assessments in India

In India, nongovernmental learning achievement surveys have become an important source of data that provide insights into student learning. For example, the Annual Status of Education Report (ASER) survey, spearheaded and facilitated by a nongovernmental organization, Pratham, was launched in 2005 to collect information on enrollment and assess the learning of rural children in reading and arithmetic. The survey covers over 15,000 villages in about 600 districts. Fieldwork is conducted every year by 25,000 volunteers, who are trained through national, state, and district-level training. This arrangement makes the initiative unique. The ASER has also been implemented in Pakistan since 2008 and in a number of Sub-Saharan African countries (Tanzania, Kenya, and Uganda since 2009; Mali in 2011; and Senegal in 2012).

Educational Initiatives (EI), jointly with Wipro, has been carrying out Quality Education Studies in urban areas. In 2006, it assessed student learning in 89 schools in five metro areas (Bangalore, Chennai, Delhi, Kolkata, and Mumbai). In 2011, EI carried out a large-scale quality assessment in 18 major Indian states, surveying over 100,000 students in grades 4, 6, and 8 in 2,000 schools. It assessed learning outcomes in math and language and examined key aspects of the education system that contribute to quality (e.g., organization of the school and student attitudes and values).

designed and implemented by Pratham, a nongovernmental organization; it is directed to rural students (box 8.4). Bottom-up system assessment, having originated in rural India, has now spread to Pakistan and into Kenya, Tanzania, and Uganda in East Africa.

Challenges of System-level Assessments and Opportunities

While most South Asian countries are off to a good start in putting in place national learning assessment programs, the information they provide is not yet yielding maximum benefits for informed decision making. Several common issues have emerged.

Quality of Assessment

National assessments are highly technical: from the design stage on, a credible framework that covers all competency domains is necessary. To monitor student progress over time, reliable trend analysis requires that instruments be unchanged or be equivalent if they are changed. In South Asian countries, the construction of assessments, the content of the questions, and the sampling framework are still evolving, making performance comparisons over time difficult.

From the baseline it is important to make sure that curricular objectives are carefully reflected in test items. It is also vital to set standards for competency or mastery levels. For instance, there is as yet no obvious basis for arriving at the point at which a standard can be said to be satisfied, and it is unreasonable to deduce that students who score just above a cut-off point differ substantially in their achievements from those who score just below (Kellaghan and Greaney 2004). To monitor progress on student competency, standards must be transparently described.

When a national assessment is conducted by sampling, having the right sampling technique is so fundamental for correctly assessing student achievement that in international assessments countries that do not follow proper sampling procedures may be disqualified from the official results. When the two Indian states participated for the first time in the PISA+ 2009, the population data they submitted did not meet PISA standards for student sampling, and the result was flagged with the caveat that the data might contain bias and the results were to be interpreted with caution (Walker 2011).

Regularity of Assessment

To be effective in tracking the progress, or regress, of educational development over time, assessments should take place on a regular schedule, especially in developing countries where educational systems are continuously evolving. If the purpose of an assessment is only to provide information on the performance of the system as a whole, assessing a sample of students in a particular curriculum area every three to five years seems adequate. Because education systems do not change rapidly, more frequent assessments are unlikely to register change. In fact, too frequent assessments probably limit the impact of the results as well as incur unnecessary costs (Greaney and Kellaghan 2008). In India, the National Achievement Survey is conducted in three phases (see table 8.3) and updates information on student performance every three to four years. While Nepal and Sri Lanka do multiple rounds of national assessments at various grades, they do not do so at regular intervals.

Government Commitment and Public Funding

Predictable and adequate funding is critical to assessments. The funding allocated should cover all core assessment activities: design, administration, analysis, reporting, research, and development. The cost varies greatly from one country to another, depending on charges for personnel and services, the number of schools and students participating, administration outlays, scoring and data entry, analytical and reporting activities, and follow-up and research and development activities (Greaney and Kellaghan 2008). Yet in South Asia, public funding is often ad hoc, which is inadequate for doing regular student assessments; often national assessments are financed in part or in full by donors and are not part of government budgets. For instance, the activities of the National Education Assessment (NEA) System in Pakistan, a World Bank-financed project, became less frequent when responsibility was transferred to provincial governments, where both commitment and public funding were inadequate.

Implementation Capacity

Setting up stable institutions to support a national assessment system is not always easy. Assessments require the involvement of a variety of stakeholders, including MOE units that deal with curriculum, examinations, textbook development, and monitoring and evaluating (M&E). Committed and continuous political support is essential to run such an institution successfully. Both the depth of national technical capacity and administrative and political circumstances influence where responsibility for national assessments is assigned. For the Primary National Student Assessment in Bangladesh, the Department of Primary Education (under the Ministry of Primary and Mass Education) coordinates and collaborates with the National Curriculum and Textbook Boards and the National Assessment Cell. In Sri Lanka, a permanent unit, the National Education Research and Evaluation Center (NEREC), is well established in the Faculty of Education at the University of Colombo. Certainly, a national assessment should be carried out by a credible team or organization whose work can command respect and enhance the likelihood that its assessments will be widely accepted.

Because assessment involves a series of specialized technical and operational work, not only assigning it an institutional home but also equipping it with skilled staff is essential. Successful national assessments require experts to act as national and regional coordinators, item writers, statisticians, data managers, and translators, and implementers to act as school liaison persons, data recorders, test administrators, and scorers (Greaney and Kellaghan 2012). Project-funded initiatives often include capacity-building activities (e.g., training, technical assistance), but because they take time, in practice drafting test items, sampling, scaling of scores, analysis, and other highly technical activities are often carried out by outside experts while tests are conducted by the national team, as with, for example, the Bangladesh National Student Assessment of 2011.

Although countries recognize the importance of having a team of technical experts to do training, high staff turnover is often a problem. In Maldives, MOE-trained officials who conducted national assessments were either promoted or transferred elsewhere within a few years, undermining the ministry's assessment capacity (Aturupane and Shojo 2012). One way of overcoming the human resource constraint could be to partner with academic bodies or research institutions. Sri Lanka, for instance, is building capacity for rigorous national assessments in NEREC at the University of Colombo, which has considerably more analytical and technical capacity than the government.

Analysis of Results

Although national assessments have huge potential to illuminate issues in education, countries often underuse the information they produce. For instance, an aggregate summary of performance, as is common, may obscure highly relevant information. Results should be presented in terms of detailed curriculum areas or a designated level of mastery. A relatively simple approach is to disclose item-level information. While such information may be too detailed for policy makers, it is vital for curriculum personnel, teacher trainers, teachers, and even textbook writers—certainly, it is imperative for both teachers and curriculum personnel.

National assessment surveys often collect additional information about schools, teachers, class environment, and student background that permits deeper analysis of factors related to learning. For example, the resources available to schools, how they are used, and how they are related to student performance is valuable for rationalizing resource allocations to schools. An analysis of student and household background information would allow policy makers to address issues about inequities in learning achievement by social group.

From Findings to Action

A variety of reasons may be advanced for the underuse of national assessment findings, such as these (Kellaghan, Greaney, and Murray 2009):

- National assessment is regarded as a stand-alone activity, with little connection to other educational endeavors.
- Stakeholders are not adequately involved in design and conduct of an assessment.
- Findings are not communicated to those in a position to act.
- There is a lack of confidence in the findings.
- Making the findings public is politically sensitive.
- There is limited political support.
- Schools fail to take action.

To make effective use of national learning assessment findings, it is necessary to take the following steps:

- Describe the current status of student achievement.
- Communicate the findings widely.
- Formulate policies and undertake intervention programs.
- Finally, monitor outcomes.

Detailed analysis of assessment results can provide valuable information for setting learning standards, identifying weaknesses in the curriculum, and targeting schools that perform less well.

International Assessments

In South Asia, participation in international assessments has been limited to the two states in India, Himachal Pradesh and Tamil Nadu, that participated in PISA 2009+. Questions from international tests, such as PIRLS, TIMSS, and PISA, have been incorporated into some national assessments in the region, but not consistently.

There are both advantages and disadvantages to participating in international assessments. Among the advantages are that the data are internationally comparable and that by benchmarking with students from a number of countries participating countries have an opportunity to identify areas for improvement. Since these assessments require all participating countries to meet high-quality technical standards, they also apply external pressure to improve the quality of the national technical team.

Box 8.5 PISA Results and Improvement in the Quality of Education in Mexico

Mexico demonstrates that participation in international assessments can positively affect learning levels quite quickly when the initiative gets government support. In mathematics, the performance of Mexico on PISA, as measured by mean scores, rose from 385 in 2003 to 406 in 2006 and 419 in 2009, making it the country with the biggest increase (33 points) over this period. Although the proportion of Mexican students below Level 2 on the PISA mathematics scale (levels range from 1 to 6) is still very high at 50.8 percent—averages in Organisation for Economic Co-operation and Development (OECD) countries are 20.8 percent, in the G-20 32.6 percent, and in countries with similar per capita gross domestic product (GDP) 38.8 percent—Mexico has been able to considerably reduce its proportion of poor performers, which stood at 65.9 percent in 2003.

Mexico achieved these performance gains after President Felipe Calderón set the government's strategies, objectives, and PISA performance targets. In 2008, the government and the National Union of Educational Workers, the largest trade union in Latin America, jointly launched the Alliance for Educational Quality to promote innovative educational policies and to mobilize human, material, and institutional resources to improve student learning. The OECD advised the Mexican government on this process. Due to the nationwide commitment to improving student outcomes, according to OECD, Mexico was on the right trajectory to reach the target of a PISA score of 435 points in reading and mathematics in 2012.

Source: OECD 2011.

Mexico, Brazil, and Poland, among other countries, have benefited from international assessments to accelerate improvements in student achievement (see box 8.5 for a case study from Mexico). International assessments can also attract political support for reforming national educational systems.

However, a word of caution about international assessments is in order, especially where there are large discrepancies between the national curriculum and what the assessments test. Test items are developed not only to measure average achievement but also to capture variances in learning. In developing countries, where average achievement is low, accurate capture of the complete range of student achievements may not be possible. Political pressures when performance is relatively unfavorable might also be a risk for policy makers, although the risk needs to be balanced against the opportunities participation in international assessments can open up for policy reforms.

Classroom Assessments in South Asia

High-quality formative classroom assessment activities are positively correlated with better student learning outcomes (Black and William 1998). Although international evidence is available, it is generally difficult to collect data on the quality of classroom assessment at the system level. School assessments take place in the daily teaching and learning process, and practices necessarily vary greatly across teachers and schools. However, it is possible to get a sense of the extent to which supportive system-level policies and conditions help teachers to acquire effective assessment practices that they can use daily. Finland and Scotland, for instance, are known as sterling examples of high-performing education systems that have established classroom assessment systems.

Country Cases in South Asia

The Bangladesh MOE formally introduced a school-based assessment (SBA) initiative in 2005 to support improvement of classroom assessment practices in grades 6–9. The Teachers Guide for SBA, issued by the National Curriculum and Textbook Board, provides system-wide guidelines for SBA in grades 6–9 but has few mechanisms to help teachers and external supervisors build skills in classroom assessment. Required outcomes of classroom assessments are diagnosing student learning issues, providing feedback to students on their learning, informing parents about their child's learning, and grading students for internal classroom use. Unfortunately, in practice, classroom assessment in Bangladesh is mainly used for administrative control.

In Nepal, the National Curriculum Framework for School Education provides guidelines for classroom assessment and a variety of mechanisms to help ensure that teachers build the necessary expertise, including in- and preservice teacher training and opportunities to participate in conferences and workshops. However, classroom assessment practices, which are generally not aligned with the national curriculum, are considered below par. It is common to see errors in the grading of student work, teachers provide little useful feedback to students, and parents are poorly informed about their children's grades.

The 2006 National Curriculum provides general but not comprehensive guidelines on classroom assessment for Punjab and other provinces in Pakistan. There are a few system-level mechanisms, such as pre- and in-service teacher training opportunities, that are meant to ensure that teachers become more skilled in assessment, but practices still vary from school to school and students and parents receive little feedback. There is no formal requirement for classroom assessment information to support student learning, and there are no mechanisms for systematically monitoring the quality of classroom assessment.

In Sri Lanka, no document provides guidelines for classroom assessment. The only mechanisms for ensuring that teachers acquire the necessary skills are pre- and in-service teacher training offered by the National Colleges of Education and the National Institute of Education. Some assessment information is also required for the external examination program (the General Certificate of Education Examination), although it is unclear whether the results from SBAs are moderated before they are combined with scores from external examination papers.

In India, until recently the concept—and actual practice—of classroom assessments involved regular class tests (weekly/monthly/quarterly/mid-yearly/annually) that mainly assessed rote memorization. While at the national level the concept of formative classroom assessments, CCE, is

Box 8.6 India: Guidelines for Classroom Assessment in the National Curriculum Framework

Early childhood development and grades 1 and 2 of the elementary stage: At this stage, assessments must be purely qualitative judgments of children's activities in various domains and an evaluation of their health status and physical development based on observations through everyday interactions. On no account should they be made to take any form of test, oral or written.

Grades 3–7 of the elementary stage: A variety of methods may be used, including oral and written tests and observations. Children should be aware that they are being assessed, but they must view this as part of the teaching process, not a fearful constant threat. Marks, along with qualitative judgments of achievement and areas requiring attention, are essential at this stage. Children's self-evaluations can be part of report cards from grade 5 on. Rather than examinations, from time to time there could be short criterion-based tests. Term examinations could be commenced from grade 7 on when children are more psychologically ready to study large chunks of material and to spend a few hours in an examination room, working at answering questions. Again, the report card must carry general observations on health and nutrition, specific observations on the progress of the learner, and information and advice for the parents.

Grades 9–12 of the secondary and higher secondary stages: Assessment may be based mainly on tests, examinations, and project reports for the knowledge-based areas of the curriculum, along with self-assessment. Other areas would be assessed through observation and self-evaluation. Reports could include a great deal more analysis about students, various skill and knowledge areas, and percentiles, for example. This would help students by pointing out areas of study that they need to focus on, and also help them by providing a basis for the choices that they make about what to study thereafter.

Source: India National Curriculum Framework 2005.

developed holistically (see box 8.6), Indian states are almost all at different stages in the process of actually using CCE. The meaning and spirit have not fully penetrated to the classroom, and there continues to be confusion about it. However, some states are making concerted efforts to roll out classroom-based formative assessments to replace test papers. While some states use the Source Books of Assessment for grades 1–5 developed by NCERT as a single CCE model, others have drafted their own handbooks based on the source books. Uttar Pradesh teachers, for example, put together a handbook on CCE. It appears that assessments are being integrated into the teaching-learning process and providing feedback for improving teaching and learning.

Challenges of Classroom Assessments and Opportunities

Although many South Asian countries have the basic elements of classroom assessment in place, in practice, assessment tends to be weak and in need of further system-level supports. Activities that can help ensure high quality and effectively support student learning might be to:

- Disseminate system-wide guidelines for teachers on classroom assessments that cover all subject areas and grade levels.
- Provide more resources and materials for teachers to use in carrying out classroom assessment, such as item banks and scoring rubrics.
- Put in place required system-wide mechanisms, such as high-quality pre- and in-service training modules, to help teachers become better at effective classroom assessment and appropriate use of assessment information.
- Institutionalize formal mechanisms to systematically monitor the quality of classroom assessment (for example, as part of school inspection or teacher supervision and evaluation).

For South Asian countries that already undertake classroom assessments, it is important to ensure that they are of high quality and are actually being done. For example, while academic supervisors and assistant inspectors are responsible for monitoring the quality of classroom assessment in Bangladesh, they reportedly focus on administrative activities. Similarly, in Nepal, resource persons responsible for monitoring the quality of classroom assessment within assigned clusters are reportedly much more likely to simply gather data than monitor classroom assessments.

A constraint on any effort to improve the quality of classroom assessment will be the quality of the teachers. Hence, improvements to classroom assessment practices are closely bound to, and affected by, general efforts to improve the recruitment, training, performance, and retention of teachers.

Policy Implications

In general, in part for historical reasons, assessment systems in South Asia lean heavily on examinations and far less on classroom and system-level assessments. However, to build up the quality and outcomes of their education systems, South Asian countries need to create more balanced assessment systems that can provide the different kinds of information on student achievement needed to meet a variety of decision-making needs.

While South Asian countries have well-established examination systems, it is still necessary to ensure alignment between curriculum objectives and how examinations measure student performance against those objectives. The role of public examinations is currently critical to what students learn; lessons tend to be extremely examination-focused, and students study only to pass examinations. Meanwhile, competence in real world critical thinking and problem solving is unmet. Despite decades-long government efforts to overcome this limitation, misconduct continues to be associated with examinations. Furthermore, improving the validity and reliability of public examinations is important for fully assessing student achievement and producing graduates with adequate knowledge and skills.

National assessments are more appropriate than public examinations for diagnosing systemic education issues and understanding student performance gaps and distributions. Although South Asian countries have embarked on a variety of national assessment initiatives, there is still confusion about the objectives and use of public examinations versus national assessments. Credible national assessments conducted regularly will enable countries to monitor the learning achievements of their students over time and will expose education system strengths and weaknesses. Examinations, on the other hand, are usually too associated with high stakes to be an effective way for policy makers to understand the positives and negatives in their national systems.

Finally, while a national assessment is the first step in accurately diagnosing the learning of students and tracking their progress over time, participation in international assessments such as TIMSS and PISA is important for benchmarking student achievement in South Asia against international standards within and beyond the region. They offer a unique opportunity for improving the quality of education by exposing the country to international curriculum and performance standards and providing an objective assessment of student performance in terms of the global knowledge economy.

Notes

1. Programme on the Analysis of Education Systems Conference of National Education Ministers in a French-speaking World (CONFEMEN).
2. Latin American Laboratory for Education Quality Evaluation.
3. Education Quality Measurement System in Chile.
4. In Bangladesh, *madrassas* (religious schools) have examinations at grade 5 (*Ibtedayee* Terminal Examination), grade 8 (Junior *Dakhil* Certificate Examination), grade 10 (*Dakhil* Certificate Examination), and grade 12 (*Alim* Certificate Examination).
5. One common threat to test score validity is a difference between the language of instruction and the language of testing, which may make it difficult for children to show what they know and can do.
6. There are also 10 examination boards for vocational training, including madrassa boards.
7. Before examination, officials, paper setters, moderators, or school administrators may leak exam content, and candidates may be improperly assigned to particular centers. During the examination, there may be (a) impersonation of a candidate; (b) external assistance (e.g., from helpers or via cellular phone); (c) smuggling of material (as in clothing); (d) copying and collusion between test takers; (e) intimidation of supervisory staff (by candidates, external helpers, government agencies, politicians, journalists, and teacher unions); (f) substitution of answer papers; and (g) use of ghost (nonexistent) centers. After examination, there may be (a) substitution of answer papers, (b) intimidation of markers (sometimes with the aid of corrupt officials), (c) bribes solicited from parents, (d) collusion between a candidate and a marker, (e) falsification of data files and results sheets, and (f) issuance of fake diplomas (Kellaghan and Greaney 2004).

8. As described in box 8.3, the census-based national assessment in Chile is used for accountability purposes and has been effective in targeting disadvantaged schools and providing public awareness opportunities.
9. Many Indian states do their own assessments to gauge how effectively large-scale initiatives promote learning, such as the 3 'R's Guarantee Programme and Educational Quality Improvement Programme (EQIP) in Maharashtra; the Integrated Learning Improvement Programme (ILIP) in West Bengal; Activity-Based Learning (ABL) and Active Learning Methodologies (ALM) in Tamil Nadu; Karnataka Schools Toward Quality Education (KSQE); Buniyad in Jharkhand, Neev in Uttarakhand, and Aadhar in Himachal Pradesh; the Children's Learning Acceleration Programme for Sustainability (CLAPS) in Andhra Pradesh; the Gujarat Achievement Profile (GAP); Nai Disha in Uttar Pradesh; the Multilingual Education Programme for tribal areas in Odisha and Andhra Pradesh; and Noottikku Noorroo in Kerala (Patnaik 2009).

Bibliography

ADB (Asian Development Bank). 2006. *Proposed Sector Development Program Loans People's Republic of Bangladesh: Secondary Education Sector Development Program.* Project Number 37307. Manila: ADB.

AERA (American Educational Research Association), APA (American Psychological Association), and NCME (National Council on Measurement in Education). 1999. *Standards for Educational and Psychological Testing.* Washington, DC: AERA.

Agrawal, M. 2004. "Curricular Reform in Schools: The Importance of Evaluation." *Journal of Curriculum Studies* 36 (3): 361–79.

Airasian, P., and M. Russell. 2007. *Classroom Assessment: Concepts and Applications.* 6th ed. New York: McGraw Hill.

Aly, J. H. 2007. *Education in Pakistan: A White Paper Revised Draft Document to Debate and Finalize the National Education Policy.* Islamabad: National Education Policy Review Team.

Aturupane, H., and M. Shojo. 2012. "Enhancing the Quality of Education in the Maldives: Challenges and Prospects." Discussion Paper 51, Human Development Unit, South Asia Region, World Bank, Washington, DC.

Black, P., and D. William. 1998. "Assessment and Classroom Learning. Assessment in Education: Principles." *Policy and Practice* 5 (1): 7–73.

CBSE (Central Board of Secondary Education). 2009. "Examination Reforms and Continuous and Comprehensive Evaluation (CCE) in the Central Board of Secondary Education (CBSE)." Circular No. 39/20-09-2009, No. CBSE/ACAD/2009, September 20.

Clarke, M. 2012. "What Matters Most for Student Assessment Systems: A Framework Paper." SABER–Student Assessment Working Paper 1, World Bank, Washington, DC.

Darling-Hammond, L., and L. Wentworth. 2010. "Benchmarking Learning Systems: Student Performance Assessment in International Context." Stanford Center for Opportunity Policy in Education, Stanford University, Stanford, CA.

Furhman, S., and D. Elmore, eds. 1994. *Governing Curriculum.* Alexandria, VA: Association for Supervision and Curriculum Development.

Greaney, V. and P. Hasan. 1998. "Public Examinations in Pakistan: A System in Need of Reform." In *Education and the State: Fifty Years of Pakistan*, edited by P. Hoodbhoy. Karachi: Oxford University Press.

Greaney, V., and T. Kellaghan. 1995. "Equity Issues in Public Examinations in Developing Countries." Technical Paper 272, Asia Technical Series, World Bank, Washington, DC.

———. 2008. *Assessing National Achievement Levels in Education*. Vol. 1 of *National Assessments of Educational Attainment*. Washington, DC: World Bank.

———. 2012. *Implementing a National Assessment of Educational Achievement*. Vol. 3 of *National Assessments of Educational Attainment*. Washington, DC: World Bank.

Hanushek, E. A., S. Link, and L. Woessmann. 2013. "Does School Autonomy Make Sense Everywhere? Panel Estimates from PISA." *Journal of Development Economics* 104: 212–32.

Hanushek, E. A., and L. Woessmann. 2008. "The Role of Cognitive Skills in Economic Development." *Journal of Economic Literature* 46 (3): 607–68.

Heubert, J., and R. Hauser. 1999. *High Stakes: Testing for Tracking, Promotion, and Graduation*. Washington, DC: National Academy Press.

Hossain, M. Z. 2009. "Creative Questions: Validity and Reliability of Secondary School Certificate Examination." *Bangladesh Education Journal* 8 (2): 33–43.

Hussain, I. 2009. "Country Case Study: Bhutan." In *Secondary School External Examination Systems: Reliability, Robustness and Resilience*, edited by B. Vlaardingerbroek and N. Taylor. Amherst, NY: Cambria Press.

Kellaghan, T., and V. Greaney. 2004. *Assessing Student Learning in Africa*. Washington, DC: World Bank.

Kellaghan, T., V. Greaney, and T. S. Murray. 2009. *Using the Results of a National Assessment of Educational Achievement*. Vol. 5 of *National Assessments of Educational Attainment*. Washington, DC: World Bank.

Mirza, M. 1999. "Examination System and Teaching and Practice of Teachers at Secondary, Higher Secondary and O-Level." *Bulletin of Education and Research* 1. Institute of Education and Research, Quaid-E-Azam Campus, University of the Punjab, Lahore.

NCERT (National Council of Educational Research and Training). 2005. *National Curriculum Framework*. New Delhi: NCERT.

———. 2006. *Position Paper: National Focus Group on Examination Reforms*. New Delhi: NCERT.

———. 2011. *What Do They Know? A Summary of India's National Achievement Survey, Class V, Cycle 3 2010/11*. New Delhi: NCERT.

OECD (Organisation for Economic Co-operation and Development). 2011. *Lessons from PISA for Mexico: Strong Performers and Successful Reformers in Education*. Paris: OECD.

Patnaik, B. 2009. "Initiatives under the Sarva Shiksha Abhiyan for Improvement in Basic Numeracy Skills among Children in the Early Grades." Proceedings of epiSTEME 3, Mumbai, January. http://cvs.gnowledge.org/episteme3/pro_pdfs/39-binay.pdf.

Rehmani, A. 2003. "Impact of Public Examination System on Teaching and Learning in Pakistan." *ANTRIEP Newsletter* 8 (1): 3–6.

Rinchen, P. 2009. "Country Case Study: Bhutan." In *Secondary School External Examination Systems: Reliability, Robustness and Resilience*, edited by B. Vlaardingerbroek and N. Taylor. New York: Cambria Press.

Shepard, L. A. 2000. "The Role of Classroom Assessment in Teaching and Learning." CSE Technical Report 517, Center for the Study of Education, University of California, Los Angeles.

Smith, M. S., and J. O'Day. 1991. "Systemic School Reform." In *The Politics of Curriculum and Testing, 1990 Yearbook of the Politics of Education Association*, edited by S. H. Fuhrman and B. Malen. Washington, DC: Falmer Press.

Walker, M. 2011. *PISA 2009 Plus Results: Performance of 15-Year-Olds in Reading, Mathematics and Science for 10 Additional Participants*. Melbourne: ACER Press. http://research.acer.edu.au/pisa/1/.

World Bank. 2013. *Kingdom of Bhutan: Human Development Public Expenditure Review*. Edited by Somil Nagpal and Susan Opper. Human Development Unit, South Asia Region, World Bank, Washington, DC.

CHAPTER 9

Private Education: Fostering Choice and Competition*

Introduction

Through financing and/or direct provision of services, the private sector can complement or supplement educational services provided by the public sector, which would expand the resources invested in the human capital of young people. In South Asia, private education has expanded rapidly and significantly in recent decades. This raises the question of what public policy should be toward private schools. Should expansion of the private sector be encouraged? If so, how? And how would private schools be regulated? Does the experience of the private sector offer any lessons that could be used in designing the reform of government schools?

Before answering these questions, it is necessary to assess whether there is robust evidence of a learning gap between private and public schools across countries and, if there is, to identify factors that could explain these differences. Can better achievement in private schools be explained by differences in inputs, management, or incentives? Or is it simply the result of the selection into private schools of children from richer socioeconomic backgrounds? A better understanding of how private schools function and perform can provide useful insights to improve learning quality in public schools.

This chapter will first describe the extent of private education in South Asia and how it has evolved over time. It will then discuss the regulatory framework within which private schools operate and the various modalities of their operation. In what follows, the chapter will present evidence on levels of learning achievements in private vs. public schools, discussing differences and factors that contribute to those differences. The fourth section will spell out implications for policy formulation and, in particular, make recommendations on how

*See box 9.1 for a summary of the chapter's key questions and findings.

Box 9.1 Questions and Findings

Questions

- How important is private education in South Asia, and what quality of learning does it provide?
- What should government policy be toward private education? To what extent should private schools be regulated?

Findings

- About one-third of children enrolled in school in South Asia attend private schools (27 percent for ages 6–10 years, 31 percent for ages 11–15 years, and 39 percent for ages 16–18 years). The only countries where private schooling is minimal are Bhutan, Sri Lanka, and Afghanistan.

- The expansion of private education is fairly recent, dating back only to the 1980s and 1990s in some countries. Although it is mainly found in urban areas, it has also reached rural areas. Over the past five years, it has been expanding faster than the public sector, so that the share of enrollment in the private sector is rising. Private tutoring is also becoming common, even in rural areas and among children in the poorest families.

- Private education reflects a variety of management and financing arrangements. Besides privately financed and managed schools, there are different types of public-private partnerships (PPPs). The most common type of PPP is privately managed schools that receive financial support from the government, mainly to pay teacher salaries.

- Overall, the general performance of private schools seems no worse—and in many cases seems better—than that of public schools once observable student and school characteristics are taken into account. Even then, learning levels in private schools remain very low; a large number of children master little more than basic literacy. It is important to note that there is a significant degree of variability in test scores within schools of both types. There are good and bad scores in both categories of schools. And since private schools generally operate with lower expenses (mostly due to lower teacher salaries), they are more cost-effective for society as a whole.

- Moving forward, it is clear that South Asia must leverage the contribution of the private sector. It cannot meet the double challenge of increasing the educational attainment of its people and improving the quality of learning without the combined effort of governments, households, and the private sector. Since the private sector has already demonstrated that it can offer access at lower social cost, with comparable or better outcomes than the public sector, countries will gain by easing barriers to entry and through well-designed PPPs. Innovative and cost-effective programs like those in Bangladesh and Pakistan could be replicated.

box continues next page

Box 9.1 Questions and Findings *(continued)*

- Available evidence does not support the view that imposing tighter regulations on private schools, in particular with respect to fees and teacher credentials, would improve quality—especially when capacity for enforcement is low. Fostering competition between private and public schools could provide an alternative. For this, better monitoring capacity and providing reliable and regular information about school-level and student-level learning quality would be critical. Competition could be stimulated if governments used stipend programs not only to promote access as they have done so far, but also to allow children from poor households to attend the school of their choice.

- If quality improvements in public schools were achieved, competition would also contribute to raising the quality of the whole sector. Public schools are the baseline upon which private schools make their investments and determine the premium that can attract students. The lower the baseline, the less private schools will need to invest in order to distinguish themselves from competitors.

to improve quality in both private and public schools. The evidence presented in this chapter draws on previous studies, school censuses, and the most recent household and educational assessment surveys conducted in countries in the region.

Trends in Private Sector Engagement

Today, a sizable proportion of children attend private schools in South Asia, except in Sri Lanka, where legal restrictions constrain its expansion since 1961, less than 1 percent of the schools in the country are private schools that were established before 1961, and in Bhutan and Afghanistan, where the sector is still incipient (see table 9.1). For the region as a whole, 27 percent of children ages 6–10 years, 31 percent ages 11–15 years, and close to 40 percent ages 16–18 years attend private schools.

Privately run schools are heavily concentrated in urban areas. In countries where the private sector is very active (Bangladesh, India, Nepal, and Pakistan), more than half the children in urban areas attend private primary and lower secondary schools (in Pakistan about 42 percent at the lower secondary level, and in Bangladesh about 39 percent at the primary level). At the higher secondary level, the proportion ranges from 29 percent in Pakistan to 70 percent in Bangladesh. However, private education is not confined to urban areas; the share of private school enrollment in rural areas ranges from 12 percent to 33 percent in India, Nepal, and Pakistan and reaches 54 percent for the 11–15 years age group and 77 percent for the 16–18 years group in Bangladesh.

There seems to be no systematic gender divide across the region (see figure 9.1). Girls are somewhat more likely than boys to attend private schools

Table 9.1 Enrollment in Private School in Rural and Urban Areas, South Asian Countries
Percent

	6–10-year-olds			*11–15-year-olds*			*16–18-year-olds*		
	Total	*Urban*	*Rural*	*Total*	*Urban*	*Rural*	*Total*	*Urban*	*Rural*
Afghanistan (2008)	1.0	2.6	0.5	0.8	1.9	0.3	1.0	1.9	0.5
Bangladesh (2010)	22.4	38.8	16.3	56.1	62.0	54.1	75.0	70.0	77.2
Bhutan (2007)	2.6	6.8	0.7	1.0	2.3	0.5	5.6	12.0	2.2
India (2010)	28.1	55.5	19.8	30.2	52.0	22.6	38.9	50.3	33.3
Nepal (2010)	30.7	66.2	24.3	19.3	53.3	12.1	21.7	48.5	13.6
Pakistan (2011)	32.0	54.3	21.3	27.7	41.8	19.1	23.6	28.9	19.1
Sri Lanka	n.a.			n.a.			n.a.		
All countries	27.0			31.1			38.8		

Source: Household surveys (survey year in parentheses).
Note: n.a. = not applicable.

Figure 9.1 Enrollment in Private Schools, by Gender, in Selected South Asian Countries

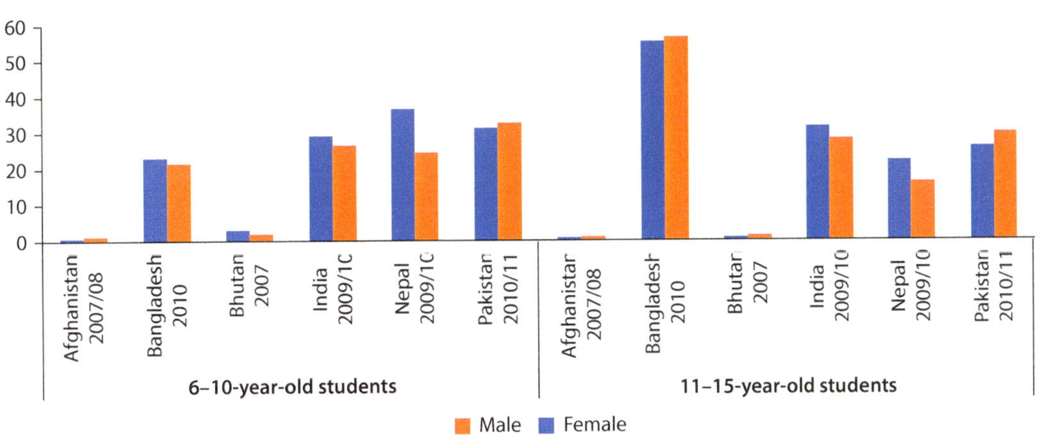

Source: Household surveys.

in Pakistan, are somewhat less likely in India and Nepal, and have practically equal chances in Bangladesh, Bhutan, and Afghanistan. Only the data for India and Nepal offer any support for the often-expressed view that parents prefer to send sons rather than daughters to fee-charging private schools because of future market returns.

The rapid expansion of private education is a recent phenomenon. As figure 9.2 shows, most of the private schools in Bangladesh were built after 1970 and in Nepal and Pakistan after 1990. In those countries, they re-emerged after a period of school nationalization. The process has been more gradual in India where private schools date back to the colonial period.

The pace of expansion has been even more rapid than total enrollment, leading to an increase in the share of private enrollment (see table 9.2). This phenomenon is particularly striking in Nepal, where private enrollment almost doubled in five years.

Tutoring by private providers also seems to have become increasingly common, even in rural areas and among the poorest children.[1] For example, data on Bangladesh (figure 9.3) show that over the span of 10 years the number of children being privately tutored—to complement school teaching—has more than doubled among children ages 6–10 years, and that currently about half of children ages 11–15 years get some tutoring whether they attend public or private schools. Even in Sri Lanka, where the number of private schools is very limited, tutoring has expanded: the 2003 National Education Survey found that about 75 percent of primary school students receive private tutoring (Glewwe and Jayachandaran 2006).

Figure 9.2 Establishment of Private Schools over Time, South Asia

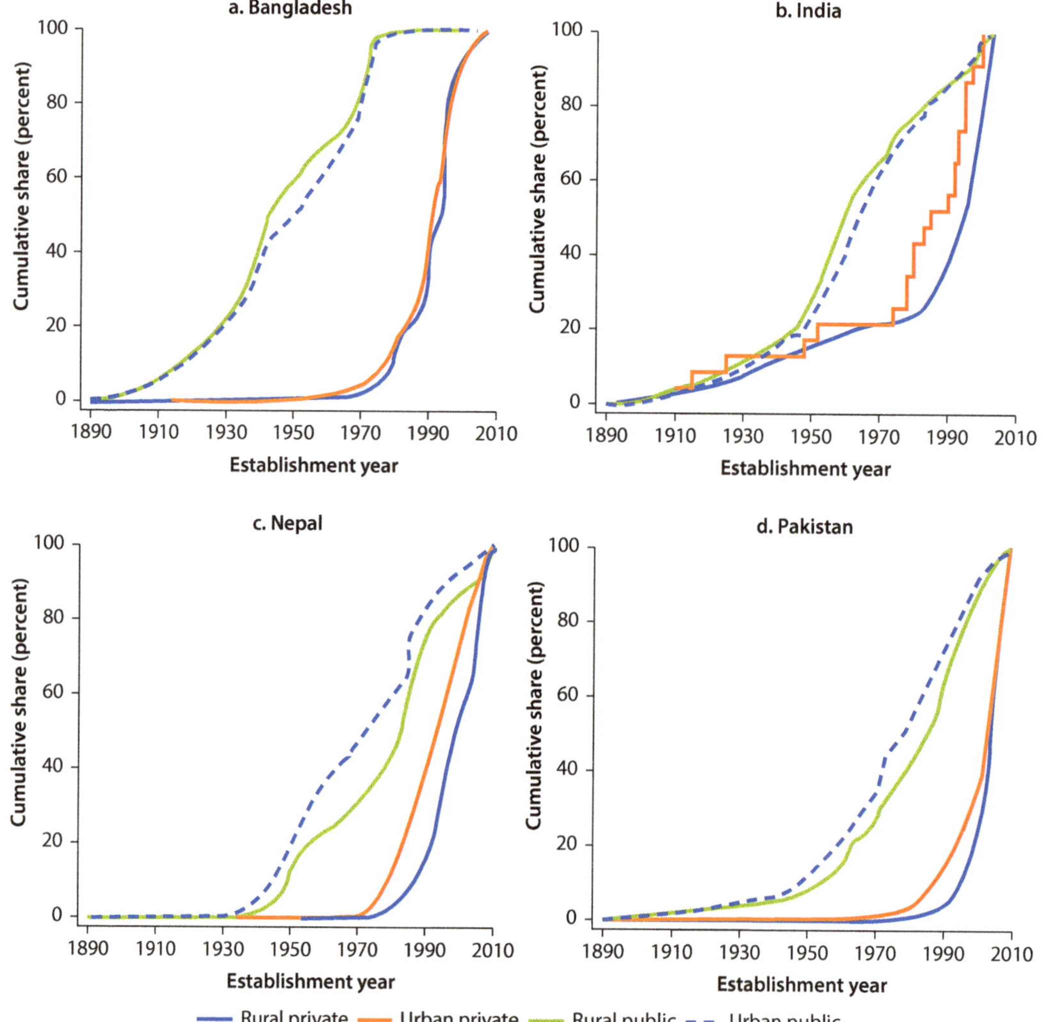

Sources: The Primary School Census 2006 (Bangladesh); the Human Development Survey 2005 (India); Flash Data 2009/10 (Nepal); and the Primary and Secondary School Census 2005 (Pakistan).

Types of Private Sector Engagement

Private education in South Asia is provided and supported in a variety of ways and the prevalence of different types of school financing and management varies across countries (table 9.3). Schools can either be privately funded and managed (unaided schools), or can operate in collaboration with the public sector.

Whenever public-private partnerships (PPPs) are in place, arrangements can vary (table 9.3). In the table, Type (2) refers to schools managed by the private sector but fully or partially financed or supported by the government (aided schools). This is the most common arrangement. It covers some primary

Table 9.2 Change in Private School Enrollment over Time, South Asia

Country and period of change	*Period 1 enrollment (%)* Total (TP1)	*Period 1 enrollment (%)* Private (PP1)	*Period 2 enrollment (%)* Total (TP2)	*Period 2 enrollment (%)* Private (PP2)	*Change in private share of enrollment (%) [i.e., (PP2/TP2)—(PP1/TP1)]*
Age group 6–10					
Bangladesh (2005–10)	80.5	12.3	85.0	19.1	7.1
India (2005–10)	87.1	22.7	91.8	25.8	2.0
Nepal (2004–10)	79.1	14.1	93.8	28.8	12.8
Pakistan (2005–11)	62.0	17.5	68.1	21.8	3.7
Age group 11–15					
Bangladesh (2005–10)	70.0	38.3	78.6	44.1	1.4
India (2005–10)	78.5	24.5	86.7	26.4	-0.9
Nepal (2004–10)	75.7	9.9	90.2	17.4	6.2
Pakistan (2005–11)	59.4	14.1	66.4	18.4	3.9

Sources: Household surveys.

Figure 9.3 Private Tutoring, Bangladesh, 2000–10

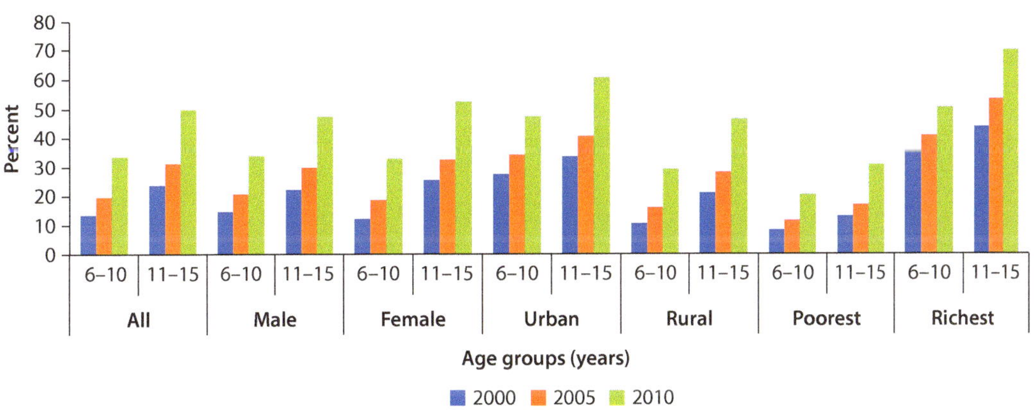

Source: Household and Income Expenditure Surveys (HIES).

Table 9.3 Private Engagement in Primary and Secondary Education, South Asia

Type of financing and management	*AFG*	*BGD*	*BTN*	*IND*	*LKA*	*NPL*	*PAK*
1. Privately funded and privately managed (unaided) schools	x	xx	x	xx		xx	xx
2. Government funded/supported, privately managed (aided) schools (sometimes coupled with direct funding to students)	x	xx		xx		xx	x
3. Government funded and managed, privately assisted schools				x			x
4. Privately funded and privately managed schools, to be transitioned eventually into the government system	x						
5. Government vouchers to students to attend school types 1, 2, and 4		x		x			x
6. Private tutoring	—	x	x	x	x	x	—

Note: xx = considerable prevalence, that is, the type is listed in household or school survey questionnaires; x = more modest prevalence (applying to at least 100 schools in government or institutional documents or peer-reviewed research papers); blank cells = a type not prevalent enough to qualify for a rating; — = no information available from any source; AFG = Afghanistan; BGD = Bangladesh; BTN = Bhutan; IND = India; LKA = Sri Lanka; NPL = Nepal; PAK = Pakistan.

schools and most secondary schools in Bangladesh and a large proportion of Indian primary and secondary schools. This category also includes community-managed schools, which are numerous in Afghanistan and Nepal,[2] but not elsewhere in the region. Finally, it includes schools managed by foundations or nongovernmental organizations (NGOs) with financial support from the government. Type (3) refers to the opposite situation: schools are publicly managed but benefit from some financing or other support from the private sector. Type (4) are schools in which government framework and policy (such as for curriculum and teacher training) are formally applied, but the private sector takes direct charge of both funding and management until the government has the capacity to take over entirely. This applies mostly to Afghanistan. Type (5) refers to provision of vouchers and scholarships to students that make private schooling more affordable, thereby increasing the student's options, and Type (6) refers to private tutoring. All PPP types often target educationally disadvantaged populations, such as the rural poor and girls. In the face of enormous education challenges and budget constraints, PPPs have become increasingly important to governments, not only in the region but also throughout the world, as a way to leverage both the efficiency objective of the private sector and the equity objective of the public sector.[3]

Though religious schools are a type of private school, they have not been considered in this report. According to available survey data there seem to be few such schools (the reported share is about 0.1 percent in Afghanistan, 1.5 percent in Nepal, 2.0 percent in Pakistan, and in the 3.0–7.0 percent range in Bangladesh), and they usually follow a curriculum and structure that differs greatly from the secular school curriculum, except in Bangladesh, where Alia Madrassas are heavily financed by the government (see Asadullah, Chaudhury, and Al-Zayed Josh 2009). It is thus quite difficult to assess the quality of education they provide and to compare them with other types of schools.

Enrollment in aided and unaided private schools (Types 1 and 2) relative to public schools is shown in figure 9.4. It varies considerably between countries. In South Asian countries other than Afghanistan and Bhutan, where it is minimal, 17–30 percent of children ages 6–10 years and 17–45 percent of those ages 11–15 years attend private schools. Aided private schools cover a significant portion of enrollment in India and Bangladesh, following a tradition inherited from the colonial period.[4] For these schools, government support consists of a subsidy to pay teacher salaries in proportion to enrollment. The proportion is highest in Bangladesh, where over 55 percent of enrolled children ages 11–15 years and 75 percent ages 16–18 years attend aided schools. In Pakistan, however, where aided schools disappeared after all private schools were nationalized in 1972, the private schools that emerged after enactment of the 1979 Education Policy are mainly unaided. Schools managed by foundations or NGOs do receive public support, but they are far fewer and are not captured by household surveys. In Nepal, the transfer of schools to communities is still not reflected in surveys and it is not possible to distinguish community from regular public

Figure 9.4 Private Education of Children Ages 6–10 Years and 11–15 Years, by Type of Institution, South Asia

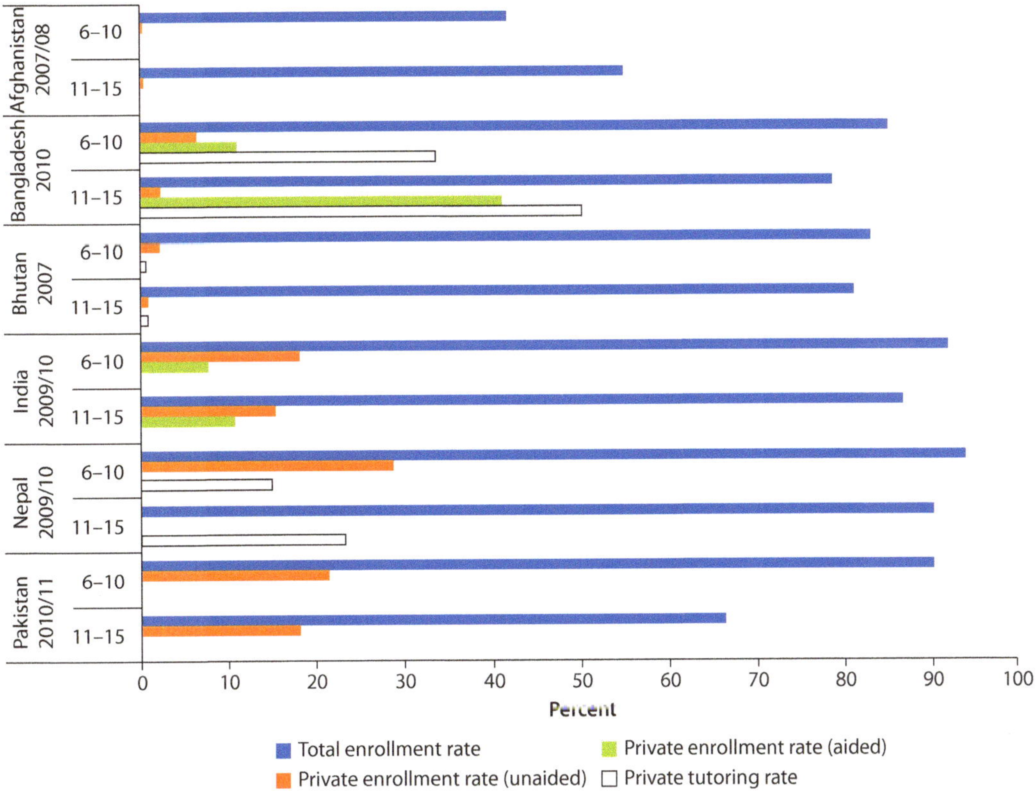

Source: Household survey data.
Note: Missing bars indicate data were not available or not applicable.

schools. Figure 9.4 also suggests that private tutoring is common in Bangladesh and Nepal, in particular for students ages 11–15 years, most likely in view of the grade 10 national exams.

Do Private Schools Offer Better Quality Education?

As explained in chapter 2, children in South Asia do not learn much in school; many acquire no more than basic literacy. The question then arises: Is this also true of children attending private schools? In other words: Are private schools performing better than public schools?

Available evidence suggests that learning outcomes are on average higher in private than in government schools, but nevertheless remain very low. A number of studies, most of them on India (Kingdon 1996, 2007; PROBE 1999; Tooley and Dixon 2005; Pandey, Goyal, and Sundararaman 2008; Desai et al. 2009; Goyal and Pandey 2009; French and Kingdon 2010) and some in Pakistan (Andrabi et al. 2007; Aslam 2009) and Nepal (Thapa 2011; Sharma 2012) with datasets limited in many cases to a few states or provinces, have found that almost always private schools fare better than public in terms of mean differences on raw scores, which supports the widespread belief that private education is of higher quality. This finding is confirmed by additional data from three countries of the region. For two, India and Nepal, the datasets are nationally representative. Figure 9.5 presents test scores for India, Nepal, and Pakistan corresponding to different age groups. In India, the first scores are those of a nationally representative sample of children ages 8–11 years tested in 2004–05, and the second are those of a sample of 15-year-olds who in 2009 were administered a Programme for International Student Assessment (PISA) test in two states, Himachal Pradesh and Tamil Nadu; in Nepal, they are 2004 nationwide school leaving certificate (SLC)[5] test scores of grade 10 students, and in Pakistan they correspond to grade 4 students in rural Punjab in 2006.

Figure 9.5 Student Performance in Public and Private Schools

a. Rural and urban 15-year-old students, Himachal Pradesh and Tamil Nadu, India, PISA 2009 Test

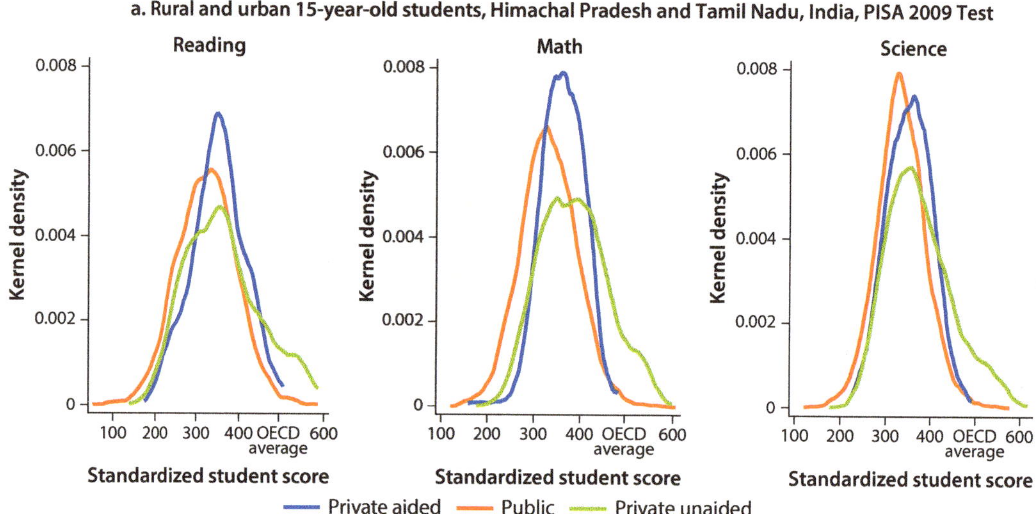

b. Rural and urban 8–11-year-old Indian students, 2004–05: Indian Human Development Survey scores

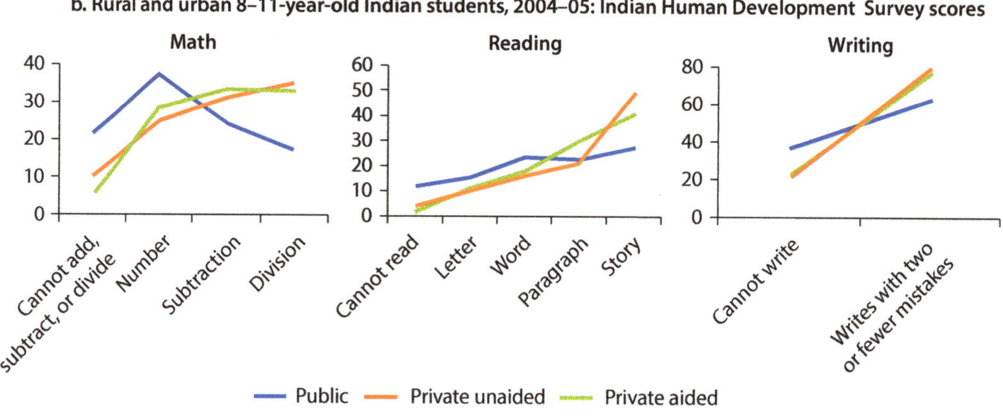

figure continues next page

Figure 9.5 Student Performance in Public and Private Schools *(continued)*

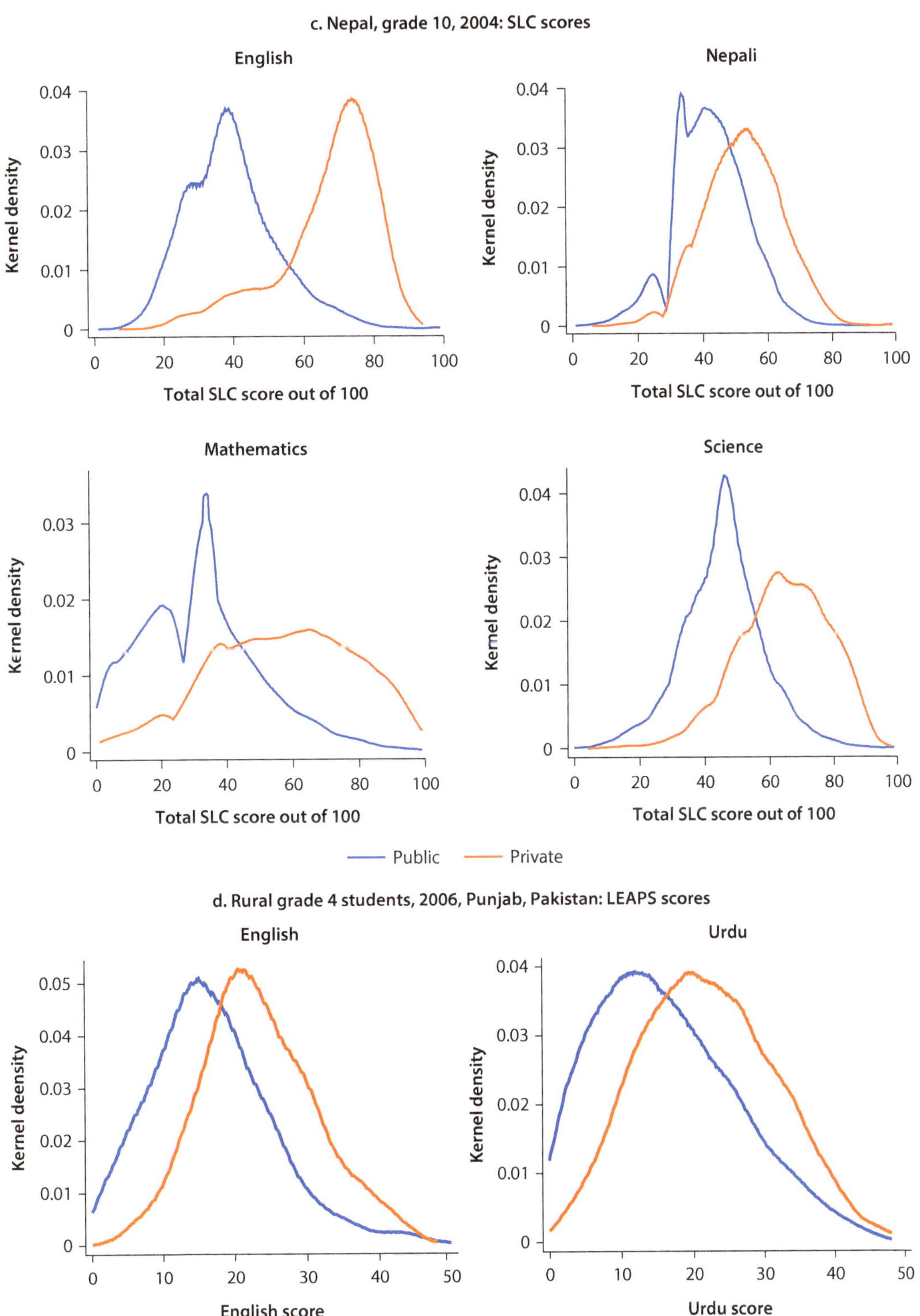

figure continues next page

Figure 9.5 Student Performance in Public and Private Schools *(continued)*

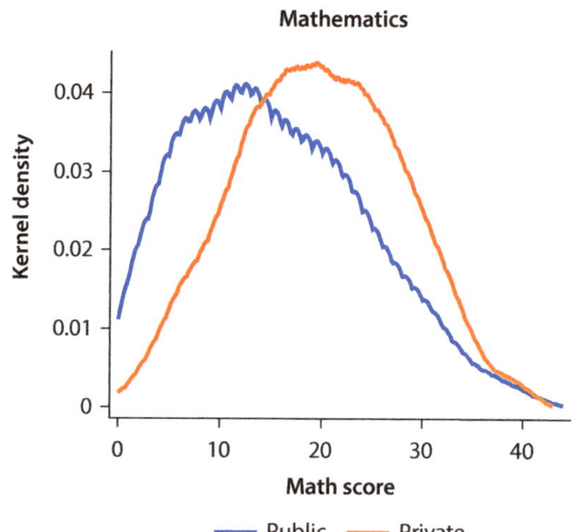

Source: Student assessments.
Note: LEAPS = Learning and Education Achievement in Punjab Schools; OECD Organisation for Economic Co-operation and Development; PISA = Programme for International Student Assessment; SLC = school leaving certificate.

Several facts stand out:

- **In all three countries,[6] private schools outperform public schools** with performance measured by raw test scores. In India, for example, while less than 20 percent of children ages 8–11 years enrolled in a public school can solve a division problem, over 30 percent of children of the same age in private school can do so. A similar observation can be made for reading and writing. In all three countries, the distribution of scores shifts to the right for children attending private schools.[7]
- **Even in private schools, learning levels are very low.** For example, in Pakistan, grade 4 students in rural private schools answer only about 45 percent of questions correctly. In India, just over 30 percent of the students ages 8–11 years can solve a division problem, and fewer than 50 percent can read a story.
- **There is considerable heterogeneity within private and public schools: good and bad scores exist in both types**, as illustrated by the Pakistan, Nepal, and India PISA data (figure 9.5). Some students in public schools obtain good scores and some in private obtain bad scores.
- **Decomposition of the scores by rural/urban residence and gender (table 9.4) shows that the outperformance of private school students over their public school peers is not just an urban phenomenon** but can also be observed in rural areas. This contradicts the common argument that location can help explain learning level differentials (public schools being located more often in remote and poor areas and catering primarily to disadvantaged children). There is no obvious gender divide, either.

Table 9.4 Student Performance–Analysis, by Gender and Urban/Rural Areas

	India, 8–11-year-olds, 2004–05			*Nepal, grade 10, 2004*			*Pakistan, grade 4, 2006*		
	India Human Development Survey			*Nepal School Leaving Certificate (SLC) Exam*			*LEAPS survey*		
	Math	*Writing*	*Reading*	*Math*	*Nepali*	*English*	*Math*	*Urdu*	*English*
Private female	68	81	74	53	53	66	n.a.	n.a.	n.a.
Private male	68	82	71	59	52	68	n.a.	n.a.	n.a.
Public female	42	64	51	29	42	38	n.a.	n.a.	n.a.
Public male	47	66	54	34	43	40	n.a.	n.a.	n.a.
Rural private	63	79	68	52	51	62	44	46	46
Rural public	42	63	50	31	42	38	35	34	33
Rural private female	60	77	68	47	51	61	43	48	47
Rural private male	65	80	69	55	51	63	45	44	45
Rural public female	39	62	49	28	41	37	32	36	35
Rural public male	44	64	52	33	42	39	36	33	31
Urban private	73	83	76	59	53	70	n.a.	n.a.	n.a.
Urban public	55	73	62	35	44	42	n.a.	n.a.	n.a.
Urban private female	75	84	79	55	54	69	n.a.	n.a.	n.a.
Urban private male	72	83	73	62	53	70	n.a.	n.a.	n.a.
Urban public female	54	72	61	31	44	41	n.a.	n.a.	n.a.
Urban public male	57	74	64	38	45	43	n.a.	n.a.	n.a.

Sources: India Human Development Survey, Nepal School Leaving Certificate Examination, and Learning and Educational Achievement in Pakistan Schools (LEAPS) survey.
Note: Measurement of student performance differs. In India, figures refer to the percentage of students who can do at least one subtraction problem, write with three or fewer mistakes, and read a paragraph or a story. Reading and writing tests in India were conducted in local languages. In Nepal, figures refer to mean scores out of a maximum of 100 in each subject. In Pakistan, figures are the percentage of questions correctly answered. n.a. = not applicable.

A topic often debated is whether unaided schools perform worse than aided. They are sometimes perceived as offering lower-quality education because they are subject to less government oversight[8] than aided schools, in particular with respect to fees and teacher credentials. The evidence presented in figure 9.5 does not support this hypothesis. In Pakistan, most private schools are unaided and still outperform public schools. National data for India show no significant difference between the two types of schools, and the PISA data even suggest that unaided schools outperform aided. Goyal and Pandey (2009) reached a similar conclusion and Kingdon (2007) found that in Uttar Pradesh only unaided schools performed better than government schools; aided schools performed about the same.

Community schools—another form of aided schools—are becoming increasingly frequent in some countries in the region. Evidence on their performance is as yet limited but preliminary findings suggest that they may provide learning opportunities cost-effectively. Two recent studies (Chaudhury and Parajuli 2010; Dang, Sarr, and Asadullah 2011) have examined the experiences of Bangladesh with the ROSC (Reaching Out-of-School Children) schools and of Nepal with the recent transfer of responsibilities to communities. The two experiences differ greatly: in Nepal, communities were empowered to take over management of existing public schools; in Bangladesh, communities receive grants and other support to set up new learning centers and attract out-of-school children. In the first case, the goal is to improve educational outcomes by changing school governance. In the second, it is to provide schooling opportunities to deeply disadvantaged children. The Bangladesh evaluation showed that ROSC schools have indeed reduced the number of out-of-school children and are providing children from poor households with a quality of education similar to that of regular government schools, at half the cost. In Nepal, schools that had shifted to community management and oversight were found to have better progression rates across grades and enhanced parental involvement, but no significant differences in student learning levels were found during the period of the evaluation (see box 9.2 for more details).

Box 9.2 Performance of Community Schools: The Experiences of Bangladesh and Nepal

Community schools, another form of private aided schools, benefit from government support but are managed by their communities.

In Bangladesh, the Reaching-out-of-School-Children (ROSC) schools were created through a 2004 government initiative with the intent of providing access to learning opportunities for out-of-school children ages 7–14 years. Learning centers (ROSC schools) are created at the demand of communities and can operate with more flexible norms than regular primary schools to cater to specific local needs of children (e.g., flexible school hours, multigrade teaching, entry at an older age). They are managed by a committee that is directly accountable to parents and students and receive financial support from the government, in the form of stipends and grants as well as from the community; and implementing partner nongovernmental organizations. Grants are per capita, and continuation of financing is contingent on a school achieving specified student attendance ratios and performance. Initial findings from an independent evaluation show that ROSC schools (now more than 15,000) have reduced the number of out-of-school children, giving learning opportunities to about half a million of them, and that their learning levels are similar to those in regular government schools at half the cost.

In Nepal, a 2001 amendment of the Education Act authorized communities to take over management of public schools by applying formally to the government and setting up a school management committee consisting of parents and local citizens. The process, which was voluntary, began in 2002 and accelerated after 2003. Community schools receive incentive grants in the year of transfer and performance grants for increasing enrollment and promotion rates; scholarships are awarded to children from disadvantaged backgrounds, and training programs are available for teachers and community members. As of July 2010, more than 10,000 of Nepal's 25,000 public schools had been transferred to community management. An evaluation found that communities that took over management of their schools had a smaller proportion of out-of-school children, better grade progression rates, and enhanced community participation and parental involvement. Within the time frame of the evaluation, there was no significant difference in learning levels.

Source: Chaudhury and Parajuli 2010.

What Contributes to Greater Learning in Private Schools?

To what extent do such factors as better students, improved inputs, or more effective teachers make private schools superior to public schools? Thus far, the mean differences in raw test scores that have been discussed have not been adjusted for other factors that may affect outcomes. One of these factors is the socioeconomic background of children, which is a proxy for a set of children's characteristics. It is well-known that children from more educated and richer families come to school better nourished and prepared and with more family support that children from poorer families. As a result, they generally do better in school (see chapter 3). If children who attend private schools come predominantly from richer and better-educated families, it is plausible that their higher learning levels are due to their own characteristics and that public schools fare no better and no worse once this is taken into account.

Table 9.5 and figure 9.6 show that across South Asia, within rural as well as urban areas, children belonging to families from the richest income quintiles are

Table 9.5 Total and Private Enrollment Rates of Different Socioeconomic Groups

	Afghanistan 2007–08		*Bangladesh 2010*		*Bhutan 2007*		*India 2009–10*		*Nepal 2009–10*		*Pakistan 2010–11*	
Enrollment (%)	*Total*	*Private*	*Total*	*Private*	*Total*	*Private*	*Total*	*Private*	*Total*	*Private*	*Total*	*Private*
6–10 years old												
All	41.7	0.4	85.0	19.1	83.0	2.1	91.8	25.8	93.8	28.8	68.1	21.8
Richest	59.1	1.2	92.3	41.4	96.5	7.9	97.8	68.1	98.8	75.0	82.2	50.3
Poorest	34.7	0.2	78.4	10.7	68.1	0.2	85.3	9.1	89.5	9.0	50.5	4.4
Urban richest	68.7	3.6	97.7	62.6	98.0	22.8	98.3	83.8	99.2	88.8	87.4	65.2
Urban poorest	50.9	1.1	84.1	14.2	94.6	1.3	88.0	24.8	87.8	22.7	71.2	26.2
Rural richest	48.9	0.3	91.5	18.9	92.4	1.6	96.4	43.5	98.3	47.6	79.6	30.7
Rural poorest	33.6	0.2	76.1	9.9	67.8	0.2	84.7	7.3	88.8	7.9	46.0	3.9
11–15 years old												
All	54.9	0.5	78.6	44.1	81.0	0.8	86.7	26.2	90.2	17.4	66.4	18.4
Richest	77.8	1.2	87.7	58.7	95.1	2.5	96.8	58.8	95.4	55.4	84.7	40.7
Poorest	43.7	0.2	68.7	30.6	66.2	0.2	77.9	9.9	82.8	3.1	43.0	3.9
Urban richest	86.4	1.4	96.8	62.8	96.3	4.2	97.9	77.4	94.0	68.5	90.4	57.1
Urban poorest	67.5	1.6	67.9	39.7	95.3	0.0	79.4	21.6	79.2	11.8	67.9	17.5
Rural richest	62.2	0.5	89.6	57.8	89.4	0.4	93.4	37.9	96.4	28.3	78.3	22.4
Rural poorest	41.9	0.1	67.5	30.8	66.0	0.2	77.3	7.8	82.2	2.3	38.9	3.4
16–18 year olds												
All	37.9	0.4	42.1	31.6	56.2	3.2	56.7	22.0	68.5	14.9	39.7	9.4
Richest	57.7	1.2	59.7	42.6	77.2	9.9	81.3	44.1	83.4	45.4	58.9	19.3
Poorest	27.2	0.1	22.0	15.0	36.2	0.1	39.1	7.6	51.2	3.7	17.3	2.0
Urban richest	71.4	1.5	72.3	49.6	76.9	14.8	90.2	57.5	73.8	51.8	68.6	28.3
Urban poorest	46.4	0.6	29.1	22.6	72.6	7.0	44.3	14.6	53.8	7.8	37.0	7.5
Rural richest	40.4	0.4	60.0	47.9	73.4	4.8	72.5	30.6	83.3	22.0	50.7	12.6
Rural poorest	24.6	0.0	19.0	14.6	35.5	0.0	38.5	6.0	45.7	2.7	13.9	1.4

Source: Household survey data.

Figure 9.6 Shares of Private School Enrollment, by Wealth Quintile, 2004–05 and 2010–11

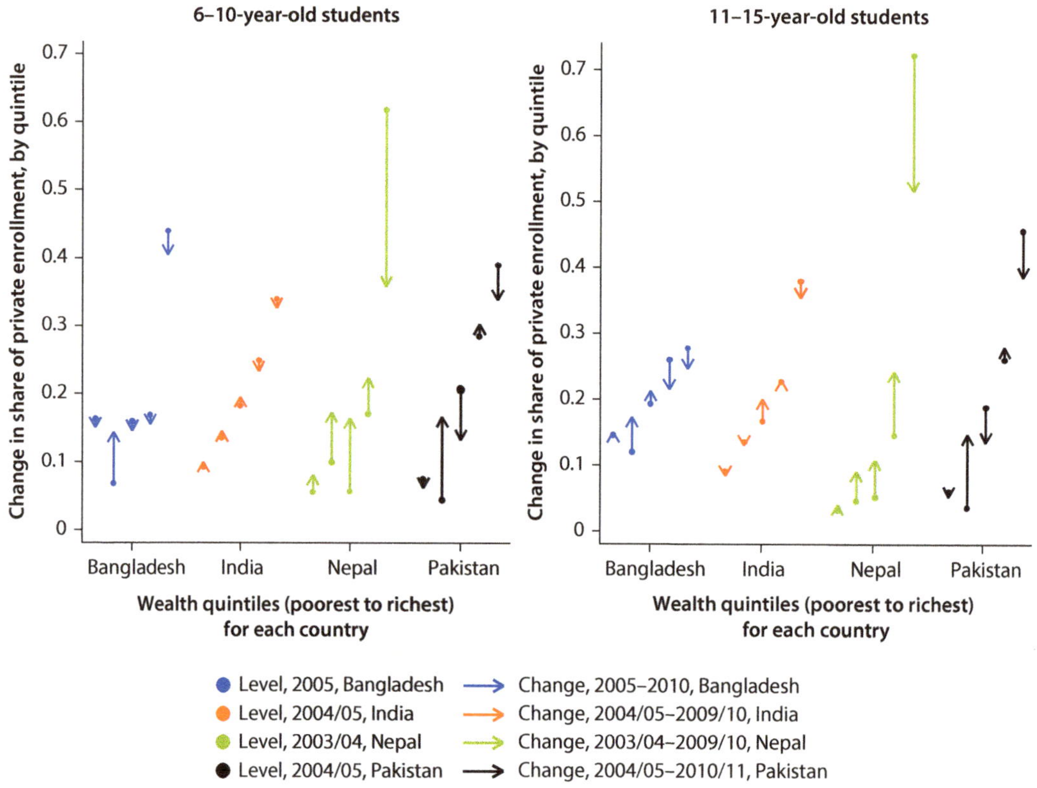

Source: Household survey data.
Note: For each country, the five arrow origin points add up to 100 percent of private school enrollment in the earlier period and the five arrow head points add up to 100 percent of private sector enrollment in the later period.

more likely to attend private schools than children from the poorest quintile. Figure 9.6, which presents more disaggregated data, further shows that the share of private school enrollment gradually increases as children move from the poorest to the highest wealth quintile (except in Bangladesh, where the share is at roughly the same level for the first four quintiles). Findings from several other studies are consistent with these observations. In rural Punjab, Pakistan, Andrabi et al. (2007) found disproportionately more private schools in larger and richer villages and in richer and more literate settlements within villages that had greater access to water and electricity.[9] In Dhaka, Bangladesh, even among slum households, children of wealthier and better educated parents are more likely to go to a private primary school (Cameron 2011).

Over time, however, the gap between rich and poor children narrows; children from poor families are increasingly attending private schools. Figure 9.6 shows a trend toward convergence over five to six years. In all four countries, the share of the richest quintile shows a decrease from 2004/05, with the largest decrease in Nepal and the smallest in India. At the bottom of the distribution, while no clear change can be observed for the poorest quintile, the share of children in private

Table 9.6 Private Tutoring in Bangladesh and Nepal by Socioeconomic Status and Urban/Rural Residence

		Private tutoring for 6–10-year-olds (%)		*Private tutoring for 11–15-year-olds (%)*	
		Private enrolled	*Public enrolled*	*Private enrolled*	*Public enrolled*
Bangladesh 2010	All	52.4	49.6	75.1	60.0
	Richest	60.3	60.5	84.7	77.9
	Poorest	35.0	36.8	60.5	40.7
	Urban richest	59.7	65.2	86.6	81.1
	Urban poorest	23.9	35.2	60.9	28.7
	Rural richest	61.2	55.7	82.4	72.9
	Rural poorest	32.1	34.7	58.5	40.9
Nepal 2010	All	30.5	10.1	38.9	23.1
	Richest	30.7	14.1	40.1	33.2
	Poorest	13.4	10.3	25.4	16.3
	Urban richest	28.9	20.2	37.3	29.4
	Urban poorest	0.0	15.4	44.4	19.9
	Rural richest	32.0	11.7	47.8	33.7
	Rural poorest	12.0	9.7	28.3	15.4

Source: Latest household survey data.

school belonging to the second wealth quintile is increasing, with the largest increases in Pakistan, and the smallest in India. This trend could accelerate in India over the next few years: The Right to Education Act of 2009 obliges private schools to set aside 25 percent of their seats for poor students. Evidence from Bangladesh and Nepal also suggests that the rich-poor divide on access to private tutoring is even less marked than for enrollment in private schools (table 9.6). While the richest can obviously afford supplementary private tutoring, the poorest may need it even more to compensate for low-quality public schools. Furthermore, for poor families becoming increasingly aware of the low quality of education and potential returns from education for their children, tutoring may be a more affordable option than paying high fees for enrollment in private schools.

Studies on India, Nepal, and Pakistan have tried to evaluate how much of the learning gap could be explained by children's background and characteristics (table 9.7). Most also attempt to simultaneously control for other factors that may affect outcomes, such as school characteristics. Private and public schools may indeed differ in terms of infrastructure, number of students, class size, proportion of female teachers, the extent of multigrade classrooms, qualification of teachers, time spent on instruction tasks, availability/quality of teaching materials, timeliness of textbook delivery, per student expenditure, location, and so forth.

All those studies confirm that raw estimates of learning differentials between private and public schools are biased upward. Once correction is done for selection bias, the premium of private schools is reduced. The magnitude of this decline varies. For example, Goyal (2009) found that the learning gap is reduced by about one-third when children's characteristics are controlled for, and Chudgar and Quin (2012) found that the remaining difference was no longer statistically significant.

Table 9.7 The Private-Public School Premium after Controlling for Student Background and School Characteristics (Estimated)

Study	*Data and coverage*	*Empirical strategy*	*Learning outcomes*	*Control variables beyond household and child characteristics*	*Findings after correction*
Bhatta 2004	Nepal 2004: Nationwide survey of 452 schools from SLC exams	Multiple regression analysis	SLC exam scores and pass rates	Per student spending, timeliness in textbook delivery, number of students, share of non-Nepali speakers in the student body (found statistically significant)	Higher pass rates and exam scores for private school students
Tooley 2009	India 2004: 150 randomly selected primary schools in poor areas of Hyderabad in Andhra Pradesh	Regression analysis	Standardized math and English tests for grades 4 and 5	School facilities and fees, number of students, teacher qualifications and average student IQ, teacher age, IQ, experience and training, availability of teaching tools	16–19 percentage points higher in math and English in private aided/ unaided recognized/unrecognized schools
Goyal and Pandey 2009	India 2006–07: All private and public primary schools in randomly selected areas in Madhya Pradesh and Uttar Pradesh	Regression analysis, district/village fixed effects	Hindi and math tests for grade 4	School characteristics (infrastructure, midday meal, free textbooks, and teacher's gender, education level, training and experience), district of location dummies and rural location dummy (or village dummies)	No private school advantage in Madhya Pradesh; Private school advantage in grade 5 and private unrecognized school advantage over private recognized schools in Uttar Pradesh
Andrabi et al. 2007	Pakistan 2003: All 812 public and private primary schools in 112 villages of Punjab	Regression analysis, village fixed effects	Grade 3 English, math, and Urdu tests	School infrastructure index and student-teacher ratio found not statistically significant	The test score gap in English/math/Urdu between public and private schools was 12 times the gap between rich versus poor, 8 times the gap between literate and illiterate fathers, and 18 times the gap between literate versus illiterate mothers
Muralidharan and Kremer 2008	India 2003: Nationally representative survey of rural primary schools	Regression analysis, village fixed effects	Short test mostly on arithmetic skills for grade 4 students	Controls for electricity, library availability, whether classrooms have roofs	0.4 standard deviation higher in test scores in private unaided recognized and unrecognized schools

table continues next page

Table 9.7 The Private-Public School Premium after Controlling for Student Background and School Characteristics (Estimated) *(continued)*

Study	*Data and coverage*	*Empirical strategy*	*Learning outcomes*	*Control variables beyond household and child characteristics*	*Findings after correction*
Chudgar and Quin 2012	India 2005: India Human Development Survey	Propensity score matching at child level	Short standardized reading, writing, and arithmetic tests for ages 8–11	No control for school characteristics	Difference but largely statistically insignificant between private unaided and public/aided schools in rural and urban areas. low-fee private schools similar to public counterparts
Thapa 2011	Nepal 2004: Nationwide survey of 452 schools from SLC exams	Propensity score matching	SLC exam scores and pass rates	Controls for number of students, science lab availability, number of school days per year, student-teacher ratio, medium of SLC exam (found statistically significant)	Higher pass rates and exam scores in private schools
Goyal 2009	India 2006: 143 public and 35 private schools, all randomly selected, in 8 districts of Odisha.	Altonji, Elder, and Taber (2005) method	Curriculum-based grade 4 reading and TIMSS math tests	Controls for midday meal provision, share of teachers receiving salaries regularly, share of teachers with a graduate qualification, multigrade teaching (found statistically significant)	15–16 percentage points higher in math and English in private schools
Desai et al. 2009	India 2005: India Human Development Survey	Heckman and Navarro-Lozano (2004) method, household fixed effects	Short standardized reading, writing, and arithmetic tests for ages 8–11	No control for school characteristics	Enrollment in private school associated with higher child outcomes by a moderate extent of a one-fourth of a standard deviation on average

Note: SLC = school leaving certificate; TIMSS = Trends in Mathematics and Science Study.

As for other factors such as school characteristics, there is not enough evidence to conclude that differences in inputs or in the quality of infrastructure can explain differences in learning between private and public schools. Some studies have found certain school characteristics to be statistically significant, which further adjusts downward the private school premium. However, the list of those characteristics is limited and varies by study, most probably depending on data availability. Moreover, results are not robust across studies. For instance, student-teacher ratios, which tend to be lower in private schools, have been found to be significant in some studies (Goyal 2009; Thapa 2011) but not others (Andrabi et al. 2007). As for differences in infrastructure, which some studies have taken into consideration, there is no evidence of a systematic difference to the advantage or disadvantage of private schools. Goyal and Pandey (2009) found no difference in their analysis of schools in the Indian states of Madhya Pradesh and Uttar Pradesh. Muralidharan and Kremer (2008) reached a similar conclusion about schools in rural India generally.

Some studies have also considered differences in teacher qualifications and experience to be possible determinants (see table 9.7). In general, private school teachers tend to be younger and less experienced than public school teachers, although there does not seem to be a systematic difference in terms of educational qualifications. In rural Pakistan, Andrabi et al. (2008) found that a typical private school teacher has completed secondary school while a typical government teacher has an undergraduate degree. Muralidharan and Kremer (2008) found that in India, private school teachers are more likely to hold a college degree but less likely to have a formal teacher training certificate. Here again, there is no evidence that this is a determinant factor. Research in other parts of the world has produced similar findings: teacher characteristics and credentials other than knowledge and behavior do not seem to have a significant impact on learning (Glewwe et al. 2011; Rockoff et al. 2011).

Overall, some studies found a non-negative private school premium and others found that a positive premium still exists after correction for students and some school characteristics. In other words, the performance of private schools seems no worse, and in many cases seems better, than the performance of public schools, once observable student and some school characteristics are taken into account. Whenever a positive premium persists after correction, the reasons for it have yet to be determined.

One of the most common hypotheses to explain the residual private school premium gives precedence to teacher behavior or effort, rather than qualifications or experience. This is consistent with findings that teachers are the most critical factor for quality (see chapters 2 and 5). Although "behavior" is not easily measurable, some proxies, such as absenteeism, can provide useful information. South Asia reports very high teacher absenteeism in public schools—25 percent in India, 16 percent in Bangladesh (see Chaudhury et al. 2006), while there is some evidence that teachers in private schools are absent less often. Muralidharan and Sundararaman (2011) found that, within the same village in rural India, private school teachers were 8 percentage points less likely to be absent.

Furthermore, there is some evidence that private school teachers are not only more likely to be present but also to teach more actively. Tooley (2009) reported that, during visits to 265 schools in slum areas of East Delhi, teachers were teaching in only 38 percent of the government schools reviewed, compared to 72 percent in the private unrecognized and 69 percent in the private recognized. Muralidharan and Kremer (2008) also found 2–8 percentage points less teacher absence and 6–9 percentage points more teaching activity in private unaided schools than in public schools in the same village in rural India. By the very nature of their fixed-term, renewable work contracts and the greater risk of being penalized or even losing their jobs, private school teachers are more likely to be accountable to school management. Headmasters can easily apply disciplinary procedures. Often hired from the local community, private school teachers may also be more accountable to parents and others in the community.

More research is required to determine the extent to which behavioral differences fully explain learning variations between private and public schools. In government schools, an increasing proportion of teachers are hired on contract, so they have much in common with private school teachers: lower pay, a greater risk of losing their job, and often local hiring. Contract teachers in government schools have also been found to be less often absent and more active in teaching than regular teachers. Over time, this trend may make the performance of public and private schools converge.

What provides strong support to the hypothesis that teacher behavior or effort may be a determinant factor is the finding that learning improves when teacher performance incentives tied to financing are in effect (see chapter 5). Indeed, PPP programs in Pakistan that condition public support to private schools to some measure of performance (student pass rate in Punjab; test scores in Sindh) were found to have a positive impact on learning achievement (Barrera-Osorio and Raju 2010, 2011; box 9.3).

Cost-Effectiveness of Private Schools

Although there is still a great deal not known about what determines learning, evidence so far suggests that private schools perform at least as well as public schools, and in some cases better. They also generally operate with lower costs using their resources, including parent fees, more effectively. While private schooling may be more expensive for households, it is cheaper for society as a whole, making private schools unambiguously more cost-effective even if test scores show no absolute advantage.

Kingdon (2008) reported that in Uttar Pradesh, India, recurrent per-pupil expenditures in private schools were only 41 percent of what public schools were spending and attributed most of the difference to teacher salaries, the largest cost component. Evidence from India further suggests that the cost differential may have increased dramatically over time: while in the mid-1990s, private teacher salaries were about 40–50 percent of government teacher salaries, by the early 2000s they were only about 20 percent (Kingdon and Muzammil 2013).

Box 9.3 Public-Private Partnerships: A Promising Mechanism for Improving the Quality of Education

Several recent public-private partnership (PPP) programs in Pakistan have proved to be cost-effective in generating gains in student participation and achievement.

Introduced in 2005, the Foundation Assisted School (FAS) program administered by the Punjab Education Foundation (Pakistan) provides conditional cash subsidies to low-cost private schools in order to offer private school opportunities for children from low-income households and raise the level of learning in those schools. There are essentially no conditions on how the monthly per-student subsidies are to be used. The amount is purposely set low (half the estimated public school per-student cost) to ensure that only low-cost private schools self-select into the program. In return for the subsidy, a school has to waive tuition and other fees for all students and ensure that the school achieves a minimum student pass rate in the Quality Assurance Test (QAT). The QAT is a curriculum-based, multisubject test designed by subject specialists and administered by independent agencies. Program schools are also eligible for group-based bonuses for teachers who achieve high QAT pass rates, and there are competitive bonuses for schools with the highest QAT rankings. Schools that fail to achieve a minimum pass rate in two consecutive attempts must leave the program.

As of June 2010, the FAS program had proceeded through six phases of expansion and supported about 800,000 students in 1,800 schools in 29 of the 36 districts in the province. Within two years, the program had generated large gains of about 40 percent in enrollment and school inputs and a gain in student achievement of 0.3–0.5 standard deviation (Barrera-Osorio and Raju 2010, 2011).

The Punjab Education Foundation runs a sister program, the New School Program (NSP), which supports the founding and operations of new schools in underserved communities. The program provides per-student subsidies to new private schools, conditional on a school's achievement in standardized, competency-based tests. The program currently covers over 20,000 students in 230 schools in 16 districts.

In Promoting Private Schooling in Rural Sindh (PPRS), a program similar to the NSP run by the Government of Sindh, Pakistan, schools in underserved rural communities get grants for construction and other school support in addition to per-student subsidies conditional on minimum student achievement. A rigorous evaluation of PPRS also found substantial gains in participation and achievement (Barrera-Osorio et al. 2011).

In other developing and developed countries, charter-type schools have been found to yield positive effects when incentives are tied to some measure of performance (see, for example, Angrist et al. [2010] for an evaluation of the Knowledge Is Power Program [KIPP] in the United States; and Barrera-Osorio [2007] and Bonilla [2010] for an evaluation of the Concession Schools program in Bogotá, Colombia).

Private teachers are usually drawn from the local workforce and paid according to local labor market rates; often they are women who are unable to travel far for work. Tooley (2009) found that in Delhi, fourth-grade teachers earned Rs 10,072 a month in public schools, Rs 3,627 in private recognized schools, and Rs 1,360 in unrecognized schools. Muralidharan and Sundararaman (2011) found that in rural India private school teachers earned even less than contract teachers in government schools. Goyal and Pandey (2009) reported that teacher salaries in private schools were just one-seventh to one-eighth of government teacher salaries in Uttar Pradesh and Madhya Pradesh. Andrabi, Das, and Khwaja (2008) documented that government teachers in rural Pakistan earned up to five times more than private school teachers.

Impact on Quality of Other Public-Private Partnership Structures

Other types of PPPs are mainly stipends or scholarships provided by the government to make private schooling affordable, or private financial or technical support for government schools (the reverse of the most common type of PPPs).

Although several South Asian countries have stipend programs, in very few are stipends given with the option of attending either a private or a public school, and most are fairly recent. The largest and oldest stipend program that allows students to attend a private school is the Bangladeshi program targeted at secondary-school girls. However, that hardly presents the option of school choice because more than 90 percent of secondary schools in Bangladesh are private-aided. Evaluation of this program[10] has shown a positive impact on girls attending school but no evidence of impact on test scores. It is worth noting, nevertheless, that in this case, the primary intent was gender parity, not improving quality through competition between the public and private sectors. Bangladesh has another stipend program, this one at the primary level, that provides the option to attend either a government school or a recognized private school, but no study has attempted to measure whether it has had an impact on test scores.

In India, the few trial voucher schemes that exist in some states are mostly run by foundations. However, the scope of such partnerships is likely to increase significantly when the 2009 Right to Education Act, which requires that private schools set aside 25 percent of their seats for poor students (with funding from the government), is fully operational. In Pakistan, the scale of the Punjab government Education Voucher Scheme expanded significantly in 2011, with 140,000 vouchers handed over in disadvantaged urban neighborhoods in 36 districts of the state capital. The government has decided that expansion of the program will depend on a rigorous evaluation.

When the private sector provides support to government schools, it is mainly through NGOs that target their attention to children falling behind in government schools or in specific fields. This is true of Pratham[11] support to government schools in India (Balsakhi, Read India, and computer-assisted learning programs). Those programs have been found (see annex 9B) to be effective in improving test scores (Banerjee et al., 2007; Poverty Action Lab–South Asia 2011).

Policy Implications

Given the region's capacity and resource constraints, South Asia cannot possibly raise the educational attainment of the population and improve the quality of learning at each level of education without a combined effort by government, households, and the private sector. Leveraging the contribution of the private sector is vital to meet those challenges and to expand the resources invested in preparing human capital.

Facilitating the Expansion of Private Education

The private sector has already contributed to the significant expansion in enrollment in the region and has demonstrated it can offer access at lower social cost, often with comparable or better outcomes than the public sector. There are also clear signs of a demand for private education and a willingness to pay for it. There is thus no reason for any government to prevent or limit private sector activity in education.

From past experience, the private sector is likely to continue to expand its role on its own, but it could also be encouraged by easing barriers to entry and PPPs. Private providers often cite lack of access to credit and excessive bureaucracy in registering and accrediting institutions as disincentives to setting up new schools. Those procedures could be made easier to facilitate new initiatives.

Given educational budget constraints, the cost-effectiveness of private schools makes them particularly attractive. Recent PPP initiatives in the region have indeed proved to be a cost-effective way to reach underserved areas and children (see box 9.2). Another model is the Bangladesh community (ROSC) schools, where school grants and student allowances are already covering half a million children at half the cost of public schools. Governments could innovate more by using this type of subsidy to induce private providers to set up new schools for very poor children.

Fostering Competition versus Tighter Regulation

Available evidence does not support the view that heavier regulation of private school fees and teacher credentials would improve quality. First, as shown earlier, there is no evidence that unaided private schools that are subject to less regulation perform worse; in fact, they seem to outperform aided private schools. Second, it would be very difficult to gauge the efficient level of fees and teacher credentials for an education market as diverse as in South Asia. For example, in areas with very poor levels of learning, a sizable number of out-of-school children, and few teachers available, it might not be wise to require high teacher credentials for some time. In other areas, needs and teacher availability could be quite different.

Third, to ensure compliance would require significant capacity; regulations that cannot be enforced add no value. A similar argument would apply to raising standards for accreditation. Nevertheless, this might be reconsidered where there is danger of political decisions and nepotism interfering with recruitment decisions; enforcement could then effectively counter partiality in decision making. For instance, Bangladesh requires that private secondary school teachers be recruited from a pool of accredited teachers. In doing so, it has managed to reduce the influence of political decisions and favoritism, bringing more transparency to the process.

Injecting into the sector a healthy dose of competition between private and public schools and between individual private schools may provide an alternative to stricter control and may be sufficient to ensure that fees remain affordable. For this, better monitoring capacity and reliable and regularly updated information about school-level and student-level learning quality would be crucial for households to make informed choices. Competition could also be enhanced by more extensive provision of stipends or vouchers to children from poor households to allow them to attend the school of their choice.[12] Although school choice already exists for the fraction of students whose parents can afford to pay fees, stipends would enlarge the number while creating even more competition between schools and students.

Although there are a number of stipend programs already in place in several parts of South Asia, their primary rationale was to improve access to schools rather than to foster competition and quality improvements. It is only very recently that initiatives in India and Pakistan seem to have been taken in this direction. Learning about their impact through rigorous evaluation would be most useful for other countries deciding whether to scale up or replicate them.

Improving Quality in Both Public and Private Schools

One useful way for governments to improve the quality of private schools would be to improve the quality of public schools. Public schools are the baseline upon which private schools make their investment and determine a premium that can attract students. The lower the baseline, the less private schools need to invest to distinguish themselves from competitors. As long as public school quality is low, there is little incentive for private schools to do much better. Enhancing the quality of public schools would give private schools an incentive to raise the bar in order to keep attracting students. Less effective private schools at the low end of the quality spectrum would be likely to leave the market, thus reducing the current high variability.

Reliable government systems of assessing learning and teaching would also give private schools the information they need to set quality-related incentives and maximize their cost-effectiveness. The flexibility that private schools have may allow them to adopt innovations and adaptations much faster than public schools can and, based on teacher responsiveness to certain incentives, lead to greater learning outcomes.

Annex 9A: Total and Private Enrollment Rates of Different Socioeconomic Groups

School	*Afghanistan 2007/08*		*Bangladesh 2010*		*Bhutan 2007*		*India 2009/10*		*Nepal 2009/10*		*Pakistan 2010/11*	
enrollment (%)	*Total*	*Private*	*Total*	*Private*	*Total*	*Private*	*Total*	*Private*	*Total*	*Private*	*Total*	*Private*
6–10 years old												
All	41.7	0.4	85.0	19.1	83.0	2.1	91.8	25.8	93.8	28.8	68.1	21.8
Urban	59.0	1.5	88.3	34.3	95.0	6.5	94.4	52.4	95.8	63.5	79.0	42.9
Rural	38.2	0.2	83.9	13.7	78.8	0.6	91.0	18.0	93.4	22.7	63.8	13.6
Male	48.7	0.4	82.7	19.2	83.8	2.6	92.8	27.1	94.1	34.7	72.8	22.9

table continues next page

School enrollment (%)	Afghanistan 2007/08		Bangladesh 2010		Bhutan 2007		India 2009/10		Nepal 2009/10		Pakistan 2010/11	
	Total	Private	Total	Private	Total	Private	Total	Private	Total	Private	Total	Private
Female	34.3	0.4	87.3	19.0	82.2	1.7	90.7	24.3	93.5	23.1	62.8	20.6
Richest	59.1	1.2	92.3	41.4	96.5	7.9	97.8	68.1	98.8	75.0	82.2	50.3
Poorest	34.7	0.2	78.4	10.7	68.1	0.2	85.3	9.1	89.5	9.0	50.5	4.4
Urban male	62.8	1.6	87.0	33.0	94.7	8.0	94.9	53.7	96.6	68.7	80.4	44.0
Urban female	55.0	1.4	89.8	35.8	95.4	4.9	93.9	50.9	95.1	58.4	77.5	41.7
Rural male	45.8	0.1	81.4	14.0	79.8	0.6	92.1	19.3	93.6	28.7	69.9	14.8
Rural female	30.0	0.2	86.6	13.3	77.7	0.5	89.7	16.5	93.2	17.0	57.0	12.3
Urban richest	68.7	3.6	97.7	62.6	98.0	22.8	98.3	83.8	99.2	88.8	87.4	65.2
Urban poorest	50.9	1.1	84.1	14.2	94.6	1.3	88.0	24.8	87.8	22.7	71.2	26.2
Rural richest	48.9	0.3	91.5	18.9	92.4	1.6	96.4	43.5	98.3	47.6	79.6	30.7
Rural poorest	33.6	0.2	76.1	9.9	67.8	0.2	84.7	7.3	88.8	7.9	46.0	3.9
11–15 years old												
All	54.9	0.5	78.6	44.1	81.0	0.8	86.7	26.2	90.2	17.4	66.4	18.4
Urban	78.8	1.5	79.6	49.3	95.2	2.2	90.2	46.9	91.0	48.5	79.4	33.2
Rural	48.3	0.2	78.3	42.3	76.2	0.4	85.6	19.4	90.0	10.9	60.3	11.5
Male	66.3	0.5	72.8	40.4	81.8	0.6	88.9	28.1	92.5	20.7	73.2	19.1
Female	42.2	0.4	84.9	48.1	80.3	1.1	84.1	23.9	87.9	14.2	58.5	17.5
Richest	77.8	1.2	87.7	58.7	95.1	2.5	96.8	58.8	95.4	55.4	84.7	40.7
Poorest	43.7	0.2	68.7	30.6	66.2	0.2	77.9	9.9	82.8	3.1	43.0	3.9
Urban male	87.8	1.9	72.6	44.8	97.1	1.4	90.4	48.8	91.8	52.4	80.6	35.0
Urban female	69.5	1.2	87.7	54.8	93.5	2.9	89.9	44.5	90.1	44.7	78.2	31.2
Rural male	60.7	0.1	72.9	38.9	77.0	0.4	88.4	21.3	92.6	14.0	69.9	12.1
Rural female	34.1	0.2	84.0	46.1	75.5	0.4	82.2	17.1	87.5	7.8	49.0	10.8
Urban richest	86.4	1.4	96.8	62.8	96.3	4.2	97.9	77.4	94.0	68.5	90.4	57.1
Urban poorest	67.5	1.6	67.9	39.7	95.3	0.0	79.4	21.6	79.2	11.8	67.9	17.5
Rural richest	62.2	0.5	89.6	57.8	89.4	0.4	93.4	37.9	96.4	28.3	78.3	22.4
Rural poorest	41.9	0.1	67.5	30.8	66.0	0.2	77.3	7.8	82.2	2.3	38.9	3.4
16–18 years olds												
All	37.9	0.4	42.1	31.6	56.2	3.2	56.7	22.0	68.5	14.9	39.7	9.4
Urban	59.1	1.1	46.5	32.6	75.3	9.1	68.3	34.4	74.6	36.2	52.6	15.2
Rural	30.7	0.1	40.4	31.2	49.5	1.1	52.3	17.4	66.9	9.1	32.9	6.3
Male	50.1	0.5	43.6	32.1	58.4	2.6	60.3	24.3	76.0	17.8	45.3	10.0
Female	24.2	0.3	40.3	31.0	54.2	3.7	52.1	19.2	62.3	12.5	33.7	8.6
Richest	57.7	1.2	59.7	42.6	77.2	9.9	81.3	44.1	83.4	45.4	58.9	19.3
Poorest	27.2	0.1	22.0	15.0	36.2	0.1	39.1	7.6	51.2	3.7	17.3	2.0
Urban male	68.0	1.7	47.3	33.5	80.8	9.1	68.7	36.2	75.6	39.7	52.7	16.6
Urban female	50.0	0.5	45.7	31.6	71.7	9.1	67.9	32.1	73.7	32.8	52.5	13.8
Rural male	44.4	0.1	42.2	31.6	52.0	0.7	57.2	19.9	76.2	11.2	41.5	6.7
Rural female	15.0	0.2	38.3	30.7	47.0	1.4	46.0	14.2	59.5	7.4	23.4	5.8
Urban richest	71.4	1.5	72.3	49.6	76.9	14.8	90.2	57.5	73.8	51.8	68.6	28.3
Urban poorest	46.4	0.6	29.1	22.6	72.6	7.0	44.3	14.6	53.8	7.8	37.0	7.5
Rural richest	40.4	0.4	60.0	47.9	73.4	4.8	72.5	30.6	83.3	22.0	50.7	12.6
Rural poorest	24.6	0.0	19.0	14.6	35.5	0.0	38.5	6.0	45.7	2.7	13.9	1.4

Annex 9B: Public-Private Partnerships in South Asia: Impact Evaluation Results

	Type and period of partnership	Financing/support conditions	Coverage	Impact evaluation	Methodology	Data	Findings
A. Public-private partnerships (PPPs) in which the government provides funding or support to the private sector (sometimes also directly to students), and the private sector is responsible for delivering education services							
Bangladesh	Service rules and salary subvention system for teachers and staff in private secondary schools (1981–present)	Service rules and full-scale salary subvention system for teachers and staff in private secondary schools	Countrywide	N/A			
	Female Secondary School Assistance Project (FSSAP) (1993–2008)	Subsidies to rural girls to attend secondary schools that are mostly privately managed and publicly funded; teacher training and other support to schools	2008: 121 disadvantaged subdistricts	Khandker, Pitt, and Fuwa 2003	Difference-in-differences on a randomized sample of subdistricts	Baseline and follow-up surveys	Substantial increase in secondary education for girls but not for boys
	Reaching Out-of-School Children (ROSC) (2005–present)	School grant, student allowance, and other support from government to set up and operate single-teacher schools; school management by parents, local personnel, and teachers	2011: Over 500,000 children in the 60 poorest subdistricts	Dang, Sarr, and Asadullah 2011	Difference-in-differences on a randomly selected sample of ROSC and non-ROSC schools	Retrospective baseline survey and follow-up survey	Enrollment gains of 9–18 percentage points for 6–10-year-olds; standardized language and math test score gains similar to non-ROSC schools; positive externalities on non-ROSC schools

table continues next page

	Type and period of partnership	Financing/support conditions	Coverage	Impact evaluation	Methodology	Data	Findings
India	Grant-in-aid (1859–present)	Subsidies for teacher salaries, in proportion to enrollment	Countrywide	N/A			
	Education Guarantee Scheme (1997–present)	Primary schools provided to remote, especially tribal, communities per their needs and request	2003: 26,571 primary schools in Madhya Pradesh	Raykar 2011	Difference-in-differences	2005–06 National Family Health Survey	Substantial positive impact on rural women's completed years of schooling and probability of attending secondary school
Nepal	Community Support Program (CSP) (2003–present)	Grants provided to school management committees (consisting of parents and influential local citizens) along with school staffing and fiscal decisions	2010: More than 10,200 out of 26,275 public schools	Chaudhury and Parajuli 2010	Instrumental variable, and difference-in-differences on 220 schools and communities in 16 districts	Program baseline and follow-up surveys	Positive impact on certain schooling access and equity outcomes; no impact on curriculum-based language and mathematics and TIMSS-type test scores; mixed impact on school governance
Pakistan	Adopt-a-School (1998–present)	Continuous technical support and monitoring provided by the Sindh Education Foundation (SEF) to the adopting agency	2008: 147 schools and 34,379 students in 11 of 23 Sindh districts	N/A			
	Leasing of public school buildings to private operators (2001–present)	Building upgrade; payment for part of operating costs; 10 percent profits; per-student fees	2008: 6,000 schools in Punjab	N/A			
	Support to Private Education Institutions (2003–present)	Technical and infrastructural support provided by SEF and partners	2011: 300 schools in 6 Sindh districts	N/A			

table continues next page

Type and period of partnership	*Financing/support conditions*	*Coverage*	*Impact evaluation*	*Methodology*	*Data*	*Findings*
Foundation Assisted Schools (FAS) (2005–present)	Minimum student pass rate on a standardized academic test; group-based teacher bonuses conditional on a minimum score in a composite measure of student test participation and mean test scores	2008: 1,082 private schools and 474,000 students in 18 of 35 Punjab districts; now covers about 1,800 schools and 800,000 students in 29 districts	Barrera-Osorio and Raju 2010 Barrera-Osorio and Raju 2011	Regression discontinuity design	Program and test records, phone interviews (only for 2011 paper)	Large learning gains due to student pass rate condition; no learning gains due to group-based teacher bonuses Large positive impacts on number of test passers, teachers, classrooms, and blackboards
Cluster-Based Training of Teachers (2006–present)	Allowance provided to teachers from clusters of private schools to attend training in knowledge	Punjab	N/A			
Balochistan Education Support Project (2006–2012)	Grants for school construction by communities and entrepreneurs, and other school-level support; per-student subsidy with priority to girls	2010: Over 50,000 students in about 850 schools in rural Balochistan	N/A			
Promoting Private Schooling in Rural Sindh (PPRS) (2009–present)	Grants for construction of private schools, and other school-level support; per-student subsidy conditional on school's achievement in standardized, competency-based test scores	2011: 481 schools in underserved rural Sindh	Barrera-Osorio et al. 2011	Randomized controlled trial on 296 schools	Program baseline and follow-up surveys	Participation increase of 51 percentage points, with 4–5 percentage points more for girls. Improvements in test scores

table continues next page

	Type and period of partnership	Financing/support conditions	Coverage	Impact evaluation	Methodology	Data	Findings
B. PPPs in which the private sector provides financing or support and the government delivers educational services							
Afghanistan	Building Education Support Systems for Teachers (2006–11)	In-service training funded and managed by USAID to improve the instructional skills and knowledge of primary and secondary school teachers and the management skills of principals	2011: About 53,000 teachers and principals in 11 of 34 provinces	N/A			
India	Balsakhi (1998–present)	A teacher provided by Pratham to children falling behind in basic literacy and numeracy in grades 3 and 4 in public schools	2004: Mumbai and Vadodara cities	Banerjee et al. 2007	Randomized controlled trial	Program baseline and follow-up surveys	Balsakhi 2001–03: increase of 0.28 standard deviation in test scores, mostly of weakest students; computer-assisted Learning 2002–03: increase of 0.47 standard deviation in math scores; in 2004, only 25 percent of initial gains
	Computer-assisted Learning (2002–03)	Instructors from Pratham to elementary students in using computer software designed to improve math skills	2003: Vadodara city				
	Read India (2007–present)	(1) Pratham training and monitoring of public school teachers, (2) specially designed learning materials, (3) village volunteer support to children in need	2009: 33 million children in 19 states	Poverty Action Lab–South Asia 2011	Randomized controlled trial in Bihar and Uttarakhand	Program baseline and follow-up surveys	Teacher training and monitoring, learning materials and volunteers, and summer camp activities significantly improve reading, writing, and math test scores
	Computer education (2009–present)	Computer and computer-aided education provided by NIIT, a global information technology firm	2011: 9,000 schools and 70,000 students in 12 states	N/A			

table continues next page

	Type and period of partnership	Financing/support conditions	Coverage	Impact evaluation	Methodology	Data	Findings
Nepal	Teacher Education Project (2002–09)	Cooperation between public institutions and private service providers to build a teacher education and training system for primary education	2009: Training provided by 99 private and other providers to 114,406 teachers	N/A			
Pakistan	Local NGO support on school management (1998–present)	Teacher and staff supervised by Cooperation for Advancement, Rehabilitation, and Education (CARE)	2008: 170 schools and 100,000 students in Lahore and Sarghoda	N/A			
	Quality Education for All (2002–present)	Operational budget and staff supervision transferred fully to National Rural Support Programme (NRSP)	2008: More than 2,400 rural primary schools in Punjab	N/A			
C. PPPs in which the government framework and policy, in terms of curriculum and teacher training, are formally applied, and the private sector takes direct charge of Both funding and delivering educational service							
Afghanistan	Partnership for Advancing Community-based Education (PACE-A) (2006–11)	Funding from USAID and management and other support from a consortium of NGOs to improve access to basic education in rural underserved areas through a variety of activities; model to be taken over by government	Countrywide	Burde and Linden 2012	Randomized controlled trial on 31 villages and 1,490 students	Program baseline and follow-up surveys	Construction of village-based schools and provision of educational materials and training to locally recruited teachers improving enrollment and math and language scores of 6–11-year-olds; significantly reduced gender disparities in enrollment and test scores

table continues next page

	Type and period of partnership	*Financing/support conditions*	*Coverage*	*Impact evaluation*	*Methodology*	*Data*	*Findings*
D. PPPs in which the government provides vouchers/scholarships to students to make private schooling more affordable							
India	Pre- and post-matriculation scholarships for minority students	Scholarships from federal government and governments of Andhra Pradesh, Bihar, and Uttar Pradesh to meritorious grades 1–10 students from economically weaker sections of certain minority communities studying in a government or recognized private school	Countrywide or statewide (with state-specific conditions)	N/A			
	Prematriculation scholarships for disabled students	Scholarships from government of Andhra Pradesh to disabled and economically disadvantaged grades 1–12 students in unaided recognized private schools	Andhra Pradesh	N/A			
	Private primary school vouchers	Scholarships from government of Andhra Pradesh to class 1 students to move to a private school of their choice	Andhra Pradesh	Kremer et al. 2011	Randomized controlled trial on 180 villages	Program baseline and follow-up surveys	No impact on average test scores, with important heterogeneity across subjects/languages of instruction; process indicators (such as teaching activity, school time, parents' satisfaction) are much better in private schools

Note: NGO = nongovernmental organization; TIMSS = Trend in Mathematics and Science Studies; USAID = United States Agency for International Development.

Notes

1. Cameron (2011) found that almost half of children living in slums in Dhaka, Bangladesh, who attended school are privately tutored.
2. In 2003, the Nepal government decided to transfer management of 10,200 public schools (of a total of 26,275) to local communities. The transfer was completed by the end of fiscal year 2009–10. In Afghanistan, NGOs with support from the United States Agency for International Development have since 2006 established some 3,000 classes in village-based schools.
3. Annex 9B presents types of partnerships as implemented in the countries of the region, their modalities and coverage, and the findings of impact evaluations where available.
4. Under British rule, a president of the Board of Control of the East Asia Company in 1854 recommended that (pre-partition) India provide grant-in-aid support to private schools.
5. SLC refers to the Annual School Leaving Certificate examination conducted by the Nepal government at the end of grade 10.
6. The case of Bangladesh may deserve a separate analysis. The majority of secondary schools are private aided, making the comparison between public and private schools meaningless. At the primary level, where government and private aided schools coexist, results from the 2011 National Student Assessment have shown higher test scores in government than in private aided schools (recognized nongovernment schools; see ACER 2012).
7. Estimates of raw learning gaps vary by country and by subject. In the three datasets analyzed, they are about 25 percent.
8. A very large proportion of unaided schools, which receive no financial support from the government, nevertheless follow the government curriculum.
9. A similar finding—that children in richer and urban areas are more likely to be enrolled in private schools—is explained with detailed data in annex 9A.
10. See Khandker, Pitt, and Fuwa 2003 for an evaluation of the Female Secondary Assistance project and annex 9B for a summary of results.
11. Pratham is a leading Indian NGO that provides education to marginalized children (see www.pratham.org).
12. See Bravo, Mukhopadhyay, and Todd (2010) and Patrinos and Sakellariou (2011) for a review of evidence on the impact of school choice programs.

Bibliography

ACER (Australian Council for Educational Research). 2012. *2011 National Student Assessment Grades 3 and 5*. Revised Report, June.

Altonji, J., T. Elder, and C. Taber. 2005. "Selection on Observed and Unobserved Variables: Assessing the Effectiveness of Catholic Schools." *Journal of Political Economy* 113 (1): 151–84.

Andrabi, T., J. Das, and A. Khwaja. 2008. "A Dime a Day: The Possibilities and Limits of Private Schooling in Pakistan." *Comparative Education Review* 52 (3): 329–55.

Andrabi, T., J. Das, A. Khwaja, T. Vishwanath, and T. Zajonc. 2007. *Pakistan: Learning and Educational Achievements in Punjab Schools (LEAPS): Insights to Inform the*

Education Policy Debate. http://www.leapsproject.org/assets/publications/LEAPS_Report_ExecSummary.pdf.

Angrist, J. D., S. M. Dynarski, T. J. Kane, P. A. Pathak, and C. Walters. 2010. "Inputs and Impacts in Charter Schools: KIPP Lynn." *American Economic Review Papers and Proceedings* 100 (2): 1–5.

Asadullah, M. N., N. Chaudhury, and S. R. Al-Zayed Josh. 2009. *Secondary School Madrasas in Bangladesh: Incidence, Quality, and Implications for Reform*. Washington, DC: South Asia Region Human Development Department, World Bank.

Aslam, M. 2009. "The Relative Effectiveness of Government and Private Schools in Pakistan: Are Girls Worse Off?" *Education Economics* 17 (3): 329–54.

Banerjee, A. V., S. Cole, E. Duflo, and L. L. Linden.2007. "Remedying Education: Evidence from Two Randomized Experiments in India." *The Quarterly Journal of Economics* 122 (3): 1235–64.

Barrera-Osorio, F. 2007. "The Impact of Private Provision of Public Education: Empirical Evidence from Bogotá's Concession Schools." Policy Research Working Paper 4121, World Bank, Washington, DC.

Barrera-Osorio, F., D. S. Blakeslee, M. Hoover, L. L. Linden, and D. Raju. 2011. "Expanding Educational Opportunities in Remote Parts of the World: Evidence from a RCT of a Public Private Partnership in Pakistan." In Third Institute for the Study of Labor (IZA) Workshop, "Child Labor in Developing Countries," Mexico City. http://www.iza.org/conference_files/childl2011/blakeslee_d6783.

Barrera-Osorio, F., and D. Raju. 2010. "Short-run Learning Dynamics under a Test-based Accountability System: Evidence from Pakistan." Policy Research Working Paper 5465, World Bank, Washington, DC.

———. 2011. "Evaluating Public Per-Student Subsidies to Low-Cost Private Schools." Working Paper, Human Development Unit, South Asia Region, World Bank, Washington, DC.

Bhatta, S. D. 2004. *A Descriptive Analysis of the Disparities in School Performance in the SLC Exams. SLC Study Report # 1*. The Education Sector Advisory Team, Ministry of Education and Sports, Katmandu, Nepal.

Bonilla, J. 2010. "Contracting Out Public Schools for Academic Achievement: Evidence from Colombia." Working Paper, Department of Economics, University of Maryland, College Park, MD. http://www.fea.usp.br/feaecon//media/fck/File/bonilla.pdf.

Bravo, D., S. Mukhopadhyay, and P. E. Todd. 2010. "Effects of School Reform on Education and Labor Market Performance: Evidence from Chile's Universal Voucher System." *Quantitative Economics* 1 (1): 47–95.

Burde, D., and L. L. Linden. 2012. "The Effect of Village-Based Schools: Evidence from a Randomized Controlled Trial in Afghanistan." Working Paper 18039, National Bureau of Economic Research, Cambridge, MA.

Cameron, S. 2011. "Whether and Where to Enroll: Choosing a Private School in Dhaka." *International Journal of Educational Development* 31 (4): 333–416.

Chaudhury, N., J. Hammer, M. Kremer, K. Muralidharan, and F. H. Rogers. 2006. "Missing in Action: Teacher and Health Worker Absence in Developing Countries." *Journal of Economic Perspectives* 20 (1): 91–116.

Chaudhury, N., and D. Parajuli. 2010. "Nepal Community School Impact Evaluation." Working Paper, Human Development Unit, South Asia Region, World Bank, Washington, DC.

Chudgar, A., and E. Quin. 2012. "Relationship between Private Schooling and Achievement: Results from Rural and Urban India." *Economics of Education Review* 31 (4): 376–90.

Dang, H., L. Sarr, and N. Asadullah. 2011. "School Access, Resources, and Learning Outcomes: Evidence from a Non-Formal School Program in Bangladesh." IZA Discussion Paper 5659, Institute for the Study of Labor, Bonn, Germany.

Das, J., P. Pandey, and T. Zajonc. 2006. "Learning Levels and Gaps in Pakistan." Policy Research Working Paper 4067, World Bank, Washington DC.

Desai, S., A. Dubey, R. Vanneman, and R. Banerji. 2009. "Private Schooling in India: A New Educational Landscape." *India Policy Forum* 5 (1): 1–38.

French, R., and G. Kingdon. 2010. "The Relative Effectiveness of Private and Government Schools in Rural India: Evidence from ASER Data." Department of Quantitative Social Science Working Paper 10-03, Institute of Education, University of London, London, UK.

Glewwe, P. W., E. A. Hanushek, S. D. Humpage, and R. Ravina. 2011. "School Resources and Educational Outcomes in Developing Countries: A Review of the Literature from 1990 to 2010." Working Paper 17554, National Bureau of Economic Research, Cambridge, MA.

Glewwe, P., N. Ilias, and M. Kremer.2010. "Teacher Incentives." *American Economic Journal: Applied Economics* 2: 205–27.

Glewwe, P., and S. Jayachandaran. 2006. "Incentives to Teach Badly? After-School Tutoring in Developing Countries." In Applied Economics Workshop, University of Chicago Booth School of Business. http://www.chicagobooth.edu/research/workshops/AppliedEcon/archive/WebArchive20062007/Jayachandran-TeachBadly.pdf.

Goyal, S. 2009. "Inside the House of Learning: the Relative Performance of Public and Private Schools in Orissa." *Education Economics* 17 (3): 315–27.

Goyal, S., and P. Pandey. 2009. *How Do Government and Private Schools Differ? Findings from Two Large Indian States*. Report 30, South Asia Human Development Unit. Washington, DC: World Bank.

He, F., L. Linden, and M. MacLeod. 2008. "How to Teach English in India: Testing the Relative Productivity of Instruction Methods within the Pratham English Language Education Program." Unpublished paper, Columbia University, New York.

Heckman, J., and S. Navarro-Lozano. 2004. "Using Matching, Instrumental Variables, and Control Functions to Estimate Economic Choice Models." *The Review of Economics and Statistics* 86 (1): 30–57.

Khandker, S., M. Pitt, and N. Fuwa. 2003. "Subsidy to Promote Girls' Secondary Education: The Female Stipend Program in Bangladesh." MPRA Paper 23688, Munich Personal RePEc Archive.

Kingdon, G. 1996. "The Quality and Efficiency of Private and Public Education: A Case Study of Urban India." *Oxford Bulletin of Economics and Statistics* 58 (1): 57–82.

———. 2007. "The Progress of School Education in India." *Oxford Review of Economic Policy* 23 (2): 168–95.

———. 2008. "School-Sector Effects on Student Achievement in India." In *Exploring Public—Private Partnerships*, edited by R. Chakrabarti and P. E. Peterson. Cambridge, MA: MIT Press.

Kingdon, G., and R. Banerji. 2009. "Addressing School Quality: Some Policy Pointers from Rural North India." RECOUP Policy Brief 5, Faculty of Education, University of Cambridge, U.K.

Kingdon, G., and M. Muzammil. 2013. "The School Governance Environment in Uttar Pradesh, India: Implications for Teacher Accountability and Effort." *The Journal of Development Studies* 49 (2): 251–69.

Kremer, M., K. Muralidharan, N. Chaudhury, J. Hammer, and F. Halsey Rogers. 2005. "Teacher Absence in India: A Snapshot." *Journal of the European Economic Association* 3 (2–3): 658–67.

Muralidharan, K., and M. Kremer. 2008. "Public and Private Schools in Rural India." In *School Choice International*, edited by P. Peterson and R. Chakrabarti. Cambridge, MA: MIT Press.

Muralidharan, K., and V. Sundararaman. 2011. "Teacher Performance Pay: Experimental Evidence from India." *Journal of Political Economy* 119 (1): 39–77.

Pandey, P., S. Goyal, and V. Sundararaman. 2008. "Commmunity Participation in Public Schools: The Impact of Information Campaigns in Three Indian States." Impact Evaluation Series 26, Policy Research Working Paper 4776, World Bank, Washington, DC.

Patrinos, H. A., and C. Sakellariou. 2011. "Quality of Schooling, Returns to Schooling and the 1981 Vouchers Reform in Chile." *World Development* 39 (12): 2245–56.

Poverty Action Lab–South Asia. 2011. "What Helps Children to Learn? Evaluation of Pratham's Read India Program in Bihar and Uttarakhand." Research Note. http://www.povertyactionlab.org/publication/what-helps-children-learn-evaluation-prathams-read-india-program.

PROBE. 1999. *Public Report on Basic Education in India.* New Delhi: Oxford University Press.

Raykar, N. 2011. "Measuring the Impact of the Education Guarantee Scheme on Schooling Outcomes of Women in India." Working Paper, International Household Survey Network. http://neharaykar.weebly.com/uploads/5/7/4/8/5748051/jmp_final_july2011.pdf.

Rockoff, J., B. Jacob., T. Kane, and D. Staiger. 2011. "Can You Recognize an Effective Teacher When You Recruit One?" *Education Finance and Policy* 6 (1): 43–74.

Sharma, U. 2012. "Essays on the Economics of Education." PhD dissertation, University of Minnesota.

Thapa, A. 2011. "Does Private School Competition Improve Public School Performance? The Case of Nepal." Unpublished PhD thesis, Columbia University, New York.

Tooley, J. 2009. *The Beautiful Tree: A Personal Journey into How the World's Poor Are Educating Themselves*. New Delhi: Penguin.

Tooley, J., and P. Dixon. 2005. *Private Education Is Good for the Poor: A Study of Private Schools Serving the Poor in Low-Income Countries.* Washington, DC: Cato Institute.

CHAPTER 10

Delivering Quality Education in South Asia: Has Decentralization Worked?*

Introduction

Student learning is complex. It is shaped by multiple factors, including school-based inputs, such as infrastructure and teacher quality; non-school-based inputs, such as family and neighborhood characteristics; and student innate ability. Of the three factors, school-based inputs have received the most policy attention. Yet increasing school-based inputs, as policy frequently proposes, does not automatically guarantee their efficient use in improving student outcomes such as retention and learning. For instance, between 2000 and 2011, the Government of India increased its financial commitment to elementary education six-fold; yet learning levels did not improve commensurately (ASER 2010; EI 2011; NCERT 2012).

How effectively policy inputs translate into educational outcomes depends upon the formal governance framework—the system of formal laws, regulations and procedures—within which decisions pertaining to designing policies, financing, implementation, and accountability are made. These formal rules interact with underlying informal norms, customs, and beliefs, generating the de facto governance framework. This framework is important because it gives rise to a series of incentives, only some of which are conducive to achieving goals, such as the incentive to exert greater effort. Others are associated with inefficiencies, waste, and leaks. An ideal governance framework should not only improve student learning, it should also minimize inefficiencies, waste, and leaks in the system.

This chapter focuses on understanding the implementation challenges and the different dimensions of education decentralization reforms in South Asia—a popular policy response for modifying the governance framework for educational programs worldwide—and the link between these reforms and school quality.

---

*See box 10.1 for a summary of the chapter's key questions and findings.

Box 10.1 Questions and Findings

Questions

- What is the pattern of decentralization reforms in education in South Asia?
- Have decentralization reforms led to improvements in the way personnel and resources are allocated to schools and in accountability processes?
- What impact have these reforms had on the quality of student learning? What lessons can be drawn from the decentralization experience of countries in South Asia?

Findings

- Countries in South Asia have shown a historical commitment to decentralization in education. By bringing governance structures closer to the people, the purpose of decentralization has been to improve quality through two mechanisms: increasing the responsiveness of policy and enhancing accountability. India, Pakistan, and Sri Lanka currently have a constitutional mandate supporting decentralization in education. Despite this commitment, decisions likely to influence school quality, such as personnel management, are rarely taken at or near the school level. These decisions are typically made at the central, state, province, or district level. This dilutes the twin goals of responsiveness and accountability that decentralization reforms attempt to address.
- Decentralization reforms in South Asia have suffered from several challenges. These include policy uncertainty and inconsistency, inadequate resources, weak political buy-in and political interventions, weak local capacity and ineffective community engagement, low ownership of reforms, and poor information systems to guide reforms.
- Despite the pitfalls, there are examples of innovative methods in countries such as Nepal and India in which communities are provided information on decentralization and their respective roles and responsibilities. Although it is too early to discern whether these innovations have improved student learning, recent evidence suggests that community members are now more motivated to demand accountability.
- Overall, the findings in this chapter suggest that the implementation of decentralization reforms in South Asia has been much weaker than is needed if they are to be effective from the perspective of student learning. Specifically, decentralization reforms have been deprived of both the time and the money needed to be implemented properly. The implementation gaps make it difficult to comment on the effectiveness of decentralization reforms in the region. These findings are generally consistent with what we see in other low- and middle-income countries.

The explicit intention of decentralization reforms in South Asia, as elsewhere, has been improving the quality of education. It achieves this through two mechanisms: increasing the responsiveness of policy and enhancing accountability (Bardhan and Mookherjee 2006). The literature does not, however, give us a complete understanding of whether decentralization programs have in fact been effective in improving educational quality in schools. In general, studies examining the impact of decentralization find greater school autonomy improves community or parental participation. Studies also find positive impacts on student enrollment, attendance, and repetition rates as well as teacher presence and effort. However, the effect on student learning—the focus of this volume—is inconclusive. What explains this?

This chapter examines the factors underpinning the effectiveness of decentralization reforms in an attempt to understand why specific decentralization reforms have not always achieved their intended outcomes. The analysis, taking into account previous studies, reveals that decentralization reforms in South Asia are frequently deprived of both the time and the resources needed to be properly effective. It shows how the formal components of the institutional framework—the written rules and policies of decentralization—interact with informal components of the system, such as norms, beliefs, and customs, and eventually lead to outcomes that could differ from those policies intended. For instance, written rules may require that school management committees (SMCs) be democratically elected, but actual practice in deeply hierarchical settings may subvert such rules. The situation created by the interplay of the formal and informal components of the system underscores the need to understand implementation challenges more completely if policy is to address them effectively.

An important contribution of this chapter is the use of new data to document and examine the effectiveness of education decentralization in South Asia. The data include case studies and interviews undertaken specifically for this chapter in Pakistan, Sri Lanka, and India. The main goal of the case studies and interviews is to throw light on the mechanisms through which decentralization and school governance reforms have led, if at all, to actual quality changes in schools. These qualitative data provide unique insight on what is happening on the ground, which may differ considerably from what policy expected. The chapter also presents analyses using the recent PISA data for two Indian states, Himachal Pradesh and Tamil Nadu, to study the relationship between student achievement and school governance reforms as currently practiced in the two states. As is discussed later, however, the procedural and implementation aspects of decentralization reforms make it difficult to make generalizable statements on the causal link between decentralization and quality improvements in education.

Decentralization: Concepts, Rationale, and Models

Concepts

Researchers have used the term decentralization ambiguously. The underlying commonality in its usage has been the transfer or reallocation of responsibility for public functions from the central government to subordinate levels of government, other government organizations, or the private sector. This chapter will focus on transfers of responsibility within the government or from the government to school and community-based groups.

Any decentralization decision, whether it involves making roads or providing education, has two components: what responsibility to reallocate and to whom. The most frequent types of reallocated responsibilities involve decision making with regard to what to do (planning), how to do it (implementation), how to finance it, and how to ensure the task is done satisfactorily (accountability). Within each, there are subcategories. These decisions cover a broad realm of dimensions, from management of the school budget and personnel and curricular choices to community involvement.

The next question is to whom, or more specifically, to what level and entity, is responsibility transferred? Two basic principles guide such transfers: political representation and administrative appointment. Functions or authority may be transferred from centralized levels of government to local institutions based on local political representation. This is known as political decentralization or devolution. Administrative decentralization, also known as deconcentration, delegates central authority from the central government to local branches of the central government. Here, authority for the implementation of rules is transferred, but not authority for making rules (OECD 2004).

The delivery of a service, such as education, involves addressing multiple dimensions, such as teacher policy, curriculum and standards, school construction and maintenance, assessment, and measures/mechanisms to hold service providers accountable. In practice, each of these may be served through a different institutional arrangement. For instance, curriculum and standards may be determined at the central level and assessment undertaken at a much lower level, such as the district. Similarly, the appointment of teachers may take place at the state or provincial level through administrative channels, but they may be accountable to political entities at the village level, as with the *gram panchayats* (district-level elected governments) in Kerala, India. Different types and levels of schooling may also have widely varying governance practices, as in Bangladesh, where primary and secondary schools fall under different ministries and have different governance structures. Government and nongovernmental schools in Bangladesh also have different governance structures.

Different institutional arrangements for different tasks build flexibility into the system but also make the system complex and difficult to characterize as either centralized or decentralized. The fact that systems are typically "mixed"—hybrids—highlights the fact that there are advantages and disadvantages in both centralized and decentralized structures and, therefore, trade-offs in choosing one over the other.

Why Decentralize?

The main argument for decentralization rather than centralization is that it brings government and governance structures closer to the people served and thereby improves the quality of service provision. Theoretically, service provision improves through at least two routes: increased responsiveness and improved accountability (Bardhan and Mookherjee 2006). By inserting more layers of government between the center and communities, information asymmetries characterizing the relationship between a distant centralized bureaucracy and communities are presumably reduced. Having government officers closer, at least geographically, makes it easier for communities to communicate what they need and for policy makers to be more flexible, and therefore responsive, with regard to heterogeneous or time-varying community needs. Additionally, decentralization, because it brings government structures closer to the ground and promotes superior community involvement, opens up multiple channels for monitoring service provision and demanding improved quality. This increases accountability in the system.

Yet, in practice, for several reasons decentralization may not improve responsiveness and accountability, thereby thwarting the attainment of superior outcomes. First, local communities lack voice, and hence the ability to make their demands known or reduce the information gaps characterizing centralized systems (Galiani, Gertler, and Schargrodsky 2008). Second, local governments may also suffer from coordination and capacity problems, and may be less technically able than central governments to administer public services. Third, elite capture could potentially diminish the monitoring and accountability advantages of decentralization (Bardhan and Mookherjee 2006). Finally, if communities pursue goals other than student achievement, maintaining national standards becomes difficult and the problem of accountability even more complex (Hanushek, Link, and Woessmann 2011).

Decentralization and School Quality

Decentralization Policies in South Asia

With the focus of policy making shifting from increasing access to prioritizing educational quality, equity, and relevance, centralized systems not just in South Asia but around the world have gradually sought greater involvement from subnational levels of government. By 1998, 85 countries were moving toward decentralization in education, including Sri Lanka, Pakistan, India, and Nepal.

Decentralization efforts in South Asia have focused mainly on shifting power to different levels of government. Historically, these countries have recognized the importance of decentralization in education to varying degrees (box 10.2). Nepal had a long history of community-managed schools until 1971, when the national government took over schools. Following poor educational performance, in 2001 the government amended the Education Act to hand schools back to communities. In post-independence Pakistan, the Constitution of 1956 gave provinces limited autonomy. In India, the Constitution, adopted in 1950, mandated that "the State shall take steps to organize village *panchayats* and endow them with such powers and authority as may be necessary to enable

Box 10.2 History of Decentralization in Education, Selected South Asian Countries

Bangladesh: The rise and fall of Bangladesh governments have affected the success of efforts to decentralize education. With the Decree of Nationalization of 1973, the central government assumed sole authority for management of primary education, disbanding all district school boards. The Primary Education Act of 1981 proposed to set up local education authorities and school management committees (SMCs) to ensure participation of local communities. Political changes post-1981 impeded these reforms. A second attempt was made in 1982–83 to decentralize through the *upazilla* system, but the education system could not survive the 1990 change in government, and primary education management reverted to central control. Even though SMCs and parent-teacher associations exist today, they have little authority and capacity.

India: The extent of decentralization in India varies from state to state. In 1950 education was deemed to be a state function, but a 1976 constitutional amendment put it on the concurrent list where state and center could both exercise control. The constitution also allowed a role for local *panchayats* to further decentralization efforts. In the 73rd Constitution Amendment in 1992, the government required all states to create a three-tiered local governance system but left each state the option to pass the Conformity Act of 1994. This left considerable room for state governments to design their own plans to decentralize to the local level, subject to internal needs and resources. As a result, some states devolved significant functions, such as budget preparation, to *panchayats;* Rajasthan and others did not.

Nepal: Nepal has shown consistent commitment to decentralization since the 1990s. After restoration of multiparty democracy, reforms initiated in 1992 gave the District Education Officer (DEO) significant authority and devolved substantial powers to head teachers and SMCs. The regional education officer was expected to intervene only during a dispute or for interdistrict functions. The commitment to decentralization was echoed in the Local Self-Governance Act (1999), the 9th Five-Year Plan (1997–2002), the 10th Five Year Plan (2003–07), and the Interim Plan (2008–10).

Sri Lanka: Four phases can be identified in Sri Lanka's history of educational decentralization. The circuit education model of the 1960–70s that advocated formation of school clusters yielded only marginal results, paving the way for reforms in 1984. Although these reforms retained clustering, they mandated reorganization and restructuring of regional departments and district offices and gave more authority to school principals. Though well intended, the initiatives were not systematically implemented. In 1987, the Provincial Council Act led to an island-wide devolution of political and administrative functions. Clustering was replaced by a system where Divisional Education Officers had direct oversight of schools. In 1996, the government declared that the process of decentralization must go all the way down to the school. The Education Sector Development Framework and Program (ESDFP) 2006–10 supported decentralization efforts in Sri Lanka; it authorized funds for school staff development.

Pakistan: Paradoxically, major decentralization reforms in education took place in Pakistan under martial law. Pre-1979, policies vacillated between giving autonomy to local or to provincial entities. In 1979, President Muhammad Zia-ul-Haq's military government introduced the

box continues next page

Box 10.2 History of Decentralization in Education, Selected South Asian Countries *(continued)*

Local Government Ordinance that gave basic municipal functions like water and sanitation, street lighting management, and solid waste collection to local governments. In 2001, the military-led government of Pervez Musharraf issued another Local Government Ordinance that established district governments and devolved to them delivery of education, among other powers. This reform could not be implemented widely. In Sindh, the system has formally reverted to the 1979 ordinance, which has far less decentralization; in Punjab, although district governments are in place, no local government elections have been held.

---

them to function as units of self-government" (Article 40). At the time, both countries considered decentralization in the context of overall system governance, not specifically education. Sri Lanka differed in this regard, with policy pronouncements in the Ministry of Education and Cultural Affairs emphasizing decentralization as far back as 1961:

> Decentralization is one of the important means of securing efficiency and speed in handling the day-to-day work of administration. Decentralization connotes delegation of authority to the regional office and lessening of concentration of power at the head office.... Inadequate delegation of authority and unnecessary concentration in the head office have been mainly responsible for administrative decisions being considerably delayed and work unnecessarily duplicated (Perera 2012).

In the 50 years after independence, Pakistan, India, Nepal, and Sri Lanka fluctuated between policies promoting more decentralization and those promoting less. Today Sri Lanka, India, and Pakistan have constitutional mandates for decentralized governance in general.[1] When education performed badly under Nepal's central government, the Education Act was amended in 2001 to hand schools back to communities. In both Sri Lanka and India, 20 years after the constitutional mandate there is a highly uneven pattern in application across provinces or states. The Sri Lanka, India, and Pakistan case studies discussed below suggest that the wavering in policy both reflects and gives rise to such challenges as the administrative problems created by roughly parallel entities charged with the same task; recipients of services not being ready to demand accountability; and the difficulty of numerous political players sharing power.

Tables 10.1–10.3 describe the governance structure in education in areas of India, Pakistan, Sri Lanka, Bangladesh, and Nepal. As the tables show, in most countries in South Asia the entirety of education decision making is not devolved to a specific level of government but, depending on the decision, to different levels of government. For instance, decisions related to curriculum and standards are made by the center and states in India, but those related to implementing school improvement plans rest with the school. Even within countries in South Asia, education decentralization reforms have taken many forms, depending on the province or state,

Table 10.1 Responsibility for Education Governance in India

Decision	*Madhya Pradesh*	*Uttar Pradesh*	*Karnataka*
Planning and management of school budgets			
Decide expenditures	State, district	State, district	State, district
Manage personnel budget	State	State	State
Manage nonpersonnel budget	District, school[a]	District, school[a]	District, school[a]
Role of school council in nonpersonnel budget	None except for funds in the council account[a]	None except for funds in the council account[a]	None except for funds in the council account[a]
Participation of school council in budget preparation	Same as above	Same as above	Same as above
School council's authority to approve budget	Same as above	Same as above	Same as above
Participation of school council in budget implementation	Same as above	Same as above	Same as above
Personnel management			
Teacher policy	State, district (hiring of contract teachers)[b]	State, school (hiring of contract teachers)	State
Hiring	State, district (hiring of contract teachers)[b]	State, school (hiring of contract teachers)	State
Deployment	State, district	State, district	District
Pay	Center, state	Center, state	Center, state
Professional development	State, district	State, district	State, district
Monitoring teacher performance	District, school	District, school	District, school
School council role in monitoring teacher performance	Verifies teacher attendance, can reduce salary if attendance is not acceptable	If not satisfied, can fire contract teachers; for civil-service teachers, can only file a complaint in block or district education office	If not satisfied, can only file a complaint in block or district education office
School council role in teacher tenure, transfer, or removal	None, except can file a complaint in block or district education office	For contract teachers, decides on renewal; for civil-service teachers none, except can file a complaint in block or district education office	None, except can file a complaint in block or district education office
Curriculum, textbooks, and learning			
Curriculum and standards	Center, state	Center, state	Center, state
Choose textbooks	State	State	State

table continues next page

Table 10.1 Responsibility for Education Governance in India *(continued)*

Decision	*Madhya Pradesh*	*Uttar Pradesh*	*Karnataka*
Determine teaching methods	State, district	State, district	State, district
Student assessment	Standardized assessment by center (grades 10, 12); state (grades 5, 8, 10, 12)	Standardized assessment by center (grades 10, 12); state (grades 5, 8, 10, 12)	Standardized assessment by center (grades 10, 12); state (grades 3, 5, 8, 10, 12)
Use of assessments for making school adjustments (pedagogy, personnel)	None formally specified	None formally specified	None formally specified
School improvement and accountability			
Monitoring student performance	State, district, school (school's own assessment)	State, district, school (school's own assessment)	State, district, school (school's own assessment)
School council role in monitoring student performance	None, except if not satisfied, can file a complaint in block or district education office	None, except if not satisfied, can file a complaint in block or district education office	None, except if not satisfied, can file a complaint in block or district education office
Publication of school and student assessments	Results of standardized assessments in grades 8, 10, 12 are made public	Results of standardized assessments in grades 8, 10, 12 are made public	Results of standardized assessments in grades 8, 10, 12 are made public
Comparisons of school and student performance reports	None, except student report card of school's own assessment shared with parents	None, except student report card of school's own assessment shared with parents	None, except student report card of school's own assessment shared with parents
Guidelines for use of school and student assessments by the school council	None	None	None
Financial accountability	District, school (school council monitors school finances)[a]	District, school (school council monitors school finances)[a]	District, school (school council monitors finances)[a]
School council authority to perform financial audits	None, except for funds that come to council account[a]	None, except for funds that come to council account[a]	None, except for funds that come to council account[a]
Guidelines for participation of school council in audits	None	None	None
Monitoring student performance	State, district, school (school's own assessment)	State, district, school (school's own assessment)	State, district, school (school's own assessment)

Sources: Béteille and Pandey 2012; Khawar 2012; Perera 2012.

a. These funds are typically small—about Rs 15,000 per school per year—and are expected to be used for teaching learning material, school development, and school maintenance.

b. Since 2004, Madhya Pradesh hires only contract teachers in primary schools.

Table 10.2 Responsibility for Education Governance in Pakistan

Decision	*Sindh*	*Punjab*
Planning and management of school budget		
Decide expenditures	Province, school	District, school
Manage personnel budget	Province	District
Manage nonpersonnel budget	Province, school[a]	District, school[a]
Role of school council in nonpersonnel budget	None, except for funds in the council account[a]	None, except for funds in the council account[a]
Participation of school council in budget preparation	Same as above	Same as above
School council's authority to approve budget	Same as above	Same as above
Participation of school council in budget implementation	Same as above	Same as above
Personnel management		
Teacher policy	Province	Province
Hiring	Province	Province
Deployment	Province	Province
Pay	Province	Province
Professional development	Province	Province
Monitoring teacher performance	Province, school	Province, district, school
School council role in monitoring teacher performance	If not satisfied, can only file a complaint in block or district education office	If not satisfied, can only file a complaint in block or district education office
School council role in teacher tenure, transfer, or removal	None, except for filing a complaint in block or district education office	None, except for filing a complaint in block or district education office[b]
Curriculum, textbooks, and learning		
Curriculum and standards	Center, province	Center, province
Choose textbooks	Province	Province
Determine teaching methods	Province	Province
Student assessment	Standardized assessment by province (grades 9–12)	Standardized assessment by province (grades 5, 8, 9–12)
Use of assessments for making school adjustments (pedagogy, personnel)	None formally specified	None formally specified

table continues next page

Table 10.2 Responsibility for Education Governance in Pakistan *(continued)*

Decision	*Sindh*	*Punjab*
School improvement and accountability		
Implementing school improvement plan (e.g., school civil-works)	Province, school	District, school
Monitoring student performance	Province, school (school's own assessment)	Province, school (school's own assessment)
School council role in monitoring student performance	None	None
Publication of school and student assessments	Results of standardized assessments for grades 9–12 are made public	Results of standardized assessments for grades 5, 8, 9–12 made public
Comparisons of school and student performance reports	None, except student report card of school's own assessment shared with parents	None, except student report card of school's own assessment shared with parents
Guidelines for use of school and student assessments by the school council	None	None
Financial accountability	Province, school (council monitors finances in its account)[a]	Province, district, school (council monitors finances in its account)[a]
School council authority to perform financial audits	None	None
Guidelines for participation of school council in audits	None	None

Sources: Béteille and Pandey 2012; Khawar 2012; Perera 2012.

a. These funds are typically small. School councils make an annual school improvement plan to be implemented through grants made to them. Councils can also raise additional funds. However, for regular budget councils have no role.

b. School councils are to be consulted if a teacher is hired through funds raised by councils.

Table 10.3 Responsibility for Education Governance in Bangladesh, Nepal, and Sri Lanka

Decision	*Bangladesh (primary only)*	*Nepal*	*Sri Lanka*
Planning and management of school budget			
Decide expenditures	Center, division, district, school	Center, school[b]	Center, province, zone, school
Manage personnel budget	Center	Center, district, school	Center, province
Manage nonpersonnel budget	Center, division, district, school	Center, district, school	Center province, zone, school
Role of school council in nonpersonnel budget	None, except for funds in the council account[a]	None, except for funds in the council account[b]	None, except for funds in the council account[a]
Participation of school council in budget preparation	Same as above	Same as above	Same as above
School council's authority to approve budget	Negligible	Same as above	None
Participation of school council in budget implementation	None, except for funds in the council account[a]	Same as above	None, except for funds in the council account[a]
Personnel management			
Teacher policy	Center, district, and subdistrict	Center, district, school[c]	Center, province
Hiring	Center, district, and subdistrict	Center, district, school[c]	Center, province
Deployment	Center	Center, district, school	Center, province, zone
Pay	Center	Center, school[c]	Center, province
Professional development	Center, subdistrict	Center, district, school	Center, province, zone
Monitoring teacher performance	Division, district, school	Center, district, school[c]	Zone, division, school
School council role in monitoring teacher performance	Not much in government schools	Yes	If not satisfied, can only file a complaint in the education office
School council role in teacher tenure, transfer, or removal	None	Yes	Can only file a complaint in the education office
Curriculum, textbooks, and learning			
Curriculum and standards	Center	Center	Center, province
Choose textbooks	Center	Center	Center
Determine teaching methods	Center	Center	Center, zone, division, school
Student assessment	Standardized assessment by center (grade 5)	Standardized assessment by center (grades 10, 12) and district (grade 8)	Standardized assessment by center (grades 5, 11, 13) and province (grades 9–11)
Use of assessments for making school adjustments (pedagogy, personnel)	None formally specified	None formally specified	None formally specified

table continues next page

Table 10.3 Responsibility for Education Governance in Bangladesh, Nepal, and Sri Lanka *(continued)*

Decision	*Bangladesh (primary only)*	*Nepal*	*Sri Lanka*
School improvement and accountability			
Implementing school improvement plan	School	School	School
Monitoring student performance	Division, district, school (school's own assessment)	Center, district, school (school's own assessment)	Province, zone, school (school's own assessment)
School council role in monitoring student performance	None	Yes	None
Publication of school and student assessments	Results of standardized assessments made public	Results of standardized assessments are made public	Results of standardized assessments made available to students online
Comparisons of school and student performance reports	None, except student report card shared with parents	None, except student report card shared with parents	None, except student report card of school's own assessment shared with parents
Guidelines for use of school and student assessments by the school council	None	None	None
Financial accountability	Division, district, subdistrict, school	Center, district, school	Zone, division, school
School council authority to perform financial audits	None, except for funds that come to the council[a]	Council can conduct social audit for funds it receives[b]	None, except council can demand audit from public or private sources for funds that come to the council[a]
Guidelines for participation of school council in audits	No	Yes	Yes

Sources: Béteille and Pandey 2012; Khawar 2012; Perera 2012.

a. Funds to school council account are typically small. School councils make an annual school improvement plan to be implemented through grants made to them based on the prepared school budget. In Sri Lanka, councils can raise additional funds from parents and alumni.

b. The responsibilities of school councils include generating resources and formulating budgets, using a combination of government incentive grants, non-tied block grants, international aid, and resources raised by the community. Significant local resources were unlocked, with every rupee of government grants leveraging NPR 1.5 in community financing.

c. Community-managed schools can send regular (government-recruited) teachers back to the district, directly hire and fire community-recruited teachers, and index teacher salaries to school performance. The government froze the number of government-appointed teaching slots and introduced salary grants to allow communities to recruit teachers locally and hold them accountable for classroom performance.

differing by the level of government to which decisions are devolved and the types of decisions devolved. For instance, in Sindh, Pakistan, decisions related to the planning and management of school budgets rest primarily with the province, with schools having some say over nonpersonnel spending. In Punjab, Pakistan, however, districts—not provinces—play the key role. Similarly, in India, decisions relating to the hiring of contract teachers are undertaken by the district *panchayat* in Madhya Pradesh but by school councils in Uttar Pradesh.

When the type of education decisions devolved to lower levels of government in South Asia is scrutinized, a disconcerting pattern emerges: key decisions likely to influence school quality, such as personnel management, are taken by entities too far from individual schools. For instance, in India such decisions are made at the state level; in Bangladesh at the central level; in Sri Lanka at the central and provincial levels; and in Pakistan at the provincial or district level, depending on the province. Only in Nepal does the school have some say in such decisions. Looking at teacher recruitment, there appears to be little in the policies of these countries that allows schools to find teachers who match their specific needs. For instance, in Sri Lanka teacher hiring takes place at the central and provincial level, and in Bangladesh at the primary level districts and subdistrict articulate their needs in terms of numbers and subjects taught, but recruitment is done centrally. In general, across South Asia decision making on big budget items, such as personnel management (for instance, teacher pay) and the organization of instruction (such as curriculum, textbooks, and assessments), has been generally retained by the central or provincial or state level. The distance between schools and decision-making entities in core big budget areas defeats the purpose of responsiveness, an important goal of decentralization reforms.

The tables also reveal that while schools and local bodies across countries in South Asia are given some discretion over accountability-related functions, such as monitoring school performance, and low-budget items, such as nonpersonnel budget expenditures, their ability to undertake the roles expected of them is compromised by limited powers in other areas and the fact that policies fail to specify clear rules for enforcement. For instance, school councils are given important powers in monitoring school and student performance in Bangladesh, but what use is this if they have little say in personnel management decisions or curriculum choices? Similarly, in India, while school councils are expected to monitor student performance, if a school is failing to help its students learn, the most a school council can do is file a complaint with a higher-level office. There is little by way of policy to ensure that complaints are systematically addressed. In this way, the goals of accountability in South Asia are compromised. The situation is in stark contrast to better-performing countries like those in the Organisation for Economic Co-operation and Development, such as Finland, the Netherlands, the United Kingdom, and Sweden, where local bodies and schools make key decisions on resource allocation, personnel management, and organization of instruction.

A final point on the pattern of educational decentralization in South Asia: As the tables show, except for Nepal and to a lesser extent Sri Lanka, South Asian countries provide little evidence of school-based management policies—policies that transfer the responsibility for key school operations to a combination of head teachers, teachers, parents, and other community members.[2]

Decentralization and Quality: Lessons from Other Countries

Quantitative studies of the effect of decentralization reforms on school quality have increased over the past 10 15 years. Although they have mainly concerned reforms in Latin America, key points from these studies are summarized because they are instructive for analyzing what has happened in South Asia.

First, the studies have consistently found a positive link between increased local and school autonomy and such variables as enrollment, attendance, retention, teacher presence, and effort (Jimenez and Sawada 1999, 2003; King, Ozler, and Rawlings 1999; Sawada and Ragatz 2005; Di Gropello 2006; Murnane, Willet, and Cardenas 2006; Skoufias and Shapiro 2006; Eskeland and Filmer 2007; Khattri, Ling, and Jha 2010). Evidence of a link with student learning is, however, mixed (Jimenez and Sawada 1999; Rodriguez 2006; Galiani, Gertler, and Schargrodsky 2008; Khattri, Ling, and Jha 2010; Bruns, Filmer, and Patrinos 2011).

The literature posits the following reasons for the uncertain link between decentralization reforms and student learning:

- Decentralization programs are typically accompanied by an increase in enrollment, which tends to come from the low end of the test score distribution, thereby lowering the average test score (Rodriguez 2006; Madeira 2007; Galiani, Gertler, and Schargrodsky 2008).

- Learning takes time. Bruns, Filmer, and Patrinos (2011) provide evidence from developed countries suggesting it can take up to eight years to see an impact of decentralization in education reforms on student learning. In a meta-analysis of the effectiveness of school-based management (SBM) models in the United States that reviewed 232 studies looking at 29 SBM programs, Borman et al. (2003) found that the number of years of program implementation is a statistically significant predictor of the magnitude of impact on student achievement. This would be especially true for decentralization reforms that affect or challenge the existing, often unequal, power structures and hierarchies. To assess impact on learning, evaluations need to take a longer time frame than most of the studies presented here.

- Finally, Béteille and Loeb (2009) note that test scores are unlikely to be the most precise measure of all that a student has learned. There are good and bad test days, and good and bad test takers. Additionally, because studies are interested in measuring student achievement gain from one time to the next, it is important that the tests measure comparable content and scores be measured on comparable scales.

The second key point emanating from the literature addresses the question of why some schools benefit more from autonomy. These studies link successful decentralization reforms with well-established institutional arrangements conducive to autonomy and parental participation (Eskeland and Filmer 2007; Madeira 2007; Hanushek, Link, and Woessmann 2011). The location of such institutional arrangements, in turn, is correlated with the income and education level of the community (Gunnarsson et al. 2009). In particular, using multiple rounds of data for 42 countries, Hanushek, Link, and Woessmann (2011) found that high-income countries benefit from autonomous schools but developing and low-performing countries may be affected negatively by autonomy. High-income countries tend to have well-established institutions that enable autonomy; developing countries typically lack such strong structures. Further, the benefit of autonomy in the study is greater in countries where schools have external accountability through centralized examinations. Put differently, local autonomy matters for school outcomes but is effective only when the necessary institutions are in place. The literature, however, tells us little about which institutions are appropriate where, how productive institutions can be created, and how unproductive ones can be replaced.

Nepal and India: Making Decentralization Work

If good institutions facilitate successful decentralization, what happens when such institutions are not in place—as is true for a majority of the poor? Studies in South Asia have examined whether addressing a specific aspect of well-functioning institutions (the availability of credible information, for instance) could improve school outcomes. Decentralization programs seeking active parental participation may, for instance, create school councils, but if parents are not aware of their own role, they are unlikely to be effective. In other words, what would actively motivate parents and promote successful decentralization?

Chaudhury and Parajuli (2010) evaluated a program in Nepal that transferred school management to the community. After Nepal nationalized schools in the early 1970s, both school accountability and the quality of education were low. In 2001, the government decided to hand schools back to the communities: SMCs consisting of both parents and influential citizens were given powers to transfer government teachers, hire and fire community-recruited teachers, and index teacher salaries to school performance. SMCs also received non-tied block grants for school rehabilitation. Although school management was an option for all communities, participation was voluntary, the study used a design where a nongovernmental organization (NGO) conducted an advocacy campaign in randomly selected communities[3] that (a) informed the community about the program and (b) offered to facilitate the process if a community decided to participate. Impact estimates two years later suggested that devolving managerial responsibilities to communities led to increased grade promotion, reduction in dropouts, and fewer out-of-school children, particularly among disadvantaged groups.[4] Community participation and parental involvement also increased. There was as yet, however, no evidence of an impact on learning.

Two recent studies, both randomized evaluations in India, looked at the impact of interventions to promote community participation via school committees by providing school-related information to the community. The first study, in Uttar Pradesh, had three levels of intervention (Banerjee et al. 2008). The first provided information solely on the role of existing school committees. The second added information on student test scores and how to evaluate a child's learning. The third had a remedial education component beyond the public school that supplemented the second by training village volunteers in simple techniques for teaching children to read. After a six-month follow-up, the researchers found no impact of the first two interventions on reading outcomes but a positive effect of the third.

The second study, in three states, provided information to communities on their oversight roles and responsibilities in school management and the services they were entitled to from schools (Pandey, Goyal, and Sundararamen 2011). The campaign was structured and repeated several times over about two years. It targeted school committee members, parents, and disadvantaged groups. In a two-and-a-half-year follow-up, the study found positive results but with important differences between states. Impacts were larger in the two lagging states and smaller in the third, which at baseline was already substantially ahead in school outcomes. Teachers were more likely to be present and teaching, especially civil service teachers with permanent jobs. Among these, impact was greater for the socially powerful ones, who had made less effort to begin with.

Pandey, Goyal, and Sundararamen (2011) reported a consistent and significant increase in learning outcomes, although mainly in mathematics. Their conjecture is that math skills may be easier to improve in the short term, especially if they are not significantly dependent on language skills. The lack of wider impact on learning is attributed to two factors: (a) If teaching skills are inadequate, extra teacher time in the classroom does not translate into large gains in learning. (b) Learning is a cumulative process; it may take some time to assess the impact.

That study also found significant increases in community participation. School committees were more active and more aware of their roles after the campaign, although participation of disadvantaged groups, such as low castes, did not seem to increase much. Focus group discussions found that a large percentage of parents discussed the information with others and actively brought up teaching and learning issues with teachers and school committees.

Provinces and states within countries have introduced innovations for engaging local governments and government schools in the educational improvement process. Box 10.3 describes an example in Kerala, India.

Box 10.3 *Haritha Vidyalayam*: A Reality Show to Help Government Schools Excel

Kerala's *Sarva Shiksha Abhiyan* program, along with the State Institute of Education Training and the IT@Schools project, has adopted a novel approach to encouraging government schools in india to do their best and learn from each other. The project has played an important role in motivating excellence by fostering competition between districts in the state. Schools are invited to participate in a reality show, *Haritha Vidyalayam*, that is widely aired on state television. To be featured, government and government-aided schools apply online describing their innovative learning techniques and achievements in infrastructure, cocurricular activities, and information technology. Three schools per district are short-listed, and students and teachers from those schools are invited to participate in a live show in which a team of nationally renowned experts quizzes them. Ten schools make it to the final round, where the winner receives INR 1.5 million, the first runner-up INR 1 million, and the second runner-up INR 500,000. The show thus (a) provides substantial reputational as well as financial gains for good performers, (b) informs other schools about innovative techniques, (c) promotes productive competition between districts, and (d) dispels the myth that government schools are declining.

Source: Béteille and Pandey 2012.

Decentralization Challenges: Lessons from India, Pakistan, and Sri Lanka

Why has it generally been difficult in South Asia to build institutions conducive to decentralization? While decentralization policies in the region have repeatedly emphasized the importance of both responsiveness and accountability, there is still a considerable gap between policy and practice. The gap has also been exacerbated by several, often related, factors that together magnify the effect of each. Case studies from Sri Lanka, Pakistan, and India commissioned specifically for this report illuminate the problems. Despite the many socioeconomic differences between the three countries, common themes underlie their relative lack of decentralization success.

A brief note on the educational structure in the three countries will help to contextualize the discussion. In Pakistan, the hierarchy is federal/central at the top, followed by provinces and then districts. In Sri Lanka, the hierarchy is center, provinces, zones, divisions, districts, and schools. In India, the hierarchy is center, states, districts, blocks/*talukas*, clusters, villages, habitations, and finally schools.

Policy Uncertainty and Inconsistency

The unstable nature of many reforms, which have oscillated between decentralized decision making and reversion to a more centralized structure, reduces the effectiveness of the original reform. The first relates to uncertainty in the policy realm, and therefore reduced commitment to any given reform at a given point in time. As Khawar (2012) notes, there is no shared understanding in any of the provinces of Pakistan about decentralization being the future course, given past wavering between decentralizing and more centralizing policies. For instance, with the repeal in 2008 of the Sindh Local Government Ordinance 2001, establishing district governments with substantial autonomy, and the subsequent reinstatement of the Local Government Ordinance 1979, giving local governments only basic municipal functions, the national government effectively recentralized education. The current 18th Amendment proposes greater decentralization, but the historical trajectory of such reforms in Pakistan may have reduced its legitimacy.

A further problem with iterative reforms is a duplication of roles, responsibilities, and structures that are difficult to dismantle later. For instance, most Indian states have guidelines for the structure and the responsibilities of school committees. In Uttar Pradesh and other states, however, two school committees exist, one mandated by and answerable to the state education office and the other the village school committee answerable to the local government (the *gram panchayat*). Typically, the state education office committee is delegated most of the responsibilities; the village committee exists in name only.

Duplication of roles also muddies the lines of accountability. For instance, Sri Lanka's Provincial Council Act of 1987 not only devolved political and administrative functions island-wide, it also led to creation of new positions, such as the provisional secretary of education and the provisional director of education. Perera and Palihakkara (1997, 281–82) identified several resultant problems:

> The provincial director was made accountable to the provincial secretary, and wherever there were strained relationships between the two, problems occurred. The divisional office was often subjected to dual control by the provincial ministry and the provincial department. The officers in the divisional office found themselves … left wondering who their real master was. The roles of the provincial secretary and the provincial director needed to have been defined more precisely.

Redundant structures create power-sharing problems that could threaten the success of decentralization. In Sri Lanka, as one zonal director said, "Decentralization has not given the zone enough authority. I have to ask everything from the authorities above." While zones had been responsible for teacher deployment, often this responsibility now rests with the province. A zonal director said, "I don't know who will be appointed at what time. I cannot appoint principals …. I have no authority to change the subject of an officer working in my office" (Perera 2012). When those closest to the ground have no say in how teachers are assigned, here is a problem matching what schools need with what they get. Some schools have a deficit and others a surplus, again leading to waste and inefficiency. Divisional officers in Sri Lanka also feel that today they are held accountable for tasks for which they have no decision-making authority. For instance, the division has no say in financial allocations to schools, but divisional officers are expected to supervise how schools spend the money.

Finally, Perera (2012) argued, the dual school system of national and provincial schools—the former run by the central government and the latter by provincial authorities—has had a polarizing influence on education in Sri Lanka, with national schools getting better-performing students and more teachers and resources. Students who perform well in the grade 5 national scholarship and the General Certificate of Education (GCE) O-level examination are moved out of provincial schools into national schools, which perpetuates the underlying problem. Interview data from two low-performing provinces, Uva and Central, suggest that better-achieving students move to popular schools, mainly in the Western province. As a result, poor-performing schools left with low-performing students are stuck in the low-performing trap.

Inadequate Resources and Limited Fiscal Decentralization

For a system to function efficiently, decision makers at different levels should have access to the resources they need to implement their decisions—in other words, financial and educational decentralization need to go together. Yet, in Pakistan, India, and Sri Lanka, decentralization has yet to allow lower levels of government to make financial decisions.

In Pakistan, where the federal government handles central taxation, provincial governments depend on resource transfers from the federal government to fund operations. There is little emphasis on revenue generation in provinces, let alone lower tiers (Khawar 2012), which implicitly limits their activities. In Punjab, provincial governments transfer school budgets to districts as a single-line transfer in the overall budget. Although districts are empowered to use the money as needed (table 10.4), their discretion has little meaning when the fiscal space is shrinking, as it has in recent years (Khawar 2012).

In India, although the Sarva Shiksha Abhiyan (SSA) and the Right to Education Act (RTE) 2009 have promoted bottom-up planning for schools, SMCs have spending powers over only about 5 percent of SSA funds, and even this spending must be based on rules set by the central government. As PAISA

Table 10.4 District Budgets and Expenditure, Punjab, Pakistan, 2007–10

	Final budget (PRs millions)			*Development budget as % of total budget*
Year	*Development*	*Recurrent*	*Total*	
2008–09	37,633	113,806	151,439	24.85
2009–10	59,128	130,302	189,430	31.21
2010–11	30,553	162,786	193,339	15.80
2011–12	17,350	180,893	198,243	8.75
	Expenditure (PRs millions)			*Development expenditure as % of total expenditure*
Year	*Development*	*Recurrent*	*Total*	
2007–08	29,226	85,049	114,275	25.58
2008–09	20,275	100,464	120,739	16.79
2009–10	30,079	113,291	143,370	20.98
2010–11	18,082	146,003	164,085	11.02
2011–12	9,254	121,507	130,761	7.10

Source: Khawar 2012.

(2011) noted, if a school wants to spend more than the norm on, say, purchasing teacher material or investing in improving children's reading abilities by drawing upon these funds, it cannot. Ultimately, these reforms have promoted a bottom-up delivery system with top-down controls and decision-making powers.

Similarly, in Sri Lanka, while responsibilities have been shifted from the center to lower units, such as zones and divisions, the pattern of revenue-sharing circumscribes their capacity to meet their responsibilities because financial, physical, and human resources are not available (Perera 2012). The central treasury allocates money to the provinces, but provinces decide on zonal allocations without consulting zones. While zonal and division officers are supposed to visit schools, for instance, they do not have enough resources to do so (Perera 2012).

Weak Political Buy-in and Political Interference

From the perspective of a politician, decentralization reforms pit the good of being more responsive to constituents against the bad of surrendering power to lower tiers of government, which because of their proximity to individual voters could pose a political threat to incumbents. The resulting shaky political buy-in is illustrated by, for example, political interventions that impede the day-to-day functioning of schools. Undue political pressure in both Sri Lanka and Pakistan have interfered with school financial and resource management. In Sri Lanka, the provincial ministry, which is part of the elected provincial council, decides on all capital allocations for, for example, playgrounds and school buildings. Capital allocation decisions are often based on political patronage rather than actual needs—another instance of informal mechanisms counteracting formal rules (Perera 2012). This situation is not new: "Extreme politicization of the system at all levels has serious consequences and [has] contributed extensively toward the development of inefficiency and incompetence and indifference of officials and principals and lack of motivation among the teachers" (National Education Commission 2003).

Similarly, while the current system in both Punjab and Sindh provinces in Pakistan envisages allocation of resources based on needs assessment, political interference is nontrivial (Khawar 2012). Previously, provincial assemblies had legitimate access to funds available through the provincial government. Since the district governments are now autonomous and take direct control of development work, the assemblies no longer enjoy transparent access to funds. To benefit their constituencies, therefore, the assemblies exert pressure in subtle ways (Khawar 2012). Again, informal mechanisms subvert the formal.

Politicians interfere in the allocation not only of resources but also of teachers to schools. Béteille (2009) documented an elaborate pattern of political patronage underlying teacher assignment in Rajasthan, Madhya Pradesh, and Karnataka in India. In a national survey in India, Béteille and Muralidharan (2011) found that over 30 percent of district or divisional education officers (DEOs) said that politicians interfere unduly in teacher appointments and transfers, and 20 percent reported that government officials also interfere (table 10.5).

Table 10.5 Interference in Teacher Appointments and Transfers (District Education Officer Responses)

	Teacher appointments (Mean)	*Teacher appointments (N)*	*Teacher transfers (Mean)*	*Teacher transfers (N)*
Politicians interfere				
Very frequently	8.33	9	11.82	13
Frequently	6.48	7	6.36	7
Occasionally	19.44	21	19.09	21
Never	65.74	71	62.73	69
Government officials interfere				
Very frequently	2.78	2	5.56	6
Frequently	5.56	6	4.63	5
Occasionally	11.11	12	11.11	12
Never	80.56	87	78.70	85

Source: Béteille and Muralidharan 2011.

Low Ownership of Reforms

Low ownership of reforms is closely related to a sense of limited power in the face of political interference. Both in policy and in practice, communities are given responsibility only over small-budget low-stakes tasks: the typical school committee in India tends to be involved in enrollment drives and managing civil works (Béteille and Muralidharan 2011).

The difficulty school committees and DEOs have in holding teachers accountable reduces any trust that such reforms can be effective. Béteille and Muralidharan (2011) found that a large percentage of DEOs in India saw teachers trying to influence their appointments and transfers with the help of politicians and government officials in return for political favors.

There is also evidence that the local elite have weak ownership of schools. Over 50 percent of village influentials, such as village council chairpersons and secretaries, send their children to private schools (Béteille and Muralidharan 2011).

Finally, even when policy clearly specifies responsibilities, as does India's SSA, it cannot be assumed that the system will accept them. For instance, in Karnataka, where village panchayats have a long history that predates the 73rd Constitutional Amendment, new structures created through SSA, such as school development committees, have limited legitimacy (Sharma 2009). While village panchayat elections are subject to State Election Commission rules, most states do not have checks and balances on how school committees are formed—and whether, as mandated, the election process is indeed democratic.

Given the political realities and limited efforts to build local capacity, it is unlikely that policies promoting school autonomy will actually promote student achievement. It appears from the latest (2009/10) Programme for International Student Assessment (PISA) data for Himachal Pradesh and Tamil Nadu that greater school autonomy has either no or a negative correlation with the achievement of public school students. Test scores appear to be no worse or no better no matter where responsibility for decision making rests. This is true for autonomy in both resources and curriculum, although the negative effects are more pronounced for autonomy in resources. Note, however, that for private schools autonomy in resources is positively correlated with test scores. Annex 10A provides details of the PISA analyses.

Poor Local Capacity

Local capacity—the ability to contribute effectively to decision making in education—is minimal in low-income communities for well-documented reasons, such as lack of access to and understanding of policy provisions due to low literacy, social distance between parents and teachers, and limited mechanisms for exercising accountability.

In a study of local participation in education in Uttar Pradesh, Madhya Pradesh, and Karnataka, Pandey, Goyal, and Sundararaman (2010) found that the school committees given oversight responsibilities, such as the Village Education Committee in Uttar Pradesh, the Parent Teacher Association (PTA) in Madhya Pradesh, and the School Development Management Committee in Karnataka, are often unaware of their responsibilities (box 10.4). Asked to

---

Box 10.4 Key Roles and Responsibilities of PTAs in Madhya Pradesh

- Ensure that the school is functioning well.
- Prepare plans for improving schools.
- Ensure that all children ages 5–14 years are enrolled in school.
- Ensure that children attend school regularly.
- Look after any construction and repair work in schools and manage existing schools.
- Manage and monitor the funds coming into the school education account.
- Decide how money is to be spent based on the school's needs and give consent for use of funds.
- Monitor the distribution of textbooks, scholarships, and uniforms.
- Implement the midday meal program, and monitor the quality of food served.
- Ensure that children are learning at appropriate levels for their grade.
- Ensure that teachers come to school regularly and teach properly.
- Verify every teacher's attendance monthly by the PTA chair signing the teacher's attendance sheet; can stop a teacher's salary by not signing the attendance sheet if the teacher does not come regularly.
- Complain to the block or district education office or to the *Jan Shiksha Kendra* (cluster resource center) and recommend disciplinary action if dissatisfied with teacher (examples: if teachers do not come or do not discharge their duties appropriately).
- Ensure at least 200 teaching days per school year, and at least five hours of teaching on average per day.

Source: Pandey, Goyal, and Sundararaman 2011.

---

list their responsibilities, 52 percent of parent members of school committees in Uttar Pradesh and 58 percent in Madhya Pradesh could not list a single one. On average, in Uttar Pradesh they could correctly name only 20 percent of their fellow committee members and in Madhya Pradesh 10 percent. Karnataka fares better, with the majority of members able to list their responsibilities.

A large proportion of committee members in all three states had received no training on their responsibilities, and where there was training, parent members were the least likely to have received any: about 20 percent of parent members in Karnataka, 8 percent in Madhya Pradesh, and 2 percent in Uttar Pradesh reported receiving any training. In any case, the quality of training is questionable. In a study of 14 states in India, most school committee members could not even recall the content of training sessions (NUEPA 2011). Of those who could, many reported that the sessions focused on enrollment and civil works. Issues of quality, such as learning and pedagogy, were not raised.

The inadequate training and capacity building of committee members is especially worrying because school committees across South Asia are mandated with such tasks as ensuring teacher performance, student learning, and appropriate use of funds (tables 10.1–10.3). For example, most Indian states list "ensuring children are learning at grade-appropriate levels" as a school committee responsibility, but committees often have little idea of what grade-appropriate learning levels are. Programs to assist parents in understanding what learning means have proved useful in improving student outcomes in other parts of the world, such as Peru (box 10.5).

Nor do school committees have clearly defined mechanisms to ensure delivery of the outcomes they must monitor. If teachers are underperforming or student learning is below par, at best parents and school committees can only complain to the local education office (NUEPA 2011). Whether this leads to substantial change is debatable.

Committees are rarely active in overseeing school management. The problem is compounded by the social distance between teachers and parents (Rawal and Kingdon 2010). The fact that the community, the final beneficiary, is often unaware that school committees exist shows a broken link in the accountability chain. The study by Pandey, Goyal, and Sundararaman (2010) found that the majority of parents do not even know that there is such a committee in their children's schools. For instance, in Madhya Pradesh, although the Parent Teacher Association chair is supposed to verify attendance monthly before a teacher gets paid, many chairpersons reported in field conversations that it was common for teachers to get attendance verification slips signed in advance to ensure their full salary. The National University of Educational Planning and Administration study also found that meetings and school visits were rare and often committee chairpersons and secretaries were making decisions themselves, including financial ones.

Box 10.5 RECURSO: Creating High Expectations among Parents

Peru's RECURSO (Rendicion de Cuentas para la Reforma Social—Accountability for Social Reform) program aimed to break the low-quality equilibrium that characterized school performance in the mid-2000s. Low expectations of performance were seen as the fundamental barrier to quality improvement efforts: although various stakeholders were actively engaged in expanding coverage, they were not focusing on improving quality. Analyses suggested that one reason stakeholders were not pressing for improved quality was because it was difficult for them to see or measure quality. While coverage is concrete and therefore easy to see and measure, the quality of education is an abstract concept. Parents who have not been to school themselves do not always know what to expect from schools. Since there are no benchmarks on how to measure their child's achievement, parents believe their children are doing well as long as they get passing grades and show some improvement. If they were to know that their child takes five years to learn to read at a level that should have been achieved after one to two years, they might demand change.

RECURSO aimed to provide stakeholders with information and methods to track whether children had the skills expected at their age. The program produced a number of instruments for the general public, many directed specifically to the parents of poor children. These included three videos, a radio theater series, and numerous brochures and posters produced in multiple languages. The videos have been especially effective in building public opinion. They demonstrate poor education quality by showing children who cannot read or struggle to read. These dramatic scenes are followed by images of high-quality education, with poor rural children of the same age reading fluently, sometimes in multiple languages. The video then defines a standard: children finishing the second grade should be able to read 60 words per minute, and the video gives clear, simple instructions on how parents can measure this with any watch. The video challenges parents to find out how well their children are reading and tells them they have the right to demand a good education.

Source: Cotlear 2008.

Lack of Information to Guide Reforms

Information is crucial if decentralization policies are to work. Policy makers need information to make effective decisions about resource allocation, personnel management, and capacity development. Citizens need information to monitor school outcomes, express their voice, and hold providers accountable. More generally, measurement and analysis form the backbone of any system, especially one for improving quality. This requires both collection of data and its appropriate use. Such education data are usually collected through student assessments, school monitoring, and censuses.

In South Asia, information on student performance is not readily available; nor is it used systematically. In Punjab, Pakistan, for instance, there are multiple sources of information (Khawar 2012): the Boards of Intermediate and

Secondary Education conduct annual standardized tests for grades 9, 10, 11, and 12, and the Punjab Examination Commission conducts standardized tests for grades 5 and 8 and reports the results.[5] Educational assessments are also conducted by the Punjab Education Assessment System, the Provincial Education Assessment Center, the Project Monitoring and Implementation Unit in Punjab and the Reform Support Unit in Sindh (Khawar 2012). Unfortunately, the data are neither consolidated nor effectively used in Pakistan. Khawar (2012) attributed this to two factors: (a) there is no systematic way to reward or penalize good and poor performers and (b) there is no uniform system to allocate resources based on such information. Resources to schools are provided primarily through regular budgets and mainly cover salaries. Additional funding through SMC grants is fixed. Teacher training is generic and does not take into account how well a teacher's students fare on assessments.

India has similar data management problems. Although Sarva Shiksha Abhiyan has created a management information system in all districts, Béteille and Muralidharan (2011) found that a sizable percentage of district education and project offices have difficulty keeping student, teacher, and school data current.[6] For instance, nearly one-quarter of DEOs did not keep records on students, and although they are the primary body responsible for teacher-related administration, a fifth do not keep any teacher service records. Further, a majority of the records kept are on paper. It is possible that such records are maintained at the block or school level, but the lack of consolidated data makes it difficult to compute district- or state-wide statistics—not to mention understanding trends in school outcomes. District project offices are more likely than DEOs to have student, school, and household data and for the data to be computerized (although that is still minimal). This may be because data collected by the district project offices feed into Sarva Shiksha Abhiyan state and district report cards. As table 10.6 shows, almost half of district project offices do not keep any teacher service records (Béteille and Muralidharan 2011).

Table 10.6 Records Maintained in District Project and District Education Offices

	District project office				*District education office*			
	Records are not available (mean)	*Written records are available (mean)*	*Computerized records are available (mean)*	*N*	*Records are not available (mean)*	*Written records are available (mean)*	*Computerized records are available (mean)*	*N*
Student data	17.78	38.52	43.70	135	23.26	51.94	24.81	129
School funds data	11.76	40.44	47.79	136	22.31	47.11	30.58	121
Household data	20.74	36.30	42.96	135	30.51	42.37	27.12	118
Service book records data	45.22	31.30	23.48	115	20.74	61.48	17.78	135

Source: Béteille and Muralidharan 2011.

The lack of information about teacher performance is troubling. As Khawar (2012) noted, although in both Sindh and Punjab teacher education was given due importance in terms of allocated resources, teachers have rarely been tested or assessed, primarily for political reasons. A few years ago, Punjab introduced a pre- and post-test for all training programs, to which teacher associations took strong exception, protesting vehemently. For similar reasons, despite a real need for it, the concept of teacher licensing has not yet been introduced in any province.

In short, there is a dearth of information to facilitate effective policy decisions and respond to parental demands for accountability. There is also a lack of mechanisms for policy makers to use information to correct educational deficits and improve quality, or for schools to make adjustments in response to parental demands. Although results of standardized assessments in specific grades are made public in individual schools or available to students online, there are no public comparisons of school and student performance. Even if there were, no policy prescriptions inform district education offices or schools on what adjustments to make in pedagogy and personnel. Similarly, school councils and parents are expected to monitor outcomes and voice concerns but have little means to do so, especially since many are not very literate. They have neither access to readily available and easy-to-interpret assessment results nor the capacity to use them to demand better outcomes.

In South Asia limited ability to motivate teacher performance through incentives and disincentives may mean that simply providing test scores to parents as a means of monitoring teacher performance is unlikely to have much impact on either teacher behavior or student performance. Evidence from the PISA data for Himachal Pradesh and Tamil Nadu suggests that giving parents information on student performance or posting achievement data publicly has little impact on school accountability. Similarly, using assessment data to monitor teachers has no effect on student performance, and using teacher peer reviews can be associated with worse outcomes (see Annex 10A).

Summary

Countries in South Asia have been undertaking decentralization reforms in one form or another for 40–50 years, with varying degrees of success. Decentralization reforms aimed at improving school performance are inherently difficult because they involve the redistribution of power. Entities typically do not like to see their power reduced, and school improvement may not be the primary goal of every player in the system. Influential teachers, for instance, often block accountability-enhancing reforms. The lack of involvement, capacity, and ownership of reforms by the larger parent community also compromises efforts to exercise oversight and demand accountability from schools. Decentralization policies may have underestimated both the importance and the difficulty of having participants own the process.

Actual implementation of decentralization reforms is much weaker than is needed if they are to be effective. To begin with, throughout the region fiscal decentralization is limited, which means that lower levels of government rarely command the resources they need to fund important decisions. Detailed evidence from India suggests that communities in several states do not fully understand the powers and decisions devolved to them, or even know that school committees exist. There is a significant lack of effective efforts to build the oversight capacity of communities (NUEPA 2011). Participation and decision making in school committee meetings is usually dominated by chairpersons and secretaries.

For decentralization reforms to be effective in improving learning, the following issues need to be addressed:

- **Greater political support and consistency in implementation of reforms:** Decentralization reforms in the region have been uncertain and inconsistent, frequently oscillating between greater and lesser centralization. Such inconsistency has not only reduced commitment and ownership of decentralization reforms, it has also led to the duplication of roles, responsibilities, and structures and to confusion about accountability.

- **Adequate resources and fiscal authority at lower levels of government:** For a system to function efficiently, decision makers at all levels should have access to the resources they need to implement decisions. In countries across the region, financial decentralization has yet to allow lower levels of governments to make effective decisions. In India, for instance, although the *Sarva Shiksha Abhiyan* and the Right to Education Act set out a bottom-up planning structure for schools, SMCs have spending power only over about 5 percent of *Sarva Shiksha Abhiyan* funds, and even these need to be spent based on central government norms (Dongre, Chowdhury, and Aiyar 2012). This limits the ability of SMCs to undertake important functions related to improving schooling outcomes.

- **Systematically build local capacity so that communities can contribute effectively to decision making:** In most parts of the region, local capacity is minimal, with low-income communities having little ability to contribute effectively to decision making in education. As an example, most Indian states list "ensuring children are learning at grade-appropriate levels" as one responsibility of school committees. Programs to assist parents in understanding what learning means have proved useful in improving student outcomes (box 10.5). Due to their low capacity, community-based groups tend to be accorded responsibility only over low-stakes tasks: the typical SMC in India is not empowered to hire and fire teachers; instead, SMCs tend to be involved in enrollment drives and managing civil works (Béteille and Muralidharan 2011). For SMCs to make meaningful contributions, they need to be assigned roles and responsibilities they have been trained to undertake.

Annex 10A: Analysis of Indian PISA 2009–10 Data

Methodology

PISA 2009–10 data were used to analyze how variables measuring school autonomy, accountability, and practices to monitor teachers are associated with school test scores. Linear regression is used to control for student background and school characteristics that can be correlated with test scores and autonomy variables. Because school autonomy rules differ for public and private schools, results are analyzed separately for public schools (table 10A.1) and private schools (table 10A.2).

Table 10A.1 Results of the OLS Regression: Public Schools[a]

	Reading	*Math*	*Science*
School autonomy in curriculum	−51.30 (0.087)*	−45.07 (0.059)*	−62.63 (0.016)**
School autonomy in resources	−149.06 (0.28)	−284.86 (0.007)***	−189.68 (0.018)**
Providing information to parents			
1. Information on student performance relative to other students in same school	−0.92 (0.96)	4.73 (0.69)	0.59 (0.96)
2. Information on student performance relative to national or regional benchmarks	−18.38 (0.065)*	−3.93 (0.66)	−12.19 (0.064)*
3. Information on student performance relative to other students in same grade	5.69 (0.52)	−10.12 (0.18)	2.98 (0.65)
Achievement data posted publicly (e.g., in the media)	12.36 (0.17)	5.82 (0.43)	0.43 (0.95)
Achievement data used in evaluation of principal's performance	−14.58 (0.30)	−17.47 (0.079)*	−24.09 (0.001)***
Achievement data used in evaluation of teachers' performance	6.98 (0.73)	3.25 (0.82)	11.10 (0.19)
Monitoring teachers through			
1. Tests or assessments of student achievement	−19.80 (0.14)	−12.87 (0.26)	2.88 (0.76)
2. Teacher peer review (of lesson plans, assessment instruments, lessons)	−8.70 (0.48)	−15.44 (0.076)*	−11.39 (0.088)*
3. Principal or senior staff observations of lessons	20.27 (0.23)	32.49 (0.008)***	25.51 (0.004)***
4. Observation of classes by inspectors or other persons external to the school	12.54 (0.38)	14.83 (0.18)	5.32 (0.54)
Constant	3.96 (0.97)	30.90 (0.76)	40.79 (0.65)
Observations	2656	2656	2656
R-squared	0.18	0.20	0.15

Source: Data from the OECD PISA+ for two Indian states.
Note: Robust *p* values in parentheses; OLS = ordinary least squares.
Significance level: * = 10 percent, ** = 5 percent, *** = 1 percent.
a. Each regression includes state fixed effects, controls for student characteristics (age, gender, dummies for parental education, index of wealth), and school characteristics (student-teacher ratio, enrollment, index of school infrastructure, percent of teachers certified, percent of teachers qualified).
p-values are based on robust standard errors clustered at school level.

Table 10A.2 Results of the OLS Regression: Private Schools[a]

	Reading	*Math*	*Science*
School autonomy in curriculum	−35.97 (0.56)	−53.12 (0.47)	−71.93 (0.44)
School autonomy in resources	223.55 (0.009)***	223.87 (0.022)**	238.03 (0.048)**
Providing information to parents			
1. Information on student performance relative to other students in same school	−23.27 (0.36)	0.92 (0.97)	−4.25 (0.90)
2. Information on student performance relative to national or regional benchmarks	23.36 (0.12)	19.23 (0.33)	−0.58 (0.98)
3. Information on student performance relative to other students in same grade	−7.51 (0.63)	0.08 (1.00)	−2.29 (0.93)
Achievement data posted publicly (e.g., in the media)	42.16 (0.039)**	79.25 (0.002)***	38.96 −0.20
Achievement data used in evaluation of principal's performance	−117.73 (0.005)***	−167.05 (0.002)***	−42.52 −0.48
Achievement data used in evaluation of teachers' performance	−16.30 (0.29)	11.78 (0.61)	−18.38 (0.49)
Monitoring teachers through			
1. Tests or assessments of student achievement	27.05 (0.46)	37.39 (0.33)	−5.59 (0.90)
2. Teacher peer review (of lesson plans, assessment instruments, lessons)	56.70 (0.064)*	50.62 (0.078)*	34.32 (0.33)
3. Principal or senior staff observations of lessons	8.36 (0.87)	-86.00 (0.10)	102.30 (0.15)
4. Observation of classes by inspectors or other persons external to the school	24.42 (0.23)	46.34 (0.059)*	1.21 (0.97)
Constant	254.56 (0.34)	145.13 (0.52)	−150.29 (0.59)
Observations	466	466	466
R-squared	0.56	0.51	0.52

Source: Data from the OECD PISA+ for two Indian states.
Note: Robust *p* values in parentheses; OLS = ordinary least squares.
Significance level: * = 10 percent, ** = 5 percent, *** = 1 percent.
a. Private schools refers to private unaided schools only. Each regression includes state fixed effect, controls for student characteristics (age, gender, dummies for parental education, index of wealth) and school characteristics (student-teacher ratio, enrollment, index of school infrastructure, percent of teachers certified, percent of teachers qualified).
p-values are based on robust standard errors clustered at school level.

Description of Variables

School autonomy consists of two variables: (a) autonomy in resources: ratio of the number of school-level decisions in areas of staff and budget to the number of such decisions at the regional or national level and (b) autonomy in curriculum and assessment: ratio of the number of school-level decisions in areas of assessment and curriculum to the number of regional or national decisions. PISA 2009 asked schools to report whether principals, teachers, a school governing board, a regional or local education authority, or a national education authority has considerable responsibility for

- Establishing student-assessment policies, choosing which textbooks are used, determining course content, and deciding which courses are offered. The ratio of the number of these four activities for which principals or teachers have responsibility to the number of these activities for which a regional or local education authority or a national education authority has responsibility is computed by PISA as the "school autonomy in curriculum and assessment variable."

- Selecting teachers for hire, dismissing teachers, establishing teacher starting salaries, determining teacher salary increases, formulating the school budget, and deciding on budget allocations within the school. The ratio of the number of these six activities for which principals or teachers have responsibility to the number of these activities for which a regional or local education authority or a national education authority has authority is computed as the "school autonomy in resources variable."

Accountability variables are whether schools provide information on achievement to parents and publicly post achievement data. Monitoring variables are whether schools use achievement data to evaluate teachers and use other ways of monitoring, such as student assessment, teacher peer review, principal's monitoring of lessons, and external monitors.

Notes

1. Sri Lanka passed the 13th Amendment in 1987, India the 73rd and 74th Constitutional Amendments in 1992–93, and Pakistan the 18th Amendment in 2010.
2. Most school-based programs work through a school committee, which may monitor school performance, for example, in test scores or teacher and student attendance; appoint or dismiss teachers; ensure that teacher salaries are paid on time; approve school budgets; and examine financial statements (Caldwell 2005).
3. This provides a source of exogenous variation in program participation.
4. The empirical strategy combined instrumental variables and difference-in-differences approaches.
5. Sindh is starting similar tests through a third party on grade 5 curricula (test will be taken by grade 6 entrants).
6. Student data relate to enrollment and attendance. School funds data track how much funding each school receives and how it is used. Household data are used to determine the number of children not in school. Teacher service records have the profile of each teacher and their salary, promotion, and performance evaluation history.

Bibliography

ASER. 2010. *The Annual Status of Education Report.* New Delhi: ASER Centre.

Banerjee, A., R. Banerji, E. Duflo, R. Glennerster, and S. Khemani. 2008. "Pitfalls of Participatory Programs: Evidence from a Randomized Evaluation in Education in India." Working Paper 14311, National Bureau of Economic Research, Cambridge, MA.

Bardhan, P., and D. Mookherjee, eds. 2006. *Decentralization and Local Governance in Developing Countries*. Cambridge, MA: MIT Press.

Béteille, T. 2009. "Absenteeism, Transfers and Patronage: The Political Economy of Teacher Labour Markets in India." PhD thesis, Stanford University, Stanford, CA.

Béteille, T., and S. Loeb. 2009. "Teacher Quality and Teacher Labor Markets." In *Handbook of Education Policy Research*, edited by G. Sykes, B. Schneider, and D. N. Plank. London, U.K.: Routledge.

Béteille, T., and K. Muralidharan. 2011. "School Governance in Rural India." Working draft, University of California, San Diego, CA.

Béteille, T., and P. Pandey. 2012. "Education Decentralization in South Asia." Background paper prepared for this study, Human Development Unit, South Asia Region, World Bank, Washington, DC.

Borman, G. D., G. M. Hewes, L. T. Overman, and S. Brown. 2003. "Comprehensive School Reform and Achievement: A Meta-Analysis." *Review of Educational Research* 73 (2): 125–30.

Bruns, B., D. Filmer, and H. A. Patrinos. 2011. *Making Schools Work: New Evidence on Accountability Reforms*. Washington, DC: World Bank.

Caldwell, B. J. 2005. *School-Based Management*. Paris: The International Institute for Educational Planning; Brussels: The International Academy of Education.

Chaudhury, N., and D. Parajuli. 2010. "Nepal Community School Impact Evaluation." Working Paper, Human Development Unit, South Asia Region, World Bank, Washington, DC.

Cotlear, D. 2008. "Making Accountability Work: Lessons from RECURSO." En breve No 135. Operations Services Department, Latin America and the Caribbean Region, World Bank, Washington, DC.

Di Gropello, E. 2006. *A Comparative Analysis of School-Based Management in Central America*. Washington, DC: World Bank.

Dongre, A., A. Chowdhury, and Y. Aiyar. 2012. "Unpacking School Finances." Draft Background Note, Human Development Unit, South Asia Region, World Bank, Washington DC.

EI (Educational Initiatives). 2011. "Student Learning Study. Status of Learning across 198 Sites of India in Urban and Rural Schools." EI, Ahmedabad, India. http://www.ei-india.com/wp-content/uploads/Main_Report-Low_Resolution-25-01.pdf.

Eskeland, G. S., and D. Filmer. 2007. "Autonomy, Participation and Learning: Findings from Argentine Schools, and Implications for Decentralization." *Education Economics* 15 (1): 103–27.

Galiani, S., P. Gertler, and E. Schargrodsky. 2008. "School Decentralization: Helping the Good Get Better, but Leaving the Poor Behind." *Journal of Public Economics* 92 (10): 2106–20.

Gunnarsson, V., P. F. Orazem, M. A. Sánchez, and A. Verdisco. 2009. "Does Local School Control Raise Student Outcomes? Evidence on the Roles of School Autonomy and Parental Participation." *Economic Development and Cultural Change* 58 (1): 25–52.

Hanushek, E. A., S. Link, and L. Woessmann. 2011. "Does School Autonomy Make Sense Everywhere? Panel Estimates from PISA." Working Paper 17591, National Bureau of Economic Research, Cambridge, MA.

Hoxby, C. 1996. "How Teachers' Unions Affect Education Production." *Quarterly Journal of Economics* 111 (4): 671–718.

Jimenez, E., and Y. Sawada. 1999. "Do Community-Managed Schools Work? An Evaluation of El Salvador's EDUCO Program." *World Bank Economic Review* 13 (3): 415–41.

———. 2003. "Does Community Management Help Kids in Schools? Evidence Using Panel Data from EL Salvador's EDUCO Program." CIRJE Discussion Papers, CIRJE-F-236, University of Tokyo, Japan.

Khattri, N., C. Ling, and S. Jha. 2010. "The Effects of School-Based Management in the Philippines: An Initial Assessment Using Administrative Data." Policy Research Working Paper 5248, World Bank, Washington, DC.

Khawar, H. 2012. "Education Decentralization in Pakistan: The Effects on the Quality of Education and Accountability." Background study conducted for this report. Human Development Unit, South Asia Region, World Bank, Washington, DC.

King, E., B. Ozler, and L. B. Rawlings. 1999. "Nicaragua's School Autonomy Reform: Fact or Fiction?" Working Paper 19, Impact Evaluation of Education Reforms Series, World Bank, Washington, DC.

Kremer, M., N. Chaudhury, F. H. Rogers, K. Muralidharan, and J. Hammer. 2005. "Teacher Absence in India: A Snapshot." *Journal of the European Economic Association* 3 (2–3): 658–67.

Madeira, R., 2007. "The Effects of Decentralization on Schooling: Evidence from the Sao Paulo State's Education Reform". University of São Paulo, São Paulo, Brazil. http://www.cid.harvard.edu/neudc07/docs/neudc07_s1_p12_madeira.pdf.

Murnane, R. J., J. B. Willet, and S. Cardenas. 2006. "Did the Participation of Schools in Programa Escuelas De Calidad Influence Student Outcomes?" Working paper, Harvard University Graduate School of Education, Cambridge, MA.

National Education Commission. 2003. National Education Commission 2003. Colombo.

NCERT (National Council of Educational Research and Training). 2012. *National Achievement Survey Class V.* New Delhi: NCERT.

NUEPA (National University of Educational Planning and Administration). 2011. *Annual Report.* New Delhi: NUEPA.

OECD (Organisation for Economic Co-operation and Development). 2004. *Raising the Quality of Educational Performance at School.* Policy Brief. Paris: OECD.

PAISA Report. 2011. *Do Schools Get Their Money? Accountability Initiative.* http://www.accountabilityindia.in/article/state-report-cards/2475-paisa-report-2011/.

Pandey, P., S. Goyal, and V. Sundararaman. 2010. "Public Participation, Teacher Accountability and School Outcomes in Three States." *Economic and Political Weekly* 45 (24): 75–83.

———. 2011. "Does Information Improve School Accountability? Results of a Large Randomized Trial." Discussion Paper Series Report 39, South Asia Human Development Unit, World Bank, Washington, DC.

Perera, W. J. 2012. "Education Decentralization in Sri Lanka." Background note prepared for this report, Human Development South Asia Region, World Bank, Washington, DC.

Perera, W. J., and H. Palihakkara. 1997. "Decentralization in Education: The Sri Lankan Experience." In *Decentralization of Educational Management: Experiences from South Asia,* edited by R. Govinda. Paris: IIEP.

Rawal, S., and G. Kingdon. 2010. "Akin to My Teacher: Does Caste, Religious or Gender Distance Between Student and Teacher Matter? Some Evidence from India." DoQSS Working Paper 10–18, Institute of Education, University of London, London.

Rodriguez, C. 2006. "Households' Schooling Behavior and Political Economy Trade-Offs after Decentralization." Working Paper, Universidad de los Andes, Colombia.

Sawada, Y., and A. B. Ragatz. 2005. "Decentralization of Education, Teacher Behavior, and Outcomes." In *Incentives to Improve Teaching,* edited by E. Vegas. Washington, DC: World Bank.

Sharma, Rashmi. 2009. *Local Government in India: Policy and Practice With Special Reference to a Field Study of Decentralization in Kerala.* New Delhi, India: Manohar Publishers.

Skoufias, E., and J. Shapiro. 2006. "The Pitfalls of Evaluating a School Grants Program Using Non-Experimental Data." Policy Research Working Paper 4036, World Bank, Washington, DC.

Environmental Benefits Statement

The World Bank Group is committed to reducing its environmental footprint. In support of this commitment, the Publishing and Knowledge Division leverages electronic publishing options and print-on-demand technology, which is located in regional hubs worldwide. Together, these initiatives enable print runs to be lowered and shipping distances decreased, resulting in reduced paper consumption, chemical use, greenhouse gas emissions, and waste.

The Publishing and Knowledge Division follows the recommended standards for paper use set by the Green Press Initiative. Whenever possible, books are printed on 50 percent to 100 percent postconsumer recycled paper, and at least 50 percent of the fiber in our book paper is either unbleached or bleached using Totally Chlorine Free (TCF), Processed Chlorine Free (PCF), or Enhanced Elemental Chlorine Free (EECF) processes.

More information about the Bank's environmental philosophy can be found at http://crinfo.worldbank.org/wbcrinfo/node/4.